D0024500

CATHOLIC SCHOOLS IN THE UNITED STATES

AN ENCYCLOPEDIA

Volume I: A–L

EDITED BY
THOMAS C. HUNT, ELLIS A. JOSEPH, AND
RONALD J. NUZZI

Foreword by Glenn Anne McPhee, OP

GREENWOOD PRESS
Westport, Connecticut • London

Library of Congress Cataloging-in-Publication Data

Catholic schools in the United States : an encyclopedia / edited by Thomas C. Hunt, Ellis
   A. Joseph, and Ronald J. Nuzzi ; foreword by Glenn Anne McPhee.
      p. cm.
   Includes bibliographical references and index.
   ISBN 1–57356–532–6 (set : alk. paper)—ISBN 1–57356–596–2 (v. 1 : alk. paper)—
   ISBN 1–57356–597–0 (v. 2 : alk. paper)
   1. Catholic schools—United States—Encyclopedias. 2. Catholic
Church—Education—United States—Encyclopedias. I. Hunt, Thomas C., 1930– II. Joseph,
Ellis A. III. Nuzzi, Ronald James, 1958–
   LC501.C3483 2004
   371.071′2′03—dc22   2004042483

British Library Cataloguing in Publication Data is available.

Library of Congress Catalog Card Number: 2004042483
ISBN: 1–57356–532–6 (set)
        1–57356–596–2 (vol. I)
        1–57356–597–0 (vol. II)

First published in 2004

Greenwood Press, 88 Post Road West, Westport, CT 06881
An imprint of Greenwood Publishing Group, Inc.
www.greenwood.com

Printed in the United States of America

The paper used in this book complies with the
Permanent Paper Standard issued by the National
Information Standards Organization (Z39.48–1984).

10 9 8 7 6 5 4 3 2 1

Ellis Joseph dedicates this encyclopedia to his children, Ellis Joseph, Jr., Laurice Joseph, Paula Joseph, and Rose Marie Joseph.

Ronald Nuzzi dedicates it to his nieces and nephews in Orlando, Florida, and Niles, Ohio, all of whom have been blessed with generous parents who provided them a Catholic school education.

Thomas Hunt dedicates the encyclopedia to his daughters, Staci and Eryn, and to Staci's husband, Derek, and their son, Nathaniel.

Contents

Alphabetical List of Entries

Guide to Related Topics

Blum, Virgil C.

Bouquillon, Thomas

Drexel, Katharine

Gibbons, James Cardinal

Greeley, Andrew M.

Groome, Thomas

Holaind, Rene I.

Hughes, John

Ireland, John

Johnson, George

Katzer, Frederick

Malone, James

Mann, Horace

Maritain, Jacques

McManus, William

McQuaid, Bernard

Mundelein, George W., Cardinal

Satolli, Francis (Francesco)

Seton, Elizabeth Ann

Shields, Thomas Edward

Spalding, Catherine

Spalding, John Lancaster

EDUCATION PROGRAMS

Bilingual education

Character education

Cristo Rey schools

Dress codes

Gifted and talented, education for

Parish School of Religion (PSR)

Retreats

School uniforms

Section 504

Sex education

Special needs

Vocational education

ETHNIC GROUPS AND CONCERNS

African Americans

Americanization

Arab American Catholics

Asian American Catholics

Cahenslyism

Catholic High Schools and Minority Students

Cristo Rey schools

Diversity

Ethnicity (and parish schools)

German American Catholics

Hispanics/Latinos

Immigration/Immigrants

Inner-city schools

Integration in Catholic schools

Irish American Catholics

Italian American Catholics

Minority students

Native Americans

Polish American Catholics

Slavic American Catholics

FINANCE

Cathedraticum

Development

Endowments

Financing of Catholic schools

Subsidies

Tuition

Tuition tax credits

Vouchers

GOVERNANCE

Bishops

Consolidated schools

Diocesan and archdiocesan schools

Diocese and archdiocese

Faribault Plan

Governance

Hierarchy

Jurisdiction

National Catholic Welfare Conference
  (NCWC)

PARENTS

Choice, parent and school
Cultural influences on parenting
Family development theory
Home schooling
Milwaukee Parental Choice Program
Parental rights
Parents as primary educators
Vouchers

PEOPLE

Aquinas, St. Thomas
Augustine, St.
Blum, Virgil C.
Bouquillon, Thomas
Carroll, John
Coleman, James S.
Corrigan, Michael
D'Amour, O'Neill C.
Darcy-Berube, Francoise
Drexel, Katharine
Ellis, John Tracy
Gardner, Howard
Gibbons, James Cardinal
Greeley, Andrew M.
Groome, Thomas
Holaind, Rene I.
Hughes, John
Ireland, John
John XXIII, Pope
John Paul II, Pope
Johnson, George
Katzer, Frederick
Leo XIII, Pope
Malone, James
Mann, Horace
Maritain, Jacques
McManus, William
McQuaid, Bernard
Merton, Thomas

Mundelein, George W., Cardinal
Newman, John Henry, Cardinal
Paul VI, Pope
Pius XI, Pope
Pius XII, Pope
Ryan, Mary Perkins
Satolli, Francis (Francesco)
Seton, Elizabeth Ann
Shields, Thomas Edward
Spalding, Catherine
Spalding, John Lancaster

PUBLICATIONS AND RESEARCH

Baltimore Catechism

Catechism of the Catholic Church

Catholic Education: A Journal of Inquiry and Practice

Catholic High Schools and Minority Students

Catholic High Schools: Their Impact on Low-Income Students

Catholic publishers

Catholic School, The

Catholic School on the Threshold of the Third Millennium, The

Catholic Schools and the Common Good

Catholic Schools in a Declining Church

Catholic Schools Make a Difference: Twenty-five Years of Research

Catholic Schools Still Make a Difference: Ten Years of Research, 1991–2000

Catholic Teacher, The

Education by Choice: The Case for Family Control

Education of Catholic Americans, The

Education: To Whom Does It Belong?

Effective Catholic Schools: An Exploration

Equality of Educational Opportunity

Giving Form to the Vision

Guidelines for Doctrinally Sound Catechetical Material

Guiding Growth in Christian Social Living

Foreword

When our national culture was still forming, Catholic education grew largely out of the convents and seminaries. Instructors and administrators were overwhelmingly religious, imbued with vocational fervor both as educators and as ministers of Jesus' teaching. Devoted and in the context of the times, highly professional, they produced substantial numbers of graduates of superior intellectual and moral quality.

Now most of the leadership and instruction in American Catholic education is carried on by laypersons, often trained in public institutions. Still, Catholic education in the United States continues to be hailed for its excellence and sophistication, avoiding many of the ailments plaguing its secular counterpart.

Much of the thought, research, and spiritual/moral foundation for this continuity is set out here in these two volumes, available as example, inspiration, and caution for those who may follow in the long tradition of Catholic education or who want to learn more about its rich and varied history.

There are resources here for educators in the inner cities where Catholic schools welcome students from virtually any family background. There are materials helpful and relevant for private education in general, whose organizations are strongly supported by our Catholic educational community, and there is much to consider for any student of education.

It will become plain, in reading this encyclopedia, that Catholic education has been a major influence in the flow of American pedagogical thought and application, a shining example of the success possible where the practice of teaching stands firmly on moral and intellectual bedrock.

Thanks are due to the many thoughtful contributors herein for their research and analysis and for their intellectual devotion to the interests of the future of American Catholic education.

Glenn Anne McPhee, OP
Secretary for Education
United States Conference of Catholic Bishops

Preface

Catholic Schools in the United States: An Encyclopedia aims to provide a single, comprehensive resource for anyone interested in Catholic education from kindergarten through twelfth grade (K–12). Its 340 entries seek to educate its readers, initiated and uninitiated alike, about the basic tenets, issues, and movements in Catholic education. It treats historical, philosophical, academic, social, ecclesiastical, and legal matters that have been and are crucial to Catholic schooling.

The encyclopedia is a comprehensive reference tool for all matters related to Catholic schooling. It seeks to inform the inquiring reader and the serious student of education about one of the most successful and effective educational agencies ever designed—Catholic schools. These schools have made and are making a vital contribution to the Church and to civic life in the United States.

The book begins with a comprehensive historical overview of Catholic schools in the United States, including a substantive bibliography. The entries in this encyclopedia, arranged alphabetically A–Z, are related to such larger topics as administration; anti-Catholicism; church documents; curriculum; education associations, issues, leaders, and programs; ethnic groups; finance; governance; government aid; identity and mission; institutions/school types; learning styles and theories; legal matters; moral education; parents; people; publications and research; religion; religious men and women; students; teachers; technology; and Vatican persons and agencies. The encyclopedia ends with a lengthy list of references and index. As such, *Catholic Schools in the United States: An Encyclopedia* is a one-stop reference source for libraries, professors, teachers, historians, pastors, principals, bishops, superintendents, policymakers, students and researchers of education, and all those interested in seeking to understand why Catholic schools have been and remain so successful in their educational mission.

Acknowledgments

Ronald Nuzzi acknowledges his administrative assistant at the University of Notre Dame, Gayle Daugherty, for her invaluable help. Ellis Joseph acknowledges Vera and Don Gast for their affirmations. Thomas Hunt acknowledges with gratitude the indispensable aid of his graduate assistant at the University of Dayton, Nicole LaSelle, and the support of Dianne Hoops and her colleagues in the Roesch Library. All three editors recognize the generous assistance provided by the Dean of the School of Education and Allied Professions at the University of Dayton, Dr. Thomas J. Lasley II, and the contributions made by the authors of the entries.

Historical Overview of Catholic Schools in the United States

THE COLONIAL PERIOD

Catholic schools were established in Louisiana and Florida as early as the seventeenth century. Religious zeal was the main reason for their establishment, and missionaries sought to spread the Catholic faith thereby. Conflict with civil authorities occurred in the pre-Revolutionary schools, especially in colonies under English (Protestant) rule.

THE REVOLUTIONARY ERA

The Catholic population in what was now the United States of America was sparse and scattered. Catholic schools were but one of many concerns of the nation's first bishop, John Carroll of Baltimore. In 1792 he issued his first pastoral letter, in which he described the "virtuous and Christian instruction of youth as a principal object of pastoral solicitude" and emphasized the "necessity of a pious and Catholic education of the young to insure their growing up in the faith" (Buetow, 1970, p. 45). Georgetown College and St. Mary's College in Baltimore were among the educational institutions opened during Carroll's tenure as bishop.

The First Amendment to the federal Constitution required that no church could be established, nor could the free exercise of religion be prohibited. Unfortunately, religious discrimination against Catholics did occur in the several states during the nation's infancy. Catholic clerical leaders were concerned with preserving the faith of Catholics in the country and looked to the establishment of Catholic schools as one means to attain this goal. Their efforts would increase as the nineteenth century arrived.

CATHOLIC SCHOOLS IN THE MID-NINETEENTH CENTURY

Catholic schools multiplied as the nineteenth century progressed. Abetted by immigration and by the pan-Protestant nature of the common school movement spearheaded by Horace Mann, the nation's Catholic bishops, both in councils and individually, supported the founding and frequenting of Catholic parish elementary schools. In early and mid-century the bishops' urging was due to what they perceived was danger to the faith posed by Protestant influence, as witnessed by the reading of the King James version of the Bible and attendant devotional exercises; as the century progressed, the secular state became the major adversary. The bishops' position, though by no means unanimous, was not always followed by the laity, even when spiritual penalties were attached to noncompliance. Ethnicity, as was the case for German Americans, for example, contributed heavily to the growing Catholic school movement. Despite the poverty that beset most Catholics, there were 1,444 parish schools in existence by 1875. The bishops who backed Catholic schools, sometimes referred to as "conservative," were bolstered by a declaration of the Congregation for the Propagation of the Faith (a Vatican body with jurisdiction over the missionary arm of the Catholic Church) in 1875. This was followed by the influential Third Plenary Council of Baltimore in 1884, which decreed that within two years every Catholic parish was to have a parish school and that all Catholic parents were to send their children there under pain of sin, unless the bishop of the diocese gave permission otherwise.

ETHNICITY, RELIGIOSITY, AND AMERICANISM AT THE TURN OF THE CENTURY

The Catholic population increased almost 300 percent from 1880, escalating from just over six million in 1880 to 17,735,553 in 1920. Catholic school enrollment increased more than 400 percent in that same period, from just over 400,000 to 1,701,219. Meanwhile, in public education, at least in urban areas, morality was increasingly divorced from religion, and citizenship education became the priority for public schools. Faced with a new adversary, secular education under the auspices of the civil state, Church authorities adopted the motto "Every Catholic child in a Catholic school." Despite all of its efforts, including persuasion and canonical penalties, the Church was to fall far short of this goal. The situation led to an intra-Church fracas, featuring Archbishop Ireland of St. Paul, on the "liberal" side, and a collection of Irish and German American bishops, labeled "conservative," on the other. Generally, the "liberals" favored cooperating with government in educational matters, and the "conservatives" held fast to the necessity of Catholic schools for the good of the faith. Neither American Plenary Council (e.g., Baltimore III in 1884) nor Vatican document nor papal legate could settle the issue; the intervention of Pope Leo XIII was required to end the open warfare. At issue was the proper relationship of the Church with the American civil state, especially in the question of who had the primary authority and responsibility for educating children and, essentially, what constituted education. Pride in, and the desire to preserve, their ethnic heritage on the part of some recent immigrants played a significant role in the conflict. The beginnings of widespread secondary schooling in the 1910s, abetted by the patriotism engendered by the war (and the hostility to anything "foreign" that the war generated), contributed to the tensions. The identification of public schools with "good citizenship" took many forms, even leading to a law (in Oregon) requiring attendance at public schools for children between the ages of 8 and 16 on the grounds that said attendance was necessary for good citizenship. The U.S. Supreme Court overturned that law in 1925, in the process holding that the "child is not the mere creature of the state" (*Pierce v. Society of Sisters*).

CATHOLIC SCHOOLS IN THE ERA OF WORLD WARS

In the years following World War I considerable emphasis was placed on the professionalism of Catholic schools. Begun by Thomas Edward Shields of Catholic University and intensified by his pupil George Johnson, Catholic schools addressed issues such as teacher certification and school accreditation. Johnson, in particular, took the lead in establishing a Catholic presence in professional educational matters at the national level. He also worked to bring together the Catholic bishops, the professional Catholic educators, and the educators at the Catholic University of America.

Two other issues surfaced during this period. The first related to the preparation of the sister-teachers who staffed the Catholic parish elementary schools. After some debate, their preparation was left to their respective religious orders. The second issue dealt with the growing secondary school movement. Beginning with the post–World War I years, public secondary education began a steep and steady increase. Prior to the war, about 10 percent of high school-age youth were in high school; this proportion climbed rapidly upward in the next two decades. This increase brought new challenges to Catholic schools; what should be the Church's response? The era witnessed the establishment and growth of the central Catholic high school, along with private high schools, usually single-gender, that were owned and operated by religious orders of men and women. Questions such as the responsibility of the Church to include terminal educational programs, such as vocational education, in Catholic secondary schools arose. Jurisdictional (interparish) issues also clouded the educational sky.

Pope Pius XI, faced with the rising tide of both fascism and communism and their assertions of control over education, authored his seminal encyclical "The Christian Education of Youth" in 1929. The encyclical, which called for the internal assent of Catholics to its teachings, held that while parents were their children's primary educators, this education must be carried out in accord with the teaching of the Church. The state, as a civil society, also had rights in schooling but must respect the more fundamental rights of parent and Church. The Pope declared that the true end of education was supernatural, eternal destiny and that the ideal was for all Catholic children to be in a Catholic school.

The 1930s saw Catholic schools confronted with the hard times brought on by the depression. The schools survived, in large measure due to the "contributed services" of their sister-teachers and the loyalty of Catholic parents. In 1940, a year before the nation entered yet another world war, the Supreme Court handed down a decision that was to affect the legal future of Catholic schools. Ruling in *Cantwell v. Connecticut*, the Court made the First Amendment applicable to the states through the Fourteenth Amendment. Subsequent legal battles over educational issues that affected Catholic schools would be fought on new terrain, the First Amendment.

IN THE WAKE OF WORLD WAR II

Catholic schools rode a wave of popularity in the aftermath of the war. Schools were overcrowded, and dioceses could not keep up with the demand of parents for Catholic education for their children. Nonpublic school enrollment increased 118 percent between 1940 and 1959, compared to a 36 percent increase in public schools. Policy issues abounded; so did financial ones. There were challenging curricular issues, as well as concerns related to personnel and relations with government and the public sector. Catholic Church authorities continued to identify attendance at a Catholic school as a religious matter. In 1958 a majority of dioceses that responded to a survey (55 of 104) had a statute that required parents to send their children to a Catholic school; 12 of the 55 imposed a reserved sin, one "reserved" to the bishop for forgiveness, on parents who failed to comply with the regulation.

In 1947 the Supreme Court adjudged, on a five-to-four ruling, that public funds could be used to transport children to Church-affiliated schools. The Court's decision, which was bitterly opposed in some quarters, was based on the "child benefit" principle and on the "public purpose" of the legislation. Financial pressures contributed to efforts in some quarters of the church hierarchy as well as to lay organizations, such as the Citizens for Educational Freedom (CEF), to obtain government financial aid (often "indirect" aid, such as assistance to parents) for Catholic schools.

In 1959 Catholic school enrollment stood at 4,101,792 in elementary schools and 810,768 in high schools. Two years prior, Archbishop Albert G. Meyer of Milwaukee, president of the National Catholic Educational Association (NCEA), lauded both the quantity and quality of Catholic schools. The feeling was widespread that Catholic schools, despite financial strains and overcrowding, were well-off. One voice who disagreed was the Catholic historian John Tracy Ellis, who felt that overemphasis of the school as an agency for moral development led to an inadequate concern for its intellectual role.

THE TURBULENT 1960s

Pope John XXIII convened the Second Vatican Council (Vatican II) in October 1962. The council was to shake the moorings of the Catholic Church and its schools in the United States. The first indication of what was to come occurred in 1964 with Mary Perkins Ryan's *Are Parochial Schools the Answer? Catholic Education in the Light of the Council.* The book, which elicited an emotional response from many Catholic educators, charged the schools with being anachronistic and an illustration of misplaced priorities. Ryan averred that the schools had well served an impoverished immigrant population in a clerical-dominated church in the nineteenth century; however, they were outdated and no longer needed in the post–Vatican II era. She called on parents to assume their God-given responsibility of educating their children, so empowered by adult education programs and emphasis on the liturgy.

Vatican II had come out in support of Catholic schools, declaring that the Church's involvement in education was "demonstrated by the Catholic school." The school, "evidenced by the gospel spirit of freedom and charity," was to prepare its students for this world and for the "advancement of the reign of God." The gathered prelates again reminded parents of their "duty to entrust their children to Catholic schools when and where this is possible."

In 1965–1966, Catholic school enrollment reached an all-time high of 5.6 million pupils, constituting 87 percent of the country's nonpublic school enrollment. The reassurances of Vatican II notwithstanding, Catholic enrollment plummeted in the years following, caused by internal doubt about its mission and identity as well as escalating costs. The doubt was publicly expressed in some unexpected quarters, including a cardinal archbishop and the leadership of teaching religious orders.

The closing of Catholic schools in the late 1960s, many of which were in the inner cities, led some to question whether the Church was abandoning its historic commitment to the poor. Some saw the maintenance of Catholic schools for non-Catholic racial minorities in the central cities as the embodiment of the Church's teaching on social justice. Others thought the schools should follow the movement of Catholics to the suburbs. The Church's educational efforts on behalf of the poor in this period were brought out in a number of ways.

Vatican II had emphasized the responsibility of laypeople in the affairs of the Church. This injunction took the form of participation on school boards in education, at the diocesan, area, and parish levels. The National Catholic Educational Association (NCEA) and the Citizens for Educational Freedom (CEF) were among those who called for increased community support on behalf of Catholic schools.

The 1960s witnessed two prestigious research studies on Catholic schools. One was conducted by researchers Andrew Greeley and Peter Rossi from the University of Chicago; the second by Reginald Neuwien under the auspices of the University of Notre Dame. The study by Greeley and Rossi focused on the effects of a Catholic education that were manifested in adulthood. The Notre Dame study evaluated religious and secular outcomes of Catholic schools and reported on the major strengths and weaknesses of Catholic schools.

Brought on at least in part by financial pressure, Catholic leaders sought increased government financial support for their schools. Their efforts met with some success, as in the New York textbook case, which allowed public schools to lend secular textbooks on the state-approved list to pupils in nonpublic schools. Attempts to fund the secular services, such as teaching reading and math, were initiated and faced judicial scrutiny in the early 1970s.

Catholic bishops, aware of the malaise that had infected Catholic schools, published "Catholic Schools Are Indispensable" in 1967. It is evident from this document that the bishops were attempting to bolster the morale of Catholic educators and the schools' patrons, which had been shaken severely by recent events. Nonetheless, as the 1960s came to a close, Catholic education was in a state of deep gloom.

THE 1970s—THE TURMOIL CONTINUES

The decline in enrollment continued in the 1970s. This decline, when combined with the loss of a sense of purpose of the schools on the part of Catholics, presented challenges of the greatest magnitude for the schools' advocates. The Catholic bishops published their influential pastoral *To Teach as Jesus Did* in 1972, in which they proclaimed a threefold ministry for Catholic schools, namely, to teach doctrine, to build community, and to serve all humankind. Above all, the bishops beseeched Catholics to avoid a defeatist attitude.

The bishops continued this message in 1977, when they penned that Catholic schools embody the purpose of Catholic education; growth in faith was central to their purpose. The schools' cause was aided by Pope John Paul II in 1979, when he declared that the quality of religious instruction integrated into the children's education was the basic reason for both the existence and frequenting of Catholic schools.

The decade of the 1970s also witnessed a turn on the part of Catholic educators, who called for concentration on their uniqueness, rather than comparing them to public schools. The school as "faith community" became a central focus of the schools. Catholic educators, especially principals, were to play a critical role in developing the "faith community." Teachers were called on to assist in this process with their students. The task was more formidable, given the significant drop in the percent of religious teachers (from 56.7 to 24.8 from 1968–1969 to 1981–1982). The drop caused significant economic problems for Catholic schools, since the religious received but a pittance in financial compensation. Additionally, new ways had to be developed to instill the indispensable religiosity in the staff, which was steadily becoming composed of laypeople.

So many lay teachers gave rise to discussions—and sometimes even strikes—over the appropriate relationship between the teachers and the schools' governing bodies. The Church was hard-pressed at times to apply the social teaching established earlier by Popes Leo XIII and Pius XI on the rights of workers to form associations to represent them and to strike, if need be, in support of their just demands.

Efforts to obtain financial support from the government continued. The "excessive entanglement" (between Church and state) criterion adjudicated in the *Lemon* decision obstructed many of these efforts. The Court reasoned that the surveillance required of teachers under religious authority constituted a violation of the Establishment Clause.

Yet, with all of the difficulties of the past decade, Andrew Greeley et al. reported in 1976 that Catholic schools had the firm support of Catholic laity, even to the extent that laity would contribute more financially to save a school in distress. Greeley, a noted sociologist, recommended that the bishops turn control of the schools over to the laity, who were both able and willing to run them, if the schools were to be successful.

RENAISSANCE IN THE 1980s

Enrollment decline continued to plague Catholic schools at the onset of the 1980s. Addressing the NCEA in 1982, Alfred McBride, a former NCEA official, identified three major challenges that confronted Catholic schools in the 1980s. The most fundamental was to keep Catholic schools Catholic in all aspects. Academic excellence constituted the second challenge, and developing a sound financial basis was the third.

Publications were directed to the growing presence of lay teachers and administrators in Catholic schools. Alfred McBride authored *The Christian Formation of Catholic Educators* in 1981, which was followed in 1982 by the Congregation's "Lay Catholics in Schools: Witnesses to Faith" and by an NCEA-sponsored booklet, *The Pre-Service Formation of Teachers for Catholic Schools*.

James Coleman and his colleagues attested to the academic achievement of Catholic schools during this period. Coleman maintained that the community support of Catholic schools, which he termed "social capital," gave them a distinct advantage over public schools. Coleman's conclusions were challenged, especially by public school backers.

Financial problems remained, especially for Catholic schools in the central cities, which were peopled by a majority of minority poor, in the main, non-Catholic. Relying on a combination of tuition and subsidy, these schools in particular had immense difficulty in meeting their growing costs. Schools looked to professional development personnel to meet these problems, with a development officer heading up public relations and fund-raising efforts. A study published by the Milwaukee-based Catholic League for Religious and Civil Rights in 1982 challenged the assertion that Catholic schools were focused on educating the elite, noting the existence of sixty-four schools in eight central cities, 54 percent of which were Title I recipients. These schools provided a safe environment, emphasized basic learning skills, and fostered moral values in their pupils, a third of whom were non-Catholic, and almost 70 percent minority.

The schools continued to receive less than total support from bishops and pastors, a phenomenon that had plagued them especially since the time of Vatican II.

The question of Catholic identity—what did it mean to be a Catholic school?— began its journey to the forefront in this era. An address by Pope John Paul II in 1987 stimulated discussion over this issue. The Pope's remarks were followed the next year by a document published by the Vatican-based Congregation for Catholic Education entitled "The Religious Dimension of Education in a Catholic School."

CATHOLIC SCHOOLS ENTER THE THIRD MILLENNIUM

In 1991–1992 there were 8,508 Catholic schools, of which 1,269 were secondary schools. Enrollment totaled 2,550,863, of which about 23 percent were minority and 12 percent non-Catholic. In 1998–1999, as the decade and century neared their conclusions, there were 8,217 Catholic schools with 36 schools having opened that year. Total Catholic school enrollment was listed as 2,648,844, with 1,990,947 in attendance at an elementary school. Forty-one percent of all schools had a waiting list for admission.

The NCEA sponsored a "National Congress on Catholic Schools for the 21st Century" in 1991. The main goals of the Congress were (1) to tell the story of the academic and religious effectiveness of Catholic schools; (2) to celebrate these schools' success and to broaden their support; and (3) to convene an assembly of key leaders in Catholic schooling to create strategies for the success of these schools. Papers were commissioned on Catholic Identity, Leadership, the Catholic Schools and Society, Catholic School Governance and Finance, and Public Policy and Catholic Schools.

An ethnographic study by Anthony Bryk et al. in 1993 heralded Catholic secondary schools for their accomplishments, namely, decentralization (with parental involvement), a shared set of moral beliefs (by parents, students, and faculty), a shared code of conduct (including human dignity and the belief that human reason can discern ethical truth), smallness of size (which promotes interaction between students, parents, and staff), and emphasis on academics (abetted by a concentration on basics).

Catholic schools experienced a slight increase in enrollment in the late 1990s. They have also been hit with the charge of "elitism," with the abandonment of the Catholic working class and the embracing of wealthy non-Catholics, people who do not consider themselves religious at all. These charges have been challenged by Catholic educators and others.

In the urban areas, where the financial crunch is felt most, Catholic schools are in the greatest danger, and, in fact, a number have been closed in recent years. Money, or lack of it, is the source of the difficulties. Where might financial help come from? One source is the government. Public vouchers have been employed in several places, most notably in Milwaukee and Cleveland. The legal standing of publicly supported vouchers has had a mixed review. The U.S. Supreme Court, in *Zelman v. Simmons-Harris*, upheld their constitutionality in 2002. It remains to be seen how state legislatures will act in light of this decision. Government aid, even indirect through parents, is no panacea. While it would alleviate the financial stress on these schools, enabling them to pay living wage salaries coupled with benefits to their staffs, and simultaneously make them affordable to families of modest and lesser means, the presence of students and professional personnel who do not espouse the religious value of Catholic schooling could well have an adverse effect on the schools' religious identity. Further, public aid, if accompanied by government control, could cause these schools to become religiously barren, as has been the case with state subsidization of churches in several European countries.

In February 2001 private sources were providing assistance to parents in seventy-nine cities across the land. Regularly employing the Federal Reduced Lunch Program as the standard for qualifiers, these programs have demonstrated a consistent growth since their inception in the late 1980s.

In 1998 the Vatican recognized that Catholic schools were in a difficult period, one that called for courageous renewal. Writing in 2000, Youniss and Convey put it this way:

> The system of education that took over in the nineteenth century and reached its quantitative peak in 1965 is unlikely ever to be reconstituted. That system produced results that have been of obvious worth to the Catholic Church and the nation at large. There are still many contributions this system can make. But to ensure that they will be made, Catholic schools must be viewed in the context of significant issues in the Church and nation. Only then can reasonable options be considered realistically from educational, social, and religious perspectives. (Youniss and Convey, 2000, p. 10)

In a follow-up book that same year, also made possible by the Lilly Foundation, which sponsored the "Legacy at the Crossroads: The Future of Catholic Schools," Youniss, Convey, and McLellan wrote:

> Our work has convinced us that Catholic schooling in the United States is indeed at a crossroads. Our hope is that in publishing the present volume, we can help educators, scholars, and policymakers focus on needs and opportunities. Catholic education has given us a legacy well worth continuing. By clarifying the current status, we want to ensure that its future will be even more worthy of respect. (Youniss, Convey, and McLellan, 2000, p. v)

The Institute for Catholic Educational Leadership (ICEL) at the University of San Francisco was host to a summit conference for researchers on Catholic schools in March 2000. The summit concluded with reflection on issues prominent today that were not ten years ago. Chief among these were public and private voucher arrangements; growth in home schooling; impact of charter schools; teacher shortage; stress on accountability and competition in the broader education sector; emergence of the Web; impact of a growing disparity between wealthy and poor; and struggles related to ecclesial identity.

What can Catholic educators look for in the future? The mission of Catholic schools will likely remain consistent but will be shaped according to the realities of time and place. Many backers of Catholic schools will join with other citizens in pursuit of school choice, obtaining government funds that they believe will empower parents to choose the school they deem appropriate for their children. Finally, Catholic education can anticipate sustained emphasis on the mission of the Catholic school in evangelization, in building community, and in apostolic service, which constitute the sine qua non of Catholic schooling: Catholic identity.

FURTHER READING

The Colonial Period

Harold A. Buetow, *Of Singular Benefit: The Story of U.S. Catholic Education* (New York: Macmillan, 1970); Timothy Walch, *Parish School: American Catholic Parochial Education from Colonial Times to the Present* (New York: Crossroad, 1996).

The Revolutionary Era

Harold A. Buetow, *Of Singular Benefit: The Story of U.S. Catholic Education* (New York: Macmillan, 1970); Timothy Walch, *Parish School: American Catholic Parochial Education from Colonial Times to the Present* (New York: Crossroad, 1996).

Catholic Schools in the Mid-nineteenth Century

Harold A. Buetow, *Of Singular Benefit: The Story of U.S. Catholic Education* (New York: Macmillan, 1970); James A. Burns, *Catholic Education: A Study of Conditions* (New York: Arno Press and the New York Times, 1969); James A. Burns, *The Growth and Development of the Catholic School System in the United States* (New York: Arno Press and the New York Times, 1969); Robert D. Cross, "Origins of the Catholic Parochial Schools in America," *The American Benedictine Review* 16 (1965): 194–200; Peter Guilday, *A History of the Councils of Baltimore, 1791–1884* (New York: Macmillan, 1932); Timothy Walch, *Parish School: American Catholic Parochial Education from Colonial Times to the Present* (New York: Crossroad, 1996).

Ethnicity, Religiosity, and Americanism at the Turn of the Century

Colman J. Barry, *The Catholic Church and German Americans* (Milwaukee: Bruce, 1953); Harold A. Buetow, *Of Singular Benefit: The Story of U.S. Catholic Education* (New York: Macmillan, 1970); Marvin Lazerson, "Understanding American Catholic Educational History," *History of Education Quarterly* 17, 3 (Fall 1977): 297–317; *Pierce v. Society of Sisters* 268 U.S. 510 (1925); Daniel Reilly, *The School Controversy, 1891–1893* (Washington, DC: Catholic University of America Press, 1944); Gerald Shaughnessy, *Has the Immigrant Kept the Faith?* (New York: Arno Press and the New York Times, 1969).

Catholic Schools in the Era of World Wars

Harold A. Buetow, *Of Singular Benefit: The Story of U.S. Catholic Education* (New York: Macmillan, 1970); James A. Burns, *The Growth and Development of the Catholic School System* (New York: Arno Press and the New York Times, 1969); *Cantwell v. Connecticut*, 210 U.S. 296 (1940); Neil G. McCluskey, *Catholic Viewpoint on Education* (Garden City, NY: Hanover House, 1959); Pope Pius XI, *The Christian Education of Youth (Divini Illius Magistri)*, in *Five Great Encyclicals* (New York: Paulist Press, 1939).

In the Wake of World War II

Virgil C. Blum, *Freedom of Choice in Education* (New York: Paulist Press, 1963); Harold A. Buetow, *Of Singular Benefit: The Story of U.S. Catholic Education* (New York: Macmillan, 1970); *Everson v. Board of Education*, 330 U.S. 1 (1947); Timothy Walch, *Parish School: American Catholic Parochial Education from Colonial Times to the Present* (New York: Crossroad, 1996).

The Turbulent 1960s

Walter M. Abbott, ed., *The Documents of Vatican II* (New York: Guild Press, 1966); Harold A. Buetow, *Of Singular Benefit: The Story of U.S. Catholic Education* (New York: Macmillan, 1970); *Central School District v. Allen*, 392 U.S. 206 (1968); O'Neill C. D'Amour, "Reconstituting Patterns of Education," in C. Albert Koob, ed., *What Is Happening to Catholic Education?* (Washington, DC: National Catholic Educational Association, 1966); James C. Donohue, "New Priorities for Catholic Education," *America* 13 (April 1968): 476–479; Andrew M. Greeley and Peter H. Rossi, *The Education of Catholic Americans* (Chicago: Aldine, 1966); National Catholic Educational Association, *Voice of the Community: The Board Movement in Catholic Education* (Washington, DC: National Catholic Educational Association, 1967); Reginald A. Neuwien, ed., *Catholic Schools in Action* (Notre Dame, IN: University of Notre Dame Press, 1966); Mary Perkins Ryan, *Are Parochial Schools the Answer? Catholic Education in the Light of the Council* (New York: Guild Press, 1964).

The 1970s—The Turmoil Continues

Andrew M. Greeley, William C. McReady, and Kathleen McCourt, *Catholic Schools in a Declining Church* (Kansas City, KS: Sheed and Ward, 1976); Pope John Paul II, "Catechesi Tradendae," *The Living Light* 17 (Spring 1980): 44–89; *Lemon v. Kurtzman*, 403 U.S. 602 (1971); National Catholic Educational Association, *Giving Form to the Vision: The Pastoral in Practice* (Washington, DC: National Catholic Educational Association, 1974); National Conference of Catholic Bishops, "Sharing the Light of Faith: National Catechetical Directory for Catholics in the United States" (Washington, DC: United States Catholic Conference, 1979); National Conference of Catholic Bishops, *To Teach as Jesus Did: A Pastoral Message on Catholic Education* (Washington, DC: United States Catholic Conference, 1973); *National Labor Relations Board v. The Catholic Archbishop of Chicago, et al.*, 99 S. CT. 1313 (1979).

Renaissance in the 1980s

James G. Cibulka, Timothy J. O'Brien, and Donald Zewe, *Inner-City Private Elementary Schools: A Study* (Milwaukee: Marquette University Press, 1982); James Coleman and Thomas Hoffer, *Public and Private High Schools: The Impact on Communities* (New York: Basic Books, 1987); James Coleman, Thomas Hoffer, and Sally Kilgore, *High School Achievement: Public, Catholic, and Private Schools* (New York: Basic Books, 1982); Alfred A. McBride, *The Christian Formation of Catholic Educators* (Washington, DC: National Catholic Educational Association, 1981); J. Stephen O'Brien, *Mixed Messages: What Bishops and Priests Say about Catholic Schools* (Washington, DC: National Catholic Educational Association, 1987); Lourdes Sheehan, "A Study of the Functions of School Boards in the Educational System of the Roman Catholic Church in the United States," Unpublished doctoral dissertation,

Virginia Polytechnic Institute and State University, 1981; Sacred Congregation for Catholic Education, "The Religious Dimension of Education in a Catholic School" (Washington, DC: United States Catholic Conference, 1988).

Catholic Schools Enter the Third Millennium

David P. Baker and Cornelius Riordan, "The 'Eliting' of the American Catholic School and the National Education Crisis," *Phi Delta Kappan* 80, 1 (September 1998): 16–23; Anthony S. Bryk, Valerie E. Lee, and Peter B. Holland, *Catholic Schools and the Common Good* (Cambridge: Harvard University Press, 1993); John J. Convey, *Catholic Schools Make a Difference: Twenty-five Years of Research* (Washington, DC: National Catholic Educational Association, 1992); Andrew M. Greeley, "The So-Called Failure of Catholic Schools," *Phi Delta Kappan* 80, 1 (September 1998): 24–25; Michael J. Guerra, Regina Haney, and Robert J. Kealey, comps., *Executive Summary: Catholic Schools for the 21st Century* (Washington, DC: National Catholic Educational Association, 1992); Thomas C. Hunt, Thomas E. Oldenski, and Theodore J. Wallace, eds., *Catholic School Leadership: An Invitation to Lead* (London and New York: Falmer Press, 2000); Thomas C. Hunt, Ellis A. Joseph, and Ronald J. Nuzzi, eds., *Catholic Schools Still Make a Difference: Ten Years of Research, 1991–2000* (Washington, DC: National Catholic Educational Association, 2002); Thomas C. Hunt, Ellis A. Joseph, and Ronald J. Nuzzi, eds., *Handbook of Research on Catholic Education* (Westport, CT: Greenwood Publishing Group, 2001); Francis D. Kelly, *What Makes a School Catholic?* (Washington, DC: National Catholic Educational Association, 1991); Terence H. McLaughlin, Joseph M. O'Keefe, and Bernadette O'Keefe, eds., *The Contemporary Catholic School: Context, Identity and Diversity* (London: Falmer Press, 1996); Sacred Congregation for Catholic Education, "The Catholic School on the Threshold of the Third Millennium" (Washington, DC: United States Catholic Conference, 1997); James Youniss and John J. Convey, eds., *Catholic Schools at the Crossroads: Survival and Transformation* (New York: Teachers College Press, 2000); James Youniss, John J. Convey, and Jeffrey A. McLellan, eds., *The Catholic Character of Catholic Schools* (Notre Dame, IN: University of Notre Dame Press, 2000); *Zelman v. Simmons-Harris*, 122 S. Ct. 2460 (2002).

Thomas C. Hunt

CATHOLIC SCHOOLS IN THE UNITED STATES

Academic organizations

The governance structures, the physical arrangement of students within school buildings, the scope and sequence of educational experiences, and the educational practices employed in schools are designed to ensure a quality education for all students. Catholic school academic organization is typified by strong local control of schools that is formalized in canon law. This governance structure effectively places a great deal of authority in the hands of the principal and minimizes the educational bureaucracy so prevalent in public schools. Catholic schools typically are smaller than public schools, have high academic expectations for students that are expressed in terms of elevated graduation requirements, and rely on a common core of academic curriculum for all students that maximizes the exposure of students of all ability levels to rigorous academic courses.

The Code of Canon Law (1983) places the oversight of the Catholic educational enterprise in the hands of ecclesiastical authorities. These authorities—bishops, heads of religious orders, and pastors—in turn, delegate to competent professionals the task of carrying out the educational mission of the Church. In practice this governance structure places a great deal of power and authority in the hands of the educational administrators. Hunt, Joseph, and Nuzzi (2001) cite several studies that indicate vast differences between Catholic school principals and public school principals in terms of their role and function, including greater autonomy and greater influence of Catholic school principals in the day-to-day decisions and management of the school, the lack of bureaucratic structures in Catholic schools that typically inhibit opportunities for instructional leadership by the principal, and the ability of Catholic school principals to reward and sanction teachers more frequently. Additional research spanning the previous decade indicates that Catholic school principals hold high expectations for all students, including low-ability students. Indeed, principals in Catholic schools understand their role to include primary responsibility for everything that happens within the school.

Catholic schools are typically organized as K–8 elementary schools, K–12 school systems, or 9–12 high schools. Between 1995 and 1999, the National Catholic Educational Association (NCEA) reported middle school data as a separate category from the elementary school data. The annual statistical report for the 1998–1999 school year revealed that of the 8,217 Catholic schools in the United States, only 127 were middle schools (McDonald, 1999).

Catholic schools also tend to be smaller in terms of student population than public schools. The United States Catholic Elementary and Secondary Schools annual statistical report for the 2000–2001 school year, drawing on data from the National Center for Educational Statistics, indicated that while more than 70 percent of public schools have a student population of 300 or more, only 35.5 percent of Catholic schools fall into this category (McDonald, 2001). This smaller size is more conducive for the development of strong interpersonal relationships among and between the faculty and students. A growing body of research is identifying both small school size and communal school environments as strong correlates of effective schools.

The most significant research on the academic organization of Catholic schools published in recent years is that of Bryk, Lee, and Holland (1993). Bryk et al. examined the common school hypothesis advanced by earlier research on Catholic schools. Their study included field research in seven secondary schools from across the country, data from the National Center for Educational Statistics, and data from the National Catholic Educational Association. Even after controlling for socioeconomic status, prior educational experience, race, and selection bias on the part of parents choosing Catholic education for their children, they found that Catholic school students are more likely to be assigned to an academic track where they encounter a more restricted and academically challenging curriculum that in turn translates into higher achievement. Bryk et al. (1993) note that the largest portion of a Catholic school student's curriculum is dictated through the prescriptive graduation requirements resulting in students from all tracks taking more academic courses than students in equivalent tracks in public schools. They conclude that "Catholic high schools take a direct, active role in deciding what their students *should* learn and deliberately create an academic structure to advance this aim" (p. 124). Furthermore, the common curriculum "exerts a strong integrating force on both students and adults, binding them together in a common round of school life that encourages each person's best efforts" (Bryk et al., 1993, p. 125). After citing copious statistical controls for selection bias, characteristics of students, teachers, and schools, the authors nevertheless declare that "we have found substantial variation among schools in teacher commitment and student engagement that is largely explained by the communal character of schools. Our results indicate that the internal organization of schools as communities fosters, *literally creates*, the engagement of school members in its mission" (Bryk et al., 1993, p. 293). They conclude with recommendations for all schools derived from their research on the success of Catholic schools in the area of academic organization: offer a delimited technical core, develop a communal organization, employ a decentralized governance structure, and adopt an inspirational ideology. *See also*: Catholic Schools and the Common Good; Community; School size.

Further Reading: Anthony S. Bryk, Valerie E. Lee, and Peter B. Holland, *Catholic Schools and the Common Good* (Cambridge: Harvard University Press, 1993); Thomas C. Hunt, Ellis A. Joseph, and Ronald J. Nuzzi, eds., *Handbook of Research on Catholic Education* (Westport, CT: Greenwood Press, 2001); John Paul II, *Code of Canon Law* (Washington, DC: Canon Law Society, 1983); Dale McDonald, *United States Catholic Elementary and Secondary Schools 1998–1999: The Annual Statistical Report on Schools, Enrollment and Staffing* (Washington, DC: National Catholic Educational Association, 1999); Dale McDonald, *United States Catholic*

Elementary and Secondary Schools 2000–2001: The Annual Statistical Report on Schools, Enrollment and Staffing (Washington, DC: National Catholic Educational Association, 2001).

John T. James

Academics

The broad range of academic subjects represents a variety of approaches to the acquisition of truth and knowledge. In addition, pedagogies abound in the world of education, with little consensus on how to best acquire truth and knowledge. Privett (2000) succinctly depicted the disarray of curriculum today and clearly identified the Catholic approach: "Today, we live with the spoiled fruits of the Renaissance focus on the content of knowledge—increasingly fragmented subdivisions of knowledge with little sense of the purpose that directs humanistic education: the full and integral development of the human person" (p. 53).

Groome (1998) proposed a humanizing pedagogical approach to the curriculum of a Catholic school that, he wrote, "suggests a community of co-learners in conversation" (p. 429). He continued, "The essential dynamic of a humanizing pedagogy is to mediate between people's lives in the world and the legacy of tradition—in the humanities, sciences, and arts; and for religious education, in the Story and Vision of its community of faith over time" (p. 430). This mediation between life and tradition, as foundational to the curriculum of a Catholic school, reverberates throughout the church documents on education. For example, the National Conference of Catholic Bishops in 1972 wrote: "The integration of religious truth and values with life distinguishes the Catholic school from other schools. This is a matter of crucial importance today in view of contemporary trends and pressures to compartmentalize life and learning and to isolate the religious dimension of existence from other areas of human life" (#105).

The Congregation for Catholic Education (1988) specifically urged educators to develop integrated curricula that will overcome fragmented subdivisions of knowledge. These Roman authors advised that teachers who instruct in discrete subject areas "all have the opportunity to present a complete picture of the human person, including the religious dimension" (#55). For example, the Congregation for Catholic Education described the religious dimension of the study of history as a progression, beginning with the cultivation of a "taste for historical truth" (#58) that would involve the development of the ability to critically analyze texts. The next step would be to assist students to perceive history as reality, "the drama of human grandeur and human misery" with the human person as the protagonist who projects onto the world the good and evil that dwell within human beings. Thus, history is represented as a global struggle between these two fundamental realities that are subject to moral decision-making. To this end, the teacher is advised to help students to view history holistically, encompassing the development of civilizations and the awareness of progress in such areas as economic development, human freedom, and international cooperation.

A subsequent step in addressing the religious dimension in the teaching of history, according to the Congregation for Catholic Education (1988), is to invite students, when they are ready to appreciate this aspect, to reflect upon the human struggle as rooted "within the divine history of universal salvation. At this moment, the religious dimension of history begins to shine forth in all its luminous grandeur" (#59). The distinctiveness of Catholic education is evident when each subject area in the Catholic school is taught from such a perspective, which, according to Groome (1998), involves a "humanizing pedagogy" that mediates between students' lives in the world and the legacy of tradition. He suggested an "overall dynamic of from Life to Tradition to Life, to Tradition to Life to Tradition, and so on—in an endless and creative exchange between learners" own lives in the world and the legacy of those before and around them" (p. 430).

Durka (2002) further elaborated upon a Christian, humanizing approach to education. She referred to Clement of Alexandria, who, toward the end of the second century, described the work of Jesus Christ as that of a *paedagogus*, a companion who nourished the heart, mind, soul, and body of those with whom he walked. She stated that those who teach in the Christian tradition "uniquely participate in the work of accompanying students in the process of education" (p. 21) and that this education is not restricted to producing lawyers, doctors, and engineers. Although careers, job specializations, and sustaining a livelihood are important, they are not sufficient. "This is not an education *for* anything; it is an education *of* someone, of a human person. Such a perspective allows us to realize that whatever furthers humanization furthers the work of the church" (p. 21). Thus, instruction in content areas, such as the sciences, literature, art, and religion, are the work of the Church, since whatever humanizes the student makes him or her more like God. Durka referred to the calling of the educator as a "holy work" with Jesus as one's companion-tutor in the process.

Groome (1998) proposed seven commitments that, in combination, constitute a humanizing pedagogy: *engaging* ("drawing learners into active participation from the beginning and to maintain their 'interest' throughout"), *attending* ("encouraging learners' attention . . . attending to everything that comes into their experience, initiative, and consciousness"), *expressing* (inviting learners' self-expression), *reflecting* (creating opportunities for learners to reflect on what they are learning), *accessing* (stimulating learners to become "active agents who rediscover the tradition for themselves more than having it 'poured in' or 'delivered' "), *appropriating* (bringing learners to their own knowledge and wisdom, "to have them appropriate from Life and Tradition what they see, understand, judge, and decide"), and *deciding* (inviting learners to choices and commitments) (pp. 431–439). He stated that, although he separates out these teaching strategies, in real-life teaching situations they occur nonsequentially and in myriad combinations. "Setting the seven out as a schema can heighten the intentionality of the educator and, while avoiding a rigid pattern, may suggest the dynamics of a humanizing pedagogy" (p. 431). *See also*: *Catholic Schools and the Common Good; Religious Dimension of Education in a Catholic School, The.*

Further Reading: Congregation for Catholic Education, *The Religious Dimension of Education in a Catholic School* (Boston: Daughters of St. Paul, 1988); Gloria Durka, *The Teacher's Calling, a Spirituality for Those Who Teach* (New York: Paulist Press, 2002); Thomas H. Groome, *Educating for Life: A Spiritual Vision for Every Teacher and Parent* (Allen, TX: Thomas More, 1998); National Conference of Catholic Bishops, *To Teach as Jesus Did: A Pastoral Message on Catholic Education* (Washington, DC: United States Catholic Conference, 1972); Stephen A. Privett, "The University and the Struggle for Justice," in Mary K. McCullough, ed., *The Just One Justices: The Role of Justice at the Heart of Catholic Higher Education* (Scranton, PA: University of Scranton Press, 2000).

Gini Shimabukuro

Academies

Academies were uniquely American educational institutions of the eighteenth and nineteenth centuries that embodied aspects of the Latin and English grammar schools and what was to become known in the future as the secondary school. The "academy" curriculum tended to be a mixture, in unpredictable proportions, of the traditional classical studies pursued in the Latin grammar school and the "realistic" or "practical" subjects and skills of the colonial English school. Academy programs also often included a religious aspect that might involve studies and/or church attendance. Regarding academies in America, Butts and Cremin (1953) observe: "The period from 1810 to 1840 . . . has often been called the age of the Academy. . . . [B]y 1850 there were probably more than 6,000 enrolling over a quarter of a million students" (p. 239).

An example of an early "academy" curriculum is the one proposed in 1751 by the famous Philadelphia Academy. Seybolt (1925) indicated, "Youth will be taught Latin, Greek, English, French, and German Languages, together with History, Geography, Chronology, Logic, and Rhetoric; also Writing, Arithmetic, Merchants Accounts, Geometry, Algebra, Surveying, Gauging, Navigation, Astronomy, Drawing in Perspective, and other mathematical Sciences; with natural and mechanical Philosophy, . . ." (pp. 98–99). Attending an academy provided schooling beyond the elementary level and was often the preference of students of middle-class origins. The comprehensiveness of the academy offerings often resulted in a democratically inclusive student body preparing for college or commerce or even to be teachers for elementary schools.

As was true of the English grammar schools, some academies continued the egalitarian practice of accepting both boys and girls. Academies dedicated to educating girls were also established. Butts and Cremin (1953) aver they "often became the basis for later foundations of colleges for women in the nineteenth century" (p. 127). It was often the practice to provide accommodations for boarding children at an academy. The quality of the level of education offered by academies varied greatly. Academies located in metropolitan areas such as Boston or New York usually provided more academically challenging courses than academies in rural localities.

Just as the Latin and English grammar school served as the curricular heritage of the academies, so the academies were the embryos for many high schools and colleges. This is the reason that the academy is often referred to as a "transitional" institution. The curriculum of some academies drifted toward an emphasis on classical course offerings whose aim was to prepare students for college. Among these are the well-known and -endowed Phillips academies of Andover, Massachusetts, and Exeter, New Hampshire. The movement from academies to high schools began in 1821 with the establishment of the first three-year high school in Boston. Lesser-known academies in the New England states became the high schools for their communities and locales. Many are still referred to by their original "academy" label, even though they were absorbed into the public school system many years ago.

In 1790, Catholics accounted for only 3.5 percent of the over 4 million residents of the newly established United States of America. From the very beginning of their work on the American continent, Catholic missionaries engaged in educational activities that ranged from catechesis, to direct attempts at schooling, to modeling and demonstrating skills that were regarded as beneficial for living. Catholic involvement in delivering education began very early in the story of the new American republic. Education was regarded by some of the religious orders that came to care for American

Catholics as their particular "apostolate" for the raising up of good and faithful Christians.

The "academy" as it had developed in America was adopted by the religious orders as an adequate model for offering and delivering education. Buetow (1970) indicates the prerequisites for admission to a Catholic academy included ". . . the ability to read and write, moral integrity, and enough money to pay the tuition fee" (p. 21). The American educational historians Butts and Cremin (1953) observe: "Particularly in the case of the Roman Catholics, the academy was an important phase of the parochial school system. Teaching orders such as the Jesuits, the Brothers of the Christian Schools, and the Sisters of Notre Dame de Namur established and conducted a number of thriving institutions during this period" (p. 278). One of the early Catholic academies was the Jesuits' Academy at Georgetown, which was launched with only two students on January 2, 1792. This academy evolved into a high school known as the Georgetown Preparatory School, into a college, and then into Georgetown University with charters from the federal Congress of the United States and the Roman Congregation for the Propagation of the Faith.

Historians have also recognized that Catholic academies established for women tended to serve as a catalyst for the advancement of the notion of "women's education" and influenced other groups to also make arrangements for the education of girls and women. The traditions and experience of members of the teaching orders had a very positive influence on the academies they established, which were often regarded as outstanding even by non-Catholics. Thus, the Nazareth Academy in Kentucky and the Visitation Academy of Georgetown were both heavily patronized by non-Catholic families of means and influence. It is also noteworthy that the tuition from academies was used by some religious orders to fund schools for the poor. As was the case with other American academies, the Catholic establishments were also supplanted by high schools, and others developed into Catholic colleges for men or women. *See also*: High schools; Private schools; *Public and Private High schools: The Impact of Communities.*

Further Reading: Harold A. Buetow, *Of Singular Benefit: The Story of U.S. Catholic Education* (New York: Macmillan, 1970); R. Freeman Butts and Lawrence A. Cremin, *A History of Education in American Culture* (New York: Holt, Rinehart, and Winston, 1953); Robert Emmett Curran, *The Bicentennial History of Georgetown University 1: From Academy to University, 1789–1889* (Washington, DC: Georgetown University Press, 1993); Robert Francis Seybolt, *Source Studies in American Colonial Education: The Private School* (Urbana: University of Illinois Press, 1925; New York: Arno Press and the New York Times, 1971).

Robert B. Williams

Accrediting agencies. *See* Regional accrediting agencies.

Administrative models
A schematic description of the governance structure that articulates how line authority is exercised within the Catholic school organization. The administrative model in use is largely dependent upon whether the Catholic school is parochial, interparochial, diocesan, or private and upon the discretion of the local ordinary or canonical administrator.

The bishop of a diocese typically delegates to the superintendent of schools the responsibility for the administration of all diocesan schools and as a coordinator of all parochial and inter-parochial schools. Pastors serve as the canonical administrator of parochial schools. For the inter-parochial schools, the bishop typically names a pastor from one of the sponsoring parishes as the canonical administrator. Diocesan, parochial, and inter-parochial schools also have principals and presidents that serve as site-based administrators of the school. Catholic schools sponsored by a religious community do not fall under the direct authority of the bishop except in those areas specifically identified in canon law. The religious congregations are juridic persons separate and distinct from the juridic person of the diocese, and therefore the governance of their schools is aligned with the dictates of the religious orders' constitution and governance structure. Religious congregations typically have a member of their order serving as the canonical administrator for a school or schools.

In most Catholic school administrative models, the administrator works collaboratively with a board that may be a consultative board, a board with limited jurisdiction, or a corporate board. A consultative board usually takes on the responsibilities of planning, policy development, financing, public relations, and evaluation. The canonical administrator or delegate typically sits on this board. The board serves as a policy-making body, while the administration of the educational program is left to the president, principal, or administrative team. The board with limited jurisdiction takes on specific governance responsibilities enumerated in the board constitution and by-laws that have been duly approved by the appropriate ecclesiastical authority. A board with limited jurisdiction has more authority than the consultative board, including the responsibility for the hiring, evaluation, and dismissal of the chief administrator, subject to the final review by the canonical administrator. The corporate board typically takes on all the responsibilities articulated in its corporate charter and bylaws and serves as the ultimate governing authority except for those areas specifically reserved for the bishop in accordance with canon law.

The most common administrative model for a single parish grade school is the pastor-principal model. In this model the principal is empowered by the pastor to provide leadership for the school in terms of its academic excellence and religious formation. The principal provides educational leadership in the areas of hiring of personnel, curriculum development, supervision of instruction, evaluation of personnel, ongoing faculty training, and the necessary administrative authority to run the school. The pastor typically retains ultimate authority in administration, especially in the area of faith formation and in those areas that pertain to the use and distribution of church goods such as fund-raising, budget development, facilities, and payroll. The board structure in a single parish school is either an education committee working as a subsidiary unit of the pastoral council, which is a consultative committee to a consultative board, a consultative board, or a board with limited jurisdiction. The role of the principal and of the boards depends in large part on the pastor, who serves as the canonical administrator of the parish.

In a multiparish school, the most common administrative model is that of pastor-principal. According to Tracy (2001), this model is used in 65 percent of multiparish or interparochial high schools. In the multiparish school, there is typically a board with representatives from the various parishes sponsoring the school, including a pastor from one of the parishes who serves as a canonical administrator. However, since the school serves the educational and religious needs of multiple parishes, the pastor who serves as the canonical administrator typically takes on a lesser role in the school administration than a pastor of a single-parish school. In most multiparish schools, the principal assumes a greater degree of the responsibility for the administration of the school than would a principal in a single-parish school. In some multiparish high schools or multiparish school systems (K–12), a president-principal model is used. Tracy (2001) notes that this model is used in 20 percent of multiparish or interparochial high schools. In this model a president serves as the chief executive officer of the school and assumes responsibility for fund-raising, financial development and school advancement, facilities management, marketing and public relations, budget development, and supervision of the principal.

In a diocesan high school, the most common administrative models are diocesan administrator-principal and diocesan administrator-president. The diocesan administrator may be a vicar for education, secretary for education, superintendent of schools, or assistant superintendent. The roles and duties assumed by the diocesan administrator are entirely dependent upon the local ordinary.

In private schools, the most common administrative model is president-principal. This model is used in 42.9 percent of private, religiously sponsored high schools and 35 percent of private Catholic high schools (Tracy, 2001). The religiously sponsored schools are governed in accordance with the dictates of the religious orders' constitution and governance structure, which may include majority membership or a controlling interest on the board of directors. Private Catholic schools operate with the permission of the local ordinary. The role of the head of school, be it president or principal, and board in these schools is typically enumerated in the articles of incorporation that are on file with the state.

Tracy (2001) notes that while the principal remains the most common title of the head of school in parochial high schools (95.8%), diocesan high schools (67.2%), and multiparish or inter-parochial schools (65%), the president-principal model grew in use among Catholic high schools from 20 percent in 1992 to 29 percent in 2000 (Tracy, 2001). This trend may be attributed to the rising complexity of secondary school administration and the increasing demand on Catholic high schools to find alternative sources of revenue to supplement tuition income in response to the rising costs of education. *See also*: Boards of education, diocesan, parish, school; (Arch) Diocesan schools; Parish (parochial) schools; Pastors; Private schools.

Further Reading: John Paul II, *Code of Canon Law* (Washington, DC: Canon Law Society, 1983); J. Stephen O'Brien, ed., *A Primer on Educational Governance in the Catholic Church* (Washington, DC: National Catholic Educational Association, 1987); Mary E. Tracy, *Mission and Money: A CHS 2000 Report on Finance, Advancement, and Governance* (Washington, DC: National Catholic Educational Association, 2001).

John T. James

Administrator shortage

School administrators in both private and public schools, like teachers, continue to be in short supply at the beginning of the twenty-first century. On the surface, this shortage has been characterized as the result of principals from the baby boom generation beginning to reach retirement age. However, the increasing complexity of the principal's job, the politicized environment in which school leadership occurs, and often the sense of being responsible, but not having commensurate authority, have increased the level of attrition and early retirement from the principalship and the inability to field qualified individuals to enter the profession (Gilman and Givens, 2001). While

Gilman and Givens were reporting primarily on the public school principalship, their evaluation certainly resonates with the experience of Catholic school administrators.

Researchers have attempted to clarify the nature of the difficulties in finding replacements for principals. The explanations fall into three categories. First, they believe the principal's pay is not commensurate with job obligations. Principals' salaries, like teachers' salaries, vary from one district to another. In many districts, the differential in pay between an experienced teacher and a beginning principal is slight. In the Catholic school system, most principals make considerably less than their public school colleagues. Second, there is a high level of stress inherent in the principal's job as he or she attempts to balance multiple responsibilities. Building administrators are required to lobby their superintendent, school board, and other legislators; coordinate and lead the instructional program in the building; maintain above-average standardized test scores; manage the budget, technology, and maintenance of the building; and provide a safe and welcoming environment for all students. Principals have multiple responsibilities, but often they are not given sufficient authority to meet their multiple challenges. In urban public systems, the bureaucracy often stands between principals and the free exercise of their responsibilities. In this regard, private school principals, especially Catholic school principals, have an advantage. The administration of private schools is often site-based. Although these principals are responsible to local school boards or pastors, they are usually granted wider authority. Finally, principals feel there are not sufficient hours in the day. They move rapidly from one activity to another, many of which were unplanned and unexpected. These factors have been the recipe for burnout and early retirement for many principals. While a shortage of administrators is equally problematic for public and private school systems, this entry deals primarily with the administrative shortage in Catholic schools.

Hansen (2001), studying the Catholic school principalship as a lay ministry, notes that formal Church documents, from both the Vatican and the Australian bishops, do not mention the unique role of the laity in the leadership of Catholic education. The presupposition in these articles is twofold: first, that religious and priests continue to lead Catholic schools and second, that it is essential to the identity of these schools that religious and priests hold that role. The reality is that the laity clearly maintains the principalship at a majority of Catholic schools throughout the English-speaking world. The Church documents studied by Hansen (2001) emphasized the pastoral role that was the responsibility of the principal in Catholic schools. This emphasis upon the pastoral role of the Catholic school principal comes at the expense of a lack of emphasis upon the educational role of the principal in these documents. In the United States, the National Catholic Educational Association along with the National Conference of Catholic Bishops developed a description of the role of the Catholic school principal that is broad-based and emphasizes three distinct areas of competence: leadership in faith, leadership in the management of temporalities, and curricular leadership (Ciriello, 1994).

Catholic school administrators must be strong educational leaders; they are also called to be leaders of a faith community and savvy business and plant managers (Ciriello, 1994). While their academic training focuses primarily on instructional leadership, the future principal's preparation in areas such as child and adult faith development and business management is considerably weaker (Hansen, 2001). The multiple challenges of the Catholic school principalship, coupled with a salary and benefits package that falls seriously below that of their public school colleagues (Helm,

2001), might make the Catholic school principalship an unattractive career path to many. Administrators in Catholic schools must be not only talented but committed as well.

Because of the array of talents required of Catholic school administrators and the level of commitment required in order to meet the challenges of the job, Catholic schools must plan ahead for leadership succession. A transition of leadership approach that is marked by waiting until the incumbent principal resigns and then beginning a search will not prove successful in an era when both public and private schools struggle to find competent and qualified leaders to head their schools. Future leaders must be sought out, encouraged, and developed. Once new leaders are in place, these leaders must be provided with opportunities to be mentored (Canavan, 2001).

The Catholic schools of the archdiocese of Chicago provide one sample of this type of leadership development program. Potential leaders are identified from among the faculty of Catholic schools. They are invited to leadership inquiry workshops, where the expectations and roles of leadership in Catholic schools are shared with individuals. A number of partial scholarships, provided in part by the archdiocese and the participating Catholic university, are awarded to those willing not only to prepare but also to serve in the schools of the archdiocese for three years after completion of their leadership preparation program. Those who are hired in administrative positions participate in a formal mentoring program with archdiocesan school officials during the course of their first year. More significantly, veteran Catholic school administrators offer support and advice to the new administrators on an ad hoc basis. Supportive programs such as this certainly have aided the recruitment process. *See also*: Administrative models; Chief Administrators of Catholic Education (CACE); Principals.

Further Reading: Kelvin Canavan, "Leadership Succession in Catholic Schools: Planned or Unplanned?," *Catholic Education: A Journal of Inquiry and Practice* 5, 1 (September 2001): 72–84; Maria J. Ciriello, *Formation and Development for Catholic School Leaders* (Washington, DC: United States Catholic Conference, 1994); David Alan Gilman and Barbara Lanman-Givens, "Where Have All the Principals Gone?," *Educational Leadership* 58, 8 (May 2001): 72–74; Paul J. Hansen, "Catholic School Lay Principalship: The Neglected Ministry in Church Documents," *Catholic Education: A Journal of Inquiry and Practice* 5, 1 (September 2001): 28–38; Claire M. Helm, "What Is My Work Worth?," *Momentum* 32, 4 (November/December 2001): 10–14.

Anthony J. Dosen, CM

Admissions

Historically, Catholic schools admitted, almost exclusively, children of Catholic families. Changing demographics and socioeconomic conditions led to the development of more complex admission polices and practices to accommodate the differences among those who desired a Catholic school education for their children. Admission policies vary from school to school depending on the type of Catholic school and the population it serves. However, some elements are common to most Catholic schools. Issues of admission priorities, maximum class size, socioeconomic diversity, and Catholic identity are all affected by school admission policies. Critics frequently accuse Catholic schools of being too selective in admitting students. While a certain amount of selectivity may be present, it is often overstated by critics. Most children who apply to Catholic schools are accepted. Good admission policies and practices will help Catholic educators meet the challenges of preserving Catholic identity and creating a school that is accessible to a wide variety of students.

The major growth of Catholic schools occurred in the early decades of the twentieth century, when parishes built schools to educate the children of Catholic immigrants. Catholic schools were for Catholic children, and parents were expected to send their children to Catholic schools. Changing demographics and shifting populations altered the terrain for Catholic schools. These changes created a situation where large school buildings existed in areas where Catholic families no longer lived and few Catholic schools existed in areas where Catholics now lived.

The post-1965 decline in Catholic school enrollment called for drastic change. Catholic schools were closed and consolidated. To survive, school doors were open to a greater variety of students—both Catholic and non-Catholic. Admissions policies were established to guide school leaders in accepting students.

A typical Catholic elementary school admission policy usually includes three elements: (1) a statement that welcomes all regardless of race, creed, sex, or national origin, (2) a list of admission priorities, and (3) a recognition that the principal makes the final decision regarding the acceptance of the student. Some schools may limit the number of admissions to control the size of classes. Principals often exercise their discretion in admitting students with special circumstances, for example, exceeding class size limits by accepting a child whose family relocated to the area in mid-year. Admission priorities frequently list the following ranked criteria for selecting students:

1. Students currently enrolled—Catholic and non-Catholic
2. Siblings of students currently enrolled
3. Children of registered parishioners
4. Registered parishioners in other Catholic parishes
5. New students from non-Catholic families by order of preregistration date.

The most important criteria for admission to Catholic high schools are successful completion of the previous academic year, completion of a standardized achievement or aptitude test, the recommendation of the elementary school administrator, and a good academic record.

In practice, assuming that the school does not have a waiting list, most students who apply for admission to a Catholic school are accepted. For high schools, which arguably include the most selective Catholic schools, the median acceptance rate is in the high 80 percent range. Selectivity is exercised more by students and parents than by schools and their policies. Families and students are opting to join a school community whose values, principles, and expectations are understood and accepted. The operative dynamic is inclusion rather than exclusion for those who want to attend a Catholic school. More often than not, the parents and students are selecting the school rather than the school selecting the student.

Critics of Catholic schools often question Catholic school admission practices. Some within the Catholic Church charge that Catholic schools are eroding their Catholic identity by admitting too many non-Catholic students. Others both within and outside the Church accuse Catholic schools of being too selective by accepting only the best, the brightest, and those who are able to pay the increasingly high tuition. This practice, critics claim, leads to the "eliting" of Catholic schools and the abandonment of what Catholic schools do best—educate disadvantaged youth.

The arguments of critics point to challenges that need to be addressed by Catholic educational leaders. Chief among these challenges are maintaining the Catholic identity of schools with an increasing non-Catholic student population, keeping Catholic schools financially affordable for lower-income families, increasing the accessibility of Catholic schools for children with special needs, and enrolling students who are culturally and socioeconomically diverse. *See also*: Enrollment; Religion (of Catholic school students and teachers); Socioeconomic status (of students).

Further Reading: Anthony S. Bryk, Valerie E. Lee, and Peter B. Holland, *Catholic Schools and the Common Good* (Cambridge: Harvard University Press, 1993); Michael J. Guerra, *CHS 2000: A First Look* (Washington, DC: National Catholic Educational Association, 1998); Michael J. Guerra, *Dollars and Sense: Catholic High Schools and Their Finances 1994* (Washington, DC: National Catholic Educational Association, 1995).

Frank X. Savage

Aeterni Patris

Aeterni Patris is an encyclical by Pope Leo XIII, written to restore the study of scholastic philosophy, particularly the works of St. Thomas Aquinas, or as Pope Leo XIII refers to him, the "Angelic Doctor."

When *Aeterni Patris* was published on August 4, 1879, Leo XIII had been Pope for only eighteen months. He encouraged Christian theologians to use faith and reason for the defense of the Catholic Church and "to bring back to a right understanding the minds of men and dispel the darkness of error" (Treacy, 1951, p. 5). The Pope goes on to state: "We exhort you, Venerable Brethren, in all earnestness to restore the golden wisdom of St. Thomas, and to spread it far and wide for the defense and beauty of the Catholic faith, for the good of society, and for the advantages of all the sciences" (Treacy, 1951, p. 22).

As a result of changes in European society, including, but not limited to, the French Revolution, the Enlightenment, and the loss of the Papal States to the Italian King Victor Emmanuel in 1870, conflicts in philosophy and theology rose. Some of these conflicting theories included Cartesian philosophy, Suarezian theology, and rationalist philosophies. The Pope wanted church scholars to study the scholastic philosophy of the thirteenth century to help face challenges caused by social and scientific developments of the late nineteenth century, such as socialism, evolution, and nihilism.

The instruction to study Thomas Aquinas represented a change in the direction of church teaching, resulting in a revival of Thomist thought called Neo-Thomism, or Neo-Scholasticism. Before *Aeterni Patris*, the study of Thomas Aquinas had fallen out of favor. There was a Thomist movement, with Jesuits, who were prescribed to study Thomas Aquinas, and Dominicans, who continued to study the works of one of their own, but the Pope was the leading figure in the revival of Thomism.

Leo XIII had a history of philosophical interests, especially in the works of St. Thomas Aquinas, to combat errors he felt were found in liberalism and traditionalism (Brezik, 1981, p. 12). Before he became Pope, he was the bishop and then cardinal of Perugia. His brother, Joseph Pecci, was a professor at the seminary in Perugia and eventually became a cardinal. Joseph Pecci was also enamored with the teachings of Thomas Aquinas, and in the seminary, taught Thomistic science of philosophy, instead of Cartesian philosophy, and Suarezian theology (Brezik, 1981, p. 13).

Thomas Aquinas was born in late 1224 or early 1225. He studied at the Benedictine Abbey at Monte Casino and enrolled at the University of Naples in 1239. He joined the new Order of Preachers, or Dominicans, in 1244 (Kretzmann and Stump, 1993, p. 12). Thomas Aquinas is considered one of the great thinkers in medieval theology and a doctor of the Church. His career was concurrent with the rise of universities such as those in Paris, Salmanca, Alcala, Douay, Toulouse, Louvain, and many others. He was influenced by Aristotle, Augustine, and, to a lesser extent, Plato. He taught at the University of Paris and other universities. In Paris, he met St. Bonaventure, a Franciscan colleague. Scholastics, such as Aquinas and Bonaventure, would discuss questions on major topics, such as truth. They would subdivide their discussions into articles, which were then examined in detail. The medieval scholastic method derives from classroom disputation, which was a more contested style of discourse than a modern classroom. A prolific writer, Aquinas' two best-known books are *Summa Theologica* and *Summa Contra Gentiles*. He died in 1274. St. Thomas Aquinas is the patron saint of Catholic schools.

Aeterni Patris was somewhat of a surprise, yet it revived interest in, and study of, Thomas Aquinas. One result of *Aeterni Patris* was that many professors of the Gregorian College, a seminary in Rome, left after the encyclical was issued because they were ordered not to teach the philosophy of Descartes. At first, there were not enough American professors in seminaries capable of complying with the encyclical. Some American Catholic and non-Catholic intellectuals expressed skepticism about Thomas Aquinas' relevance to modern philosophy, science, and social and economic problems (Brezik, 1981, p. 30). According to J. Loewenberg in an article in *Commonweal* ("Fifty Years of St. Thomas," January 8, 1930, pp. 272–274), *Aeterni Patris* revived interest in the scholastics and increased cooperation between Catholic and non-Catholic philosophers. *Aeterni Patris* sparked a return to the study of historical sources. Since the Second Vatican Council, Thomas Aquinas has been less in favor with ecclestical scholars (Kretzmann and Stump, 1993, p. 1). *See also*: Aquinas, St. Thomas; Leo XIII, Pope.

Further Reading: "Aeterni Patris," *New Catholic Encyclopedia*, vol. 1 (New York: McGraw-Hill, 1967–1979): 165; Victor B. Brezik, ed., *One Hundred Years of Thomism: Aeterni Patris and Afterwards, a Symposium* (Houston, TX: Center for Thomistic Studies, University of St. Thomas, 1981); Claudia Carlen, ed., *Papal Encyclicals* (Wilmington, NC: McGrath, 1981); Norman Kretzmann and Eleonore Stump, eds., *The Cambridge Companion to Aquinas* (Cambridge, England, and New York: Cambridge University Press, 1993); *Scholastic Philosophy: Encyclical Letter of Pope Leo XIII: Aeterni Patris* (New York: Paulist Press, 1951); *Scholastic Philosophy: Encyclical Letter of Pope Leo XIII: Aeterni Patris with Discussion Club Outline by Rev. Gerald C. Treacy, SJ* (New York: Paulist Press, 1951).

Jack O'Gorman

Affective learning

Affective learning embraces the emotional aspect of the learner and is intrinsic to Catholic pedagogy, which is dedicated to the formation of the whole child. Reimer, Paolitto, and Hersh (1983) wrote, "Affect develops parallel to cognition; the emotions we experience change as we develop new abilities to interpret our social situations" (p. 39). Hence, emotions and cognition cannot be separated. In addition, emotions are critical to memory in that they enable the storage and recall of information (Rosenfield, 1988). Bluestein (2001) reinforced this point, in citing research on the brain as it relates to learning. She claimed that even learning that is relegated to simple recall of factual information relies on the "emotional brain" for transfer to the "thinking brain."

She continued, "In fact, without the element of emotion, most new information will not remain in storage in the brain for long" (p. 26).

Caine and Caine (1991) emphatically stated, "Teachers need to understand that students' feelings and attitudes will be involved and will determine future learning. Because it is impossible to isolate the cognitive from the affective domain, the emotional climate in the school and classroom must be monitored on a consistent basis, using effective communication strategies and allowing for student and teacher reflection and metacognitive processes" (p. 82).

Bluestein (2001) suggested more than sixty ways in which learning may be sabotaged for students through affective means. A sampling included "not having enough time to think about a question or process new information"; "overhearing teachers or other significant adults discussing you negatively within earshot (either deliberately or accidentally)"; "unpredictable or inconsistent teacher behavior"; "not being positively recognized or acknowledged for positive behavior, achievement, effort, cooperation, etc."; "little variety in day-to-day curriculum"; "feeling little love in school in general"; "being told you're not applying yourself"; "teachers' hollering, explosive behavior"; "not being allowed to express problems openly and verbally to a teacher"; "teachers' inability or unwillingness to help the slow learners or kids who need extra help"; and "poor match of learning style to teaching style; learning styles and preferences not accommodated" (pp. 34–36).

The Congregation for Catholic Education (1982) acknowledged the existence of a variety of pedagogical theories but insisted that the Catholic educator must base his or her pedagogy on the Christian concept of the human person, "a pedagogy which gives special emphasis to direct and personal contact with the students" (#21). This emphasis on "direct and personal contact" from educators who, through every aspect of their behavior, witness to their faith clearly addresses the affective dimension of students. It also provides the means by which teachers learn about their students in order to guide them effectively in their learning. Church authors recommended that relationships with students be "a prudent combination of familiarity and distance" (#33), which must be adjusted to the needs of individual students. "Familiarity will make a personal relationship easier, but a certain distance is also needed: students need to learn how to express their own personality without being pre-conditioned; they need to be freed from inhibitions in the responsible exercise of their freedom" (#33).

The Congregation for Catholic Education (1988) depicted students as "active agents in their own formation process" (#105) and asserted that the cooperation of students "with their intelligence, freedom, will, and the whole complex range of human emotions" in this process is essential. The Congregation warned, "The formation process comes to a halt when students are uninvolved and unmoved." Church authors suggested ways for teachers to establish rapport with their students: to simply talk with them and let them talk; to tackle the serious questions that may emerge in conversation "that make a calm study of the Christian faith very difficult" (#72); to respond with patience and humility and to avoid the type of peremptory statements that close down communication; to provide opportunities for students to become involved in their own formation, such as the development of educational goals; to trust students and to give them responsibility; to take advantage of every opportunity to support students in those areas that will help them to reach their goals in the educational process; to pray for students; and to encourage students to pray for their teachers.

The behavior of the teacher is critical to student formation. According to the Congregation for Catholic Education (1988), students should be able to recognize authentic human qualities in their teachers. They are teachers of the faith; however, like Christ, they must also be teachers of what it means to be human. This includes culture, but it also includes such things as affection, tact, understanding, serenity of spirit, a balanced judgment, patience in listening to others and prudence in the way they respond, and, finally, availability for personal meetings and conversations with the students" (#96).

The Congregation (1988) exhorted that students should come to regard the school as an extension of their homes "and therefore a *school-home* ought to have some of the amenities which can create a pleasant and happy family atmosphere. When this is missing from the home, the school can do a great deal to make up for it" (#27). Students can sense the atmosphere in the school and are more willing to become engaged in learning when they feel respected, trusted, and loved. A school climate that is warm and friendly, with teachers who are ready to help, reinforces student cooperation. *See also*: Character education; Cognitive moral development; Congregation for Catholic Education, The; Emotional intelligence; Moral education, history of.

Further Reading: Jane Bluestein, *Creating Emotionally Safe Schools, a Guide for Educators and Parents* (Deerfield Beach, FL: Health Communications, 2001); Renate Nummela Caine and Geoffrey Caine, *Making Connections, Teaching and the Human Brain* (Alexandria, VA: Association for Supervision and Curriculum Development, 1991); Congregation for Catholic Education, *Lay Catholics in Schools: Witnesses to Faith* (Boston: Daughters of St. Paul, 1982); Congregation for Catholic Education, *The Religious Dimension of Education in a Catholic School* (Boston: Daughters of St. Paul, 1988); Daniel Goleman, *Emotional Intelligence* (New York: Bantam Books, 1995); Joseph Reimer, Diana Pritchard Paolitto, and Richard Hersh, *Promoting Moral Growth, from Piaget to Kohlberg* (Prospect Heights, IL: Waveland Press, 1983); Israel Rosenfield, *The Invention of Memory* (New York: Basic Books, 1988).

Gini Shimabukuro

African Americans

The relationship between the Catholic Church and the African American community has been a troubled one. To be sure, the Church in America has always been concerned about the religious salvation of the Black American community, but few Catholics took it upon themselves to reach out to African Americans and invite them to become Catholics. Not surprisingly, therefore, few African Americans chose to convert to Catholicism, and those who did were segregated from the rest of the Church.

The response of the Church to the education of African American Catholic children was mixed at best. There were tentative efforts to establish black Catholic schools at Mount St. Mary's in Maryland and at Charleston in South Carolina in the early nineteenth century. These primitive schools had a limited impact.

Another early black Catholic school was in Baltimore in 1825. In that year, Fr. James Joubert, a Sulpician priest, established an order of black nuns called the Oblate Sisters of St. Francis. Among the first activities of the order was to establish a school for African American children in Baltimore. At first the curriculum focused on the industrial arts but later included reading and writing as well as sewing, embroidery, washing, and ironing.

Perhaps the biggest challenge faced by the Church in the education of African

A typical Catholic school classroom in Philadelphia in the 1960s. © The Robert & Theresa Halvey Collection, Philadelphia Archdiocesan Historical Research Center.

American children in the years before the Civil War was the animosity of southern society to any black educational opportunities. When Bishop John England established a black Catholic school in Charleston, his efforts were undermined by laws prohibiting anyone from teaching African American children. England was reluctantly forced to close his school.

In the years after the Civil War the bishops became more concerned about the education of the newly freed slaves. Archbishop Martin Spalding of Baltimore spoke out forcefully in 1867, when he encouraged his fellow bishops to establish "schools for the colored" because literacy was needed if these African Americans were to become Catholics. Spalding was true to his word and established a number of black Catholic schools in Baltimore and Washington in the late 1860s.

One of the first national efforts to reach out to African Americans and the education of their children came in 1871 with the arrival of the Josephite Fathers from England. The Josephites took as their mission the education of African Americans. They were later joined in their efforts by several orders of teaching sisters, including the Fran-

Catholic school students work with their teacher in a computer lab. © The Robert & Theresa Halvey Collection, Philadelphia Archdiocesan Historical Research Center.

ciscans, the Mission Helpers, Servants of the Sacred Heart, and the Sisters of the Blessed Sacrament. This last order was established by St. Katharine Drexel of Philadelphia.

The first efforts of these religious orders were modest indeed when it came to education. For the most part, educational activities rarely extended beyond instruction in reading, writing, and religion. Beginning in the early years of the twentieth century, however, these religious orders did establish parishes and schools for blacks in many major cities in the East and Midwest.

The Church's interest in the education of African Americans was, however, inconsistent. At the Third Plenary Council of Baltimore in 1884, the bishops did include a chapter of their pastoral letter on African Americans, and the bishops did call on priests to focus on the education of African Americans. "It is our will," wrote the bishops, "that bishops exert every effort to provide the Negro, wherever possible, with churches, schools, orphanages, and homes for the poor."

It was a noble sentiment, and there was some progress over the next thirty-five years. Statistics compiled by the Negro and Indian Mission Fund indicated a growth in the number of black Catholic schools from 98 in 1890 to 141 in 1917, and enrollment growth was even more impressive with a jump from 6,093 students in 1890 to 14,997 by 1917. This achievement was the direct result of a desire by black Catholics for better educational opportunities for their children and a correlate willingness of sister-teachers to serve the African American people.

As the African American population moved north to take jobs in the big industrial cities of the northern states, they clashed with whites, many of them Catholics. The story of Chicago was typical of most major archdioceses in the country. The increasing number of black Catholics in Chicago, for example, taxed the few parishes and schools open to them. Blacks in the 1930s began to protest the archdiocesan policy of segregated parishes, and one Catholic complained to the Apostolic Delegate. The delegate wrote to Cardinal George Mundelein asking for an explanation of his policy. The archbishop claimed that "the doors of any church in Chicago are open to all Catholics," but he was not so forthright on the schools: "I have found it in the best interest of religion to leave it to the prudent judgment and priestly zeal of individual pastors to act in each case" (James Sanders, *Education of an Urban Minority: Catholic in Chicago, 1833–1965* [New York: Oxford University Press, 1977], p. 231).

Mundelein refused to admit what was obvious to all: his policy of separation of the races allowed white Catholics to sustain their racism without fear of contradiction from their Church. There is no doubt that black children suffered as a result of this policy. Even the *New World* acknowledged the plight of the black Catholic child. "Worst of all, they are handicapped in the Catholic education of their children," noted the paper. "What are they to do when there is no Catholic school within reasonable distance or when the Catholic school is not available?" (*New World*, November 2, 1937). Mundelein had no answer; it would not be until the 1940s, under Mundelein's successor, Samuel Stritch, that any progress in race relations was made in Chicago.

The hostility of white ethnic Catholics across the country had a chilling effect on the conversion of African Americans who chose to join the Catholic Church and send their children to parochial schools. The average number of black children who attended Catholic schools in the 1940s hovered around 45,000. The majority of black Catholic schools were in the South and staffed by the Sisters of the Blessed Sacrament and the Josephite Fathers.

The first stirrings of the civil rights movement in the late 1940s had the beneficial effect of desegregating Catholic schools in archdioceses as diverse as Chicago, Indianapolis, St. Louis, San Antonio, and Washington, DC. In each of these archdioceses, archbishops came out forcefully against segregation and ordered reluctant pastors and hostile laity to accept their commands. Other prelates in other dioceses followed this lead, and the Catholic schools were desegregated in the 1950s.

Racism, though, was pervasive within the Catholic Church, and efforts to convert blacks were modest at best. To be sure, liberal Catholics marched with Martin Luther King in the civil rights struggles of the 1960s, but the number of blacks who joined the Catholic Church in the 1960s and 1970s was small. Even smaller was the number of African American children attending Catholic schools. More progress has been made in the past thirty years than was made in the previous seventy years. Many barriers to integration have come down, and overt racism is on the decline. The number of African American Catholics has grown, and the number of black children in Catholic schools also has increased. But overall, the experience of African Americans in the Catholic Church and its schools has been difficult at best. Those African Americans who chose to send their children to Catholic schools did not make the decision lightly. They were committed to their Church and its school. *See also*: *Inner-City Private Elementary Schools: A Study*; Inner-city schools; Minority students.

Further Reading: Harold A. Buetow, *Of Singular Benefit: The Story of U.S. Catholic Education* (New York: Macmillan, 1970); Cyprian Davis, *Black Catholics in the United States*

(New York: Crossroad, 1990); William A. Osborne, *Segregated Covenant: Race Relations and American Catholics* (New York: Herder and Herder, 1967).

Timothy Walch

Agostini v. Felton

In *Agostini v. Felton*, a bitterly divided Supreme Court, in a five-to-four decision, essentially reversed its 1985 judgment in *Aguilar v. Felton* and upheld the on-site delivery of Title I services for students enrolled in religiously affiliated nonpublic schools. In so doing, the Court continued its revitalization of the child benefit test, opening the door for major changes in the delivery of remedial services for underprivileged students who attended religious schools.

Agostini began in 1978, when six taxpayers in New York City challenged the use of funds under Title I, an expansive federal statute that provides remedial education specifically targeting underprivileged at-risk children, on-site in their religiously affiliated nonpublic schools. The funds were used to pay the salaries of public school personnel who taught remedial classes in reading, mathematics, and English as a second language as well as those professionals who provided guidance services in religious schools, of which about 90 percent were Roman Catholic. The New York City Board of Education (NYCBOE) created safeguards to avoid entanglement between public school personnel and religious educators such as having volunteers serve only in the religious schools, where they were supervised by field personnel who made frequent unannounced visits. In addition, Title I assignments were made without regard to the religious affiliations of public school employees, most worked in religious schools that were not of their own faith, and most moved among different nonpublic schools while usually not spending a full week in one location.

After a federal trial court in New York upheld the NYCBOE's delivery system, the Second Circuit reversed its finding that it violated the Establishment Clause. On further review, even in the absence of an allegation of a constitutional violation, the Supreme Court in *Aguilar v. Felton* affirmed that the program was unconstitutional based on the fear of excessive entanglement. The Court vitiated the program, thereby imposing massive costs on school systems, based on the fear of violating the excessive entanglement clause of the *Lemon* test.

On remand, in September 1985, a federal trial court enjoined the NYCBOE and federal government from providing Title I services on-site in religiously affiliated nonpublic schools. Consequently, the NYCBOE and school systems throughout the country developed alternative delivery systems. In fact, the NYCBOE spent more than $100 million between 1986–1987 and 1993–1994 school years on computer-aided instruction, leasing sites and mobile instructional units, and transporting students to these locations.

In 1995, parents, joined by the NYCBOE and federal Department of Education, sought to dissolve the injunction based largely on newly discovered evidence relating to the significant additional cost of providing services and rendered its ongoing enforcement inequitable. Both a federal trial court and the Second Circuit rejected a request for relief. The Supreme Court agreed to revisit *Aguilar* and ultimately took the unusual step of dissolving the earlier injunction, thereby essentially overruling itself and permitting the on-site delivery of services.

Writing for the Court, Justice O'Connor, author of a scathing dissent in the original *Aguilar*, held that the NYCBOE's Title I program did not violate any of the three standards that it used to consider whether state aid has advanced religion since there was no governmental indoctrination, there were no distinctions between recipients based on religion, and there was no excessive entanglement. She held that a federally funded program that provides supplemental, remedial instruction and counseling services to disadvantaged children on a neutral basis is not invalid under the Establishment Clause when they are provided on-site in religiously affiliated schools by government employees pursuant to a program containing safeguards such as the NYCBOE had implemented. Having concluded that *Aguilar* was not good law, Justice O'Connor observed that since the Court's Establishment Clause jurisprudence changed over the previous decade, *Agostini* was grounded on far more than a present doctrinal disposition to come out differently from *Aguilar*. As such, she asserted that all that remained for the Court was to consider the request to dissolve the injunction. She commended the lower courts for recognizing that the motion for relief had to be denied until the Court ruled on the merits of the case, especially in light of the fact that a majority of justices had expressed their displeasure with *Aguilar* in an earlier case. In deciding that there was no reason to wait for another case to question the ongoing viability of *Aguilar*, Justice O'Connor granted the requested relief by reversing the judgment of the Second Circuit and returned the case to the trial court with instructions to vacate its 1985 order.

Dissenting opinions by Justices Souter and Ginsburg feared that the Court's permitting the on-site delivery of Title I services misinterpreted the Court's earlier rulings on aid that did not present a sufficient basis under which to rule in *Agostini*. Further, Ginsburg professed that the integrity of the Court's interpretation of its procedural rules required it to wait for a more appropriate case under which to review *Aguilar*. *See also*: Establishment Clause; Separation of Church and state.

Further Reading: *Agostini v. Felton*, 521 U.S. 203 (1997); *Aguilar v. Felton*, 473 U.S. 402 (1985).

Charles J. Russo

Alliance for Catholic Education (ACE)

The Alliance for Catholic Education (ACE) is a teaching-service program of the University of Notre Dame, serving twenty-five dioceses across the United States. ACE seeks to develop a corps of highly motivated and committed educators to meet the needs of the country's underserved Catholic elementary and secondary schools.

The 1990s witnessed an unprecedented and growing awareness of the strengths of American Catholic schools. Despite population shifts and financial pressures, Catholic schools have made heroic efforts to stay open in inner cities and to serve mainly poor and minority students, many of them non-Catholic.

At the same time, many leading Catholic educators recognize an impending crisis. The numbers of men and women choosing religious vocations, many of whom in the past served Catholic education as teachers and administrators, are diminishing. There is a real need to attract and prepare talented and committed young people to teach and lead the 8,500 Catholic schools across the nation. Such preparation requires not only academic depth and excellence but also understanding about how to foster community in schools, especially in ways that stimulate the intellectual and ethical development of students.

In 1993, in an effort to respond to these opportunities and challenges, the University of Notre Dame, under the leadership for Fr. Timothy Scully, CSC, forged ACE with

Alliance For Catholic Education—Group Photo July 21, 2003. © University of Notre Dame Archives.

the U.S. Catholic Conference's Department of Education, the National Catholic Educational Association (NCEA), and the University of Portland. ACE now annually places over 160 college graduates in over 100 parochial schools in twenty-five dioceses within fourteen states, primarily in the South and Southwest.

The Alliance for Catholic Education is an outgrowth of the mission of service of the University of Notre Dame and is based on the three pillars of professional teaching, community, and spirituality.

Professional teaching. From the outset, ACE has held the conviction that its teachers must be prepared for the challenges of classroom teaching. Therefore, their two-year service commitment is grounded in an innovative teacher-preparation program that culminates in a master's degree in education (M.Ed.) and initial licensure. During eight weeks of course work in the first summer, ACE teachers serve as practicum students in the South Bend public and diocesan schools in the morning. Then, they integrate their experiences with current educational theory during graduate classes in the afternoons. After completing the summer's educational experience, ACE teachers travel to the parochial school systems of the South. There, they teach full-time as teachers of record in schools that report a chronic shortage of well-trained teachers, especially in math, science, the social sciences, and theology. During this time they take Internet courses and are enrolled in the supervised teaching course. They return the second summer for an additional seven weeks of course work and return to their schools the second year with continued support in supervised teaching and Internet courses.

ACE places great emphasis on supporting its teachers through the challenges and rewards of beginning teaching. Faculty supervisors formally observe each ACE teacher each semester and maintain close contact with the new teachers through regular e-mail correspondence. In addition, during the two-year supervised teaching experience, trained on-site clinical supervisors, usually the building principal, provide immediate supervision and guidance. The ACE teachers are also paired with an experienced mentor teacher in the school where they serve. This professional mentorship is augmented by the peer support ACE teachers gain by living together in community.

Community life. Central to the mission of ACE is the belief that community living draws out the person of Christ in all individuals and calls them to a deeper understanding of their service to God and to one another. Community life is central to both the professional and the spiritual growth of ACE teachers as they attempt to imitate Christ in their everyday lives.

Community life provides a valuable support network for beginning teachers. ACE teachers living in community are able to share and reflect upon the daily struggles and rewards inherent in the first years of teaching. As intentional communities bringing together persons of differing gifts and talents, ACE communities are able to promote the positive and personal growth of individual members. Life in community challenges ACE members to deepen their understanding of self and thus to live a life of greater compassion for others. This understanding and compassion ultimately strengthen the community as a whole and help to advance the mission of ACE.

These communities serve not only to benefit themselves. They are a sign of hope and witness to a larger society, especially one of faith in action, apparent through the example of these young persons dedicating themselves to a life of service, to God and to neighbor, through the ministry of teaching.

Spirituality. As Catholic school teachers and members of an intentional Christian community, ACE participants are continually invited to a deeper identity with the primary model of the ACE Program—Christ the Teacher. The goal is for the ACE participants themselves to embody increasingly more fully Christ's person and teachings, both to the students they serve and to the peers with whom they live. This third pillar of the ACE program—building a spiritual relationship with Christ the Teacher—receives its life and direction on a regular basis from the sacramental dimension of the Church, in which the ACE teachers participate. Especially through the Eucharist, the ACE teachers receive nourishment, consolation, and inspiration from the person of Christ. Also through a series of retreats, as well as the development of their own personal and community prayer life, the ACE teachers are called continually to reflect upon and deepen their commitment to the ongoing development of their spiritual lives and their witness to others to the life and teachings of Christ the Teacher.

ACE participants are invited to develop their own personal spirituality in the context of their local community and to share with one another the journey of becoming committed Catholic school teachers. Given this program goal, ACE faculty and staff strive to provide ACE teachers with the tools to become reflective professional educators and people of faith. ACE supports many formal and informal opportunities for students to reflect on their lives and work during the summer and during the two years of service in their community. The ACE program seeks to develop its students as genuine and effective role models of moral and ethical lives.

To carry out its core teaching mission ACE recruits talented graduates from the University of Notre Dame and a number of select colleges and universities. ACE teachers represent a variety of undergraduate disciplines and a diverse set of backgrounds and experiences. Graduates of the ACE program receive an M.Ed. and an initial teaching license. More than 95 percent of the students who enter ACE complete the program, and 75 percent of the graduates have remained in the field of education; 55 percent have remained in Catholic education.

In 1999, ACE made a programmatic decision not to expand beyond a total of 170 teachers, in order to maintain the professional standards and intimacy necessary to educate and support quality teachers. With this in mind, alternative methods of expansion have been explored, and Notre Dame moved to support the replication of the ACE concept of teacher education by other universities. With the support of both the federal government and several independent foundations, ACE has begun working with eleven higher education institutions as they design innovative and intensive teacher-service programs.

In the summer of 2002, ACE expanded its program to include the preparation of Catholic school administrators. This state-approved licensure program is a fourteen-month preparation, beginning in June, that allows Catholic school teachers with masters' degrees to remain in their Catholic schools during the academic year as members of an administrative team and to complete their formal course work in the second summer. *See also*: Christian service; Lalanne Project; Teacher shortage; Teaching as ministry.

Further Reading: ACE Website: http://ace.nd.edu; Michael Pressley, ed., *Teaching Service and Alternative Teacher Education: Notre Dame's Alliance for Catholic Education* (Notre Dame, IN: University of Notre Dame Press, 2002); Alicia Roehrig, Michael Pressley, and Denise Talotta, *Stories of Beginning Teachers* (Notre Dame, IN: University of Notre Dame Press, 2002).

Joyce V. Johnstone

Americanization

Americanization is a process by which millions of immigrants and their children and grandchildren became Americans. Catholic schools played a large role in this process.

Americanization is a socializing mechanism ranging from the distinctly American upbringing of colonial American Catholics, like John Carroll, to the recent arrival of Latin American, Southeast Asian, and other Catholic immigrants. Because of the over nine million immigrants, the majority of whom were Catholic, that came to the United States between 1880 and the onset of World War I, Americanization is often associated with the late nineteenth and early twentieth centuries.

The American Heritage Dictionary of the English Language defines "Americanize" as to make American in form or to absorb or assimilate into American culture or to bring under American influence or control. But what is an American? What is distinct about American culture? An American usually speaks the English language and participates in a capitalist economy and democratic electoral process. American society is perceived as a somewhat egalitarian society, and for the immigrants in the nineteenth and early twentieth centuries it was largely urban. American-style food, clothing, culture, and sports are also components of the society. In contrast, many immigrants came from non-English-speaking countries. Many were peasants, either under a monarchy or with little input into the governmental process. They often came from rural environments. Immigrants' food and music have contributed to American society, for example, hamburgers from Germany and pizza from Italy. So, Americanization is a process of acculturation by which immigrants and their children and grandchildren join the mainstream of American life. Examples of this include Al Smith's 1928 bid for the presidency, as the first Catholic American candidate, or the popularity of baseball among immigrants and their children. Although "Casey at the Bat" was fictional, Casey represents the immigrant's embrace of urban American culture.

Most immigrants may have arrived in the United States poor, but they worked to make a better life for their children or grandchildren. Their story is the American Dream; with hard work they could improve their economic and social situation. Immigrants grasped the value of education for their children. Many of them valued English-language instruction but wanted an education that was consistent with their values, specifically, their religious values.

Public schools were begun in the 1830s with Horace Mann's concept of "common schools." These schools were supposed to be nondenominational, but the reading of the Protestant version of the Bible, singing Protestant hymns, and anti-Catholic rhetoric in the textbooks all led Catholics to desire separate schooling for their children.

For the immigrants, Catholic schools served as the bridge between their European past and their American future. Many of the teachers were from the same ethnic group and had the same religious values as the parents. Also, the Catholic schools taught civics, democracy, and American government and stressed patriotism in the curriculum. Thus, "while Catholic schools consciously sought to preserve Catholic values and ethnic identities, they also facilitated the assimilation of immigrants into American public life" (Bryk et al., 1993, p. 27).

Many of the immigrants sought to establish ethnic schools, which at first were taught in a language other than English. A 1912 publication on Catholic schools entitled *The Growth and Development of the Catholic School System in the United States* discusses separate German, French Canadian, Italian, and Polish schools, as well as Spanish-language Catholic schools in the American Southwest. It also considers Bohemian, Lithuanian, Slovak, Greek Rite, Portuguese, Hungarian, and Belgian schools as well as schools for Indians, African Americans, orphanages, and schools for the deaf and dumb.

As the demographics changed at the end of the nineteenth century, there were more American born Irish Americans and German Americans than immigrants. This fact and the understanding by the immigrant community that the use of English led to better economic success and did not limit them to low-wage and low-status jobs, led to more instruction in English. Even after the use of English become more common, some schools continued their pride in their ethnic origins.

Although critics stated that Catholic schools prevented absorption into American life, Andrew Greeley and Peter Rossi (1966) write: "Far from being divisive, it is possible that Catholic schools have accelerated the acculturation of Catholic immigrant groups partly because they have consciously promoted 'Americanization' in a fashion that the public schools could not have done without stirring up trouble from the ethnic communities" (p. 161).

These diverse European ethnic groups made vital and vibrant contributions to American culture. Examples of this are celebrations, such as St. Patrick's Day, or the feast of St. Joseph. This ethnic identity persists long after the immigrant experience, as a fourth-generation American might say, "I'm Italian." The Catholic schools acted as a conduit through which descendants of immigrants achieved higher economic status, greater political participation, and life in the mainstream of American culture. *See also*: American Protective Association (APA); Anti-Catholicism; Cahenslyism; Catholic School Question, The; Ethnicity (and parish schools); Immigration/Immigrants; Ku Klux Klan.

Further Reading: "Americanize" http://www.bartleby.com, *The American Heritage Dictionary of the English Language*, 4th ed., 2000. Accessed September 30, 2002; Anthony S. Bryk, Valerie E. Lee, and Peter B. Holland, *Catholic Schools and the Common Good* (Cambridge: Harvard University Press, 1993); James A. Burns, *The Growth and Development of the Catholic School System in the United States* (New York and Cincinnati: Benziger Brothers, 1912); Andrew Greeley and Peter Rossi, *The Education of Catholic Americans* (Chicago: Aldine, 1966); Timothy Meagher, "Ethnic, Catholic, White: Changes in the Identity of European American Catholics," in James Youniss, John J. Convey, and Jeffrey A. McLellan, eds., *The Catholic Character of Catholic Schools* (Notre Dame, IN: University of Notre Dame Press, 2000).

Jack O'Gorman

American Protective Association (APA)

Henry Bowers called seven men to his office on Sunday afternoon, March 13, 1887, in Clinton, Iowa, to discuss the "Catholic menace." Clinton, at the time Iowa's largest industrial city, had an immigrant population of approximately 40 percent, chiefly Irish and German. Sparked by the results of a recent local election, the meeting resulted in the founding of the APA to "defend American institutions against foreign aggression."

The organization was directed more against Catholics than against foreigners in general. Bowers saw Catholic conspiracies everywhere. A self-taught lawyer, he blamed his educational deficiencies on Jesuit subversion of the public schools in Baltimore, where he grew up. Ultimately, the APA stretched nationwide; its strength, however, was in the Midwest. By 1890 it had established units from Omaha to Detroit; by 1893 it claimed 500,000 members.

As a secret society, the APA administered an oath to its members. The oath's chief features included provisions to prevent Catholics from joining the association; not to employ Catholics; not to enter into any agreement with Catholics, including workers' associations or strikes; and not to vote for any Catholics for any public office. The ultimate goal was to break the power of "Romanism" in the country.

The APA resented the growing strength of the Catholic Church in the United States, as witnessed by the Church's swelling numbers, increased political strength, and its failure to embrace public schools and its commitment to parochial schools. It looked to the public schools as the bulwark of democracy; hence, it saw the parochial schools, especially those that held to Old World language and customs (e.g., as it interpreted the contemporary Bennett Law struggle in Wisconsin) as evidence of the hold of "Romanism" on Catholic Americans, an influence that was anti-American.

In 1892 William J. H. Traynor became its head. This was the beginning of the APA's "boom years," as it achieved national influence. The organization published the *A.P.A. Magazine*, and Traynor edited the *Patriotic American*. It reached the zenith of its power around 1893. That year it published two forgeries, the first being an "Instruction to Catholics" that it alleged was from the Pope instructing Catholics to remove "heretics" (Protestants) from jobs and replace them with Catholic immigrants. The second was a bogus encyclical, attributed to Pope Leo XIII, that stated that it was the duty of Catholics to exterminate all heretics found within the United States. This forgery of a forthcoming massacre carried out by Catholics under the orders of a foreigner caused considerable concern in certain parts of the nation; the date for the uprising passed, but the scare remained for a period.

In 1894, under the banner of the "Supreme Council of the American Protective Association of the World," in a gathering at Des Moines, Iowa, position statements were made in opposition to: any non-American ecclesiastical power irreconcilable with American citizenship; any ecclesiastical power having absolute control over the education of children growing up "under the stars and stripes"; Catholics serving as administrators or teachers in public schools; and the expenditure of any public funds for sectarian schools. The meeting produced affirmations on behalf of sectarian-free public schools as the "bulwark of American institutions" and the restriction of immigration to those who demonstrated their ability and honest intention to become self-supporting American citizens. In 1894 the APA reported members in every state and was at the peak of its membership; 1894 also witnessed several nativistic anti-Catholic riots, in two of which the APA was directly involved. These resulted in several fatalities, including several Catholics and one APA leader.

The organization began to decline in 1895. Consistently opposed by the Democratic Party, its recommendations for the platform of the Republican Party in 1896 were rejected, and it was discredited. In the mid-1890s it unsuccessfully opposed the government contract system between the commissioner of Indian affairs and the Catholic bureau for the education of American Indians. Its efforts in opposition to the placing of a statue of the Jesuit explorer, Father Marquette, representing the state of Wisconsin in the nation's capital, came to no avail. Its attempts to form an independent political party failed.

In 1895 Traynor claimed that there were twenty members of the APA in Congress. The decline in the APA's popularity had set in, and one by one, its newspapers, which were located mostly in the Midwest, ceased to exist until there were but three left in 1900. The organization's political influence declined proportionately.

The APA has been judged a success if the measuring rod is applied to immigration restriction, elimination of appropriations for sectarian institutions, and extension of state control over charitable activities. It is of less significance in its influence as a secret lodge, dedicated to discrimination against hiring Catholics. As Catholics moved into the middle class, the APA lost some of its leverage. It died for no apparent reason other than that the times were not ripe for an organization of its kind to flourish. *See also*: Americanization; Anti-Catholicism; Immigration/Immigrants; Ku Klux Klan.

Further Reading: Harold A. Buetow, *Of Singular Benefit: The Story of U.S. Catholic Education* (New York: Macmillan, 1970); Humphrey J. Desmond, *The A.P.A. Movement* (Washington, DC: New Century Press, 1912); John Higham, *Strangers in the Land: Patterns of American Nativism* (New York: Atheneum, 1970); Donald L. Kinzer, *An Episode in Anti-Catholicism: The American Protective Association* (Seattle: University of Washington Press, 1964); Gerald Shaughnessy, *Has the Immigrant Kept the Faith? A Study of Immigration and Catholic Growth in the United States* (New York: Macmillan, 1925).

Thomas C. Hunt

Anti-Catholicism

Between 1840 and 1960, Catholics and non-Catholics argued over who would control the education of Catholic children. Occasionally, the arguments escalated into violence, and for most of those 120 years, there was a strong anti-Catholic bias against parochial schools.

During the nineteenth century, native-born Americans focused on the Catholic Church as the symbol of all that was wrong with the foreign-born. There were attacks against Catholic churches, priests, nuns, and the laity in Boston, New York, Philadelphia, Baltimore, Cincinnati, Detroit, and St. Louis, among other cities.

The violence was the result of an anti-Catholicism deeply rooted in the American mind. Catholicism had been anathema since the establishment of the British colonies. The Catholic Church was mocked in both the popular and religious press, in novels, histories, children's books, and even almanacs. Using the pulpit and the press, Protestant ministers and social reformers warned the nation to be on the watch for Catholic conspiracies to deprive America of its liberties. Exposing Catholicism as a national threat did nothing, however, about millions of Catholic immigrants already in the country. Native-born Americans searched for ways and means of transforming the Catholic foreigner into productive, God-fearing citizens.

Among the social institutions that promised to "homogenize" Catholics was the common school. Even though they had no proof that this transformation process would work, common schoolmen spoke as if it were only a matter of time before immigrant children were acting and thinking like native-born children.

Catholic leaders accused common schoolmen of incorporating large doses of Protestant doctrine into the "nonsectarian" common school curriculum. Catholics further accused common schoolmen of a subtle campaign to win the allegiance of Catholic children and at the same time to denigrate the Catholic Church. The end result, noted Catholic leaders, was a generational conflict between these "Americanized" children and their immigrant Catholic parents. In response, local Catholic parishes opened their own schools.

Non-Catholics viewed the growth of parochial schools with alarm. Many public school advocates had hoped that Catholics would abandon their parish schools if public schools became nonsectarian, but it became increasingly clear in the decades after the Civil War that parish schools were not going to die out and would become a significant part of the American educational system.

Non-Catholics sought ways to end the Catholic campaigns to gain state funds for their schools. Throughout the 1870s and 1880s, many state legislatures amended their constitutions to prohibit the use of public funds for religious institutions. Between 1877 and 1917, some twenty-nine states incorporated the amendment into their constitutions. Indeed, some state legislatures looked for ways to exert public control over portions of the parish school curricula.

In the late nineteenth century, non-Catholics were fixated on the persistence of foreign nationalism and culture in the United States, and parish schools were considered to be part of the problem. Some thought there ought to be a law that required parochial schools to conform to public school standards. The implication of these laws—state control over private schools—was unprecedented, but the vigor of the Catholic backlash came as a surprise to many Americans.

In the 1920s, Catholic educators became increasingly concerned about a growing antagonism toward parochial education on the part of many state legislatures. Legislation under consideration in several states threatened the very existence of parish schools, and when the citizens of Oregon passed a referendum requiring all children to attend public schools, the bishops swung into action.

Courts at all levels agreed that Oregon had no power to force Catholic children to

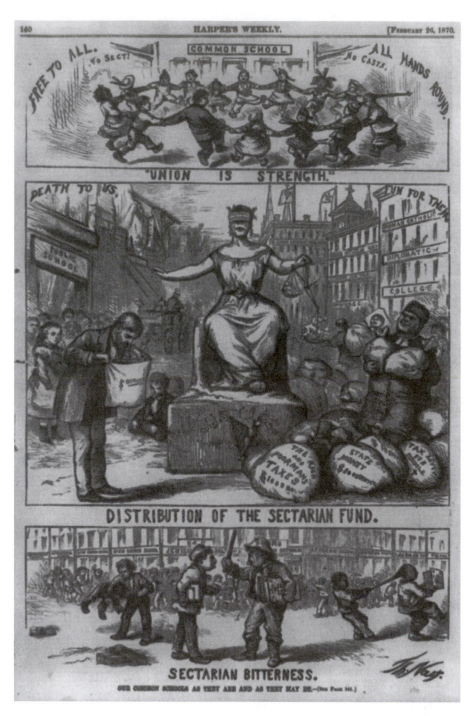

Anti-Catholic cartoon showing (1) "Union is Strength"—children of all races and religions playing together; (2) "Distribution of the Sectarian Fund"—all to Catholic and none to public schools; (3) "Sectarian Bitterness" of private schools. Courtesy of the Library of Congress.

attend public schools. Yet the Supreme Court, in a decision known as *Pierce v. Society of School Sisters*, was careful not to proscribe "the power of the state to reasonably regulate all schools." Following the Supreme Court decision, church leaders devoted their energies to encouraging Catholic schools to bring themselves up to the standards set by the state boards of education.

The contours of anti-Catholic attacks on parochial schools shifted in the years after the *Pierce* decision. At the root of the Catholic–Protestant conflict from 1930 to 1960 was the relationship between Church, state, and school under the Constitution. In 1930, only five years after it had upheld the right of Catholic schools to exist, the Court upheld a Louisiana law that provided schoolbooks to all children in the state attending either private or public schools. The Court agreed that such a law was in the best interest of the state and did not breach the wall separating Church and state. This decision (*Cochran v. Louisiana*) encouraged Catholics to think that other forms of state aid also might be ruled constitutional.

The devastation of the Great Depression followed by World War II temporarily ended the acrimony and argument between Catholics and Protestants over education, but a boom in parochial education after the war caused the tension to emerge once again. The opening round came in 1947, when the U.S. Supreme Court, in *Everson v. Board of Education*, permitted school districts to provide free bus transportation to parochial as well as public school students. In May 1949, Catholics protested a bill to provide federal aid to public schools because of a gratuitous provision of the bill prohibiting the states from using any portion of the funds to provide bus transportation for parochial school students as permitted in the *Everson* decision. Neither side was very happy in the struggle over aid to parochial schools.

The strain between Catholics and Protestants also was intensified by the establishment of Protestants and Other Americans United [POAU] for the Separation of Church and State, an organization opposed to any public aid to parochial schools. The POAU proclaimed that its goal was "to enlighten and mobilize public opinion in support of religious liberty." Legislative petitions and court action by the POAU were thinly veiled attacks on the Catholic Church.

The POAU did not represent mainstream Protestant opinion of Catholicism. In spite of serious disagreements with various Catholic positions, a number of Protestant groups sought a rapprochement with Catholicism during the latter 1950s. By the end of the 1950s the POAU no longer was a force in interfaith relations. Catholics and Protestants had come to accept and tolerate their respective rights in a pluralistic American society.

The anti-Catholic protests against Catholic education dissipated with the rapid decline in the number and enrollment in Catholic schools starting in the 1960s. To be sure, non-Catholics—led by the refurbished group now called Americans United for the Separation of Church and State—opposed both direct and indirect public aid for parochial schools. But by the turn of the twenty-first century, virtually all Americans—non-Catholic as well as Catholic—embrace the value of parochial education in American society. *See also*: Americanization; American Protective Association (APA); Ku Klux Klan; Protestants and Other Americans United (POAU) for Separation of Church and State.

Further Reading: Ray Allen Billington, *The Protestant Crusade* (New York: Macmillan, 1938); Michael Feldberg, *The Philadelphia Bible Riots of 1844: A Study of Ethnic Conflict* (Westport, CT: Greenwood Press, 1975); Fayette Veverka, *For God and Country: Catholic*

Schooling in the 1920s (New York: Garland, 1988); Timothy Walch, *Parish School: American Catholic Parochial Education from Colonial Times to the Present* (New York: Crossroad, 1996).

Timothy Walch

Aquinas, St. Thomas (1225–1274)

St. Thomas has provided for the Catholic Church a worldview to underpin an educational philosophy; a method of study; and an understanding of the person and the learning process. Together with the extraordinary character of his life, these have provided a unique source of inspiration for Catholic educators.

St. Thomas is best known for his synthesis of the Christian faith in the *Summa Theologica*, which, despite its length and complexity, was intended as a basic tool for catechists and teachers of the Catholic faith. This remarkable work, unsurpassed in Catholic writings for its imaginative scope and breadth of understanding, has remained the single most influential synthesis of faith and reason in the Catholic tradition. The work remains unfinished as the result of a vision that St. Thomas had toward the end of his life, after which he reported that all of his work seemed "like straw."

St. Thomas also authored a significant companion work, *Summa Contra Gentiles* (Summa against the Pagans), which was conceived as more of a work of apologetics and evangelization. His other writings that have been important signposts for Catholic educationalists include *de Veritate* (Truth), a defense of the objective nature of truth.

As a member of one of the new mendicant orders, the Dominicans, leaving the rich and well-established Benedictine Abbey of Monte Cassino at the age of 15 and, at 19, adopting the life of an itinerant preacher and evangelizer, his life has an appeal to students who can readily identify with his embracing of voluntary poverty and simplicity of life.

Students in Catholic schools are also interested to learn of the innovative character of his work. St. Thomas was twice professor of philosophy at the University of Paris, one of the new centers of learning in Europe. While the study of Aquinas' thought might at first appear a mere venture in antiquarianism, in St. Thomas' own day many of his ideas met with strong opposition from a number of clerics and theologians who regarded him as too radical and creative a thinker, especially in the use he made of the works of Aristotle. Aristotle's writings had been banned several times by the Church, and Aquinas horrified many members of both the Church and the university because of his enthusiastic engagement with this pagan philosopher's writings that were purely rational in origin and outlook.

Moreover, others studying Aristotle at the time were proposing that there exists an antagonism, or at least a deep division, between the worlds of reason and faith. One of St. Thomas' chief concerns, then, was to demonstrate both the integral place of reason in the study of the faith and also its insufficiency and limitations. For Aquinas there is a place for philosophical reasoning as well as science, for the truths of reason as well as the truths of revelation. Just as grace builds upon nature and brings it to fulfillment, so he argued that faith builds upon reason and perfects the natural work of the mind.

He also held that it is the truth of any proposition that must be judged and not its provenance, thus enabling students to be truly "catholic" in their research and in their investigations into reality: "whatever its source, truth is of the Holy Spirit" (*Summa Theologica*, 1–11, 109, 1 ad 1).

One of the chief contributions of Aquinas to education, then, lies in the breadth of his vision. His interpretation of the world was dynamic, whole, and all-embracing. The structure of the *Summa Theologica* is circular, an *exitus-redditus*, beginning with God, one and three, from whom everything is made, including people; and then treating of human action and the restoration of the human person through the work of Christ and the salvation He offers to bring humankind, as the microcosm of creation, back to God, our destiny and fulfillment. St. Thomas emphasizes the unity of knowledge, and this overall vision of reality provides a context for appreciating the place of the subject disciplines being studied, as well as their role in a coherent understanding of the human person and the nature of human fulfillment.

As well as holding firmly to a sense of the unity of truth from different sources of knowledge, he was convinced that all knowledge begins with the senses and that philosophy cannot be detached from the real world. Existence is grasped by the mind through the senses. Aquinas opposed both subjectivism and agnosticism, stressing that we can know reality and insisting that all reality shares in the transcendental properties of Being: unity, beauty, truth, and goodness. All of reality, then, is *knowable* and is *worth knowing*. Aquinas was a philosophical realist, arguing for a trust in the powers of the human mind to know not only appearances but reality.

St. Thomas' teaching method has been hugely influential. It was based on the belief that truth is reached through dialogue, *disputatio*, following Aristotle's maxim: "If one wishes to find truth one must first consider the opinions of those who judge differently" (*Metaphysics* 3, 1; 995a). This method was one already established in the universities of his time, but it had become overelaborate: St. Thomas toned the method down to a calm, precise, and disciplined dialogue. This framework of dialogue characterizes the whole of his work. The basic building block in the *Summa Theologica*, for example, is the article in which a question is presented that can be answered only through a simple "Yes" or "No." It is not the opinion of St. Thomas that follows, but rather the voices of those opposed to his position. St. Thomas allows these views to be articulated before stating his own conviction and then offering arguments to support his position. He then goes on to answer the particular arguments raised by "the opposition." It is a vigorous and tightly argued system of investigation into reality that is widely used and encouraged in contemporary school studies. Students of all persuasions benefit from the intellectual clarity, rigor, and economy of this approach.

The intellectual generosity and spirit of openness encouraged by this way of pursuing knowledge have also made it very attractive. St. Thomas believed in giving full weight to the arguments of an opponent and treating these arguments with utter seriousness. He also held that, because the mind necessarily attaches itself to truth, even a view that is fundamentally in error must contain some element of truth within it. St. Thomas held that it is not enough to refute the argument of an opponent—one must also know what is right within that view.

Aquinas' view of the human person is one that takes account of both the body and senses and also the immortality of the soul and power of the intellect to grasp universal truths, building upon, but transcending, immediate sense data. He also emphasized the social character of the person, in line with the Aristotelian heritage he was integrating into Christian thinking. He treated at length the character of the intellect and the will in the human person, the two main "powers" of the human soul. He also gave an important role to the imagination in the formulation of knowledge, considering it to be a type of interior sense faculty, providing objects for the intellect to contemplate and adjust.

In his exposition and discussion of the nature of the person, then, Aquinas is supremely rounded and complete, providing the philosophical and theological basis not only for an adequate appreciation of the equality, dignity, and rights of the person but also for the various academic disciplines available to the human being as a composite of matter and form, body and soul, earth and spirit.

Several strands of Thomism have emerged that have proved influential on Catholic education. Foremost among these was neo-Thomism, at the end of the nineteenth century, which highlighted the importance of returning to the writings of St. Thomas himself rather than the commentaries on Aquinas that had dominated seminary training, and thus theological formation, since the Council of Trent in the sixteenth century.

In the nineteenth century Pope Leo XIII made strenuous efforts to restore the study of St. Thomas to the central place in both clerical and university education (see *Aeterni Patris*, 1879, on the permanent value of Thomism, and his letter, *Quod in novissimo*, April 10, 1887, to the Archbishop of Baltimore). *See also*: *Aeterni Patris*; Catholic philosophy of education; Leo XIII, Pope.

Further Reading: Frederick Charles Copleston, *Aquinas* (Harmondsworth, Middlesex, England: Penguin Books, 1955); John Paul II, *Faith and Reason* (Boston: Pauline Books and Media, 1998); Peter Kreeft, ed. and annotator, *Summa of the Summa*, *I* (San Francisco: Ignatius Press, 1990); Josef Pieper, *Guide to Thomas Aquinas* (San Francisco: Ignatius Press, 1986).

Petroc Willey

Arab American Catholics

About three million Arab Americans reside in all fifty states, with one-third concentrated in California, Michigan, and New York. While the Arabic language, with its different dialects, is the unifying language, Arab Americans are Christians, Catholics, Orthodox Christians, Muslims, Druze, and others. Most immigrated to the United States between 1875 and 1920. A second wave began in the 1940s. The first wave came from Syria and Lebanon, and most were Christians. Later, many were Muslims and students from many Middle Eastern countries.

While early immigrants were workers in places such as Dearborn, Michigan, and Lawrence, Massachusetts, Arab Americans have become successful professionals and businesspeople. They have contributed such personages as Kahlil Gibran, artist and poet; Sen. George Mitchell, former majority leader of the Senate; Ralph Nader, consumer advocate; Dr. Michael DeBakey, pioneering heart surgeon; Najeeb Halaby, head of the Federal Aviation Administration; Sen. Spencer Abraham of Michigan; Sen. James Abourezk of South Dakota; James Jabara, America's first jet ace; Donna Shalala, longest-serving secretary of health and human resources; Helen Thomas of the White House Press Corps; Danny Thomas, entertainer; and many prominent leaders of business and industry. In southern states (such as North Carolina) with sparse Catholic populations, Lebanese Americans are credited with building and preserving Roman Catholic churches.

According to Alexa Naff's (1985) definitive work on the early Arab immigrant experience, the Maronite Church has been identified with the Lebanese who employed Syriac as their liturgical language. Melkites and Orthodox used Arabic as their liturgical language and identified with Greater Syria. In most locations, no Maronite or Eastern-rite church existed; therefore, a great many Arab immigrants formed an affinity with the Roman Catholic Church. Muslims in the 1920s and 1930s came together to pray at home or work to compensate for the lack of religious institutions. Currently, many mosques and schools for Muslims have been built, alleviating a lack of locations for worship and study.

Arab Americans at various times have formed clubs and organizations first for social reasons and later for political purposes. These organizations have never become a potent force perhaps because Arab Americans have Lebanese, Syrian, or other nationalities as places or origin. Further, some immigrants are Christian or Muslim or are members of other religious groups. Moreover, many Christian denominations are represented, and several Muslim viewpoints are extant.

The *Harvard Encyclopedia of American Ethnic Groups* reports that Arab Americans have a high rate of achievement. A sizable percentage are professional and semi-professional people in all fields. Second-generation Arab Americans are strongly urged to pursue academic pursuits by their families. Most parents see education as a means to a better life for their children than the hardships endured by the older generation.

This emphasis upon education is made possible by close family ties, including a strong devotion to children. The Arab American family is characterized by generosity and hospitality to guests and visitors. Children are encouraged to show respect for family guests and to be present when visitors are present.

The foundation for family identity, education, and generosity was provided by the hard work of pioneers. Many Arab Americans started as individual entrepreneurs, often selling dry goods from horses and carts from house to house. They were thrifty, saved their earnings, and created successful businesses that provided future generations the best of educations. Self-sufficiency was prized, and welfare was frowned upon. *See also*: Immigration/Immigrants.

Further Reading: Alexa Naff, *Becoming American: The Early Arab Immigrant Experience* (Carbondale and Edwardsville: Southern Illinois University Press, 1985); A. Tannous, "Acculturation of an Arab-Syrian Community in the Deep South," *American Sociological Review* 9 (1942): 264–271; S. Thernstrom et al., eds., *Harvard Encyclopedia of American Ethnic Groups* (Cambridge: Belknap Press of Harvard University Press, 1980).

Ellis A. Joseph

Asian American Catholics

The Asians present in the United States trace their origins to China, the Philippine Islands, Japan, India, Korea, and Vietnam. The 2000 U.S. Census Bureau cited these groups and "Other Asian" (Other Asian Alone, e.g. Cambodian, or two or more Asian categories) in the 2000 Census. Of the total U.S. population of 281,421,906, Asians numbered 10,242,998, or 3.6 percent.

The following numbers describe the Asian American population: Asian Indian 1,678,765 (0.6%), Chinese 2,432,585 (0.9%), Filipino 1,850,314 (0.7%), Japanese 796,700 (0.3%), Korean 1,076,872 (0.4%), and Other Asian 1,285,234 (0.5%). There are no specific numbers available about the Asian American Catholic population.

From 1989 to 1990 hearings on Asian Americans were conducted by the National Catholic Educational Association, the United States Catholic Conference's Office of Migration and Refugee Services, and the Archdiocese of New York's Office of Pastoral Research and Planning. This seminal meeting gathered representatives from various Asian communities and cities to reflect upon their experience in the United States and the Catholic Church. Among the many topics discussed and reported upon were the Asian American experience and perceptions of Catholic schools.

A major finding of these hearings asserted the diversity of the various groups but also found some generalizations that can be made regarding the Asian American attitudes toward Catholic schools. First and foremost, Asian Americans voiced the importance that education held in their families. They perceive Catholic schools as safe, structured learning environments where moral values are taught and the Catholic faith is lived.

While wanting their children to assimilate and succeed in U.S. society, Asian Americans want Catholic schools to assist them with maintaining cultural identity through customs, history, and language. Parents expressed a desire for their children to be fluent in English as well as their native language but prefer that instruction be completely in English.

Generally speaking, the previous experience of Filipinos and Vietnamese with Catholic schools in their particular country of origin was positive and had favorably disposed these Asian communities to see the value of Catholic education as experienced in elementary and secondary schools, as well as in institutions of higher education. The Asian Americans see the schools as places to grow in their faith, build bonds of community, and be immersed in the knowledge and spirit of the Second Vatican Council.

Catholic school teachers note the excellent academic performance of Asian American students. They are seen as highly motivated and demonstrate exceptional language acquisition skills when English is not the native language. Reflecting cultures that honor elders, structure, and community, Asian students are seen as cooperative and productive students.

Asian Americans represent small numbers of administrative leadership and faculty in Catholic schools. A common theme and value in all education circles, both public and private, is that a faculty and staff should be a reflection of the general population and especially a representation of a particular student body. Efforts should be encouraged for Asian Americans to consider careers and ministry in Catholic education.

The United States Catholic Elementary and Secondary School 2001–2002: The Annual Statistical Report on Schools, Enrollment, and Staffing on ethnic groups and minorities stated that the number of minorities has more than doubled in the past thirty years. The organization's records indicated that of the total U.S. Catholic school student populations in 1970, 1980, and 2002, minorities accounted for 10.8 percent, 19.4 percent, and 26.1 percent, respectively. NCEA (2002) statistics noted that Asian Americans in elementary and middle schools numbered 76,727 students, or 3.8 percent of the total elementary and middle Catholic school population of 2,004,037. Asian American students in Catholic secondary schools numbered 26,473, representing 4.1 percent of the 643,264 students in these schools.

While Asian American families place high value on a quality education for their children, many find Catholic school costs in tuition and fees to present a formidable obstacle to sending their children to Catholic schools. Unlike immigrant groups of the past who benefited from a Catholic school system that was highly subsidized by the contributed services of women and men religious and parishes, Asian Americans experience a different situation. Most schools are staffed by laypeople, for whom their respective schools struggle to pay a just and living wage. With the escalation of expenditures to operate a Catholic school, Asian Americans, along with many other newly immigrated groups, face a difficult choice in having the ability to provide a Catholic education for their children. *See also*: Immigration/Immigrants.

Further Reading: Suzanne E. Hall, Ruth Narita Doyle, and Peter Tran, eds., *A Catholic Response to the Asian Presence*, A Report on Asian Hearings conducted by NCEA, USCC Office of Migration and Refugee Services, Pastoral Care of Migrants and Refugees, and New York Archdiocesan Office of Pastoral Research and Planning (Washington, DC: National Catholic Educational Association, 1990); Dale McDonald, *United States Catholic Elementary and Secondary School 2001–2002: The Annual Statistical Report on Schools, Enrollment, and Staffing* (Washington, DC: National Catholic Educational Association, 2002); United States Catholic Conference, *Asian and Pacific Presence: Harmony in Faith* (Washington, DC: Author, 2001); James Youniss and John J. Convey, eds., *Catholic Schools at the Crossroads; Survival and Transformation* (New York: Teachers College Press, 2000).

Michael P. Caruso, SJ

Assessment

The American Federation of Teachers in 1990 described assessment as "the process of obtaining information that is used to make educational decisions about students, to give feedback to the student about his or her progress, strengths, and weaknesses, to judge instructional effectiveness and curricular adequacy, and to inform policy" (p. 2). Wiggins (1998) further delineated the purpose of assessment, which, he claimed, is to *improve* student learning, not solely to *audit* it. *Auditing* describes an inventory of activities when they are completed, as in the case of accountants who audit a corporation's books at the end of the fiscal year to check that all the financial records match for accuracy. Individuals do not run their businesses solely for a successful audit. However, according to Wiggins, schools too often are concerned about the equivalent: "[W]e focus on teaching students to pass simplistic, often multiple-choice tests composed of 'items' that neither assess what we value nor provide useful feedback about how to teach and how to learn" (p. 7).

Lazear (1994) compared the traditional with the new assessment paradigm, along with the instructional consequences of each approach. For example, he identified the traditional assessment paradigm as promoting (1) standardized instruction and testing since all students are perceived as learning in basically the same way; (2) standardized tests as the most accurate indicators of student learning; (3) a clearly defined body of knowledge that students acquire in school and then demonstrate or reproduce on a test; and (4) the perspective that if learning cannot be objectively tested in a standardized way, then it is not worth teaching or learning. In contrast, the new assessment paradigm advocates that (1) there are no "standard students," that each student learns in unique ways; therefore, instruction and assessment must be diversified and individualized; (2) performance-based assessment, involving a variety of testing instruments, provides a more comprehensive and accurate profile of student learning; (3) teaching students to be lifelong learners, that is, teaching them how to learn, to think critically and creatively, and to be intelligent in as many ways as possible, is the main purpose of education; and (4) the process of learning is as critical as the content of the curriculum, and not all learning can be objectively tested.

When teachers test what is easy to test, rather than the complex and important tasks that they value in their classrooms and that are at the heart of their curriculum, they sacrifice their primary purpose as educators, as well as their students' intellectual needs. In such instances, Wiggins (1998) identified teachers as settling for score accuracy and efficiency, rather than striving to gather more valuable information about student learning. This practice is based upon a misunderstanding of the role of assessment in learning. Wiggins elaborated: "In other words, the greatest impediment to achieving the vision described is not standardized testing. Rather, the problem is the reverse: we use the tests we do because we persist in thinking of assessment as not germane to learning, and therefore best done expediently" (p. 7). He further made the point that once assessment becomes integrated into teaching and learning, that is, no longer separate from instruction, it will become an educative aspect of the curriculum.

Critical to Wiggins' (1998) perspective on the integration of assessment with teaching and learning is effective teaching practice. Parkay and Stanford (1995) stated, "Successful teachers continually evaluate the effectiveness of their teaching because they recognize that how well students learn depends on how well they teach" (p. 382). A synthesis of current research on best educational practices was introduced by Zemelman, Daniels, and Hyde (1998). These educators summarized the research into thirteen interrelated principles, assumptions, or theories that characterize best teaching practices. They are (1) "Schooling should be STUDENT-CENTERED, taking its cues from young people's interests, concerns, and questions"; (2) "As often as possible, school should stress learning that is EXPERIENTIAL"; (3) "Learning in all subjects needs to be HOLISTIC"; (4) "Learning activities need to be AUTHENTIC"; (5) "Students need to learn and practice many forms of EXPRESSION to deeply engage ideas"; (6) "Effective learning is balanced with opportunities for REFLECTION"; (7) "Teachers should tap into the primal power of SOCIAL relations to promote learning"; (8) "Some of the most effective social learning activities are COLLABORATIVE"; (9) "Classrooms can become more effective and productive when procedures are DEMOCRATIC"; (10) "Powerful learning comes from COGNITIVE experiences"; (11) "Children's learning must be approached as DEVELOPMENTAL"; (12) "Children's learning always involves CONSTRUCTING ideas and systems"; and (13) "Following all these principles means that school is CHALLENGING" (pp. 9–15).

The Congregation for Catholic Education, in its 1977 document, *The Catholic School*, declared that the specifically Catholic character of the school lies in its intention to foster the growth of the whole person. Catholic pedagogy rests upon teaching to the whole child, individualizing instruction, and personalizing the learning, which necessitate holistic assessment practices. Catholic educators who are learner-focused must continue to value the learner through their assessment methods. This necessitates expanding one's assessment practices beyond standardized means and incorporating qualitative measures of identifying students' academic strengths and weaknesses.

Although the new assessment paradigm demonstrates a shift to qualitative measures of student performance, it does not dictate that quantitative approaches should be abandoned. Rather, a combination of quantitative with qualitative measurements should be utilized thoughtfully in the pursuit of a comprehensive, holistic learning plan for each student. *See also*: Outcomes.

Further Reading: American Federation of Teachers, National Council on Measurement in Education, and National Education Association, *Standards for Teacher Competence in Educational Assessment of Students*, ERIC Document No. ED 323 186, 1990; Congregation for Catholic Education, *The Catholic School* (Washington, DC: United States Catholic Conference, 1977); David Lazear, *Multiple Intelligence Approaches to Assessment, Solving the Assessment Conundrum* (Tucson, AZ: Zephyr Press, 1994); Forrest W. Parkay and Beverly H. Stanford,

Becoming a Teacher (Boston: Allyn and Bacon, 1995); Grant Wiggins, *Educative Assessment, Designing Assessments to Inform and Improve Student Performance* (San Francisco: Jossey-Bass, 1998); Grant Wiggins and Jay McTighe, *Understanding by Design* (Alexandria, VA: Association for Supervision and Curriculum Development, 1998); Steven Zemelman, Harvey Daniels, and Arthur Hyde, *Best Practice, New Standards for Teaching and Learning in America's Schools* (Portsmouth, NH: Heinemann, 1998).

Gini Shimabukuro

Association of Catholic Leadership Programs (ACLP)

The Association of Catholic Leadership Programs, commonly referred to as the ACLP, is an organization of Catholic colleges and universities that offer formal programs and degrees to prepare leaders for Catholic education at the elementary and secondary levels. The history of this organization highlights the desire of Catholic colleges and universities to be in dialogue with one another about the vision and direction of the Church's schools.

The organization cites the document *Catholic Higher Education and the Pastoral Ministry of the Church* (1980) as a summons "to provide Christian formation programs for educators who are evangelizers by call and covenant and mission. Only those who have been formed theologically and spiritually can respond adequately to the call of professional ministry in Christian education according to the vision of Jesus Christ and the Church" (p. 6). The ACLP would also anticipate the harmonious relationships between dioceses and Catholic higher education, as delineated in the Apostolic Constitution *Ex Corde Ecclesiae* (1990), in which Catholic higher education places its resources in service to the needs of the local church.

Throughout the 1980s several scholars from various universities met periodically to discuss their particular leadership programs and how they might cooperate in a more organized manner to share experience and perspectives. The participants of these discussions included Rev. Edwin McDermott, SJ, and Sr. Mary Peter Traviss, OP, representing the University of San Francisco's Institute of Catholic Educational Leadership (ICEL); Thomas McCarver and Karen Ristau of the University of St. Thomas' Murray Institute, St. Paul, Minnesota; Donald Frericks of the University of Dayton; and Sr. Rosemary Hocevar, OSU, of Ursuline College, Pepper Pike, Ohio.

While the organization maintains 1983 as its year of foundation, at the April 1991 National Catholic Educational Association's (NCEA) annual convention in Boston, the ACLP adopted the final drafts of its bylaws and constitution. Sr. Mary Peter Traviss, OP, was elected as the first president of the organization, with Donald Frericks elected as the first secretary. The organization meets twice a year in conjunction with the NCEA's Easter week national convention and at the fall meeting of NCEA's Chief Administrators of Catholic Education (CACE).

ACLP is loosely affiliated with CACE. Since the vision of the ACLP has direct bearing upon the work of diocesan superintendents in finding qualified principals and leaders for their schools, ACLP determined that their work and presence should be showcased at CACE's annual meeting. The ACLP is configured to assist the member schools but primarily to be of service to the Church's elementary and secondary schools.

Each year the ACLP members exhibit their work at the NCEA's national convention and meet with people interested in the programs from the ACLP schools. Another popular feature at the NCEA convention is the presentation of recently completed doctoral dissertations about Catholic education. Many members of the ACLP are regular presenters at the convention, offering their expertise and the findings from their research.

Training competent, scholarly professionals is the chief aim of the ACLP. The founders' vision promotes the belief that formal training in a university degree or credential program would provide greater breadth and depth than workshops could render. The organization is committed to the conviction that "leaders of Catholic educational institutions are best served through regular studies in degree programs designed for that specific purpose."

There are 236 Catholic colleges and universities in the United States. Some of these institutions have distinct programs for developing Catholic school leaders. Among these institutions are the following members of ACLP, listed regionally: California, Loyola Marymount University, University of San Francisco; Florida, Barry University; Illinois, Dominican University; Indiana, Marian College, University of Notre Dame; Maryland, Loyola College in Maryland; Massachusetts, Boston College; Minnesota, St. Mary's University of Minnesota, University of St. Thomas; Missouri, St. Louis University; Nebraska, Creighton University; New Jersey, Caldwell College; New York, Fordham University, Manhattan College, University of Rochester; Ohio, University of Dayton, Ursuline College, Xavier University; Oregon, University of Portland; Pennsylvania, Villanova University; Texas, Saint Mary's University, University of Dallas; Washington, Seattle University; Washington, D.C., Catholic University of America; Australia, Australian Catholic University. The NCEA and diocese of Sioux City, Iowa, also maintain memberships in the organization. *See also*: *Chief Administrators of Catholic Education (CACE); National Catholic Educational Association (NCEA).*

Further Reading: United States Catholic Conference, *Catholic Higher Education and the Pastoral Ministry of the Church* (Washington, DC: Author, 1980).

Michael P. Caruso, SJ

At will employment

The doctrine of at will employment is based on English master–servant law, which held that the master had the right to hire and fire whomever he wished for whatever reason he wished. Concepts such as tenure, an expectation of continuing employment, were not recognized by the English system of law in the ordinary employer–employee relationship. Thus, an employer could hire anyone he pleased and could fire that same person for no reason, a good reason, or even a bad reason, although there existed no clear definition of what constituted a bad reason. The at will employment doctrine dominated employment law until fairly recent times, although an early California case, *Petermann v. International Brotherhood of Teamsters Local 396*, held that the employer could not escape liability for firing an at will employee who declined to commit perjury. *Petermann* and its progeny began the tort theory of wrongful discharge. Petermann actually brought suit on a breach of contract theory; the Court examined the demands of public policy, which would militate against forcing employees to commit perjury, and began judicial consideration of the tort of wrongful discharge.

The case of *Wagenseller v. Scottsdale Memorial Hospital* provides one example of the tort of wrongful discharge. A nurse who had participated in a white-water rafting trip with some doctors and other nurses in the hospital refused to participate in a "talent show" that required her to expose her unclothed backside to others. She also refused to participate when she was later asked to perform for other doctors and nurses in the hospital. She had an exemplary employment record, but after her refusals, she was fired for lack of a cooperative attitude. The Court declined to extend the at will doctrine to cover such a situation and held that the firing violated public policy. In essence, the Court ruled that an employer could fire for no reason or a good reason but not for a bad reason. A bad reason would be anything that violates public policy. One example of this would be whistle-blowing legislation, which protects persons who bring problems to the attention of management or law enforcement authorities.

Employers in Catholic institutions have long availed themselves of the protections of the at will doctrine. Since significant state action has to exist in a nonpublic institution to such an extent that the contested action can fairly be said to be that of the state before a court will recognize the existence of constitutional due process protections, it is extremely difficult for an employee of a nonpublic institution to succeed in a claim for wrongful termination. The 1982 U.S. Supreme Court case *Rendell-Baker v. Kohn* held that a private school that received 99 percent of its funding from the state did not have state action in the firing of employees; thus, a nonpublic employee trying to win a termination case on the grounds of state action has little chance of being considered anything but an at will employee. If the employee has a contract, breach of contract damages may be sought. Without a contract, the employee is considered to be at will.

Contract law seemed to provide an assist to employees protesting termination. Promises made in employee handbooks and sometimes promises made at hiring were found to be contractual and limited employers' ability to terminate. More recent times have witnessed employers placing disclaimers, stating that the handbook is not a contract, in the handbook.

Institutions that offer employees contracts do not have to utilize the at will doctrine since declining to renew a contract is not the same thing as terminating someone. Numerous cases involving Catholic institutions have held that not renewing a contract is the prerogative of the employer who does not offer renewal of contract to an employee so long as no laws are violated in the nonrenewal.

Many sectarian institutions, including Catholic ones, have moved to eliminate contracts for employees. Without contracts, in the vast majority of states, employees have at will employment status. Employers are free to hire and fire whom they wish when they wish so long as no public policy is violated.

Tenure, the expectation of continuing employment, is one way that teachers have been given job protection. The case of *NLRB v. Catholic Bishop of Chicago* ruled that Catholic schools did not have to recognize labor unions, which foster tenure. Without unions, since the concept of de facto tenure, in fact, has been largely abandoned by the courts, teachers find their employment status governed by contract law or in the absence of a contract, by the at will doctrine. *See also*: Contract law; *National Labor Relations Board v. The Catholic Bishop of Chicago et al.*

Further Reading: Deborah A. Ballam, "Employment-at-Will: The Impending Death of a Doctrine," *American Business Law Journal* 37 (Summer 2000): 653–687; *NLRB v. Catholic Bishop of Chicago*, 440 U.S. 490 (1975); *Petermann v. International Brotherhood of Teamsters*, 344 P.2d 25 (Cal. 1959); *Rendell-Baker v. Kohn*, 102 S.Ct. 2764 (1982); *Wagenseller v. Scottsdale Memorial Hospital*, 710 P.2d 1025 (1985).

Mary Angela Shaughnessy, SCN

Augustine, St. (384–430)

The influence of St. Augustine of Hippo (A.D. 384–430) upon Christian education has been highly significant, both through the religious orders involved in Catholic schools that have adopted his *Rule* and through the enormous impact of his theological and spiritual writings, which provide foundations for the Church's understanding of itself and its mission, especially in the West.

In the first place, it is important to note that, standing in direct descent from St. Augustine are numerous religious orders, many of which have an educational apostolate, that have looked to his *Rule* for inspiration. The Dominicans, the Servites, and the Premonstratensians are among the orders that have adopted his *Rule*, and countless religious orders of women, both active and contemplative, are guided by it. This *Rule*, the first to be drawn up in the West, "recapitulates Augustinian spirituality" (Clark, 1994, p. 92), and those orders following this *Rule* that are involved in school education have thus been able to provide for those in their care an ethos imbued with an Augustinian spirit.

More fundamentally, as holding the acknowledged primary place among the Latin Fathers of the Church, St. Augustine has left an immense legacy in his writings. These bear witness to a complex, towering figure of genius whose personality and thought have impacted upon the development of the Christian faith, especially in the Western Church, more than any other single figure save St. Thomas Aquinas. His contribution to the shaping of culture and thought has had a direct bearing upon the notion of Christian education.

His work *De catechizandis rudibus* is a milestone in the Church's understanding of the methodology and content of an adult catechesis. This work, written in about A.D. 400, covers both the vocation and spirituality of the catechist and outlines what needs to be covered in any catechesis for an adult wishing to be received into the Catholic faith.

Augustine's best-known work is his *Confessions* (c. 397–401), an autobiographical account of his childhood, growth to maturity, conversion to the Catholic faith after numerous explorations and struggles, and subsequent settling to the newly discovered joy of the limitless grace and mercy of God, which is unparalleled in the ancient world in its scope, power, and character, accenting as it does the intensely personal nature of the dialogue between the individual Christian and God. In this unique work, he can be seen as the precursor to the more recent interest in the subjectivity of the person and the realm of religious experience.

Augustine forged a vital synthesis between contemporary philosophical thought, in the form of Neoplatonism, and the Christian scriptural heritage. In doing so he set the basic orientation for spiritual and cultural development in the West for almost the next thousand years, when scholasticism, especially through the work of St. Thomas Aquinas, provided a new synthesis between the Augustinian legacy and the work of "the Philosopher," Aristotle.

The founder of Neoplatonism, which revived Plato's teaching, was Plotinus (A.D. 205–270). Though Augustine parted company with Neoplatonism at certain key points and was at pains to distinguish genuine Christian wisdom from this movement (O'Meara, 1982), especially in its assessment of the value of the historical, contingent world, in particular, in the light of the incarnational character of the Christian faith, Neoplatonism was deeply influential in his overall conception of reality.

The Neoplatonist conception of God was that He could be described as the One,

Saint Augustine. Courtesy of the Library of Congress.

the True, the Good, and the Beautiful. St. Augustine, together with the majority of the early church fathers, found such a metaphysic congenial to Christian thought. The Lord is One, and Augustine believed that He is rightly approached along the paths of truth seeking, goodness, and the appreciation of beauty.

Alongside his developing doctrine of God, Augustine was also meditating deeply upon the Christian understanding of the human person, and here again he achieves a synthesis of elements of the Neoplatonist metaphysic with scriptural accounts. Augustine offered the Church an anthropology rooted in an understanding of the person as imaging the Divine Trinity. In *De Trinitate*, written between 399 and 419, Augustine explored analogies to the Trinity in the person. He believed that the whole of creation, as the work of its Creator, reflected the Trinity in some way—there are "traces" of the Trinity everywhere (*De Trinitate* VI, 10, 12). But the peak of creation, the human being, shows an image of the Trinity in the threefold capacity of the soul to memorize, to know, and to will. The person comes to fulfillment as an image of God in the activity of remembering, understanding and loving God (*De Trinitate* XIV, 8, 11–12; XV, 27, 49).

For Augustine, all educational practice is rooted, more or less explicitly, in a philosophical understanding of reality, especially ultimate reality and an understanding of the human person. These contribute the framework for educational aims and set out the desired and anticipated achievements of the intellectual quest. In this respect, then, in setting a framework for educational discovery, we can see Augustine's most important contribution to Catholic schooling.

The understanding of God as One and as Creator leads Augustine to the conviction that all knowledge must cohere and that, therefore, educational disciplines can be brought into harmony with one another. There is one God who creates a single, coherent world.

God as Truth is the foundation of Augustine's theory of knowledge, while the human capacity for understanding ensures that intellectual effort can reach its "end." In the light of the current prevalence of relativist understandings of truth, at both popular and scholarly levels, Augustine's thinking on this matter is perhaps of particular importance. Two early works are concerned with a defense of the objectivity of knowledge. Against the Skeptics, Augustine set out to establish the possibility of attaining truth. What is at stake, he argued, is "our life, our morals, our soul." *De Magistro* (*On the Teacher*), written in 389, also sets out to establish the human capacity to know truth and includes an investigation into the causes of learning. While he wished to defend the ability of the human person to find truth, Augustine was also anxious to show that human reason has its limitations in the ascent to truth and that it must prepare the way for the act of faith. His defense of the reasonableness of the act of faith and, therefore, of an educational philosophy rooted in faith premises is a vital contribution in this area (Bubacz, 1981).

God as the Good is the foundation for Augustine's theory of happiness, and his understanding of the capacity and limitations of the human will is also of key importance here. Neoplatonists regarded all that exists as a kind of overflow of the Good. A longing for union with what is higher and ultimately with the Good itself pervades all reality. This longing for wholeness and union is the source of that divinely human discontent which cannot find rest until it unites itself with what is highest. Augustine, therefore, shared with Neoplatonism the conviction that education is not a purely intellectual activity but is also a path of formation, a cultivation of the capacities of the whole person, including the bodily and affective dimensions. The goal is participation in the life of God, who is the Good as well as the True. Education must help us to discern where true happiness can be found, which is not finally in any created reality but only in God. But here also Augustine parted company with Neoplatonism in his stress on the absolute necessity of grace. Augustine established the conceptual theological framework that has underpinned antipathy to any form of "pedagogic naturalism" in educational theory or practice.

God as Beauty provides Augustine with the foundation for his aesthetics. Created realities can attract us by evoking a love for what is beautiful, and they can lead us back to their source in God, who is the all-beautiful, ever ancient, and ever new. This movement toward God requires conversion in the human being because beauty can distract us from its divine source as well as lead us to it, and so the ascent to God through beauty involves the response of the will to grace as well as the involvement of the senses, memory, and intellect. An appreciation of the place of beauty in Augustine's thought, then, enables us to see the ways in which he stresses the need for graced religious and moral, as well as intellectual, conversion and growth in the educational development of the person. *See also*: Catholic philosophy of education.

Further Reading: Augustine, *De catechizandis rudibus* (*On instructing the unlearned*), Ancient Christian Writers Series 2 (Westminster, MD, 1946; available: Mahwah, NJ: Paulist Press); Augustine, *De Trinitate*, Fathers of the Church Series 45 (New York and Washington: Catholic University of America Press, 1947); Bruce Bubacz, *St. Augustine's Theory of Knowledge* (New York: Edwin Mellor Press, 1981); Mary T. Clark, *Augustine* (London: Geoffrey Chapman, 1994); Dominic O'Meara, ed., *Neoplatonism and Christian Thought* (Albany: State University of New York Press, 1982).

Petroc Willey

B

Baltimore Catechism

Among the catechisms available, the *Baltimore Catechism* was the best-known Catholic religious education text in use in the United States from the time of its initial publication in 1885 until just prior to the Second Vatican Council (1962–1965). The text presents doctrine and theology in a "catechism" question-and-answer format. It recommended, "You should . . . learn the Catechism by heart . . . even when you do not fully understand it; because afterwards, when you read books on religion or hear sermons, all these questions and answers will come back to your mind."

What came to be known as the *Baltimore Catechism* was an initiative of the Third Plenary Council of Baltimore in 1884 by the U.S. bishops. The catechism was part of the armamentaria, or equipment, along with parish parochial schools, that the bishops advocated to sustain the faith of American Catholics. Some historical information about the *Baltimore Catechism* noted in the extensive documentation by Bryce points out that it was Bishop John Lancaster Spalding of Peoria and Reverend Januarius de Concilio of Jersey City, New Jersey, who authored the first edition of the catechism. The intent of a common catechism was to maintain doctrinal orthodoxy. Theologians such as Bishop Spalding and Rev. de Concilio wrote all the editions of the catechism without consulting educators. During the first ten years, there was little enthusiasm for the *Baltimore Catechism*; this is revealed by diocesan ecclesiastical endorsements of seven other catechisms. Some of the critical reviews of the catechism were published by clerical authors of catechisms and religion texts in competition with the *Baltimore Catechism*. By 1896, a special committee was to be assigned by the bishops to revise the catechism. Recurring concerns expressed about the catechism were theological errors, language that children found difficult, and vagueness of ecclesiastical endorsements. Beginning in 1898, religion texts directed at grade levels, in expository formats with illustrations and enlarged print, became available. Bryce observes, "By 1918, at least 72 new texts had appeared; and by 1941, the year when the revised edition of the *Baltimore Catechism* finally did come out, at least 109 additional volumes had been published" (p. 143). Revision of the catechism was an ongoing process up to the time of the Second Vatican Council. A revision of the catechism being prepared prior to the council was never issued. It was intended to be a resource document for catechists rather than a text for students.

The *Baltimore Catechism* has survived its many critics and continues to be available in the twenty-first century. It has found a considerable following among those identified as "traditionalist" Catholics. There are several versions of the *Baltimore Catechism* in print, including reproductions of the original catechisms by TAN Books and Publishers. The publisher describes them as the well-known "phoneticized words and meanings" versions of the *Baltimore Catechisms, Nos. 1, 2, 3*, and Fr. Thomas L. Kinkead's (1994) *Explanation of the Baltimore Catechism, No. 4*, originally issued in 1891. In the preface of the *Explanation of the Baltimore Catechism*, Fr. Kinkead makes the observation that there are religion teachers who are not able to explain what they are teaching and unable to inspire their students. Fr. Kinkead added informative commentary, clarifications, or definitions to each of the 421 questions and answers of the second version of the catechism that included the 100 questions of the first version.

Another version of the catechism is edited by Allan R. Kucera and entitled *Baltimore Catechism No. 3: Fr. Connell's Confraternity Edition*. There are also the three age-group level texts of the *Saint Joseph Baltimore Catechisms* explained by Fr. Bennet Kelley, CP. They are designated as No. 0, *First Communion Catechism*, for grades 1–2, No. 1 for grades 3–5, and No. 2 for grades 6–8. These catechisms are in the revised 1941 text of the "official" *Baltimore Catechism* and include prayers, scriptural texts, liturgy, pictures, and discussion questions to reinforce the traditional lessons of the catechism. Also, still available are Catholic religious education textbooks such as the *Our Holy Faith Series* developed in the 1950s and based on the *Baltimore Catechism*. The series includes texts for each of the eight grades at the elementary level and is offered by the Neumann Press of Long Prairie, Minnesota (cf. http://www.neumannpress.com/ourholfaitse.html. Accessed June 24, 2002).

Regarding the appropriateness of the use of the *Baltimore Catechism* in the contemporary Church, it is noteworthy that as of June 1, 2002, it was not listed among the catechetical materials voluntarily submitted for review and found to be in conformity with the *Catechism of the Catholic Church*, which is the catechism currently in use, by the Ad Hoc Committee to Oversee the Use of the *Catechism of the Catholic Church* of the National Conference of Catholic Bishops. *See also*: Bishops; Bishops, in the nineteenth-century conflict over Catholic schools; Plenary Councils of Baltimore.

Further Reading: Mary Charles Bryce, "The *Baltimore Catechism*—Origin and Reception," in Michael Warren, ed., *Sourcebook for Modern Catechetics, Volume 1* (Winona, MN: Saint Mary's Press, Christian Brothers, 1983); Mary Charles Bryce, "The Influence of the Catechism of the Third Plenary Council of Baltimore on Widely Used Elementary Religion Text Books from Its Composition in 1885 to Its 1941 Revision," unpublished doctoral dissertation, Catholic University of America, 1970; Mary Charles Bryce, "Religious Education in the Pastoral Letters and National Meetings of the U.S. Hierarchy," in Michael Warren, ed., *Sourcebook for Modern Catechetics, Volume 1* (Winona, MN: Saint Mary's Press, Christian Brothers, 1983); Bennet Kelley, *Saint Joseph Baltimore Catechism*, rev. ed. No. 2 (New York: Catholic Book, 1969); Thomas L. Kinkead, *An Explanation of the Baltimore Catechism, No. 4* (Rockford, IL: Tan Book and Publisher, 1994).

Robert B. Williams

Bennett Law

The educational activities of states increased in the years following the Civil War. Catholic authorities perceived a tendency toward what they felt was undue interference in the operation of their schools, which they believed was a divine right, by the civil state. The strife over the Bennett Law in Wisconsin is a most fitting illustration of the conflict between the Church and the civil state over education.

In the 1880s, state superintendents of schools felt that existing compulsory school attendance legislation was inadequate. In 1889, Gov. William Dempster Hoard, a Republican, called for legislation that would empower local superintendents of schools to inspect all schools in their districts to ensure that all children were being taught to read and write English, thus guaranteeing their right to full citizenship. Hoard looked upon the English language as an indispensable agent in forging loyalty to the country's heritage and in developing a true American nationality, especially among immigrants and their descendants.

The Bennett Law was enacted in the spring of 1889. Its key features required attendance in the town or district of a child's residence and defined a school as a place where English would be the language of instruction. The Lutherans were first to oppose the law. The Catholic hierarchy was quick to follow suit. The bishops termed the law unnecessary, offensive, and unjust. They claimed that the law constituted state interference with Catholic schools. The conflict escalated, with the bishops insisting their position emanated from natural and divine law, and Gov. Hoard and his backers arguing that it was the right of the state to demand that all schools within its borders develop citizenship and to ascertain whether that citizenship education was taking place.

The census of 1890 reported that there were 249,164 Catholics and 160,919 Lutherans in the state, constituting approximately 75 percent of the communicants of religious bodies in Wisconsin. Wisconsin ranked first of the north-central states in parochial school enrollments with 66,065 students; of this number there were 37,854 in Catholic schools and 26,359 in Lutheran schools.

The Bennett Law was the central issue in the Milwaukee mayoral election in the spring of 1890. It has been estimated that in 1890 over one-half of Milwaukee's population either had been born in Germany or had at least one parent born there. Governor Hoard contended that the Catholic and Lutheran church leaders were interfering with the legitimate rights of the state. He maintained that there were 50,000 young Wisconsites who were not receiving any instruction. Democrat George W. Peck, an opponent of the Bennett Law, swept to victory in the election.

The German Catholic Convention opened in Milwaukee in May 1890. Bishop Frederick W. Katzer of Green Bay, soon to become archbishop of Milwaukee, delivered the keynote address, in which he asserted that the law amounted to a usurpation of parental rights and a state monopoly of schooling.

Catholic and Lutheran authorities were united in opposition to the law, because they viewed it as an attack on their schools. Other Protestants, with few schools of their own and with a historic adherence to the public school and to the English language as a vehicle to instill patriotism and build citizenship, generally supported the law. The Unitarians were particularly supportive, regarding the public school as the fundamental safeguard to American liberty. They interpreted the Catholic position as subjecting the secular state to ecclesiastical control, and they urged Wisconsin's Catholics to throw off what they deemed was the yoke of the Roman, foreign-spirited hierarchy.

The Democratic candidate, George W. Peck, soundly defeated Gov. Hoard in the fall gubernatorial election. The Bennett Law played a major role in determining the election's outcome. Commentators attributed ethnic and religious forces as critical in the election. The acrimony that arose was due in part to those nativists who claimed that the public school was under attack. Others argued that the haste to "Americanize" everything had led to a resurgence of German nationalistic spirit.

Catholic leaders in Wisconsin had maintained that the Bennett Law was directed against Catholicism and sought to destroy Catholic schools. All Catholic sources agreed that the Church had won a victory in the election, which most deemed crucial for the Church's educational mission. Some Catholics maintained that the state had no right or competence in education but should financially support the educational endeavors of parent and Church. At the very least, they thought, the state should leave the Catholic parents and Catholic schools alone.

The repeal of the Bennett Law was the first action of the Wisconsin legislature in 1891. Governor Peck had urged its repeal, holding that the state should uphold the right of citizens to educate their children in accord with their conscience without interference by the state. In its stead an act was passed that eliminated the district clause of residence and the definition of a school as one that taught certain subjects in English. The Catholic Church had successfully protected its schools from what church leaders considered an attempt by the secular state to control, and perhaps eradicate, them. As a result, they had achieved a measure of independence for their schools, which they considered to be essential for the preservation of the faith. *See also*: Ethnicity (and parish schools); German American Catholics; Katzer, Frederick; Parental rights.

Further Reading: Colman J. Barry, *The Catholic Church and German Americans* (Milwaukee: Bruce, 1953); Harry H. Heming, *The Catholic Church in Wisconsin* (Milwaukee: T. J. Sullivan, 1896); Thomas C. Hunt, "The Bennett Law: Focus of Conflict between Church and State," *Journal of Church and State* 23, 1 (Winter 1981): 69–93; George W. Rankin, *William Dempster Hoard* (Fort Atkinson, WI: W. D. Hoard and Sons, 1923); Roger E. Wyman, "Wisconsin Ethnic Groups and the Election of 1890," *Wisconsin Magazine of History* 4 (Summer 1968): 269–293.

Thomas C. Hunt

Bible-reading in public schools

The devotional reading of the Bible, King James version, was a hallmark of nineteenth-century public education and continued on into the twentieth century. Bible-reading was the visible sign of Protestant ascendancy in American public education. The practice was a focal point of conflict between Catholics and Protestants over educational policy, conflict that was sometimes bitter and on occasion violent.

As early as 1786 Benjamin Rush, a leader in the Revolutionary era, advocated the use of the Bible in schools, arguing that no other book contained half as much useful knowledge for civil governments or for individuals. Bible-reading was the linchpin of Horace Mann's argument that the common school he advanced was religious but not sectarian. It was the "authoritative expounder" of Christianity, and wherever it was, there was Christianity. Described as having provided an "invaluable blessing" to the Christian world, the Bible was regarded by mainstream Protestants as a book of principles that contained the true standards of character and the best motives and aids to virtue but was not a sectarian book; rather, it belonged to all Christians and must be present in schools.

Historians of American education are generally in accord that moral education was the overriding purpose of the nineteenth-century common school. Ministers occupied positions of leadership; teachers had a moral calling, guiding the students in sound moral character, utilizing Bible-reading, hymns, and prayers that were common to most Protestant creeds. The growth of the Catholic population in the United States, especially in the Northeast and Midwest, led to Protestants closing their ranks on educational issues, such as devotional Bible-reading in schools.

Compulsory Bible-reading in public schools was a major Catholic grievance in the 1840s. In New York in 1840 Archbishop John Hughes spoke out against the indiscriminate reading of the Scriptures, to be interpreted privately by the reader. Catholic teaching held that the truths of Scripture are to be taught by church authority. In Philadelphia, compulsory reading of the King James version of the Bible led to a proclamation by the bishop of Philadelphia, Francis P. Kenrick, that Catholics did not seek to oust the Bible from the schools; rather, Catholics sought to use the Catholic version of the Bible, the Douay for the Catholic children. The Philadelphia school board concurred with Kenrick's request; a group of nativists responded by initiating a riot against Catholics that included the burning of Catholic property worth over $150,000 at the time. These nativists and their allies were successful nationally in portraying the Catholic position as opposed to the Bible, not just to the Protestant version of the Bible with private interpretation. Their success in establishing this view led to increased tensions between Catholics and their fellow citizens over schooling issues.

In the 1860s the practice of Bible-reading in public schools began to be challenged in court. Decisions were mixed. Most Protestants maintained that the common school system was the offspring of the Bible and that popular education existed only among evangelical Protestants, who had a sacred duty to maintain the place of the Bible in the schools it had created. Students who refused to participate in the practice were, on occasion, expelled, whipped, or otherwise sanctioned.

After the Civil War, legal challenges continued. Some Protestants contended that the government of the United States rested on the Bible, that the government would fall without the Bible as its foundation, and that those who opposed it in the public schools were un-American. In the 1880s in Wisconsin a successful challenge to the use of the Bible was mounted. The conflict resulted in the decision of the Wisconsin Supreme Court in 1890 that devotional Bible-reading in public schools constituted sectarian instruction, made the school a place of worship, and thus was illegal. Some of Wisconsin's Protestants, especially Congregationalist, Methodist, and Presbyterian, strongly opposed the decision and predicted dire calamities for the state as a consequence. Generally, their position involved the following points. Morality rested on religion, and the Bible was *the* book of religious belief. The Bible was necessary for children to reverence God and their fellow humans and accept the responsibilities of self-government. The American people owed their liberties to the Bible. The religion of the Bible was every citizen's birthright, and without it, the republic itself would be in peril. The schools would be irreligious, unsatisfactory, and incapable of forming the young in Christian virtue without the indispensable aid of the Holy Scriptures.

Wisconsin, with a high percentage of immigrants, many of whom were Catholic, was not representative of all of the states of the union. Many, especially in what became known as the "Bible Belt" in the South, continued the practice. Those who advocated the practice claimed that the situation in the nation and the world required religious exercises in the schools that were Bible-based. They claimed that the secularization of American education that resulted from the absence of the Bible had led to the social and moral degeneration of the country, including increased crime and assorted other evils. The lofty ideals of Christianity could be communicated to the children in America's schools via the Bible with the result that these evils would be eradicated and virtue would return.

In 1962 the Supreme Court of the United States ruled that school-sponsored prayer in public schools was unconstitutional. The Court followed up that decision with one in 1963 that adjudged devotional Bible-reading of a voluntary nature (i.e., with objecting children having the right to excuse themselves from the room), with attendant exercises to be in violation of the Establishment Clause of the First Amendment and hence illegal. At the time of the decision, thirty-seven states permitted Bible-reading in public schools, and thirteen of those states mandated the practice. Prior to the *Schempp* decision, judicial decisions had been handed down in twenty states. Only seven of those prior decisions had declared the practice illegal. The public outcry that greeted the decision, coming one year after the Court's ruling on school-sponsored prayer, was loud and bitter. It paralleled on a national scale the outburst in Wisconsin seventy-three years earlier. Denunciations included allegations of atheism and communism. The public schools were, in these people's eyes, Godless and had abandoned their heritage, which had made them both great and successful. Baleful predictions were made as to the nation's future, at a time in which it was locked in a "cold war" with the Soviet Union. Others argued that as a result of these two decisions the issue of the role of religion in public education, especially prayer and Bible-reading, would disappear from the national scene. That prediction has proved to be inaccurate, and the place of religion in public education, including the role of the Bible, continues to be at issue as of this writing. *See also*: Edgerton (Wisconsin) bible case; Establishment Clause; *School District of Abington Township v. Schempp* and *Murray v. Curlett*.

Further Reading: Donald E. Boles, *The Bible, Religion, and the Public Schools*, 3rd ed. (Ames: Iowa State University Press, 1965); Harold A. Buetow, *Of Singular Benefit: The Story of U.S. Catholic Education* (New York: Macmillan, 1970); Thomas C. Hunt, "The Edgerton Bible Decision: The End of an Era," *The Catholic Historical Review* 67, 4 (October 1981): 589–619; Horace Mann, *Twelfth Annual Report Covering the Year 1848* (Boston: Wentworth and Dutton, State Printers, 1849); Warren A. Nord, *Religion & American Education: Rethinking a National Dilemma* (Chapel Hill: University of North Carolina Press, 1995); *School District of Abington Township v. Schempp*, 374 U.S. 203 (1963).

Thomas C. Hunt

Bilingual education

The schooling of language-minority students that includes elements of both first (native) language and English language. Bilingual education is distinguished from English as a second language (ESL) education in its orientation toward literacy development. While bilingual education aims to enhance English-language development through literacy instruction in two languages (the student's first language and English), ESL seeks chiefly to develop students' fluency in English. Bilingual education has been a feature of public and Catholic schooling throughout much of the nation's history. It can be found in schools in a variety of programmatic formats. Demographic changes in Catholic school enrollments over the past century have continued the need to serve multilingual communities, particularly in the present context of a growing population whose first language is Spanish.

Bilingual education takes place in several programmatic forms in schools. Features common to all types are the use of students' first language for instruction, the focus on this one first language for grouping students in classes, and a local community setting in which a single language other than English predominates. Early-exit bilingual programs are designed to rapidly phase out the students' first language in instruction and to mainstream students into English-only classrooms. The first language is used primarily for clarification and initial literacy instruction. Late-exit bilingual programs are designed to facilitate the maintenance of students' first language as they learn English. The focus is on dual-language fluency and literacy. These programs are generally greater in length in terms of both use of the first language for instruction and time spent in the bilingual classroom before entrance into mainstreamed, English-only classes. Two-way bilingual programs (sometimes referred to as developmental bilingual programs) place language minority students (non-English-speaking) into classrooms with language-majority students (English-speaking) with the goal of mutual cultural understanding and bilingual language development. Ideally, classrooms comprise an equal number of students representing both languages. Instruction takes place in both languages in a variety of formats: one language alternating every other day; one language for mornings or afternoons; one language for particular subjects; dividing students by native language for particular subjects. Programs may be taught by a single teacher who is bilingual or through team-teaching.

Bilingual education has been a feature of schooling in the United States since the eighteenth century, particularly in regions of the North (Scandinavian), East and Midwest (German and Polish), Southeast and Southwest (Spanish), and Louisianan territories (French). Schools that provided instruction in a first language were typically situated in a non-English-speaking ethnic community. The schools provided a vital social link between the protective ethnic community and the greater multiethnic and English-speaking commercial and legal entities at the local, state, and national levels. Bilingual education dissipated during the late nineteenth and early twentieth centuries as programs of Americanization and the world wars encouraged the primacy of English in education for social change.

Renewed growth in bilingual programs in schools began in the 1960s. New immigration and passage in 1968 of the Title VII Bilingual Education Act provided incentives for programs in schools. Programs serving Spanish-speaking communities in California, Florida, New Mexico, and Texas represented the largest proportion of these programs. The 1978 Supreme Court decision, *Lau v. Nichols*, further contributed to growth of these programs. This decision held that school programs conducted exclusively in English denied students who spoke other languages equal access to education. Although it stipulated that all students be served in some meaningful way, the decision stopped short of mandating bilingual education.

Reauthorization of Title VII in 1988 provided funding for multiple programmatic types of bilingual education and, in particular, for ESL as an alternative to dual language development. Several prominent states repealed (California and Colorado) or revised (Illinois and Texas) bilingual education laws in the 1980s in favor of English immersion and ESL programs limited to a number of years. ESL programs are often used in school settings where the language-minority population is diverse and represents many different languages. These programs may pull out students from regular classroom for a portion of the day, consist of a regularly scheduled class period in middle or high school, or take the form of a resource center that functions as a pull-out program for several students throughout the school day.

Bilingual and ESL education represents an issue increasingly relevant to Catholic education and works of social justice. The proportion of parishioners and students in Catholic schools whose first language is Spanish has increased with each decade. Many are from first-generation American and immigrant families. Catholic education may serve as a societal link between the Church and social services within the bilingual context of these demographic changes, much as it has done in the previous century. *See also*: Hispanics/Latinos; Immigration/Immigrants.

Further Reading: James Crawford, *Bilingual Education: History, Politics, Theory, and Practice*, 4th ed. (Los Angeles: Bilingual Educational Services, 1999); Fred Genesee, *Learning through Two Languages: Studies of Immersion and Bilingual Education* (Cambridge, MA: Newbury House, 1987); *Lau v. Nichols*, 414 U.S. 563 (1974); Carlos Ovando, Virginia Collier, Mary Combs, and Jim Cummings, *Bilingual and ESL Classrooms: Teaching in Multicultural Contexts*, 3rd ed. (Columbus, OH: McGraw-Hill, 2003).

John L. Watzke

Bishops

Bishops are the legal and canonical leaders of the Catholic Church, assigned by the Pope to exercise jurisdiction in a particular geographical area, known as a diocese. The office of bishop holds the fullness of authority in all matters pertaining to the pastoral life of the Church, the administration of temporal goods, and the celebration of sacraments. According to the Second Vatican Council (*Christus Dominus*, Decree on the Pastoral Office of Bishops, 1987), bishops exercise a threefold responsibility: teaching, governance, and sanctification.

Bishops exercise their ministry of teaching most clearly in their preaching the Gospel and in their oversight of all religious education that occurs in their diocese. Part of this responsibility includes the approval of all catechetical materials in use in classroom and religious education programs, certification of teachers and catechists, and the religious and spiritual formation of all educational and catechetical leaders in the diocese. Bishops share these responsibilities with other competent professionals and delegate the authority to operate programs and certify personnel to qualified leaders. Bishops also serve as the guardians of the tradition and teaching of the Church, often speaking out as defenders of the faith. Some bishops have understood this aspect of their role to include the public chastisement of theologians who disagree with church teaching or the upbraiding of Catholic politicians who vote for legislation that is contrary to church teaching.

In relationship to the Catholic school, the bishop is the first teacher of the diocese. No institution in a diocese can even call itself Catholic unless the local bishop approves (*Code of Canon Law, Canon #803.3, 808*). Thus, public use of the adjective "Catholic" is, by Church law, under the purview of a bishop's teaching authority. While it would be highly unusual for any bishop to remove the designation "Catholic" from a school, hospital, or social service agency without grave cause, canon law gives bishops authority to do so, to appoint or remove teachers and catechists, and to do whatever is necessary to safeguard, protect, and uphold Gospel values and authentic church teaching.

The governance responsibility of bishops includes the management and care of the temporal goods of the local church. In this regard, bishops have tremendous fiduciary duties involving the funds, properties, personnel, and business aspects of the operation of the entire diocese. While most bishops delegate these responsibilities and share them with qualified professionals, the ultimate responsibility for all temporal matters remains with the bishop. In the case of diocesan high schools and parish elementary schools, the local bishop is final authority in all administrative matters. Private Catholic schools and those owned and operated by religious communities have their own internal governance structures, distinct from the diocese in which they reside, and therefore follow their own policies regarding governance. However, in matters pertaining to religious education and the faith, the bishop still maintains ultimate responsibility.

Sanctification means "to make holy." Bishops are charged to help sanctify or make holy the people in the diocese, mostly through the preaching of the Gospel and the celebration of the sacraments. Indeed, most of a bishop's time is filled with such sacramental celebrations: Mass with different parishes and schools, confirmation celebrations, reconciliation services, weddings, ecumenical prayers, ordinations to the priesthood, and a variety of liturgical events that invite people to prayer and to participate in the ritual, sacramental life of the Church. Bishops help to sanctify the Church by presiding at these various celebrations and by ensuring that they are well planned and executed. In their role of sanctification, bishops also function as teachers and as administrative heads of the diocese. Thus, the threefold responsibility that bishops have is a dynamic, ongoing ministry, with one area overlapping with, and reinforcing, another.

Historically, bishops have been strident supporters of Catholic schools. At the Third Plenary Council of Baltimore (1884), the U.S. bishops declared that all parishes must have Catholic schools. It was also not uncommon for bishops to enact penalties for parents who willfully refused to send their children to Catholic schools. In modern times, the place of the Catholic school in the wider society has become more easily accepted, and bishops' support has taken on new forms. U.S. bishops did praise Catholic schools in their 1972 pastoral message, *To Teach as Jesus Did* (National Conference of Catholic Bishops, 1972). Most bishops are generally supportive of Catholic schools and Catholic educators in their respective dioceses, but to varying degrees. Some researchers maintain that given the verifiable success of Catholic schools, bishops have been relatively silent regarding their importance to the life of the church (Greeley, 1977, 1998, 1999). *See also*: Bishops, in the nineteenth-century conflict over Catholic schools; Governance; Hierarchy.

Further Reading: *Christus Dominus: Decree on the Pastoral Office of Bishops*. In Austin Flannery, ed., *Vatican Council II: The Conciliar & Post-Conciliar Documents* (Northport, NY: Costello, 1987); *Code of Canon Law: Text & Commentary* (Mahwah, NJ: Paulist Press, 1983); Andrew Greeley, "A Preliminary Investigation: The Profitability of Catholic Schools," *Momentum* 8, 4 (1977); 43–49; Andrew Greeley, "More Assertions Not Backed by Data," *Phi Delta Kappan* 80, 6 (1999): 463: Andrew Greeley, "The So-called Failure of Catholic Schools," *Phi Delta Kappan* 80, 1 (1998): 24–25; Thomas C. Hunt, Ellis A. Joseph, and Ronald J. Nuzzi, eds., *Catholic Schools Still Make a Difference: Ten Years of Research, 1991–2000* (Washington, DC: NCEA, 2002); National Conference of Catholic Bishops (NCCB), *To Teach as Jesus Did: A Pastoral Message on Catholic Education* (Washington, DC: United States Catholic Conference, 1972).

Ronald J. Nuzzi

Bishops, in the nineteenth-century conflict over Catholic schools
From 1829 to 1884, the American Catholic bishops met periodically to discuss the issues affecting the Roman Catholic Church in America. The resulting pastoral letters were meant to guide both the temporal and the spiritual lives of American Catholics. As was the custom in such letters, the advice was very general, reflecting the bishops' concern for various social problems but offering no specific solutions. It remained for the Catholic laity to interpret what the bishops wanted done.

The first pastoral letters on education warned Catholic parents about the dangers of public schooling. Throughout the 1830s, the messages from the bishops reminded the laity of their duties as parents and implied that their only possible choice was Catholic education.

The response from the laity was lackluster, and the bishops became alarmed at the large number of Catholic children who attended public schools or no schools at all. But the bishops were not so much concerned with illiteracy as they were with religion. "The great evil," they concluded in 1840, "is the danger to which [the children] are exposed, of having their faith undermined." In 1843, the bishops were even more direct and stressed that the eternal salvation of all children rested with their parents. "Let them avail themselves of their natural rights," concluded the pastoral letter of 1843, "and see that no interference with the faith of their children be used in the public schools." The bishops were quite explicit on what parents could do to protect the spiritual lives of their children. "It is no easy matter to preserve the faith of your children in the midst of so many difficulties," noted the pastoral of 1840. "We are always better pleased to have a separate system of education for the children of our communion."

The message became even more direct in succeeding councils, particularly in the Plenary Councils of 1852, 1866, and 1884. Catholic parents had a moral responsibility to provide for the spiritual lives of their children, and the best means of providing that spiritual life was through parish schools. Catholic parents were never *required* to send their children to parish schools until 1884, but not to do so was to incur the displeasure of the organized Church.

Were the pastoral letters and the subsequent editorials effective tools in rallying the support of the Catholic population? The answer has to be a qualified "yes," for without the strong support of the hierarchy, there would have been few parish schools. But the influence of the bishops was limited; even with all their cajoling, only about half of all Catholic children ever attended Catholic schools.

In 1852, after two decades of anti-Catholic violence, the Catholic bishops met in Baltimore to address the state of Catholicism in the nation. Time had not resolved the issues of contention. Catholic leaders were still determined to obtain their share of public funds to support their own schools, and public school advocates were just as determined to resist any effort to divide tax moneys or to change the public school curriculum to accommodate Catholic concerns.

There was one notable difference. The bitter violence and confrontation of the 1830s and 1840s had given way to relative calm at mid-century. Growth in the number of communicants and growth in the number of dioceses and provinces meant that by 1852 American Catholicism was truly national—from the archdiocese of Baltimore in the East to the archdiocese of Oregon City in the West.

One message that certainly came through clearly was the firm resolve of all the bishops to support and establish parochial schools. "Encourage the establishment and support of Catholic schools," the bishops warned; "make every sacrifice which may be necessary for this object." The words of the bishops encouraged Catholic school advocates to redouble their efforts to establish a Catholic school in every parish.

The development of Catholic parochial education after the Civil War caused serious concerns within the Catholic community. Many Catholic leaders were pleased with the rapid growth of parish schools, but some Catholics were angry that many of their brethren spurned these institutions. In fact, conservatives were appalled with the large number of Catholic parents who continued to send their children to public schools. They looked for a way to force reluctant pastors to build more schools and require recalcitrant Catholic parents to send their children to these schools.

The campaign to force Catholic parents to send their children to parochial schools was spearheaded by James McMaster, the editor of the *Freeman's Journal* of New York. Ignoring the bishops altogether, McMaster presented a formal memorandum to Vatican officials in February 1874 asking if Catholic parents could send their children to schools "not under the supervision of the Catholic clergy." In an effort to influence the answer, he sent along several articles on the horrors of public education in the United States.

The Vatican responded quickly, asking the archbishops of the United States about the "evils" of public education. Specifically, the Vatican wanted to know why some Catholic parents sent their children to public schools. Was there an effective way to reverse this trend? Why did some Catholics advocate the denial of sacraments to parents who sent their children to public schools? Could such a policy be instituted without harm to the Church, and would it be effective?

Concerned about this Vatican effort to influence American education, the American archbishops gathered in Cincinnati to respond to these questions and counter conservative allegations about public schools. Most important, the archbishops rebuffed a Vatican proposal to deny absolution to parents who sent their children to public schools. Such a policy, the archbishops argued, would only alienate Catholics from the Church.

They responded to each of the Vatican's questions. Why did Catholics send their children to public schools? The archbishops noted that many rural communities had no Catholic schools and that in many large cities, parochial schools were clearly inferior to public schools. This trend would change in time, they argued, as the quantity and quality of parish schools caught up with the Catholic population. This was the only effective solution to the problem.

The response from Rome, in the form of an "instruction," did not please the American hierarchy. Issued in November 1875, the eight-point document, "The Instruction of 1875," strongly supported the position taken by McMaster and his conservative colleagues. The Vatican called on the bishops to do everything in their power to prevent Catholic children from attending public schools.

The Vatican did acknowledge that certain circumstances might permit Catholic parents to send their children to public schools, but only in cases where no Catholic school existed or where the Catholic school was clearly inferior to the public school. On the question of absolution, the document was evasive. Absolution could be denied to "obstinate" parents who sent their children to public schools, even though they could afford to send them to a "good and well-equipped Catholic school" in the same neighborhood. The document did not define any of the many vague terms in its statement, preferring that the bishops set standards for their own dioceses.

Yet few American bishops had the economic resources to provide a desk in a parish school for every Catholic child in their diocese. It just was not possible, regardless of the Vatican's instruction for every Catholic child to attend a Catholic school. The status quo prevailed, and the document was largely ignored, regarded by many of the bishops as an embarrassment. Yet the "Instruction of 1875" was not without impact, for it later served as the framework for the discussion of parochial education that took place at the Third Plenary Council of Baltimore nine years later.

The intervening years between the publication of the Vatican "Instruction" and the Baltimore Council in 1884 did little to resolve the conflict within Catholic education. To be sure, Catholic schools continued to grow at unprecedented rates. In fact, the number of parish schools jumped from 1,400 in 1875 to over 2,500 in less than a decade. In spite of this growth, hundreds of thousands of Catholic children continued to attend public schools. What could be done to change this latter trend? Could the Church ever provide enough schools for an ever-expanding Catholic population? These were among the questions facing the bishops as they arrived in Baltimore in 1884.

Much of the discussion of parochial schools was tactical. How could the bishops convince the laity of the vital importance of parish schools? Should the council take a clear-cut stand and require pastors to build parish schools? Should they require recalcitrant parents, under the pain of sin, to send their children to parish schools? It was clear to all the bishops present that the tone of their message would be as important as the content.

The result was an effort to take the middle ground. The pastoral letter on the "education of youth" was gentle. "No parish is complete," concluded the letter, "till it has schools adequate to meet the needs of its children and the pastor and the people of such a parish should feel that they have not accomplished their entire duty until the want is supplied." There were no harsh words in the pastoral concerning pastors and parents who did not agree with the bishops or follow their advice.

The decrees of the Baltimore Council were another matter, however, and reflected a firm commitment to the belief that every Catholic child belonged to a Catholic school. The first decree stated bluntly that a parish school must be built near every Catholic Church. The second decree provided for the removal of parish pastors who were "gravely negligent" in erecting parish schools. The third decree promised spiritual "punishment" for any parish that failed to support their pastor's effort to build a school. A final decree stressed that "all Catholic parents are bound to send their children to parochial schools unless at home or in other Catholic schools, they provide sufficiently and fully for their Christian education." The implementation of the four decrees was reserved for the bishops themselves.

The decrees were a setback for the liberal prelates who wanted to encourage Catholic parents to send their children to parish schools but stop short of imposing sanctions on those parents who chose not to follow. But the conservatives had argued persuasively that decades of "encouragement" had not stopped the tide of Catholic children from attending public schools. It was time, the conservatives argued, to require these so called fair-weather Catholics and recalcitrant pastors to build and support parish schools.

Yet, there was a vast chasm between this new policy and its implementation, and the education decrees had only limited impact on the pattern and rate of parochial school development during the balance of the century. Like the "Instruction of 1875," the education decrees of the Third Plenary Council of Baltimore in 1884 failed to face the clear fact that the American Church lacked the economic resources to provide a Catholic education for every child.

The decrees did, however, have a significant impact on the organizational structure of parochial schools. For more than a century the Catholic schools had been administered at the parish level by pastors and trustees. Most dioceses were patchworks of semiautonomous parish schools as different from one another as the cultures that made up American Catholicism itself.

But the educational discussions of the Third Plenary Council gave momentum to an effort to coordinate parish schools through diocesan school boards. The establishment of boards in most dioceses in the years from 1885 to 1920 was the first major step in the long campaign to standardize and establish control over parochial schools.

The deliberations of the American Catholic bishops at Baltimore were vital in shaping the future of Catholic education in the nineteenth century. Speaking with one voice, the bishops articulated rationale for the establishment and support of Catholic education. Indeed, the bishops clearly believed—and restated as much at every council—that the future of American Catholicism was closely tied to the success of parochial schools. In the minds of the bishops, Catholic schools were the one effective means of protecting Catholic children against both the hostility and the temptation of American society. *See also*: Bishops; Catholic School Question, The; Gibbons, James Cardinal; Ireland, John; Plenary Councils of Baltimore; Satolli, Francis (Francesco).

Further Reading: Gerald P. Fogarty, ed., *Patterns of Episcopal Leadership* (New York: Macmillan, 1989); Bernard Julius Meiring, *Educational Aspects of the Legislation of the Councils of Baltimore, 1829–1884* (New York: Arno Press, 1978); Hugh J. Nolan, ed., *Pastoral Letters of the American Catholic Hierarchy*, 4 vols. (Huntington, IN: OSV, 1971); Timothy Walch, *Parish School: American Catholic Parochial Education from Colonial Times to the Present* (New York: Crossroad, 1996).

Timothy Walch

Blaine Amendment

On August 4, 1875, Rep. James G. Blaine of Maine introduced a constitutional amendment that would prohibit public support of sectarian schools. The proposed amendment, commonly known as the Blaine Amendment, subsequently failed to receive the support needed to amend the federal Constitution.

Although the proposed measure failed, the fervor behind the amendment spread through the states. The same year that Blaine proposed the initial amendment Pennsylvania passed a Blaine Amendment to its state constitution. Three decades later thirty-four states had Blaine or Blaine-like amendments in their constitutions. Presently, thirty-eight states have Blaine constitutional provisions. Blaine amendments have had an enduring impact, even in this early part of the twenty-first century, on issues of school choice and school funding.

The original Blaine amendment was developed in a context of political ambition, political struggle, and heightened anti-Catholic sentiment. President Ulysses Grant (R) in a bid for re-election appealed to Protestant Republican voters by calling for a constitutional amendment that would prohibit the use of public money for sectarian schools. Rep. Blaine, who also sought the 1876 Republican presidential nomination, introduced the type of amendment Grant had advocated. Though not always mentioned, Catholic schools were the target for the proposals of Grant and Blaine. Both

Grant and Blaine were among a growing number of Americans who were vocal about their anti-Catholic positions. Furthermore, the congressional record on the Blaine amendment debates reveals (1) the underlying anti-Catholic sentiment among amendment advocates and (2) the focus of the amendment on Catholic schools.

The proposed measure sought to apply the Establishment and Free Exercise Clauses of the First Amendment directly to the states and prohibit public support of sectarian schools (H.R. 1, 1875). The Blaine Amendment stated that "no public property, and no public revenue of . . . the United States, or any State, Territory, District or municipal corporation, shall be appropriated to, or made or used for, the support of any school, educational or other institution, under the control of any religious or anti-religious sect, organization, or denomination" (Amendment, Congressional Record, 44th Congress, 1st session, December 14, 1875).

In August 1876, the proposed Blaine Amendment easily passed through the House of Representatives with a vote of 180 to 7. There were, however, ninety-eight abstentions. Passing the amendment through the Senate proved to be a harder challenge. The amendment did not receive the necessary two-thirds-majority vote to take the measure to the states. The Senate vote was strictly partisan. Republicans supported the amendment, and Democrats opposed the amendment. Some of the Democratic opposition, though, was not because Catholic schools were targeted, but rather because of the power the federal government would have over states.

The legacy of Blaine's amendment did not end with the 1876 Senate vote. The Blaine Amendment was a catalyst to statewide movements limiting sectarian school funding. Blaine's amendment served as a model for subsequent state "Blaine amendments," which commonly posited that education must be free from sectarian control. Pennsylvania amended its constitution in 1876 with a Blaine provision. Other states followed suit, adding to their constitutions the restrictions advocated in the original Blaine Amendment. In addition, as new states entered the union, Congress insisted on education clauses and state restrictions of public aid to sectarian schools. By 1917, twenty-nine states either had Blaine amendments or Blaine language in their constitutions. Three decades later thirty-four states had such provisions, and presently such language exists in thirty-eight states.

Residual effects of the Blaine Amendment continue to be felt. Issues of school choice, private school funding, and state constitutional revisions are intertwined with the controversy associated with Blaine amendments. For example, the Blaine Amendment resurfaced as an issue in the 1960s, when New York rewrote its state constitution. During the rewrite, suggestions were made to eliminate Blaine provisions that prohibited state funding of religious education. More recently, it was present in the Cleveland school voucher program, upheld in *Zelman v. Simmons-Harris* (2002).

The anti-Catholic goals behind the Blaine amendment have also received contemporary attention. In *Kotterman v. Killian* (1999), the Arizona Supreme Court made reference to Blaine amendments and their legacy. In this particular case the Arizona court ruled that tuition tax credits to individuals for contributions made to nonprofit school tuition organizations were constitutional. The majority opinion stated that the amendments were "a clear manifestation of religious bigotry . . . to counter what was perceived as a growing Catholic menace." *See also*: Americanization; American Protective Association (APA); Anti-Catholicism.

Further Reading: Marie C. Klinkhammer, "The Blaine Amendment of 1875," *Catholic Historical Review* 21 (1965): 15–49; Robert P. Lockwood, "Anti-Catholicism and the History of School Funding," On-line research paper (Milwaukee: Catholic League for Religious and Civil Rights, February, 2000), http://www.catholicleague.org/research/researchpapers.html. Accessed January 13, 2003. F. William O'Brien, "The Blaine Amendment, 1875–1876," *University of Detroit Law Journal* 41 (December 1963): 137–205; http://www.catholicleague.org/research/schoolfunding.htm. Accessed July 18, 2002.

Yolanda Hart

Blum, Virgil C. (1913–1990)

Virgil C. Blum, SJ, was a leader on behalf of parental rights in education. He also was a defender of the rights of Catholics in the marketplace.

Born in Defiance, Iowa, on March 27, 1913, Virgil Blum was ordained a priest in the Society of Jesus in 1947. Father Blum was a professor of political science at Marquette University from 1956 until 1978, when he was named professor emeritus. He continued to teach courses until 1990. Blum entered the national arena when he became one of the founders of the Citizens for Educational Freedom (CEF) in 1959. In this lay organization with chapters throughout the United States, Fr. Blum functioned as the organization's adviser through the years.

Under the motto "A Fair Share for Every Child" Blum advanced the cause of the CEF by speeches and writing. In one of his major works, *Freedom of Choice in Education*, Blum put forth the thesis that the chief asset of the state is its youth, to whom the state must maintain an active role in their total development. The purpose of government in education is to seek the good of the whole child, which will benefit the common good and the child. The child's right to be treated equally by government is a personal, constitutional right based on the Fourteenth Amendment. No child should have to surrender her or his individual freedom of mind to share in government's benefits. Thus, if government financially subsidizes only one kind of school (the public), its action is arbitrary, unreasonable, and discriminatory. The state must uphold the constitution that demands the equal protection of each child and is obliged to be neutral to religion. Were the state to shirk its responsibility to the child under the Fourteenth Amendment because of religion, that would make the state hostile to religion, because the student's religion would become a liability to her or him. Thus, students who attend church-related schools may not in justice be denied sharing in the common benefits dispensed by the state, including government's bearing the cost of their education in "God-centered" schools.

Blum argued that Christian and Jewish schools were "God-centered" because they endeavored to give their students an understanding of:

1. The central truths of religious faith;
2. The moral values that are rooted in religious commitments;
3. Man's relation to God and to his fellowman; and
4. The meaning and purpose of life, and ideals that inspire the religious man. (Blum, 1967, p. 35)

The public schools were secular, Blum held, because God was officially dead in them and thus in the education of their students. Students in institutions such as these were required to conform to the ethic of this world or "humanistic" thought.

Blum exhorted parents to become involved in the political process, doing battle for

Virgil C. Blum. © Marquette University Libraries.

their rights and for those of their children in education—hence, his participation in and support of CEF.

Fr. Blum continued his struggle on behalf of constitutional rights for Catholics in the civil arena. In 1973 he founded the Catholic League for Religious and Civil Rights in Milwaukee. He continued as the organization's president until his death in 1990. *See also*: Choice, parent and school; Citizens for Educational Freedom; Parental rights.

Further Reading: Virgil C. Blum, SJ, Bibliographic information, Wisconsin Province of the Society of Jesus, Milwaukee; Virgil C. Blum, SJ, *Catholic Education: Survival or Demise?* (Chicago: Argus Communications, 1969); Virgil C. Blum, SJ, *Education: Freedom and Competition* (Chicago: Argus Communications, 1967); Virgil C. Blum, SJ, *Freedom in Education: Federal Aid for ALL Children* (Garden City, NY: Doubleday, 1965); Virgil C. Blum, SJ, *Freedom of Choice in Education*, rev. ed. (New York: Paulist Press with Macmillan, 1963); Virgil C. Blum, SJ, Midwest Jesuit Archives, St. Louis; Virgil C. Blum, SJ, *Quest for Religious Freedom II* (Milwaukee: Catholic League for Religious and Civil Rights, 1986); Edward Maron, ed., *Anti-Catholicism in the United States* (Milwaukee: Catholic League for Religious and Civil Rights, 1978).

Thomas C. Hunt

Board of Education of Central School District No. 1 v. Allen

Board of Education of Central School District No. 1 v. Allen involved a dispute over a New York state statute that required public school boards to purchase and loan textbooks for secular instruction to all students in grades 7 to 12 who lived within district boundaries regardless of whether they attended public or nonpublic schools. The Board of Education of Central School District No. 1 (BECSD) successfully challenged the statute in a suit against the state commissioner of education, alleging that it violated the state and federal constitutions by requiring it to provide publicly funded textbooks to students who attended religious schools. After an intermediate appellate court and the New York State Court of Appeals reversed and upheld the statute's constitutionality, the BECSD sought further review.

The Supreme Court, in a six-to-three decision, with one justice writing a separate concurring opinion, affirmed that since the textbook loan law was part of a general statutory initiative designed to further the secular education of all children, regardless of where they went to school, it was constitutional. At the outset of its analysis, the Court placed great reliance on *Everson v. Board of Education* as the case most nearly applicable to the dispute in noting that the Establishment Clause does not prevent a state from extending benefits to all of its citizens without regard for their religious affiliations.

In addition to *Everson*, the Court cited the so-called purpose and effects test that it enunciated in the companion cases of *School District of Abington Township v. Schempp* and *Murray v. Curlett*. The Court was satisfied that the textbook statute had a secular legislative purpose and a principal or primary effect that neither advanced nor inhibited religion since, in making textbooks available to all children free of charge, it furthered educational opportunities available to the young. In language revealing its ongoing reliance on the emerging child benefit test, the Court expanded its rationale in explaining that although the books technically remained state property, no funds or books were furnished to the religious schools and that any financial benefit accrued to parents and children, not the schools. The Court was also untroubled by the fact that even if the statute made it more likely that some students would attend religious schools, this alone was insufficient to demonstrate an unconstitutional degree of aid to a religious institution.

Readily conceding that books are different from buses, the Court placed significant emphasis on the fact that regulations overseeing the statute's implementation specified which books on lists approved by public school officials could be used for instruction in secular courses in the nonpublic schools. Further, in rejecting the BECSD's argument that textbooks could be distinguished from buses insofar as the former are critical to the teaching process, the Court cited its own precedent-setting cases that long recognized that religious schools serve two goals: religious instruction and secular education. At the same time, the Court reasoned that the statute authorizing the textbook loans reflects "a recognition that private education has played and is playing a significant and valuable role in raising national knowledge, competence, and experience" (Allen, p. 247). Against this background and based on the lack of evidence to the contrary, the Court rebuffed the BECSD's claims either that all teaching in nonpublic schools is religious or that the processes of secular and religious education were so intertwined that the secular textbooks were instrumental in teaching religion.

The Court summarily disposed of the BECSD's final allegation, that the law authorizing the textbook loans violated the Free Exercise Clause, in observing that its members had not contended that the law in any way coerced them as individuals in the practice of their religions. The Court thus affirmed that the textbook loan statute passed Establishment Clause muster.

The lengthy dissenting opinion feared that upholding the statute would inevitably have led to religious leaders seeking to provide their schools with publicly funded textbooks that best reflected their particular "theocentric or other philosoph[ies]" (Allen, p. 265). As such, the dissent unsuccessfully argued that the statute was unconstitutional because it violated the Establishment Clause's principle of separation of Church and state, words that do not appear in the text of the Constitution.

Until its decision in *Agostini v. Felton*, permitting the on-site delivery of Title I services in religiously affiliated nonpublic schools, *Allen* was generally accepted as the outer limit of permissible aid to religiously affiliated nonpublic schools. *See also*: Establishment Clause; Separation of Church and state.

Further Reading: *Agostini v. Felton*, 521 U.S. 203 (1997); *Board of Education of Central School District No. 1 v. Allen*, 392 U.S. 236 (1968); *School District of Abington Township v. Schempp* and *Murray v. Curlett*, 374 U.S. 203 (1963).

Charles J. Russo

Board of Education of Kiryas Joel Village School District v. Grumet

Board of Education of Kiryas Joel Village School District v. Grumet (1994) illustrates the difficulties that arise when public officials try to accommodate the needs of religious parents who wish to direct the education of their children.

During the early 1970s, members of the Satmar Hasidic sect of Judaism moved from New York City to a suburban enclave not far from the city limits. Following a zoning dispute, members of the group who practiced a strict form of their faith left the original community and created the Village of Kiryas Joel. While most children in Kiryas Joel attended religiously affiliated Hebrew day schools, there were no plans for providing special education services for students with disabilities. Further, even though the local public school board made special education services available in the Hebrew day schools, it had to discontinue the practice in light of *Aguilar v. Felton*'s (1985) preventing the on-site delivery of Title I services to children who attended religiously affiliated nonpublic schools. Although parents could have sent their children to public schools outside the village to receive special education, they stopped doing so because their offspring had difficulty leaving their community and being with people whose ways were different from their own.

As controversy arose over meeting the educational needs of Satmar children with disabilities, in 1989 the New York state legislature created a special school district with boundaries that were coextensive with those of the Village of Kiryas Joel. Even before it began to operate, the New York State School Boards Association and others challenged the statute's constitutionality. All three levels of the New York state courts agreed that the statute authorizing the creation of the district violated the *Lemon v. Kurtzman* (1971) test.

On further review, the Supreme Court, in a six-to-three decision, affirmed that the statute creating the Village of Kiryas Joel School District was unconstitutional. Even though the lower courts relied heavily on *Lemon*, the Supreme Court focused on its 1982 decision in *Larkin v. Grendel's Den*. In *Larkin* the Court struck down a Massachusetts law that granted the governing bodies of local religious organizations veto power over applications for liquor licenses that were to be used within 500 feet of a church, synagogue, or school. The Court followed *Larkin* in determining that its prohibiting a state from delegating civic authority to a religious group made it closer to *Kiryas Joel*. Even so, the Court contended that two major distinctions between *Larkin* and *Kiryas Joel* were not substantial.

The Court brushed aside the first distinction on the basis that there was essentially no difference between *Kiryas Joel*'s inappropriately vesting state authority in a religious community and *Larkin*'s placing such power in religious governing. The Court explained that there was a difference without a distinction between the two cases because, in any event, a state cannot delegate its civic power to a group that is selected on the basis of religious criteria.

Second, although making provisions for the delivery of special education for qualified students was not an expressly religious action, the Court was concerned that the legislature failed to exercise governmental authority in a religiously neutral manner. More specifically, since Kiryas Joel was the only district covered by the law, the Court was uncertain whether other similarly situated communities would have received their own school systems. In rounding out its opinion, even in recognizing that states can accommodate religious needs, the Court feared that the New York state legislature exceeded acceptable limits. The Court concluded that since alternatives such as transporting the children to public schools or neutral sites were available, the statute was unconstitutional.

A lengthy dissent would have upheld the statute as a reasonable accommodation to parents, especially since no direct financial assistance went to a religious organization.

Within days after the Supreme Court vitiated the statute, the New York state legislature amended it in an attempt to eliminate the Establishment Clause problem. Yet, the Court of Appeals of New York twice struck down the revised statute for violating the Establishment Clause because it had the impermissible effect of advancing one religion (*Grumet v. Cuomo*, 1997; *Grumet v. Pataki*, 1999a). The Supreme Court refused to hear a further appeal (*Grumet v. Pataki*, 1999b). *See also*: Establishment Clause; Separation of Church and state.

Further Reading: *Aguilar v. Felton*, 473 U.S. 402 (1985); *Board of Education of Kiryas Joel Village School District v. Grumet*, 512 U.S. 687 (1994); *Grumet v. Cuomo*, 659 N.Y.S.2d (N.Y. 1997); *Grumet v. Pataki*, 697 N.Y.S.2d 846 (N.Y. 1999a), cert. denied, 528 U.S. 946 (1999b); *Larkin v. Grendel's Den*, 459 U.S. 116 (1982); *Lemon v. Kurtzman*, 403 U.S. 602 (1971); Charles J. Russo, "The Curious Case of *Kiryas Joel*: Untangling Church–State Relations," *School Business Affairs* 61, 1 (1995): 62–64.

Charles J. Russo

Boards of education, diocesan, parish, school

According to O'Brien (1987), a Catholic school board is "a body whose members are selected or elected to participate in decision-making" for a diocesan, local, or area school. The same definition can be applied to a diocesan school board that governs all the elementary and secondary schools under the leadership of the local bishop. Throughout the United States, these governing groups differ in authority, structure, and areas of responsibility that are allowed within the canonical mandates of the Church and the spirit of Second Vatican Council.

Even though historical records indicate that Catholic education boards were operative in the mid 1800s, the most significant time for Catholic educational governance followed the close of the Second Vatican Council in 1965. The council called for subsidiarity and coresponsibility. Bishops were encouraged to seek greater involvement of other clergy, the religious community members, and laypersons to participate in decision-making. The development of Catholic education boards, commissions, and councils was seen as one way for members of the local community to take a significant role in the governance of Catholic education. More importantly, involvement of more people in the community would build greater support for the school's mission that ultimately would enhance the quality of education and stability of the schools they served.

Around the close of the Council, Msgr. O'Neill D'Amour promoted participatory decision-making through boards and established the first parish board on record, St. Mary Parish School Board in Norway, Michigan. D'Amour, therefore, is considered the "Father of the Catholic Board Movement in the United States." He was joined by Msgr. Olin Murdick, who assisted with the furtherance of school boards nationwide throughout the 1960s and 1970s. Some benefits of the involvement of these governing groups were the inclusion of parental insights of children's needs and capabilities; an extensive understanding and promotion of the school's mission; a broader base of financial support; the engagement of a wide range of skills and experience to address the growing demands of education in general and Catholic education in particular; and the contribution of members' personal time devoted to organizing projects that benefit the schools. Based on the realities of today, these benefits most likely were part of D'Amour's and Murdick's motivation for promoting the establishment of boards.

The groundwork laid by D'Amour and Murdick was substantially enhanced and advanced by the research of Lourdes Sheehan. Her work presents structures that are appropriate for Catholic education on the elementary and secondary school levels. Influenced by Sheehan's study, *A Primer on Educational Governance in the Catholic Church* (O'Brien, 1987) was published, which continues to provide a common frame of reference and universal vocabulary for educational governance at all levels.

The primer provides a definition of a board (commission or council) as a body whose members are selected or elected to participate in decision-making in education at the diocesan, regional, interparish, or parish level. O'Brien provides the following common descriptions of three models of board authority that the publication advocates:

1. Advisory board advises the bishop/pastor on educational polices and other educational matters. The diocese/pastoral leader develops and enacts the policy.
2. Consultative board operates in the policy-making process by formulating and adapting

policy but never enacts policy. The person with final authority establishes the areas in which the board is to be consulted and enacts the policies it recommends.

3. Limited jurisdiction board has power limited to certain areas of educational concerns established by the entity that has the final jurisdiction. Its jurisdiction is limited to the areas in which its authority is established.

The National Congress for Catholic Schools for the 21st Century, a two-year process to plan for the future of Catholic schools, was another mile marker for the development of boards. At the concluding event in Washington, D.C., delegates developed belief and directional statements to ensure the viability of Catholic schools. Guerra, Haney, and Kealey (1992) report two belief statements related to governance:

1. Effective Catholic school governance requires the preparation, empowerment, and collaboration of the community that it serves.

2. Governance with the full participation of the laity is the key to the future of Catholic schools.

Related to these two belief statements, Guerra, Haney, and Kealey offer the following statement that provides direction or vision for boards in today's Church: "to establish governance structures which give all those committed to the Catholic school's mission the power and authority to achieve it" (p. 26). These statements speak to the call of the Second Vatican Council and the vision of the earlier leaders of the Catholic education board movement, which is to empower the laity and to collaborate with others who are committed to the mission of the school/s.

Currently, Catholic education leaders collaborate with members of governing groups responsible for diocesan, local, and regional schools to provide leadership and direction that will ensure their institution's future. For example, ultimate authority in a diocesan school is vested in the bishop, while the authority of a local school is vested in the parish corporation or the religious congregation or parent group that owns the school. In the case of regional schools, the authority would be vested in all the parishes served or a corporate board representative of the area pastors. As the board movement grows, so do the variations of the structural models originally put forth in O'Brien's primer. Leaders have creatively stayed within the parameters allowed by church authority to provide governance structures that unleash the energy of members to effectively lead the schools for which they are responsible.

In 1993–1994, the National Association of Boards, Commissions, and Councils (NABCC) conducted a national survey to assess the status of diocesan, elementary, and secondary school boards, commissions, or councils. Using the definitions for board authority models set forth in *A Primer on Educational Governance in the Catholic Church*, the survey revealed that only 9 percent of diocesan boards have limited jurisdiction, 32 percent are consultative, and 54 percent are advisory. One-fifth of the local boards are boards of limited jurisdiction, and 2 percent are boards of trustees. Like the diocesan boards, the majority of local boards are advisory, while 35 percent of local boards are consultative.

In addition to identifying the numbers of each authority model nationwide, the survey identified eleven statistically significant characteristics of effective or achieving boards. According to the survey, as reported by Convey and Haney (1997), effective boards have members that include businesspeople and alumni; take ownership of issues under their jurisdiction; are involved with issues pertaining to budget, policy, mission, philosophy, and planning; have goals, which are reviewed or updated annually and used as a basis of self-evaluation; have active committees such as finance, nominating, policy, marketing, development, facility, and executive committees; communicate with their constituencies; assess their progress periodically; have effective meetings; are dedicated and committed to the school's mission; train new members and conduct annual in-service for all members; and demonstrate achievement in the areas of development/fund-raising, budget/financial stability, long-range planning, marketing/public relations/recruitment, and plant upgrade. These serve as benchmarks or standards for other Catholic elementary and secondary boards to match or surpass.

Boards that have implemented these standards have contributed to their school's success. Each year the National Association of Boards, Commissions, and Councils of Catholic Education (NABCCCE) recognizes outstanding boards that can demonstrate that they have been successful according to the standards listed above. Award-winning boards have been credited with the following success stories:

1. A school in financial trouble is now on a strong financial foundation.
2. A decreasing enrollment trend in a school was reversed that necessitated expanding the faculties to accommodate additional grades.
3. The board conducted a needs assessment, space audit, constituent survey, and feasibility study that required building renovations around curriculum needs and student services to enhance the quality of education.

These and the numerous other successes of award-winning boards over the last twelve years emphasize the necessity and importance of Catholic school boards.

Those Catholic leaders in the past and present who responded to the council's called-for subsidiarity and coresponsibility by involving board members in participatory decision-making have seen benefits of their invitation. Catholic education board, commission, and council members at the diocesan, area, and local levels have taken part significantly in the governance of Catholic education and, therefore, enhanced the quality of education and stability of the schools that they served. *See also*: D'Amour, O'Neill C.; Governance; National Catholic Educational Association (NCEA).

Further Reading: John Convey and Regina Haney, *Benchmarks of Excellence: Effective Boards of Catholic Education* (Washington, DC: National Catholic Educational Association, 1997); Michael Guerra, Regina Haney, and Robert Kealey, eds., *National Congress Catholic Schools for the 21st Century: Executive Summary* (Washington, DC: National Catholic Educational Association, 1992); J. Stephen O'Brien, ed., *A Primer on Educational Governance in the Catholic Church* (Washington, DC: National Catholic Educational Association, 1987); Lourdes Sheehan, "A Study of the Functions of School Boards in the Educational System of the Roman Catholic Church in the United States," unpublished doctoral dissertation, Virginia Polytechnic Institute and State University, Blacksburg, VA, 1981.

Regina M. Haney

Bodily-kinesthetic intelligence
One of seven intelligences identified in Howard Gardner's Multiple Intelligence Theory—a theory that has gained wide acceptance in education and instruction since the middle of the 1980s. Bodily-kinesthetic intelligence involves the use of the body to

create, express ideas, perform functions, and manipulate objects. Its core operations include the ability to control body movement and the ability to skillfully handle objects. Individuals with high bodily-kinesthetic ability are able to solve and fashion problems through gross motor movement of the body or fine motor movement of the hands. Athletes, actors, dancers, and sculptors are examples of individuals who display high ability in this intelligence. This intelligence has also been applied as a means to understand and participate in religious studies and the mass.

According to Gardner, bodily-kinesthetic intelligence meets the criteria of an independent intelligence because it is culturally significant and has biological origins. Every normally functioning adult develops some degree of competence in bodily-kinesthetic operations. The relationship between the brain and body movement involves complex coordination of the nervous and muscular system. Research shows that humans have a tendency to have one dominant half of the body and brain. Brain damage to the left hemisphere can produce impairments, called apraxias, in which the individual lacks the ability to carry out a sequence of motor events, use either hand, or control body parts. These apraxias are not related to the aphasias that affect language but instead relate directly to motor actions. The independence of this intelligence is also demonstrated by individuals who have lost their verbal memory but can remember sequences of motor action and patterns of behavior. Some idiot savants and autistic children maintain normal bodily actions, although they lack language and interpersonal skills.

Evolutionary studies look at the relationship between human and primate body movement and use of tools. Primates develop the ability to use tools through sensory-motor development, discovering uses for objects in the environment and realizing they have control over the environment. Distinct differences are noted between primates and humans, notably that primates operate primarily with only one hand. Further evolutionary research traces humans' development of tool use beginning with stones, axes, the discovery of fire, and the crafting of weapons. Humans also developed symbols, pictures, and decorative objects, all ancient products of bodily-kinesthetic functioning.

Bodily-kinesthetic intelligence follows a pattern of development in normally functioning individuals. Children begin with basic reflexes and progress to more goal-oriented activities. The development of understanding symbols contributes to the development of bodily skills. Although most individuals develop the basic motor skills necessary for daily living, individuals with high bodily-kinesthetic ability show a command over body movement and fine motor skills that can be shown through dance, acting, or athletics.

Although some cultures value body skill more than others, bodily-kinesthetic abilities are utilized across cultures. Some cultures value individuals skilled in dance, while others value strength for manual labor. Other cultures emphasize the fine-motor skills needed for weaving and other crafts. Although bodily-kinesthetic intelligence is identified as an independent intelligence, it overlaps with the other intelligences in certain areas. Logical-mathematical intelligence and spatial intelligence are related to the ability to use and transform objects. Bodily-kinesthetic intelligence also depends on interpersonal awareness and intrapersonal communication.

Bodily-kinesthetic intelligence can be easily incorporated into religious education. Physical activity is not often a focus of the traditional classroom, yet it can enhance a student's experience and ability to remember material. Hands-on activities, acting out biblical stories, and content-based learning experiences are some interactive ideas to develop and use bodily-kinesthetic skills. Catholic tradition has long understood the importance of gestures and movement in shaping and solidifying religious faith. Each of the seven sacraments involves a physical act, a public ritual gesture that is considered a sign of God's presence. This outward sign necessary for a sacrament is an appeal to, and engagement of, the bodily-kinesthetic intelligence.

The Lenten prayer of the Stations of the Cross is, perhaps, the most bodily-kinesthetic prayer in Catholicism. Participants walk to each station, sing, read, genuflect, and bless themselves and move on to repeat the gestures at each station or stop.

The Catholic mass incorporates bodily-kinesthetic intelligence in several ways. Throughout the mass, participants genuflect, sit, stand, kneel, and make the sign of the cross. Posture is important during the liturgy as the assembly looks toward the altar together and focuses on the act of thanksgiving. The Rite of Peace involves shaking hands, and the Communion Rite involves approaching the altar and receiving the body and blood of Christ.

The fact that the reception of Holy Communion involves the eating and drinking of bread and wine that has been consecrated (blessed) and changed into the Body and Blood of Christ demonstrates that the use of the bodily-kinesthetic intelligence is essential to Catholic tradition. *See also*: Gardner, Howard; Multiple Intelligence Theory (MI).

Further Reading: Howard Gardner, *Frames of Mind: The Theory of Multiple Intelligences* (New York: Basic Books, 1983); Howard Gardner, *Intelligence Reframed: Multiple Intelligences for the 21st Century* (New York: Basic Books, 1999); Howard Gardner, *Multiple Intelligences: The Theory in Practice* (New York: Basic Books, 1993); Ronald J. Nuzzi, *Gifts of the Spirit: Multiple Intelligences in Religious Education* (Washington DC: National Catholic Educational Association, 1999).

John L. Watzke

Bouquillon, Thomas (1840–1902)

A prominent theologian who was born May 16, 1840, in Warneton, Belgium, and died in Brussels on November 5, 1902, Dr. Bouquillon gained recognition as the leading moral theologian of his time for his composition *Theologia Moralis Fundamentalis*.

His parents were small landowners, and he attended local schools until his studies at the College of St. Louis at Menin. He then studied philosophy at Roulers and attended the seminary at Bruges. In 1863, he went to Rome to attend the Georgian University. He was ordained a priest in 1865 and became a doctor of theology in 1867. Bouquillon spent the next ten years at the Bruges seminary (1867–1877) and the next eight years at the Catholic University of Lille, France, as professor of moral theology.

Due to poor health, he retired to the Benedictine monastery at Maredsous, where he focused his energies on a second edition of his noted work *Theologia Moralis Fundamentalis*. Later, enjoying improved health, he accepted a chair in moral theology at the Catholic University of America (1889–1902) in Washington, D.C., which he held until his death.

Early in his tenure at Catholic University, Bouquillon became embroiled in a Catholic education controversy ignited by Archbishop John Ireland's speech at the 1890 National Education Association meeting in St. Paul, Minnesota. Archbishop Ireland presented an argument that seemed to many in the church hierarchy as an abdication of Catholic parish schools and a direct contradiction of the bishops' statements at the Third Plenary Council of Baltimore.

The publication of Dr. Bouquillon's *Education: To Whom Does It Belong* pamphlet followed soon after Ireland's speech. Many suspected that Bouquillon and Ireland worked together on the text. In fact, Cardinal Gibbons suggested that Bouquillon, as an eminent moral theologian, provide a theoretical argument that might help to end the controversy. The result was just the opposite. Since the pamphlet appeared to provide theoretical underpinnings for Ireland's position, Bouquillon was drawn into the fray. Considerable debate followed, which became known as the "Bouquillon controversy."

In his pamphlet, Bouquillon wrote that education "belongs to the individual, physical or moral, to the family, to the state, to the Church, to none of these solely and exclusively, but to all four combined in harmonious working" (Buetow, 1970, pp. 171–172). Bouquillon was known for his clear, logical presentation in the pamphlet. He took the position of a dispassionate academic providing a researched argument.

However, responding in a subsequent series of articles, Bouquillon became increasingly agitated by critiques of his position, especially from Rev. R. I. Holaind, SJ, who wrote a counterpamphlet, *The Parent First*. Some critiques charged that Bouquillon should not write on the topic since he was a newcomer to the United States and did not understand the school question. Bouquillon remained stalwart and did not waver from his established position, charging his detractors with a lack of understanding of his viewpoint.

The controversy surrounding the pamphlet and the ensuing questions about American Catholic education ultimately led to an appeal to Rome. An intervention by the Apostolic Delegate, Archbishop Satolli, followed, whose statements vindicated Bouquillon and supported Archbishop Ireland. The opposition camp appealed to the Pope again, but the Holy Father pleaded for the American Church to reconcile on this topic, finally issuing a letter stating that there was no disparity between the edicts of the Baltimore Council and Satolli's settlement.

Dr. Bouquillon dedicated his academic life to the improvement of moral theology as a discipline. He developed a clear scientific approach to render to moral theology legitimacy comparable to studies in sociology and history. He advanced the teaching methods used to present moral theology as a critical field of study. He was known as a powerful teacher in every setting where he displayed his depth of thinking and clarity. In addition, he was recognized for the capacity to render a practical approach to academic and legal problems. Though not a hardy person, he worked tirelessly in a simple lifestyle that supported his academic commitments. He contributed greatly to the development of the Catholic universities in Lille and Washington.

Throughout his life, Dr. Bouquillon was a confidant of foremost churchmen, including Pope Leo XIII. His prolific writings made him a pivotal figure in shaping modern church thought. He is credited with nearly fifty articles and pamphlets, including his most famous work, *Theologia Moralis Fundamentalis*. *See also*: Catholic School Question, The; *Education: To Whom Does It Belong?*; Holaind, Rene I.; *Parent First, The*.

Further Reading: Thomas Bouquillon, *Education: To Whom Does It Belong?* (Baltimore: John Murphy, 1892); Harold A. Buetow, *Of Singular Benefit: The Story of U.S. Catholic Ed-*

ucation (New York: Macmillan, 1970); C. Joseph Nuesse, *The Catholic University of America: A Centennial History* (Washington, DC: Catholic University of America Press, 1990); Daniel F. Reilly, *The School Controversy 1891–1893* (Washington, DC: Catholic University of America Press, 1943).

Merylann J. "Mimi" Schuttloffel

Bus transportation

The controversy surrounding church–state–school relationships reached the U.S. Supreme Court for a third time in 1947 over the issue of publicly subsidized transportation of students to religious schools. The constitutionality of assistance to students in private and religious schools was first brought before the Court in the 1930 *Cochran v. Louisiana State Board of Education* case concerning the provision of nonsectarian textbooks to students in religious schools. The Court ruled affirmatively, articulating a liberal interpretation of the First Amendment concept of separation of Church and state. The decision ruled that the intent of the statute was to benefit the schoolchildren rather than the schools, even though the religious schools were spared the expense of providing textbooks for the students.

Ruling that indirect aid to schools was constitutionally permissible, the Court invigorated advocates to pursue legislative efforts to secure a portion of tax dollars for students in private and religious schools. By the end of World War II, more than 350 Catholic schools across the nation were receiving some indirect public assistance, and more than half a dozen states were providing subsidized transportation to students in religious schools.

The busing of private school children at public expense was the subject of a 1947 U.S. Supreme Court decision in *Everson v. Board of Education* that became a landmark case in Church–state relations and established precedents for interpreting the First Amendment when considering school aid. The Court agreed to hear *Everson* with the intention of clarifying the constitutionality of indirect aid to religious schools vis-à-vis the First Amendment and religious liberty.

At issue in *Everson* was a challenge to a New Jersey statute providing parents reimbursement for costs incurred by them to transport their children on regular, publicly operated buses to attend religious schools. The New Jersey Supreme Court had invalidated the law based on its interpretation of the New Jersey state constitution and the federal First and Fourteenth Amendments. The lower court accepted the plaintiffs' contentions that the law violated due process by (1) taking, through taxation, the private property of some to bestow it on others for their own private purposes (Fourteenth Amendment) and (2) ignoring both state and federal prohibitions against the establishment of religion by forcing taxpayers to support and maintain religious schools.

The five-to-four affirmative decision reached by the Court revealed a level of acrimony and divisiveness that was indicative of some anti-Catholic bias that endured in the nation. The majority opinion went to great lengths to explicate its interpretation of the meaning of the First Amendment and the applicability of the Jeffersonian metaphor of a "wall of separation" between Church and state. Examining the New Jersey statute, the Court found no bias toward or against religious groups, noting that the free exercise interpretation precluded exclusion purely on religious grounds. The decision pursued the interpretation that the state must be neutral regarding religion, not taking an advocacy or adversarial position. The justices affirmed that the wall of separation must be kept impregnable, declaring that the New Jersey law did not breach it.

In reaching that decision, the justices drew the analogy between the state providing police and fire protection with its funding transportation for parochial school children. The justices were persuaded that the legislation did nothing more than provide a general program to help parents get their children, regardless of their religion, safely to and from parochial schools that met New Jersey's requirements to provide secular education.

While all nine justices agreed on the concept of strict separation of Church and state, they differed sharply in its interpretation, as evidenced by the dissenting opinions. An anti-Catholic bias surfaced in many of the latter arguments that focused on the fact that regular religious instruction conforming to the religious tenets and modes of worship of the Catholic faith was provided and that the superintendent of the schools was a Catholic priest. They argued that Catholic school children would not be discriminated against if the law were invalidated because their parents decided to forgo the right to attend a public school. Since they were exercising a "free" and merely "private" choice in sending their children to their schools, they should not be reimbursed, even if the religious school fulfilled a public function of preparing an educated citizenry. They opposed any aid to parochial schools, citing canon law to defend the assertion that the schools are "parochial only in name—they, in fact, represent a worldwide and age old policy of the Roman Catholic Church" and that provision of any tax aid to its schools was tantamount to aiding the church directly.

Rather than end the controversy by defining the limits to aid for religious schools, the *Everson* decision sparked forty more years of legislative and judicial activity defining the parameters of the decision.

By the end of the twentieth century, more than thirty states were providing subsidized transportation to students in private schools. More than half a million students in over 4,000 Catholic schools received such benefits in the 2002 school year. For the most part, transportation is provided by means of buses owned by the local public school districts. Religious school children are accommodated along the same routes as the public school students, resulting in logistical coordinating problems for private schools whose students come from multiple districts with varying schedules and school holidays that differ from those of the private school.

The most significant and controversial case dealing with bus transportation as a tool of educational policy, *Swann v. Charlotte-Mecklenburg Board of Education*, did not impact the transportation of students in private schools. That case affirmed the mandatory busing of students as a remedial measure to achieve racial integration in public schools. In response, most Catholic bishops forbade their schools from accepting students transferring from public schools to avoid the integration mandate. *See also*: Establishment Clause; *Everson v. Board of Education of Ewing Township*; Parental rights.

Further Reading: *Everson v. Board of Education*, 330 U.S. 1 (1947); Charles R. Morris, *American Catholic: The Saints and Sinners Who Built America's Most Powerful Church* (New York: Times Books/Random House, 1997); *Swann v. Charlotte-Mecklenburg Board of Education*, 402 U.S. 1 (1971); Timothy Walch, *Parish School: American Catholic Parochial Education from Colonial Times to the Present* (New York: Crossroad, 1996).

Dale McDonald, PBVM

C

Cahenslyism

Viewpoint represented by a minority group of German American Catholics, promoted in a plan by the German Peter Paul Cahensly. In 1891, Cahensly carried a Memorial to Pope Leo XIII that suggested that the ecclesiastical needs of immigrants entering the United States would be better served by organizing the American Catholic Church according to European nationalities. The plan required the appointment of bishops and priests of the same race and language as the majority of the members of a diocese or congregation. The plan was successfully opposed by American church leaders, including Archbishop John Ireland, who stated that Cahensly's premise was contrary to American principles.

Peter Paul Cahensly was a member of the Reichstag, the German parliament, and a prominent merchant of Limburg, Prussia. In 1866, at a Catholic Congress held in Trier, Cahensly suggested the establishment of the St. Raphael Society to provide for the protection of German immigrants at their port of departure in Europe and their landing point in America. Cahensly was unhappy that the German Society of New York focused its efforts on assisting immigrants exclusively with their relocation. He argued that the society was not adequately supporting the immigrant population's religious needs. Within three years a St. Raphael Society committee was under way in New York but received little support in Germany. To build his case, in 1883, Cahensly himself traveled to New York in steerage class to experience the typical immigrant's crossing. He lobbied shipping companies and hotels to improve the conditions for immigrants. Bishop Winand M. Wigger of Newark became the first president of the St. Raphael Society. Still, little progress was made until Rev. John Reuland came from Germany to manage the New York office. Eventually, German priests collected sufficient funds to build a home for German immigrants. The house was entitled Leo House.

Cahensly was highly critical of the American hierarchy, as he believed that they did not respond adequately to the immigrant's plight. He communicated that message in September 1890 to a general European Catholic congress held in Liege, Belgium. Abbe Villeneuve of Canada claimed during a session devoted to American immigration that twenty million Catholic immigrants had left the Church. The shock of this news precipitated another conference in Lucerne, Switzerland, December 9 and 10,

1890. Representatives of the St. Raphael's Society presented a description of the immigrants' predicament. The Lucerne Memorial was to be presented to Pope Leo XIII by Peter Paul Cahensly and Volpe-Landi.

The Lucerne Memorial was signed by ten members of the German St. Raphael's Society, nine Austrians, eight Italians, seven Belgians, and one Swiss. All were men of considerable influence. Premier Mercier of Quebec also endorsed the plan.

The document stated that the American Catholic Church had lost ten million Catholics, a reduction from earlier claims. The plan included the following elements: (1) establishment of separate churches for each nationality, (2) appointment of priests representative of parishioner nationality to these churches, (3) religious instruction in the national language of origin even when the numbers did not indicate a separate Church, (4) establishment of separate parochial schools for every nationality, (5) guarantee of equal privileges for priests of every nationality, (6) the foundation of Catholic mutual aid associations, (7) inclusion of bishops of every nationality in the American episcopate, when possible, and (8) papal encouragement to train missionary priests to serve in the United States and establish St. Raphael's Society in European countries.

Reaction to the plan was swift and strong from the United States. Archbishop John Ireland challenged Cahensly's view of German immigrant conditions and the Church's care for this group. Ireland questioned the motives of the Lucerne group and ultimately encouraged them to stay out of American affairs. Other responses attacked the Lucerne assembly's lack of understanding that American bishops were eager to have European immigrants integrated into American life as Americans as soon as possible. Critics of Ireland's appraisal, in turn, argued that the Irish immigrant model was not suitable to all immigrants. The Lucerne plan did not become the model for the American Church. Though Cahensly's plan was not formalized, attributes of the plan were engaged in every argument between those in favor of Americanism and those who considered assimilation a threat to the Church. With the advent of World War I, the German Catholic community severed its benevolent affiliation with the fatherland. State Department officials and President Harrison himself credited Archbishops Ireland and Gibbons with saving the country from a serious threat—Cahenslyism. *See also*: Catholic School Question, The; German American Catholics.

Further Reading: Coleman J. Barry, *The Catholic Church and German Americans* (Milwaukee: Bruce, 1953); John Tracy Ellis, *American Catholicism* (Chicago: University of Chicago Press, 1955); Daniel F. Reilly, *The School Controversy 1891–1893* (Washington, DC: Catholic University of America Press, 1943); A. S. Will, *The Life of Cardinal Gibbons* (Baltimore: E. P. Dutton, 1911).

Merylann J. "Mimi" Schuttloffel

Cantwell v. State of Connecticut

Cantwell v. State of Connecticut stands out as the first case wherein the U.S. Supreme Court applied the First Amendment religion clauses, through the Fourteenth Amendment's Due Process Clause, to a dispute involving state action.

In *Cantwell*, a father and his two sons, members of the Jehovah's Witnesses, were charged with violating a state statute against public solicitation and the common-law offense of inciting a breach of the peace. On the day of their arrests, the plaintiffs, who went house-to-house soliciting funds in a neighborhood that was heavily populated by Roman Catholics, asked residents for permission to play a record on a portable phonograph player. The record described *Enemies*, a book that included a general

attack on all organized religious systems as instruments of Satan before harshly singling out the Roman Catholic Church. If a person agreed, the plaintiffs offered to sell
the individual a copy of *Enemies*. If an individual refused to make a purchase, the
plaintiffs solicited a contribution for one of their informational pamphlets. Donors
were given a copy of a pamphlet on the condition that they would read its contents.
Another aspect of the case involved one of the sons having approached two Catholic
men on the street who granted him permission to play the record. However, both men
were so angered by the record's contents that they were tempted to strike the plaintiff.
Insofar as the plaintiff followed the suggestion from one of the men that he walk
away in order to avoid trouble, by all accounts, this incident did not give rise to a
public disturbance of the peace.

The three men were convicted of violating the state statute that required them to
seek the approval of the secretary of the Public Welfare Council, who had to determine
whether they were engaged in a legitimate charitable or philanthropic activity and the
common-law offense of breach of the peace. On further review, the Supreme Court
of Connecticut affirmed the three convictions for violating the solicitations statute but
upheld the breach of peace conviction only with regard to the plaintiff, who approached the two Catholics.

In its brief, but unanimous, opinion, the Supreme Court reversed in favor of the
plaintiffs. The Court began its review of the conviction of the plaintiffs for violating
the state solicitation statute by indicating that just as the First Amendment prohibits
the federal government from making a law respecting an establishment of religion or
prohibiting the free exercise thereof, the Fourteenth Amendment rendered state legislatures equally as unable to do so. The Court reflected on the double aspect of the
religion clauses to the extent that while the Free Exercise Clause represents an absolute
right to believe, the freedom to act on such beliefs is not an absolute. Rather, the
Court explained that a state may subject individuals to regulation with regard to the
time, manner, and place that are designed to protect society even where individuals
solicit funds to further their religious perspectives. The Court determined that the statute at issue was not such a safety regulation since, absent state approval, the plaintiffs
were prohibited from soliciting funds. In fact, the Court agreed with the plaintiffs that
the regulation amounted to an unconstitutional prior restraint on their right to the free
exercise of religion because the secretary of the Public Welfare Council had the authority to evaluate whether their cause was religious. The Court described this practice
as "a denial of liberty protected by the First Amendment and included in the liberty
which is within the protection of the Fourteenth" (p. 305). Further, the Court rejected
the state's claims that sufficient safeguards were in place if the secretary acted arbi-
trarily, capriciously, or corruptly. The Court responded that even if an aggrieved party
could seek judicial review, it still would have amounted to a restraint on the exercise
of a constitutional right.

Turning to the conviction of the one plaintiff for common-law breach of peace,
the Court acknowledged the presence of two conflicting interests. On the one hand
was the right that neither the free exercise of religion be prohibited nor that freedom
to communicate information and opinion be abridged. On the other hand was the
state's interest in the preservation and protection of peace. In weighing these two
important interests in light of the facts, the Court held that other than offending the
two men with whom he spoke, the plaintiff did not breach the peace. As such, the
Court concluded "that in the absence of a statute narrowly drawn to define and punish

specific conduct as constituting a clear and present danger to a substantial interest of the State" (p. 311), the breach of peace conviction was to be reversed. *See also*: Establishment Clause; Separation of Church and state.

Further Reading: *Cantwell v. State of Connecticut*, 310 U.S. 296 (1940).

Charles J. Russo

Carroll, John (1736–1815)

John Carroll (January 8, 1736–December 3, 1815), first bishop and archbishop of Baltimore, was a shaper of American Catholicism and of American Catholic education. Spalding (2000) writes that:

> Carroll was the architect of the "Maryland tradition" in American Catholicism. He accepted without qualification such American principles as freedom of conscience and separation of Church and state and sought in his relationship with the Holy See a measure of autonomy for the American Church. Totally committed to interfaith harmony, he contributed more than anyone to the public's acceptance of Roman Catholicism. (p. 6)

John Carroll was the son of Daniel Carroll, a wealthy merchant, and Eleanor Darnall, daughter of a distinguished Maryland family. As a boy, he was enrolled at a short-lived Jesuit school in Cecil County, Maryland. In 1748, he went to the English Jesuit College of St. Omer in French Flanders. In 1753, he entered the Jesuit novitiate at Waten. At the Jesuit College at Liege, he studied philosophy and theology. In 1761, the auxiliary bishop of Liege ordained him. Carroll taught philosophy and theology at the English College until 1767. He was broadened by the experience of chaperoning the son of an English nobleman traveling in Europe.

International events caused a change his life when, in 1773, the Jesuits were suppressed. Carroll went to England and then returned to Maryland in the spring of 1774. In 1776, the Continental Congress asked Carroll to go on a mission to Canada. Carroll anticipated the difficulties but decided the trip was a patriotic duty. He, along with his cousin, Charles Carroll of Carrollton, Benjamin Franklin, and Samuel Chase, went to Quebec. They were unsuccessful in achieving the goals of their mission, but Carroll's friendship with Franklin would later prove important.

In 1783, Carroll called together six American clergy to deal with the issues of the former Jesuit properties and other ecclesiastical questions. He communicated to Rome the need for an American Catholic Church free of foreign influences. Congress, responding to Carroll's inquiry, stated it had no interest in the ecclesiastical structure of American Catholics, provided that the person in charge made no claim to temporal jurisdiction.

During the peace process that ended the American Revolution, Vatican officials approached the American delegation in Paris. Benjamin Franklin recommended Carroll to be the first American bishop. As a missionary Church, the Church in the United States reported to the Commission of the Propagation of the Faith. In 1789, Carroll was named the bishop of the new diocese of Baltimore and he was installed as bishop in Dorset, England, in 1790. Carroll advocated equal rights for Roman Catholics in the new republic in an article written in 1784 called *Address to the Roman Catholics of the United States of America*.

Religious and secular education were a priority for Carroll. He invited religious orders to work in the United States. In 1805, he persuaded English Dominicans to open a college and priory in Kentucky to serve Marylanders settling there. Carroll encouraged the Sisters of the Visitation to take charge of a school in Georgetown and the Sisters of Charity to establish a motherhouse and academy in Emmitsburg, Maryland. He was a mentor to Elizabeth Ann Seton.

Under his auspices, Catholic colleges for men were founded in Maryland at Georgetown (1788), Baltimore (St. Mary's, 1799), and Emmetsburg (Mt. St. Mary's, 1808). Academies for girls were begun at Georgetown (Visitation, 1799), Emmitsburg (St. Joseph's, 1809), and Bardstown, Kentucky (Nazareth, 1814).

Carroll was president of the board of the Baltimore Library Company from its founding until his death. In 1784 he became a member of the board of St. John's College in Annapolis and in 1788 became its president. In 1801, he joined the board of directors of the nonsectarian Female Humane Association Charity School. He also served as president of the board of Baltimore College. The University of Maryland elected him provost in 1812, but he declined because of his other responsibilities.

Carroll established dioceses in Boston, New York, Philadelphia, Kentucky, and Louisiana. In 1811, he was appointed archbishop of Baltimore. He tried to prevent influence by European bishops in the selection of bishops for New York and Philadelphia. Under Carroll's leadership, the Church grew, but growth of native clergy was slow, so Carroll relied upon clergy from Ireland, France, and Germany. He worked with Benjamin Henry Latrobe (1764–1820), architect of the U.S. Capitol Building, for the construction of a cathedral in Baltimore. John Carroll received the last sacraments on November 23, 1815, and died on December 3, 1815. *See also*: Catholic philosophy of education; Parental rights.

Further Reading: Joseph Agonito, *The Building of an American Catholic Church: The Episcopacy of John Carroll* (New York: Garland, 1988); "John Carroll," *New Catholic Encyclopedia*, Vol. 2 (New York: McGraw-Hill, 1967–1979): 151–154; F. Michael Perko, SJ "John Carroll: Founding Father of American Catholicism," *Religion and Public Education* 14, 4 (Winter 1987): 350–354; Thomas W. Spalding, "Carroll, John," http://www.anb.org/articles/08/08-00239.html, *American National Biography Online*, February 2000. Accessed February 8, 2002.

Jack O'Gorman

Catechesi Tradendae

A document issued by Pope John Paul II in 1979 that describes a vision for catechesis or religious education. It is one of a number of documents issued between 1970 and 2000 that have tried to reshape the understanding and practice of Catholic religious education in light of the insights of the Second Vatican Council.

Catechesi Tradendae recognizes the constant need for catechesis to renew and revise its understanding of mission, teaching methods, the best language to reach people, and new ways of transmitting the message of the Gospel, but it is also aware such constant reevaluation and change can cause a loss of continuity with the Church's ancient traditions of faith and faith formation.

Catechesi Tradendae hopes to establish principles for staying faithful to the past, while continuing to struggle to make religious education relevant and effective in a constantly changing world. The document identifies family catechesis as preceding, accompanying, and enriching all other forms of catechesis, and the parish community as the pre-eminent place for catechesis, though most parishes need to rediscover this vocation. Like the *General Catechetical Directory* before it, *Catechesi Tradendae* affirms that catechesis of adults is the principal form of catechesis, because only adults have the full capacity to live the Christian message in its fully developed form. It also notes the importance of linking catechesis at different age levels. It must be linked with the hopes, questions, anxieties, and struggles of each generation.

Catechesi Tradendae, an apostolic exhortation, had its origin in a 1977 synod entitled, "Catechesis in Our Time," which produced thirty-four propositions that the bishops felt the Pope should include in his apostolic exhortation. Popes Paul VI and John Paul I worked on the document before its completion by John Paul II.

A critical dimension of the document is its definition and explanation of the ancient process of passing on faith, known as catechesis. Once a faith response has been elicited from a person, catechesis attempts to gradually deepen this first step in faith. Through reflection and study, it helps a person understand the consequences of the message of salvation and its repercussions on one's personal life, eventually initiating the hearers into the fullness of Christian life.

Catechesis Tradendae builds on the *General Catechetical Directory*, issued in 1971, and Paul VI's 1975 apostolic exhortation *Evangelii Nuntiandi*, which described catechesis as a moment in the process of evangelization. *Catechesi Tradendae* adds to the previous works an emphasis on educational catechesis, the actual teaching of doctrine, salvation history, and many of the facts of the faith. It also highlights the need for systematic catechesis, which demonstrates how biblical, moral, liturgical, scriptural, and pastoral concepts and perspectives fit together to make a total religious meaning system.

A systematic emphasis calls for programmed efforts to achieve precise learning goals, rather than relying on improvisation in the classroom. These goals include dealing seriously with the essentials of faith in as complete a way as possible and the reasons for believing in the Christian message, but it also incorporates learning how to connect faith with the experience of Christian living, how to truly celebrate the sacraments, how to become integrated into the faith community, and how to open oneself to a process of ongoing, lifelong conversion.

Catechesi Tradendae seeks a new balance between content and process, cognitive material and affective experience, and formal and informal learning. Prior to Vatican II, the primary textbook used by many religious educators to accomplish catechetical learning objectives was a question-and-answer catechism. To accomplish their goal of passing on the faith, most teachers relied heavily on memorization of doctrinal information. The Council called this strategy into question and unleashed new energy and excitement by the late 1970s, but, ten to twelve years after the Council, many bishops were also becoming concerned about limitations and deficiencies. They feared that catechists were presenting their personal opinions as Church teaching and that increasing numbers of people were coming to believe that Church doctrine and life experiences had little to do with each other.

Catechesi Tradendae challenges catechists to learn how to recognize and separate their personal opinions from Christ's teachings and the lessons of his life. They are asked to take great care in identifying and separating their ideological views, especially social and political ones. The document states that this maturity in self-knowledge requires deep study of the word of God and the deposit of faith, a spirit of prayer, and the learning of a sense of detachment from self.

Catechesi Tradendae has nine chapters. The first four establish the philosophical principles guiding catechesis. Chapters 1 and 2 lay out the foundations. Catechesis is Christocentric (Chapter 1) and has roots deep in the historical tradition of the Church (Chapter 2). Chapters 3 and 4 explain the place catechesis has in all the activities of the Church. It is a dimension of evangelization (Chapter 3) and has Scripture and tradition as its main source of inspiration and information (Chapter 4). Launching from these principles to some of the practical concerns of catechesis, the document describes the different types of people in need of catechesis—infants, children, adolescents, the young, the handicapped, and adults (Chapter 5). Next, *Catechesi Tradendae* comments on the more common catechetical tools used to reach these groups, such as homilies, catechetical textbooks, and catechisms (Chapter 6), and some of the methods used, with a special mention of memorization (Chapter 7). The last two chapters highlight the potential joy the message of the Gospel can bring to the world (Chapter 8) and the necessity of all Christians taking part in the mission (Chapter 9). *See also*: John Paul II, Pope; Religion, Teaching of; Total Catholic Education.

Further Reading: The Bishop's 1977 synod is summarized and interpreted in *Living Light* 15, 1978, pp. 1–128; Cesare Bonivento, " 'Going, Teach . . . ': Commentary on the Apostolic Exhortation *Catechesi Tradendae* of John Paul II" (Boston: St. Paul Editions, 1980); Anna S. Campbell, "Toward a Systematic Catechesis: An Interpretation of *Catechesis Tradendae*," *Living Light* 17 (1980): 311–320; John Paul II, *Catechesi Tradendae, on Catechesis in Our Time* (Washington, DC: United States Catholic Conference, 1979); Jane E. Regan, "Principles of Catechesis from Ecclesial Documents," in Thomas H. Groome and Michael J. Corso, eds., *Empowering Catechetical Leaders* (Washington DC: National Catholic Educational Association): 29–54.

Mark S. Markuly

Catechism of the Catholic Church

The aim of the *Catechism of the Catholic Church*, published in 1992, is to "provide a sure and authentic reference text for teaching Catholic doctrine and particularly for preparing local catechisms" (John Paul II, 1992).

The primary concern of the authors of the *Catechism* was to articulate the content of the Church's faith, focusing upon "the exposition of doctrine" (paragraph 23). Nonetheless, some of the choices made concerning the manner of presentation, together with the careful structuring of the content, have pedagogical implications.

First, the authors stress that the *Catechism* is an "organic presentation" of the entirety of the Catholic faith around the hierarchy of truths (paragraphs 18 and 90). Curricula are expected to highlight the central doctrines of the faith: the Trinity, the person and work of Christ, the priority of grace in the Christian life, and the dignity and value of the human person. They are also expected to provide a balanced presentation of the Catholic faith in terms of the four "pillars" of doctrine, celebration, the moral life, and prayer. A careful attention to each of these "pillars" within catechetics ensures holistic faith development.

Second, the catechism lays especial emphasis on the renewal of catechesis through acquainting readers with the sources of the faith, in particular the Scriptures, primary liturgical texts and the works of the leading Fathers of the Church, who were early theological authors. Care has been taken in drawing attention to the dynamic sources of the faith from both the Eastern and Western traditions and from classic works of spirituality as well as council documents and statements from the Church's Magisterium. The main source drawn upon by the authors is sacred Scripture, indicating the need for catechetical presentations to be deeply biblical. In this commitment to renew catechesis "at the living sources of the faith" (John Paul II, 1994, p. 3) the catechism continues the impetus of the "ressourcement" (the recovery of foundational theological themes and approaches from the Bible, the Fathers and medieval scholarship) that was prominent during the twentieth century and was influential on the thinking of the Fathers of the Second Vatican Council. It also encourages the use of contemplation and analysis of original texts in religious education.

Third, the authors include "In brief" paragraphs at the conclusion of each of the major sections of the text. These are offered to "suggest to local catechists brief summary formulas that could be memorized" (paragraph 22). The *Catechism of the Catholic Church* was written partly in order to encourage the writing of local and national catechisms, including shorter catechisms that contain material for memorization. In this way, the authors are encouraging catechists to reconsider the role of memorization within religious learning and to broaden the appreciation of its role beyond the caricature of mere "rote-learning."

Fourth, the authors have selected works of art to accompany the text of the *Catechism*, not as adornment but as a mode of catechesis. Instruction through art is presented not simply as a preliterate catechetical methodology but one especially pertinent for alerting the believer to God as "the Beautiful One" (St. Augustine, quoted in paragraph 32).

Finally, the importance of uniting an *integral catechesis* to *the integrity of the catechist* is emphasized through the attention given to the saints, especially Mary, the mother of God, as the primary "witnesses" to the Faith. The exposition of each section is typically crowned with an example of a saint who exemplified the doctrine in his or her own life and teaching. In this way holiness is presented as the supreme mode of catechesis.

In the United States the publication of the *Catechism* has led to the drawing up, by the National Conference of Catholic Bishops, of a National Adult Catechism and to the establishment of an "Ad Hoc Committee to Oversee the Use of the Catechism." This Ad Hoc Committee examines the content of religion texts and curricula against "The Protocol for Assessing the Conformity of Catechetical Materials with the *Catechism of the Catholic Church*." The protocol consists of 114 statements on "The Profession of Faith," 70 items on "The Celebration of the Christian Mystery," 132 statements in the area of "Life in Christ," and 19 on "Christian Prayer." Publishers are invited to submit catechetical materials for scrutiny against these statements. One of the results of this scrutiny has been the identification of "a pattern of doctrinal deficiencies" in catechetical materials. The deficiencies include insufficient attention to the Trinity and the Trinitarian structure of Catholic beliefs and teachings, an obscured presentation of the centrality of Christ in salvation history, and an insufficient emphasis on the divinity of Christ, and an indistinct treatment of the ecclesial context of Catholic beliefs and magisterial teachings. Specific problems noted, which have affected the presentation of Catholic teaching over the past thirty years, also include an inadequate sense of a distinctively Christian anthropology, an overemphasis on human action compared to the action of God, and an underdeveloped sense of the efficacy of grace.

As of June 1, 2002, fifty-one catechetical series, including student texts and teacher manuals, have been reviewed and found to be in conformity with the *Catechism of the Catholic Church*. *See also*: Religion, teaching of; Total Catholic Education.

Further Reading: Ad Hoc Committee to Oversee the Use of the Catechism of the Catholic Church of the National Conference of Catholic Bishops/United States Catholic Conference, "The Protocol for Assessing the Conformity of Catechetical Materials with the Catechism of the Catholic Church," 1998, http://www.nccbuscc.org/catechism/document/protocol.htm. Accessed July 21, 2002; Daniel Buechlein, "Oral Report to the General Assembly of Bishops," June 1997, http://www.nccbuscc.org/catechism/document/oralrpt.htm. Accessed July 27, 2002; *Catechism of the Catholic Church*, 2nd ed. (Washington, DC: United States Catholic Conference, 1997); John Paul II, *Fidei Depositum*, On the Publication of the *Catechism of the Catholic Church*, in *Catechism of the Catholic Church* (Boston: St Paul Books and Media, 1992); Petroc Willey, "Teaching with the Catechism, Part 1," *The Sower* 21, 3 (April 2000): 21–24.

Petroc Willey

Cathedraticum

The term *cathedraticum* describes the monetary contribution assessed by the bishop of a diocese from the various parish and lay organizations. These funds are typically used to maintain the bishop and the ministries of the diocese. At its inception, the *cathedraticum* was a tribute that all the bishop's benefices—that is, parishes and other religious and lay organizations—paid to the bishop as a sign of their loyalty to him. Since the revision of the Code of Canon Law in 1983, the term has commonly been used to describe the tax imposed by a diocese on its parishes.

The *Decree of Gratian* (c. 1140) gives the earliest description of the nature of the *cathedraticum*, calling it an honorific gift of a "moderate sum" of money given to the bishop from the parishes and other benefices within his diocese. Bishops, by custom, could also receive a third of the offerings from a local church when the bishop was present and celebrated with them. According to *Gratian*, the bishops, much to their credit, often did not accept this added gift but accepted only the *cathedraticum* for the benefit of their ministry (Kealy, 1986, p. 126).

While the Council of Trent did not mention the *cathedraticum*, the Holy See's response to inquiries about the *cathedraticum* following the Council of Trent provides sufficient evidence that its practice continued in the years following that council. Pope Benedict XIV determined that the traditional amount prescribed for the *cathedraticum* should be determined by each diocese and that all were to pay it unless they were given an exemption by the Pope.

The 1917 Code of Canon Law gave *cathedraticum* legal status, requiring every parish and lay confraternity under the jurisdiction of the diocesan bishop to pay a moderate tax. The rate of tax was to be determined by a gathering of all the bishops within the metropolitan province. In 1920, French bishops, in need of money, sought permission from the Sacred Congregation of the Council to raise the *cathedraticum*, adjusting it proportionately to the population of the parishes and other institutions in their dioceses. The Congregation denied their request, stating that the *cathedraticum* was honorific in nature, and therefore its rate was to remain nominal. They reminded the bishops that any attempt to turn the *cathedraticum* into a head tax would be in direct violation of the intent of the law.

There is no mention of the term *cathedraticum* in the 1983 revision of the Code of Canon Law. According to canonist Robert Kealy (1986), since the New Code remains silent about the *cathedraticum*, it can no longer be considered as having the force of law. However, Archbishop John Myers and other canonists continue to use the term *cathedraticum* to describe the diocesan tax that Canon 1263 of the New Code of Canon Law permits bishops to collect from parishes and lay confraternities in their respective dioceses (Myers, 1985).

Thus the term *cathedraticum*, as it has been used since the promulgation of the 1983 Code of Canon Law, is now defined as an assessment imposed by the diocesan bishop on all parishes and certain other works in his diocese for the purpose of supporting the administration and works of the diocese. Each diocese has its own particular regulations and customs about who is assessed, the rate of the assessment, and what sorts of parish income are subject to the assessment. The tax assessment is a percentage of the parish's income, including their regular collections, any endowments the parish may have, and profits from any parish-related fund-raising events, such as bingo or the parish carnival. Showing their support for Catholic education, tuition moneys collected from parish schools are exempt from the diocesan tax in many American dioceses. Some dioceses also provide parishes a limited refund from the assessment for each child who is enrolled in their parish school.

According to canon law (Canon 1263), diocesan bishops may authorize this moderate tax within their own dioceses, proportionate to the parish or institution's income. The bishop can authorize this tax once he has consulted with both his financial and presbyteral councils. Typically, the diocesan tax is assessed at a rate of 7 or 8 percent. The proceeds from this tax cover the operational expenses of the pastoral center, the preparation of seminarians from the diocese for ordination, and works that transcend parish boundaries such as diocesan regional high schools and various charitable activities. A number of dioceses also provide financial subsidies to inner-city parishes and schools. Parishes are assessed separately for their share of insurance and priest retirement payments. Beyond the assessment, dioceses also meet their financial needs by authorizing a special collection, known as the diocesan appeal, or by engaging in other types of fund-raising activities, such as capital campaigns and pledge drives. *See also*: Financing of Catholic schools; Governance.

Further Reading: Robert L. Kealy, "Diocesan Financial Support: Its History and Canonical Status," unpublished doctoral dissertation, Pontifical Gregorian University, Rome, 1986; John J. Myers, "Commentary on the Temporal Goods of the Church," in James A. Coriden, Thomas J. Green, and Donald E. Heintschel, eds., *The Code of Canon Law: A Text and Commentary* (New York: Paulist Press, 1985); Thomas J. Reese, *Archbishop: Inside the Power Structure of the Roman Catholic Church* (San Francisco: Harper and Row, 1989).

Anthony J. Dosen, CM

Catholic Education: A Journal of Inquiry and Practice

A peer-reviewed, scholarly periodical dedicated exclusively to issues in Catholic education, including elementary and secondary schools as well as Catholic colleges and universities.

Catholic Education was founded in 1997 as a result of the collaboration of four Catholic institutions of higher learning: Fordham University, the University of Dayton, Saint Louis University, and the University of San Francisco. Administrators at these universities secured the financial support of each institution and worked together to acquire a grant from the Lilly Foundation to cover the initial operating costs. Key players from each institution included Rev. James Heft, SM, author of the Lilly grant, from the University of Dayton; Sr. Mary Peter Traviss, OP, from the University of San Francisco; Rev. Michael Garanzini, SJ, Saint Louis University; and Gerald Cattaro, Fordham University. Representatives of Boston College were involved in these foundational discussions but chose not to participate in beginning the journal. At the time of its origination, *Catholic Education* was the only refereed journal of its kind with an exclusive focus on the educational mission of the Catholic Church. Refereed in this context refers to the publication process used to evaluate manuscripts for pub-

The University of Notre Dame, the most recognizable Catholic educational image in the world. © Getty Images.

lication. In refereed or peer-reviewed journals, all submitted manuscripts are reviewed by a panel of experts, who offer feedback, criticism, suggestions for revisions, and a judgment about a particular manuscript's worthiness for publication and dissemination. Peer reviewers work without knowing the identity of the author under review. This is often called a blind review. Peer-reviewed journals are held in higher esteem than nonpeer-reviewed journals, especially at the university level. For purposes of promotion and tenure, most colleges and universities require significant publications by professors in peer-reviewed journals. For this reason, *Catholic Education* is not only an important scholarly resource for researchers, principals, superintendents, diocesan officials, and clergy but it also a venue for scholars and professors of Catholic educational leadership to publish the results of their research.

The purposes of *Catholic Education* are to support Catholic education and its contribution to the culture; to contribute to the creation of a new vision of Catholic education by exploring important issues that challenge the field; to draw upon the philosophical and theological traditions of Catholic education in analyzing significant educational issues; to examine selected research studies that relate to the purposes and practices of Catholic education; to nourish the ministerial role of educators by exploring the relationship between Christian faith and professional practice; and to challenge Catholic educators to rethink from an inquiry orientation their positions on the major questions confronting their institutions and their unique traditions.

The original plan for the administration of *Catholic Education* was for each of the four founding institutions to house the editorial offices in turn and to be responsible for the maintenance of journal operations, including publication, for a period of five years. The University of Dayton was the first home of the editorial offices in 1997 and, because of financial exigencies, continued as host to the journal past the five-year term until 2003.

Because of increasing costs related to publication, *Catholic Education* began to expand its support base in 2000. Sponsors were sought to help maintain the mission of publishing a research quarterly dedicated to Catholic educational concerns. Several new sponsors were found, including Seton Hall University, Saint Bonaventure University, the Archdiocese of St. Louis, the Archdiocese of San Antonio, and the Dufferin-Peel Catholic School District in Ontario, Canada.

In 2002, many Catholic universities and colleges in the United States joined the effort to support and maintain *Catholic Education* by committing to participation in its newly formed governing board. These institutions include Barry University, Boston College, Creighton University, DePaul University, Loyola Marymount University, Loyola University of Chicago, Marquette University, Seton Hall University, Spalding University, the Catholic University of America, and the University of Notre Dame, as well as the original four founding institutions. Marywood University joined the governing board in 2003. Each of the universities designates a representative to serve on the board. The board is responsible to set policies for the journal, including the confirmation of the editors, the price of subscriptions, and the movement of the editorial offices.

As a refereed journal, *Catholic Education* accepts a limited amount of advertising, preferring to focus on scholarly research, doctoral dissertations, and new books relevant to those who serve as educators. Each issue of the journal follows a similar structure. A series of feature-length articles begins each issue. Articles are typically 6,000–7,500 words. Exceptions are not uncommon for longer essays of particular merit or interest. Articles in any given issue often constitute a focus section. A focus section is a series of four or five articles all addressing the same general topic from a variety of vantage points. *Catholic Education* has published focus sections on school law, vouchers, Catholic identity, students with special needs in Catholic schools, *Ex Corde Ecclesiae*, spirituality, and a variety of other topics.

A Review of Research follows the focus section. This section typically provides a summary of current research on a narrow topic. The primary source for these reviews is doctoral dissertations. The final section of each issue is reserved for book reviews, where select leaders are invited to offer their insights about the relative value of newly published books in education, theology, law, spirituality, and learning theory.

The editorship of *Catholic Education* rotates among the universities that constitute the governing board. The founding editor of the journal was Joseph Rogus of the University of Dayton, who shared those responsibilities for a time with Dayton colleague William Losito. In 1999, Thomas Hunt and Ronald Nuzzi became co-editors. The editorial offices relocated in May 2003 to the University of Notre Dame. *See also*: Catholic publishers; Effectiveness of Catholic schools.

Further Reading: *Catholic Education: A Journal of Inquiry and Practice* 6, 1 (September 2002); Thomas C. Hunt, Ellis A. Joseph, and Ronald J. Nuzzi, eds., *Catholic Schools Still Make a Difference: Ten Years of Research, 1991–2000* (Washington, DC: NCEA, 2002); Thomas C. Hunt, Ellis A. Joseph, and Ronald J. Nuzzi, eds., *Handbook of Research on Catholic Education* (Westport, CT: Greenwood Press, 2001).

Ronald J. Nuzzi

Catholic Educational Association

The Catholic Educational Association (CEA), renamed the National Catholic Educational Association in 1927, was established in St. Louis in July 1904. The new association was a hybrid organization, the merger of three separate and distinct Catholic educational associations: the Educational Conference of Seminary Faculties, the Association of Catholic Colleges, and the Parish School Conference. After the merger, these associations became departments within the CEA.

The driving force behind the establishment of the CEA was Thomas J. Conaty, the rector of the Catholic University of America. The major obstacle faced by Conaty was the fact that Catholic education had traditionally been a parish and diocesan matter. The bishops guarded their independence and autonomy and were wary of a national organization that aspired to speak for them.

The task of implementing Conaty's plan fell to Fr. Francis Howard, the CEA's first secretary. Experience had taught Howard that control could never be forced on parish schools, and he resisted efforts by the bishops to take over the new association. The CEA was to be a forum for the exchange of educational methods and ideas, not an episcopal policy-making agency.

One of the major issues facing Howard during his tenure was the length and content of the parish school curriculum in an increasingly industrialized society. The progressives saw the need for the introduction of vocational education in the parish school curriculum, but the traditionalists feared that vocational instruction would undermine the general curriculum.

The members of the Catholic Educational Association—even its most progressive members—were not very innovative in their approach to elementary education. Yet Catholic educators could not reject modern educational ideas out of hand without risking the loss of more children to the public schools. The 1920s, a decade of modern ideas, challenged Catholic educators to modernize the Catholic schools without abandoning their traditional curriculum.

In 1928 the CEA became the National Catholic Educational Association (NCEA), and the following year Howard turned over his position as NCEA secretary to Fr. George Johnson, a professor of education at the Catholic University of America (CUA) and the director of the Education Department of the National Catholic Welfare Conference. *See also*: National Catholic Educational Association (NCEA); National Catholic Welfare Conference (NCWC).

Further Reading: Donald C. Horrigan, *The Shaping of NCEA* (Washington, DC: National Catholic Educational Association, 1978); Timothy Walch, *Parish School: American Catholic Parochial Education from Colonial Times to the Present* (New York, Crossroad, 1996).

Timothy Walch

Catholic High Schools and Minority Students

Catholic Schools and Minority Students, written by Andrew Greeley and published in 1982, used longitudinal data from the *High School and Beyond* study (HS&B; sponsored by the National Center for Education Statistics) to focus on minority students attending Catholic secondary schools. Specifically, Greeley was interested in why "black and Hispanic students who attend Roman Catholic secondary schools display much higher levels of academic effort and achievement than black and Hispanic young people attending public schools" (1982, p. 3). In essence, Greeley's work attempted to tease out whether the positive effects of a Catholic secondary education are due to "input" variables (i.e., a student's background characteristics) or a "school effect" explanation (i.e., quality of instruction). After an opening chapter describes the overall research question and plan of analyses, the remaining nine chapters of the book are arranged as a systematic examination of minority students' performance in Catholic schools.

Greeley examined the demographic, environmental, and economic differences among youth attending Catholic versus public schools. Families that selected Catholic schools for their children were more affluent and better educated. Parents' college aspirations for their children were greater for Catholic versus public school families. Greeley reported that Catholic school minorities had more physical resources in the home for learning than their public school counterparts. Hispanic and black children in Catholic schools also reported higher levels of parental monitoring and supervision of homework.

Greeley used the HS&B data to examine the disciplinary and academic environments of Catholic versus public secondary schools. Public school students reported more acute disciplinary problems (almost one standard deviation greater than Catholic school students) according to a discipline scale reflecting students' perception of disciplinary problems in their school. More Catholic than public school students reported that the disciplinary system in their school was fair and effective. Greeley also found that disciplinary effectiveness was related to school control by a religious order. The academic environments of Catholic and public schools were examined using several methods. One, for example, found that students' reaction to quality of instruction and teacher interest was greater in Catholic schools. In other measures of academic experience, "those who attend Catholic schools are more likely to say that they have participated in laboratory work or field project, that they have written essays, poems, or term papers for their classes, that they have received individual instruction, and that they are satisfied with the academic effort made by their high school" (Greeley, 1982, pp. 43–44). Greeley noted that more homework was both demanded and obtained by teachers at Catholic schools.

After the consideration and review of both "input" (i.e., demographic, environmental, and economic) and "school effect" (i.e., discipline and academics) variables, the question becomes, To what extent does *each* of these factors account for differences in academic achievement and college aspirations? Greeley developed various statistical models to examine these effects. His conclusions indicated that college aspiration differences between black and Hispanic Catholic and public school youth are largely accounted for by student background (i.e., an input effect). In contrast, a school effect (manifest through ownership by a religious order, disciplinary control, and quality of instruction) better accounted for differences in homework and academic performance. Greeley (1982) clarified, "Of the three school environment dynamics which seem to contribute to the superior performance of black and Hispanic students in Catholic schools, the most important is the apparent superior quality of academic instruction in these schools—even when the other two environmental factors are held constant" (p. 71).

Some educators contended that one reason for the success of minorities in Catholic schools is that they likely attract the most upwardly mobile families and most ambitious minority students. Greeley's (1982) analyses, however, did not support this contention. In fact, correlations between social class and achievement are much lower among Catholic school students. The educational effectiveness of Catholic schools is more evenly distributed among social-class groups than is the effectiveness of public schools" (p. 74). Moreover, social class differences on academic achievement diminished or were almost entirely eliminated by the time the students were high school seniors. Some final evidence for a Catholic school effect in explaining minority students' achievement is found in analyses directed at the effect of academic tracking. Greeley found that although Catholic schools were twice as likely to place minority students in academic tracks, the greatest impact of Catholic schools was on those students in a general track, a powerful effect that increased between sophomore and senior years. In sum, Greeley (1982) noted that Catholic schools seem to have their most notable effect on those students who are not in the college-oriented track and their most powerful effect on multiply disadvantaged students—members of minority groups whose fathers did not attend college and who themselves are not sufficiently equipped in educational experience to be admitted to academic track programs" (p. 96). *See also*: *Catholic High Schools: Their Impact on Low-Income Students*; Greeley, Andrew M.; Inner-city schools.

Further Reading: Andrew M. Greeley, *Catholic High Schools and Minority Students* (New Brunswick, NJ: Transaction Books, 1982); James Youniss and John J. Convey, eds., *Catholic Schools at the Crossroads: Survival and Transformation* (New York: Teachers College Press, 2000).

James M. Frabutt

Catholic High Schools: Their Impact on Low-Income Students

The effectiveness of Catholic schools for low-income high school students has been demonstrated through a series of empirical research projects that began in the mid-1960s. These research initiatives were undertaken by several sources: the federal government, university-based researchers, foundations, and the National Catholic Educational Association (NCEA). The results of these data, spanning almost forty years of investigation, yielded similar conclusions: low-income and minority students in Catholic schools attain higher achievement levels than do their peers in public high schools.

The mission of the Catholic school, derived from that of the Church itself, is to offer students an experience of an education community that challenges and empowers all students, regardless of their race, ethnicity, or socioeconomic background. The research project *Catholic High Schools: Their Impact on Low-Income Students*, undertaken by the National Catholic Educational Association with a grant from the Ford Foundation, analyzed the success of the mission from several perspectives. The research focused on the organizational aspects of U.S. Catholic high schools with large numbers of low-income students, evaluating the academic and social aspirations and outcomes of the students, and it identified specific characteristics (curriculum, resources, school climate) that contributed to desirable student outcomes. The research built on several previous works.

The early studies of Catholic schools, conducted in the 1960s and 1970s, looked at various social, religious, and personal outcomes of students. *Catholic Schools in Action*, known as the Notre Dame study, released in 1966, offered a comprehensive, descriptive look at Catholic school outcomes that measured student attitudes and religious values and reported favorable results concerning the impact of multiple variables such as religious, civic, and family values and educational aspirations. A more analytic and quantitatively based study, *The Education of Catholic Americans*, conducted by Greeley and Rossi at the National Opinion Research Center (NORC), presented data that evidenced the effectiveness of Catholic school attendance on their graduates in terms of academic outcomes and predictable adult religious behavior.

A 1966 controversial study, *Equality of Educational Opportunity*, commissioned by the federal government and conducted by James Coleman, focused on the factors that contributed to the success of some high schools in educating diverse populations. He surveyed both public and private schools, and a surprising result was that Catholic high schools had greater success than their public counterparts in creating an environment conducive to learning, particularly when educating disadvantaged youth. Subsequently, the federal government commissioned Coleman to conduct a comparison of the outcomes of public and private school using a federal longitudinal database, *High School and Beyond* (HS&B). The 1982 release of *High School Achievement: Public, Private and Catholic Schools Compared* (Coleman, Hoffer, and Kilgore) indicated that Catholic high school students consistently demonstrated higher academic achievement than their public school counterparts regardless of the socioeconomic status of the family and that the structure of the high school and its quality of instruction, discipline, and faculty expectations of students contributed to the academic and social successes of students.

Andrew Greeley's *Catholic High Schools and Minority Students* (1982) also used the HS&B database to measure the impact of Catholic high schools on Hispanic and African American students. The data concluded that the most disadvantaged students (defined by level of family income and parental levels of education) experienced higher levels of achievement than those similarly situated in public schools and attributed that success to the environment and sense of community they experienced in a Catholic high school.

The 1986 NCEA study, *Catholic High Schools: Their Impact on Low-Income Students* (Benson et al.), presented descriptive data about Catholic secondary schools. It compared the characteristics of Catholic schools that had large percentages of low-income students with other Catholic schools serving students with higher levels of income, providing descriptions of effective programs and learning environments for low-income students. This study demonstrates the impact of educational aspirations of minority students regarding future levels of academic attainment and success in college. Minority students who graduate from Catholic schools were more likely than those from public school to complete college degrees. The data indicate that about a quarter of minorities who graduate from Catholic schools attained at least a bachelor's degree, compared with fewer than 9 percent of public school graduates who attend college.

The Catholic school effect, the better performance of low-income and minority students than public school graduates on school outcomes, when comparing for background variables, has been explored by Bryk, Lee, and Holland (1993). Their research demonstrates the institutional influence of Catholic schools over student attainment and aspirations by means of a controlled academic orientation and expectations for these students who are more likely to remain in school and to attend college than similarly at-risk students in public schools.

The cumulative research reveals that Catholic schools are particularly effective for students from low-income families and minority backgrounds and for those whose parents have the least education. The data indicate higher achievement levels of students in Catholic schools and show that differences in test performance over that of public school peers increased at every grade and significantly so in high school, while the achievement gap between minority and white students in Catholic schools decreased across the grade levels. Catholic high schools place higher expectations on all students, resulting in more rigorous course work and homework and lower absenteeism and fewer disciplinary problems than public schools. The caring environment and discipline in Catholic schools are the reasons most often cited by minority parents when selecting a Catholic school for enrolling their children. The incorporation into a school community in which students are placed in an academic curriculum in which they are expected to do well is the primary reason that minority students attain the levels of academic success. *See also*: *Catholic High Schools and Minority Students*; *Catholic Schools and the Common Good*; *Catholic Schools in Action*; Inner-city schools; *Public and Private High Schools: The Impact of Communities*.

Further Reading: Peter Benson et al., *Catholic High Schools: Their Impact on Low-Income Students* (Washington, DC: National Catholic Educational Association, 1986); Anthony Bryk, Valerie Lee, and Peter Holland, *Catholic Schools and the Common Good* (Cambridge: Harvard University Press, 1993); James Coleman, *Equality of Educational Opportunity* (Washington, DC: U.S. Government Printing Office, 1966); James Coleman, Thomas Hoffer, and Sally Kilgore, *High School Achievement: Public, Private and Catholic Schools Compared* (New York: Basic Books, 1982); John Convey, *Catholic Schools Make a Difference: Twenty-five Years of Research* (Washington, DC: National Catholic Educational Association, 1992); Andrew M. Greeley, *Catholic High Schools and Minority Students* (New Brunswick, NJ: Transaction Books, 1982); Andrew M. Greeley and Peter H. Rossi, *The Education of Catholic Americans* (Chicago: Aldine, 1966); Reginald A. Neuwien, *Catholic Schools in Action: A Report* (Notre Dame, IN: University of Notre Dame Press, 1966).

Dale McDonald, PBVM

Catholic identity

Literature about identity, personal or institutional, typically flourishes in times of rapid change and confusion. Otherwise, identity is mostly taken for granted. In the United States, Catholic authors rarely raised questions about their religious identity or that of their educational institutions until the Second Vatican Council (1962–1965). Before then, Catholics lived mostly in coherent Catholic subcultures. Authors worried more about the quality of their educational institutions, about the professional preparation of their teachers, and about the money needed to support them than about who they were.

Even now, at the beginning of the twenty-first century, in no country have Catholics made a greater investment in Catholic schools and universities than in the United States. Though U.S. Catholics represent only 6 percent of the world population of Catholics, they have established one-quarter of all the Catholic colleges and universities in the world. Much of this institutional building began in the middle of the nineteenth century, when immigrant Catholics established hundreds of primary schools. Moreover, the new democracy had high expectations of its citizens: all were expected to read and write. Such high expectations meant that they had to confront the Protestantism that then pervaded the common schools. Over the next 100 years, the rapid development of industry, more and more sophisticated technology, and the general professionalization of the workforce required longer periods of education for citizens who intended to compete for jobs. To meet this need for the growing Catholic population and to protect their Catholic faith, great numbers of religious brothers, sisters, and priests founded and staffed educational institutions, making them both affordable and visibly Catholic.

Catholics wrestled with their identity from the time they arrived in the New World. At the time of the founding of the republic, Catholic leadership found ways to contribute to its political identity. By the latter part of the nineteenth century, prominent Catholics (e.g., John Ireland and John Lancaster Spalding) promoted an American form of Catholicism that conservative Catholic thinkers, supported by their interpretation of Leo XIII's 1899 encyclical *Testem Benevolentiae*, strongly opposed. At the same time, the bishops in the United States declared in 1884 at the Third Plenary Council of Baltimore that every parish should have a Catholic school, and the building boom in Catholic education institutions commenced.

After World War II, some Catholic intellectuals argued that Leo XIII's encyclical had misunderstood efforts of American Catholics to adapt to American culture and led an effort to shape a more indigenous form of American Catholicism. In 1955, John Tracy Ellis generated an intense national debate among leading Catholics about the quality of Catholic intellectual life. However, few Catholic thinkers then focused on what ought to be distinctive about Catholic scholarship.

Once the 1960s arrived in the United States, several factors converged to intensify the debate. By then, a huge generation of "baby boomers," children of World War II veterans who went to college on the GI Bill of 1944, flooded the nation's campuses. Their middle-class parents had moved into the cultural mainstream, which was becoming increasingly nonsectarian. A cultural revolution, kicked off in the 1950s with the birth of rock 'n' roll and television, intensified in the 1960s with a growing civil rights movement and a more widespread use of drugs. By the late 1960s, opposition to the war in Vietnam exploded on many campuses.

Besides increasing demographics and affluence and the cultural revolution and the war in Vietnam, Catholics had to deal in that same decade with the far-reaching changes called for by Vatican Council II. Protestants, instead of heretics, became "separated brethren." The eucharistic liturgy underwent sweeping changes, sometimes imposed without sufficient explanation or preparation. The council declared that all the baptized, not just the religious alone, were called to holiness. Finally, all Americans experienced an especially difficult year in 1968, when two American leaders were assassinated (Martin Luther King, Jr., in April and Robert F. Kennedy in June) and violent street protests scarred the Chicago National Democratic Convention. That same summer, the confusion of many Catholics about their Catholic identity increased when Pope Paul VI published the encyclical *Humanae Vitae* condemning artificial forms of birth control.

Many religious left their orders in the late 1960s, and laypersons, typically without theological preparation, took their places in the schools. Affluent Catholics moved to suburbs, where many sent their children to good public schools, hoping that religious education classes at the local parish would satisfy passing on the Catholic tradition to their children. Fewer of the religious who stayed wanted to remain in teaching, and inner-city schools often accepted an increasing number of non-Catholic students.

At the university level, increased professional requirements meant that many professors, now more highly trained with Ph.D.s in their disciplines, became more interested in their academic work than in the religious mission of the university. How disciplinary work and religious identity could be combined while respecting the integrity of each was rarely explored then. Where once a Thomistic synthesis seamlessly shaped the curriculum in both philosophy and theology, a greater pluralism in content and method rapidly emerged in the 1960s. By the 1970s, most Catholic universities had established policies of academic freedom and tenure, made provisions for faculty governance, and appointed predominantly lay boards of trustees who brought considerable skills in management and finance but left the Catholic identity to the dwindling number of religious, one of whom typically was still the president. Finally, most Catholic colleges and universities offered stronger professional programs (business, education, and law) than liberal arts degrees, precisely where one might expect to find the best context for articulating a clear Catholic identity.

Taken together, all these developments created considerable confusion over Catholic identity. Since the 1960s and 1970s, however, a slow, but steady, and often contested movement toward a clearer Catholic identity may be discerned. The 1967 Land O'Lakes statement affirmed not only the importance of institutional autonomy and academic freedom but also a Catholic identity and mission of Catholic colleges and universities. Primary and secondary schools benefited from the U.S. bishops' 1972 pastoral on Catholic education, *To Teach as Jesus Did*. Seven years later, the bishops published "Sharing the Light of Faith: National Catechetical Directory for Catholics of the United States." Catholic colleges and universities, after a period of neglect, began to establish programs in Catholic school leadership for lay administrators. More faculty at the university level began to rethink their academic work in relation to Catholic intellectual traditions. Though few philosophers and theologians wanted to return to an exclusive reliance on Thomistic thought, a number of them began to press for more coherent undergraduate degree programs, asking in the process what philosophy and theology should be in a Catholic university. By the mid-1980s, an international discussion on the identity and mission of Catholic colleges and universities helped shape John Paul II's 1990 Apostolic Constitution, *Ex Corde Ecclesiae*. Books by Catholic theologians such as Lawrence Cunningham, Dennis Doyle, and Cardinal Avery Dulles, sociologists such as Andrew Greeley and James Davidson, and philosophers such as Alasdair MacIntyre and Charles Taylor helped clarify further the contours of a full Catholic identity. They stressed, among other things, that Catholic identity not only rests on catechetical and apologetic formation but also requires intellectual work and cultural engagement. The affirmation of the creed and the doctrinal basis of Catholicism include a wide range of social teachings, including those that commit Catholics to social justice, a special and politically astute care for the poor, and respect for subsidiarity in the Church. In a highly individualistic culture, Catholicism retains a strong emphasis on community, a liturgical celebration of the sacraments. In a culture dominated by the market and consumerism, Catholic tradition emphasizes simplicity of life, contemplation, and appropriate leisure. Lay leadership need not lead to secularization, anymore than the affirmation of a distinctive role for the hierarchy necessarily means centralization of authority or the diminishment of the role of the laity. A Catholic imagination sees the world in sacramental and communal terms. Finally, American Catholics carry within them a sense of international history and a tradition replete with saints of many cultures, despite the widespread emphasis in American culture on the present and its immediate concerns. While the internalization of these elements of Catholic identity vary widely, Catholics now affirm them with increasing frequency. *See also*: Catholic philosophy of education; Ellis, John Tracy; Vatican Council, II.

Further Reading: William D'Antonio et al., eds., *American Catholics: Gender, Generation, and Commitment* (Walnut Creek, CA: AltaMira Press, 2001); Avery R. Dulles, *The Catholicity of the Church* (Oxford, England: Clarendon Press, 1985); Andrew M. Greeley, *The Catholic*

Imagination (Berkeley: University of California Press, 2000); James Heft, SM, ed., *A Catholic Modernity?* (New York: Oxford University Press, 1999); James Provost and Knut Walf, eds., *Catholic Identity* (Concilium Series, London: SCM Press, 1994).

James L. Heft, SM

Catholic philosophy of education

When one treats the topic of the philosophy of Catholic education, several considerations are in order: (1) whether theology instead of philosophy guides Catholic education; (2) the ultimate end and purpose of the curriculum; (3) the notion of knowledge as its own reward; (4) the speculative and the practical intellect; (5) prudence as an intellectual and moral virtue; (6) theocentric humanism; (7) Catholic faith as a countercultural faith; (8) transformative leaders as products of Catholic schools; (9) the centrality of theology and religion in the curriculum; (10) importance of the notion of habit; (11) Aquinas on potency and act and their influence on the act of teaching; (12) the abyss between the social claim and the individual claim; and (13) the contrast with pragmatism.

The Catholic philosophy of education has been so influenced by Catholic theology that it is probably more accurate to speak of a theology of education. Philosophy is concerned with ends, and the proclaimed ultimate end of Catholic education is eternal salvation. The end or the purpose of the curriculum is very much related to eternal salvation. In this way the Catholic school curriculum differs from curricula in other schools.

The treatment of aesthetics, art, and literature, for example, recognizes that God and religion have been the most frequent subjects. Art is viewed as having redemptive value. Students are encouraged to view the vertical line in the *Castelfranco Madonna* with a great sense of majesty for verticals.

History is seen as a subject that is beyond time and not merely containing events within time. Since it is seen as a subject beyond time, then each event within historical time is considered in terms of salvation and disaster. That is, what is perceived as being beyond time has a profound influence upon behavior within time. Students in Catholic schools are encouraged to reflect upon the meaning of this view of history for their self-understanding.

Language aids a student in the discovery and ordering of reality. Catholic students reflect on the kind of reality being ordered. They see language as related to the dignity of persons.

Physicists pursue generalizations leading to essences. Catholic philosophy has long pursued essences, or, as physicists put it, the meaning of it all.

In addition to learning taxonomies and functionalism in biology, in Catholic schools a focus stresses that the most important topic in biology is the meaning of life.

Statistics, namely the coefficient of correlation, is the rod and staff methodological tool for social science. Value judgments are not appropriate, for a coefficient of correlation is merely a degree of similarity between two variables. For example, a high correlation exists between school achievement and poverty. A social scientist will not claim that one causes the other. Neither will the Catholic school student. However, the Catholic school student will use the findings of social science as a guide in making proper and God-centered decisions in accord with social justice. These are but a few examples of how the Catholic school curriculum is influenced by a theocentric attitude.

The philosophy of the Catholic school curriculum has long been under the influence of Cardinal John Henry Newman and the philosopher Jacques Maritain. Both of these thinkers were influential in eliciting assent to the notion that knowledge is its own reward and that learning should be characterized by a disinterested joy in knowledge and beauty. These notions are often misinterpreted and misunderstood. Learning for its own sake in Catholic educational philosophy comes *before* specialization and vo-cationalism. Specialization and vocationalism are thought to hinder learning for its own sake, which is another way of labeling liberal education as an education of the mind that frees the mind.

This tradition of liberal education has roots in the works of Aristotle and St. Tho-mas Aquinas. Both posited the importance of what they called the *speculative intellect*. The speculative intellect is at work attempting to discover what is, what things are without a regard to what one ought to make with such discovery. To put it another way, the speculative intellect is concerned with what one finds and does not make. It is for the *practical intellect*, according to Aristotle and St. Thomas, to be concerned with making from what one finds. Catholic philosophy (not necessarily Catholic school practice) sees the speculative intellect as properly prior to the practical. The reason for this is obvious. How can one make from what one finds unless a prior effort is made to find? Rockets cannot be made to go to the moon unless basic research sup-ports the practical aspects of rocket construction. Medical cures are not possible with-out basic scientific discoveries in chemistry and biology. In the long run, when primacy is placed upon practical activity, practical learning, to the exclusion of knowl-edge developed by the speculative intellect, then practical application suffers.

In the philosophy of Catholic education the intellectual virtues of the practical order are art and prudence. Art involves the right reason about things to be made. Prudence refers to the right reason about things to be done. The moral order contains the virtues of temperance, fortitude, justice, and prudence. The profound strength and beauty of the Catholic philosophical position on the virtues of the practical and moral spheres is that prudence is *both* an intellectual *and* a moral virtue. This, theoretically, should be the great strength of Catholic education.

Catholic school students have a commendable record of academic achievement. While achievement is related to success in life and a degree of self-sufficiency, the philosophy of Catholic education cautions its products not to fall into the fatal error of thinking that financial and professional success is enough to reach one's destiny. Reaching one's destiny unaided by transcendence is seen by Catholic educators as an assent to the notion of an anthropocentric humanism. Catholic schools teach a hu-manism that is theocentric (God-centered). It is a humanism that states that persons by themselves alone, unaided by transcendence, cannot achieve their destinies. The intention, therefore, is for students to develop a humility in relation to what academic achievement has enabled them to do in life. The power of knowledge and high com-petence is placed in proper perspective by a theocentric humanism.

The belief in a theocentric humanism creates a unique framework for the use of academic competence in furthering social justice. The motivation to render each per-son his or her due with a constant and perpetual will is thought to have a deeper foundation if it emanates from a theocentric humanism, which is often called a hu-manism of the Incarnation.

The philosophy of Catholic education is mindful that the Catholic faith is a coun-tercultural faith. Secularism, materialism, abortion, sexual promiscuity, and many other aspects of the wider society are contrary to the Magisterium of the Church.

Catholic schools, then, are not freestanding entities unrelated to the mission of the Church. They are sacramental places and participate in the Church's overall ministry. In an ultimate sense, this is the central purpose of the Catholic school. Catholic schools, because of allegiance to the Magisterium, see themselves as educating students to be faithful and to be responsible citizens for Christian witness and action in the world.

In this sense, Catholic schools are institutions educating transformative leaders with a heroic and self-transcending vision. This vision excludes cheap politics, utilitarianism, lack of respect for life and the environment, ignoring conditions of poverty, and all forms of injustice. It excludes ignoring needs of the poor for health care, taking sexual advantage of children, and marginalizing the elderly. In short, the philosophy of Catholic education mandates a descent into temporal affairs.

Catholic schools are committed to the notion that all the realms of meaning are worthy of study. Accordingly, empirics (science and social science), symbolics (grammar, mathematics, and nondiscursive forms), aesthetics (literature, performing arts, and visual arts), and synthetics (history, philosophy, and theology) are all considered worthy of inclusion in the course of studies. Theology and religion are pursued in as qualitative and serious a manner as other subjects. More importantly, theology and religion are not considered only as separate subjects, but an attempt is made to have them permeate all disciplines. This makes the course of studies in a Catholic school unique. It is in accordance with the formation of the kind of visionary, heroic leaders Catholic schools hope to produce in order to counter secular society.

Aquinas and Aristotle, in their consideration of the notion of habit, left a legacy for the philosophy of Catholic education. This legacy is related to the inclusion of theology and religion as vital components of the course of studies. In addition to studying theology and religion, students in Catholic schools are asked to engage in certain practices that emanate from their faith. Prayer, spiritual formation, mass attendance, and, in general, caring for others in practical ways are logical extensions of the study of theology and religion. These spiritual rituals and practices are stressed as habits of character. Habits of character involve the ability to act with facility in a certain way. This Aristo-Thomistic view of habit accounts for many spiritual and, indeed, other formation activities in the Catholic school.

Another Aristo-Thomistic position, that on potency and act, has had a great influence upon the way Catholic schools teach students. For Aquinas, act delineates potency, and potency limits act. The interplay of perspectives of potency and act has led Catholic schools to make inferences about students based upon their actions over time. This is in contrast to onetime labeling of students based upon a single psychometric instrument or a few of them. In the philosophy of Catholic education, the student's mind is not regarded as a blank slate to be filled. Indeed, in the Catholic philosophical tradition the act of teaching is making explicit what is implicit in the mind of the learner. Current emphases on discovery learning, problem solving, and so-called constructivism are congruent with this view of the teaching act.

One of the greatest Catholic philosophers of education, Jacques Maritain, has placed what he calls a super-added burden on Catholic education: to bridge the abyss between the social claim and the individual claim. Since Catholic educators use the term "community" often, and since they are committed to the uniqueness and dignity of each individual person, bridging such an abyss is quite a challenge, as it is for other institutions of society.

Pragmatism, or progressive education, has been America's contribution to philosophy, thanks largely to John Dewey in educational circles. Catholic schools have been stereotyped as traditional places where religious faculty demands strict discipline and inflexibility. On the other hand, progressive education and the pragmatic philosophy that undergirds it are seen as "modern" and innovative. Catholic educators see their schools guided by a theology and philosophy that are contemporary with all the ages. They see Dewey as substituting inquiry for truth as the fundamental concept in logic and the theory of knowledge. Thus, for them, Dewey is more interested in seeking than in finding, more interested in process than in achievement. Of course, progressive education and pragmatism cannot be given adequate treatment here, but an attempt has been made to briefly indicate the perceptions of Catholic educators. In actual practice, Catholic schools employ the same innovative and modern methodologies of instruction and learning advocated by progressive thinkers. However, the principles from which these methodologies emanate are regarded as immutable, that is, good for all persons over all the ages. *See also*: Aquinas, St. Thomas; Augustine, St.; Catholic identity; Maritain, Jacques.

Further Reading: Jacques Maritain, *Education at the Crossroads* (New Haven, CT: Yale University Press, 1943); Jacques Maritain, *The Range of Reason* (New York: Charles Scribner's Sons, 1952); John Henry Newman, *The Idea of a University* (New York: Holt, Rinehart, and Winston, 1960).

Ellis A. Joseph

Catholic publishers

In the fifteenth century, Johann Gutenberg's development of movable type for printing led to a timely and expanded capacity to produce books and other printed materials. In 1455, the first printed edition of the Vulgate Bible was issued. The Church clearly recognized the benefits of applying this new technology to the mission of evangelization. A Vatican Press was established by Pope Sixtus V in 1587 to continue the publication of the Vulgate Bible and to publish the writings of the fathers and church documents. This event represents the beginning of a tradition of Catholic publishing.

One of the earliest and continuous Catholic publishing ventures in the United States is the diocesan newspaper. *The New Catholic Miscellany*, which was published in 1822 in the diocese of Charleston, South Carolina, was the first such publication. The tradition of diocesan publishing has continued, and there were 169 diocesan newspapers being published on either a weekly, biweekly, monthly, or quarterly basis throughout the United States in 1998. The focus of Catholic publishing in the United States includes diocesan and general circulation newspapers, general circulation magazines, scholarly journals, religious education and catechetical texts, liturgical and devotional texts, and scholarly theological books and resources. The remainder of this entry reviews selected exemplars of Catholic publishers who have been recognized as having a significant impact on one or more segments of the Catholic community in America.

A tradition of publishing that was to become the Paulist Press was initiated by Father Isaac Hecker, who founded the American missionary society known as the Paulist Fathers in 1858. Father Hecker's intention was to reach those who were unlikely to have anything to do with religion or a church. The first publication of the Paulists was a monthly magazine entitled *Catholic World*. Concerned that many Catholics could not afford the cost of a magazine subscription, Father Hecker established the Catholic Publication Society in 1866 to create and publish penny-pamphlets on the teachings of the Catholic Church that were distributed nationwide. By 1870, Father Hecker's press was issuing an illustrated publication for children known as *The Young Catholic*, whose readership by the end of the first year was 50,000. Since Fr. Hecker's death in 1888, the Paulist Fathers have continued and expanded their publishing ministry. The Paulist Press was the largest Catholic publisher and distributor in the world by 1966. In the 1960s, the Paulist Press arranged with some European publishers to provide the fifty volumes of *Concilium: Theology in the Age of Renewal*, whose contents were the origins of theological thinking at the Second Vatican Council and after it. The Paulist Press also published the first elementary school-level religious education texts to be influenced by the most contemporary advances in catechetics when it issued the *Come to the Father* series in 1967. A very well known series of the Paulist Press is its *Classics of Western Spirituality*, which includes original documents by authors from the Catholic, Eastern Orthodox, Protestant, Jewish, Islamic, and Native American traditions.

Ave Maria Press was established by Fr. Edward Sorin in 1865 at the campus of the then-fledgling University of Notre Dame, a university that he had launched in November 1842. It is a ministry of the Priests of the Holy Cross and one of the oldest Catholic publishers in the United States. The press focuses on five categories of books: prayer and spirituality, adolescent catechesis, pastoral care and guidance, parish ministry resources, and elementary catechetical resources. Religion and sacramental preparation texts published by the Ave Maria Press have been used by millions of high school students.

Another of the early and well-known Catholic publishers in the United States was Benziger Brothers. It was founded in Switzerland in the late eighteenth century, when Joseph Charles Benziger added devotional books to the religious souvenirs sold by the family near the Marian shrine of Einsiedeln. The elder Benziger was succeeded by his sons Charles and Nicholas Benziger in 1833. By the middle of the nineteenth century there was an extensive emigration of German-speaking Catholics to America. Learning of the needs of these immigrants induced the Benzigers to establish an office in New York City. The American branch of the Benziger Company became totally independent in 1897. It published Catholic theological, liturgical, and educational texts. Among Benziger's educational texts were the *American Cardinal Readers*, published in the 1930s, and *Land of Our Lady Series*, Catholic American history texts, published in the 1950s for the fourth to eighth grades. Benziger was purchased by Crowell Collier Macmillan in 1968. The Benziger name and identity continue as an affiliate of Macmillan/McGraw-Hill.

Our Sunday Visitor Publishing Company was named for the Catholic newspaper *Our Sunday Visitor*, whose first issue was dated May 5, 1912. Father John Francis Noll published *Our Sunday Visitor* in response to the extensive number of anti-Catholic publications that were being distributed. By the end of the first year of its distribution, *Our Sunday Visitor*'s circulation reached 160,000 and 400,000 by 1914. The Our Sunday Visitor Publishing Company has expanded to producing a line of religious periodicals including *New Covenant* launched in 1971 and, since 1987, *The Catholic Answer*. Religious books and educational materials are also offered. Among the religious education materials are the first preschool religious education program in the United States, a series of sacramental texts for baptism, first communion, first confession, and Confirmation, and, for adults, *Exploring the Teaching of Christ*.

Sheed and Ward was originally established in London in 1926 by Francis Joseph Sheed, an Australian lawyer, and Maisie Ward, his British wife. It was likely their membership in the Catholic Evidence Guild inspired them to this endeavor. A New York office of Sheed and Ward was established in 1933. In 1940, as a result of the turmoil of World War II, the Sheeds themselves moved to the United States. Among all the Catholic publishers, Sheed and Ward came to be regarded as having the greatest impact on the English-speaking Catholic community. Sheed and Ward focused on publishing the writings of many distinguished luminaries and theologians such as John Tracy Ellis, Hans Kung, John Courtney Murray, Jaroslav Pelikan, Edward Schille-beeckx, Dorothy Day, Clare Booth Luce, and Jacques Maritain. Sheed and Ward was purchased by the Universal Press Syndicate in 1973 and became Sheed, Andrews, and McMeel. In 1984, the files of Sheed and Ward were donated to the archives of University of Notre Dame. In that same year, Sheed and Ward was sold to the *National Catholic Reporter*, an independent Catholic newspaper. In 1998, Sheed and Ward was purchased by the Theological Book Service of the Priests of the Sacred Heart.

Liguori Publications was established in the United States by the Congregation of the Most Holy Redeemer, or Redemptorists, in 1913, when they launched the *Liguorian* magazine. By 1947, Liguori Publications expanded to include the production of books and parish materials. The *Liguorian* magazine has been listed among the Catholic periodicals with the largest circulation. In 1999, the Priests of the Sacred Heart sold Sheed and Ward to the Redemptorist Fathers, who absorbed it into their Liguori Publications. Sheed and Ward retains its identity and continues the aims of its founders to publish worthwhile and significant books.

In 1919, the bishops of the United States established the National Catholic Welfare Council, which was renamed the National Catholic Welfare Conference (NCWC). It was the precursor of the National Conference of Catholic Bishops (NCCB) and the United States Catholic Conference (USCC). Among their activities was a significant publishing component involving the distribution of a periodical whose designations evolved with the organization from *The National Catholic Welfare Council Bulletin*, to *The National Catholic Welfare Conference Bulletin*, to *Catholic Action*. It also issued useful historical documents relating to the development of the Church in the United States such as *The National Pastorals of the American Hierarchy, 1792–1919*, which was edited by the Catholic historian Msgr. Peter Guilday. At the millennium, the NCCB and USCC were merged into the United States Conference of Catholic Bishops (USCCB), which sponsors USCCB Publishing and is recognized as the official publisher of the U.S. Catholic bishops. Its offerings in English and Spanish are extensive and include publications on every aspect of Catholic life in the United States and the most recent documents issued by the U.S. bishops and the Vatican.

Another significant Catholic publisher has been the National Catholic Educational Association (NCEA), originally known as the Catholic Educational Association, which emerged from the 1904 summer meeting of the Education Conference of Catholic Seminary Faculties, the Association of Catholic Colleges, and the Parish School Conference. In 1927 the appellation "national" was included in the title of the NCEA. The publications of the NCEA focus on administration, legal concerns related to education, research, development, elementary and secondary education, religious education and catechesis, Catholic school boards, curriculum, technology, and seminaries, colleges, and universities.

In August 2002, the Catholic publishers listed by the National Association of Parish

Catechetical Directors (NPCD) of the National Catholic Educational Association included Claretian Publications, GIA Publications, Harcourt Religion Publishing, Ignatius Press, Liturgical Press, Loyola Press, Oregon Catholic Press, Peter Li Education Group Publications, RCL (Resources for Christian Living), Silver Burdett Ginn, St. Anthony Messenger Press, St. Mary's Press, St. Paul Books and Media, Twenty-Third Publications, William H. Sadlier, and some of the publishers whose brief histories have been included above. Several of the publishers on the NPCD list are noteworthy. The Peter Li Education Group Publications offers several well-known Catholic educational periodicals. Listed among those with the largest circulation are *Today's Catholic Teacher*, *The Catechist*, and the *Religion Teacher's Journal*. Also worthy of note is Twenty-Third Publications, owned by Bayard U.S.A., which has purchased the *Catholic Digest*, which is among the Catholic magazines with the greatest number of subscriptions.

There is a group of publishers who are dedicated to reviving and preserving by reprinting traditional Catholic resources such as catechisms, Catholic school readers, lives of the saints, novenas and devotional booklets, liturgical texts, prayer books, and even the traditional Catholic Douay-Rheims Bible. Among the publishers offering these traditional Catholic resources are TAN Books and Publishers, Catholic Book Publishing Company, and Neumann Press.

Another category of Catholic publishers in the United States includes the university presses of the Catholic University of America, Duquesne University, Fordham University, Franciscan University, Georgetown University, the University of Scranton, and the University of Notre Dame.

For access to the most current information about Catholic publishers in the United States, the Catholic Press Association's annual *Catholic Press Directory* can be consulted. The importance of Catholic publishers for the apostolate of the Church has been recognized by Vatican Council II in its Decree on the Means of Social Communication (*Inter Mirifica*). This decree includes a plea:

> If . . . one really wants to form readers in a truly Christian spirit, an authentically Catholic press ought to be established and supported. Such a press, whether it be established and directed by the ecclesiastical authority or by individual Catholics, would have for its manifest purpose to form, to consolidate and to promote a public opinion in conformity with the natural law and with Catholic doctrines and directives. (paragraph 14)

By 1971, the Pontifical Council for the Instruments of Social Communication issued the Pastoral Instruction on the Means of Social Communication (*Communio et Progressio*). In this Pastoral Instruction, "Catholics are encouraged to read Catholic publications regularly. Naturally these must deserve the name of being Catholic. It is hard to see how people can keep in touch with what is happening in the Church without the Catholic Press" (paragraph 140). *See also*: National Catholic Educational Association (NCEA); United States Conference of Catholic Bishops (USCCB).

Further Reading: *A Brief History of Sheed and Ward Publishing* (Ashland, OH: Sheed and Ward [An Apostolate of the Priests of the Sacred Heart], 2002); *About Ave Maria Press* (Notre Dame, IN: Ave Maria Press, 2002); *Liguori Publications: Company Overview* (Liguori, MO: Liguori, 2002); Patrick A. Metress, "Catholic Periodicals Published in the United States," *Serials Review* 25, 3 (1999): 35–46; *The History of Paulist Press* (Mahwah, NJ: Paulist Press, 2002); *To Serve the Church: The Story of Our Sunday Visitor Publishing Company* (Huntington, IN: Our Sunday Visitor, 1998–2002).

Robert B. Williams

Catholic School, The

An official church document written and published by the Sacred Congregation for Catholic Education in 1977. The Congregation for Catholic Education is a department, or dicastery, at the Vatican dedicated to overseeing the various aspects of Catholic education present in the universal Church. Because this document emanated from the Vatican office, it is understood to be addressed to all Catholics in the world and to offer teaching that is of benefit to all.

This document is noteworthy for several reasons. First, *The Catholic School* is the first document of its kind from the Congregation for Catholic Education. Prior to this time, this Vatican office typically was engaged with Catholic education at other levels. Most of their juridical activity, publications, and oversight tended to be with ecclesiastical faculties, pontifical colleges, seminary formation programs, and Catholic colleges and universities. This is the first time in its over 400-year history that the Congregation for Catholic Education has turned its attention toward Catholic schools at the pre-university level. The new solicitude for K–12 Catholic schools was made possible by the Apostolic Constitution of Pope Paul VI, *Regimini Ecclesiae Universae*, promulgated in 1967. In *Regimini*, Paul VI established a schools' office within the Congregation, charging it with the care and promotion of Catholic schools for the universal Church. *The Catholic School*, published ten years later, is the first major publication of the Congregation dealing with schools. While ten years may seem like a long time to be writing a promotional document, it should be noted that the process for writing this document was highly consultative, with several drafts of text being shared repeatedly with bishops and Catholic educational leaders in dozens of countries. While such a consultation could be expedited today via technology, in the 1970s, this took more time. Thus, a ten-year time frame for the publication of its first document on schools is noteworthy.

Second, as the title indicates, the document is explicitly concerned with Catholic schools and stands as the historical first in a steady line of publications on Catholic education that have come from the Congregation. While Vatican documents on Catholic schools now appear with some regularity, *The Catholic School* represents the first comprehensive treatment provided by the Vatican of the place of Catholic schools in the overall educational mission of the Church.

Third, the document is highly theological and ties the mission and purpose of Catholic schools to the ministry of Jesus, to the salvific mission of the Church, and to the broader good of life in community. As such, the document moves beyond pedagogical and academic arguments for Catholic education and provides a philosophical framework for the unique and essential religious dimensions of Catholic schools.

The Catholic School is organized into seven separate sections and, following standard practice for Vatican documents, comprises numbered paragraphs, ninety-seven in all. The seven sections are: (1) the Catholic school and the salvific mission of the Church; (2) present difficulties over Catholic schools; (3) the school as a center of human formation; (4) the educational work of the Catholic school; (5) the responsibility of the Catholic school today; (6) practical directions; and (7) courageous and unified commitment.

Historically, the document can be read in the light of the Second Vatican Council and in particular as a response to the renewed emphasis placed on the Church in the documents of Vatican II, especially *Lumen Gentium* and *Gaudium et Spes*. Furthermore, the council's declaration on education, *Gravissimum Educationis*, merits considerable attention and citation in *The Catholic School*, for the Congregation sees this 1977 document as a development of, and deeper reflection on, Vatican II (*The Catholic School*, #1). Though not cited formally in the text, *To Teach as Jesus Did*, a popular pastoral message from the bishops of the United States, is also part of the historical context of *The Catholic School*. The United States Conference of Catholic Bishops published *To Teach as Jesus Did* in 1972.

The document affirms that Catholic schools provide a privileged environment for Christian education and formation and, in so doing, offer a highly important service to the human family (#16). Nonetheless, many objections are raised relative to the existence of Catholic schools, and the document acknowledges them forthrightly: (1) the Church ought not to operate schools at all but should focus solely on religious matters; (2) the Catholic school can be highly sectarian and a place of proselytism; (3) Catholic schools have outlived their usefulness now that the state can assume responsibility for education; (4) some Catholic schools have been obliged to restrict their educational activities to wealthier social classes; and (5) educational results are often mixed. The document does not address each challenge individually but rather asserts that such views of Catholic schooling are not only contrary to the directives of the Second Vatican Council but also inimical to the Church's mission.

The document recognizes that many schools face financial struggles and urges bishops, pastors, and all of the people of God to work tirelessly to support and finance this important aspect of the Church's ministry. The document also praises those Catholics who work and teach in state schools throughout the world, encouraging them to bear witness to the Gospel in their work.

The Catholic School was published on March 19, 1977, the Feast of St. Joseph, and carried the signature of Gabriel-Marie Cardinal Garrone, then prefect or department head of the Congregation, and Antonio M. Javierre, secretary and titular archbishop of Meta. *See also*: Congregation for Catholic Education, The; *Regimini Ecclesiae Universae*; *To Teach as Jesus Did*.

Further Reading: *Annuario Pontificio* (Citta' Del Vaticano: Libreria Editrice Vaticana, 2001); Congregation for Catholic Education, *The Catholic School* (Washington, DC: United States Catholic Conference, 1977); Congregation for Catholic Education, *The Religious Dimension of Education in a Catholic School* (Washington, DC: United States Catholic Conference, 1988); Austin Flannery, ed., *Vatican Council II: The Conciliar and Post Conciliar Documents* (Northport, NY: Costello, 1988); National Conference of Catholic Bishops, *To Teach as Jesus Did: A Pastoral Message on Catholic Education* (Washington, DC: United States Catholic Conference, 1972); Thomas C. Hunt, Ellis A. Joseph, and Ronald J. Nuzzi, eds., *Handbook of Research on Catholic Education* (Westport, CT: Greenwood Press, 2001).

Ronald J. Nuzzi

Catholic School on the Threshold of the Third Millennium, The

A Vatican document, issued by the Congregation for Catholic Education in late 1997, in support of the contributions Catholic schools are making to the overall educational mission of the church.

The Congregation for Catholic Education is the Vatican office charged with oversight and promotion of Catholic education at every level. This document is part of the Congregation's solicitude and proper jurisdiction. The Congregation was not always attentive to, or involved in, the needs of K–12 Catholic schools. At its inception, the Congregation focused exclusively on seminary education and the proper formation of clergy. Later, it came to be concerned with ecclesiastical universities and faculties and eventually with all Catholic universities. These particular developments spanned over 400 years. Only recently has the Congregation begun to address issues concerning Catholic schools at the preuniversity level. *Regimini Ecclesiae Universae*, an Apostolic Constitution of Pope Paul VI published in 1967, reorganized this Congregation and, for the first time in its history, established an office for K–12 Catholic schools.

Since this reorganization that followed upon the Second Vatican Council, the Congregation has issued numerous official documents pertaining to Catholic schools. Among these are *The Catholic School* (1977); *Lay Catholics in Schools: Witnesses to Faith* (1982); and *The Religious Dimension of Education in a Catholic School* (1988). *The Catholic School on the Threshold of the Third Millennium* should be seen as the most recent addition to this group, as an example of the ongoing concern of the Vatican for Catholic schools since 1967.

While the text of the document is short, twenty-one paragraphs, easily read in a single sitting, its importance should not be underestimated. As a Vatican document, it addresses the needs and convictions of the universal Church regarding Catholic schools. As such, it merits attention and reflection from all Catholics, especially those involved in educational ministries.

The document states that Catholic schools "participate in the evangelizing mission of the church" and thereby constitute "the privileged environment in which Christian education is carried out" (#11). The Congregation sees Catholic schools as an essential part of the overall educational mission of the Church and as a true example of what it means to be Church. Catholic schools are not additions to the ministry of the Church; they are not expensive, optional extras. They are authentic manifestations of the Church, sharing in the Church's mission. Where Catholic schools exist, the Church exists, for schools are dedicated to the work of evangelization.

Said another way, the Church should not be understood as an institution that somehow subsidizes schools, as if schools were something foreign to its mission. It is not a question of subsidy but, rather, a proper understanding of the place of the schools as a bona fide manifestation of the Church. As the document states at #11, "The Catholic school [is] at the heart of the church." The document has a high regard for Catholic schools and affirms their unique, privileged, and essential contribution to the life of the Church.

This insistence of the ecclesial nature of the Catholic school is an important contribution of the document, one that has not gone unnoticed by Catholic leaders. Tobin et al. (1998) noted that while the document uses obtuse prose, the point is clear that Catholic schools are not accidental to the mission of the Church. Rather, they have a privileged place "within the organic pastoral work of the Christian community" (#12). Even more dramatically, the document concludes that "the work of the school is irreplaceable and the investment of human and material resources in the school becomes a prophetic choice" (#21).

The document also calls for Catholic schools to embrace a spiritual renewal of their energy and vision in preparation for the third millennium of Christianity. Many challenges confront Catholic education, including a crisis of values influenced by subjectivism, moral relativism, nihilism, rapid structural changes, technological advances, the globalization of the economy, and the growing marginalization of Christianity.

Another important emphasis in the document is its affirmation of the school's mission to those who are poor and weak. Historically, Catholic schools have been effective among disadvantaged students, immigrants, the urban poor, and other communities that were underresourced. The document challenges Catholic educators to pay special attention to the weakest and to those whose material poverty might otherwise prevent them from having access to formal education. As Tobin noted, "[T]his stirring mandate presents a critical challenge to bishops and pastors and to all those who are a part of the Catholic school community: where to find the political will and temporal resources to provide Catholic education for all our families, particularly those unable to pay their own way" (Tobin, 1998, p. 226).

The document makes a general reference to "true equality for non-state schools," asking that such equality remain "respectful of their educational project" (#17). Given the ongoing interest in voucher programs in the United States and in other ways of securing public support for private schools, this statement seems especially timely.

While this document was well received and promoted as a vision statement for schools moving into the third millennium, some commentators were hoping for more explicit direction. Tobin (1998) remarked that the document would have been more complete had it addressed pastors of the Church, especially bishops and priests, since the work of finding the resources and promoting the schools often falls to them. Kambeitz (1998) expressed appreciation for the document's acknowledgment of the dedicated service of vowed religious men and women in the history of Catholic schools but wondered why the document failed to mention or recognize the large numbers of dedicated laity who today staff Catholic schools. Further, Kambeitz noted that while extolling the roles of teachers and parents, the document neglected to point out the crucial need for leadership in Catholic schools and the growing demand for qualified, faith-filled principals. Hoyt (Tobin, 1998) noted that the publication of the document coincided serendipitously with the thirtieth anniversary of the establishment of the schools' office within the Congregation and the twentieth anniversary of the publication of *The Catholic School*. While appreciative of the focus on Catholic schools, Hoyt found little that was new in the document but read it as an affirmation of the history of Catholic schools and their importance in today's global world. Hoyt faulted the document for failing to give directives to bishops and pastors on prioritizing Catholic schools among their ministerial responsibilities.

The full text of the document has been published by *Origins*, the publication arm of the United States Conference of Catholic Bishops (USCCB), *Catholic Education: A Journal of Inquiry & Practice*, the Daughters of St. Paul, and is available online at the Vatican's Web site. *See also*: Congregation for Catholic Education, The; *Lay Catholics in Schools: Witnesses to Faith*; *Religious Dimension of Education in a Catholic School, The*; *Catholic School, The*.

Further Reading: Congregation for Catholic Education, "The Catholic School on the Threshold of the Third Millennium," *Catholic Education: A Journal of Inquiry & Practice* 2, 1 (September 1998): 4–14; Thomas Tobin, Dale Hoyt, Teresita Kambietz, and Patricia Kelly-Stiles, "Responses to the Vatican Document: *The Catholic School on the Threshold of the Third Millennium*," *Catholic Education: A Journal of Inquiry & Practice* 2, 2 (December 1998): 225–234.

Ronald J. Nuzzi

Catholic school question

Question refers to the quest by Catholics in the mid- to late 1800s to establish an appropriate system of education to prepare their children both academically and religiously in an environment of nationalism, increasing secularization, and anti-Catholic prejudice.

The heart of the Catholic school question rested on the ability of the common schools to provide an education suitable for Catholic children. The religious bias in these schools was intolerable for Catholics; the First Provincial Council of Baltimore (1829) promulgated the importance of establishing Catholic parish schools.

Even before the funding of religious schools was challenged, Catholic schools did not receive their fair share of tax appropriations. Historically, from the colonial through the early national periods, church and private schools regularly received public funds. Catholics did not typically share this benefit due to their lack of status and influence along with a general religious prejudice.

In July 1840, Archbishop John Hughes of New York began a campaign to receive proportionate funding for Catholic schools. It was soon apparent that it was not possible to have a reasonable discussion on the Catholic school question. A series of raucous public debates was held where Archbishop Hughes solely stood his position against a field of Protestant protesters. Hughes' funding plan was defeated, but soon after, the sectarian commission that regulated public schools was replaced by an elected body. Unfortunately, a secular press used the debates and their results as further evidence of how unpatriotic and dangerous Catholicism was.

The First Plenary Council of Baltimore (1852) reiterated the necessity of Catholic parish schools. Martin John Spalding, bishop of Louisville, wrote, "The great question of the day for us Americans, is, undoubtedly, that of Common School Education" (Reilly, 1943, p. 17), and he attempted to build a case for public funding by using European education as an example. Non-Catholic groups had but a single objective in response, to keep Catholics from securing a portion of state school funds.

The general alienation of religion from public education, promoted by Horace Mann in the mid-1800s as a positive development, solidified the loss of tax support for all denominational schools. Mann argued that a single-tax-supported school system was necessary to transform a nation of immigrants into a strong United States of America. The burgeoning number of Protestant denominations solved their financial strains by a unified claim to the public school system. Catholic parents were left to support financially two school systems: one public and one parochial. Finances increasingly put a strain on parish schools, particularly as the number of poor Catholic immigrants swelled.

This funding problem beleaguered the hierarchy of the Catholic Church. Numerous approaches were proposed to relieve the Catholic community of the double taxation burden. In 1890, Archbishop Ireland used the occasion of a speech to the National Education Association in St. Paul, Minnesota, to approach public educators with the Catholic school question. He began by commending the state for establishing schools. Ireland noted that the availability of free public schools was necessary for the common good of society.

Ireland then made two proposals to the state in an attempt to remove the double tax burden from Catholic parents. His first option was the establishment of a denominational system of state-supported schools. If this was rejected, his second option was to supplement public education with religious education, generally referred to as the Poughkeepsie Plan.

The Poughkeepsie Plan allowed for a Catholic school building to be leased by the public school district for a minimal amount. There would be no religious instruction during the school day but given either before or after regular school hours. Catholic school teachers, even religious, would be retained to teach in the schools. They would meet state requirements and be paid by the public school district.

Ireland's speech received broad criticism among Catholics for his support of public education, but he continued to argue that his position merely reflected the reality in a state with few Catholics who could support parochial schools in addition to bearing public school taxes. Ireland became associated with the "Americanism of the Church," a term used to describe the assimilation of Catholics into the nation while retaining their attachment to the Catholic faith and Church. Pope Leo XIII appeared to refer to this concept in his Apostolic Letter *Testem Benevolentiae* (1899). Archbishop Ireland continued to argue that Catholics must demonstrate an allegiance to the United States if they are to remove the prejudice against them. Ireland believed that it was not advantageous for Catholics to alienate either Protestants or public schooling.

Archbishop Michael Corrigan and his colleagues represented another approach to the Catholic school question. They vigorously supported the establishment of parish schools that served the religious needs of immigrants within their ethnic heritage. Corrigan's camp demonstrated some sympathies to Cahenslyism. Cahenslyism was a plan proposed to the Pope by Peter Paul Cahensly (1891) to meet the ecclesiastical needs of immigrants entering the United States by organizing the American Catholic Church according to European nationalities. The plan would require bishops and priests of the same race and language as the majority of the members of a diocese or congregation. This plan was robustly opposed by some American bishops, led by Archbishop Ireland.

Predominantly, Corrigan's agenda was to extinguish the efforts to bring American Catholics into mainstream American ideology. He believed that by becoming a part of the social and political scene, American Catholics would lose their religious identity. Corrigan supported the separation of Church and state because he believed that ultimately was favorable to the Catholic Church. He represented a belief that by developing Catholic institutions, Catholics would receive the necessary supports to preserve the faith in the United States.

The Catholic school question, documented through the struggle of influential archbishops, portrays a period in American history before Catholics were accepted into mainstream society. Unfortunately, the issue of double taxation and school funding was never resolved to the satisfaction of most American Catholics. *See also*: Bouquillon, Thomas; Gibbons, James Cardinal; Holaind, Rene I.; Ireland, John; Katzer, Frederick; Leo XIII, Pope; McQuaid, Bernard; Satolli, Francis (Francesco).

Further Reading: John P. Bland and John O'Brien, *The Public School Question: Roman Catholicism and Americanism* (Cambridge: Harvard University Press, John Wilson & Sons, 1880); Harold A. Buetow, *Of Singular Benefit: The Story of U.S. Catholic Education* (New York: Macmillan 1970); Richard J. Gabel, *Public Funds for Church and Private Schools* (Washington, DC: Catholic University of America Press, 1937); Thomas S. Preston, *The Catholic View of the School Question* (New York: R. Coddington, 1870); Daniel F. Reilly, *The School Controversy 1891–1893* (Washington, DC: Catholic University of America Press, 1943).

Merylann J. "Mimi" Schuttloffel

Catholic Schools and the Common Good

Catholic Schools and the Common Good is a 1993 book by Anthony S. Bryk, professor of education at the University of Chicago; Valerie E. Lee, associate professor of education at the University of Michigan at Ann Arbor; and Peter B. Holland, superintendent of the Belmont School System in Belmont, Massachusetts. The authors presented the findings of their research on Catholic secondary schools, which began in 1981, citing a twofold purpose: first, to present a portrait of Catholic high schools at the particular time that these studies were conducted, and second, to provide an analysis of the structures of these seven schools that support student achievement across a variety of demographic variables.

The chapter titles in the book provide a glimpse into the substance and scope of their investigations: "The Tradition of Catholic Schools," "Research Past and Present," "Classroom Life," "Curriculum and Academic Organization," "Communal Organization," "Governance," "The Transition to High School," "Variations in Internal Operations," "Single-Sex versus Coeducational Schools," "The Impact of Academic Organization," "The Impact of Communal Organization," "Catholic Lessons for America's Schools," and "Epilogue: The Future of Catholic High Schools."

The methodology of the book involved historical research on the background and development of Catholic education in the United States, extensive fieldwork and observations in the seven selected high schools, and statistical data gathered from the *High Schools and Beyond* survey, managed by the National Center for Education Statistics.

Each high school was carefully described and given a new name: St. Richard's Diocesan/coed, Suburban Boston, enrollment of 855; St. Frances' Private/girls, Urban Baltimore, enrollment 540; St. Cornelius' Diocesan/coed, Urban Cleveland, enrollment 950; St. Madeleine's Private/girls, Urban Los Angeles, enrollment 660; St. Edward's Private/boys, Suburban Louisville, enrollment 1,500; St. Peter's Inter-parish/coed, Urban San Antonio, enrollment 350; Bishop O'Boyle Private/coed, enrollment 130.

The findings demonstrated a Catholic high school record of universally higher academic achievement than could be found in public schools. This conclusion was particularly encouraging because its higher level of learning is representative of various races and classes. The study also noted a core curriculum that every student was expected to complete no matter what his or her personal background might have been or what his or her aspirations were. Closely linked to the development and stability of this core curriculum is the presence of a faculty who support this educational design through a shared vision about fundamental curriculum that an educated person must learn.

A second set of findings concerned the communal organization of the Catholic high schools. The authors cited numerous activities at these schools and the large number of participants in such areas as athletics, drama, and campus ministry. These activities also provide a way of being socialized into the culture of the various schools and a bond of connection with former students. The positive influence of administrators and teachers as role models is noted especially in the area of collegiality. The research underscores the dual importance of these adults competently fulfilling their duties, while being available to the students in numerous ways. The authors also noted how the philosophical emphasis and vision of these schools imbue the organization with respect for the dignity and value of each person. This vision is particularly characterized by its communal nature. The extensive presence and importance of social capital, that is, the web of supportive constituencies, are a theme that runs throughout the book.

A third set of findings noted the importance of decentralized governance, sometimes described as site-based management. Mirroring the Catholic Church's emphasis on subsidiary governance found in the documents and spirit of Vatican II, these schools make most major decisions locally. The principal at each school, whether it is parish, diocesan, or private, is primarily responsible for the operations and vision of the school.

The final set of findings focuses upon the inspirational ideology that guides these schools. The authors cite a heavy emphasis upon Christian personalism that recognizes the value of each person made in the image and likeness of God. Christian personalism charges faculty and staff to be concerned about the acquisition of knowledge and facts and extends to concern about moral choices made by students and the kind of people they strive to become. The researchers further explain how the presence of subsidiarity impacts the ideology of the school and sets a context for social ethics.

Catholic social ethics contribute to the inspirational ideology of the schools studied. The research indicated the importance of understanding and living moral truths while creating a public place that acknowledges the wisdom of such truths. The real and symbolic importance of Jesus Christ as a model for one's life was evident. Theological themes such as the Kingdom of God and the triumph of the Resurrection inspire both hope and the moral necessity of addressing poverty and injustice.

This study was widely reviewed and contributed to the ongoing conversation of culture and climate of Catholic education in the United States. Enthusiastic reviews were written in mainstream Catholic periodicals, professional journals, and daily newspapers. In particular, it assisted Catholic secondary schools in strengthening their sense of resolve in mission and identity, at a time when changing demographics, diminishment of religious, and escalating costs contributed to a general sense of uncertainty.

Research continues to draw upon the findings of this book and build upon the insights described. The quality of this study and the impact of its findings have furthered the research on Catholic schools. This book benchmarked many anecdotal assertions and hypothesis while instilling a sense of confidence and hope in the mission of secondary education. *See also*: *Catholic High Schools and Minority Students*; *Catholic High Schools*: *Their Impact on Low-Income Students*; Community; Effectiveness of Catholic schools; Enrollment.

Further Reading: Anthony S. Bryk, Valerie E. Lee, and Peter B. Holland, *Catholic Schools and the Common Good* (Cambridge: Harvard University Press, 1993).

Michael P. Caruso, SJ

Catholic Schools in Action

A 1966 publication of the University of Notre Dame, reporting the results of a four-year study of Catholic schools in the United States. Also known as the Notre Dame Study of Catholic Elementary and Secondary Schools in the United States, the report was for many years the most exhaustive and comprehensive study of Catholic schools ever undertaken.

Data were gathered from 1962 to 1966 by Notre Dame with the support of a $350,000 grant from the Carnegie Corporation of New York. The first director of the effort, William H. Conley, was granted a leave of absence from his position at Marquette University in Milwaukee in order to lead the study. Conley resigned, however, in May 1963 to become president of Sacred Heart University, Bridgeport, Connecticut. Reginald Neuwien, one of Conley's associates, then became director of the study and served as editor of *Catholic Schools in Action* (CSIA).

CSIA focused the attention of the national media, church leaders, educators, and civic leaders on the strengths of Catholic schools. At that time, the nation's Catholic elementary and secondary schools had an excellent academic record, but they enrolled less than half of the nearly 11.5 million Catholics students eligible to attend. CSIA saw this as problematic.

CSIA showed that students enrolled in Catholic schools scored superior on the scale of national norms both in academic achievement and in learning potential. This indicated superiority, CSIA argued, was attributed to the relatively selective admissions policies of Catholic schools that, during 1962–1963, admitted 5,351,354 students, representing 46.74 percent of those eligible through infant baptism to enroll.

In releasing the study, the report's executive committee—Rev. Theodore Hesburgh, CSC, president of the University of Notre Dame; Rt. Rev. Msgr. Frederick Hochwalt, executive secretary of the National Catholic Educational Association; and Dr. George Shuster, former president of Hunter College in New York City—called attention to the valuable information the study contained, much of it available for the first time. Among these findings were that (1) the attitudes of Catholic school children on a variety of subjects differs not only with their individual backgrounds but also with the region, the diocese, and the peculiar local circumstances; (2) lay teachers feel that they are not accepted as professional co-equals by the religious teachers (sisters, priests, and brothers) or by the parents of children in Catholic schools, even though there is one lay teacher to every 2.24 religious teachers at the elementary level; and (3) parents of children in Catholic schools attach more importance to the school's religious-moral goals than to their intellectual or vocational objectives.

The study had the benefit of a high level of participation, an exceptional response rate to surveys, and the support of many church leaders. The research involved 92 percent (9,451) of the nation's Catholic elementary schools and 84 percent (2,075) of Catholic high schools. Surveys were completed by 103,000 elementary teachers, 40,000 high school teachers, 9,450 elementary principals, 2,075 high school principals, and 24,000 parents, in addition to the standardized testing of thousands of students and depth studies (focus groups) in thirteen dioceses. Official church support for the effort, including the granting of access to schools and school personnel, came in the form of national leadership from Archbishop Lawrence Shehan of Baltimore, chairman of the Department of Education of the National Catholic Welfare Conference, Msgr. William McManus, then the superintendent of Catholic schools for the Archdiocese of Chicago, and Albert Cardinal Meyer, the archbishop of Chicago. Other contributors to the study were Donald N. Barrett, John Darby, SM, Terry Denny, Xavier J. Harris, OFM, Robert F. Harvanek, SJ, Leonard J. Kazmier, Mary Emil Penet, IHM, Mary James Rau, OP, and John E. Walsh, CSC.

Convey (1992) noted that the most distinctive contribution of CSIA was the development of the *Inventory of Catholic School Outcomes* (ICSO), a standardized measure of religious knowledge, values, and attitudes. Because the ICSO measured understanding of church law, church doctrine, and liturgy, it was of great interest to educators and bishops alike. Few such tests of religious knowledge were available prior to this time. The students tested did equally well on the three areas of law, doctrine, and liturgy, with girls in all-girls' high schools earning the highest scores. Seniors in high school showed significant gains and higher scores than eighth graders, indicating a measure of growth in religious knowledge through the high school years.

CSIA received some criticism for being descriptive in nature, rather than evaluative, and for being focused at a popular, rather than a scholarly, audience. Convey (1992) found much of that criticism valid, pointing out that although the text of the study often refers to statistical analyses, the statistics themselves are absent from the report. Even with these serious limitations, however, CSIA represents a significant moment in research on Catholic schools because of its scope and its attempt to measure values and content that remain at the heart of the Catholic schools' mission. *See also*: *Education of Catholic Americans, The*; Vatican Council II.

Further Reading: William Conley, "Catholic Schools in Action—A Critique," *The Catholic School Journal* 66, 9 (1966): 27–30; John Convey, *Catholic Schools Make a Difference: Twenty-five Years of Research* (Washington, DC: National Catholic Educational Association, 1992); Neil McCluskey, *Catholic Education Faces Its Future* (Garden City, NY: Doubleday, 1968); Reginald A. Neuwein, ed., *Catholic Schools in Action: The Notre Dame Study of Catholic Elementary and Secondary Schools in the United States* (Notre Dame, IN: University of Notre Dame Press, 1966).

Ronald J. Nuzzi

Catholic Schools in a Declining Church

A book containing the results of a study about Catholic schools conducted by Reverend Andrew Greeley and several colleagues, published in 1976 (Greeley, McGready, and McCourt, 1976). The inspiration for the study was actually an earlier project by Greeley and Peter Rossi, *The Education of Catholic Americans* (Greeley and Rossi, 1966). Convey reported that this earlier study was the "most ambitious study of Catholic education up until that time" (Convey, 1992, pp. 12–13). *The Education of Catholic Americans* was undertaken with a grant from the Carnegie Corporation, and Greeley and Rossi set out to study the effects of a Catholic school education. Specifically, they asked whether Catholics who attended Catholic schools were more involved in the Church, more economically successful, and more tolerant socially and politically than were Catholics who did not attend Catholic schools. They were interested to see if Catholic schools had a measurable effect in dividing American society by creating an exclusive ghetto mentality among their alumni and whether or not attendance at a Catholic school had any relationship to church attendance and other religious behaviors in adult life.

Catholic Schools in a Declining Church was, in large measure, an attempt to replicate the study contained in *The Education of Catholic Americans*. Convey (1992) judged the replication effort as important because the earlier study, while a landmark in many respects, suffered from design limitations regarding the measure of association employed to analyze certain relationships. Convey noted that the earlier study appeared at a time when helpful statistical procedures such as regression analyses and path models were not as yet popular in educational research. Hence, Greeley and Rossi were not able to avail themselves of a statistical model to predict the cumulative effects of their chosen predictors of adult religious behavior. *Catholic Schools in a Declining Church* was able to correct that limitation.

In the new study, Greeley and his colleagues concluded that Catholic schools were even more important than they were in the earlier study a decade before. They argued that schools were actually increasing their influence on graduates as both the Church and the wider society experienced dramatic changes. The Church was experiencing internal challenges in the wake of Vatican II and the reaction to Pope Paul VI's encyclical banning artificial birth control, *Humanae Vitae*. American society had its own struggles to confront in dealing with the Vietnam War, the Civil Rights Movement, and the sexual revolution. Convey (1992) believed that this widespread unrest in the Church and in society created an entirely different national context for the new study.

Greeley and his colleagues came to several important conclusions: (1) years in Catholic school was more important than parental religious behavior in predicting adult religious behavior; (2) the relationship between the years of attendance in Catholic schools and financial contributions to the Church as an adult was stronger than ever; and (3) Catholic school attendance continued to provide economic advantages in adult life.

The study noted that this success was occurring despite declining enrollment and increasing costs. In fact, the study concluded that support for Catholic schools was strong among American Catholics. An overwhelming 80 percent of Catholics surveyed indicated their abiding support for Catholic schools, as well as their readiness to increase their monetary contributions at the local level in order to support the parish school. Among respondents with more than ten years of Catholic education, 86 percent indicated a willingness to contribute more. Among those with no Catholic schooling, 79 percent would give more. As to the size of the increased monetary gift anticipated, responses ranged from $5 to $500. The researchers extrapolated the results, projecting these response rates widely to include the entire Catholic population at the time, in order to estimate the potential size of increased contributions. They reported that approximately 28 percent would be willing to contribute between $51 and $100 more, 2 percent would give $500 more, and 3 percent under $5.

At the time of the study, average tuition was $343, representing approximately 3.32 percent of family income. Still, 24 percent of respondents indicated that Catholic schools were too expensive.

As Greeley has stated many times before, the effectiveness of Catholic schools is unparalleled in any other church educational initiative, especially the CCD (Confraternity of Christian Doctrine) effort. The 1976 study repeated what Greeley and Rossi (1966) had stated earlier, namely, that CCD was neither a comparable project nor a viable alternative to Catholic schools, for it was without any of these measurable effects. In today's Church, varied structures and programs exist, both at the diocesan and parish level, to respond to the religious education needs of the Christian faithful. Most parishes and dioceses have numerous formal and informal ways that people may choose to learn more about the faith, develop their own spirituality, involve themselves in various ministries, and so deepen their relationship with God and the Church. However, as Greeley has noted (1982), Catholic schools participate in this great heritage of the Church's evangelical mission and became, in the 1900s, the most effective catechetical tool the Church has ever experienced. *See also*: *Education of Catholic Americans, The*; Effectiveness of Catholic schools; Greeley, Andrew M.

Further Reading: John J. Convey, *Catholic Schools Make a Difference: Twenty-five Years of Research* (Washington, DC: NCEA, 1992); Andrew M. Greeley, *Catholic High Schools and Minority Students* (New Brunswick, NJ: Transaction Books, 1982); Andrew Greeley, William C. McCready, and Kathleen McCourt, *Catholic Schools in a Declining Church* (Kansas City, MO: Sheed and Ward, 1976); Andrew Greeley and Peter H. Rossi, *The Education of Catholic Americans* (Chicago: Aldine, 1966); Thomas C. Hunt, Ellis A. Joseph, and Ronald J. Nuzzi, eds., *Catholic Schools Still Make a Difference: Ten Years of Research, 1991–2000* (Washington,

DC: NCEA, 2002); Thomas C. Hunt, Ellis A. Joseph, and Ronald J. Nuzzi, eds., *Handbook of Research on Catholic Education* (Westport, CT: Greenwood Press, 2001).

Ronald J. Nuzzi

Catholic Schools Make a Difference: Twenty-five Years of Research
An overview and summary of the research on kindergarten through grade 12 Catholic schools in the United States, written by John Convey and published by the National Catholic Educational Association (NCEA) in 1992. The book was intended as an original compilation and review of the research and scholarly work conducted on Catholic schools during the period 1965–1990. The author himself called the text, "a study of the studies on Catholic schools" (Convey, 1992, p. vii).

Convey undertook the effort to write the book at the invitation of the research board of the Chief Administrators of Catholic Education (CACE), a department of the NCEA for diocesan superintendents, vicars of education, directors of total Catholic education, secretaries of education, and diocesan directors of religious education. At the time, Convey was the chair of the Department of Education at the Catholic University of America, where he has since become provost.

The book was highly anticipated and well received. Because research on Catholic schools grew remarkably between 1965 and 1990, Convey had at his disposal national research studies that addressed the effectiveness of Catholic schools. Thus, the audience for the book was highly diversified: professional educators, Catholic school teachers and principals, diocesan superintendents, pastors, university professors, educational researchers, parents, and public policy leaders interested in what could be learned from Catholic schools that would be helpful to public education.

Among the more provocative findings from Catholic school research between 1965 and 1990 are that (1) Catholic schools are particularly effective for minorities and (2) Catholic schools are "generally able to create a climate characterized by discipline and order, a strong sense of community, high academic standards, a highly committed and collegial faculty, and high levels of parental interest and participation, each of which the research has shown to be associated with effective schools" (Convey, 1992, pp. 1–2).

The major studies that come under discussion in the text for both review and analysis include *Catholic Schools in Action* (Neuwien, 1966), commonly referred to as the Notre Dame Study of Catholic Education; *The Education of Catholic Americans* (Greeley and Rossi, 1966); *Catholic Schools in a Declining Church* (Greeley, McCready, and McCourt, 1976); *High School Achievement: Public, Catholic, and Private Schools Compared* (Coleman, Hoffer, and Kilgore, 1982); and various data mined from the *National Education Longitudinal Study of 1988.*

Convey (1992) offered a balanced interpretation in reviewing various studies, especially in his treatment of the comparative study of Coleman, Hoffer, and Kilgore (1982). This study was particularly controversial in academic and political circles because the authors concluded that Catholic schools were doing a consistently better job of educating students than public schools. Their study revealed that, even after applying statistical controls for differences in family background, students in Catholic high schools and other private schools attained higher scores in mathematics and in verbal skills at both the tenth and twelfth grade levels than did similar students in public schools. Coleman and his colleagues argued that the higher achievement in Catholic schools was due to strong discipline, high expectations of the teachers, and the structured curriculum that characterized these schools. Convey (1992) reported the "furious debate" (p. 17) that ensued, as major journals, including the *Harvard Educational Review* (November 1981) and the *Sociology of Education* (April/July 1982; October, 1982; July, 1985) devoted special issues to the topic. Convey found merit in many of the criticisms of Coleman and his associates and reported that the majority of researchers eventually agreed that the overall Catholic school advantage, or the "Catholic school effect," was actually much smaller than originally suggested. Nonetheless, "whatever the size of the effects, the Catholic school advantage that did occur . . . was due to a homogeneous and rigorous curriculum, good discipline, and a supportive school climate, which produced positive results for students of all backgrounds" (Convey, 1992, p. 18).

Other areas of research where Convey summarizes and reviews available data include demographic variables such as minority enrollment, family income, and market share; academic outcomes; school climate variables such as discipline and order, the presence of a faith community, and a strong academic emphasis; teacher preparation and experience; parental involvement; student demographics such as disadvantaged students in Catholic schools and the ongoing debate about single-sex versus co-educational Catholic high schools; and the relative effectiveness of Catholic schools in terms of both academic and religious outcomes.

Convey (1992) offered several recommendations for further research and suggested that Catholic education would be better served if future studies could incorporate some methodological modifications in their design. Specifically, Convey called for (1) the increased use of ethnographic studies of particular schools as a way to study those variables that relate to the unique, Catholic character of schools, such as the transmission of values, the experience of a faith community, and the spiritual leadership of the principal and faculty; (2) the use of longitudinal designs rather than cross-sectional designs; and (3) the adoption of new statistical models to analyze data.

Because of the popularity and helpfulness of Convey's work and its practical utility for both scholars and practitioners, the NCEA commissioned a follow-up study of the studies in 2000. The ever-increasing body of research on Catholic schools made a twenty-five-year overview somewhat unwieldy, so the new text deliberately focused on the period 1991–2000. Compiled by three editors and a variety of authors, the new text follows Convey's approach for the most part, while updating research in all the relevant fields. Published by the NCEA in 2002, the new study of the studies is called *Catholic Schools Still Make a Difference* (Hunt, Joseph, and Nuzzi) to signify the ongoing impact of Convey's work and the enduring success of Catholic schools. *See also*: *Catholic Schools Still Make a Difference: Ten Years of Research, 1991–2000*; Effectiveness of Catholic schools.

Further Reading: James Coleman, Thomas Hoffer, and Sally Kilgore, *High School Achievement: Public, Catholic, and Private Schools Compared* (New York: Basic Books, 1982); John J. Convey, *Catholic Schools Make a Difference: Twenty-five Years of Research* (Washington, DC: NCEA, 1992); Andrew Greeley, William C. McCready, and Kathleen McCourt, *Catholic Schools in a Declining Church* (Kansas City, KS: Sheed and Ward, 1976); Andrew Greeley and Peter B. Rossi, *The Education of Catholic Americans* (Chicago: Aldine, 1966); Thomas C. Hunt, Ellis A. Joseph, and Ronald J. Nuzzi eds., *Catholic Schools Still Make a Difference: Ten Years of Research, 1991–2000* (Washington, DC: NCEA, 2002); Reginald Neuwien, *Catholic Schools in Action* (Notre Dame, IN: University of Notre Dame Press, 1966).

Ronald J. Nuzzi

Catholic Schools *Still* Make a Difference: Ten Years of Research, 1991–2000

An overview and summary of research on kindergarten through grade 12 Catholic schools in the United States, published by the NCEA (National Catholic Educational Association) in 2002. The book was intended as a follow-up and updating of an earlier text published by the NCEA in 1992 and written by John Convey, chair of the Department of Education at the Catholic University of America in Washington, D.C. Convey was the first to provide this "study of the studies" approach by reviewing all available research on Catholics schools from the period 1965 to 1990. The Convey text was named *Catholic Schools Make a Difference* (Convey, 1992). In order to express the close connection between the two volumes, the new text was named *Catholic Schools Still Make a Difference* (Hunt, Joseph, and Nuzzi, 2002).

During his preparation for the first book, Convey discovered that no comprehensive review of the research on Catholic schools had ever been assembled (Hunt, Joseph, and Nuzzi, 2002). While a variety of significant studies existed, no effort had been made to synthesize available knowledge or to compile the results of the studies in a publication. Convey singled out the work of Andrew Greeley, perhaps the best-known Catholic school researcher, and the work of James Coleman, particularly his study *High School Achievement: Public, Catholic, and Private Schools Compared* (Coleman, Hoffer, and Kilgore, 1982).

As Convey's original work addressed research up to 1990, there was a manifest need to update the compendium and provide a current synthesis of available research on Catholic schools. This was especially important as the decade of the 1990s produced important research on Catholic schools. In the preface to the 2002 volume, Convey stated that at least three factors contributed to researchers' interest in Catholic schools: (1) the support of Catholic schools by families, clearly seen in the growth of Catholic school enrollments during this period; (2) the increased publicity about Catholic school effectiveness, especially regarding minority and disadvantaged students; and (3) the general political climate, which has focused national attention on policy issues such as school choice, vouchers, and charter schools (Convey in Hunt, Joseph, and Nuzzi, 2002, p. vii).

While *Catholic Schools Still Make a Difference* was modeled on the approach taken by Convey, several important differences separate the two books. First, Convey was the sole author of the first "study of the studies." While the successful undertaking and completion of such an extensive research project are laudable, the growing body of research on Catholic schools made the effort to update the book a larger, more complicated process than could be handled well by one researcher. Thus, several editors, working with colleagues across the United States, solicited the participation of Catholic educational scholars and invited them to review the research in their respective areas of expertise. The result was a more in-depth treatment of a variety of topics and an extensive, comprehensive bibliography.

A second and significant difference between the two books involves the topics that are the focus of each chapter. While most of Convey's original chapters are revisited and updated, several new chapters did not appear in the original Convey work. This is not because Convey declined or neglected to review such research. It is because research on these topics as they related to Catholic schools did not exist during the period 1965–1990. These new topics and chapters include faith leadership, Catholic identity, gifted education, learning styles, technology, school choice and vouchers, finance and development, and serving students with special needs in Catholic schools.

Of major concern to the NCEA and to the editors was the chapter on serving students with special needs in Catholic schools. The authors of that chapter, H. Roberta Weaver and Mary F. Landers, both of the University of Dayton, are nationally recognized leaders in inclusive education and have worked with dozens of Catholic schools and dioceses across the United States to help design and support inclusive Catholic schools. In their treatment of the history of serving students with special needs in Catholic schools, the authors were critical of the NCEA for its slowness to provide leadership in this area. Even before publication, the editors worked extensively with the authors and the publisher to reach a precise agreement about language, meaning, and implications in what would become Chapter 9 of the book. After repeated discussions and communications, all parties agreed to certain revisions in the text. However, when the book was finally printed, the NCEA had made a number of changes to the written agreement, editing the original work of the authors without permission and circumventing the work of the editors and its own liaison. As published, the chapter does not accurately reflect the work of the authors. Furthermore, all of the unapproved changes come at points in the text where the authors were criticizing the NCEA, and the published version contains no criticism whatsoever of the NCEA. Both the authors and the editors strongly objected, but the book went to press without the required approval for the changes delineated above.

Authors and topics found in the book include Ellis Joseph (faith leadership); Ronald Nuzzi (Catholic identity); Richard Jacobs (environment); Maria Ciriello, Elizabeth Meegan, and James Carroll (outcomes); Timothy Cook (teachers); James Frabutt (parents); Richard McGrath (students); Leslie Rebhorn (gifted); H. Roberta Weaver and Mary F. Landers (special needs); Dorothy Miles, Linda Bufkin, and Ann Rule (learning styles); Jeanne Hagelskamp (technology); Frank Savage (demographics); Patricia Kelleher (governance); William Davis (school choice and vouchers); and Theodore Wallace (finance and development). *See also*: *Catholic Schools Make a Difference: Twenty-five Years of Research.*

Further Reading: James Coleman, Thomas Hoffer, and Sally Kilgore, *High School Achievement: Public, Catholic, and Private Schools Compared* (New York: Basic Books, 1982); John J. Convey, *Catholic Schools Make a Difference* (Washington, DC: NCEA, 1992); Thomas C. Hunt, Ellis A. Joseph, and Ronald J. Nuzzi, eds., *Catholic Schools Still Make a Difference: Ten Years of Reearch, 1991–2000* (Washington, DC: NCEA, 2002); Mary F. Landers and H. Roberta Weaver, *NICE* (Network for Inclusive Catholic Education) *Newsletter* (Dayton, OH: University of Dayton, Fall 2002); Ronald J. Nuzzi, *NICE* (Network for Inclusive Catholic Education) *Newsletter* (Dayton, OH: University of Dayton, Fall 2002).

Ronald J. Nuzzi

Catholic Teacher, The

A papal allocution given by Pope Pius XII to the Italian Catholic Elementary School Teachers' Association on November 4, 1955. A papal allocution is a formal address delivered by the Pope on an important subject or to mark the anniversary or inauguration of a special event. In this case, Pius XII was marking the tenth anniversary of the teachers' association.

The occasion was noteworthy because for the first time, all of the dioceses and provinces in Italy had been organized to work together for the good of Catholic education. At the time, there were over 1,300 sections of the organization, representing about 80 percent of Italy's teachers.

Pius XII delivered his remarks as a response to three questions that he felt were at the heart of being a Catholic teacher: (1) what should a teacher be? (2) what should a teacher know? and (3) what should a teacher want? His responses are instructive for teachers even today.

What should a teacher be? "Teacher" is the highest title that can be given to an instructor. In fact, the Pope distinguishes between the instructor as the mere imparter of knowledge and the teacher who is a person who knows how to create a close relationship between his own soul and the soul of a child. He claims that elementary teachers deserve the complete respect of their country because it is at this level of education that crucial, lifelong formation occurs, providing the foundation for all future intellectual and spiritual development. True teachers, therefore, must be "complete persons and Christians. That is, they must be imitators of the only Divine Master, Jesus Christ" (*Papal Teaching: Education* [*PTE*], p. 514). The Pope lamented the lack of attention to Christian principles in many Italian schools and spoke of his deep grief that "in a seemingly harmless way under specious pretexts, Jesus is in reality ignored or, worse still, where pupils are taught to fight Him and to exclude Him wherever He is found" (*PTE*, p. 514). In a clear statement of the importance of the role of teacher as witness, Pius XII told the teachers that it is not enough that they have declared themselves Catholic; living up to one's faith is required of teachers. It is insufficient, claimed the Pope, to expound the truths of the faith and point out the way to be followed; children must see their teachers practice their faith. In a quaint rhetorical flourish, the Pope indicated that teachers must be role models for their students so that students will desire to be like them. This will, in turn, have the effect on the teachers of making them like little children: "To enter the kingdom of heaven, become as these children—efficiamini sicut parvuli: pure, simple, humble, and generous" (*PTE*, p. 515).

What should a teacher know? Pius XII cautions teachers not to think that their service can be mediocre simply because their charges are young of mind. On the contrary, he urges diligence and care in the teaching of children because they are so open and capable of learning. He encourages patient listening, active learning, and respect for the childlike thirst to learn. He warns teachers to avoid monotony, excessive lengthiness, and too many explanations and encourages them to neglect nothing that can aid the imagination.

What should a teacher want? Teachers should want their students to acquire all the knowledge that is absolutely indispensable to life. They should be particularly careful that their religious education is clear and consistent. The teaching of religion must be lively, "not only in the sense of interesting, but also in the sense that religion is life" (*PTE*, p. 517). Teachers must mold their students and urge them to exercise the human virtues of loyalty, courage, devotion to duty, family, and country. Above all, teachers must do all in their power to make every person a good Christian. "Jesus wants saints among the children of today" (*PTE*, p. 519), so it is vital that students look upon Christ both as a model of every virtue and as a friend.

The Pope sees Catholic school teachers as carrying out an important mission of salvation, of evangelizing youth, and of contributing to the overall good of society. This mission is, by divine plan, an essential part of the activity of the Church and "in happy accord with the right interests of families" (*PTE*, p. 521). Thus, like teaching in a Catholic school, many of "the measures taken by the Church in the various fields of public life prove themselves in time to be right, that is to say, in accordance with God's wishes" (*PTE*, p. 521). *See also*: Gospel values; Pius XII, Pope; Teaching as ministry.

Further Reading: Pius XII, The Catholic Teacher, *L'Osservatore Romano* (November 5, 1955) 743–759 (Rome: Vatican Press); Benedictine Monks of Solesmes, eds., *Papal Teaching: Education* (Boston: Daughters of St. Paul, 1960).

Ronald J. Nuzzi

Certification (licensure) of teachers

"Certification" is a word frequently used as the process for acquiring a teaching license or teaching certificate. Acquiring a teacher license is a complex and often over-whelming task for the newly graduated teacher and the veteran alike. Because the responsibility for education was deemed a state function when the Constitution was written, each state determines not only the curriculum for schools in that state but also the qualifications of the teachers who will be licensed to teach within its boundaries. Likewise, each state accredits the schools and departments of education located within that state that prepare teachers for that state's schools. As a result, a teacher may graduate from a teacher education program in Ohio; apply for and receive an Ohio license, since the teacher education program was accredited by the state of Ohio; and yet need to take additional course work to obtain a license in Minnesota.

Generally, states license teachers using one of two methods: they have listed credits and courses that are required for a specific license, or they have performance standards that a candidate must meet in order to receive a license in a particular subject. The agency within a state, which is responsible for the licensing of teachers, is usually a state teachers' professional standards board or a division within a state department of education.

The process for obtaining a license is as follows. A candidate completes an approved teacher education program within that state and requests from the state's professional standards board or state department of education an application for a license. The majority of states, forty-seven at last count, also require a satisfactory score on some form of competency test. Most states test the subject matter competency, like math or biology. Many also require a test of basic competency in reading, writing, and math. Many also require tests of basic pedagogical skills. Candidates need to contact the teacher licensing board or department in a particular state to determine which tests need to be completed. Many states (thirty-six) use praxis tests developed by Educational Testing Service (ETS). However, if states use the exact same test, they may have different cutoff scores. To add further confusion, ETS also has several different tests in some content areas, like math, so a candidate may take a Praxis II math test for one state and find out that another state requires a different Praxis II math test.

When candidates register for a test, they must "code" their teacher education program to receive their test scores as well as "code" the state or states where scores should be sent. These scores are then checked when the candidate applies for a license. Most states have a section of the application that must be completed by the licensing adviser at the university where the candidate received his or her education. Generally, states also require some kind of criminal background check before the license can be issued, and again this must be initiated by the candidate. Once all paperwork is in to the state agency, it usually takes two to six weeks to obtain a license.

For candidates who complete their preparation at a university outside the state where they wish to teach, the process can be a bit more daunting. However, state directors of teacher certification have begun working together so that licenses received in one state have reciprocity with other states. The National Association of State Directors of Teacher Education and Certification (NASDTEC) is the organization that represents professional standards boards and commissions and state departments of education in all fifty states, the District of Columbia, the Department of Defense Education Activity, the U.S. territories, Alberta, British Columbia, and Ontario that are responsible for the preparation, licensure, and discipline of educational personnel. NASDTEC promotes high standards for educators, teacher mobility across state lines, comprehensive personnel screening, and a clearinghouse on teacher discipline.

NASDTEC publishes a comprehensive manual on certification requirements and practices in the United States and Canada. NASDTEC has also developed an Interstate Contract agreement. The Interstate Contract facilitates the movement of educators among the states and other jurisdictions that are members of NASDTEC and have signed the contract. Although there may be conditions applicable to individual states, such as their own testing requirements, the contract makes it possible for an educator who has completed an approved program and/or who holds a certificate or license in one state to earn a certificate or license in another state. Receiving states may impose certain special requirements that must be met in a reasonable period of time. For example, a state may require a history teacher to have course-work in that state's history. As of January 2002, forty-eight states or jurisdictions had signed the Interstate Contract for teaching licenses, thirty-one for administrator licenses, twenty-nine for support personnel, and nineteen for vocational teachers.

Licenses in states may vary in the length of time for validity. More and more states are moving to a provisional or probationary license, usually valid for one or two years, during which time the new teacher must demonstrate competence. Even "regular" or "standard" licenses must be renewed every five or ten years. Generally, additional course work or professional experiences are required for renewal of the license. Again, the state agency responsible for licensing will have that information.

Due to teacher shortages, many states now have alternative routes to teacher licensing. These vary greatly and generally are advantageous for those who hold content area degrees (e.g., math) but did not take undergraduate education courses. It must be noted, however, that alternative licenses are most often valid only in the state from which they are issued. *See also*: Teacher preparation; Teacher qualifications.

Further Reading: Willis D. Hawley, *The Alternative Certification of Teachers* (Washington, DC: ERIC Clearinghouse, 1992); National Association of State Directors of Teacher Education, http://NASDTEC.org; National Association of State Directors of Teacher Education, *The NASDTEC Manual*, 2002 (Dubuque, IA: Kendall/Hunt, 2002).

Joyce V. Johnstone

Character education

According to many public sector definitions, the task of character education is to lead students to a knowledge of, and commitment to, applying ethical and other values that communities regard as worthy and essential. Among these values are self-discipline and self-control, a sense of right and wrong, honesty, fairness, respect for others, courtesy, industry, frugality, chastity, moderation, temperance, accepting responsibility for one's actions, love of country, and community service.

Character education was an essential part of the school experience in America from the very beginning. The Bible was the primary resource for providing moral guidance and teaching. Lessons in popular schoolbook texts, such as the McGuffey Readers, had moral and patriotic themes woven within their lessons. An erosion of commitment to moral and character education seems to have begun in the 1900s. As is true of many trends, there was minimal awareness of this until the symptoms of the decline of personal, moral, civil, and social responsibility could no longer be ignored. There is evidence that even during the decline some educators in the public sector continued to prepare textbooks with character education content. One example of such a text is *Personality and School: Accent on Youth* by Walton B. Bliss. While the content of this text primarily discussed being a successful student, it also explicitly dealt with such topics as personality, manners, and conduct in and out of school, personal morals, and even a discussion of the value of religion in one's life.

Thomas Lickona (1991) has explicated the trends that contributed to the abandonment of the teaching of values in public schools beginning in the mid-1950s. First, there was the influence of "evolution" that resulted in a sense of moral flux. Then, Einstein's theory of relativity regarding physical matter was wrongly applied to moral issues that came to be regarded as relative to one's point of view. Third, a "personalism" with an emphasis on rights and freedom over responsibility and commitment emerged in the 1960s. By the mid-1960s, personalism under the rubric of "values clarification" was initiated to assist students in clarifying their own values. Classroom deliberations about "moral dilemmas" and "rational decision-making" were initiated in the 1970s with the intent of cultivating thinking skills, not genuine morality. Bennett, Finn, and Cribb observe that "moral relativism had displaced traditional virtue in America's schools. In 1985, for example, the *New York Times* ran an article quoting educators explaining that they deliberately avoid trying to tell students what is ethically right and wrong" (p. 524). The cumulative impact of neglecting to teach values has also become an issue at colleges and universities. In 1997, Diane Halpern, president of the Society for the Teaching of Psychology, advised the members that her theme for 1997–1998 is: "What works in helping students become (more) honest?"

The trend of the interest in "values clarification" and "moral dilemmas" can be validated via a query of the U.S. Department of Education's Educational Resources Information Center (ERIC) database, which cites no articles on "values clarification" prior to 1971, 108 from 1971 to 1980, 258 from 1981 to 1990, and 139 during 1991 to 2002. The ERIC database cites 21 articles related to "moral dilemmas" published between 1978 and 1980 and 124 from 1981 to 2002. Sixty-three, or 51 percent, of these were cited in the ERIC database during the period 1991 to 2002.

During the 1980s an interest in character education reemerged as an aspect of the public sector's educational reform movement under a variety of labels such as "citizenship," "core life skills," "social and moral development," and "character and citizenship education." To establish the legitimacy and veracity of character education in the public sector schools, school boards and state departments of education had to give their approbation and support. In some states character education was explicitly identified as a professional development requirement for the renewal of one's state certification to teach. The recency of interest in the notion of "character education" is easily demonstrated by the fact that no journal articles on the topic are cited in the

ERIC database prior to 1981. Interestingly, of the 360 journal articles on "character education" cited for the period from 1981 to 2002, 311, or 86 percent, of these were included in the database between 1991 and 2002. Other developments in support of character education were the initiation in 1995 of the Partnerships in Character Education Pilot Projects, and in 1999 the U.S. Department of Education distributed $2.3 million in grants for character education to local school districts in nine states.

The elements of what educators in the public sector have identified as character education have always been an integral aspect of the curriculum and climate of Catholic schools. Catholic school personnel recognize that non-academic complementary things such as student government, athletics, modeling of the adult community, and the practice of respect do more to foster moral maturity, or the lack of it, than didactic teaching. In 1972, the United States Catholic Conference made the observation in *To Teach as Jesus Did* that "the commitment of Catholic schools to Christian values and the Christian moral code renders a profound service to society which depends on spiritual values and good moral conduct for its very survival" (paragraph 111). Character education, along with challenging academics, was an assumed benefit of a Catholic education.

Guerra, Donahue, and Benson (1990) conducted a retrospective study of character education outcomes such as social and educational values, concern for people, at-risk behaviors, self-perceptions, and religiousness. The subjects were Catholic students in their senior year in Catholic and public high schools who were among the participants in a survey of high school seniors by the *Monitoring the Future* project during the years 1976 to 1985. Some notable differences between these groups were: (1) Under social and educational values, Catholic high school seniors were higher in their endorsement of pro-marriage attitudes and college plans, whereas public high school seniors were more supportive of militarism and reported more cutting of school. (2) Regarding concern for people, Catholic high school seniors indicated greater community involvement, contributions of money, and concern for others than did Catholic seniors in public high schools. (3) At-risk behaviors found to be higher among Catholic high school seniors were alcohol use and binge drinking, whereas Catholic seniors attending public high schools reported greater cigarette, cocaine, and illicit drug use. (4) Perceptions of self were more pessimistic among Catholic seniors at public high schools. (5) Regarding religiousness, Catholic seniors at Catholic high schools reported higher church attendance, contributions, and regard for the importance of religion than did Catholic seniors at public high schools.

While there has never been a hiatus from the inclusion of objective morality, values, or character education among Catholic educators, a consensus emerged under the leadership of Sr. Catherine McNamee, CSJ, president of the National Catholic Educational Association (NCEA), that a comprehensive program of character development ought to be articulated for Catholic schools, teachers, and children. A committee of the NCEA initiated and envisioned a three-step program beginning with the preparation of a foundational statement on character development in a Catholic school context, identification of standards of character for children from preschool through the high school grades, and training in character development for Catholic educators. Patricia H. Cronin, Ph.D., at the time principal of St. Polycarp Grade School in Stanton, California, prepared the foundational statement on character development in a Catholic school.

Cronin (1999) notes: "Character is that lasting and distinctive part of the inner person that governs behavior through informed choices and good habits." She identified three goals or tasks of character development that, in a paraphrase format, are as follows: (1) nurturing goodness manifested in care and concern for self and others, (2) learning to examine one's behavior to gain an awareness of how one is treating oneself and others, and (3) gaining an understanding of why one should be good and how one can be good.

In *Character Development in the Catholic School*, Cronin (1999) presents a useful scheme that addresses the pedagogical tasks of character development at the various age and grade levels. The years of kindergarten through the third grade are the time when the foundations of character are established. During these years, children are most amenable to learning new academic material and social skills and behaviors. Cronin proposes that teachers work with the youngest children in the school on their mastery of "honesty, obedience, self-discipline, orderliness, respect, generosity, empathy and compassion" (p. 12). Success with the kindergarten and primary grade children provides basis for the tasks of character development in the fourth through the sixth grades. According to Cronin, the tasks of character development for children in the fourth to sixth grades involve the mastery of decision-making skills. The opportunities for learning about, and applying, decision-making skills in the school setting are innumerable and may include making choices about responsibilities such as behavior at school, homework, chores, handling money, what to watch on television, language, and even religious practices.

Youngsters in grades 7 through 12 work at consolidating the essentials of their character. The most significant challenge to youngsters during these years is physical maturation accompanied by the emergence of significant emotional and social issues related to sex, dating, and relationships. Concurrently, there are the tasks of deciding on a career and further education. This is also a time for youngsters to volunteer to help others in their communities, and this enables them to try out and evaluate roles. The teacher's role from grades 4 through 12 is to be vigilant in providing cues, support, and guidance during discussions of issues and topics related to character development. While the impact that Catholic schools and teachers have had on the character development of children is impressive, Guerra, Donahue, and Benson (1990) feel it is important to recall that Catholic schools are "part of a larger setting in which strength is drawn from a common moral language, a common history, and a shared vision of the human journey" (p. 39). *See also*: Cognitive moral development; Moral education, history of; Values clarification.

Further Reading: William J. Bennett, Chester E. Finn, Jr., and John T. E. Cribb, Jr., *The Educated Child: A Parent's Guide from Preschool through Eighth Grade* (New York: Free Press, 1999); Walton B. Bliss, *Personality and School: Accent on Youth* (Boston: Allyn and Bacon, 1951); Patricia H. Cronin, ed., *Character Development in the Catholic School* (Washington, DC: National Catholic Educational Association, 1999); Michael J. Guerra, Michael J. Donahue, and Peter L. Benson, *The Heart of the Matter: Effects of Catholic High Schools on Student Values, Beliefs and Behaviors* (Washington, DC: National Catholic Educational Association, 1990); Diane Halpern, "President's Message: The Great Society," *Newsletter of the Society for the Teaching of Psychology* (Fall 1997); Thomas Lickona, *Educating for Character: How Our Schools Can Teach Respect and Responsibility* (New York: Bantam Books, 1991); National Conference of Catholic Bishops, *To Teach as Jesus Did: A Pastoral Message on Catholic Education* (Washington, DC: United States Catholic Conference, 1972); Nan Robinson, "Character Education in Public Schools: Memories, Theories, and Hope," *Momentum* 30, 3 (August/September 1999): 28–31.

Robert B. Williams

Charism

Charism is a Greek word that is translated as a "free gift given to someone by God." The word charism is used frequently in the Epistles of Saint Paul to describe the various gifts alive in the early Christian communities. Paul made it clear that all these gifts were from God and were to be used for the good of the community. Throughout the history of the Church, a charism has been defined as the special spiritual gifts or insights given by God to individual members of the community for the good of the whole community.

The history of the founding of religious congregations is the history of charisms lived out in time and space in response to the needs of the community. Throughout the history of the Church some extraordinary men and women have felt a call to live out some specific aspect of the life, message, and ministry of Jesus. Their charismatic personalities and the quality of their lives and works attracted others to join them. As these groups became larger and larger, it became necessary to describe and define each group in terms of its mission, its spirit, its spirituality, and the process whereby one became a member. This was the usual process by which a charism became institutionalized as a religious congregation or order.

One of the first religious orders to be founded was the Benedictines. The rule of this order, which guides the lives of these monks and nuns, was developed in the sixth century by St. Benedict of Nursia in Italy. Central to this rule is an ordered or balanced life lived in community. The motto of the Benedictines is "Ora et Labora" (prayer and work), which highlights the balance in the lives of Benedictines between their ministry and their prayer life. Another essential aspect of the lives of Benedictines is community life. In addition to the three vows of poverty, chastity, and obedience, the monks take a fourth vow of stability, which means the religious promise to remain members of a specific monastery for life.

In the thirteenth century two mendicant religious orders were founded that would have a profound effect on the Church into the twenty-first century. These were the Franciscans and the Dominicans. The Franciscans were founded by Francis of Assisi, who had a profound religious experience that led him to forsake a life of wealth for a life of voluntary poverty. Francis took very seriously the message of Jesus in the Gospel and lived a simple life of begging, caring for lepers and the poor, and preaching the love of God. By the time of his death, thousands of men and women had been drawn to follow his example. St. Dominic Guzman inaugurated a program of preaching against the heresies of his time. The men who followed him were sent out to preach not only in churches but wherever they could gather a group of listeners. The motto of these Dominicans (who are also called the Order of Preachers) is "Veritas," which is the Latin word for truth. Through study and preaching these men sought to teach the truths of the Catholic Church throughout Europe and beyond. Both St. Francis and St. Dominic established orders of women who were cloistered and whose lives were dedicated to praying in support of the friars. The establishment of Third Order sisters, who lived the spirit of the order in doing good works while living outside the monasteries, quickly followed.

The Jesuits were founded by St. Ignatius of Loyola in the sixteenth century. The

Jesuits were tied to no specific work, but the members were to do all "for the greater glory of God" in seeking to ensure the salvation of souls. Central to the Jesuit spirituality and ministry were the "Spiritual Exercises" written by Ignatius. The Jesuits were a kind of "shock troops" placed at the disposal of the Pope and were to respond to whatever needs to which he wanted them to attend. In fact, the Jesuits' two major apostolates for which they were best known were education and missionary work.

The Ursulines, also founded in the sixteenth century, were the first religious congregation founded specifically for the education of women. Established by St. Angela Merici in Italy, they lived in their own homes and wore no religious habit. While they originally took no vows, they lived in the spirit of the vows. They consistently escaped attempts by church authorities to place them in the cloister until 1612, when the Ursulines of the Congregation of Paris finally accepted to live in the cloister and to take solemn vows on condition that they be permitted to take a fourth vow to educate young girls. The driving vision of Angela Merici was her belief that the faith is passed on most effectively in the home. Therefore, the education of young girls in the faith would ensure that future homes would be filled with faith and religious practice.

In France, Sts. Francis deSales and Jane Frances de Chantal founded the Visitation Order of Nuns, who would, while remaining contemplative, but not cloistered, visit the sick and the poor for several hours each week. Central to their Salesian spirituality was devotion to the Sacred Heart, which for them was the concrete image of the love that God had for His people. Modeled after God's love, these religious were to make present that love in their own acts of charity and care. Eventually, they were cloistered by the Church, and their only active ministry would be the education of girls within their convents. Also in France at about the same time, Sts. Vincent de Paul and Louise de Marillac founded the Company of the Daughters of Charity as a secular institute in order to avoid the cloister and to remain active in their ministries of social service in the care of the poor and the infirmed. Vincent de Paul's love for the poor became the foundational spirituality of the Daughters of Charity.

In the eighteenth and nineteenth centuries an explosion in the foundation of religious communities sought to address many of the needs of the people at this time. Many were dedicated to the education of children; some focused their lives on the care of the sick; others took care of orphans or the aged or engaged in other forms of social service. Some were established to attend to the needs of a particular ethnic group. Some began in Europe and were invited to the United States to help in this growing missionary country, and many were actually founded in the United States. The history of each of these religious communities is the story of charismatic leaders who saw needs and responded to them with the particular gifts with which they were blessed.

The needs of the ethnic Catholic minority in a country that was openly anti-Catholic were many. Orphanages were needed to ensure that Catholic orphans would be raised in the faith. Since many of the "public" schools were actually anti-Catholic, bishops desperately needed religious to found and staff Catholic schools to preserve and pass on the faith. The needs of the Church came before charism even to the extent that the first bishop of the United States, Archbishop John Carroll, tried repeatedly to convince the Carmelites to leave their cloister and open a school in Baltimore.

As young men and young women entered a religious congregation, they would undergo a process of formation usually involving a two- or three-year period of postulancy and novitiate. During that time, the young person would be introduced to the history, spirit, spirituality, and works of the congregation. This would begin a lifelong process by which the religious would take on the identity of the congregation and do its work. The works of the congregation, whether in education, health care, or social service, were to be influenced and impacted by the spirit of that congregation.

In the United States, as the Catholic population grew in the nineteenth and twentieth centuries, the needs of the Church demanded more and more religious, and many men and women responded to the call to religious life in service of the Church. Along with the development of the spiritual lives of the individual religious, the religious congregations focused on their works. Little reflection was done on the charism of the congregation. This was to radically change in the middle of the twentieth century with the convening of the Second Vatican Council.

While addressing the renewal of religious life, the council required that all religious congregations enter into a period of reflection and renewal. To do this, the council suggested that the religious get in touch once more with the charism of their founders and seek to renew their life and ministries in light of the charism and the exigencies of the modern world. Thus began a process of self-study, a re-examination of the writings of the founder in an attempt to understand the world in which the founder lived, and the nature of the founder's response to the needs of his or her own time. This was coupled with an examination of the present needs of the world and the Church. The study of these two realities often concluded with the question: "What would the founder do today?" In doing so, many religious congregations began to question their current lifestyles and ministries. Dress, customs, regimen of prayer, community life, and ministries and apostolates were changed, sometimes radically. In this process thousands of sisters, brothers, and priests sought dispensation from their vows. Many more chose to leave the "traditional" ministries of their community to address other needs they saw in the Church and in the world that they believed were more in conformity with the "spirit" or charism of the founder.

In the 1980s and 1990s, as the number of religious in the schools, academies, and colleges of the religious communities began to decline, they began to reflect on how the charism of the community would be carried forward into the future in these institutions with minimal or no presence of the religious sisters, brothers, or priests on the faculty or in administration. A number of steps were taken by various religious communities. Some developed programs in which the lay faculties were introduced to the charism of the community in such a way as to help them to internalize and live that charism in their own life and ministry. Another was to develop mission and vision statements for the school that incorporated the charism of the community. Since the vision and mission statements were to guide and direct the philosophy and programs of the schools, it was hoped that these mission and vision statements would help to keep the charism alive. Some religious communities developed the position of the director of mission effectiveness. This person was usually a member of the religious community and would have the responsibility of visiting the community-owned or -sponsored institutions to assist the school in preserving and passing on the charism of the community in the school.

In the last years of the twentieth century and in the first years of the twenty-first century, as the average age of the members of religious congregations grew considerably older, there was much discussion on charism and how to preserve and pass it on to the next generation. The engaging spiritualities and the great work that has been realized by the living out of the charisms of the religious communities have had a profound effect on the shape of Catholicism in the United States. How these charisms will continue to influence the development of Catholicism in this country is yet to be played out. *See also*: Religious orders of men; Religious orders of women.

Further Reading: A Collaboration by the Sisters of St. Joseph of Carondolet, St. Paul Province, *Eyes Open on a World: The Challenges of Change* (St. Cloud, MN: North Star Press of St. Cloud, 2001); Philip Hughes, *A History of the Church*, 3 vols. (New York: Sheed and Ward, 1952); Bernard L. Marthaler, OFM, ed., *New Catholic Encyclopedia*, 2nd ed. (Washington, DC: Catholic University of America Press and the Gale Group, 2002); Annabelle Raiche, CSJ and Ann Marie Biermaier, OSB, *They Came to Teach: The Story of Sisters Who Taught in Parochial Schools and Their Contribution to Elementary Education in Minnesota* (St. Cloud, MN: North Star Press of St. Cloud, 1994); George C. Stewart, Jr., *Marvels of Charity: History of American Sisters and Nuns* (Huntington, IN: Our Sunday Visitor Publishing Division, 1994).

Patrick J. Riley

Charter schools

Charter schools are independent public schools of choice that are freed from most of the bureaucratic and regulatory mandates that impact other public schools. The charters creating these schools provide for a clear, focused mission, a smaller student population that facilitates creation of community, more innovative teaching practices, greater parental and local community involvement, defined educational and fiscal standards, and accountability measures. Functionally, they are a hybrid with characteristics of both public and private education.

The federal government has taken an active role in support of parental choice in public schools through legislation and federal funds to spur charter school development. However, states must enact the charter school legislation that determines if and how charters will be granted. There are substantial differences among the states in the governance, oversight, and fiscal structures established in their charter laws. The state may retain a role in approving charters, as an approving agency or in an appellate position, or may delegate it to the local school board to grant or approve particular charters. Parents, teachers, universities, community organizations, and others may apply for a charter and, if granted, open a school.

The charter is a legal contract binding the school operators to achieve the accountability measures described in the charter in order to retain their existence and public funding. The creation of charter schools stems from the general education reform movement of the late twentieth century in the United States. A National Commission on Excellence in Education was created by President Ronald Reagan, and a national summit of state governors endorsed six educational goals targeted to improving the performance of America's schools through higher standards and greater accountability for results. Their recommendations included the idea of freeing schools from bureaucratic control at the state and district levels and investing greater authority in local control and decision-making with attendant mandates for accountability for results. Inherent in this concept was an intentional paradigm shift that was postulated to reinvent American education by challenging old assumptions about the nature of the purpose of schooling that seemed to be no longer producing effective results. One of the first proponents of charter schools was Albert Shanker, the late president of the American Federation of Teachers, who initially favored the introduction of charters as a means of improving the quality of the public schools.

Charter schools are public entities that represent a variety of different philosophical and political concepts involving new governance models, innovation, competition, and choice. A high degree of independence is given to the professionals at the school level in determining key issues such as curriculum, hiring, and fiscal responsibilities. Charter schools can be created in two ways: as start-up enterprises (new school is created) or by means of conversions of existing public schools. Generally, state law prohibits a religious school from converting to a charter school. Once the structure is approved, the school is entitled to all or some of the public funds that would have been allocated to the school district for the enrolled students. However, in most charter school authorization, funding is not provided for the acquisition and capital expenses incurred with renovating older buildings to serve the needs of the charter school. The charter school is obliged to observe state and federal regulations pertaining to health, safety, and civil rights issues, but not most of the districtwide bureaucratic and administrative regulations. In exchange for the stipulated autonomy pertaining to the operational standards and financial, organizational, and academic parameters, the school agrees to specified accountability measures that must be met in order to avoid rescinding of the charter.

Ideally, the localization of the governance role within the charter school was to promote parental choice and involvement and school improvement through competition and accountability when parents could exercise an exit option and seek better alternatives at public expense. The politics of creating and maintaining charter schools are complex. Politically, legislators are pressured by special interest groups that oppose as well as favor legislation creating them. Local school boards have a vested interest in retaining power over the funds that traditional public school student enrollment generates for the schools under their control. Since charter schools have autonomy in hiring personnel, teacher unions fear loss of members and control of contractual agreements reached outside their purview, resulting in the unions lobbying for greater control over personnel and work conditions as part of state authorizing legislation for charter schools. Since charter schools are a largely urban phenomenon created to offer parents relief from dismal academic outcomes, most tend to have a largely minority enrollment, promoting concerns about charter schools increasing racial and economic stratification that are not easily remedied due to the societal compositions of the neighborhood where schools are located or from which they draw their students.

Catholic and other religious schools are usually precluded by law and/or their own religious mission from converting to a charter school status that would render them public schools subject to First Amendment scrutiny. Because charters are public schools, they may not charge students tuition and fees. Consequently, in many urban areas religious schools are being negatively impacted by transfers, particularly among non-Catholic students, to charter schools where parents can obtain some of the same benefits, sans religion, without the burden of tuition.

At the start of the 2002 school year, thirty-nine states and the District of Columbia had enacted legislation allowing charter schools to exist. Almost 3,000 schools were in operation, serving more than half a million students. The Center for Education Reform, a Washington, D.C.-based charter school advocacy organization, has tracked developments in the charter school movement and reports that about 2.6 percent of the existing charter schools had their charters revoked for a variety of reasons: fiscal mis-management, improper authorization, low enrollments, or lack of community support. *See also*: Choice, parent and school; Parental rights.

Further Reading: Chester Finn, Jr., Bruno Manno, and Gregg Vanourek, *Charter Schools* *in Action* (Princeton, NJ: Princeton University Press, 2000); Paul Peterson and David E. Campbell, eds., *Charters, Vouchers and Public Education* (Washington, DC: Brookings Institution Press, 2001); Joseph Viteritti, *Choosing Equality: School Choice, the Constitution and Civil Society* (Washington, DC: Brookings Institution Press, 2001).

Dale McDonald, PBVM

Chief Administrators of Catholic Education (CACE)

The Department of Chief Administrators of Catholic Education (CACE) of the National Catholic Educational Association provides programs and services to any person who exercises major administrative responsibilities for Catholic education and catechetical ministry. CACE members serve at the diocesan, interdiocesan (e.g., State Catholic Conference), religious order provincial, or interprovincial level.

According to the Mission Statement of the Chief Administrators of Catholic Education, the scope of Catholic education includes Catholic schools, parish religious education programs, and other programs designed to foster lifelong growth in faith and the realization of God-given human potential. CACE professes the uniqueness and interdependence of the various and diverse efforts that constitute the ministry of Catholic education and catechetical ministry from diocese to diocese.

The Department of Chief Administrators of Catholic Education exists to:

- Exert leadership on, and in behalf of, Catholic education
- Influence the development of leadership
- Be a strong advocate for Catholic education at the national level
- Offer resources and services to members in order that they will be supported in their ministry, mobilized for local and national action, networked with one another, and linked with government and church agencies as well as civic and business communities when appropriate.

Based on a constituent member's job description, an administrator may elect to join one of three divisions: Total Catholic Education, Catholic Schools, or Religious Education. Associate membership is offered to those who hold positions in central diocesan offices and those who hold positions in the education departments of colleges and universities. Honorary membership is conferred upon past presidents of CACE and past executive directors of CACE.

An advisory committee consisting of members elected from a defined region guides each CACE division. The Executive Committee is selected from representatives of the three advisory committees. The CACE Executive Committee coordinates the strategic actions of each division, while championing the vision of total Catholic education.

CACE also sponsors the CACE Research Center, which assists in the funding of research in all aspects of Catholic education.

Each fall, CACE conducts a five-day conference to provide spiritual, professional, and social opportunities for its members. In the spring, *CACE Conversations* is scheduled as part of the NCEA Convention. This is an opportunity for the members to hear a major presentation and participate in discussions on a topic of critical importance to Catholic education and catechetical leaders. In collaboration with other NCEA departments, strategic planning, financial management, and other professional services are provided for dioceses, parishes, schools, and religious congregations. Through the efforts of CACE, Catholic education, catechetical ministry, and the mission of the National Catholic Educational Association are furthered. *See also*: National Catholic Educational Association (NCEA).

Further Reading: John J. Augenstein, *Lighting the Way, 1907 to 1935, the Early Years of Catholic School Superintendency* (Washington, DC: National Catholic Educational Association, 1996); John J. Augenstein, Christopher J. Kauffman, and Robert J. Wister, *Leadership, Charism, Ethos, and Ethnicity* (Washington, DC: National Catholic Educational Association, 2002).

Daniel F. Curtin

Child benefit theory

Decisions of the U.S. Supreme Court involving efforts to secure some form of public assistance for private schools gave rise to the conceptual framework of the child benefit theory that is predicated upon judicial distinctions between direct and indirect school aid.

The constitutionality of taxpayer assistance to students in private and religious schools was first brought before the Court in the 1930 *Cochran v. Louisiana State Board of Education* case concerning the provision of nonsectarian textbooks to students in religious schools. The Court ruled affirmatively, noting that the intent of the statute was to benefit the schoolchildren rather than the schools, even though the religious schools were spared the expense of providing textbooks for the students. This ruling helped to energize advocates of taxpayer aid to private schools to pursue legislative efforts to secure a portion of tax dollars for students in private and religious schools.

In subsequent years, several other cases decided by the Supreme Court expanded the scope of constitutionally permissible aid to children as long as it is provided in a manner judged not to directly benefit institutions. The busing of private school children at public expense was the subject of a 1947 U.S. Supreme Court decision in *Everson v. Board of Education* that became a landmark case in Church–state relations and established precedents for interpreting the First Amendment and the scope of religious liberty in relation to school aid. In reaching that decision, the justices drew the analogy between the state providing police and fire protection with its funding transportation for parochial school children. The justices were persuaded that the legislation did nothing more than provide a general program to help parents get their children, regardless of their religion, safely to and from parochial schools that met New Jersey's requirements to provide secular education. This opened possibilities for the further extension of similar types of aid under the rubric of promoting the general welfare of children.

The extent to which the child benefit theory could be extended was tested in several cases in which the opinions produced a legal ambiguity that made it impossible to predict judicial outcomes in court decisions. The Court upheld programs that provided aid for the administration of state-prepared tests, speech and hearing services, and tax benefits to reimburse parents for tuition and other educational expenses yet denied salary assistance for teachers of secular subjects, provisions of instructional materials other than books, and the financing of student field trips.

Following World War II, the child benefit theory also appeared in federal legislation as the government began to link education policy with other national interests, including general welfare issues. At the national level, the government adopted a policy orientation that led to a federal role in education through programs of direct aid to the states. As early as the 1940s, attempts were made to enact federal legislation to provide general assistance to elementary and secondary schools. Such general aid was to be distributed to the states to be used for the construction of new schools and teacher salaries.

These attempts failed because of the lack of agreement on several issues: ideological differences pertaining to state and local autonomy, civil rights, and the inclusion of private and religious schools in the programs. Traditionally, the American Catholic bishops had vigorously opposed the concept of any federal aid to education but by the 1950s realized that it was inevitable and decided to cooperate and become involved in the formulation of such legislation.

Early in his administration, President John F. Kennedy proposed a program of general education aid for the states. He specifically excluded nonpublic schools from participation, declaring that it would be unconstitutional to provide any sectarian school with public money. The Catholic Church fought the exclusion and, through a series of negotiations with the commissioner of education, the highest national education officer who served in the Department of Health, Welfare, and Education, produced a compromise with President Johnson, who succeeded Kennedy.

Johnson changed the construct, shifting from a program of general aid to one of categorical assistance. Using the rationale of the *Everson* child benefit theory, this approach focused on specifically delineated programs with defined objectives and was targeted to specific populations of disadvantaged students in both public and private schools.

The Elementary and Secondary Education Act (ESEA) of 1965 was the first step in the passage of federal aid legislation directed to elementary and secondary school education. As a significant component of President Johnson's national priority of declaring a War on Poverty, the legislation authorized categorical programs to benefit educationally needy elementary and secondary students living in areas with high concentrations of children from low-income families.

The struggle to overcome the concerns about religion and First Amendment issues that would allow for the inclusion of nonpublic school children in the legislation was resolved through a compromise that established two principles for providing services to students in public, private, and religious schools. These principles, child benefit and public trusteeship, remain the operational framework for participation of private and religious school students in federal programs.

The child benefit concept views the provision of categorical assistance or services as serving needy students based on a poverty formula. That any of the benefits might be construed as accruing to the school they attend would be only incidental and not vitiate the primary purpose of the aid. To circumvent the constitutional hurdles of public moneys reaching the religious school directly, the aid is distributed through public trustees or public authorities who receive and manage the ESEA funds and act as accountable trustees on behalf of all the eligible children in their community, regardless of the type of school they attended. In turn, the public trustees provide the services, through public employees or publicly negotiated and executed contracts.

Under the child benefit theory, students and faculty members in private schools have received benefits in the form of remedial math and reading services to needy students, professional development programs for teachers, technology training and equipment, violence and drug prevention programs, counseling, and instructional, library, and media materials.

ESEA programs provide services only to students and teachers in nonpublic schools. No money is channeled to the schools so as to avoid First Amendment issues regarding separation of Church and state. Private school officials work through the local public school district to arrange for the delivery of programs and services for the students and faculty.

For almost forty years the inclusion of private and religious school students and their teachers in federal aid programs has endured, but not without controversy and legal challenges. The national teacher unions and public school interests have consistently opposed the inclusion of nonpublic schools in additional aid programs and, along with civil liberties groups and taxpayer organizations, sought to eliminate or minimize participation in all or parts of the federal programs. Some problems with implementation have occurred at the local level due to miscommunication or hostility on the part of some of the local school districts that are reluctant to share resources despite their obligation to private school students as their public trustees.

Although the U.S. Supreme Court upheld the right of taxpayers to have legal standing to sue the federal government for the passage of legislation on Establishment Clause grounds (*Flast v. Cohen*), no lawsuit has ever been brought to enjoin the participation of children in religious schools in categorical programs. Three legal challenges to the participation of private school students in some parts of ESEA have reached the U.S. Supreme Court. An attempt to exclude students in religious schools from participation in Title I services was remedied in *Aguilar v. Felton* (1985), when the Court ruled that services were permissible as long as they were delivered at a neutral site so as not to create the impression that religion was being endorsed by the presence of public school teachers on religious property. For more than a decade, millions of dollars of program moneys were spent on the acquisition and maintenance of trailers and rental of neutral sites apart from the religious school campus in which children were provided with remedial instruction. This was overturned in *Agostini v. Felton* (1997), when the Court changed its views on the Establishment Clause and allowed services to be delivered back in the religious schools in rooms that would meet the neutrality standard if they were devoid of religious symbols. In *Mitchell v. Helms* (2000) the Court ruled that the use of Title VI funds that supplies instructional materials, including computers and software, to both public and private schools did not violate the Establishment Clause. In doing so, it rejected arguments that computers might be diverted for religious purposes to further the religious mission of the schools.

While continuing the fundamental philosophy directing federal education aid to benefit children through public trusteeship, subtle shifts in program focus occurred in the 1990s. During that time, emphasis shifted away from individual student remediation to programs for improving schools, focusing on improving academic outcomes across the entire school as a means of aiding the educationally disadvantaged. This construct excludes private schools that must continue with "pull-out" programs that remove individual students from regular classes to receive remedial aid in neutral settings. *See also*: Blum, Virgil C.; Choice, parent and school; Citizens for Educational Freedom; Parental rights; Parents as primary educators; Vouchers.

Further Reading: *Agostini v. Felton*, 521 U.S. 203 (1997); *Aguilar v. Felton*, 473 U.S. 402 (1985); *Cochran v. Louisiana*, 281 U.S. 370 (1930); *Everson v. Board of Education*, 330 U.S. 1 (1947); *Flast v. Cohen* 392 U.S. 83 (1968); Dale McDonald, "Pluralism and Public Policy: Catholic Schools in the United States," in Thomas C. Hunt, Ellis A. Joseph, and Ronald J. Nuzzi, eds., *Handbook of Research on Catholic Education* (Westport, CT: Greenwood Press,

2001); *Mitchell v. Helms*, 530 U.S. 793 (2000); Timothy Walch, *Parish School: American Catholic Parochial Education from Colonial Times to the Present* (New York: Crossroad, 1996).

Dale McDonald, PBVM

Child Protection Policy

An official statement governing the conduct of adult employees of parishes, schools, and dioceses in their work with, and relationship to, children of minority age who have been placed in their care. Child Protection Policies (CPP), though already existing in a variety forms, have become mandatory for all dioceses in the United States following the sexual abuse scandals of recent years.

In 2003, the United States Conference of Catholic Bishops (USCCB) commissioned the John Jay College of Criminal Justice to study the nature and scope of the problem of sexual abuse of minors by Catholic priests and deacons in the United States. The report, distributed in February 2004, chronicled allegations of sexual abuse against a total of 4,392 priests during the period 1950–2002 (John Jay College, 2004). Moreover, a total of 10,667 individuals made allegations against priests of child sexual abuse.

The USCCB directed all dioceses in the U.S. to establish safe environment programs in an effort to prevent child abuse of any kind. The safe environment program is at the heart of the wider effort to have every diocese clearly articulate, publish, and enforce a set of policies designed to protect children from harm. The general norms established by the USCCB (2002) include a written code of conduct signed by employees and volunteers, mandatory background checks utilizing the resources of law enforcement and other community agencies, and the training of parents, ministers, educators, church personnel, occasional volunteers, and any others regularly involved with minors, so that they are aware of the child protection policies and the standards of conduct necessary in ministering to children.

A controversial element of the national charter included the provision that diocesan policies will provide that for even a single act of sexual abuse of a minor—past, present, or future—the offending priest or deacon will be permanently removed from ministry, not excluding dismissal from the clerical state, if the case so warrants (USCCB, 2002, art. 5). This is a new standard and an important one, for it no longer allows an individual bishop discretion in deciding whether to return an offending priest to active ministry. To further the reach of the policy and to safeguard against any administrative oversights, Article 14 prohibits the transfer of any priest or deacon who has committed an act of sexual abuse of a minor from one diocese or religious province to another.

The implementation of safe environment programs and child protection policies is being monitored by a special group of experts known as the National Review Board. The first director of the newly established board was Kathleen McChesney, who came to the board from a high-profile position in the Federal Bureau of Investigation (FBI). Implementing child protection policies and establishing safe environments are proving costly to dioceses and parishes, but the cost is an investment not only in protecting children but also in preventing expensive litigation often associated with abuse cases. In fact, the costs seem small in comparison to dealing with the costs—both financial and spiritual—of dealing with sexual abuse cases. For example, one medium-sized diocese reported an expense of $30,000 during the previous year for conducting criminal background checks on all employees and volunteers who work with children (Feuerherd, 2003).

Because of the increased attention to child protection and the need for policies and programs, establishing safe environments has become something of a growth industry. In 2002, an Illinois-based insurance company, the National Catholic Risk Retention Group, successfully marketed its program—known as Virtus—to over sixty dioceses. The program includes training for every level in the chain of command, consulting services for drafting policies, videos, simulations, problem-solving techniques, a self-audit instrument, and a victim advocacy program.

Catholic schools have not been immune to the problem of sexual abuse. A 2004 report (John Jay College, 2004) found that during the period 1950–2002, over 900 incidents of sexual abuse were reported to have occurred in school. Moreover, priest-teachers accounted for over 7 percent of all reported abuse cases. The current policies try to ensure that educators do not become complacent in their efforts, and they mandate such things as training, background checks, and multiple adult supervisors when dealing with minor children. Schools especially have more work to do in screening administrators, teachers, coaches, volunteers, drivers, playground help, teachers' aides, and fund-raisers, in providing proper training and adequate supervision, and in maintaining high standards of professional conduct for all who work with children.

The National Review Board began a process in 2003 of evaluating what each diocese has done to implement policies and programs aimed at child protection and safe environments. The goal of the audit is to measure diocesan compliance with the bishops' charter, and it represents the first time that any national effort has been undertaken to measure compliance and agreement on any issue.

Further Reading: Jason Berry, *Lead Us Not Into Temptation: Catholic Priests and the Sexual Abuse of Children* (New York: Doubleday, 1992); The Boston Globe, *Betrayal: The Crisis in the Catholic Church* (Boston: Little, Brown, 2002); Diocese of Youngstown, *Child Protection Policy* (Youngstown, OH: Author, March 1, 2003); "Dismissing All Abusive Priests Is Ineffective Strategy, Vatican Told," *America* 188, 14 (April 24, 2003): 4–5; Joe Feuerherd, "Catholic Church Takes Lead in Child Protection Industry," *National Catholic Reporter* 39, 24 (April 18, 2003): 11; John Jay College of Criminal Justice, *The Nature and Scope of the Problem of Sexual Abuse of Minors by Catholic Priests and Deacons in the United States* (Washington, DC: United States Conference of Catholic Bishops, 2004); United States Conference of Catholic Bishops, *Promise To Protect, Pledge To Heal: Charter for the Protection of Children and Young People* (Washington, DC: USCCB, 2002).

Ronald J. Nuzzi

Choice, parent and school

Historically, debates about the right of parents in determining the type of education their children would receive have centered around two concepts: compulsory government education and the financing of alternatives. The ideological content of these debates about parental rights and school choice are often polarized, volatile, and politically partisan.

The concept of parental choice in education is embodied in a range of options that allows parents to select the type of schooling they want for their children. These options can be grouped into five major categories:

1. Tax relief in the form of tax credits and tax deductions. A tax credit provides a direct reduction of an individual or corporate tax liability; a refundable credit allows for a

tax refund if the credit exceeds the liability. A tax deduction allows for a reduction of the portion of taxable income made prior to the calculation of tax liability.

2. Publicly or privately funded vouchers or scholarships. With a publicly funded voucher the government makes payment to a parent, or an institution on a parent's behalf, to be used for all or some of a child's education expenses. With a privately funded voucher, a private organization provides the funding.

3. Public school choice. Choices are restricted to public school options that include interdistrict/intradistrict enrollment across attendance area boundaries or at a magnet school that is organized around a specific program or philosophy and enrolls students across attendance areas.

4. Charter schools. These are public schools that have been established and operated by an entity apart from the local public school district with public funds and fewer state and local school board bureaucratic regulations.

5. Home schooling. This is a growing movement whereby a parent chooses to educate a child in the home using instructors and curriculum in accord with family philosophy rather than in an established public or private school. These families are from a variety of religious, economic, political, and philosophical backgrounds. There are local, state, and national home-schooling support groups that network and share information via the Internet to expand options for their children. In most states, there are no laws governing this educational option. Estimates place about two million children in this form of education in the United States.

The exercise of parental choice in selecting the type of education they want for their children has had an evolving and controversial history. In colonial America, schooling children was an established part of neighborhood society. No single model prevailed, and regional differences were evident, reflecting the founding charters for the individual colonies. Most schools were established by religious or charitable organizations and were financed through tuition charges or philanthropic trusts. In some towns, schools were quasi-public, supported by a combination of tuition charges and local taxes; others were independent establishments set up by a teacher who was supported by paying pupils. The common denominator was that parents had a great deal of control over the schools, choosing teachers, textbooks, and the curriculum.

In the nineteenth century a social movement began in which reformers sought to homogenize large masses of newly arriving immigrants into American societal values through public education. Originating in the 1830s, the common school movement purported to serve distinct social and political goals: a common body of knowledge was to be transmitted in a common schoolhouse. In the public schools, the social ideals embodied in Protestantism and the Social Gospel converged to shape a common moral and religious ideal to produce a political consensus. Public education and religious values were bound together, and to avoid contentious situations, trustees of the free schools attempted to respect the general values of all sects in a concept of nondenominational Christianity.

Initially, direct aid to religious schools was provided in Connecticut, New York, Pennsylvania, Virginia, South Carolina, Maryland, Delaware, Georgia, Tennessee, Ohio, Illinois, and Indiana. The funds were to be used to educate the poor; parents who could afford to do so were required to pay a fair share. As the society expanded, particularly in the urban areas, conflicts that were charged with religious, ethnic, and class animosities erupted over control of the schools. Religious and nonsectarian school leaders debated publicly about the nature of the schools and their funding sources. Ongoing strife and litigation resulted in reinterpretations of the First Amendment to effectively eliminate direct support for nonpublic schools.

The U.S. Supreme Court decision in *Pierce v. the Society Sisters* (1925) conferred legal standing on the exercise of parental rights in education. This decision established a dual system of schools in the United States by protecting the right of the nonpublic schools to exist and the freedom of parents to choose from among alternatives for their children. While the creation of this duality resulted in a diversity of educational opportunities and a variety of ideologies concerning the role of education in a democratic and pluralistic society, it did not address the controversy surrounding the question of whether or not there should be public financial support for the choices exercised by parents in educating their children. That unresolved issue often surfaced in public policy debates in the nation before and after *Pierce* but has been receiving more vigorous attention as part of the education reform debates of the latter part of the twentieth century.

In the past century, private schools began to reflect upon their service to the common good and examined the fiscal costs in providing such public service; they began to challenge the inequities inherent in denial of funding because of educational choices exercised by parents. Ultimately, their lobbying efforts resulted in acquisition of some benefits for students in the form of provisions for school lunches, public transportation, student textbook loans, and participation in the *Elementary and Secondary Education Act*. Other attempts to secure direct public assistance for nonpublic schools resulted in a series of Supreme Court decisions that became increasingly unfavorable in the 1970s. The Court struck down attempts to reimburse schools for secular educational services, payment of salaries for teachers of secular subjects, and tuition tax credits for private school parents.

The movement to obtain more direct aid for parents in support of their exercise of choice has several origins and philosophical and political motivations. Within the ranks of choice supporters, there are differences in ideological underpinnings: market-based proponents focus on competition to spur improvement; equity-based advocates concentrate on fair access for all, especially the poor, to a quality education; and libertarians want little or no government role in education.

In 1955, Milton Friedman, a Nobel Prize-winning economist, called for the radical reform of American education through the creation of a privatization and market-based approach that would give vouchers to all parents to freely choose the schools their children would attend. Private organizations began to build coalitions to influence state legislatures and the federal government to obtain financial assistance for nonpublic schools. Lobbying efforts began at state levels to obtain tax relief and vouchers for parents who faced the dual hardship of taxation to support public schools and tuition to finance their choice to educate children in nongovernment schools. In the early 1970s, these efforts were expanded through legislative and judicial activity and in public policy debates and political campaigns.

The development of political action on school choice issues has been rooted in the exercise of political influence and the ability to pressure lawmakers directly and through their constituents. As political contexts changed (new elections that resulted in shifts in control of legislatures and/or changed administrations), opportunities for leadership to make new policy initiatives were attempted. Evolving judicial standards also contribute to policy shifts and revisions of past laws or enactment of new laws.

Legislative activity in support of, or opposition to, school choice has centered on efforts to obtain federal and state education taxpayer relief and publicly funded vouchers. During the 1972 presidential campaign the option for inclusion of private schools in federal government funding proposals began to surface as a viable issue. In the twenty years thereafter, several tax credit initiatives were introduced into Congress with bipartisan support but ultimately failed to be enacted into law. Attempts to enact legislation that would have provided federal funds for a small demonstration pilot program of voucher aid for students in the District of Columbia were defeated. Over time, the issue became increasingly politicized and identified as a Republican cause that Democrats opposed.

Efforts to secure state tax credit legislation proved to be more successful than federal initiatives. Currently seven states—Iowa, Illinois, Louisiana, Minnesota, Arizona, Florida, and Pennsylvania—offer state tax relief to individuals and/or corporations for educational expenses incurred for children or for donations to organizations that provide education scholarships.

Five states—Ohio, Wisconsin, Florida, Maine, and Vermont—offer publicly funded vouchers to families under limited conditions. Each of these programs has been under judicial scrutiny; two have been validated by the U.S. Supreme Court, and the others are in process.

State ballot initiatives to provide vouchers have been the most unsuccessful of all efforts. Voucher initiatives were on the ballots in Michigan in 1978 and 2000, Oregon in 1990, Colorado in 1992, and California in 1993 and 2000, and all were voted down by ratios of at least two to one.

Currently, the *No Child Left Behind Act*, the latest reauthorization of the *Elementary and Secondary Education Act*, gives parents greater control over where their children attend school, allowing them to move from designated failing public schools to higher-performing public schools without incurring personal expense for tuition or transportation. Political pressure by interest groups opposed to choice prevented this program from including private and religious options.

Evolving jurisprudence in interpretations of the First Amendment concept of separation of Church and state has resulted in a shift away from a strict and narrow view of the nonestablishment of religion prohibitions in state action to a more expansive view of the free exercise provision of that same amendment. Recent U.S. Supreme Court decisions have upheld the constitutionality of programs of aid that would indirectly benefit religious schools if the intent of the law authorizing them was to accomplish a genuine secular purpose whose primary effect neither advances nor prohibits religion or fosters excessive government entanglement with religion in its implementation. School voucher programs that follow that rubric have been ruled constitutional by the Court.

Although federal constitutional law is clear, there is no guarantee that obtaining similar aid elsewhere may be possible. Thirty-seven states have constitutional provisions that exclude aid to nonpublic schools under three categories: public money can be spent only on public schools, public money cannot be spent on religious schools, and taxpayer "compelled support" of religious worship or instruction is prohibited.

Judicial interpretations of how broadly or narrowly to apply these state provisions and whether or not state constitutions can be more restrictive than the federal Constitution is the next battleground in the school choice wars. With the First Amendment issue resolved regarding parameters within which federal funds may be used to assist parents in selecting school choice, the issue has moved into the public policy arena where questions surface about whether or not it is good for the nation to finance such choice even if it is legal to do so. Today the parental choice debate is often framed in emotional rather than intellectual terms and poses policy questions that erroneously dichotomize public and private education as conflicting entities rather than as parts of a comprehensive education reform agenda. *See also*: Blum, Virgil C.; Charter Schools; Child-benefit theory; Citizens for Educational Freedom; Parental rights; Parents as primary educators; Vouchers.

Further Reading: John E. Coons and Stephen D. Sugarman, *Education by Choice: The Case for Family Control* (Berkely: University of California Press, 1978); Andrew J. Coulson, *Education: The Unknown History* (Washington, DC: Brookings Institution Press, 1999); Dale McDonald, "A Chronology of Parental Choice in Education," *Momentum* 32, 2 (April 2001): 10–15; Terry Moe, *Schools, Vouchers and the American Public* (Washington, DC: Brookings Institution Press, 2001); Joel Spring, *The American School: 1642–1990* (New York: Longmans, 1990); Joseph Viteritti, *Choosing Equality: School Choice, the Constitution, and Civil Society* (Washington, DC: Brookings Institution Press, 1999).

Dale McDonald, PBVM

Christian Education of Youth, The (Divini Illius Magistri)

This encyclical was written by Pope Pius XI (1922–1939) and promulgated on December 31, 1929, the year he celebrated his Golden Jubilee of priesthood. The modern reader of this encyclical must recognize the historical context in which it was written. In 1929, the stock market crashed, the rippling effects of which were felt all over the world. During this period, the world was moving from the Victorian era with its strict social rules into the modern era. A large group of people felt the changes that were taking place (Prohibition, flappers, modern dance, and cinema) were eroding traditional values of the time. Totalitarian "isms," namely, communism and fascism, were claiming to have total control of humans, including their education. It is against this background that the document, reflecting a pre–Vatican II paradigm, is more clearly understood.

Having suffered through the ravages of World War I and the crash of the stock market, people more readily recognized that earthly goods would not produce happiness or perfection. Rather, they sought to acquire this perfection through education. The Pope proposed that because all education is directed to preparing men and women for their final end, there can be no perfect education that is not Christian.

In his encyclical, he stated that three groups lay claim to the preparation of individuals for this ultimate purpose: the family, civil society, and the Church. The first educators are parents and family members. It is their natural right and obligation to educate children until they are capable of providing for themselves. The family lays the foundation for formal education and faith formation and does so most effectively through their good example. The Pope notes that there is often a lack of preparation of parents and family members to meet these responsibilities. He admonishes pastors to teach parents about their grave obligation regarding the religious, moral, and civil training of their children. In fact, the document says that "the Church . . . is the educational environment most intimately and harmoniously associated with the Christian family." Pope Pius XI reiterates the writings of Pius IX (1846–1878) and Leo XIII (1878–1903) forbidding Catholic children from attending non-Catholic schools, with any exceptions subject to the local bishop's approval.

To assist parents in the education of their children, civil society formed schools that taught civil responsibilities as well as science, literature, and art. These schools, however, did not provide for faith formation, and the Holy Father, in his encyclical, emphasizes that parents must refuse to send their children to schools in which there is the danger of influence from evils in the secular world. For example, the document warns against the dangers of naturalism (the assumption that nature is the supreme guide of human actions). This theory was prevalent at that time in education. Vatican Council I (1869–1870) affirmed that faith and reason cannot be at odds with one another but should be of mutual help. Right reason establishes the foundations of faith and, with its help, develops knowledge that is free from error. The Church, therefore, supports the development of arts and sciences but cautions them from opposing divine doctrine and disturbing the domain of faith. The Pope also stresses that the state has an obligation to protect, in its legislation, the moral and religious education of youth. While the state has an interest in providing education (for the formation of good citizens), it cannot force parents to choose public education but must protect the right of the parents to provide a Christian education for their children and respect the inherent right of the Church to provide such education.

Of the three groups, pre-eminently the responsibility of education falls to the Church. In the Gospels, Jesus Christ admonishes his disciples to "teach all nations, baptizing them in the name of the Father, Son, and Holy Spirit" (Matthew 28:19). Jesus thereby established the teaching ministry of the Church since all men and women, by baptism, are called to enter God's kingdom and reach eternal salvation. As a sharer in the divine Magisterium, the Church has been gifted with infallibility regarding doctrines of the faith. The Church is independent from any earthly power in exercising its mission as an educator and therefore has the independent right to decide what may help or harm Christian education.

Pope Pius XI references the Code of Canon Law, which established the right of the Church to found and maintain schools of every type and, at the same time, reiterates the willingness of church schools to comply with legitimate dispositions of civil authority. He further emphasizes the duty of the Church to guard the education of its children in public and private institutions in the areas of religion and morality and that such supervision should not be viewed as undue interference but as assistance in the right ordering and well-being of families and society. The aim of the Church is to form good Christians for its own purposes and in so doing, form good citizens, preparing them to meet their obligations as members of society. It is impossible to produce good citizens through methods that would militate against the formation of good Christians.

Having established the Church's role in the Christian education of its youth, the encyclical then elaborates on two major related ideas: teacher preparation and curriculum.

When the issue is the education of youth, those who impart knowledge have the obligation to provide instruction in harmony with the teachings of the Church, whether the teacher be in the public or private sector. This concept was further developed by Pope Paul VI (1963–1978) in his address to the Council of the World Federation of Catholic teachers in 1997. Teachers must be well grounded in their knowledge of the faith and morals. By their example, they must reflect a Christ-like attitude in their actions and speech.

The subject of Christian education is the whole person, soul united to nature. The mind must be enlightened and the will strengthened from early years in order to attain the level of perfection in education intended by the Church. Any form of naturalism in teaching methods that might weaken the Christian formation of youth is false. No method of education should promote the sole reliance on human nature, the result of which is unbridled freedom on the part of the child. Some educators and philosophers search for a universal moral code of education as if there were no precedence in the Ten Commandments, in the Gospel, or in revelation by God Himself. In attempting to emancipate the child, these educators enslave the child to their own mistaken tendencies. Teachers must be thoroughly prepared in their subject area. They must be morally qualified and demonstrate a pure and holy love for young people. Laypeople, working side by side with priests and religious, are powerful witnesses of Catholic action.

Catholic educators aver that it is necessary that the curriculum, the school's program, and faculty be regulated by the Christian Spirit under the supervision of the Church at every grade level so that religion may be the foundation of the student's entire training. In Catholic schools, the study of secular subjects will not be at odds with religious instruction. When it is necessary to engage students in the study of authors promoting false doctrine for the purpose of refuting it, sufficient preparation will be given so that the students' faith is not only untested but strengthened. Greater stress must be placed on alignment of literature, science, and philosophy with the Catholic faith.

The document also addresses evils in society that adversely affected adolescents in 1929: immoral books, cinema, and radio (the encyclical was written prior to the development of television). Young people need not be sheltered from these influences but should be more than adequately prepared through their Christian education to withstand such allurements.

The encyclical does, however, take a cautious stance regarding sex education and coeducation in schools. Regarding sex education, the Holy Father warns against the school of thought that promotes providing detailed information at a very early age. As weakened human beings, such information might be the cause for young people to act upon their newfound knowledge. Moreover, the Pope advises that those who provide information in sex education be firmly grounded in the faith and promote the ideas in conformity with the Church's teaching and God's will.

In view of the social climate of the time, the document speaks about the potentially harmful effects of coeducation on the Christian education of adolescents. It specifically addresses physical education activities and standards of behavior.

The following quote summarizes the spirit of the encyclical:

> Christian education takes in the whole aggregate of human life, physical and spiritual, intellectual and moral, individual, domestic and social, not with a view of reducing it in any way, but in order to elevate, regulate and perfect it, in accordance with the example and teaching of Christ. Hence the true Christian, product of Christian education, is the supernatural man who thinks, judges, and acts constantly and consistently in accordance with right reason illumined by the supernatural light of the example and teaching of Christ.

See also: Catholic philosophy of education; Parental rights; Pius XI, Pope.
Further Reading: Harold A. Buetow, *Of Singular Benefit: The Story of U.S. Catholic*

Education (New York: Macmillan 1970); Robert J. Cuddihy and Verona M. Murray, "An Analysis of the Principles of Education Contained in the Encyclical of Pius XI, The Christian Education of Youth," unpublished master's thesis, St. John College of Cleveland, 1951; Pius XI, Pope, *Christian Education of Youth (Divini Illius Magistri)* (New York: American Press, 1930); Gerald C. Treacy, SJ, *Five Great Encyclicals—With Discussion Club Outlines* (New York: Paulist Press, 1939).

Joseph D. Massucci

Christian service

The call to Christian service is a primary responsibility of the Catholic school and a fundamental aspect of the spiritual development of its students. Christian service is the application of Gospel principles to daily life. The Church today is convinced that Christian service is one of the major tasks of catechesis. "Christian education is intended to make men's faith become living, conscious, and active" (National Conference of Catholic Bishops, 1972, #102). Participation in service to others, especially the poor and disenfranchised, is critical to efforts aimed at guiding students into a Christ-like way of living. Guided by the Gospel message, Catholic schools instruct students in the values Jesus taught and assist them in performing acts of Christian service such as feeding the hungry and clothing the naked. Through being of service to God, school, parish, and the larger community, the Catholic school student develops a deeper spirituality and demonstrates both understanding and acceptance of the Gospel message. Christians provide service by prayer and worship as well as direct participation in the cause for social reform. Each member of the Catholic school community is called to be an active and creative agent in service to society.

Service to others is a tradition reaching back to the beginning of Christianity. Jesus modeled service to others throughout His life. He manifested service with gentleness and a caring manner that viewed washing feet, healing the sick, and feeding the hungry as natural and necessary. His power was a form of compassion nurtured for centuries before Him in His own Jewish tradition. Jesus saw Himself as a fellow sufferer. The great care and compassion for others taught by Jesus himself became an identifying factor of the community of believers who followed Him.

The Second Vatican Council stressed the necessity of Christian service as a key element of living the Christian life. All educational ministries of the Church were charged with taking an active role in modern society and in solving societal injustices. Education is regarded as one of the most important ways by which the Church fulfills its commitment to the dignity of each person and the building of community.

The Catholic school is the most effective means available to the Church for the education of children and young people. The relationship between the Gospel message and the Catholic school is described in the documents of the Church. (The documents of the Church are official policy statements on important issues, written by the Pope, the Vatican Curia, bishops, or the conferences of bishops.) The threefold ministry of Catholic education is (1) to teach doctrine, the message revealed by God (*didache*); (2) to build community, fellowship in the life of the Holy Spirit (*koinonia*); and (3) to serve the Christian community and all humankind (*diakonia*). These essential elements of message, community, and service are integrated into daily life in the Catholic school.

Since Catholic schools find their true justification in the mission of the Church, Catholic schools are based on an educational philosophy in which faith, culture, and life are brought into harmony. Deeply rooted in Catholic social teaching, the notion of Christian service flows naturally as the tangible expression of religious attitudes and knowledge. "Doing faith" leads to developing faith. Service to others is an essential part of Christian spiritual development. The adults in Catholic schools, especially the teachers and parents, model the care and concern taught by Jesus for all members of the school community. Students become active in Christian service to others because this is what they are taught through both instruction and example.

The integration of religious values with life is a distinctive characteristic of Catholic schools. Grounded in the Gospel message of peace, love, patience, and respect for human dignity, the Catholic school has the task to deepen students' social concern and develop their sense of responsibility in working toward a just society. The opportunity to connect Gospel teaching with modern-day life is present in the Catholic school and allows students to address contemporary social issues through service.

The Catholic school, by its design, fosters the total spiritual development of all members of the school community. By actively engaging in Christian service on a regular basis, Catholic schools help students develop skills, virtues, and habits of the heart and mind required for living a life modeled after the care and compassion of Jesus. Students learn of human needs in their parishes, neighborhoods, and the world and have an opportunity to respond to those needs through Christian service.

Christian service is a responsibility of all Christians. It is especially appropriate as an element of the Catholic school curriculum. Christian service benefits not only the receiver but also the doer. Caring for others makes the one who is caring a real part of the caring activity and contributes positively to the social order and social fabric. Christian service takes place in many familiar ways: sheltering the homeless, feeding the hungry, giving drink to the thirsty, clothing the naked, tending to the needs of those who are sick or dying. Christian service is the Beatitudes embodied in everyday practice. At its best, Christian service is aimed at freeing people from dependence and helping them help themselves.

Catholic schools model and support service as an important philosophical outgrowth of their basic purpose. The Catholic school provides a unique setting that supports the development of Christian values, including service to others. *See also*: Evangelization; *To Teach as Jesus Did*.

Further Reading: Maria J. Ciriello, ed., *Formation and Development of Catholic School Leaders: The Principal as Spiritual Leader* (Washington, DC: United States Catholic Conference, 1996); Congregation for Catholic Education, *The Religious Dimension of Education in a Catholic School* (Washington, DC: United States Catholic Conference, 1988); National Conference of Catholic Bishops, *To Teach as Jesus Did: A Pastoral Message on Catholic Education* (Washington, DC: United States Catholic Conference, 1972).

Louise P. Moore

Citizens for Educational Freedom

The Citizens for Educational Freedom (CEF) was founded in 1959 by a group of St. Louis-based laymen, who set forth the following constitution:

> The purpose of this corporation shall be to undertake and promote whatever activities shall contribute to the fair and just treatment of all citizens of the United States of America, including student citizens, in the distribution of government tax monies for the purpose of education, with a view to assuring freedom of choice in education, to the end

that the civil liberties of our citizens shall be secured. (Mae Duggan and Martin Duggan, p. 199)

The introduction of legislation in the Congress of the United States, in particular the Murray-Metcalf bill of 1959, was the immediate cause of CEF's founding. The bill would have counted all schoolchildren to the federal allotment each state would receive, but those attending nonpublic schools would have been left out in the distribution of funds.

CEF chapters were organized across the nation. A newsletter, "The Fair Share News," was printed monthly. A publication named "Freedom in Education," which CEF described as upholding parents' rights in education, was distributed. An estimated 7,000 persons attended its first national conference in 1960. A CEF supporter in Congress offered a bill, which was not enacted, the "Junior G. I. Bill"; CEF efforts in state legislatures included support for pupils in nonpublic schools in the form of transportation, textbooks, and scholarships.

Heavily Catholic at the outset, CEF strove to include other denominations in its ranks. Lutherans, Orthodox Jewish, and Christian Reformed groups joined the organization as the 1960s progressed. CEF identified itself as a national organization, nonsectarian, nonpartisan, and nonprofit, that sought "A Fair Share for Every Child." It held that its common desire was to "achieve equality, freedom and excellence in education for all children." It aimed to represent the "fundamental rights and liberties of parents in the education of their children," which by constitutional law and by the nature of the family are "prior" to the rights of the state in education. These rights, since they are "God-given and inalienable," cannot be lawfully "usurped by the state." Parental choice must be upheld, CEF averred; to exclude nonpublic school children from being recipients of aid that resulted when parents exercised their God-given and constitutional rights would force "conformity to state-established moral and religious values," is "divisive and undemocratic," and is destructive of "God-centered education in America" (CEF, 1969). Parents, not the state, must have the fundamental right to decide how and where their children are educated; the state should not have a monopoly in schooling.

CEF's efforts for diversity bore fruit as the 1970s progressed. In 1978, Robert Baldwin, a Baptist, became its president. He contended that the "religion of secular humanism," which he said was dominant in public education, had led to the willingness of some Fundamentalist and Evangelical Christians to join with Catholics and others to influence the government to recognize the primacy of parental rights (*The National Catholic Reporter*, November 3, 1978, p. 20).

Over the years CEF and its allies scored some successes at the state and national levels. CEF has not ceased to labor, by means of newsletters and other attempts to get its message across, to advance its program on behalf of its deeply held cause. Currently, some 4,000 active members from a broad spectrum of race and creed work to provide freedom of choice in education for all. In recent times, CEF, which gave great impetus to the initial drive for vouchers to parents that would provide them with choice in the selection of the school their children would attend, added its voice to the chorus of those supporting the voucher movement, including the contests in Milwaukee and Cleveland. In the wake of the decision by the U.S. Supreme Court in June 2002 (*Zelman v. Simmons-Harris*, 122 S Ct. 2460) that upheld the constitutionality of vouchers that originated from the practice in Cleveland, CEF joined with the

Educational Freedom Foundation to host a "Victory Celebration" in St. Louis. Mae Duggan, one of the organization's founders, was featured in a *St. Louis Post-Dispatch* article, entitled "School Voucher Fight Began Here" (June 30, 2002, p. B-1). There is little question but that the CEF will be heard from in the many struggles that will occur in the several states as those states take up the question of the voucher in the years to come. *See also*: Blum, Virgil C.; Choice, parent and school; Parental rights; Vouchers.

Further Reading: CEF Newsletter, "Freedom in Education," Spring 1969; "Citizens for Educational Freedom: An Interview with Sister Renee Oliver," *Ligourian* 73, 2 (February 1985): 27–30; Mae Duggan and Martin Duggan, "Fight for Freedom," *Educational Freedom* (Milwaukee: Bruce, 1966); Educational Freedom Foundation, *The ABC's of Promoting Educational Choice* (St. Louis: Educational Freedom Foundation, 1995); Daniel D. McGarry, *Public Schools Teach Religion without God and Should Not Have a Monopoly* (St. Louis: Educational Freedom Foundation, n.d.); Daniel D. McGarry and Leo Ward, eds., *Educational Freedom and the Case for Government Aid to Students in Independent Schools* (Milwaukee: Bruce, 1966); Raymond McLaughlin, *The Liberty of Choice: Freedom and Justice in Education* (Collegeville, MN: Liturgical Press, 1979); School Reformers.com, "About Citizens for Educational Freedom." http://www.schoolreformers.com/cef/about.html. Accessed January 27, 2003.

Thomas C. Hunt

Climate (Catholic school)

According to Johnson and Johnson (1975), classroom climate depicts "the ways in which the people within the classroom interact with each other" (p. 26). This definition may apply to the entire school, as well, inclusive of administrators, pastors, faculty members, students, parents, school board members, and anyone else who influences the operation of the school. Wheatley (1999) depicted climate as a "field," containing forces that are invisible but immediately perceptible by anyone entering the environment and, more importantly, "unseen but real forces that influence people's behavior" (p. 15).

The climate of the Catholic school and/or classroom is distinctive in that it is grounded in Christian faith and Gospel values. The Second Vatican Council marked the beginning of a series of documents on education that stressed the importance of the learning atmosphere in the Catholic school. In 1965, this unique learning environment was characterized as "a special atmosphere animated by the Gospel spirit of freedom and charity" (#8). The National Conference of Catholic Bishops in 1976 wrote "that the atmosphere and relationships in the school are as much the focus of the Catholic school as is the formal religious education class" (pp. 7–8). In 1988, in the Congregation for Catholic Education's *The Religious Dimension of Education in a Catholic School*, a landmark document on Catholic school climate, the Catholic educator was called to create a "school-home," a learning environment that is "humanly and spiritually rich," that "reproduces, as far as possible, the warm and intimate atmosphere of family life" and exudes a "common spirit of trust and spontaneity" (40).

M. Scott Peck (1987) illuminated the concept of an authentic climate. It is

integrative. It includes people of different sexes, ages, religions, cultures, viewpoints, life styles, and stages of development by integrating them into a whole that is greater— better—than the sum of its parts. Integration is not a melting process; it does not result in a bland average. Rather, it has been compared to the creation of a salad in which the identity of the individual ingredients is preserved yet simultaneously transcended. . . . [It] does not solve the problem of pluralism by obliterating diversity. Instead it seeks out diversity, welcomes other points of view, embraces opposites, desires to see the other side of every issue. It is "wholistic." It integrates us human beings into a functioning mystical body. (p. 234)

The Congregation for Catholic Education (1988) delineated some of the conditions for creating a positive school climate: "that everyone agree with the educational goals and cooperate in achieving them; that interpersonal relationships be based on love and Christian freedom; that each individual, in daily life, be a witness to gospel values; that every student be challenged to strive for the highest possible level of formation, both human and Christian" (#103). In addition, the Congregation stated that the school climate must welcome families, that the local church be an active participant, and that outreach to civil society on the local, national, and international levels be active and ongoing.

On the other hand, educators were urged to eliminate conditions that threaten a positive school climate. The Congregation (1988) offered examples of potential problems, such as:

the educational goals are either not defined or are defined badly; those responsible for the school are not sufficiently trained; concern for academic achievement is excessive; relations between teachers and students are cold and impersonal; teachers are antagonistic toward one another; discipline is imposed from on high without any participation or cooperation from the students; relationships with families are formal or even strained, and families are not involved in helping to determine the educational goals; some within the school community are giving a negative witness; individuals are unwilling to work together for the common good; the school is isolated from the local Church; there is no interest in or concern for the problems of society; religious instruction is *routine*. (#104)

These authors claimed that whenever a combination of these threats is present, the "religious dimension," that is, a school climate based on Christian values, is endangered.

The Committee on Developments in the Science of Learning (Bransford, Brown, and Cocking, 1999), reporting on current research on how people learn, illuminated some practical areas for consideration when examining a school's climate, such as the following.

Classroom Norms and Expectations

Norms and expectations vary among classrooms and schools. Researchers have found that learning is often enhanced by social norms that value understanding and allow students and teachers the freedom to err in order to learn. An unwritten classroom norm may be to never get caught making a mistake or to be perceived as not knowing an answer. Such a norm deters students' willingness to ask questions when they do not understand the material or to creatively explore new questions. Also, there may be a different set of expectations for different students, with teachers conveying high expectations for school success to some students and lowered expectations for others.

Grading Practices

Grading practices can affect the sense of community in a classroom and, in some instances, may impede learning. Researchers believe this can be the case when individual competition is perceived as being at odds with a community ethic in which individuals contribute their strengths to the community. For example, a "high achiever" bulletin board may provoke student embarrassment, for both low and high achievers, thus discouraging the formation of community among learners and teacher.

Teachers

Barth (1990) found that the relationships among the adults of a school affect the character and quality of the school, as well as the accomplishments of the students, more than any other factor. Hence, teachers and administrators who strive to create a learning community among themselves may be far more effective in contributing to the needs of students in the long run than a teacher's isolated attempts.

There are many other factors to consider in the creation of learning communities in Catholic schools, such as recognition of diverse student learning styles, positive discipline strategies, physical arrangements of classrooms, and teacher–student and student–student relationships. From a Catholic school perspective, the pedagogical challenge lies in translating Gospel values into classroom practices in the attempt to build on the strengths, interests, and needs of the learners. *See also: Religious Dimension of Education in a Catholic School, The.*

Further Reading: Roland S. Barth, *Improving Schools from Within* (San Francisco: Jossey-Bass, 1990); J. Bransford, A. Brown, and R. Cocking, eds., *How People Learn, Brain, Mind, Experience, and School* (Washington, DC: National Academy Press, 1999); Congregation for Catholic Education, *Lay Catholics in Schools: Witnesses to Faith* (Boston: Daughters of St. Paul, 1982); Congregation for Catholic Education, *The Catholic School* (Washington, DC: United States Catholic Conference, 1977); Congregation for Catholic Education, *The Religious Dimension of Education in a Catholic School* (Boston: Daughters of St. Paul, 1988); "Declaration on Christian Education" (*Gravissimum Educationis*), in Austin Flannery, ed., *Vatican Council II*, vol. 1, rev. ed. (Northport, NY: Costello, 1988); David W. Johnson and Roger T. Johnson, *Learning Together and Alone: Cooperation, Competition, and Individualization* (Englewood Cliffs, NJ: Prentice Hall, 1975); National Conference of Catholic Bishops, *To Teach as Jesus Did: A Pastoral Message on Catholic Education* (Washington, DC: United States Catholic Conference, 1972); M. Scott Peck, *The Different Drum* (New York: Simon and Schuster, 1987); Margaret J. Wheatley, *Leadership and the New Science, Discovering Order in a Chaotic World* (San Francisco: Berrett-Koehler, 1999).

Gini Shimabukuro

Cochran v. Louisiana State Board of Education

Cochran v. Louisiana State Board of Education (1930), along with *Pierce v. Society of Sisters* (1925), is one of only two Supreme Court cases implicating Roman Catholic and other nonpublic schools prior to the evolution of its modern Establishment Clause jurisprudence in *Everson v. Board of Education of Ewing Township* (1947). As in *Pierce*, the Court resolved the dispute based on the Due Process Clause of the Fourteenth Amendment rather than the First Amendment's Establishment Clause. *Cochran* is important because in reaching its decision, the Court employed analyses that would mature into the child benefit test that emerged in *Everson*. According to the child benefit test, the Court has permitted a variety of forms of aid to students such as transportation, textbooks, and other instructional materials on the basis that the assistance is afforded the students rather than the religiously affiliated nonpublic schools that they attend.

At issue in *Cochran* was a state statute that allowed public tax revenues to provide textbooks for all students regardless of where they attended school. Citizens and taxpayers initially filed an unsuccessful challenge to the act on the grounds that it violated both the federal and state constitutions. After the Supreme Court of Louisiana upheld the statute's constitutionality, the plaintiffs sought further review. A unanimous Supreme Court affirmed that the law passed constitutional muster.

As to the merits of the claim, the Court rejected the allegation that the statute violated the Fourteenth Amendment as a taking of private property for the private purpose of aiding religious and other sectarian schools by furnishing students with free textbooks. In its analysis, the Court conceded that some of the children attended religious schools. However, in language that presaged the child benefit test, the Court reasoned that the students, rather than their schools, were the true beneficiaries of the statute. To this end, the Court pointed out that the statute contemplated that the state provide children in private schools with the same texts that were used in public schools and that it was expected that these would not be adapted to religious instruction. In conclusion, the Court applied language similar to that which it would use in the companion cases of *School District of Abington Township v. Schempp* and *Murray v. Curlett* (1963), wherein it enunciated the first two parts of the seemingly ubiquitous *Lemon v. Kurtzman* (1971) test. As such, the Court held that it was satisfied that since the statute did not have the impermissible effect attributed to it, there was no doubt that the taxing power of the state was used for an appropriate public purpose. *See also*: Child benefit theory; *Pierce v. the Society of Sisters*; Separation of Church and state.

Further Reading: *Cochran v. Louisiana State Board of Education*, 281 U.S. 370 (1930); *Everson v. Board of Education*, 330 U.S. 1 (1947); *Lemon v. Kurtzman*, 403 U.S. 602 (1971); *Pierce v. Society of Sisters*, 268 U.S. 510 (1925); *School District of Abington Township v. Schempp, Murray v. Curlett*, 374 U.S. 203 (1963).

Charles J. Russo

Coeducation

Coeducation is the term used to describe the practice of educating boys and girls in the same classes within the same school. Most Catholic schools today are coeducational. However, the earliest Catholic schools were single-sex schools that educated boys and girls in separate settings. The official teaching of the Church as late as the 1950s opposed the practice of coeducation. Catholic educators in the United States have struggled to provide Catholic schools for both boys and girls that are financially feasible, educationally sound, and faithful to the spirit of Church teaching. Proponents of coeducation argue that coeducational schools offer a learning environment that is more conducive to social maturity. Proponents of single-sex schools claim that a single-sex school provides a more beneficial learning environment, especially for girls.

Early Catholic schools provided different types of education for boys and girls. Schools for boys offered training for the priesthood, while schools for girls emphasized preparation for marriage and family life. At the beginning of the twentieth century, the demand for education intensified. Consequently, enrollment in Catholic high schools also increased. More Catholic colleges were established. As college enrollments increased, Catholic secondary schools for both girls and boys shifted their programs toward college preparation.

Even though the mission of Catholic secondary schools expanded, most Catholic secondary schools continued to operate as single-sex until after World War II. The official teaching of the Church argued against coeducation. Pope Pius XI in his 1929 encyclical *Divini Illius Magistri* ("The Christian Education of Youth"), described co-education as "false and harmful" (paragraph 68). In 1957, the Vatican Congregation for Religious issued an instruction warning of the moral dangers of coeducation. However, the same instruction stated that Catholic schools were so crucial that coeducation could be tolerated if a community could support only one Catholic school. The practice of co-institutional education was suggested as a compromise where both girls and boys were educated in the same school but in separate classes. Catholic educators were challenged to provide college preparatory schools that were financially feasible and in conformity with the teaching of the Church.

In the 1960s and 1970s, sweeping changes affected the Church in the aftermath of Vatican II. Attitudes in society were also changing, particularly in regard to gender equity. The shift from religious to lay personnel had a profound impact on the financial viability of Catholic schools. The Title IX legislation enacted in 1972 effectively abolished single-sex public schools. This legislation probably had an indirect affect on Catholic schools as well. Financial contingencies, an educational climate that favored coeducation over single-sex education, and social policy strongly supporting gender equity contributed to the building of new coeducational Catholic schools and led many historically single-sex Catholic schools to accept students of the opposite sex.

Virtually all Catholic elementary schools are coeducational. The majority of Catholic secondary schools are coeducational; however, single-sex schools constitute a significant proportion of Catholic secondary schools. While the number of Catholic secondary schools has declined, the relative proportion of Catholic coeducational and single-sex secondary schools has not significantly changed since 1940. According to data reported by the National Catholic Educational Association for the 2001–2002 school year, coeducational schools, regardless of grade level, accounted for 94 percent of all Catholic schools. Slightly over 99 percent of elementary schools and 64.6 percent of secondary schools were coeducational.

Obviously, coeducational schools are the norm for Catholic schooling. However, gender equity issues may present challenges to Catholic educators in coeducational schools. Equal educational opportunities for both boys and girls are not necessarily ensured by attending the same school facility. *See also*: *Christian Education of Youth, The (Divini Illius Magistri)*; Co-institutional high schools; Enrollment; Pius XI, Pope.

Further Reading: Anthony S. Bryk, Valerie E. Lee, and Peter B. Holland, *Catholic Schools and the Common Good* (Cambridge: Harvard University Press, 1993); Thomas C. Hunt, "The History of Catholic Schools in the United States: An Overview," in Thomas C. Hunt, Thomas E. Oldenski, and Theodore J. Wallace, eds., *Catholic School Leadership: An Invitation to Lead* (London: Falmer Press, 2000); Dale McDonald, *United States Catholic Elementary and Secondary Schools 2001–2002: The Annual Statistical Report on Schools, Enrollment and Staffing* (Washington, DC: National Catholic Educational Association, 2002); Richard J. McGrath, "Students in Catholic Schools," in Thomas C. Hunt, Ellis A. Joseph, and Ronald Nuzzi, eds., *Catholic Schools Still Make a Difference: Ten Years of Research, 1991–2000* (Washington, DC: National Catholic Educational Association, 2002); *Papal Teachings: Education*, trans. Aldo

Robeschini (Boston: Daughters of St. Paul, 1960); Pius XI, *Divini Illius Magistri* ("The Christian Education of Youth"), from *The Catholic Educational Review* 28 (1930): 133–134.

Frank X. Savage

Cognitive moral development

The cognitive development approach to moral education is based on a psychological theory first postulated by Jean Piaget that claimed that moral growth moves through stages of development based on three levels defined by John Dewey. In the mid-1950s, Lawrence Kohlberg, to whom this approach is principally attributed, conducted longitudinal and cross-cultural research on the theoretical rationale and redefined and validated the Dewey-Piaget stages. Despite objections from the Catholic right, this approach has been used in Catholic school classrooms across the nation as Catholic scholars have written about its congruence with the Catholic philosophy of education (Duska & Whelan, 1975; Power, 1985; Traviss, 1985).

Cognitive moral development is a complex theory that attempts a synthesis of philosophy, psychology, sociology, and education, and yet it is compelling enough to attract thousands of teachers to its use in place of indoctrination and inculcation. It does, however, contrary to its critics' charges, encourage the use of some indoctrination at particular ages, especially in very young children. While it is scornful of the "bag of virtues" approach, it does incorporate didactic instruction as a way of providing disequilibrium.

Dewey's three levels were theoretical; he called them (1) pre-moral or conventional, (2) conventional, and (3) autonomous. Piaget used the material from the interviews and observations that he had gathered for his work on the cognitive growth stages and suggested that the same process of disequilibrium, assimilation, and accommodation, which he had earlier shown to lead to cognitive growth, also apply to moral growth. Lawrence Kohlberg began his research (which he called "validation") with several longitudinal and cross-cultural studies in 1955 as he commenced work on his doctoral dissertation at the University of Chicago.

With Piaget, Kohlberg (1978) claimed that the stages of moral growth "are 'structured wholes,' or organized systems of thought. Individuals are consistent in levels of moral development." For Kohlberg the stages were structures of moral judgment or moral reasoning and were distinguished from the content of moral judgment. Both Piaget and Kohlberg held that stages form an invariant sequence. Under all circumstances except extreme trauma, movement is always forward, never backward. Individuals never skip stages to the next stage up. The two theories are based on the belief that "stages are 'hierarchical integrations.' Thinking at a higher stage includes or comprehends within it lower-stage thinking. There is a tendency to function at or prefer the highest stage available" (Kohlberg, 1978, p. 37).

Kohlberg's work involved the integrating and building on the contributions of many scholars before him, and he surfaced as "a dominant mid-late twentieth-century figure in the theory and practice of moral development. He has increasingly become the starting point from which most new theories emerge and/or react" (Chazan, 1985, p. 90).

Besides using the research of Piaget and the framework of Dewey, Kohlberg also employed the philosophy of Immanuel Kant and the writing on justice of his colleague at Harvard, John Rawls. Kohlberg's conclusions are often seen as a response to values relativism, explaining why Catholic school educators, in part, have found his work attractive.

The cognitive development approach views the child as taking an active part in his or her own moral development rather than being a passive recipient of external influences and teachings. It suggests that young people formulate moral ideas from organized patterns of thought, and these patterns do not come directly from the culture. It also maintains that these patterns go through a series of qualitative transformations of stages as the child develops, which may be described in the following way:

Stage One: Punishment and Reward

Right is seen as power. Moral decisions are made based on the physical consequences of the act and out of respect for power, that is, the decisions are good if one is rewarded, and bad decisions if one is punished. The child is particularly responsive to the power of parents and teachers and other adults who have authority over him or her.

Stage Two: Instrumental Relativist Orientation

Right is perceived as what satisfies one's needs, and sometimes the needs of others. Reciprocity is a key factor in the moral decision, but it is reciprocity characterized by selfishness. Even when there are notions of equal sharing and fairness, they are marked by "I'll scratch your back, if you scratch mine." The reciprocity does not flow from notions of loyalty, gratitude, or justice.

Stage Three: Good Boy-Nice Girl Orientation

The moral decision is made in light of the approval of others and of self. One wishes to think well of oneself. There is much conformity to what is majority or natural behavior and what pleases others or is perceived as acceptable to them. Societal norms are important.

Stage Four: Law and Order Orientation

At stage four the person is beginning to mature as far as making moral decisions. It is important to obey established rules and law and to do one's duty. A person on stage four shows respect for legitimate authority and maintains the social order for its own sake. There is a concern for the common good.

Stage Five: Social Contract, Legalistic Orientation

Decisions are made according to general individual rights and standards that have been critically examined and agreed upon by the whole society. The emphasis is working within the law but making changes when the need is present. This stage sometimes sees a conflict between the common good and individual good that must be resolved. This stage is the accepted moral position of the U.S. Constitution.

Stage Six: Universal-Ethical-Principle Orientation

Decisions are based on conscience in accordance with self-chosen ethical principles. Actions must be good in themselves, consistent, and universal. These principles are abstract, example, the Golden Rule, the categorical imperative. (Chazan, 1985; Modgil and Modgil, 1984; Traviss, 1985)

There have been a number of criticisms of Kohlberg's work. Of the three most serious critisms, one is that he opts for only one tradition of moral reasoning when there are several that others think are better, depending on who is criticizing. The second major criticism is that his theory is less procedural than he claims it is and that he actually imposes a particular ethic. Rather than encouraging open reflection on moral alternatives, as Socrates did with Meno, Kohlberg manipulates an acceptance of a moral response. The third criticism focuses on his neglect of the affect. Kohlberg has addressed all three criticisms in his book, *Moral Stages: A Current Formulation and a Response to Critics* (with C. Levine and A. Hewer [Basel, Switzerland: Karger, 1983]).

The cognitive developmental approach to moral education assigns the teacher four tasks. First, the teacher must assist the student to reflect on genuine moral dilemmas. Second, the student should be helped to think about alternative ways to resolve the dilemma. Third, the student should be led to think about the adequacies and inadequacies, the consistencies and inconsistencies in the moral reasoning about the alternatives. Finally, the teacher should suggest to the student that there is a procedure of reflection and resolution that is more efficient than his or her current method. *See also*: Character education; Moral education, history of; Values clarification.

Further Reading: Barry Chazan, *Contemporary Approaches to Moral Education: Analyzing Alternative Theories* (New York: Teachers' College Press, 1985); William Damon, *The Moral Child: Nurturing Children's Natural Growth* (New York: Free Press, 1988); Ronald Duska and Mariellen Whelan, *Moral Development: A Guide to Piaget and Kohlberg* (New York: Paulist Press, 1975); Lawrence Kohlberg, "The Cognitive-Development Approach to Moral Education," in V. Lois Erickson and Peter Scharf, eds., *Readings in Moral Education* (Minneapolis: Winston Press, 1978); Sohan Modgill and Cecilia Modgil, eds., *Lawrence Kohlberg: Consensus and Controversy* (Philadelphia: Falmer Press, 1984); F. Clark Power, "Democratic Moral Development in a Large High School: A Case Study," in Marvin W. Berkowitz and Fritz Oser, eds., *Moral Education: Theory and Application* (Hillsdale, NJ: Lawrence Erlbaum); Mary Peter Traviss, OP, *Student Moral Development in the Catholic School* (Washington, DC: National Catholic Educational Association, 1985).

Mary Peter Traviss, OP

Co-institutional high schools

Catholic co-institutional schools date back to the nineteenth century, when some pastors brought in religious orders of men (brothers) to teach the boys and religious orders of women (nuns) to teach girls within the same parish schools in several cities. Co-institutional high schools' peak was in the early 1960s, following an "Instruction" by the Sacred Congregation of Religious in 1957.

Catholic secondary education was carried out in single-sex schools. The Church had been opposed to coeducational schools, especially for adolescents, for decades. The Holy See had issued norms in 1901 that opposed congregations of religious women who taught in mixed schools and followed that up in 1921 with the position that "approbation shall not easily be given" to nuns for that same end. The "Magna Carta" of the Catholic position on coeducation was handed down in 1929 by Pope Pius XI in his encyclical letter, *Divini Illius Magistri* ("The Christian Education of Youth"), in which the Pontiff pointed to moral dangers present in coeducation and termed it "false" and "harmful" to Christian education.

In 1957 the Congregation of Religious issued an "Instruction" that gave impetus to the co-institutional high school. Recognizing that some economic situations dictated against the establishment and operation of single-sex schools and mindful of the Church's constant opposition to coeducation, the Congregation identified co-institutional schools as an option to be preferred over coeducational ones for Catholic secondary schools.

The key features of co-institutional schools called for men (the majority brothers or priests) to teach the boys, and women (the majority nuns) to teach the girls, unless necessity required common instruction. Then, close supervision of the two was required. Schools would have common laboratories and gymnasiums, but with separate instruction by gender, especially in physical education, in those facilities. Instruction in courses that dealt with human reproduction was to be separate by gender. Separate entrances and exits for boys and girls were to be put in place.

There were potential problems connected with the administration of this kind of school. Should it have one or two principals? If the former, the principal of the girls was invariably "second in command." In either instance, but especially the latter, the two principals absolutely had to be able to work together. What do the religious personnel who administer or staff the school think of a multistaffed school? What will their morale be like? In the case of a diocesan-supported school, how will the religious orders react to a diocesan priest, especially if he is not a professional educator, serving as overall head? How will the various orders get along with each other in this format? Those considering establishing such a school were advised to think through the potential staffing and building problems *before* beginning such a venture.

Co-institutional high schools experienced a rapid growth in the early 1960s. There were fifty-one such institutions in 1959–1960 and ninety-two in 1964–1965, and 60 percent of these had enrollments in excess of 1,000. Their numbers dwindled along with the decline of religious men and women who staffed Catholic schools. *See also*: *Christian Education of Youth, The (Divini Illius Magistri)*; Coeducation; Pius XI, Pope.

Further Reading: Harold A. Buetow, *Of Singular Benefit: The Story of U.S. Catholic Education* (New York: Macmillan, 1970); Paul F. Curran, "The Coinstitutional High School—A Study of the Problems and Rewards," *NCEA Bulletin* 62, 2 (November 1965): 1–69; Anthony H. Dorn, "Administrative Patterns in the Coinstitutional High Schools," *Catholic School Journal* 60, 9 (November 1960): 37–41; Basil Faison, *Coeducation in Catholic Schools: A Commentary on the Instruction on Coeducation* (Boston: Daughters of St. Paul, 1959).

Thomas C. Hunt

Coleman, James S. (1926–1995)

James Samuel Coleman, a noted sociologist and researcher, formulated educational policy during the second half of the twentieth century. Over the course of his academic career, he wrote over 100 articles and thirty books; the most popular was *Equality of Educational Opportunity*, popularly known as *The Coleman Report*.

Coleman was born on May 12, 1926, in Bedford, Indiana, spending most of his childhood between Bedford and Louisville, Kentucky. Coleman spent two years in the U.S. Navy (1944–1946), returning home to begin undergraduate studies in chemical engineering at Purdue University, graduating with a B.S. in 1949. After two years of employment with the Eastman Kodak Company, in 1951 Coleman changed his life course, beginning graduate study in sociology at Columbia University, where he was awarded a Ph.D. in 1955. He joined the faculty at the University of Chicago after graduation, where he remained for three years. Through the 1960s, Coleman was on the faculty at Johns Hopkins University, working in the area of social relations. During his tenure at Johns Hopkins the Coleman Report was released and subsequently published as *Equality of Educational Opportunity* (Coleman et al., 1966). Coleman returned to the University of Chicago in 1973, where he remained until his death from cancer on March 25, 1995 (Ohles et al., 1997).

Coleman's primary research was in the area of social change and collective action. It was from this work that he examined and influenced educational policy. His insights in the field of education led him to the conclusion that the social makeup of a school was ultimately more important to the school's success than the school's level of funding; that socioeconomic integration was more important than racial integration in schools; and that the public schools would benefit from examining those Catholic school policies that promote the mutual welfare of students and society. Among the numerous articles and books written by Coleman, two stand out as especially influential in educational policy. *Equality of Educational Opportunity* (1966) became the basis for decisions about busing minority students during the latter 1960s. *High School Achievement: Public and Private Schools* (Coleman, Hoffer, and Kilgore, 1982), described Catholic schools as more successful than public schools because Catholic schools provided students with discipline, homework, and high standards.

The text *Equality of Educational Opportunity* (1966) was the published report of Coleman's study on the state of schools in the United States that was commissioned by Congress in the Civil Rights Act of 1964. The study attempted to answer four questions about American schools. (1) What is the level of segregation among various racial and ethnic groups within public schools? (2) Do the schools offer equal educational opportunities? This was determined by looking at a number of programmatic characteristics such as types of programs, facilities, and characteristics of both faculty and students. (3) How much did students actually learn? This was measured through the use of standardized achievement tests. (4) What are the possible relationships between student achievement and the type of schools that the students attended? The results of this study proved not only that public schools were racially segregated but also that they were segregated by socioeconomic factors. Coleman hypothesized that segregation by socioeconomic class was the critical factor in the differences among students in public schools. Those students from lower socioeconomic classes who attended school with a majority of middle-class students tended to be more successful than those who were all from the lower socioeconomic class. Coleman also concluded that the quality of school facilities had less of an impact upon majority students than minority students. The success of minority students was more dependent upon the type of schools they attended than was the case for majority students.

In *High School Achievement: Public and Private Schools* (1982), Coleman posited that the evidence that he collected demonstrated that Catholic schools functioned much closer to the American ideal of the common school. He backed this proposition with evidence that the Catholic schools showed a greater homogeneity of achievement than the public schools, while maintaining student bodies from more diverse socioeconomic backgrounds. Students of parents with different educational backgrounds achieved at a comparable level in Catholic schools, while the difference in the educational backgrounds of parents impacted the achievement level of public school students. Coleman found that high school sophomores of color in Catholic schools achieved at a level much closer to that of white sophomores in Catholic schools compared to a similar group of sophomores in the public schools. Coleman also discovered that the achievement gap between minority students and white students in their senior year decreased slightly in Catholic schools, while in public schools the gap increased slightly. Coleman believed that the quality of student behavior and the level of academic engagement in Catholic schools were the determining factors in their success.

One colleague eulogized Coleman as a scholar who stood by his research and would not allow popular opinion to sway his beliefs or research. One of the conclusions that Coleman reached in *Equality of Educational Opportunity* was that integration of various socioeconomic groups had a profound impact upon school improvement and educational opportunity for those living in poverty. As a result of his study, busing policies were mandated within school districts in order to achieve integration in the nation's public schools. In the 1970s, Coleman declared busing to be a failure because the purpose of busing was never really accomplished because of the flight of middle-class whites to the suburbs. Therefore, the possibility of a racial and socioeconomic class integration of the public schools became an impossibility. Those who championed integration and busing saw Coleman as a traitor to the cause. Some of his colleagues in the American Sociological Association fought to remove him from the association. Cooler heads prevailed, and they did not expel Coleman from the association. His vindication was complete in 1991, when the American Sociological Association selected him as their president (McFadden, 1995; Kahlenberg, 2001). *See also*: Effectiveness of Catholic schools; *Equality of Educational Opportunity*; *High School and Beyond*; *Public and Private High Schools: The Impact of Communities*; Social capital.

Further Reading: James S. Coleman et al., *Equality of Educational Opportunity* (Washington, DC: U.S. Government Printing Office, 1966); James S. Coleman and Thomas Hoffer, *Public and Private High Schools: The Impact of Communities* (New York: Basic Books, 1987); James S. Coleman, Thomas Hoffer, and Sally Kilgore, *High School Achievement: Public, Catholic, and Private Schools Compared* (New York: Basic Books, 1982); Richard D. Kahlenberg, "Learning from James Coleman," *Public Interest* #144 (2001): 54–72; Robert D. McFadden. "Dr. James Coleman, 68, Dies," *New York Times*, March 28, 1995; Frederik Ohles et al., *Biographical Dictionary of Modern American Educators* (Westport, CT: Greenwood Press, 1997).

Anthony J. Dosen, CM

Collective bargaining

Collective bargaining in American Roman Catholic schools began shortly after its spread in public schools in the 1960s. Bargaining by teachers' unions began almost simultaneously in high schools in urban centers in the Northeast and Midwest, most notably in Brooklyn, Philadelphia, and Chicago.

Unionization in Brooklyn progressed smoothly as the first bargaining sessions took place in the spring of 1967. The same was not true in Philadelphia and Chicago. The first "strike" in American Catholic education history took place on April 17, 1967, in Philadelphia, lasting twenty minutes before the union and archdiocese reached an agreement. Four days later, teachers in three Catholic schools in Chicago went on apparently unrelated strikes, lasting from one day to several weeks, the last of which led to the firing of twenty-three teachers in one of the schools in May 1967 (Russo, 1990).

Teacher unions in Catholic high schools grew at a steady pace. By 1973, 25 of 145 dioceses reported having recognized associations or unions (NCEA Symposium,

1976, p. 277). Yet, a study in the summer of 1979, shortly after *Catholic Bishop*, revealed that the growth of unions slowed as only 27 of 162 Catholic school systems reported having teacher organizations (Augenstein, 1984).

Catholic teachers' unions received support in 1975, when the National Labor Relations Board (NLRB) asserted jurisdiction over union-organizing activities in cases involving Catholic high schools in Chicago and Ft. Wayne–South Bend. Even so, school officials refused to comply with the NLRB's order directing them to bargain. On appeal, the Seventh Circuit held that the NLRB improperly exercised its discretion (*Catholic Bishop of Chicago v. NLRB*, 1977).

On further review, in 1979, the Supreme Court's five-to-four decision in *NLRB v. Catholic Bishop of Chicago* affirmed that the NLRB lacked jurisdiction over the dispute based on its concern that judicial inquiry into labor and employment relations in religiously affiliated schools posed too great a risk of excessive governmental entanglement into their internal theological matters. A brief dissent would have extended the jurisdiction of the NLRB to protect lay teachers employed in Church-operated schools.

The publication of *Economic Justice for All*, the United States Catholic Conference 1986 pastoral letter of the American bishops on Catholic social teaching and the American economy, offered hope for the future of unions since it explicitly recognized the rights of workers in church institutions to organize and bargain collectively. Despite the promise of *Economic Justice for All*, bargaining has decelerated. Disputes over bargaining continued. For example, in *Catholic High School Association of the Archdiocese of New York v. Culvert* (1985), the Second Circuit held that the First Amendment did not prohibit the New York State Labor Relations Board (NYSLRB) from asserting jurisdiction in a conflict between lay teachers in Catholic schools and their employer. The court distinguished *Culvert* from *Catholic Bishop* in explaining that, unlike the NLRA, the New York State Labor Relations Act (NYSLRA) explicitly covered employees of educational or religious associations.

Along with *Culvert*, the NYSLRB resolved two other disputes involving Catholic high schools. In *The Matter of St. John's Preparatory School and Lay Faculty Association* (1984), the NYSLRB found that school officials unlawfully refused to bargain in good faith with the teachers' association, that the ensuing strike was precipitated by their unfair labor practices, and that they acted improperly in dismissing seventy-six striking teachers. Similarly, a second case, involving a 1981 strike at Christ the King High School in New York City, was resolved in favor of the teachers after more than fifteen years of litigation.

Starting in 1976, the union representing the lay faculty at Christ the King and management repeatedly failed to reach a contract agreement. When bargaining failures led to a 1981 work stoppage, school officials fired all ninety-six of the striking teachers and summarily ended negotiations. After years of fighting in the federal courts, the case was transferred to state court on the ground that the NYSLRB had the authority to enforce state labor law.

In *New York State Employment Relations Board v. Christ the King Regional High School* (1997), the Court of Appeals of New York unanimously affirmed that the NYSLRB could enforce an order directing management to bargain in good faith and reinstate the striking teachers. The court reasoned that the NYSLRB's inquiry did not impinge on the school's First Amendment right to free exercise of religion since the NYSLRA is neutral and has no implications of adverse or unconstitutional restrictions on religious beliefs or activities. The court concluded that since state labor law was not directed toward religion and the effect of the NYSLRB's compelling good faith negotiation only incidentally affected religion, it did not violate the First Amendment.

About six weeks after *Christ the King*, the Supreme Court of New Jersey ruled that lay teachers in Catholic schools can pursue their state constitutional right to bargain collectively over secular aspects of employment in *South Jersey Catholic School Teachers Organization v. St. Teresa of the Infant Jesus Elementary School* (1997). When the union representing teachers in St. Teresa's, a diocesan elementary school, sought certification as their bargaining representative, a Board of Pastors, acting as agent of the diocese, conditioned it on the union's signing a document entitled "Minimum Standards for Organizations Wishing to Represent Lay Teachers in a Parish or Regional Catholic Elementary School in the Diocese of Camden." The non-negotiable "Minimum Standards" vested complete and final authority to dictate the outcome of disputes in the Board of Pastors while prohibiting the union from assessing dues or collecting agency fees from nonmembers. Following the union's refusal to accept the "Minimum Standards," the diocese withheld recognition. The union sued based on language in the state constitution expressly granting public and private workers the right to organize and bargain collectively, charging that the standards would have amounted to a premature bargaining away of teacher rights.

In *St. Teresa*, the Supreme Court of New Jersey unanimously affirmed that the state constitution gave the teachers the enforceable right to unionize as long as the scope of bargaining only incidentally impacted the schools' First Amendment rights under the religion clauses and remained limited to secular terms and conditions of employment.

Current data on bargaining in Catholic schools are inconclusive. The National Association of Catholic School Teachers, headquartered in Philadelphia, is the largest Catholic teachers' organization, representing about 5,000 teachers in twenty-one affiliated unions (Archer, 1996). Further, an NCEA report indicated that 23 percent of schools have some type of negotiating group (Guerra, 1994, p. 14).

In light of the complex issues surrounding bargaining in Catholic schools, *Christ the King* and *St. Teresa* may point the way to a balancing of the labor rights of teachers with the religious prerogatives of management in Catholic schools to require teachers to comply with the Church's fundamental moral teachings. Even though unionization may not be a major force in Catholic education, it is an issue that is likely to continue to draw some attention. *See also*: Free Exercise Clause; *National Labor Relations Board v. The Catholic Bishop of Chicago et al.*

Further Reading: Jeff Archer, "Catholic Teachers Start Union in St. Louis," *Education Week* (October 6, 1996): 6; John J. Augenstein, "Teacher Unions, the Courts, and the Catholic Schools," in Robert J. Yeager, ed., *Contemporary Issues in Catholic High Schools* (Washington, DC: National Catholic Educational Association, 1984): 77–82; *Catholic Bishop of Chicago v. N.L.R.B.*, 559 F.2d 1112 (7th Cir. 1977); *Catholic High Sch. Ass'n of the Archdiocese of N.Y. v. Culvert*, 753 F.2d 1161 (2d Cir. 1985); Michael J. Guerra, *Dollars and Sense: Catholic High Schools and Their Finances* (Washington, DC: National Catholic Educational Association, 1994); NCEA Symposium: "Unionism in Catholic Schools," *Origins* 6 (1976): 287; *New York State Employment Relations Bd. v. Christ the King Reg. High Sch.*, 660 N.Y.S.2d 359 (N.Y. 1997); *NLRB v. Catholic Bishop of Chicago*, 440 U.S. 490 (1979); *The Matter of St. John's Preparatory School and Lay Faculty Association*, 47 SLRB No. 115 (N.Y. 1988); Charles J. Russo, "*NLRB v. Catholic Bishop of Chicago*: Collective Bargaining in Roman Catholic Secondary Schools Ten Years Later," *Education Law Reporter* 57, 4 (1990): 1113–1121; *South*

Jersey Catholic Sch. Teachers Org. v. St. Teresa of the Infant Jesus Elementary Sch., 696 A.2d 709 (N.J. 1997); United States Catholic Conference, *Economic Justice for All: Pastoral Letter on Catholic Social Teaching and the United States Economy* (Washington, DC: USCC, 1986).

Charles J. Russo

Come, Follow Me

A popular kindergarten through eighth grade catechetical program during the 1990s produced by Benziger Publishing Co. The series had two versions, *Come, Follow Me I*, which was issued in the early 1990s, and *Come, Follow Me II*, the series for the second half of the decade.

Come, Follow Me was an integrated K–8 program, designed to invite students to follow Jesus Christ as disciples. The program was organized to achieve four objectives: religious literacy, which consisted of knowing the basic facts of the Catholic faith tradition, such as terminology, Scripture, doctrines, and history; a sense of wonder about God, life, and the mysteries of faith; a vision of the Christian life to guide their daily living; and a commitment to putting their faith in action. Lastly, the program sought to create in the student a sense of religious imagination, knowing and owning the tradition well enough to apply it creatively to the unique details of the students' lives.

Come, Follow Me materials included the student's textbook, student activity books, a Teacher's Wraparound Edition text, and a Teacher's Support Package. The support package contained materials the teacher could reproduce for classes, like worksheets and maps, and included prayer, liturgy, and music ideas, as well as the answer key to the quizzes in the student activity books.

The series integrated activities, prayers, and practices around key learning objectives. Each year, the educational materials focused on different aspects of the Catholic faith tradition, with the treatment of various aspects of Catholic belief and practice becoming more sophisticated and more obviously linked to the specific developmental issues of the students. This is shown in Table 1, which offers a simple overview of the scope and sequence of the series.

Perhaps the most distinguishing feature of the *Come, Follow Me* series is the use of the Catechism of the Catholic Church as the chief source for content material in the textbooks. The entire series is cross-indexed with the Catechism and went through an elaborate evaluation process for conformity and consistency with the Catechism. The evaluation was conducted by the Office of the Catechism at the United States Conference of Catholic Bishops (USCCB), which checked the materials for accuracy and completion in presenting the Catholic faith.

Another unique feature of *Come, Follow Me* is the amount of space in the texts devoted to the education of religion teachers. The emphasis on teacher education or formation was a response to the realization in the 1980s and 1990s that growing numbers of women and men teaching the Catholic faith in schools and parishes had weak religious upbringings. Materials focused on teacher education were embedded in the Teacher's Wraparound Edition. The educator's manual had the student's text placed in smaller print in the center of the page, with lesson plan suggestions for the teacher, as well as the teacher education materials, wrapped around the student materials.

For instance, in Chapter 23 of the eighth grade teacher's manual, the learning objective is focused on the Church's continual need to reform itself. As part of this

Table 1
Curriculum Sequence: *Come, Follow Me*

Grade Level	Some Themes for the Year
Kindergarten	Focused on creation, especially the creation of humans, and the natural curiosity and wonder children have for the world.
One	Concentrated on knowing Jesus and celebrating the Kingdom of God.
Two	Explored the Eucharist, the nature of celebration, the saving actions of Jesus, and the moral choices of following Jesus.
Three	Emphasized the Church as the sign of God's Kingdom, the mission and structure of the Church, and Christian heroes (especially the saints).
Four	Explored issues of justice and fair play, a covenant relationship with God, and responsibility to the community.
Five	Studied the Christian heritage of belief by presenting the Creed, the sacraments, and Church history.
Six	Explained the role of the Word of God in a believer's life, highlighting the nature and purpose of salvation history.
Seven	Highlighted the differences between the Jesus of history and the Christ of faith as demonstrated in the Scriptures, the Church's teachings, and the witness of faithful disciples.
Eight	Delved into the issues of a young teen's universe, exploring them from the perspective of the Church's collective experience, wisdom, and mission.

theme, the Protestant Reformation is explored. At the bottom of the page, a special teacher's section called Catechist Background provided basic information that teachers with a strong religious education would have known in previous generations. For this particular chapter, the teacher is informed of the contributing factors leading up to the Reformation: the huge number of deaths in the Black Plague, when bubonic plague swept through Europe, and the condemnation by Renaissance humanists, like Erasmus, of the Catholic hierarchy for discouraging people from reading the Scriptures in order to keep the people ignorant and obedient to the Church. The teacher education section also had a Vocabulary Development section, which defined terms like Christendom, Black Death, and superstitious.

The *Come, Follow Me* program is the fourth generation of religious education materials to be released by Benziger Publishing since the conclusion of the Second Vatican Council in the mid-1960s. The Benziger catechetical programs, released on a ten-year cycle, include:

1. *Word and Worship* (1960s)
2. *The Word Is Life* (1970s)
3. *In Christ Jesus* (1980s)
4. *Come, Follow Me* (1990s)
5. *Christ Jesus the Way* (2000–2010)

Bengizer launches a new series every ten years to rework its educational materials in light of new church documents that are constantly being issued by the Vatican or the USCCB. Each new catechetical series presents the Catholic tradition in light of the new insights of these documents, as well as new movements within the Catholic Church, such as the Rite of Christian Initiation of Adults (RCIA) in the 1970s or the family ministry movement in the 1980s. Another factor creating the need for a new series is changes in pedagogical theory, such as an emphasis on storytelling, arts, and crafts or a new awareness of how to reach students with different learning styles. *See also*: Catholic publishers; *Guiding Growth in Christian Social Living*.

Further Reading: Benziger Publishing Co., 15319 Chatsworth Street, P.O. Box 9509, Mission Hills, CA 91395-9509. Web page: http://www.mhschool.com/benziger/; John Paul II, *Fidei Depositum*, Apostolic Letter on the Publication of the Catechism of the Catholic Church. Rome: Libreria Editrice Vaticana, October 11, 1992; John Paul II, *Laetamur Magnopere*, Apostolic Letter Promulgating the Latin Typical Edition of The Catechism of the Catholic Church (Rome: Libreria Editrice Vaticana, August 15, 1997); United States Catholic Conference, *Policies and Guidelines for Use of the Catechism* (Washington, DC: USCC, July 1994); United States Catholic Conference, *Revised Statement of Principles and Guidelines for Use of the Catechism* (Washington, DC: USCC, October 1996).

Mark S. Markuly

Commission on American Citizenship

The Commission on American Citizenship was a unique collaboration between the Vatican, the Catholic University of America (CUA), and the American Catholic hierarchy. In 1938, on the occasion of the golden anniversary of the establishment of the Catholic University of America, Pope Pius XI sent a letter to the American Catholic hierarchy urging them to take a greater role in "guarding the natural and supernatural heritage of man." The bishops chose to interpret this charge as a call to promote the Christian concept of citizenship and directed CUA to develop a comprehensive series of textbooks to be introduced into the Catholic school curriculum across the United States.

From this ambitious beginning emerged the Commission on American Citizenship. To head the commission, the bishops chose two social scientists from the CUA faculty: Msgrs. George Johnson and Francis J. Haas. Starting in 1938 and over the next thirty years, the commission developed a comprehensive curriculum on citizenship entitled *Guiding Growth in Christian Social Living* and reached millions of young Catholics with a series of "Faith and Freedom" textbooks.

The commission also sponsored other educational activities to encourage good citizenship. For example, the commission published weekly newspapers for students under the titles of *Young Catholic Messenger*, *Junior Catholic Messenger*, and *Our Little Messenger*. It also sponsored Catholic Civics Clubs for students in the seventh and eighth grades.

Johnson was primarily responsible for the commission's agenda. He worked closely with the staff to develop themes of emphasis and then turned over specific assignments to individual staff members. Staff members would, for example, use the themes to develop outlines for textbooks and select a few stories or illustrations to support their claim that the outline would develop the theme. Johnson reviewed the outlines, discussed them with his colleagues, and then turned them over to outside curriculum specialists for comment. Johnson's mark was evident on every phase of the project.

The materials prepared by Johnson and his staff had an enormous impact on the content of the Catholic curriculum right from the start. In 1938, for example, the commission reported that it was sending citizenship information to classroom weeklies "which reach over 700,000 school children weekly and preparations are underway for the writing and distribution of textbooks and other materials to effectuate the principles of Christian Democracy" (Maria Giovanni Vidoni, SND, "Monsignor George Johnson: His Principles and Their Application to the Curriculum of the Catholic Schools," Unpublished master's thesis, Catholic University of America, 1952, pp. 91–93). The textbooks were enormously popular. By early 1944 the first two volumes were ready, and eventually the eight-volume series was adopted by more than 5,000 of the 8,000 Catholic parochial schools in the United States at that time.

The success of the commission was evident long before the sales records on the textbooks were available, however. "It has been the hope of the commission from the beginning," wrote Haas in 1943, "that its work would help to make social education a living moral force and would take Catholic education far toward the goal set for it by the bishops of the United States. It is now our belief that we have accomplished a large part of our work" (Thomas Blantz, *A Priest in Public Service: Francis J. Haas and The New Deal* [Notre Dame IN: University of Notre Dame Press, 1982], p. 177).

The work of the commission also was enhanced with the success of Johnson's 1943 book, *Better Men for Better Times*, a scholarly volume published by the Catholic University of America Press. The book was written for Catholic educators and encouraged them to develop children's basic relationship with themselves and with others. Although intended for a narrow audience, *Better Men for Better Times* became a best-seller when it caught the attention of David Lawrence, who reviewed the book in his popular weekly magazine, *United States News*. Orders poured in from thousands of individuals in the armed forces and other organizations, and the book became a best-seller for the university press.

The sudden death of George Johnson in June 1944 was a shock to all and left a void at the commission. Johnson's friend and colleague, Francis J. Haas, had recently been appointed bishop of Grand Rapids and was not able to assume more responsibilities for the commission. Msgr. Frederick Hochwalt, one of Johnson's assistants and later director of the National Catholic Educational Association, would assume the directorship of the commission. Msgrs. Thomas O. Martin and Joseph A. Graham would succeed Hochwalt.

The onset of the Cold War in the late 1940s and early 1950s made the work of the commission all the more important as a centerpiece of the Catholic school curriculum. That work was best expressed in the sixty-three volumes in the "Faith and Freedom" series. The first two readers had been published in 1942 with a modest print run of 10,000 copies. Twenty years later, however, sales had increased to 3.6 million volumes per year and were being used in 11,000 Catholic elementary schools across the United States.

Perhaps the most extraordinary aspect of the evolution of this textbook series is that the five-dozen volumes were written and edited largely by a tight-knit team of sister educators who worked for the commission. Sr. M. Marguerite SSND, wrote the volumes for the primary grades, Sr. Thomas Aquinas, OP, wrote for the middle grades, and Srs. Mary Charlotte and Mary Brendan, RSM, wrote the readers for the upper grades. Other sister educators were called on to write teachers' manuals, and all these women religious were assisted by two laywomen, Mary Synon and Katherine Rankin.

The sisters more than reached their goal of producing textbooks that built "an enlightened, contentious citizenship" in the hearts and minds of the nation's Catholic youth.

In tandem with the Faith and Freedom textbooks were the commission-sponsored "Catholic Civic Clubs of America." The purpose of these clubs was to provide opportunities for seventh and eighth grade students to apply the principles of good citizenship that they had learned through the textbooks. The commission published and distributed a handbook on how to organize and run these clubs and provided monthly supplemental civics instruction in the pages of the *Young Catholic Messenger.* Like the readers, the clubs became very popular. From a few dozen clubs in 1940, the number climbed to 5,000 by 1965, and they were in every diocese in the United States. Chicago alone had nearly 200 clubs.

The work of the commission declined in the years after Vatican II. Catholic parochial schools closed in unprecedented numbers, and the need for extensive civics instruction among young Catholics seemed less compelling in the years after the election of John F. Kennedy as the first Catholic president. The work of the commission from 1938 to the late 1960s was an important chapter in the evolution of the American Catholic school curriculum. *See also*: Catholic publishers; Johnson, George.

Further Reading: Harold A. Buetow, *Of Singular Benefit: The Story of U.S. Catholic Education* (New York: Macmillan, 1970); *The Commission on American Citizenship of the Catholic University of America* (Washington, DC: Catholic University of America Press, 1946).

Timothy Walch

Common school

The common school is an institution whose history is inextricably connected with the man known as the "Father of the Common School," Horace Mann. It originated in Massachusetts with the entry of Mann into the position of secretary of the State Board of Education in 1837.

The common school originated in a society that was faced with rapidly increasing urbanization, which resulted from industrialization, and the accelerating numbers of immigrants and migrants from rural areas. Crime and poverty were on the rise; leading Whigs in Massachusetts were alarmed at the number and depth of social problems that they saw occurring in their state. Gov. Dwight convinced Horace Mann to give up a promising political career and assume the position of secretary of the board, thence to lead the movement that has been termed the "common school crusade."

The common school was to be common to rich and poor, boy and girl, alike. It called for the entrance of the state into what had been heretofore a local affair, primary or elementary schooling. Supported by taxes on property, it established a common curriculum for all. Its primary focus was on moral education, which would be based on the reading of the King James version of the Bible (without note or comment), and the "common core" truths of Christianity. Mann and those who agreed with him argued that by avoiding the divisive effects of sectarianism, the common school could bring unity to a society beset with rifts of separation and division. Being universal, the common school was a necessary instrument for the survival, prosperity, and progress of a republican government. It would eliminate poverty and crime and would ensure social stability and harmony. In Mann's words, it would be the "great equalizer of the conditions of men—the balance-wheel of the social machinery" (Mann in Cremin, 1964, p. 87). The common school would lead to the perfectibility of human life and institutions; "there was no end to the social good which might be derived from the common school" (Cremin, 1964, p. 9).

There were other ardent advocates of the common school ideology in the mid-nineteenth century, men such as Henry Barnard in Connecticut, Thaddeus Stevens in Pennsylvania, James G. Carter and Horace Bushnell in Massachusetts, and Calvin Wiley in North Carolina. The movement also had its opponents, with some opposed on religious grounds and others who favored local autonomy. As a form of conservative reform the common school movement reflected a Whig mentality. Its moral position stemmed from Unitarian beliefs.

As an instrument of pan-Protestantism, common school ideology and practice were at odds with Catholic views on education. Controlled and administered in the early years by Protestants, the movement swept across the country (in the South after the Civil War). The attention given education by plenary and provincial councils is testament to the concern American bishops felt over the common school, leading, in some instances, to prohibitions for Catholics from attending these supposed nondenominational schools. (The Protestant dominance in the common school was to be replaced after the Civil War in many areas of the nation by secular ascendancy.)

Many Americans in the past and present attribute the existence and progress of the nation to the influence and presence of the common school. For many, it is the symbol of patriotism, support of which makes one a good and loyal American. *See also*: Bible-reading in public schools; Mann, Horace.

Further Reading: Lawrence A. Cremin, ed., *The Republic and the School: Horace Mann on the Education of Free Men* (New York: Teachers College Press, 1957); Ellwood P. Cubberley, *Public Education in the United States* (Boston: Houghton Mifflin, 1919); Michael B. Katz, *The Irony of Early School Reform: Educational Innovations in Mid-Nineteenth Century Massachusetts* (Boston: Beacon Press, 1968); Horace Mann, *Lectures on Education* (Boston: Ide and Dutton, 1855); Horace Mann, *Annual Reports on Education (First through Twelfth)* (Boston: Dutton and Wentworth, state printers, 1838–1849).

Thomas C. Hunt

Community

The combined manner in which members work, learn, pray, and play together in common is known as community. Strong community life is at the heart of the Catholic school. With a fundamental belief in the dignity of each member, Catholic schools must build and maintain a strong voluntary association of all members based on a common bond of faith, hope, and love. Interdependence, reconciliation, and hospitality are hallmarks of the Catholic community. Community is a reality to be lived in every aspect of Catholic school life. Building and living in community are prime and explicit goals of the Catholic school.

Research on effective schools points to a strong sense of community as having a positive effect on the quality of life for teachers and students as well as everyone involved in the school. German sociologist Ferdinand Tonnies provides two ways to look at personal interactions in a social setting: Gesellschaft and Gemeinschaft. Tonnies describes casual, expedient relationships as Gesellschaft. Such relationships are often temporary and convenient. Gemeinschaft relationships occur when people feel they belong to a community of people who share values and traditions. Gemeinschaft relationships are close, intentional, and resistant to change. Both types of relationships exist in a Catholic school. Gesellschaft, or associative, relationships are evident in the administrative regulations and norms of the school. They provide for the smooth functioning of the day-to-day operations of the school. The Catholic school community also promotes closer, more personal (Gemeinschaft) relationships. The relationships that exist in the Catholic school community are the result of voluntary membership in a group of people who share values and traditions. The community formed in Catholic schools exhibits Gemeinschaft relationships. The Catholic school rituals, symbols, and traditions promote a sense of belonging. This deeper, more personal relationship builds community—an attribute of effective schools.

Social researcher James Coleman (1996) identified key components of community as they relate to schools. Coleman recognized Catholic schools as "functional communities." Within the framework of life in the Catholic school, Coleman cites qualities of value consistency and functional community. Value consistency is present in a community that shares common values and exposure to a particular environment. Value consistency can be found in any school with common values and a particular educational philosophy. A school can have value consistency without being a functional community. In addition to exhibiting value consistency, researchers found that Catholic schools operate as functional communities. Functional communities seek to effect a particular outcome. In a school that is a functional community, special, close relationships exist between students and those whom they know and to whom they relate both in the school and outside it. The adults know each other and each other's children. The values children learn at school are also the values of the adults in the community.

A carefully woven fabric of relationships between children, between children and adults (teachers and parents), and between adults is created in a functional community. These strong support relationships produce an effect Coleman calls social capital. Social capital is an intangible benefit of a functional community. It is the empowerment of individuals that develops as a result of the close relationships between persons. Coleman identified the Catholic school as a functional community that benefits from the strong social capital it generates. Specifically, the actual social relationships between parents of different children, the parents' relationship with the school, and the relationships among the individuals within the school contribute to the social capital. Social capital is recognized as a key component of Catholic school effectiveness.

The Second Vatican Council stressed the critical role of community in the life of the Church and redefined Catholic schools as essentially a community of people rather than simply an institution. This calls the Catholic school to integrate all persons into the mystical body of Christ. Recent church teachings on education emphasize the necessity of collaboration between school personnel and pastors, parents, and the larger community in the forming of a truly Christian community. This includes collaboration with public schools in areas such as technology and curriculum. It is the task of Catholic school leadership to develop curricula that welcome and support diverse cultural and economic populations, as well as students with special needs and exceptionalities. This is an extension of the Catholic school mission to be of service to others. School activities must encourage cultural awareness, ecumenism, and reconciliation. With a focus on the dignity of each individual, a welcoming spirit, and an attitude of compassion, the Catholic school seeks to strengthen its sense of community and build the People of God, the Church on earth.

The Catholic school is unique because it is a faith community within a learning community. Grounded in the teachings of the Catholic Church, the members of the Catholic school strive to become the Church for one another and for others. The vision of the Church on earth provides a powerful bond for members of the Catholic school community. Mutual commitment, feeling part of something greater than oneself, and sharing hopes and values all contribute to the strong collaboration that is identified with Catholic schools. Often students participate in service activities as a tangible way of expressing these values. By being of service to others within the school, parish, or larger community, children are able to see their faith in action and contribute to the strength of the school community. *See also*: *Catholic Schools and the Common Good*; Coleman, James S.; *To Teach as Jesus Did*.

Further reading: Anthony S. Bryk, Valerie E. Lee, and Peter B. Holland, *Catholic Schools and the Common Good* (Cambridge: Harvard University Press, 1993); Maria J. Ciriello, ed., *Formation and Development of Catholic School Leaders: The Principal as Spiritual Leader* (Washington, DC: United States Catholic Conference, 1996); James Coleman, "Schools and Communities," in Maria J. Ciriello, ed., *Formation and Development of Catholic School Leaders: The Principal as Spiritual Leader* (Washington, DC: United States Catholic Conference, 1996): 119–125; John J. Convey, *Catholic Schools Make a Difference: Twenty-five Years of Research* (Washington, DC: National Catholic Educational Association, 1992); Thomas C. Hunt, Thomas E. Oldenski, and Theodore J. Wallace, eds., *Catholic School Leadership: An Invitation to Lead* (London and New York: Falmer Press, 2000).

Louise P. Moore

Computer accessibility

Computer accessibility and use in Catholic schools have followed the pattern of society at large. In recent years, Catholic schools have dramatically improved computer accessibility in classrooms, media centers, and administrative offices.

Until 1995, large-scale data about computer accessibility were unavailable. Beginning in 1995, the National Catholic Educational Association (NCEA) and the National Center for Education Statistics (NCES) began acquiring data on a regular basis to track the accessibility and use of different kinds of technology in K–12 schools nationwide. Several measures of availability have been compiled, based on averages or ratios and location and intended use of the hardware.

In 1995, Catholic schools were among the leaders of private schools in the mean numbers of computers available for either instructional or administrative use. In the Catholic sector, there were, on the average, thirty-one computers in Catholic schools, lagging only slightly behind the private nonsectarian schools, which reported a mean of thirty-two computers. However, both of these groups enjoyed nearly double the number of computers available in other religious schools, whose mean number of computers was only sixteen. When compared with the seventy-two computers per school in the public school system, however, Catholic schools (and all private schools) were significantly behind.

When the total enrollments in schools are taken into consideration, the Catholic schools made a less respectable representation. There were, on the average, about ten students per computer in the K–12 Catholic schools, slightly behind the nine-to-one ratio enjoyed by other religious schools and substantially worse than that of nonsectarian schools, which reported about six students per computer. Researchers have suggested that the ideal ratio would be four or five students per instructional computer.

According to data compiled by NCEA during the 1994–1995 academic year, over two-thirds of Catholic elementary classrooms had computers, and a typical classroom had two computers. In addition, approximately 83 percent of U.S. Catholic elementary schools had at least one computer lab available for student use. Those in the mid-eastern section of the country were most apt to have at least one lab, with 89 percent reporting one or more labs, whereas only 79 percent of those in the Southeast had them. The typical computer lab had eighteen computers, and students spent, on the average, about fifty-one minutes per week in the lab. Similar data for the secondary schools were not available.

In only two years, the percentage of Catholic elementary schools with computer labs had grown to 87 percent. The number of computers in the typical lab had risen to twenty, and students spent an average of fifty-two minutes per week in the lab. There was a more dramatic increase in computer accessibility within classrooms. In just two years, the percentage of classrooms with computers available had increased from 68 percent to 75 percent. Again, most of those classrooms had two computers.

By the 1998–1999 academic year, 90 percent of the schools had computer labs, with extraordinary growth in the New England states, where 96 percent of schools reported the presence of at least one computer lab. Across the nation, lab size remained fairly constant, with about twenty computers per lab; however, average time spent in the lab increased to about sixty-three minutes per student per week. Furthermore, the average number of computers per classroom had risen from two to three.

During that same year, K–12 Catholic schools nationwide reported an average of forty-nine computers per building for either administrative or instructional use, an increase of over 50 percent from three years previous. This number was more than double the average number of computers in other religious schools (twenty-four), but it lagged behind the number of computers available in nonsectarian schools (fifty-three). Of these computers, most were used for instructional purposes, with Catholic schools taking the lead in the proportion designated for instructional use. Nearly 84 percent of computers in Catholic schools were for academic purposes, whereas 79 percent of those in other religious schools and 74 percent of those in nonsectarian schools were so designated.

When ratios of numbers of computers to total enrollments in the schools were taken into account, again Catholic schools were less well represented. Among Catholic schools, there were seven students per computer overall and eight students per instructional computer. While these ratios were approximately the same as those in other religious schools (seven students per computer and nine students per instructional computer), they paled in comparison with the ratios in nonsectarian private schools, which reported four students per computer and six students per instructional computer. Public schools also boasted a six-to-one ratio of students to instructional computer.

According to a survey done for NCEA by Quality Education Data (QED), by the 2001–2002 academic year, there were, on the average, 98.5 instructional computers per Catholic school and 18.9 administrative computers per Catholic school. NCES indicated that in that same year, the typical public school had 124 instructional computers. The ratio of students per instructional computer remained at eight to one. Additionally, about 6 percent of Catholic schools reported using handheld computing devices such as Palm, iPAQ, and Visors for either teaching or administration. Data gathered by NCEA in 2001 indicated that 89 percent of elementary classrooms had computers, and the typical elementary classroom had two computers.

Between 1995 and 1998, the percentage of Catholic schools with Internet access increased dramatically. In 1995, 35 percent of all Catholic schools had at least some

Internet access within their buildings, but only 4 percent of classrooms had Internet access. By 1998, about 80 percent of Catholic schools had Internet access, and the percentage of classrooms with Internet access had increased to 27 percent. By 2000, according to QED, nearly all Catholic schools had Internet access in computer labs and/or media centers, and 84 percent of classrooms had connections. In comparison, in the public sector, by the year 2000, 98 percent of all schools had Internet access, and 77 percent of all instructional rooms were Internet-accessible.

In 2001–2002, QED reported that 98 percent of Catholic schools provided Internet access, with 76 percent of classrooms having Internet access. (This percentage was significantly smaller than the 76 percent of classrooms reported to be connected to the Web in 2000 and was not explained.) Additionally, 69 percent of *all* computers in Catholic schools were connected to the Internet by that time. However, NCEA's 2001–2002 survey of Catholic elementary and secondary schools found that only about 85 percent of Catholic schools had Internet access, with those in New England least apt to provide connections. As in 1999–2000, NCEA noted that not every diocese provided this information. By comparison, in the *Digest of Education Statistics, 2002*, NCES reported that during the 2001–2002 academic year, 99 percent of public schools had Internet access, with 85 percent of classrooms having at least some access. In a different survey (*Internet Access in U.S. Public Schools, Fall 2001*) NCES reported that 87 percent of classrooms had Internet access.

This pattern of increases in computer hardware in Catholic schools will likely continue. A 1999 survey of administrators in Catholic schools found that they planned to purchase an average of slightly more than nine computers each year for the next two years. Although E-Rate funding cannot be utilized for such purchases, some schools have reported using moneys saved in telecommunications costs to offset expenditures for computer hardware.

Catholic schools have utilized a mix of platforms, with the predominant platform being Windows-based. By 2000, on the average, the ratio of Windows-based to Apple-brand computers was approximately three to two. This larger percentage of Windows computers was prevalent for both administrative and instructional purposes. By 2001–2002, the Windows:Apple ratio had widened to five to three.

Not only have Catholic schools enjoyed a respectable record in terms of total numbers of computers and ratio of students per computer, but they also have kept up-to-date with hardware, replacing the outdated hardware as quickly as possible.

By 2000, schools had more PowerMacs, G3s, and iMacs for instructional purposes (with about twenty-four machines per school) than they did Macintosh machines with older processors (about sixteen per school). By 2001–2002, there were more than twice as many newer Macs (about twenty-three) used for instructional purposes per school as there were older Macs (about ten). Among Windows-platform machines being utilized for instruction, the newer machines also predominated, with about two and one-half times as many Pentium-processor machines in use as there were 486 or older machines in 2000. By the 2001–2002 academic year, that ratio had increased even more, with about forty-two newer Windows-based machines per school for instruction, compared with about thirteen older Windows-based machines. *See also*: E-Rate; Internet accessibility; Telecommunications.

Further Reading: Sheila Heaviside and Elizabeth Farris, *Advanced Telecommunications in U.S. Private Schools, K–12, Fall 1995* (NCES Rep. No. 97394) (Washington, DC: U.S. Department of Education, National Center for Education Statistics, 1997); Robert Kealey, *Balance*

Sheet for Catholic Elementary Schools: 2001 Income and Expenses (Washington, DC: National Catholic Educational Association, 2001); Dale McDonald, *United States Catholic Elementary and Secondary Schools 1998–1999: The Annual Statistical Report on Schools, Enrollment, and Staffing* (Washington, DC: National Catholic Educational Association, 1999); Dale McDonald, *United States Catholic Elementary and Secondary Schools 1999–2000: The Annual Statistical Report on Schools, Enrollment, and Staffing* (Washington, DC: National Catholic Educational Association, 2000); Dale McDonald, *United States Catholic Elementary and Secondary Schools 2001–2002: The Annual Statistical Report on Schools, Enrollment, and Staffing* (Washington, DC: National Catholic Educational Association, 2002); Basmat Parsad, Rebecca Skinner, and Elizabeth Farris, *Advanced Telecommunications in U.S. Private Schools: 1998–99* (NCES Rep. No. 2001-037) (Washington, DC: U.S. Department of Education, National Center for Education Statistics, 2001); Thomas Snyder and Charlene Hoffman, *Digest of Education Statistics 2002* (NCES Rep. No. 2003-060) (Washington, DC: U.S. Department of Education, National Center for Education Statistics, 2003); Terian Tyre, *The State of Technology in Catholic Schools* (Dayton, OH: Peter Li, 2000, 2002).

Jeanne Hagelskamp, SP

Confraternity of Christian Doctrine (CCD)

The organizational structure beginning in the sixteenth century that provided religious education for those normally denied an opportunity to learn about the Catholic faith. The CCD provided the first Sunday schools and served as a predecessor to Catholic schools. The Confraternity began to lose its prominence in the late 1950s, when the catechetical renewal in Europe was brought to the United States. After Vatican II, the ministry of catechesis or religious education began to take on new forms and go by new names like Parish School of Religion (PSR).

If still used, CCD now stands for the parish religious education programs offered to youth attending public schools. But, through most of its history, the CCD provided instruction for children and adults. Laity also did the majority of the teaching in the CCD, with planning and administration conducted by clergy and religious.

The confraternity began in 1536 in Milan, Italy. A young priest, Castello de Castellano, began setting up schools of trained and zealous lay cathechists, with the goal of providing religious education for children, youth, and uneducated adults, especially those in poor neighborhoods. By 1597, St. Dorothea was already offering other elementary subjects with the religious instruction offered to poor children in Rome through the CCD, creating a prototype of the Catholic school.

Castellano's schools of religion were in response to the Protestant Reformation and the religious illiteracy of medieval Europe, which reached a low point in the late fourteenth and fifteenth centuries. When the Council of Trent (1545–1563) issued the *Catechism of the Council of Trent* in response to Martin Luther's and other reformers' catechisms, the Church began an era of focusing on religious instruction through books, with the CCD providing the educators and educational structure. The more ancient method of religious formation known as catechesis, which was rediscovered in the twentieth century, had provided a more holistic religious formation, mostly through the force of a community united in liturgical worship and a shared life of faith.

The CCD grew in stature and importance in the Catholic Church when St. Charles Borromeo was named archbishop of Milan in 1565 and began organizing Castellano's religious education effort. Borromeo wrote an important guide for the Confraternity.

The guide set the template for the CCD by setting down principles and practical methods teachers could use and outlining an organizational structure for the ministry.

When the Confraternity made it to Rome in 1536, it became popular almost immediately, attracting the attention of future saints, like Philip Neri and Robert Bellarmine. In 1571, St. Pius V ordered the establishment of the Confraternity throughout the world, and in 1607, Pope Paul V gave his full official approval to laity teaching in the CCD schools, granting spiritual benefits to those participating in its work.

Despite the strong start and committed organizational efforts, the CCD has often had a difficult time retaining its place of importance in the Church's activities. From the beginning, one of the biggest challenges has been the image of the lay catechist. Through the Middle Ages the tradition had grown that only priests should be allowed to teach doctrine. Several synods and Popes tried to defend the mission of the lay religious educator, but, Pope St. Pius X (1903–1914), often known as the "Pope of the Catechism," elevated most effectively the dignity of the lay catechist. Pius X's encyclical, *Acerbo nimis*, "On Teaching Christian Doctrine," has been called the Magna Carta of the confraternity. It elaborates many practices still governing parish formation programs, such as the practice of one hour of instruction and preparation for the sacraments beginning around the age of seven.

In the United States the growth of the Confraternity of Christian Doctrine was slower in development. The first bishop in the United States, John Carroll, was committed to Catholic education for youth but focused on the building of schools and colleges. The first reference to the CCD in American documents appeared in documents of the Second Plenary Council of Baltimore in 1866. The bishops demanded that the CCD be set up when establishing Catholic schools was not possible. This commitment to developing the CCD was reaffirmed again at the Third Plenary Council of Baltimore in 1884, which also established the Baltimore Catechism. Despite heightening the awareness of the need for religious instruction by the councils, the first official parish CCD did not open in the United States until 1902, at Our Lady of Good Counsel in New York City.

The major American force in establishing the CCD was Rev. Edwin V. O'Hara, a priest from Eugene, Oregon, who popularized religious vacation schools, which he began in his parish in 1921. O'Hara was named bishop of Great Falls, Montana, in 1930 and five years later became chair of the Episcopal Committee of the CCD, which founded the National Center of the CCD in Washington, DC.

Under O'Hara's guidance, *The Manual of the Parish Confraternity of Christian Doctrine*, originally published in 1937, became the organizational manifesto of the Confraternity. By 1954, the 122-page booklet offered a complete overview for structuring a parish CCD. The manual included specific suggestions for preparing teachers, which initiated the tradition of providing formal training for lay catechists.

Another dynamic leader of the CCD in the United States was Rev. Joseph B. Collins, who directed the national office for twenty-five years. Much of the history of the CCD was penned by Collins, as was the tradition of providing practical materials for teachers. Under his leadership the CCD heightened its influence in American Catholic life and established more sophisticated teaching materials, including teacher manuals. *See also*: Parish School of Religion; Religion, teaching of; Total Catholic Education.

Further Reading: Joseph B. Collins, "The Beginnings of the CCD in Europe and Its Modern Revival"; "Religious Education and CCD in the United States: Early Years (1902–1935)," in Michael Warren, ed., *Sourcebook for Modern Catechetics*, Vol. 1 (Winona, MN: St. Mary's Press, 1983); Confraternity of Christian Doctrine, *The Confraternity Comes of Age* (Paterson, NJ: Confraternity, 1956); Confraternity of Christian Doctrine, *Manual of the Parish Confraternity of Christian Doctrine* (Paterson, NJ: Confraternity, 1954); Anne M. Mongoven, AM, *The Prophetic Spirit of Catechesis: How We Share the Fire in Our Hearts* (New York: Paulist Press, 2000).

Mark S. Markuly

Congregation for Catholic Education

The Vatican office charged with administrative oversight for Catholic schools, colleges, universities, and seminaries worldwide. Vatican offices are commonly referred to as curial offices and the members as belonging to the Curia. The Latin cognate (*curia*, meaning "care") suggests that curial officials are charged to care for a particular area of administration. Vatican departments are known as congregations. Hence, the Congregation for Catholic Education is a department of the Vatican administrative organization whose focus is the care of Catholic education in all of its institutionalized forms.

The official delineation of the hierarchical structure of the Roman Catholic Church can be found in the annual publication *Annuario Pontificio* (Citta Del Vaticano: Libreria Editrice Vaticana, 2001). Published every year in Rome with continually updated information, the *Annuario Pontificio* lists the offices as well as the names of the current officeholders for all Vatican departments. Although the Italian title roughly translates as "Pontifical Annual" or "Pontifical Yearbook," it is simply known as the *Annuario*. Since the text of the *Annuario* is by custom written in Italian, the Congregation for Catholic Education is listed as the *Congregazione Per L'Educazione Cattolica* (*Dei Seminari e Degli Istituti Di Studi*), which translates as the Congregation for Catholic Education, for Seminaries and Other Institutes of Study. The Latin title for this congregation, often used in official congregational documents, is *Congregatio de Institutione Catholica de Seminariis atque Studiorum Instituti*.

The *Annuario* indicates that the Congregation has had a long, historical development. Initially concerned only with seminary education and the formation of priests, its influence and concern grew over the years to embrace Catholic universities and, eventually, Catholic elementary and secondary education. This rich history can be traced by analysis of church documents that outline the development of the Congregation. Eight documents in particular are cited in the *Annuario* as having relevance: five Apostolic Constitutions, two documents issued *motu propio* by Popes, and one conciliar decree from the Second Vatican Council. The Apostolic Constitutions are *Immensa*, promulgated by Pope Sixtus V, January 22, 1588; *Quod divina sapientia* by Leo XII, August 28, 1824; *Sapienti consilio* by Pius X, June 29, 1908; *Regimini Ecclesiae Universae* by Paul VI, August 15, 1967; and *Pastor Bonus* by John Paul II, June 28, 1988. The two documents issued *motu propio* are *Seminaria clericorum* by Benedict XV, November 4, 1915, and *Cum Nobis* by Pius XII, November 4, 1941. The only conciliar decree is *Optatam totius*, a document of the Second Vatican Council, published by Paul VI on October 28, 1965. All of these documents and their contribution to the development of the Congregation are discussed in detail in the *Handbook of Research on Catholic Education* (Hunt, Joseph, and Nuzzi, 2001, pp. 1–25).

The Congregation is currently structured in three separate divisions or offices: seminaries, Catholic universities and pontifical faculties, and parochial and diocesan schools. While the Congregation clearly possesses a form of universal oversight for all matters pertaining to Catholic education, several distinctions limit its jurisdiction. In particular, educational institutions in developing countries and those found throughout the Oriental churches are excluded from its purview. Developing countries, still considered mission fields, are typically given special attention at Vatican offices and fall completely under the jurisdiction of another Vatican office, the Congregation for the Evangelization of People. Oriental churches, because of their unique status, typically have all of their Vatican business handled by a separate office, the Congregation for Oriental Churches.

The Congregation for Catholic Education also has a special authority over, and interest in, what are known as ecclesiastical or pontifical faculties. These are institutions or even departments within institutions that have a direct, canonical relationship to the Vatican and grant pontifical degrees. While very often housed at universities, these ecclesiastical faculties are governed exclusively by church law. There are over 100 of these faculties in existence today, including, in the United States, programs at Berkeley, California; Weston, Massachusetts; Mundelein, Illinois; St. Mary's, Baltimore; the Josephinum, Columbus, Ohio; and the Marianum in Dayton, Ohio. The Catholic University of America in Washington, D.C., also has an ecclesiastical faculty. The distinction between Catholic universities, which enjoy a certain degree of autonomy and self-governance, on the one hand, and ecclesiastical faculties, which have a much closer, direct link to the Holy See, on the other, is important. While this Congregation would still claim jurisdiction over Catholic matters at all Catholic institutions of learning, it bears a special responsibility to ecclesiastical faculties. Since intervention into the internal affairs of institutions recognized in civil law is likely to produce protracted litigation, Vatican action is more likely within ecclesiastical faculties.

The school office of the Congregation has been supportive of the mission of K–12 Catholic schools through the publication of various documents for the universal Church, highlighting the unique purpose of Catholic schools and affirming their success. Among these documents are *The Catholic School* (1977), *The Religious Dimension of Education in a Catholic School* (1988), and *The Catholic School on the Threshold of the Third Millennium* (1997), all published by the Congregation in Rome and distributed throughout the world.

Historically, the Congregation has appeared to be more involved in matters pertaining to seminaries and Catholic universities. In the 1980s, the Congregation initiated a worldwide study of seminaries, an effort that is to be repeated in the first decade of the new millennium. The Congregation was also highly involved in the process of writing, revising, and implementing the Apostolic Constitution *Ex Corde Ecclesiae*, promulgated by John Paul II in 1990. *Ex Corde Ecclesiae* was addressed to Catholic colleges and universities and contains a widely discussed and debated norm, requiring Catholic professors of theology to receive a *mandatum* from their local bishop. In 2002–2003, the Congregation circulated a draft of a new church document, detailing the standards of admissibility for candidates to the priesthood. Early reports indicated that the Vatican wanted a new document clearly stating that those with a homosexual orientation were not qualified candidates for the priesthood and that such an orientation would be an impediment to holy orders. This draft has been seen as a reaction to the scandal of sexual abuse that shook the Catholic Church in the United States throughout 2002.

A modicum of supervisory activity directed toward K–12 Catholic schools is found in the Congregation in its collection of school-related data for the *ad limina* visits, required of diocesan bishops every five years. Chapter 10 of the *ad limina* summary deals with all aspects of Catholic education within a diocese, including priestly formation in seminaries, enrollment in Catholic schools, colleges, and universities, and the teaching of religion to students not enrolled in Catholic schools.

The increased number of school mergers and closings in the United States has resulted in an increase in correspondence to the Congregation in recent years. While the majority of these communications request an appeal of the decision of the local bishop, the Congregation does not entertain appeals from individuals or groups who seek to overturn the decisions of a diocesan bishop to close, merge, or move a school. The Christian faithful possess rights in this regard (*Code of Canon Law*, canons 208–222), but appeals of episcopal decisions are made formally to the Apostolic Signatura, the highest church court, not directly to individual congregations.

As of 2004, the head of the Congregation is its Cardinal Prefect, His Eminence Zenon Cardinal Grocholewski. Until December 2003, the secretary of the Congregation was Archbishop Giuseppe Pittau, SJ, who was succeeded by Archibishop J. Michael Miller, CSB. The congregation offices can be found at Piazza Pio XII, #3 at the Vatican. *See also*: *Catholic School on the Threshold of the Third Millennium, The*; *Religious Dimension of Education in a Catholic School, The*; *Catholic School, The*.

Further Reading: *Annuario Pontificio* (Citta' Del Vaticano: Libreria Editrice Vaticana, 2001); *Code of Canon Law* (Washington, DC: Canon Law Society of America, 1983); John Paul II, *Ex Corde Ecclesiae* (Washington, DC: USCC, 1990); Thomas C. Hunt, Ellis A. Joseph, and Ronald J. Nuzzi, eds., *Handbook of Research on Catholic Education* (Westport, CT: Greenwood Press, 2001).

Ronald J. Nuzzi

Congregation for the Doctrine of the Faith

The Congregation for the Doctrine of the Faith (CDF), originally known as the Office of the Inquisition, is one of nine congregations that make up the Roman Curia. According to the Apostolic Constitution *Pastor Bonus* (1988), the role of CDF is first to foster the study of the faith, so that new questions raised by human culture and the sciences may be examined in the light of faith. It is to help the bishops in their role as teachers and defenders of the faith and to safeguard the Church's faith and morals from error. CDF also examines offenses against the faith and serious offenses in behavior or the celebration of the sacraments. It may impose the sanctions of canon law on those who are found at fault (Provost, 1985). Since the work of the CDF is central to the life of the Church, it must often collaborate with the other congregations of the Roman Curia.

The Congregation for the Doctrine of the Faith also has responsibility for processing Privilege of the Faith marriage cases, petitions for dispensations from the vow of celibacy, and dismissal of clerics from ordained ministry. It has also been responsible for issues centering upon abuses within the Sacrament of Penance, including, but not limited to, breaking the seal of confession and allegations of solicitation in the confessional. The practice of assigning ancillary activities, such as those mentioned above, to the various congregations of the Roman Curia is common. In some cases, the congregations attempt to maintain these added duties as a way of enhancing their prestige; at other times, the congregation will attempt passing particular tasks to another congregation within the Curia (Reese, 1996).

The precursor of the Congregation for the Doctrine of the Faith, the Sacred Congregation of the Universal Inquisition, is the oldest of the Curia's nine congregations. There were earlier versions of the Inquisition, the most notorious example being the Spanish Inquisition, which also sought to fight heresy, making liberal use of punishment and torture in order to rehabilitate heretics. The Roman Inquisition, founded by Pope Paul III in 1542, became a serious tool for fighting heresy during the Reformation era. It acted as a centralizing force within the Catholic Church superseding the jurisdiction of the local diocesan bishop. While the Roman Inquisition, like the Spanish Inquisition, made use of corporal punishment, it actually was much more protective of the rights of indicted heretics. According to Bireley (1999), the due process followed by the Roman Inquisition was more enlightened than that practiced in secular courts of the era. Their concern was with those among the baptized who persistently clung to teachings contrary to the Church. The Roman Inquisition was not intended to be a means of forcing conversions from among the Muslim or Jewish peoples.

During the pontificate of Pope Paul IV (1555–1559), the Inquisition was given wide-ranging authority to fight heresy. Paul IV's use of the Inquisition was draconian to many. Refusing to call the Council of Trent back into session, Paul IV pushed his reform agenda through, making use of the Inquisition. His abuse of the Inquisition included raising suspicions of heresy from those who would not follow his lead, such as Cardinal Reginald Pole, and imprisoning others, such as Cardinal Giovanni Morone for his criticism of the treatment of Romans who were accused of heresy. In 1559, the Inquisition was given responsibility for gathering a list of books considered heretical and published it as *The Index of Forbidden Books*. The reaction to Paul IV and the repressive policies of the Inquisition became manifest upon the Pope's death. Protesting Paul IV's policies, Romans rioted and set fire to the offices of the Inquisition, destroying them. The most harmful effects of the Roman Inquisition in the early modern era were the fear it engendered in the faithful and its systemic intimidation of intellectuals.

At the beginning of the twentieth century, the 1917 Code of Canon Law delegated the determination of theological truth to the Supreme Sacred Congregation of the Holy Office. As the Roman Inquisition struggled against heresy in the era of the Counter Reformation, the Holy Office became Pope Pius X's front line against the modernist heresy. One can measure the effectiveness of the Holy Office in countering modernism by examining its fruits. The ecumenical movement was delayed for decades; a number of Spanish, Portuguese, and, later, Italian Catholics were excommunicated for their participation in the Communist Party, and a number of the theologians who were instrumental in formulating the documents of the Second Vatican Council were looked at with suspicion and, in some cases, actively persecuted (Collins, 2000).

The Second Vatican Council called for the reform of the Roman Curia and its various congregations. Pope Paul VI issued the document *Pastor Bonus* which overhauled the Roman Curia, renaming the Holy Office the Congregation for the Doctrine of the Faith. *Pastor Bonus* reconstituted the CDF in order to make it more pastoral. However, the membership of the Curia remained the same and its processes continued to be secretive. Critics often cite the cases of Fr. Charles Curran and Fr. Edward Schillebeeckx as examples of the CDF's repressive policies (Collins, 2000).

In the end, the role of the CDF is to act as a balance between the Church and theologians. The role of the theologian is to explore the limits of theology, while the role of the CDF is to assist the theologian in remaining within the boundaries of the faith. An examination of the history of the CDF demonstrates that at times this relationship between theologians and the CDF has proven to be a difficult balancing act. *See also*: Paul VI, Pope; Vatican Council, II.

Further Reading: Robert Bireley, *The Refashioning of Catholicism: 1450–1700* (Washington, DC: Catholic University of America Press, 1999); Paul Collins, *Upon This Rock* (Victoria, Australia: Melbourne University Press, 2000); John Paul II, "Apostolic Constitution: Pastor Bonus" (1988); James H. Provost, "Commentary on the Hierarchical Constitution of the Church," in James A. Coriden, Thomas J. Green, and Donald E. Heintschel, eds., *The Code of Canon Law: A Text and Commentary* (New York: Paulist Press, 1985); Thomas J. Reese, *Inside the Vatican* (Cambridge: Harvard University Press, 1996).

Anthony J. Dosen, CM

Conscience, formation of

The formation of conscience is one of the primary aims of moral development and is paramount in the religious education efforts of Catholic schools and parishes. The formation of conscience is considered a developmental core throughout Catholic education and, strangely, is almost completely absent from other programs of moral education.

Formation indicates that the conscience under construction requires more than the imparting of information. While a conscience needs to be properly informed and educated, the formation of conscience points to the need for a spiritual foundation of moral education and acknowledges the primary role that spiritual and religious values play in the successful formation of an individual's conscience.

Timothy O'Connell, a contemporary Catholic moral theologian, provides a helpful framework for understanding the formation of conscience that resonates with lived experience and has proven helpful to Catholic educators. O'Connell suggests that there are three different levels of conscience, levels that he has termed conscience/1, conscience/2, and conscience/3 (O'Connell, 1978).

Conscience/1 is a sense that to be human is to be accountable. It assumes that every person is in charge of his or her own life and that there is a desire to pursue a good direction in life. Conscience/2 concentrates more on the discrete values individuals deem important and become those values on which the individuals base their behavior. This aspect of conscience needs nurturing and attention, for this level of conscience is fallible. It can be in error through ignorance, lack of sensitivity, or neglect. Conscience/2 is in need of consultation with family, parents, teachers, the Church, the Scriptures, and moral others. Because of this part of the conscience, one must always be open and in some sense on guard, ready to learn more, develop, nuance a previously held position, and integrate new knowledge into a system of moral reasoning. Thus, assuming responsibility for informing one's own conscience might include regular reading of the Scriptures, prayer, knowledge of the teachings of the Church, and the support and counsel of moral men and women of goodwill.

Conscience/3 galvanizes a person into action based on the judgment finally made. While there is always the humble realization that the conscience may be wrong, conscience/3 serves as the end point of conscience/2, where an individual arrives at a judgment that feels fitting, proper, and responsible, based on the evidence gathered in conscience/2. It is an action that comes directly from the judgment because the person sees the merit in the judgment and embraces it freely. Conscience/3 summons or calls one to do the good one loves and to avoid the opposite evil. This is the reason that educators and theologians speak of "examining one's conscience," or "obeying one's conscience." Conscience/3 has a judgmental capacity to move one to action.

Secular research, especially in the area of psychology, has offered many competing views of conscience formation, moral education, and human development. Some theorists, like Freud, viewed the conscience as under the control of the unconscious and irrational superego. He taught that moral thinking was the result of largely unconscious forces over which an individual had little control. Thus, for Freud, moral thinking was primarily a matter of conditioning and reinforcement. This view of moral development is not unpopular.

On the other hand, Piaget viewed moral maturation as a natural process that paralleled the physical development of the person. As a person ages, argues Piaget, the individual takes on more and more responsibility for behaving morally. Kohlberg elaborated on Piaget's hypothesis and described the moral maturation process in six stages. Kohlberg also relied on the work of John Dewey and took inspiration from the writings of John Mark Baldwin. Both of these authors had emphasized that human beings develop philosophically and psychologically in a progressive fashion.

Kohlberg believed and eventually was able to demonstrate through controlled studies that people progressed in their moral reasoning and in their bases for making ethical judgments through a series of stages. He identified six stages, which could be more generally classified into three levels. Level 1/Pre-Conventional includes the stages (1) obedience and punishment and (2) individualism, instrumentalism, and exchange. Level 2/Conventional includes stages (3) "Good boy-Good girl" and (4) Law and order. Level 3/Post-Conventional includes stages (5) Social Contract and (6) Principled Conscience.

The Church teaches that because Christians have a personal faith relationship with Jesus Christ that is shared by the entire Christian community, access to the spiritual resources of that community is absolutely essential to the formation of their consciences. Christians rightly rely on the community, prayer, study, the Scriptures, wise advice and counsel of friends and family, and an understanding of the teachings of the Church in order to form their conscience properly. In fact, all of Christian education, religious education, and Catholic school education can properly be conceived as a form of postbaptismal formation of conscience. *See also*: Moral education, history of.

Further Reading: Bernard Haring, *Free and Faithful In Christ*, vol. 1 (New York: Seabury Press, 1978); Richard Hersh, *Promoting Moral Growth: From Piaget to Kohlberg* (Prospect Heights, IL: Waveland Press, 1983); Timothy O'Connell, *Principles for a Catholic Conscience* (New York: Doubleday, 1978).

Mary Peter Traviss, OP

Consecrated Persons and Their Mission in Schools

A document written and published by the Congregation for Catholic Education, the Vatican office dealing with all educational matters in the Church, released on October 28, 2002, the thirty-seventh anniversary of the publication of *Gravissimum Educationis*, the Declaration on Christian Education that was one of the official documents emanating from the Second Vatican Council.

The Congregation for Catholic Education published *Consecrated Persons and Their Mission in Schools* (CPMS) as part of its regular oversight and promotion of Catholic education. CPMS represents the most recent official church document that addresses K–12 Catholic education and the first such document of the third millennium of Christianity. For centuries, the Congregation for Catholic Education limited its interest to seminaries, ecclesiastical faculties, and Catholic universities. Only since the 1960s has it turned its attention to Catholic schools at the pre-university level. CPMS is the result of this relatively new solicitude on the part of the Vatican for K–12 Catholic education.

CPMS was promulgated by both chief officers of the Congregation—Zenon Cardinal Grocholewski, prefect, and Archbishop Giuseppe Pittau, SJ, secretary—accompanied by the superior general of the Daughters of Mary Help of Christians, Sr. Antonia Columbo. The stated purposes of the document are (1) to aid consecrated persons to reflect on their educational presence in schools; (2) to offer guidelines that help to motivate and sustain consecrated persons in their educational mission today; and (3) to offer an official expression of ecclesial gratitude to consecrated persons for having dedicated their lives and ministries to the education of youth. Although the document does not provide a definition of the term "consecrated persons," it is clear that the text is referring to vowed religious women and men, members of religious communities, commonly known as sisters (nuns), brothers, and priests.

The document notes that education is a vital function of a civilized society and that even in culture at large, there has been an increasing interest in the role of education as it relates to economic development, human dignity, care of the environment, and world peace. Recent data from the United Nations indicate that 135 million children between the ages of 6 and 11 years do not go to school and that more than 280 million children and young people are illiterate or have had no more than minimal schooling. In fact, the majority of illiterate persons worldwide, numbering in excess of 800 million, have not had the opportunity to attend school.

Schools face a myriad of other difficulties today—the weariness of teachers and administrators, violence, the loss of meaning, all of which make the witness of consecrated persons more urgent and necessary. Catholic schools play a special role in fostering an integral formation, a holistic education, which addresses the spiritual and moral dimensions of the person as well as the academic, psychological, and emotional maturity of young people. Consecrated persons have a privileged role in that special environment, for they not only educate by serving as teachers and administrators but also evangelize by the power of the witness of their consecrated lives.

CPMS relies heavily upon the 1996 Post-Synodal Apostolic Exhortation of Pope John Paul II, *Vita Consecrata*. This document was published as a summary of a meeting of bishops who gathered in 1995 to reflect upon the mission of consecrated life in the church. In eleven different notes in its eighty-four paragraphs, CPMS cites *Vita Consecrata*, highlighting the importance of the presence and service of consecrated persons in Catholic schools. Both CPMS and *Vita Consecrata* view consecrated persons as making essential contributions to developing the vertical dimension in schools, namely, the openness to God, along with the horizontal dimension, an education for living responsibly with others.

With the dramatic decline in the available numbers of consecrated persons to serve in Catholic schools in the United States, one might argue that this Vatican exaltation of the role such vowed religious men and women have in schools is long overdue. However, one might also argue that with the future of Catholic education so clearly being the province of lay leadership, the document is not timely. In fact, several

Catholic educators have expressed this view, wondering about the manifest need to cultivate and affirm Catholic lay teachers and principals for their service to Catholic schools and so to solidify the future, rather than simply being complacent with thanking consecrated persons for their service in the past (*Catholic Education: A Journal of Inquiry & Practice*, 7, 1).

Catholic schooling is not homogeneous, however, throughout the world. In Asia, for example, it is estimated that roughly 90 percent of baptized Catholics come from Catholic schools. Pittau himself remarked that nearly 50 percent of his students in Japan were baptized during their school years or after they graduated (Pittau, 2002).

Several founders of religious communities and their community's *charism* received special mention at the publication of the document. Among them are St. Jerome Emiliani, founder of the Congregation of the Somascan Fathers; St. Anthony Mary Zaccaria, founder of the Barnabites (Clerks Regular of St. Paul); St. Ignatius Loyola, founder of the Society of Jesus (Jesuits); St. Joseph Calasanz, founder of the Piarists; St. John de la Salle, founder of the Brothers of the Christian Schools; St. William Chaminade, founder of the Marianists; Marcellin-Joseph-Benoit Champagnat, founder of the Marists; Don Bosco, founder of the Salesians; St. Domenica Maria Mazzarello of the Daughters of Mary Help of Christians; and St. Julie Billiart, foundress of the Sisters of Notre Dame.

While CPMS represents the work of the Congregation for Catholic Education and therefore merits serious attention and study, its focus is clearly on religious life and on the mission of vowed religious men and women. Because of this overriding focus on consecrated persons, the document will most likely receive more attention from vowed religious than from lay Catholic educators. *See also*: Congregation for Catholic Education, The; Religious orders of men; Religious orders of women.

Further Reading: Congregation for Catholic Education, *Consecrated Persons and Their Mission in Schools* (Rome: Libreria Editrice Vaticana, 2002); Zenon Grocholewski, *Intervention on the Occasion of the Presentation of Consecrated Persons and Their Mission in Schools*, in *Catholic Education: A Journal of Inquiry & Practice* 7, 1 (2002); John Paul II, Apostolic Exhortation *Vita Consecrata*, 25 March, *Acta Apostolica Sedis* 72–73 (1996): 377–474; Giuseppe Pittau, *Intervention on the Occasion of the Presentation of Consecrated Persons and Their Mission in Schools*, in *Catholic Education: A Journal of Inquiry & Practice* 7, 1 (2002); http://www.vatican.va.

Ronald J. Nuzzi

Consolidated schools

Consolidated schools can be defined in two ways. A consolidated school can be a single regional school that serves pupils from several parishes. For example, Our Lady of the Valley Regional School in the diocese of Worcester, Massachusetts, provides elementary Catholic education for students from more than a dozen parishes. Or consolidated schools can be several area schools for which common functions such as governance, finances, business management, and efforts to acquire sources of funding other than tuition and parish support are centralized for efficiency. This entry focuses on the latter.

Buetow (1970) in his book, *Of Singular Benefit: The Story of U.S. Catholic Education*, chronicled the beginning of the consolidation movement as a way to meet the modern challenges faced by Catholic schools. In an increasingly interconnected and mobile world, consolidation would decrease expenses and broaden the scope of the schools' vision, resources, and support. He cited a report published by the National Catholic Educational Association (1967) suggesting that parish boards of education would provide truly informed direction for the schools that they governed by naturally concluding that there is a need to move from local control to an area structure. The primary rationale at that time was that as "school funds from the government increase, more detailed reporting will be necessary" (Buetow, 1970, p. 395) and government involvement will increase. The consolidation of multiple parish reporting and management systems into a single management staff would reduce cost and increase efficiency. More than thirty years later, the movement from parochialism to regionalization or consolidation has grown, but for reasons other than the oversight of government involvement and funding.

Diocesan superintendents who have spearheaded the development of a consolidated school system cite declining enrollments, teacher compensation, and school funding as the rationale for their search for alternatives to the parish school. Upon recommendations of planning committees or task forces, schools spanning pre-K through twelfth grade levels have been centralized to address the difficulties facing individual schools in their particular contiguous areas.

Usually the consolidated system is governed by a board of education. The board provides leadership and direction by developing or setting policy, creating a strategic plan, and assuming other responsibilities as stipulated in its constitution. The board relates to the diocesan administrator and to the principals of the schools that are within the system. The diocesan administrator of the program may be the superintendent of schools or some other administrator responsible for diocesan education programming.

Just as governance is centralized, so is the system's administration. The most common shared administrative areas are tuition collection, salaries and benefits, regulation of parish financial support, operating budgets, curriculum, building and grounds, student recruitment, and marketing. The number of system administrators is related to the size of the system and the number of centralized areas. One system that includes ten early childhood centers, eight elementary schools, one intermediate school, and one high school has these administrators: a chief executive officer, curriculum director, business manager, director of development, director of buildings and grounds, director of student enrollment and public relations, director of annual fund and alumni relations, special event manager, network administrator, and technology coordinator. By consolidating efforts and personnel, the consolidated schools benefit from the economy of scales, as well as the expanded effort through collaboration that will ensure the schools' future. *See also*: Boards of education, diocesan, parish, school; (Arch)Diocesan schools; Governance.

Further Reading: Harold A. Buetow, *Of Singular Benefit: The Story of U.S. Catholic Education* (New York: Macmillan, 1970); Patricia Feistritzer, "The Phoenix of Brooklyn," *Momentum* 7, 2 (May 1976): 39–46; *Voice of the Community: The Board Movement in Catholic Education*, rev. ed. (Washington, DC: National Catholic Educational Association, 1973); James Youniss and John J. Convey, eds., *Catholic Schools at the Crossroads* (New York: Teachers College Press, 2000).

Regina M. Haney

Contract law

The administration of Catholic and other nonpublic schools is grounded largely in the law of contract. Put another way, unlike public education, which affords faculty, staff, parents, and students a wide array of defined rights, insofar as Catholic schools are generally not subject to the same laws, personnel in these schools generally have only those rights explicitly afforded in contracts, whether for employment or as contained in faculty and/or student–parent handbooks.

Simply stated, a contract is an agreement between two or more parties to do or not to do something. Moreover, a contract can be in oral or in written form; clearly, a written contract is easier to enforce. A valid contract includes five basic elements, each of which is discussed below. While these elements are discussed in relation to individual contracts between and among school officials, teachers, and parents, the same principles generally apply, subject to state and possibly federal laws, when dealing with collective bargaining agreements.

The first element of a contract is mutual agreement between parties including offer and acceptance. This means that the party making an offer must intend to create a legal obligation to do (or not to do) something that is definite and certain, such as providing an education in return for a parent's payment of tuition. In return, the party accepting the offer must explicitly agree to its clear and definite terms and conditions. At the same time, there must be a genuine agreement, or assent, between the parties. If there is fraud or undue influence by one party, then no contract has been formed. In order for a mistake to render a contract invalid, it must be mutual, meaning that both sides must be in error about a term. If only one party is in error, and the other party did not deceive or trick the person into accepting an offer, then a valid contract is probably present. Further, it is important to note that a counteroffer is technically a rejection. That is, if an administrator offers a prospective teacher a position and, rather than accept the offer, the prospective teacher asks for a higher salary, the individual has actually rejected the offer. In such a situation, even if it is uncommon, a prospective employer is free to end an interview.

Capacity, the second element of a contract, means that individuals must have the legal ability, ordinarily being of legal age, having actual or apparent authority to act, or not possessing any legal impediments, such as being of unsound mind, that would otherwise prevent them from entering into an agreement. Thus, for example, tuition agreements in K–12 schools are typically between school officials and parents since children lack the ability to enter into binding contracts. Additionally, where an individual has the reasonable apparent authority to make an offer, its acceptance ordinarily leads to the existence of a valid contract. That is, if an applicant meets with a school principal and accepts that person's job offer, which is later rescinded when another official claims that the first administrator did not have the ability to act as he did, then the prospective teacher may be able to pursue a breach of contract suit.

The third element of a contract is consideration, meaning that there must be a bargained-for exchange between the parties wherein one person offers something of value in return for performance or a promise of performance, such as teaching for the next school year, according to the terms of their agreement. While an agreement need not necessarily be for an equal exchange of value, if only one party benefits from a prospective contract, such as where one promises to make a gift to another, then it may be difficult to enforce.

According to the fourth element, in order to be enforceable, a contract must involve legal subject matter. Although it is unlikely that parties to a school contract would intentionally agree to do something illegal, such a contract may not be enforceable. If, for example, an administrator in a Catholic school tries to hire a faculty member on terms that violate either the school's collective bargaining agreement or a federal or state antidiscrimination law with regard to employment, a contract may well be void and unenforceable.

The fifth element of a contract is that it must be in the proper form. Put another way, even though oral contracts may be as binding as written ones, in order to be enforceable, certain types of contracts must be in writing. Under the common-law principle known as the statute of frauds, four types of contracts that are important for schools must be in writing in order to be enforceable by their makers. First, an agreement that cannot be performed in one year, such as where a teacher is hired in April 2003 on a one-year contract to teach from September 2003 to June 2004, must be in writing; this contract cannot be performed in one year because a period of fourteen months will have elapsed between the date when the parties entered their agreement and its expiration. Second, an agreement to purchase or sell an interest in real property, such as a building site for a school, must be in writing. Third, a contract for the purchase of goods worth more than $500 must be in writing. Finally, a promise to answer the debt of another, such as where schools merge and the newly created entity agrees to pay the debts of the predecessor school such as mortgages and salaries, must be in writing.

Once the parties have performed according to the terms of their agreement, a contract is discharged, thereby ending their legal relationship. This is important in Catholic (and other nonpublic) schools because insofar as teachers and administrators often work on one-year contracts with no expectation of continuing employment as under tenure, their contract expires at the agreed-upon termination date. A contract can also be discharged by one party becoming incapacitated such as due to illness or when the parties agree to cancel the original agreement and enter into a new contact.

In the event that one party refuses to perform a contract, then a breach has occurred, thereby giving the injured party the opportunity to seek redress. Among the options that an injured party has is seeking legal damages, such as lost wages, which would place the person in the same position that he or she would have been in but for the breach. An injured party may also seek the equitable remedy of specific performance such as reinstating a teacher whose contract was improperly terminated or admitting a child to a school or program. *See also*: At will employment; *National Labor Relations Board v. The Catholic Bishop of Chicago et al.*

Further Reading: John D. Calamari and Joseph M. Perillo, *The Law of Contracts*, 4th ed. (St. Paul, MN: West Group 1998); *Chady v. Solomon Schlecter Day Schs.*, 645 N.E.2d 983 (Ill. App. Ct. 1995); *O'Brian v. Langley Sch.*, 507 S.E.2d 363 (Va. 1998); *Wall v. Tulane Univ.*, 499 So. 2d 375 (La. Ct. App. 1986); *Willitts v. Archbishop of Boston*, 581 N.E.2d 475 (Mass. 1991).

Charles J. Russo

Contributed services

Contributed services is the term used to describe the ministry done by women and men religious in founding and running Catholic schools during the era in which they received only a small stipend for their work. It is virtually impossible to determine an exact monetary worth of the contributed services of these religious, especially women, who have staffed the Catholic schools of the United States over the past 200 years. Experts who have looked at the numbers estimate the figure to be in the billions of dollars.

When John Carroll reported on the state of the Church in the United States to the Congregation for the Propagation of the Faith in 1785, he estimated the Catholic population to be about 23,000. By 1850 it numbered 1,500,000. Ten years later the Catholic population more than doubled to 3,103,000. Immigration continued at a rapid pace well into the twentieth century.

The bishops of the United States were overwhelmed by this flood of continuous immigration from Canada, Europe, and Mexico, as well as from Asia. They knew that it was their responsibility to provide pastoral and spiritual care to the immigrants. Their task was made all the more difficult because of the strong anti-Catholic feeling among the native-born Protestant majority of the country. Teachers in the "public schools" were overwhelmingly Protestant and were often antagonistic to Catholic beliefs. Many of the textbooks used had anti-Catholic materials in them. Archbishop John Hughes of New York, looking at the situation in his diocese, proclaimed that if there were not sufficient Catholic schools for the Catholic children, they would be so negatively influenced by the anti-Catholicism of the public schools that within a generation the Catholic churches would be empty.

In addition to building churches in which the immigrants could worship, many bishops began a massive building program of Catholic schools in which they could preserve and pass on the Catholic faith to the children of the immigrants. In order to staff these schools, bishops knew that they needed religious sisters. Many went to Europe and visited convents begging for sisters to come to the United States. Other bishops founded their own religious communities or convinced sisters from other parts of the country to send a few of their number to their dioceses.

For the most part, the immigrants who arrived in the United States were poor. They came to this country fleeing religious or political persecution or to seek a new life for themselves in a country with so much promise. The Irish who came to the United States in the mid-nineteenth century were fleeing the devastating results of the potato famine as well as British persecution. They swelled the slums of the major cities of the Northeast. French Canadians came south to work in the textile mills that dotted the landscape of New England. The German Catholics who were fleeing the religious persecution that reached its apex in the *Kulturkampf* (1871–1878) went west and settled in what became known as the German Triangle (St. Louis, Cincinnati, and Milwaukee). The Polish and other Eastern European immigrants later followed the Germans to the Midwest, while the Italians would settle into the major cities of the East Coast, moving into the ghettos as the Irish moved out.

While the Irish saw the Catholic schools as a way to avoid the anti-Catholicism and later the general secularism of the public schools, the Germans and later the Poles and many other non-English speaking immigrants saw the Catholic school as the only way to preserve the threefold guardians of their self-identity: the Catholic faith, their native language, and ethnic culture. So bishops not only had to provide religious sisters for their schools but also had to be sensitive to the ethnic character of the sisters they were able to secure for the widely diverse populations of their diocese.

The sisters who arrived from Europe brought little with them but their missionary zeal. Often, in spite of the promises made to them by priests and bishops, they found little waiting for them in terms of school buildings and convents. They settled with the poor whom they served and drew many of their vocations from these poor families. Whether it was in the cramped quarters of the big cities or the rough frontiers of the West, the sisters lived the same lives of poverty and hardship as the families who sent their children to the Catholic schools. The Sisters of the Humility of Mary came from France in 1864 to Cleveland, where they were given 250 acres of almost uninhabitable swampland south of Cleveland. They worked it into productive farmland. When the Sisters of Saint Joseph were asked to come from St. Louis to St. Paul, Minnesota, they reported that the bishop housed them in his own "palace," which was nothing more than a one-room log cabin with an attic open on all sides.

Since the people were poor, they had little to contribute financially to the support of their parishes. Surprisingly enough, these poor gradually built the sometimes modest and sometimes massive parish plants in cities and towns throughout the country. These remain a testament to their faith and their love of their Church. The sisters were also the object of the people's generosity. In a kind of barter system, the people of the parish would provide food, wood for the fireplace, and services to the sisters who taught their children. In addition to teaching in the schools, the sisters would give private music lessons, do sewing, or paint ceramics to earn some extra income. Later, parishioners would drive the sisters around on their errands since the sisters had no cars. In many cities the sisters used public transportation free of charge. Many Catholic, as well as non-Catholic, doctors and dentists would treat the sisters gratis. Many parishes had "pantry days" in which the people of the parish would donate food items for the convent.

As the Church in United States moved into the twentieth century and as many Catholics moved out of poverty and into the middle class, their contributions to the Church increased. As the parishes had more funds available, they began to pay modest stipends to the sisters in the parish. In the beginning this stipend amounted to no more than $25 a month per sister (only for the ten months she taught). Gradually, depending on the diocese or the local pastor, these stipends were gradually increased to where some sisters were receiving $250 a month. It is a testament to the frugality of the sisters of the local convents that most of this stipend was sent back to the motherhouses to pay for the education of the younger sisters and the care of the aged. This money was also saved and invested to be used to build and add additions to the motherhouses and the houses of formation of the various communities.

The background to this concept of contributed services rests on three understandings. First, the education of young children in Catholic schools was the primary work of many religious communities of women. It was why they existed, why they were founded, and why they attracted other young women to join their community. Since it was so central to who they were, it was commonly understood that they did not do this for money, but for the love of God, for the salvation of their own souls, and for the salvation of the souls of the children they taught. Additionally, they had a vow of poverty, which called them to work for the good of the Church seeking nothing in return. Finally, most of the vocations that swelled the ranks of the religious communities of women came from the families of the people the sisters served. They were the poor. The nuns lived the same simple and poor lives as did the people of the parish.

While there were many young sisters working in the parishes to support the few elderly sisters living in the motherhouses, a kind of social security system developed. There was a continual flow of funds into the motherhouses from the many local communities, which allowed the sisters to care for the elderly. Many religious congregations further ensured that they would continue to have funds to care for the elderly by actually buying into the Social Security system in the early 1970s. This was the result of the passage of a federal law that through a complicated formula allowed religious to buy into the Social Security system based on the fair market value of the estimated value of collective earnings of their wage-earning members. This ensured that there would be at least some source of continuous funding for the retired religious.

A severe crisis developed in the 1970s through the 1990s as thousands of sisters left religious life. One religious congregation that in 1965 had 1,750 sisters teaching in Catholic schools reported that, in 2000, 154 of their sisters were so engaged. During the same time period, another congregation dropped from 2,300 sisters in education to 226. Most religious communities experienced similar decreases in their membership. In most cases it was the young and the middle-age sisters who left the congregations. The smaller number of younger sisters working could no longer support the increasing number of retired sisters on the stipends they were receiving. By the mid-1980s it was obvious something had to be done. Many dioceses raised stipends for religious to more realistic levels. Some religious communities established a minimum salary that their sisters had to be paid. Congregations that owned their own schools from which they traditionally received no salaries for their sisters who worked in them required that the sisters be paid on a scale that reflected their educational and experiential background and was equal to the salaries earned by their lay counterparts. Even with these advances, some religious congregations estimated that their resources fell short by millions of dollars of the anticipated needs of caring for their aging religious. This problem was exacerbated because the median age of the members of most religious congregations at the end of the twentieth century was in the mid-70s.

Recognizing that the financial plight of the religious congregations of women was a direct result of over 200 years of donated services to help to staff the Catholic schools of this country, the United States Catholic Conference mandated that each year from 1988 to 2007 a special collection would be taken up in every parish of the country. This collection for religious was a clear recognition that the entire Catholic Church in this country owed a debt of gratitude to the sisters for their service to Catholic education. Between 1988 and 2002 a total of $384,606,677 was raised by this collection, which is distributed to religious communities based on the number of retired sisters in each community and their current level of need.

In 1884 the bishops of the United States at the Third Plenary Council of Baltimore mandated that within two years every parish was to have a Catholic school as part of its mission. While that goal was never reached, millions of Catholics have enjoyed the benefit of a Catholic education in the thousands of grade schools and high schools that stretch from shore to shore. This massive undertaking would never have been possible were it not for the estimated more than 300,000 religious women who gave their lives to this ministry with little financial remuneration over the past 200 years. *See also*: *Consecrated Persons and Their Mission in Schools*; Religious orders of men; Religious orders of women.

Further Reading: Harold A. Buetow, *Of Singular Benefit: The Story of U.S. Catholic Education* (New York: Macmillan, 1970); Carol K. Coburn and Martha Smith, *Spirited Lives: How Nuns Shaped Catholic Culture and American Life: 1836–1920* (Chapel Hill: University of North Carolina Press, 1999); John Fialka, *Sisters: Catholic Nuns and the Making of America* (New York: St. Martin's Press, 2003); Annabelle Raiche and Ann Marie Biermaier, *They Came to Teach: The Story of Sisters Who Taught in Parochial Schools and Their Contribution to Elementary Education in Minnesota* (St. Cloud, MN: North Start Press of St. Cloud,

1994); Timothy Walch, *Parish School: American Catholic Parochial Education from Colonial Times to the Present* (New York: Crossroad, 1996).

Patrick J. Riley

Core curriculum

Core curriculum is a group of essential courses or learning experiences that form the curriculum for all students at a school (Parkay and Stanford, 1995). Critical to this definition is the determination of *essential* subject matter and learning experiences, which ultimately relate to the educational institution's operational philosophy. *Essentials* are based upon a foundational curricular question: *What knowledge is of most worth to student learning?* The response to this critical question requires the creation of a learning community that routinely engages in reflection and curricular decision-making.

In the early 1980s, several national reports (such as the National Commission on Excellence in Education, 1983) asserted that curriculum standards in the public sector were severely lacking in rigor. Consequently, by the end of 1987, U.S. Secretary of Education William J. Bennett challenged all high schools to adopt an academically rigorous core curriculum, consisting of four years of English literature; three years each of mathematics, science, and social studies; two years of foreign language; two years of physical education; one semester each of art and music history; and, a remaining quarter of the program to be devoted to electives.

In the Catholic school, the core curriculum is distinctive from other forms of education through the integration of religious truth and values into every aspect of the curriculum, which subsequently promotes the integral formation of each student. Religion "is not one more subject alongside the rest, but instead it is perceived and functions as the underlying reality in which the student's experiences of learning and living achieve their coherence and their deepest meaning" (National Conference of Catholic Bishops, 1972, #103). As the National Conference of Catholic Bishops asserted in 1979, "Belief can . . . be expressed in the visual arts, in poetry and literature, in music and architecture, in philosophy, and scientific or technological achievements" (#59). The Congregation for Catholic Education (1982), in its educational document *Lay Catholics in Schools: Witnesses to Faith*, elaborated additional components of this approach:

> the school must be concerned with constant and careful attention to cultivating in students the intellectual, creative, and aesthetic faculties of the human person; to develop in them the ability to make correct use of their judgment, will, and affectivity; to promote in them a sense of values; to encourage just attitudes and prudent behavior; to introduce them to the cultural patrimony handed down from previous generations; to prepare them for professional life, and to encourage the friendly interchange among students of diverse cultures and backgrounds that will lead to mutual understanding. (#12)

Thus, the purpose of the Catholic school, to be realized through the core curriculum, is not restricted to the attainment of knowledge but further embraces the student's acquisition of values and the discovery of truth (Congregation for Catholic Education, 1977).

The integration of faith and values throughout the core curriculum remains a current challenge in Catholic schools. Routine dialogue among teachers and administrators on this topic is necessary for its effective implementation. This dialogue must embrace two aspects: (1) those specific teaching methodologies that support the development of Gospel values in students and (2) the actual content of the core curriculum to reflect the integration of faith and values.

In regard to the first aspect, the Catholic school teacher is expected to offer students *integral, formational* learning experiences, learning that potentially *transforms* them. A model to emulate in this area is the master of instructional delivery, Jesus Christ, who was effective in his teaching practices with a staff who were illiterate and of questionable backgrounds. A dynamic question to explore with faculty could be: *What learning techniques did Jesus incorporate with his students that we could emulate with ours?* The Schultzes (1993) identified four learning techniques of Jesus: (1) He started with the learner's context; (2) He allowed learners to discover truth, rather than lecture to them about faith; (3) He took advantage of teachable moments; and, (4) He provided learners with opportunities to practice what they learned. Jesus' methods promoted interactive, personalized, relevant learning that led to the transformation of His students and, ultimately, the world.

The second aspect, that the actual content of the core curriculum reflect an integration of the religious dimension, is of prime importance. Much of the documentation on Catholic education alluded to ways teachers can inspire students to perceive subject areas, such as history, science, and literature, in the context of "the divine history of universal salvation" (Congregation for Catholic Education, 1988, #59). For example, in regard to the disciplines of science and technology, the Congregation for Catholic Education emphatically stated,

> Those teaching these subject areas must not ignore the religious dimension. They should help their students to understand that positive science and the technology allied to it, is a part of the universe created by God. Understanding this can help encourage an interest in research: the whole of creation, from the distant celestial bodies and the immeasurable cosmic forces down to the infinitesimal particles and waves of matter and energy, all bear the imprint of the Creator's wisdom and power. (1988, #54)

Other core subject areas, such as mathematics and economics, could, for example, inspire students to grapple with issues pertaining to social justice in the world, ultimately encouraging students to become, from a Jesuit Ignatian perspective, *men and women for others.*

Curriculum specialists in the Office of Catholic Schools of the Archdiocese of Sydney, Australia, developed supplementary curriculum materials, entitled *A Sense of the Sacred*, to assist teachers to integrate faith and values into twelve secondary-level curricular areas. This curriculum could serve as a model for future curriculum development for Catholic elementary and secondary schools in the United States. *See also*: *Catholic Schools and the Common Good*; *Lay Catholics in Schools: Witnesses to Faith*; *Religious Dimension of Education in a Catholic School, The.*

Further Reading: Congregation for Catholic Education, *Lay Catholics in Schools: Witnesses to Faith* (Boston: Daughters of St. Paul, 1982); Congregation for Catholic Education, *The Catholic School* (Washington, DC: United States Catholic Conference, 1977); Congregation for Catholic Education, *The Religious Dimension of Education in a Catholic School* (Boston: Daughters of St. Paul, 1988); Thomas H. Groome, *Educating for Life* (Allen, TX: Thomas More, 1998); National Conference of Catholic Bishops, *To Teach as Jesus Did: A Pastoral Message on Catholic Education* (Washington, DC: United States Catholic Conference, 1972);

Forest W. Parkay and Beverly H. Stanford, *Becoming a Teacher* (Boston: Allyn and Bacon, 1995); Thom Schultz and Joani Schultz, *Why Nobody Learns Much of Anything at Church: and How to Fix It* (Loveland, CO: Group, 1993).

Gini Shimabukuro

Corrigan, Michael (1839–1900)

Named the third archbishop of New York in 1885, Corrigan was born August 13, 1839, in Newark, New Jersey, to Irish immigrant parents, and died May 5, 1900. He graduated from Mount St. Mary's College, Emmittsburg, Maryland, in 1859.

Corrigan was one of twelve students who formed the founding class at the North American College in Rome on December 8, 1859. After ordination he returned to New Jersey, where he became a professor of dogmatic theology and Scripture at Seton Hall College and Seminary, subsequently becoming vice president and then president of the college and seminary. He also served as vicar-general of the diocese until 1873, when he was installed as bishop of Newark.

Corrigan was named coadjutor with right of succession for New York, on October 1, 1880, due to Cardinal McCloskey, Archbishop of New York, suffering from poor health. Cardinal McCloskey died later in October, and Corrigan assumed his role as archbishop of New York.

Corrigan was an active participant in the Third Plenary Council of Baltimore (1884) and proceeded to implement the charges of the council within his diocese. He began the process by invoking a synod in November 1886. He advocated the building of Catholic schools to serve immigrant populations in order to preserve their ethnic identity and religious commitment.

The several outcomes of Corrigan's tenure include the construction of a new theological seminary at Dunwoodie to replace St. Joseph's in Troy. The towers of St. Patrick's Cathedral in New York City were completed, and the Lady Chapel was begun. Orphan Asylums were moved to a new suburban site at Kingsbridge. In both episcopates Corrigan was recognized for his ability to move a diocese into accordance with the recommendations of the plenary councils of the United States.

Corrigan became an unlikely participant in a political debate that involved one of the New York mayoral candidates. Corrigan perceived that the candidate's writings had socialistic tendencies. He did not believe that the candidate's economic theories were consistent with the Church's position on the rights of property. Adding to the incident, Rev. Dr. Edward McGlynn, rector of St. Stephen's Church, New York City, became an outspoken supporter of the candidate. McGlynn's association with the Academia, a group of priests holding liberal political views, conflicted with Corrigan's conservative position. Corrigan suspended McGlynn from his parish and forbade Catholics from attending his lectures. McGlynn then was summoned to Rome but did not comply. As a result, McGlynn incurred the sentence of excommunication. This incident became embroiled in other public debates, including the Catholic school question, as evidenced by the Bouquillon controversy.

The McGlynn incident was relieved when his censure was lifted by the Apostolic Delegate, and McGlynn proceeded to Rome. In 1894 Archbishop Corrigan appointed Dr. McGlynn pastor of St. Mary's Church, Newburgh, where he served until his death in 1901.

The Bouquillon controversy divided Catholic bishops into rival camps; Corrigan sided with his colleague, Bernard McQuaid of Rochester. Their position opposed im-

Michael Corrigan. © University of Notre Dame Archives.

plicit or explicit support of public schooling by Catholics. This position would be consistent with Corrigan's interpretation of the Third Plenary Council's statements on Catholic schooling.

Archbishop Corrigan's disagreements with Archbishop Ireland of St. Paul took a public stage when Corrigan wrote a letter to the Pope commenting that the Holy Father must have misinterpreted Ireland's argument for the Faribault–Stillwater plan, when he gave a decision of *tolerari potest*. Corrigan was faced with questions about his right to take issue with the Pope's position. Corrigan denied any attempt to disrespect the Pope but maintained his position that Archbishop Ireland was wrong to believe that the Vatican's interpretation indicated approval of his plan by the Pope. Ireland continued to argue that he had never asked to extend the plan beyond the two schools and the Vatican's decision was adequate for his plans. One major result of these events was a further polarizing of the so-called American liberal and conservative camps of bishops.

On May 4, 1898, Archbishop Corrigan celebrated the twenty-fifth anniversary of his episcopal consecration. He was widely praised for his work in providing services to immigrant populations. One hundred eighty-eight churches, chapels, and stations were built during his seventeen-year tenure as archbishop of New York. He added seventy-five schools and increased the clergy by 284.

Archbishop Corrigan's impressive career as an administrator limited his opportunities for scholarly writing. He did publish a "Register of the Clergy Laboring in the Archdiocese of New York from Early Missions to 1885" for the United States Catholic Historical Society (1889).

In 1900, while returning from a confirmation visit to the Bahamas, he became ill from a cold that worsened from an accident. He died May 5, 1900. He was saluted for his devotion to Catholicism and to his country. *See also*: Catholic School Question, The; Ireland, John; Katzer, Frederick; McQuaid, Bernard.

Further Reading: Harold A. Buetow, *Of Singular Benefit: The Story of U.S. Catholic Education* (New York: Macmillan, 1970); John M. Farley, *The History of St. Patrick's Cathedral* (New York: Society of the Propagation of the Faith, 1908); Daniel F. Reilly, *The School Controversy 1891–1893* (Washington, DC: Catholic University of America Press, 1943).

Merylann J. "Mimi" Schuttloffel

Cristo Rey schools

A Cristo Rey school is a designation for a private or diocesan Catholic high school that represents an educational initiative to underserved communities. Students from low-income families who otherwise would not be able to afford a Catholic education are offered access to this network of schools. The title Cristo Rey is also the name of the first school founded in Chicago and serves as the symbolic flagship for this educational reform movement. ·

Cristo Rey translates into Christ the King; this expression was particularly cherished by Mexican Catholics during the savage persecutions inflicted upon the Church during the Mexican Revolution and authorized by its Constitution of 1917. The Mexican people signified resistance to the abusive government by ascribing honor to Jesus Christ under the title Christ the King. On December 11, 1925, Pope Pius XI established the feast of Christ the King to assert the rights of organized religion within states. A champion of this insurgency was Blessed Miguel Augustine Pro, priest and martyr (1891–1927, feast day November 23). Pro was a Jesuit who clandestinely ministered to the people but was ultimately executed for being a priest; like many other martyrs of this period, his dying words were: "Viva! Cristo Rey!" This motto and martyr offer a foundational background for the establishment of a secondary high school serving a Hispanic population by the Jesuits.

Joseph Cardinal Bernardin of Chicago, along with the provincial leadership of the Jesuits, had identified the growing needs of the Hispanic community as a ministerial priority. The first Cristo Rey high school was inaugurated by the Chicago province of the Society of Jesus in September 1996. It was the first new high school to open in the archdiocese of Chicago in thirty-three years. The school was established in St. Stephen's grade school building, which had closed the previous spring. Cristo Rey is located in the predominantly Hispanic southwest Chicago neighborhood called Pilsen-Little Village and offers a dual-language curriculum in Spanish and English. The coeducational high school opened with eighty-five students who were sophomores and juniors. From its inception under the leadership of its first president, Fr. John P. Foley, SJ, the school envisioned a maximum capacity of 550 students.

The school's unique structure and organization have offered the possibility of a Catholic education to many who might not otherwise be able to afford it. The Cristo Rey school developed partnerships within the local business community in the form of corporate internships. Some of the initial corporate sponsors illustrate the range of investment from corporate Chicago and nonprofit organizations: Arthur Anderson Accounting, the Chicago Board of Trade, Clifford Law Offices, First Chicago Bank, Loyola Press, McGuire Engineers, Quaker Oats, the Chicago Tribune, and St. Anthony Hospital.

A business provides a full-time, entry-level clerical position to be shared by a team of five different students. The salary for this position serves directly as a work-study subsidy toward the cost of a college preparatory education; the remaining student costs are met through fund-raising efforts, scholarships, financial aid, and family tuition payments. In addition to the obvious financial benefit, the work experience would open the students' world beyond their immediate neighborhood. Lessons about professional life, dress, and decorum are essential parts of the Cristo Rey education. Classes at the school are structured in such a way to accommodate the rotating days at work.

In 2000 a new classroom building was blessed and dedicated by Cardinal George. In 2003 the school's enrollment was 450 with a faculty comprising six religious and thirty-five lay faculty. The innovative structure of the school has been replicated by other Jesuit provinces across the United States, as well as other dioceses, and religious communities such as the Christian Brothers and Daughters of Charity. There are currently eleven Cristo Rey schools and feasibility studies being conducted on an additional three by the Cassin Foundation (2003).

The Cassin Educational Foundation is committed to funding feasibility studies and providing initial help for Cristo Rey high schools. This foundation's motto summarizes its philosophical mission as "transforming urban America one student at a time." The foundation carries out the vision of B. J. Cassin, who was impressed that 80 percent of Cristo Rey graduates continued to college; Cassin wanted this educational opportunity replicated in other urban areas. The foundation also assists a similar network of Jesuit Nativity middle schools and the LaSallian San Miguel grade, middle, and secondary schools. These schools are open to all faiths and like Cristo Rey, are not tuition-driven. *See also*: African Americans; Hispanics/Latinos; Inner-city schools; Socioeconomic status (of students).

Further Reading: Cassin Educational Initiative Foundation, http://cassinfoundation.org/. Accessed September 17, 2003; John P. Foley and Geoffrey Richard Hammond, "We Do It Our Way," *Momentum* 29 (February-March 1998): 27–28; Rita George, "The Business of Education," *Company: The World of Jesuits and Their Friends* 16 (Fall 1998); Lynn Shankman, "Cristo Rey Jesuit High School," http://www.jesuits-chi.org/educational/cristo.htm; Thomas C. Widner, "The Dream of Cristo Rey," *America* 176 (February 1997): 4–5.

Michael P. Caruso, SJ

Critical pedagogy

Critical pedagogy is that amalgam of thought, critique, and action that challenges the assumptions of schooling in an effort to transform society by challenging the dominant, oppressive ideologies that silence those who are not considered part of the power structure. The role of critical pedagogy is to name the oppression and one's experience of the oppression and to engage in dialogue as to how to rectify this situation and then move to some sort of action.

Among critical pedagogues, Paulo Freire is the best known. A Brazilian educator who spent his life working among the poor, he not only taught them literacy skills but through his approach also helped them find the tools that were within them to transform their world. In his work, *Pedagogy of the Oppressed* (1972), Freire sought to transform the metaphor of schooling from a banking pedagogy where students gathered and stored knowledge for later use, to a pedagogy of dialogue and critique that leads them and their oppressors to liberation. Freire's work is one example of critical pedagogy.

According to Giroux (in Oldenski, 1997), critical pedagogy developed through four phases in the course of the twentieth century. The first phase is associated with progressive educators such as John Dewey and George Counts during the 1930s and 1940s. Their work as social reconstructionists promoted a type of democratic education that would lead students to act freely and purposefully. The second phase in the development of critical pedagogy is its interaction with the critical theorists of the Frankfort School. Examining culture and society through the lens of critique and developing an understanding of how society and culture reproduce themselves provided critical theorists with tools to name the embedded and hidden values, beliefs, and prejudices in the dominant society. During the later 1970s, critical pedagogy's third phase was marked by studies of conflict and resistance. In this phase, researchers examined how students can and do act in ways that can be transformative of both education and society. Educators first employed the concept of the *hidden curriculum* during this time. At the end of the twentieth century and the beginning of the twenty-first century, critical pedagogy has moved from issues of social reproduction and resistance to issues that focus upon particular identities. Aronowitz and Giroux (1991) have named this particular type of critical pedagogy border pedagogy. In this approach, issues of power and identity construction as defined by race, gender, sexuality, and ethnicity form the base of a dialogue that moves the participants toward acceptance of differences and thereby lays the foundation for the transformation of society.

Br. Thomas Oldenski (1997) studied how critical pedagogy and liberation theology—a Latin American theological methodology similar to the methodology of critical pedagogy—affected the mission of Catholic education, specifically at a Catholic alternative high school in East St. Louis, Illinois. Admitting that critical pedagogy is a complex matter, encompassing a wide range of viewpoints, Oldenski believes that critical pedagogy and liberation theology have the potential to provide an appropriate framework for understanding the social justice mission of Catholic education. His model of integration has three parts: (1) critical discourse describing my present situation, (2) developing a method for changing "my current reality," and (3) work to implementing that change (Oldenski, 1997, p. 93).

McLaren (2001), Aronowitz and Giroux (1991), and Freire (1970) all admit some relationship between critical pedagogy and Marxism. However, they also posit that critical pedagogy has moved beyond classical Marxism. Freire warned readers that both "Marxists and Christians" would disagree with some, if not all, of what he wrote. His concern with both Marxists and Christians was that their sectarian presuppositions would not allow the critical pedagogue to truly hear their students (1970). In contrast, McLaren informs his definition of critical pedagogy with Marxist thought, especially when examining the most appropriate way of rectifying social inequity (2001). The uncritical acceptance of Marxist philosophy as a panacea on the part of some critical theorists creates the potential for unexamined presuppositions, such as those that critical pedagogy seeks to expose, that always fix capitalism as unjust and socialism as just. Critical pedagogy can certainly provide all educators with a framework for reflecting upon one's practice and acting in an ethical and just manner. While critically reflecting on one's practice, one should be careful not to accept pat answers. *See also*: Social justice.

Further Reading: Stanley Aronowitz and Henry Giroux, *Postmodern Education: Politics, Culture & Social Criticism* (Minneapolis: University of Minnesota Press, 1991); Paulo Freire, *Pedagogy of the Oppressed* (New York: Continuum, 1970); Barry Kampol, "Critical Pedagogy for Beginning Teachers: The Movement from Despair to Hope," *The Journal of Critical Pedagogy* (1998); http://www.lib.wnc.edu/pub/jcp/issueII-I/kampol.html; Peter McLaren, "Che Guevara, Paulo Freire, and the Politics of Hope: Reclaiming Critical Pedagogy," *Cultural Studies/Critical Methodologies* 1, 1 (February 2001): 108–131; Thomas Oldenski, *Liberation Theology and Critical Pedagogy in Today's Catholic Schools* (New York: Garland, 1997).

Anthony J. Dosen, CM

Cultural influences on parenting

Human development occurs in a cultural context; therefore, all aspects of parenting children—from beliefs and attitudes to behaviors—are influenced by culture. Bornstein wrote, "At the very heart of the concept of culture is the expectation that different peoples possess different values, beliefs, and motives and behave in different ways" (1991, p. 6). Culture influences parenting practices such as which child behaviors parents appreciate and emphasize as well as how parents care for their children. Parents from various cultural groups differ, for example, in their beliefs regarding the ages when children should reach particular developmental milestones.

"It is a particular and continuing task of parents and other caretakers to enculturate children, that is to prepare them for socially accepted physical, economic, and psychological situations that are characteristic of the culture in which they are to survive and thrive" (Bornstein, 1991, p. 6). For culturally diverse families in the United States, then, parenting shares some overlap with, but is also quite distinct from, parenting in the dominant, mainstream U.S. culture (Garcia Coll, Meyer, and Brillon, 1995). Parenting in minority families involves a complex interplay of several factors that impinge upon the nature and quality of parenting. Several critical areas are germane to the issue of parenting in culturally diverse families, namely, the roles of poverty, social support, racism and prejudice, and acculturation.

Culturally diverse, minority families are overrepresented among lower socioeconomic strata when compared to the U.S. population at large. Unemployment, underemployment, and lower educational attainment rates are greater among Hispanic American, Native American, and African American populations. Accordingly, the resource environments that minority families occupy often lead to differential rates of access to safe neighborhoods, quality medical care, and educational opportunities. Moreover, macrostructural factors—such as the dominant political conservatism of the 1980s—exert negative ramifications disproportionately on minority families. As a result of the higher rates of chronic and persistent poverty that exist among minority families, considerations of economic context must be at the core, rather than the periphery, of conceptualizations of minority family functioning.

Extended family social support is a salient characteristic of parenting for African American, Native American, and Hispanic American families. Research has highlighted the role of social support as a buffer acting upon parental behavior and the parent's level of psychological distress. Social support has a direct influence on parental adjustment and is a correlate of economic well-being and neighborhood attributes. The role of kin networks and extended family social support has long been described as a culturally distinctive aspect of African American family functioning.

Racism, prejudice, and discrimination are factors that must be considered in any discussion of culturally diverse parenting. An area of study that addresses these issues, both indirectly and directly, is racial socialization. Racial socialization includes both verbalized messages and modeled behaviors that minority parents convey to their children about their own ethnic and racial group, the mainstream culture, and the reality of their existence as a minority in a dominant culture. Minority children have the challenging task of acquiring a sense of respect for their own culture while often living in a dominant culture that may malign, discredit, or outwardly discriminate against it. A unique challenge of culturally diverse parenting is to instill a sense of ethnic identity and group knowledge and to prepare children to function competently in a society in which they will likely face prejudice, racism, and discrimination.

Acculturation is another factor that exerts an influence on minority parenting in the United States. In contrast to immigration, which reflects physical mobility and movement, acculturation is a psychosocial phenomenon that captures the degree to which an individual identifies with the majority or minority culture. Acculturation is affected by such things as generational status, length of time in the host country, and potential for returning to the home country. Much variability exists in parents' efforts to integrate themselves into mainstream society and to adapt to, or even adopt, dominant cultural values. Another possible scenario is that minority parents and their children adopt the values of dominant culture that might serve them well (e.g., emphasis on education), while maintaining their own ethnic beliefs, attitudes, and customs in other areas. *See also*: Parental rights; Parents as primary educators.

Further Reading: Marc H. Bornstein, "Approaches to Parenting in Culture," in Marc H. Bornstein, ed., *Cultural Approaches to Parenting* (Hillsdale, NJ: Lawrence Erlbaum, 1991); Cynthia Garcia Coll, Elaine C. Meyer, and Lisa Brillon, "Ethnic Minority Parenting," in Marc H. Bornstein, ed., *Handbook of Parenting, Vol. 2, Biology and Ecology of Parenting* (Mahwah, NJ: Lawrence Erlbaum, 1995); Sara Harkness and Charles Super, "Ethnic Minority Parenting," in Marc H. Bornstein, ed., *Handbook of Parenting, Vol. 2, Biology and Ecology of Parenting* (Mahwah, NJ: Lawrence Erlbaum, 1995); Teresa W. Julian and Patrick C. McHenry, "Cultural Variations in Parenting: Perceptions of Caucasian, African-American, Hispanic, and Asian American Parents," *Family Relations* 43 (1994): 30–38.

James M. Frabutt

Curriculum, definitions of

Curriculum theorists and researchers have suggested various definitions for curriculum, without consensus on any one definition. Parkay and Stanford (1995) provided five definitions in current usage: (1) a course of study; (2) course content, that is, the knowledge that students are to learn; (3) planned learning experiences; (4) intended student learning outcomes, that is, the results as distinguished from the means of instruction; and (5) everything that a student experiences while at school. According to Parkay and Stanford, no one of these definitions is the "right" one. Rather, one's definition is contingent upon the situation. For example, the operational definition for curriculum when advising a high school student in course selection for a college preparatory program would be "a course of study." On the other hand, when constructing a school philosophy statement, the operational definition for curriculum would more appropriately be "everything that a student experiences while at school," inclusive of extracurricular and cocurricular programs.

Parkay and Stanford (1995) offered an additional definition of curriculum: "Curriculum refers to the experiences, both planned and unplanned, that enhance (and sometimes impede) the education and growth of students" (p. 396). This definition embraces the overall purpose of the curriculum, that is, to educate, to promote student growth. In addition, when considering the countless experiences of students in schools, not all student experiences are educative or promote growth. Elliot Eisner (1985), eminent educational researcher, wrote that "schools teach much more—and much less—than they intend to teach. Although much of what is taught is explicit and public, a great deal is not" (p. 87). Thus, there are discrete aspects of the curriculum that either enhance or impede student learning. These are the "explicit," the "hidden," and the "null" curricula.

The explicit, or "overt," curriculum refers to that which a school intends its students to learn. This curriculum consists of several distinct dimensions: student learning goals and outcomes as delineated by the school; the actual subject areas/courses that constitute each student's educational plan; and the knowledge, skills, and attitudes that teachers desire their students to acquire. Usually, when a teacher or administrator is asked to describe the curriculum, it is the explicit curriculum that is discussed. Parkay and Stanford (1995) summarized this: "In short, the explicit curriculum represents the publicly announced expectations the school has for its students" (p. 395). These expectations are visible in the school's written documents, such as curriculum guides, course descriptions, teachers' written plans, texts, and other curricular materials.

The hidden, or "implicit," curriculum, includes aspects of the school culture that students unintentionally learn. Cornbleth (1990) defined the hidden curriculum as "aspects of schooling that are recognized only occasionally and remain largely unexamined, particularly the school's pedagogical, organizational, and social environments, and their interrelations" (p. 48). An example of a hidden curriculum could lie within the physical organization of a classroom. A teacher who strongly articulates a collaborative teaching/learning approach but restricts students to a seating arrangement in which they face each other's backs in desks in straight rows for the majority of the class time is conveying a mixed message. The hidden curriculum in such a classroom conveys an authoritative, noncollaborative teaching/learning approach. Likewise, students who are taught Gospel values but who are allowed to degrade each other publicly in the school are victims of a hidden curriculum that teaches the denigration of students.

The null curriculum, according to Parkay and Stanford (1995), represents "the intellectual processes and subject content that schools do not teach" (p. 398). Eisner (1985) elaborated this aspect of the curriculum that is not found in the school as "the options students are not afforded, the perspectives they may never know about, much less be able to use, the concepts and skills that are not a part of their intellectual repertoire" (p. 107). This dimension of the curriculum may be as important as the explicit curriculum and begs one of the most critical questions today in the area of curriculum and instruction: *What knowledge is of most worth to students?* Curricular decision-makers are compelled to carefully weigh this question in light of many contemporary factors, such as an unprecedented implosion of information, the myriad skills needed in a changing workplace, global education, and other areas of knowledge that characterize the current technological age, while balancing the curriculum with subject matter representative of tradition. The Catholic school educator has the added challenge of not only deciding *What knowledge is of most worth?* but also integrating his or her curricular decision-making with Christian faith and values. Student acquisition of information and knowledge is not a sufficient curricular goal for the Catholic educator; student formation and transformation in a Christian context are the ultimate goals. Thus, the null curriculum, areas that are not taught, may be critical to examine in seeking the most effective curriculum possible for today's students.

Ozar (1994) recommended that educators collaboratively formulate a school philosophy statement, as well as a "Profile of the Graduate," as first steps in the instructional design process. Primary work in these foundational areas assists faculty to become intentional in their teaching and to realize that when student learning outcomes emanate from these primary sources, congruence exists in the curriculum. *See also*: Hidden curriculum; Null curriculum.

Further Reading: Catherine Cornbleth, *Curriculum in Context* (London: Falmer Press, 1990); Elliot W. Eisner, *The Educational Imagination: On the Design and Evaluation of School Programs* (New York: Macmillan, 1985); Thomas H. Groome, *Educating for Life* (Allen, TX: Thomas More, 1998); Lorraine Ozar, *Creating a Curriculum That Works, a Guide to Outcomes-Centered Curriculum Decision-Making* (Washington, DC: National Catholic Educational Association, 1994); Forest W. Parkay and Beverly H. Stanford, *Becoming a Teacher* (Boston: Allyn and Beacon, 1995); Peter Senge, N. Cambron-McCabe, Timothy Lucas, Bryan Smith, Janis Dutton, and Art Kleiner, *Schools That Learn, a Fifth Discipline Fieldbook for Educators, Parents, and Everyone Who Cares about Education* (New York: Doubleday, 2000); Steven Zemelman, Harvey Daniels, and Arthur Hyde, *Best Practice: New Standards for Teaching and Learning in America's Schools* (Portsmouth, NH: Heinemann, 1998).

Gini Shimabukuro

Curriculum development

In spite of the fact that there are no established guidelines for developing curriculum, experts in the field (Tyler, 1949; Taba, 1962; Wiggins and McTighe, 1998) have suggested various approaches to this critical task. One such approach, known as the "Tyler Rationale," consists of four fundamental questions that must be addressed in designing any instructional plan. They are as follows:

1. What educational purposes should the school seek to attain?
2. What educational experiences can be provided that are likely to attain these purposes?
3. How can these educational experiences be effectively organized?
4. How can we determine whether these purposes are being attained? (Tyler, 1949, p. 1)

Shimabukuro (2000) synthesized some of these past approaches and designed a curriculum development model that integrates the Catholic pedagogical dimension (Figure 1). This model incorporates seven dimensions of curriculum development with the integration of faith and Gospel values present in each aspect. The curriculum development process is not always sequential; it is dynamic and geared to the growth of learners.

Figure 1
Model for Curriculum Development in the Catholic School

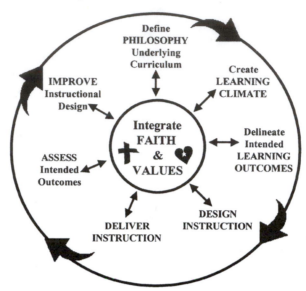

The Catholic educator's beliefs about teaching and learning are essential to the curricular development process. Beliefs underlie the teacher's educational purpose, the selection of methods of instructional delivery, and the roles of individuals involved in the educational endeavor. Intrinsic to the development of a philosophy of Catholic education is an understanding of the distinctiveness of Catholic education. Although Catholic schools are urged to promote lifelong learning for both students and teachers, academic excellence, personalized student learning, social skill development of students, service, and other factors implicit in the effective education of youth, these elements contribute to the productive education of students of many other orientations as well. The distinctiveness of the Catholic approach to educating students is the explicit integration of faith and values throughout each aspect of the curriculum. The Roman authors of *The Religious Dimension of Education in a Catholic School* (Congregation for Catholic Education, 1988) captured the essence of the mission of Catholic education in the following:

> Intellectual development and growth as a Christian go forward hand in hand. As students move up from one class to the next, it becomes increasingly imperative that a Catholic school help them become aware that a relationship exists between faith and human culture. Human culture remains human, and must be taught with scientific objectivity. But the lessons of the teacher and the reception of those students who are believers will not divorce faith from this culture; this would be a major spiritual loss. (#51)

The essence of Catholic education lies in the building of a nurturing, faith-based community. It is within a community that Christian faith is conceived and nourished. Thus, Church authors have consistently stressed that the primary role of the teacher is that of a community builder and that the learning climate and the relationships in the classroom are as important as the formal religion class. Although this step in the curriculum development process sometimes may be minimized due to a variety of academic pressures, it is essential to the Catholic identity of the school, not to mention its critical relationship to effective learning.

Educators need to know in behavioral, performance-based terminology *where they're going* with student learning, articulating intended learning outcomes with students from the outset and deciding, prior to embarking upon instruction, methods of assessing whether students *arrived* at the intended destinations. Wiggins and McTighe (1998) suggested an instructional development model that they refer to as *backward design*. They wrote, "Effective learning and school improvement are possible only when we grasp that curricula must be built backward from authentic assessment tasks, the latter providing a rationale and a basis for selecting content, skills, modes of instruction, and sequence" (p. 205). This approach advocates that the educator begin with the end, the desired results, in mind rather than from the isolated logic of the textbook. These results, or student learning outcomes, must be formulated in performance language, terminology that is measurable rather than abstract. (See Ozar [1994] for an excellent discussion of learning outcomes.) In order to progress to Wiggins' next step, that of determining acceptable evidence that the desired result has been achieved, the intended outcome must describe a performance that the student is expected to exhibit in order to be assessed competent in a particular area. Wiggins proposed that it is *after* learning outcomes and assessment methods have been determined that the educator should, then, plan the instruction and learning activities.

Curriculum that is beautifully designed, geared to the learner, with carefully crafted outcomes, must be delivered well. Instructional delivery addresses the *how* of what the teacher does, his or her actual practice, and can either advance or obstruct learning in students. In the Catholic school, the teacher is expected to offer students *integral, formational* learning experiences, learning that *transforms* them.

Effective teachers are reflective practitioners who remain open to new knowledge and routinely reflect on their classroom practices in relationship to current research. It is through reflection on one's practice, by studying one's effects in the classroom and initiating appropriate changes, that improvement is possible. Teachers who neglect this step, particularly those who mindlessly repeat their lesson plans year after year, subvert their potential for effectiveness.

This model of curriculum development embraces a holistic understanding of curriculum among teachers. For example, to simply offer professional development to educators in one aspect of the curriculum process, such as "assessment," without reflecting on, and collectively understanding, how "assessment" fits into the larger curricular picture can prove counterproductive. Improving educational practices should be a key aspect of professional development. However, efforts toward change may be sabotaged if educators are not clear on how one component, such as "assessment," fits into the larger curricular picture and connects to other important aspects of curriculum and instruction. *See also*: Faith community; *Religious Dimension of Education in a Catholic School, The.*

Further Reading: Congregation for Catholic Education, *The Religious Dimension of Education in a Catholic School* (Boston: Daughters of St. Paul, 1988); Lorraine A. Ozar, *Creating a Curriculum That Works, a Guide to Outcomes-Centered Curriculum Decision-Making* (Washington, DC: National Catholic Educational Association, 1994); Gini Shimabukuro, "Teaching and Learning in the Catholic School: Grounded in Sacred Soil," in Thomas C. Hunt, Thomas E. Oldenski, SM, and Theodore J. Wallace, eds., *Catholic School Leadership, an Invitation to*

Lead (London, England: Falmer Press, 2000); Hilda Taba, *Curriculum Development: Theory and Practice* (New York: Harcourt, Brace, and World, 1962); Ralph W. Tyler, *Basic Principles of Curriculum and Instruction* (Chicago: University of Chicago Press, 1949); Grant Wiggins and Jay McTighe, *Understanding by Design* (Alexandria, VA: Association for Supervision and Curriculum Development, 1998).

Gini Shimabukuro

Curriculum standards

At the outset, curriculum standards must be distinguished from content standards. The former relate to the overarching goals of the learning environment; the latter pertain to the specific knowledge and skills that students should attain. Curriculum standards are essential in that they establish the learning expectations for students. As a result, teachers and learners are able to communicate a common set of learning expectations.

Curriculum standards in the public sector tend to focus exclusively on outcomes of an academic nature. As academic institutions, Catholic schools also must be concerned with the academic expectations of students. However, Catholic schools are concerned about more than academic subjects. As stated by Convey (1992), "Catholic schools are faith communities that strive to develop in their students an understanding of the Catholic faith, a commitment to the practice of their religion, and a set of values that will influence the students' present and future lives" (p. 59). Thomas Groome (1998) similarly stated that Catholic schools are called to educate the very beings of their students, "to inform, form, and transform . . . who they are and how they live—with the meaning and ethic of Christian faith" (p. 118). Thus, when considering curricular standards, Catholic schools must address, in addition to traditional academic standards, their expectations in the areas of religious education and the moral development of their students.

Paramount to the academic development of students is the formation of the whole child. The task of the Catholic educator extends well beyond the mere transmission of knowledge and involves the integral formation of students. The Congregation for Catholic Education, in its 1982 document, *Lay Catholics in Schools: Witnesses to Faith*, described the distinctiveness of curricular standards of the Catholic school:

> In virtue of its mission, then, the school must be concerned with constant and careful attention to cultivating in students the intellectual, creative, and aesthetic faculties of the human person; to develop in them the ability to make correct use of their judgment, will, and affectivity; to promote in them a sense of values; to encourage just attitudes and prudent behavior; to introduce them to the cultural patrimony handed down from previous generations; to prepare them for professional life, and to encourage the friendly interchange among students of diverse cultures and backgrounds that will lead to mutual understanding. (#12)

In addition, the National Conference of Catholic Bishops in 1972 advised Catholic educators to prepare students for lifelong learning, as well as the ethical use of technology.

Extending beyond academic preparation, the National Conference of Catholic Bishops (1972) delineated the threefold purpose of Catholic education: message, community, and service. In 1978, the Congregation for Catholic Education wrote, "It is . . . widely recognized that Catholic schools are to be communities of faith in which the Christian message, the experience of community, worship, and social concern are integrated in the total experience of students, their parents, and members of the faculty" (#9).

Throughout Church documentation on education, Catholic schools have been urged to integrate religious truths and values throughout their curricula. In 1977, the Congregation for Catholic Education illuminated the task of the Catholic school as "fundamentally a synthesis of culture and faith and a synthesis of faith and life: the first is reached by integrating all the different aspects of human knowledge through the subjects taught, in the light of the Gospel" (#37). Thus, the purpose of academic subjects was "not merely the attainment of knowledge but the acquisition of values and the discovery of truth" (#39). The National Conference of Catholic Bishops (1988) further elaborated this critical curricular goal of Catholic schools, that is, of integrating the religious dimension into academic areas. They stated that "the Catholic school . . . is based on an educational philosophy in which faith, culture and life are brought into harmony" (#34) and that academic areas are expanded when integrated with a religious dimension. They strongly claimed that when Catholic schools dilute this dimension that students unfortunately "run the risk of living the best years of their lives at a shallow level" (#48).

The authors of *The Catholic School* (Congregation for Catholic Education, 1977) reminded educators of the essential component that distinguishes the Catholic school from others, the Christian element that must be primary and explicitly stated in the curricular standards of a Catholic school: "It is precisely the Gospel of Christ, taking root in the minds and lives of the faithful, that the Catholic school finds its definition" (#9) and "In Him [Jesus Christ] the Catholic school differs from all others which limit themselves to forming men [and women]. Its task is to form Christian men [and women], and, by its teaching and witness, show non-Christians something of the mystery of Christ Who surpasses all human understanding" (#47).

Aligned with the religious dimension, Catholic schools are urged to instill a sense of Christian service in students and to assist them in developing a global concern for others. According to the American bishops, Christian service not only involves a response to needs when asked but also takes the initiative to seek out the needs of persons and communities. They suggest that students be introduced to Christian service at the early levels of their schooling. *See also*: Faith community; *Lay Catholics in Schools: Witnesses to Faith*; *Catholic School, The.*

Further Reading: Congregation for Catholic Education, *The Catholic School* (Washington, DC: United States Catholic Conference, 1977); Congregation for Catholic Education, *Lay Catholics in Schools: Witnesses to Faith* (Boston: Daughters of St. Paul, 1982); John Convey, *Catholic Schools Make a Difference, Twenty-five Years of Research* (Washington, DC: National Catholic Educational Association, 1992); Thomas H. Groome, *Educating for Life: A Spiritual Vision for Every Teacher and Parent* (Allen, TX: Thomas More, 1998); National Conference of Catholic Bishops, *The Religious Dimension of Education in a Catholic School* (Washington, DC: United States Catholic Conference, 1988); National Conference of Catholic Bishops, *To Teach as Jesus Did: A Pastoral Message on Catholic Education* (Washington, DC: United States Catholic Conference, 1972); Lorraine A. Ozar, *Creating a Curriculum That Works, a Guide to Outcomes-Centered Curriculum Decision-Making* (Washington, DC: National Catholic Educational Association, 1994).

Gini Shimabukuro

D

D'Amour, O'Neill C. (1919–1968)

Born in 1919 and ordained in 1943, O'Neill C. D'Amour was appointed superintendent of schools for the diocese of Marquette, Michigan, in 1954. He reportedly began the first parish board of education in the United States in Norway, Michigan. Msgr. D'Amour was special assistant on boards of education for the National Catholic Educational Association (NCEA) from 1957 to 1964. He was chairman of the NCEA commission that was to become the National Association of Boards of Catholic Education.

D'Amour believed that a radical change needed to take place in the administration of American Catholic education. He felt that Catholic schools had fulfilled their purpose in the past (protecting the faith of a besieged, poor immigrant people), but their administration had become "hopelessly anachronistic" in the 1960s. Contending that a move from the pastoral and defensive postures to the professional was required to bring the administration and governance of Catholic schools into modern times, D'Amour (citing such things as having choir practice during school hours) called for the establishment of a system of Catholic education and an end to the relative autonomy of the parish school. The identification of the parish with its school caused confusion, he held.

Relying on documents of the Second Vatican Council, example, "The Dogmatic Constitution of the Church" and "The Declaration on Christian Education," which supported an increased role for the laity in the Church, D'Amour advocated for the creation of boards of education to govern Catholic schools. The members of these boards, at the parish, regional, and diocesan level, would be democratically elected and would be truly the representatives of the Catholic community. Bishops would have their representatives on the diocesan boards. Bishops and pastors would retain their authority in "matters of faith and morals."

It was time for the Church to adjust its structures to the realities of social and political U.S. society, he averred. There was no time to waste: "bold, daring and radical structural reform" must take place immediately. In 1965 D'Amour predicted that within five years at least 90 percent of Catholic schools in the nation would be operating under parish school boards.

The (arch)diocesan superintendent of schools would have a primary leadership role in the system of Catholic education that would include a standard pupil and financial accounting system, the merging of convents, schools, and the sharing of personnel between schools and areas, the central hiring of teachers, reasonable protection of teacher rights, adequate salary and fringe benefits for professional personnel, and a system of financing apart from parish collections. The challenge for the Catholic Church in the United States was whether it would take the legacy of Catholic schools and "make of it a dynamic force for the shaping of the future."

O'Neill D'Amour died of a heart attack while attending the NCEA Convention in April 1968. He is widely regarded as the "Father of the Catholic Board Movement in the United States." *See also*: Boards of education, diocesan, parish, school; Governance.

Further Reading: O'Neill C. D'Amour, "Catholic Schools Must Survive," *NCEA Bulletin* 65, 2 (November 1968): 3–7; O'Neill C. D'Amour, "Parochial Schools without Parochialism," *Ave Maria*, April 24, 1965, pp. 12–14; O'Neill C. D'Amour, "Restructuring Patterns of Catholic Education," in C. Albert Koob, ed., *What Is Happening to Catholic Education?* (Washington, DC: National Catholic Educational Association, 1966); O'Neill C. D'Amour, "School Boards of the Future," *America* 113, 13, September 25, 1965, pp. 316–317; O'Neill C. D'Amour, "Structural Change in Catholic Schools," *Catholic School Journal* 66, 6 (June 1966): 27–29.

Thomas C. Hunt

Darcy-Berube, Francoise (1922–   )

Francoise Darcy-Berube is a renowned author, speaker, and leader in the field of religious education and the ministry of catechesis. Francoise Darcy-Berube was born in Paris, France, and spent her early childhood years in England. She did her undergraduate work in psychology at La Sorbonne and L'Institut Catholique in Paris. Her studies continued at the Lumen Vitae Catechetical Institute in Brussels. After arriving in Canada, she earned a master's degree from Montreal University and a doctorate from the University of Ottawa.

A 1961 article on curriculum design published in *Lumen Vitae* brought her international attention and led to an invitation to serve as a member of a curriculum development team in Quebec. Also on this team was her future husband, John-Paul Berube, with whom she has co-authored several books (Groome, 1995).

The list of her publications in the area of religious education is extensive. She was a primary author of the *Come to the Father* religion curriculum (in Canada: *The Canadian Catechism*) published by Paulist Press in 1967. She co-authored, in collaboration with her husband, a two-book series designed to be used as part of a sacramental preparation course for children entitled *On Our Way with Jesus: We Share in the Eucharist* (2001) and *On Our Way with Jesus: We Discover God's Paths* (2001). Some of the other books that she has authored include *Children of Light* (1986), *Growing Up a Friend of Jesus: A Guide to Discipleship for Children* (2000), *Religious Education at a Crossroads: Moving on in the Freedom of the Spirit* (1995), *Practical Catechesis: Visions and Tasks for Catechetical Leaders* (2001), *Day by Day with God: Prayer Book for Children* (1982), and *Come Let Us Celebrate* (1984).

In one of her more recent works, *Religious Education at a Crossroads: Moving on in the Freedom of the Spirit* (1995), Darcy-Berube contends that religious education in the United States has made great strides forward but that it is in danger of regressing back toward a one-dimensional academic orientation toward catechesis. She identifies the progress made in the last twenty years through a powerful and significant paradigm shift: a movement away from a one-dimensional intellectual focus on content mastery and the instructional aspect of religious instruction that places a primary emphasis on orthodoxy and completeness in curriculum design, to a more holistic focus with a strong emphasis on the pastoral, personal, and existential aspects of faith formation. The need for a holistic view of catechesis is a fundamental guiding principle that permeates much of her work and is captured most poignantly in a story about Francoise Darcy-Berube related by Rev. Terry Odien: "While teaching at Fordham University, she surveyed adolescents from a Catholic high school to find out who God was for them, and what prayer meant to them after ten years of Catholic education. One student responded that he didn't pray. He went on to say that for ten years catechists and teachers had been talking to him *about* God, but that no one had ever introduced him *to* God" (Odien, 1999, p. 1).

According to Thomas Groome, a onetime student of Francoise Darcy-Berube who currently serves as a professor of theology and religious education at Boston College, Darcy-Berube is one of the pioneers who forged this paradigm shift that has emerged in the last fifty years. Groome (1995) credits Darcy-Berube with creating and establishing many of the elements of catechesis that are now taken for granted, such as the Trinitarian focus in catechesis with an emphasis on the experience of the Triune God rather than grappling with the doctrinal mystery in an intellectual fashion; the partnership with parents in the sacramental preparation of their children; the focus on family and early childhood catechesis; the partnership of liturgy and catechesis; the use of religious ritual in the religious formation of children; the use of contemplative exercises that engage the contemplative capacity in children; and the centrality of biblical and liturgical language in catechesis. Groome refers to her as "one of the great 'mothers' of contemporary Catholic catechetics" (Groome, 1995, p. x). *See also*: Groome, Thomas; Religion, teaching of; Total Catholic Education.

Further Reading: Francoise Darcy-Berube, *Religious Education at a Crossroads: Moving On in the Freedom of the Spirit* (New York: Paulist Press, 1995); Thomas Groome, "Wisdom from the Heat of the Day," in *Religious Education at a Crossroads: Moving On in the Freedom of the Spirit* (New York: Paulist Press, 1995); Terry Odien, Harcourt Religion, 1999 http://www.harcourtreligion.com/cresearch_wbf_2_cnt.html. Accessed November 12, 2002.

John T. James

Declaration on Christian Education, The

The Declaration on Christian Education, promulgated by Pope Paul VI on October 28, 1965, is one of sixteen documents (four constitutions, nine decrees and three declarations) resulting from the Second Vatican Council. The council was convened by Pope John XXIII on October 11, 1962, and concluded on December 8, 1965. General Councils in the Roman Catholic Church have occurred twenty-one times since A.D. 325. They are gatherings of bishops together with the Pope convened in a time of great crisis in the Church or the world. The Second Vatican Council's purpose was to update and adapt the Church to the challenges facing the modern world.

In 1965, American Catholic schools were experiencing the peak of their student population. At the same time, society was in the midst of turmoil and upheaval over issues such as the United States' involvement in the Vietnam War, political unrest, drug culture, widespread sexual experimentation, and general rebellion against established traditions and authority.

Although Catholic schools were flourishing, Vatican II recognized the urgency of educating individuals, children and adults, to enable their active participation in social, economic, and political affairs by issuing *Gravissimum Educationis* (*The Declaration on Christian Education*). In this document, the council put forth fundamental principles of Christian education, particularly in schools.

The Council Fathers assert that all men and women have the inalienable right to an education that enables each person to pursue his or her ultimate end and the good of the society in which he or she shares. Education is the tool that provides necessary skill development (social, physical, moral, and intellectual) and should motivate individuals to view moral questions with properly formed consciences. Christians, moreover, have a right to knowledge about the mystery of salvation, the gift of Faith, worship in spirit and truth, and an awareness of their calling to participate in the Christian formation of the world in which they live. This constitutes the mandate for Catholic schools and programs of religious education for both young people and adults.

Responsibility for providing this Christian education falls to bishops and pastors. Parents, who as the primary educators of their children, bear a serious obligation in this matter must recognize that the atmosphere fostered within the home should reflect the social virtues needed by our society. Moreover, parents have a duty to avail themselves of the help provided to them by the Catholic school in educating their children in the Faith. Civil society and the Church must protect parents' duties and rights to educate their children and provide assistance in carrying out the work of education.

Even in schools that are not specifically Catholic, the Church provides its presence through Catholic teachers who witness the principles and moral values inherent in the followers of Christ. However, Catholic schools that pursue cultural goals and human formation in the same manner as their public counterparts should have as a primary function to create a special atmosphere animated by the Gospel spirit of freedom and charity. The Catholic school depends almost entirely on the teachers to accomplish these goals. By their daily living and classroom activity they give witness to Christ. In today's society, with the decrease in number of priests and religious teachers in Catholic schools, it is imperative that lay Catholic school teachers ground themselves in their faith and pursue continued study and reflection. These teachers determine to the greatest extent whether the Catholic school succeeds in its purpose.

Changes in society necessitate a changing view of the Catholic school. The traditional primary and secondary schools will continue to be fostered. The council, however, recognizes the need for a broader view that includes different types of schools: college prep, vocational, adult education centers, special education centers, and facilities of training teachers for religious and other types of instruction. Pastors are encouraged to spare no sacrifice in assisting Catholic schools to achieve their purposes and to provide educational opportunities to those who are poor in spirit as well as in material goods.

The document goes on to address the needs and responsibilities of Catholic higher education institutions. These institutions are expected to prepare intelligent young men and women to live in today's society as true witnesses of the faith. Here too, the council encourages Catholic higher education institutions to assist in the matriculation of promising individuals regardless of their means. Furthermore, those colleges and universities that are not under the sponsorship of the Catholic Church should provide on-campus ministry programs to accommodate the faith needs of students and faculty.

Local bishops are charged with the responsibility to implement and monitor the progress and activities of these programs. By providing clergy to serve in this ministry, bishops guarantee that students in these secular institutions have the opportunity to continue growing in the knowledge and practice of their faith.

In all institutions of higher learning, faculties are encouraged to pursue collaborative activities. They should join together to support each other in their academic pursuits, promote opportunities for international conferences and dialogue, engage in, and share, research discoveries, and temporarily exchange professors to the extent that it is mutually helpful within the institution.

The council further entreats young people to be cognizant of the need for, and importance of, education. Although today's society seems to lack a true appreciation for the teaching profession, the council exhorts young people to be open to, and willingly embrace, a vocation to this noble profession. *See also*: Bishops; Catholic philosophy of education; Vatican Council, II.

Further Reading: "The Declaration on Christian Education," in Austin Flannery, ed., *Vatican Council II—The Conciliar and Post Conciliar Documents* (New York: Costello, 1977); George F. Donovan, *Vatican Council II, Its Challenge to Education; Proceedings* (Washington, DC: Catholic University of America Press, 1967); Michael J. Guerra, Regina Haney, and Robert J. Kealey, *Catholic Schools for the 21st Century—Executive Summary* (Washington, DC: National Catholic Educational Association, 1992); Joseph D. Massucci, "The Unique Identity of Catholic High Schools: A Comparison of the Church's Expectations and a School Community's Experience and Beliefs," unpublished doctoral dissertation, University of Dayton, 1993; Louise A. Mayock, *The Influence of the Second Vatican Council on the American Catholic School: A Report* (Ann Arbor, MI: University Microfilms International, 1992).

Joseph D. Massucci

Demographics

This entry on the demographics of Catholic school students briefly examines the major changes in the characteristics of Catholic school students from 1970 to the present.

The National Catholic Educational Association (NCEA) in reporting its data on Catholic schools divides the country into six geographical regions: New England, Mideast, Great Lakes, Plains, Southeast, and West/Far West.

The majority of Catholic school students attend schools in the Mideast and Great Lakes regions (see Table 2). The two regions combined accounted for 52 percent of Catholic school enrollment in 2001 (McDonald, 2002). This percentage is down 3.4

Table 2
Catholic School Enrollment Changes by Regions 1991–92 and 2001–2002 School Years Compared

Region	1991–92		2001–2002	
Mid East	767,879	30.1	744,297	28.4
Great Lakes	645,984	25.3	617,865	23.6
Southeast	311,630	12.2	364,692	14.0
Far West	428,584	16.8	471,657	18.0
New England	155,500	6.1	165,991	6.4
Plains	241,286	9.5	251,828	9.6
Totals	2,550,863	100.0%	2,616,330	100.0%

Source: NCEA.

Table 3
Increase in Catholic School Ethnic Enrollment in Selected School Years from 1970–1971 to 2001–2002

1970–1971	1980–1981	1990–1991	2000–2001	2001–2002
10.8%	19.4%	23.2%	25.6%	26.0%

Source: NCEA.

percent from the 55.4 percent of total enrollment reported ten years earlier in 1991. During this same ten-year period, the Southeast and the West/Far West regions increased their combined share of total enrollment from 29 percent in 1991 to 32 percent in 2001. This slight regional shift in overall enrollment percentages reflects the migration of populations to the Southern and Western areas of the United States (McDonald, 2002).

The percentage of total enrollment from the top ten states has decreased 4.5 percent from 68.4 percent in 1982 to 63.9 percent in 2001. The top ten states in 2001 listed in order of total Catholic school enrollment are New York, California, Pennsylvania, Illinois, Ohio, New Jersey, Louisiana, Florida, Michigan, and Massachusetts (McDonald, 2002). In 1992, Florida was not ranked among the top ten, California was ranked third behind Pennsylvania, and Louisiana was eighth behind Michigan. These shifts also reflect the migration of people to the South and West.

With regard to ethnic diversity of Catholic students, it is not startling to find the great majority of students to be white, of non-Hispanic ancestry. In 2001, 74 percent of all Catholic school students were white and non-Hispanic (McDonald, 2002). What is interesting is the significant increase in the percentage of students from ethnic minorities during the last three decades of the twentieth century. In 1970, students from minority groups represented 10.8 percent of total Catholic school enrollment. By 2001, these students accounted for 26 percent of total enrollment—an increase of over 15 percent (McDonald, 2002). Most of the increase in minority enrollment occurred prior to 1990 in the years of declining total enrollment. Table 3 illustrates this growth.

In addition to the increase in ethnic minority enrollment, the designation of ethnic minority categories became more refined to reflect a changing ethnic diversity. In 1990, NCEA used five categories to report ethnic minority enrollment: Black Americans, Hispanic Americans, Asian Americans, American Indians, and all others. Beginning with its statistical report for 1999–2000 school year, eight categories were used: American Indian/Native Alaskan, Asian, black, Hispanic, Native Hawaiian/Pacific Islander, multiracial, white, and unknown.

The two largest ethnic categories, exclusive of white, in the NCEA reporting classification are black and Hispanic. In 1995, black and Hispanic students constituted 76.1 percent of the minority Catholic school student population—35.6 percent black; 40.5 percent Hispanic (Savage and Milks, 1996). By 2001, the percentage of black and Hispanic students declined 3.2 percent to 72.9 percent of the minority Catholic school student enrollment (McDonald, 2002). Of this number, the proportion of black students declined almost 5 percent to 30.5 percent while Hispanic students increased almost 2 percent to 42.4 percent.

Minority enrollment varies greatly according to regions. In the 2001–2002 school year, the Plains region had the lowest percentage of ethnic enrollment and the West/

Figure 2
Change in Black and Hispanic Catholic School Enrollment

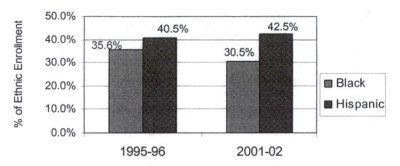

Far West region the highest. Using enrollment figures from the 2001–2002 school year, the percentages of minority Catholic school student population from lowest to highest by region are presented in Table 4.

While the large majority of students in Catholic schools are Catholic, the percentage of non-Catholic students has increased significantly since 1970. In 1970, the percentage of non-Catholic students enrolled in Catholic schools was 2.7. By 2001, the percentage had increased to 13.2 percent (McDonald, 2002). Table 5 illustrates this increase for selected years between 1970 and 2002.

The socioeconomic profile of Catholic school students changed in the latter part of the twentieth century. Catholic schools, known for their service and achievements in educating the poor and economically disadvantaged, appear to be increasingly less diverse in terms of the socioeconomic makeup of their student population (Greene and O'Keefe, 2001). According to an analysis by Cornelius Riordan (2000), the percentage of Catholic secondary school students from the lowest socioeconomic quartile decreased from 12.3 percent in 1972 to 5.5 percent in 1992—a decline of 6.8 percent. During the same period the percentage of students from families in the highest soci-

Table 4
Ethnic Enrollment as a Percentage of Total Catholic School Enrollment by Region—2001–2002 School Year

Plains	New England	Great Lakes	Southeast	Mideast	West/Far West
9.9%	15.3%	17.0%	21.3%	28.3%	48.9%

Source: NCEA.

Table 5
Changes in Non-Catholic Enrollment in Catholic Schools for Selected School Years 1970–1971 to 2001–2002

1970–1971	1980–1981	1990–1991	2000–2001	2001–2002
2.7%	11.2%	11.9%	13.6%	13.2%

Source: NCEA.

Table 6
Socioeconomic Status Makeup of Catholic Secondary
Schools—1972, 1980, 1992

	1972	**1980**	**1992**
Lowest quartile	12.3%	15.2%	5.5%
Highest quartile	29.7%	35.5%	45.8%

Source: Riordan, 2000, p. 40.

oeconomic quartile increased 16.3 percent from 29.7 percent to almost 46 percent (Greene and O'Keefe, 2001).

Historically, Catholic schools have shown great capacity to adapt to changing environments. The demographic changes highlighted here have and will continue to challenge Catholic school leaders to join clarity of mission with creative adaptation. *See also*: Enrollment; Minority students.

Further Reading: John J. Convey, *Catholic Schools Make a Difference: Twenty-five Years of Research* (Washington, DC: National Catholic Educational Association, 1992); Jessica A. Greene and Joseph M. O'Keefe, "Enrollment in Catholic Schools in the United States," in Thomas C. Hunt, Ellis A. Joseph, and Ronald J. Nuzzi, eds., *Handbook of Research on Catholic Education* (Westport, CT: Greenwood Press, 2001), 161–182; Dale McDonald, *United States Catholic Elementary and Secondary Schools 2001–2002: The Annual Statistical Report on Schools, Enrollment and Staffing* (Washington, DC: National Catholic Educational Association, 2002); Cornelius Riordan, "Trends in Student Demography in Catholic Secondary Schools, 1972–1992," in James Youniss and John J. Convey, eds., *Catholic Schools at the Crossroads: Survival and Transformation* (New York: Teachers College Press, 2000): 33–54; Frank X. Savage and Mary Jo Milks, *United States Catholic Elementary and Secondary Schools 1995–1996: The Annual Statistical Report on Schools, Enrollment and Staffing* (Washington, DC: National Catholic Educational Association, 1996).

Frank X. Savage

Development

Development can refer to several activities. In Catholic schools development refers to all the activities that help schools expand, grow, strengthen, and improve in quality. Most Catholic schools dedicate a staff or office of people strictly for development activities. Typical development office responsibilities include the following: fund-raising, endowment cultivation and management, alumni organization and communication, and strategic planning. The development office's goal is to coordinate these activities so that the school can continuously improve.

The practice of fund-raising is extremely essential to modern Catholic schools. In fact, no Catholic elementary school surveyed by the National Catholic Educational Association (NCEA) for the 2000–2001 school year failed to conduct some form of fund-raising. The cost of education continues to increase for most Catholic schools. Per pupil costs in 2000–2001 averaged $2,823 for elementary schools and $5,700 for secondary schools (McDonald, 2001). Most Catholic schools simply cannot charge students tuition equivalent to these costs. Therefore, in order to remain financially solvent, most Catholic schools engage in various fund-raising activities to help offset their operating costs. In 2000–2001, fund-raising activities on average accounted for 8.4 percent of schools' revenue (Kealey, 2001). These fund-raising activities ranged from candy sales and raffles to auctions and annual funds. The trend has been for schools to move away from time-intensive, low-profit activities such as candy sales and focus efforts on high-profit potential activities that generate larger sums of money. A Catholic school development office coordinates these activities so that they are spaced out over the school year and do not conflict with one another. The development office also needs to monitor activities so that the same volunteers are not asked to work every function and the school is not continually soliciting funds from the same contributors.

One essential fund-raising activity is the establishment of an annual fund. An annual fund is a fund-raising campaign conducted yearly with specific monetary goals. Ideally the money generated by this campaign will increase annually at least at the rate of inflation so that the revenue generated will constitute a constant percentage of a school's operating costs. Annual giving should be viewed as the primary annual development program, the one that has unlimited potential to grow in volume and in gift size. Ideally, it would raise 8–10 percent of annual operating revenue. The annual fund should be a twelve-month comprehensive, solicitation-based program (Haney and O'Keefe, 1999).

The second major activity of most Catholic school development offices is soliciting money for, and managing, the school endowment. An endowment is a sum of money invested by a nonprofit organization for long-term growth and income, from which a percentage of the profit is allocated to the organization's general operational budget or a specific program. The remaining profits along with the principal dollar amount of the investment stay unused and are continually reinvested so that the endowment grows and lasts into perpetuity. The advantage of an endowment is that donations are made once and last for the life of the school. Today, 51 percent of Catholic grade schools have an endowment fund. In 2001, the average amount of a Catholic grade school endowment fund, including only those schools with endowments, was $1,187,703. On average these Catholic schools were able to glean only 1.7 percent of their operating budgets from the unrestricted interest income from these endowments (Kealey, 2001). A development office's responsibility concerning an endowment is continually raising money to build the amount of the principal investment and contributing to the decision-making process concerning the amount of interest that is distributed to the school. Many times these decisions will also be made by the school board. The actual investing of this money should be entrusted to a professional investment adviser or to an experienced board.

The third major activity of a typical development office is alumni organization and communication. Catholic schools are obviously dependent on a variety of fund-raising activities. An essential group of potential donors for schools to call on is the alumni. In order to maximize its ability to raise money, a school must keep alumni connected to the school. This is accomplished by having accurate contact information such as telephone numbers and addresses for each individual school graduate and then frequently updating them with school news and inviting them to school events. In doing so, the school strengthens the bond between alumni and alma mater. The development office is the key link in the bond between school and alumni. This bond allows the development office to more easily and successfully approach alumni with its various fund-raising opportunities.

The final area of responsibility that a development office has in a Catholic school is to contribute to a school's strategic planning process. In order for the development office to effectively market the school and raise money, it is essential for the school to have a clear identity and vision for the future. Clarifying identity and establishing vision are two tasks that are best performed in the context of a strategic planning process. Since the development office is primarily responsible for a school's public communications, it is valuable to involve the development office in any sort of strategic planning effort. As the main link with school contributors, the development office is generally the most aware of public perceptions and desires for a school. The input that a representative from the development office brings to a strategic planning process is irreplaceable. *See also*: Financing of Catholic schools; Subsidies; Tuition.

Further Reading: Regina Haney and Joseph O'Keefe, *Creatively Financing and Resourcing Catholic Schools Conversations in Excellence* (Washington, DC: National Catholic Education Association, 1999); Robert J. Kealey, *Balance Sheet for Catholic Elementary Schools: 2001 Income and Expenses* (Washington, DC: National Catholic Educational Association, 2001); Dale McDonald, *United States Catholic Elementary and Secondary Schools 2000–2001* (Washington, DC: National Catholic Educational Association, 2001).

Jeffery M. Boetticher, Jr.

Developmental contextualism

Developmental contextualism is a theory of human development that takes an integrative, change-oriented approach to human life. As an instance of developmental systems theory, it posits that human development results from changing relations between organismic (biological) and environmental (contextual) levels of organization. In that regard, developmental contextualism contrasts with mechanistic and organismic models of development. Human behavior is both biological and social. Multiple components (e.g., historical time period, culture, society, community, family, social network, biological characteristics) influence, and are influenced by, one another, a process termed dynamic interactionism. Human development is viewed as extremely plastic; consequently, humans possess a tremendous capacity for change. Developmental contextualism has been applied in various settings to better understand child and adolescent development as well as program and policy implications for children and families.

Lerner (2002) described three key themes of developmental contextualism. First, individuals are the producers of their own development. Humans are active agents of change. Individuals bring a host of their own influential characteristics, attitudes, and behaviors to everyday interactions with others. These individual differences naturally evoke differential reactions in others. Consequently, the individual reactions feedback through a circular function to influence further development. Bidirectionality in parent–child interactions has long been a familiar idea in socialization research. Children, for example, engage in reciprocal relations with significant members of their daily lives including caregivers, teachers, and peers. Through these bidirectional interactions, a parent and child mutually influence one another through reciprocal cycles of exchange. Lerner explained, "How we behave toward our children depends a lot on how they have influenced us to behave. By influencing the parents that are influencing him or her, the child is shaping a source of his or her own development. In this sense, children are producers of their own development" (2002, p. 91).

A second key theme of developmental contextualism is that development is a life-span phenomenon. Development is not a process that occurs only in childhood and adolescence; rather, variation in developmental pathways continues across the life course. A life-span orientation espouses a concern for time, context, process, and meaning on both human and family development. The temporal focus of life-span perspectives typically delineates several levels of time—ontogenetic, generational, and

historical time—and are keenly attuned to the interactions between these three temporal levels.

A focus on development in its ecological context is the third key theme of developmental contextualism. Contextual levels, defined from the viewpoint of the developing person, range from proximal environmental features to more distal,
macro-oriented environmental variables (e.g., peers, family, school, community, culture, historical time). Urie Bronfenbrenner, a key proponent of studying contextual-
izing human behavior in context, compared these nested layers of context to a set of
Russian dolls, with the smallest layer encompassed by successively larger ones. The
microsystem identifies the immediate setting in which a child, for example, engages
in face-to-face interactions. The mesosystem includes an interlinked group of microsystems in which the developing child participates, such as the overlap between home
and child-care center. The third contextual level, the exosystem, again necessitates
interrelations and linkages between two microsystems. However, the designation of
exosystem further requires that one of the settings does not physically contain the
developing child, although events that occur in that microsystem can have an effect
on the child, for example, the linkage between the child's home and parent's workplace. The macrosystem is the overarching and encompassing contextual level that
includes a given culture's ideals, values, and beliefs. Comprising resources, hazards,
lifestyles, opportunity structures, and life-course options, the macrosystem provides a
society's general blueprint for living (Bronfenbrenner, 1988). In sum, an emphasis on
the ecological context of human development allows for an empirical focus on bidirectional relations between person and context. *See also*: Cultural influences on parenting.

Further Reading: Urie Bronfenbrenner, "Interacting Systems in Human Development. Research Paradigms: Present and Future," in Niall Bolger, Avshalom Caspi, Geraldine Downey,
and Martha Moorehouse, eds., *Persons in Context: Developmental Processes* (New York: Cambridge University Press, 1988); Richard M. Lerner, *Concepts and Theories of Human Development* (Mahwah, NJ: Lawrence Erlbaum, 2002); Richard M. Lerner, "Developmental
Contextualism," in Neil J. Salkind ed., *Child Development* (New York: Macmillan Reference
USA, 2002): pp. 88–96.

James M. Frabutt

Diocesan and archdiocesan schools

Catholic schools can be divided into three types—(arch)diocesan, parish, and private—based on how they are governed. (Arch)diocesan schools are part of the educational mission of the (arch)diocese, function as an agency of the (arch)diocese, and
are operated and financed by the (arch)diocese. Administrators of (arch)diocesan
schools are accountable to the (arch)bishop through the superintendent or vicar of
education. An archdiocese, also called the metropolitan diocese, is the diocese in the
particular region that is the oldest and is the mother diocese for other, smaller dioceses
in the area. Archdioceses, by virtue of their seniority and stature, are headed by archbishops.

(Arch)dioceses establish schools when there are educational needs that are not met
by existing parish or private schools. Many (arch)diocesan schools were established
to serve multiple parishes, either because of rapid enrollment increases or significant
enrollment declines. In these cases, schools operated by the (arch)diocese achieved
economies of scale not achievable by individual parishes.

Some archdiocesan schools were established to provide a particular type of education. Examples include coeducational schools in areas where private schools are

predominantly single-sex schools, comprehensive schools in areas where private schools predominantly have selective admissions policies, and special function schools such as those that educate children with severe special needs.

In many (arch)dioceses, the (arch)bishop has established a consultative board to advise him about matters particular to education. Some boards are also given limited jurisdiction to establish policies that guide the actions of the administrators of (arch)diocesan schools.

According to the *Private School Universe Survey* published by the U.S. Department of Education, in the fall of 1999, there were approximately 27,200 nonpublic schools in the United States, of which approximately 30 percent or 8,100 were Catholic schools. The report indicated that (arch)diocesan schools constituted 9.5 percent of the total of all nonpublic schools and 32 percent of all Catholic schools.

The numbers and proportions of (arch)diocesan schools reported by the federal government are significantly higher than those reported by the National Catholic Educational Association (NCEA). NCEA statistics for the same time period indicate that only 9 percent of Catholic schools are (arch)diocesan; if interparish schools are included with (arch)diocesan schools, the proportion is still only 21 percent. Therefore, part, but not all, of the discrepancy is likely due to different methods of categorizing schools affiliated with more than one parish. *See also*: Bishops; Boards of education, diocesan, parish, school; Consolidated schools; Pastors.

Further Reading: CACE/NABE Governance Task Force, *A Primer on Educational Governance in the Catholic Church* (Washington, DC: National Catholic Educational Association, 1987); Dale McDonald, *United States Catholic Elementary and Secondary Schools 1999–2000: The Annual Statistical Report on Schools, Enrollment, and Staffing* (Washington, DC: National Catholic Educational Association, 2000); Dale McDonald, *United States Catholic Elementary and Secondary Schools 2001–2002: The Annual Statistical Report on Schools, Enrollment, and Staffing* (Washington, DC: National Catholic Educational Association, 2002); National Center for Education Statistics, *Private School Universe Survey: 1999–2000* (Washington, DC: U.S. Department of Education, 2001); United States Conference of Catholic Bishops, *A Statistical Profile of the Church in the United States 1789 to 2000*, October, 2001. http://www.usccb.org/comm/profile.htm. Accessed July 15, 2002.

Karen L. Tichy

Diocesan sisters colleges

After World War I, the Church in the United States became interested in the professional preparation of the teachers in Catholic schools. This was occasioned by the drive for professionalism in the teaching profession in the public sector and the Church's own desire to ensure that Catholic schools were perceived by the public to be at least as good as the public schools. In order to assist the members of religious congregations in the diocese to achieve the minimum standard of a college diploma as a teaching credential, some bishops established diocesan sisters colleges.

After the war there was an phenomenal increase in the number of public high schools in the country. This reality caused the Church in this country to respond with a drive of its own to establish more and more Catholic high schools. At the same time, the states began to set minimum standards for elementary and high school teachers. By 1920, the growing movement for the accreditation of high schools had become a reality for public schools. Catholics knew that if their schools were to be considered at least as good as public schools, then they, too, had to at least meet the minimum standards for teacher certification and school accreditation.

In 1925, Rev. Edward Jordan of the Catholic University of America, speaking at the Annual Meeting of the National Catholic Educational Association, recommended that all high school teachers should have earned a college degree. In point of fact, his study found that 75 percent of the sisters teaching in Catholic high schools had already earned a college degree.

To achieve this goal, religious congregations sought out a number of options. Some religious congregations had founded their own colleges for women in which their own sisters would then earn their degrees. This was true for Ursuline College in Cleveland, Ohio, which was chartered by the state of Ohio in 1871.

Since canon law and the rules of many religious congregations prohibited women from attending colleges in which men were also enrolled, many Catholic colleges provided special sessions during the school year late in the afternoon and on Saturdays. They also offered summer sessions specifically for women religious. By 1923, there were already twenty-three Catholic colleges and universities offering summer school classes for sisters. They stretched across the country from New York to San Francisco and included colleges in Kansas, Massachusetts, Louisiana, Iowa, Nebraska, and Missouri. Where Catholic colleges were not available, some sisters, out of necessity, attended secular colleges, although this was contrary to canon law. Some religious communities circumvented the restrictions against their members attending secular colleges by creating extensions of these colleges in their own motherhouses. The professors then came to motherhouses to teach their courses.

In 1911, the Catholic University of America established the Catholic Sisters College near its own campus. Twenty-nine sisters from eleven different congregations were the first to enroll. Soon the sisters were being awarded not only bachelor of arts degrees, but also master's degrees. In 1914, two sisters were awarded doctorates. To enroll in classes at the main campus of the Catholic University, the sisters needed the permission of their own superiors. Such permission was usually granted only if a specific course was not available at Sisters College. By 1934 Archbishop Michael Curley of Baltimore would argue for the full acceptance of sisters into the Catholic University. He stated that the sisters "meant more to the Church in America, in one sense, than all its hierarchy and its priests" (Nuesse, 1990, p. 259).

Bishops who were trying to meet the needs of a growing Catholic population that wanted Catholic schools for their children felt a particular responsibility to do what they could to assist religious congregations in the education of their sisters who staffed the schools of the diocese. For a number of bishops, that concern was translated into the creation of a diocesan college whose sole purpose was the education of sisters to teach in Catholic schools.

The first such college was opened in 1871 in connection with Saint Francis Seminary near Milwaukee. It was called the Catholic Normal School or Teacher's Seminary. Other dioceses that began such institutions included the Diocesan Normal School of Brooklyn (1920), Diocesan Teachers College in St. Paul, Minnesota (1927), Sisters College (later renamed St. John College in Cleveland, Ohio (1928), the Catholic Teachers College of Providence, Rhode Island (1929), Diocesan Teachers College in Hartford, Connecticut (1949) and St. Mary's College, Wilmington, Delaware (1958).

In 1928, when new requirements were issued regarding teacher certification, the state of Ohio worked with the four Ohio dioceses to help the teachers of these dioceses to meet the new requirements. Each diocese was to combine all of its small-teacher training schools, which, for the most part, were located in congregational motherhouses, and to select one college as its official teacher-training institution through which the state would award its teacher certification. The bishops willingly agreed, and DeSales College (Toledo), St. Mary of the Springs (Columbus), Sisters College (Cleveland), and Teacher's College under the supervision of the Atheneum (Cincinnati) became the official sisters colleges of Ohio.

In his doctoral dissertation, *The Diocesan Teachers College: A Study of Its Basic Principles*, written in 1932, John Hagan, who was the first president of Sisters College in Cleveland, Ohio, argued for the superiority of the education offered at teachers college when compared to that offered by a liberal arts college in the preparation of teachers. He noted that many liberal arts colleges and universities, Catholic, private and public, had begun to develop departments or schools of education. He listed three essential differences between the liberal arts college and the teachers college. First, the teachers college offers a unity of purpose. Everyone who teaches in a teachers college knows that he or she is teaching teachers. This not only impacts those who are teaching pedagogy and other educational theory and practice courses but also impacts the way an art teacher teaches art and a math teacher teaches college math. Since they all know that they are teaching teachers, this is the lens through which they view their curriculum. This is not so in a liberal arts college.

Second, but related to the first, is the kind of instructor that is hired at a teachers college. Such a person is not a pure academician. Certainly, these instructors must have advanced degrees in their subject areas and be able to communicate effectively, but they are also to be persons who can *apply* the particular subject area to the life and work of the teacher. In liberal arts colleges, the emphasis of the instructor is to *discover* and *develop the science he or she is teaching*. This same point was central to the Diocesan Teachers College in Hartford, Connecticut. It was imperative that all the instructors at the college had at one time or another taught in elementary schools. This ensured that they had not only the pedagogical theory but also the invaluable hands-on experience of the classroom in which the students were destined to live out their religious lives.

Finally, integral to the teachers college is the laboratory of the classroom. It has schools integrally related to the college in which the students put into practice what they have learned in the college. They do this under the supervision of trained teachers. There is a constant interplay between theory and practice, between the college and the school.

Hagan outlines an educational model in which postulants take courses during this period of their formation. The second year novices are back at the college after their first year of spiritual formation in their novitiates. After taking their vows, the sisters then complete their education while they are teaching by taking courses in the late afternoon, on Saturdays, and in the summer sessions. In order for this to work, according to Hagan, all the congregations that were to take advantage of this program had to have identical dates for the beginnings of postulancy, novitiate, and final vows. He was able to work this out in the diocese of Cleveland.

In 1941, Sr. Bertrande Meyers published a study she did on sixty congregations of teaching sisters whose total population of sisters was 64,056. The object of her study was to determine the best form of education/formation for religious teachers that would take into account the religious, social, cultural, and professional ideals that the religious congregations sought for their members. The design of her study was to interview the provincials, the mistresses of novices, and the dean of sisters' studies of each of the sixty religious congregations since they would have the clearest sense of what they wanted in the education/formation of their sisters.

Her study had as its foundation that education was at the heart of the life of the religious teaching sister. Sisters who entered congregations whose primary focus was to provide teachers in Catholic schools knew that their lives were centered around the ministry of Catholic education. The "good of the children" would occupy their minds and their hearts for the rest of their lives. In order to do this most effectively, they knew that their own education had to be constantly enhanced and developed.

Sr. Bertrande's study included the variety of educational settings that the sixty religious congregations used to educate their sisters. Her study revealed that many of the congregations had strong reservations about the diocesan sisters college. These had to do with the mingling of sisters, especially younger sisters, with members of other congregations. Several congregational leaders stated that the younger sisters were not yet sufficiently grounded in the spirit of their own congregation to be able to understand the differences in customs, traditions, and practices of other congregations. They often create problems at home in questioning their own congregational traditions and customs. But these same leaders readily assent to the value of the diocesan teachers college for older sisters. In such cases the intermingling of various congregations has helped to break down parochialism and to lessen the spirit of competition that some congregations manifest.

The experience of the sisters at the Diocesan Teachers College in St. Paul, Minnesota, seemed to be a bit more positive than those in Sister Bertrande's study. A dozen different communities were educated there. The experience of these sisters helped them to realize that they were not only members of a particular religious congregation but part of a greater enterprise in the ministry of Catholic education. fMany sisters worked collaboratively with sisters of other religious congregations in the development of curriculum for the archdiocese.

In the mid-1950s the Sister Formation Conference radically changed the way religious sisters were educated in the United States. Some of the Diocesan Teachers Colleges became part of this movement, but many congregations founded or attended Sister Formation colleges like St. Teresa College in Winona, Minnesota, Providence Heights in Seattle, Washington, and Marillac College in St. Louis.

As the number of religious sisters seeking education began to dwindle, the diocesan teachers colleges either expanded their curricula to attract more students, merged with other colleges, or just closed. While they once had met a real need and performed a valuable service for the teaching congregations of sisters, they were simply no longer needed. *See also*: Religious orders of women; Sister Formation.

Further Reading: Harold A. Buetow, *Of Singular Benefit: The Story of U.S. Catholic Education* (New York: Macmillan, 1970); John Hagan, *The Diocesan Teachers College: A Study of Its Basic Principles* (Washington, DC: Catholic University of America, 1932); Bertrande Meyers, *The Education of Sisters: A Plan for Integrating the Religious, Social, Cultural, and Professional Training of Sisters* (New York: Sheed and Ward, 1941); C. Joseph Nuesse, *The Catholic University of America: A Centennial History* (Washington, DC: Catholic University of America Press, 1990); Annabelle Raiche and Ann Marie Biermaier, *They Came to Teach: The Story of Sisters Who Taught in Parochial Schools and Their Contribution to Elementary Education in Minnesota* (St. Cloud, MN: North Star Press of St. Cloud, 1994).

Patrick J. Riley

Diocesan teacher institutes

As the Catholic educational enterprise became larger and more complex at the turn of the twentieth century, Catholic dioceses became more structured in the administration of their schools and in the education of their administrators and teachers.

At the 1884 Third Plenary Council of Baltimore, the American bishops passed many pieces of legislation on Catholic schools. They mandated that within two years each parish was to have a Catholic school attached to it, unless the local bishop decided otherwise. Bishops were to ensure that these schools were to be as good as, if not better than, the public schools. To help ensure the quality of these schools, each bishop was to name one or more priests to form a "Diocesan Commission of Examination." In practice, these commissions evolved into diocesan school boards comprising priests who were to oversee the schools of the diocese.

The Archdiocese of New York was the first to implement this decree by naming a group of priests to its school board in 1886. In 1888, New York named its first superintendent. Philadelphia followed New York's example and named its superintendent in 1889. Within a few years the dioceses of Omaha, Brooklyn, Boston, and Buffalo would all follow suit.

These early superintendents took on their new posts with no training and with no place to go to get training. Each learned how to be a superintendent by being one. Later, as new superintendents were named, these men would go to those already in the job to learn how to be a superintendent.

In the first two decades of the twentieth century much changed. By then most dioceses had superintendents, and many of them were going to the Catholic University of America to seek formal training in this new field. In 1904 the Catholic Educational Association, later known as the National Catholic Educational Association (NCEA), was founded, and in 1908 a special department was created for diocesan superintendents. In 1921 the National Catholic Welfare Conference (NCWC) established a Bureau of Education, and one of its first acts was to invite the Catholic diocesan superintendents to visit their office in Washington, DC, to learn about the services this new bureau could offer to the dioceses. The superintendency had come into its own.

The work at the Catholic University, at the Superintendents' Department of the CEA, and at the Bureau of Education of the NCWC provided the superintendents throughout the country with many ideas and resources as they sought to organize their schools into school systems and to provide their teachers and administrators with training and education.

In a paper written for the Catholic Educational Association Bulletin in 1923, entitled, "The Superintendent and the Professional Improvement of His Teachers," Rev. Augustine Hickey, superintendent of the schools of the archdiocese of Boston, suggested that the improvement of teachers was one of the foremost responsibilities of the superintendent. He offered five ways in which that could be done: (1) the superintendents' conference, (2) classroom supervision, (3) teachers' visiting day, (4) lecture courses, and (5) the diocesan teachers' institute. Hickey described the Teachers' Institute as a four-or five-day gathering of his teachers for a professional retreat. The advantage of such an institute, according to Fr. Hickey, was that "the religious teacher feels the thrill of the great getting-together, and profits exceedingly by the learning and guidance of the distinguished educators who have a place on the program." The teachers took what they learned from this institute back to their classrooms renewed in knowledge and spirit (Hickey, 1923, p. 373).

Two years earlier, in the *National Catholic Welfare Council Bulletin*, Fr. Hickey explained in more detail the advantage the Diocesan Institute provided the teachers of his diocese. Such institutes had been initiated in his diocese in 1910 and had been held every year since. Hickey stated that it helped to develop and maintain an excellent spirit of diocesan cooperation. He went on to write that many religious congregations had been working in the diocese for years but had never had the opportunity to meet and mix with teaching religious of other congregations to share ideas and insights. This event helped to broaden the professional vision of the teachers, intensify mutual appreciation, and demonstrate that each sister was part of a larger picture in the work of Catholic education.

Hickey also noted that in the ten years that the institute had been in existence, the diocese was able to secure the services of men well known as experts in different aspects of Catholic education as lecturers in the institute. These men were mostly Jesuits or superintendents from other dioceses. Some of the topics they addressed included the pedagogy of education, the teaching of composition, modern social problems and their relation to educational work, principles and methods in literature, theory and practice of education, the parochial school in principle and practice, religion in the elementary curriculum, and the process of supervision and methods in penmanship. In addition to these keynote speakers, there were time and opportunity for teachers to share among themselves special topics of interest to them.

This institute was able to bring to all the teachers of the diocese what Hickey believed was the best in progressive educational thought presented by the leading Catholic educators of the country. In addition to this intellectual formation that the institute brings to the teachers of the diocese, Hickey notes once again that it also helps to develop that esprit d'corps, or work-together spirit, among all the religious teachers of the archdiocese.

While the Boston Diocesan Teachers' Institute began in 1910, it was predated by the Diocesan Institute for Teachers in the Diocese of Columbus, Ohio, where the first institute was held in 1902. Rev. Francis Howard, the diocesan superintendent of schools for that diocese, writing in 1908, explained that their institute was "official" and that all the principals were required by the bishop to attend the two-day meeting. Teachers were also invited, and many came each year. The program was planned by the members of the diocesan school board, who sought ideas and suggestions from teachers and administrators. Unlike some of the other diocesan institutes, those in Columbus did not invite well-known national speakers. The talks were given by the teachers of the diocese. These talks provided the basis for discussions in which, according to Howard, "the teachers give their experiences and opinions freely and candidly" (1908, p. 382). Among the usual topics on the agenda were curriculum and textbooks. In 1908 topics included the teaching of reading, the importance of good teaching in the primary grades, and the age and time on entrance and promotion.

Hartman notes that the bishop began each day of the institute by celebrating mass for the teachers. He remained throughout the sessions and gave a closing address to the teachers at the end of the two days.

The benefits that Howard saw in the institute were quite similar to those expressed by Hickey in Boston. It helped to bring the various religious congregations teaching in the diocese together to share ideas and to feel part of a larger enterprise than the work of the individual sister or religious congregation. The teachers were also inspired by the institute with new ideas and returned to teaching with renewed vigor.

Also writing in 1908 was Rev. H. C. Weinker, superintendent of the diocese of Erie in Pennsylvania. In "Value of Teachers' Meeting and Methods of Conducting Them," he explained that his diocese held a two- to four-day institute at the beginning of the teachers' summer vacation. That gave the teachers the whole summer to integrate into their lesson plans and teaching techniques what they had learned at the institute. He believed that such a meeting always created "new life, zeal, enthusiasm" (1908, p. 384) in the teachers of the diocese. He suggested that the speakers for the institute should be "interesting, practical, experienced lecturers, if possible real teachers and educators" and that the talks given should be of "an uplifting, cheerful nature" (p. 386). In selecting lecturers, Weinker also cautioned that superintendents "beware of advocates of fads and the oily-tongued advocates of men and firms that have something to sell" (p. 387). Weinker saw the institute as an excellent tool for the superintendent's addressing any pedagogical problems he might have witnessed as he visited the school during the previous year.

The Diocesan Teachers' Institute seems to have been a very effective resource for diocesan superintendents at the beginning of the twentieth century. The same seems to be true for many dioceses at the beginning of the twenty-first century, according to a survey conducted of all the dioceses of the United States in 2002. Dioceses were asked if they sponsored diocesan teacher institutes. Of those who responded, sixty dioceses stated that they did, and twenty replied in the negative.

The diocese of Columbus in Ohio noted that its Diocesan Teacher Institutes were held annually from 1925 (actually it was since 1902) but were discontinued in 1980. The diocese of Helena in Montana has held them annually since 1920. The diocese of Buffalo stated that its began in 1940, and Springfield in Illinois has had them without interruption since 1945. The archdiocese of New York responded that they have held teacher institutes every year for over fifty years. Monterey in California, Lansing in Michigan, and Seattle in Washington all initiated their teacher institutes in the 1960s.

This same survey revealed that the length of these institutes varied widely from diocese to diocese. While some are two and three days in length, most are one day. Some dioceses reported that they held several one-day institutes twice a year. Some combined with other dioceses for these institutes, and several stated that because of the size of their dioceses they ran the same institute several times in different geographical locations.

The shape of the institute hasn't changed much from those described by the superintendents of almost 100 years ago. Most dioceses bring in a keynote speaker who is an expert in some area of Catholic education. This is followed by smaller break-out sessions that are led by local teachers and administrators on current topics of interest in Catholic education. Many institutes also include the celebration of the Eucharist led by the diocesan bishop or the superintendent of Catholic schools. This Eucharistic celebration always includes a homily in which the leaders of the diocese express their appreciation for the work of the teachers and administrators in their Catholic schools and offer them encouragement in this ministry. Many dioceses also noted that since religious education has become a specialty of its own since the 1970s, often that, too, is the focus of their teacher institutes and break-out sessions.

The reason for dioceses holding these teacher institutes hasn't changed much since

1902. The idea is to bring the teachers of the diocese together in order for them to hear and learn about the latest trends in Catholic education. It is a time in which they can share new ideas and learn new techniques. It is a time for them to pray together and be refreshed and renewed. It is also an opportunity for the teachers from individual schools to experience and feel a part of the greater work of the diocese in its ministry of Catholic education. *See also*: Catholic Educational Association; National Catholic Welfare Conference (NCWC); Teacher preparation.

Further Reading: Harold A. Buetow, *Of Singular Benefit: The Story of U.S. Catholic Education* (New York: Macmillan, 1970); Augustine F. Hickey, "A Diocesan Institute for Religious Teachers," *The National Catholic Welfare Council Bulletin* (December 1921): 2–3; Augustine F. Hickey, "The Superintendent and the Professional Improvement of His Teachers," *The Catholic Educational Association Bulletin* (November 1923): 367–374; Francis Howard, "Diocesan Teachers' Meetings," *The Catholic Educational Association Bulletin* V, 1 (July 1908): 380–382; Timothy Walch, *Parish School: American Catholic Parochial Education from Colonial Times to the Present* (New York: Crossroad, 1996); H. C. Weinker, "Value of Teachers' Meetings and Methods of Conducting Them," *The Catholic Educational Association Bulletin* V, 1 (July 1908): 383–387.

Patrick J. Riley

Diocese and archdiocese

A diocese (archdiocese) designates an ecclesiastical territory or jurisdiction governed by a bishop or archbishop in the Roman Catholic Church. Similar terminology is used among some Protestants, while Orthodox Christians have different designations. An archdiocese is a metropolitan diocese that usually has a larger population. This archbishop has some responsibility for the dioceses, called suffragan dioceses, in his area. Attributes of a diocese are also applicable to an archdiocese.

A diocese is divided into territorial parishes. A bishop, who is believed to be a successor of the apostles, is given pastoral responsibility and leadership for these jurisdictions. While a diocese is often associated with geography, the designation is more accurately applicable to designate the people of that place.

In apostolic times a group of Christians were referred to as a church based upon the city where they lived. The Scriptures witness to such titles as the Church at Corinth or the Church in Rome. The word "diocese" comes from the Greek *dia*, through, and *oikos*, house, imparting the notion of keeping house or administrating a household. Hence, the bishop as chief pastor of a diocese has the responsibility of keeping his house or diocese in good order. St. Paul's First Letter to Timothy 3: 1–13 outlines the responsibilities of the bishop and deacon.

Just as the early Christians used public Roman buildings (basilicas) for their first churches, they also used the structures already operative in the Roman Empire. One such adaptation was the jurisdiction of a diocese. The emperor Diocletian (245–313), perhaps best known for the savage persecutions he orchestrated against the early Church, is credited with dividing geographical districts known as dioceses into provinces, with a desire for local governors to be closer to the people they served. It is the responsibility of the Pope to establish a new diocese, consolidate existing dioceses, or suppress a diocese.

In the United States there are thirty-three archdioceses, 149 dioceses, and the Military Archdiocese, which ministers to men and women serving in the armed forces throughout the world.

The administrative offices and headquarters of a diocese are located at the chancery office. Each diocese would have similar offices such as the bishop's office, the chancellor's office, the vocation office, and the tribunal, plus a variety of offices that might be of particular importance in a specific diocese. Because one of the chief responsibilities of a bishop is to teach, there are various offices and department heads to assist him in carrying out this mission. These offices would include one for religious education and one for Catholic education or schools. The chief administrative officer of the Catholic school office is usually known as a superintendent. A larger diocese may have a school office with numerous subdivisions such as separate superintendents for both elementary and secondary schools. There may be directors of special education, regional coordinators, fund-raisers, professional staff members who work with public school districts to access available moneys for various special programs, diocesan sport leagues, and directors of curriculum. Each diocese would vary in how these services are delivered. In a smaller diocese there might be one person performing the duties of several people, contrasted with a larger archdiocese and a full bureaucracy.

The superintendent serves as a liaison between the local bishop and elementary and secondary schools of a diocese. The diocesan school office assists the elementary and secondary schools in fulfilling their missions through some centralization of resources. A diocesan school office may help in serving as a clearinghouse of teacher applications, offering workshops, assisting financially strapped schools, and recommending certain textbooks. The diocesan school office can also assist families or school administrators when conflicts arise that cannot be resolved at the local level. Canon law (Canons 793–806) places most administrative authority for running the schools with bishops, who in reality delegate the pastor, parish administrator, or principal, to carry out the administration of a school. Private Catholic schools within a diocese serve at the invitation of a bishop but would not be as reliant upon the services provided by the diocesan offices.

As Catholics moved out of urban centers where most Catholic schools were established, many of these schools faced survival problems. Diocesan school offices have been instrumental in organizing foundations, endowments, and drives to assist older schools serving families that may not be able to afford Catholic school tuition. As Catholic families migrated to suburban areas, diocesan officials faced challenges presented by shifting demographics.

Among the chief responsibilities within a diocese is to identify the need for Catholic schools when new parishes are established. In 2002 the National Catholic Educational Association noted that there were 8,114 Catholic schools in the United States with 6,886 elementary and 1,228 secondary schools. This report noted that 93 schools were consolidated or closed and 49 opened.

In a research project by Meitler Consultants on Catholic School Growth from 1985 to 1999 Marquette University dean John Augenstein and Neal Meitler noted that new Catholic schools were opening at the rate of twenty-one each year. Between 1985 and 1999, 204 new elementary schools opened along with twenty-six new high schools. Their research noted that parent groups and pastors exerted the most influence on establishing a new elementary school, while bishops were the most instrumental in promoting a new high school. This report also tracked trends across the country. They reported that there were increased enrollments in the Plains, Southeast, West, and Far West of the United States contrasted to decreases in New England, the Mideast, and the Great Lakes region. In those areas where there are increased enrollments there is a parallel demand for more Catholic schools to be established. These findings highlight the challenges and work that a bishop and diocese must analyze and act upon. *See also*: Bishops; Governance; Hierarchy.

Further Reading: Thomas S. Bokenkotter, *A Concise History of the Catholic Church* (New York: Image Books, 1990); Richard M. Jacobs, *Authority and Decision Making in Catholic Schools* (Washington, DC: National Catholic Educational Association, 2002); National Catholic Educational Association, http://ncea.org. Accessed July 23, 2002.

Michael P. Caruso, SJ

Director of religious education (DRE)

A person given authority by a parish pastor to direct, organize, resource, and administer the religious education or faith formation in a parish and/or school. The director of religious education (DRE) is a relatively new position in the Catholic Church, becoming popular in the late 1960s and early 1970s as religious education attempted to adjust to the theology of Vatican Council II. Many directors of religious education have entered the field after working as teachers and principals in Catholic elementary and high schools.

The DRE position is a difficult one to describe, taking a variety of forms in dioceses throughout the United States. In many areas, the position requires a master's degree in religious education, theology, or a related field. Directors with graduate training are usually responsible for all forms of religious education in a parish. This may include a consulting or supervisory role in matters of religious education in the Catholic school.

The first generation of DREs, many of whom were religious sisters, inherited the administration of the parish Confraternity of Christian Doctrine (CCD), a religious education structure dating back to the sixteenth century that focused primarily on teaching religion to children attending public schools. Early DREs concentrated on sacramental preparation programs and classroom religious education for young people and arranged for the ongoing training of the catechists in parishes or schools.

The role of the DRE began to expand quickly in the years after the council, especially after the release in 1971 of the *General Catechetical Directory* (GCD), a philosophical statement of the nature, purpose and goals of religious education. The GCD called for creativity in response to the signs of the times, which complemented the new ministries arising from the Vatican II vision of faith and parish life. Religious educators were soon involved in youth retreats, liturgical planning, new social justice and service experiences, and the outreach to marginalized groups like divorced, alienated, or gay Catholics.

The experiences convinced many DREs that the most powerful lessons about their faith are often learned in experiences outside of classrooms and formal education. About the same time, religious education started reclaiming an older word for their ministry, catechesis, which means literally, "to echo." For many DREs, catechesis seemed to capture the learning occurring in the new ministries, a more holistic faith and spiritual formation of the entire person—heart, mind, and soul.

Meanwhile, a national catechetical directory based on the GCD, *Sharing the Light of Faith* (1978), apostolic exhortations, papal encyclicals, like *Evangelii Nuntiandi* (1975) and *Catechesi Tradendae* (1979), and pastoral letters by the United States Catholic Conference (USCC), such as *To Teach as Jesus Did* (1972), continued to explore the dynamics of faith formation and the rapidly changing world. These documents endorsed some of the new models of religious education, like family-centered catechesis and liturgical or lectionary-based catechesis. One of the most important shifts in the new vision of these documents was a heightened importance for adult religious formation.

Religious education with adults became the model for all catechesis, and the DRE was expected increasingly to commit a large amount of time and energy to faith formation with this older population. In many parishes this new adult focus came primarily through the Rite of Christian Initiation (RCIA), an adult process of learning and conversion rediscovered in the documents of Vatican II. However, it has become clear that other forms of adult education are also critical to a vibrant parish community.

The developments since Vatican Council II have made it clear that an effective DRE must serve a vast number of formal and informal roles in a parish or school. In 1996 the National Conference of Catechetical Leadership (NCCL), an organization dedicated to promoting the ministry of the DRE in the United States, developed certification standards for the parish director of religious education. The NCCL standards surfaced 122 sets of abilities needed to administer a religious education program. These abilities include such complex skills as conducting procedures for educational needs assessment and analysis; utilizing appropriate teaching and learning methodologies for adults, adolescents, and children; preparing creative, spirit-filled liturgies; and being able to teach persons the foundations of Catholic faith and doctrine and current teachings of the Church.

Many of the DRE's formal duties are similar to those of a school principal, like program administrator, curriculum planner and developer, fund-raiser, and legal resource, although unlike a principal, the DRE must work with volunteer teachers, requiring advanced skills in volunteer recruitment, motivation, and retention. The DRE also has informal duties similar to those of the pastor, the primary one being to serve as a nurturer of faith, creating community through active listening, inspiration leadership and action, and going about the ministry with a personal touch that makes children and their parents feel valued and loved. In addition, the DRE often serves in the role of the persuader, helping to move the parish community to a deeper engagement and appropriation of their faith. In this capacity the DRE works with the pastor as a change agent in the parish, initiating new programs and perspectives and getting caught in the tension of a diverse community trying to let go of the old and embrace the new.

The future of the DRE position is uncertain. Protestant churches began promoting the position of DRE in the early 1900s, hoping to create a new church profession. But, by 1940 there were less than 1,000 people serving in the field, and most churches changed the name to director of Christian education or minister of Christian education.

In the meantime, national organizations, like NCCL and the National Parish Coordinators and Directors (NPCD), and state and diocesan DRE associations, keep directors of religious education networked with each other, sharing resources and support and providing hope the field will one day come more fully into a full professional status. *See also*: Parish School of Religion; Total Catholic Education.

Further Reading: Donald G. Emler, *Revisioning the DRE* (Birmingham, AL: Religious Education Press, 1989); Maria Harris, *The D.R.E. Book* (New York: Paulist, 1976); Robert J. Hater, *New Vision, New Directions: Implementing the Catechism of the Catholic Church* (Allen, TX: Thomas More, 1994): 1–17; National Association of Parish Catechetical Directors (NPCD), www.ncea.org; *National Certification Standards for Professional Parish Directors of Religious*

Education (Washington, DC: National Conference of Catechetical Leadership, 1996); National Conference of Catechetical Leadership, www.nccl.org.

Mark S. Markuly

Disadvantaged students

Disadvantaged students face obstacles due to particular characteristics, personal background, or other factors. Disadvantaged students comprise a diverse population, ranging from racial minorities to children with emotional or learning problems. These students may face increased difficulties in scholastic endeavors based upon characteristics or factors that are beyond their control. The many reasons for these disadvantages include teacher bias, lack of parental education or income, a home life that is not conducive to learning, societal ignorance, limited resources available both at home and in school, and internalized lower expectations.

Children from poor socioeconomic backgrounds have long been discriminated against. Not only do these children lack important resources, but they are more likely to be ignored or dismissed in the classroom. For example, impoverished children have more limited educational resources because their families cannot afford to purchase extra material to strengthen and reinforce skills taught in school. The parents of these students often work long hours, thereby making child monitoring and parental involvement more difficult. Socioeconomic status is often intertwined with racial and ethnic minority status, producing a child that is doubly disadvantaged in the educational system.

Almost without exception, racial and ethnic minorities are faced with centuries of prejudice, discrimination, lowered expectations, and stereotypes. Asians are the one exception, often outperforming Caucasian students. Children for whom English is a second language face enormous difficulties competing with their peers. There has been no consensus in the educational field about the best way to break the language barrier and educate these children. Many schools simply do not have the resources to provide the much needed extra learning assistance.

Historically, males have been considered the more intelligent sex. Although this bias has lessened, women are still considered less intelligent. This, in turn, lowers expectations, and less attention is given to females in the classroom, especially in science and mathematics. Even class materials, especially literature, may contain biases toward males and establish and uphold rigid gender roles.

Children with physical disabilities, learning difficulties, or emotional problems also face disadvantage within the educational system. Administrators and teachers are charged with providing a good education for the majority of students and caring for the special needs of these children. Students with these problems often require individualized attention and do not succeed well in an average classroom.

Whether intentionally or subconsciously, children are discriminated against by the very teachers and administrators who are paid to help them. Teacher bias affects every student and varies depending on the educator's background. Teachers often underestimate a child's potential based solely on the background of that child, not on the child's past performance or ambition. It is sometimes believed that high socioeconomic status students are smarter, but low socioeconomic status children do not have lower IQs than their counterparts. Minority students and low socioeconomic status students are also more likely to be placed on a nonacademic track instead of a curriculum that is meant to prepare students for college.

Low levels of parental education can also place a child at a disadvantage. Some parents cannot help their children with their schoolwork because they do not have a strong educational background themselves. Parents who lack education may also de-emphasize the importance of education to their children. Without strong parental support, some children give up on themselves. Intrinsically linked to parental education is the fact that some children grow up in homes that are not conducive to learning. This can mean that education is not only viewed as important but also impacts the physical characteristics of the home. Unstable family circumstances, poor nutrition and health care, violence both inside and outside of the home, and drug use by family members can detract from a child's educational potential.

The availability of educational tools can also greatly affect a child's ability, especially those with physical or mental problems, to learn at the same pace as their peers. Children who have not been read to or who did not attend preschool are already behind when they start school. Even in poor school districts, upper- and middle-class students receive more assistance at home, compensating for the paucity of educational resources provided by the school district. Lower-class students are left with very few options.

Societal expectations for a child can have an enormous influence on the achievement of a disadvantaged student. Some minority students cave into the lower expectations from society and surrender, feeling that they will never win. Whether negative ideation comes from a parent, teacher, or friend, some students internalize these notions and give up. When a child constantly sees others putting forth effort and not receiving any benefits, they become passive themselves.

Not only do younger disadvantaged students face increased hardships, but they are also likely to continue to face these problems throughout their academic and work careers. Lower standardized testing scores for college admissions, a decreased likelihood of continuing their education, and adversity in acquiring stable employment are all potential outcomes for disadvantaged students who do not receive the necessary help. Along with the challenge of obtaining college admission, students who do not complete high school or attend college have more difficulty obtaining stable employment. Even in cases where a company hires them, without a competitive education or skills, the likelihood of upward mobility is minimal.

Many disadvantaged students learn to cope and succeed in life. There are several programs to give these students an extra boost. By increasing awareness of false stereotypes and by designing more programs that address the problems that plague youth, disadvantaged students can overcome their challenges, and every child will have an equal opportunity to succeed. *See also*: African Americans; Cristo Rey schools; Inner-city schools; Minority students; Socioeconomic status (of students).

Further Reading: Bruce M. Mitchell and Robert E. Salsbury, eds., *Encyclopedia of Multicultural Education* (Westport, CT, and London: Greenwood Press, 1999); Cecil R. Reynolds and Elaine Fletcher-Janzen, eds., *Encyclopedia of Special Education* (New York: John Wiley and Sons, 2000); Leslie R. Williams and Doris P. Fromberg, eds., *Encyclopedia of Early Childhood Education* (New York and London: Garland, 1992).

Rebecca Gaines and James M. Frabutt

Diversity

Diversity refers to differences in human qualities among groups of people and individuals. Diversity becomes manifest in the broad spectrum of demographic and philosophical differences created by individuals and groups. Primary and secondary dimensions of diversity exist. Primary dimensions, which are mainly biological and usually visible, include age, ethnicity, gender, race, sexual orientation, and physical abilities/qualities. Secondary dimensions of diversity are psycho/sociological characteristics and are typically those that can be changed. A nonexhaustive list of examples includes income, educational background, religious beliefs, parental status, geographic location, marital status, and work experiences. In a Catholic context, diversity may be viewed as a radical call to embrace the richness of the human experience. This call is a challenge to appreciate, respect, promote, and learn from the differences and variations of humankind.

Grant (1995) wrote that within an educational context, diversity "promotes both the appreciation of human differences and the belief that, in order for students to think critically—especially about life circumstances and opportunities that directly impact their lives and the lives of their family members, community, and country—they must affirm both *social* diversity (cultural pluralism) and *human* diversity" (p. 4). Social diversity, or cultural pluralism, refers to the notion that variety leads to strengths and that "the United States as a whole benefits from the contributions of different groups of people" (p. 4). Social diversity at the school level means that students are presented with a range of social and academic choices, students seek out and critically examine alternative choices and viewpoints, and students are taught that there is strength in diversity. Racism, classism, and sexism embedded in the larger society are naturally represented in the microcosm of the school. For this reason, direct instruction, pedagogical methods, and curriculum must be shaped in a manner so that students can effect positive social change to address these inequalities.

Human, or individual, diversity must also be accepted and valued at the school level. Grant (1995) noted that an especially critical aspect of individual diversity that must be understood and respected in schools is the variation in body size (height and weight) and the standards of physical beauty. Advertising, television programs, and movies—virtually all aspects of media—provide constant commentary and visual confirmation of what constitutes an ideal image of beauty. As Grant noted, it is possible for schools to "reflect and perpetuate these ideas mainly through their hidden curriculum (e.g., members of the cheering squad or golf team) of the model person and the model sport" (p. 11). Conscientious efforts must be made to highlight multiple models of human diversity by focusing on healthy persons rather than a so-called beautiful person or by sponsoring a variety of athletic teams that allow a broad array of students to participate.

"Prizing human diversity requires understanding the 'double consciousness' that many children of color experience as they enter schools with a large population of White students and teaching staff" (Grant, 1995, p. 12). The echoes of W.E.B. Du Bois' classic articulation of "two warring ideals within one dark body" (Du Bois, 1953, p. 3) are evident in that students of color have the challenging task of acquiring a sense of respect for their own culture while often living in a dominant culture that may malign, discredit, or outwardly discriminate against it. Teachers and school staff must be aware of, and sensitive to, the challenges that students face as their socialization unfolds on three fronts: into their own ethnic and racial group, the mainstream culture, and the reality of their existence as a minority in a dominant culture.

Gender and language are especially significant to any discussion of valuing human diversity. Within the school students develop and refine the meanings associated with gender, which consequently influence their understanding of power relationships and career paths, for example. Grant (1995) acknowledged that "schools must be alert to the way in which society socializes students because of their gender, and offer policies and practices that encourage socialization and development based on a student's ability and career goals, not on gender" (p. 13). Individual diversity is also shaped by a student's language. Language influences self-concept development, academic achievement, and teacher–student communication. For these reasons, schools must be prepared to deal with the language diversity that students possess so that students' native language becomes an asset, not a detriment, to their educational aspirations.

Nieto (2002) described several domains to which schools must be attentive in order to have a positive climate for diversity. First, schools and teachers must actively confront institutional racism and other forms of discrimination. Teachers from a dominant group must acknowledge their own privilege, or else will develop dysconscious racism, "a limited and distorted view of racism based on a tacit acceptance of dominant White norms and privileges that fails to take into account the basic structural inequities of society" (p. 188). Second, teachers and schools must maintain high expectations for student achievement regardless of gender, race, social class, or other differences. One strategy to address this issue is to ensure that teacher education curricula expose teachers to history and research on teacher expectancy effects. Third, a focus on curriculum and pedagogy is crucial to supporting diversity. "There is a distinct mismatch between the curriculum of the school and the lives of many children. . . . Add to this the fact that the joys, dilemmas, and conflicts of communities are seldom brought into the classroom in significant ways, and the result is that students report being bored because they see little in school that is of relevance to their lives" (p. 190). Curriculum is a powerful mechanism of engagement and must reflect the diversity of students' backgrounds, life experiences, and talents. Similarly, pedagogical strategies must be varied enough—perhaps including student-centered and empowering characteristics—to provide a culturally responsive educational environment. Fourth, critical questions must be asked about tracking and ability grouping since the deleterious consequences of such practices are disproportionately experienced by students who are culturally marginalized or economically disadvantaged. Nieto (2002) suggested that "teacher educators need to present future teachers with concrete suggestions for making detracking work, including skills in cooperative learning, alternative assessment, and empowering pedagogy" (p. 195). Fifth, teachers and schools must constantly engage in a critical assessment of their testing practices so that students from linguistically or culturally diverse backgrounds are assessed in an equitable manner. Finally, teacher, parent, and student involvement are ultimately key to building a school atmosphere that is supportive of diversity. Teachers must realize their powerful role as agents for change; parents must be made aware of the strong impact of involvement on student achievement; and students must be viewed as integral to the two-way process of learning, complete with experiences, ideas, and interests that can enliven the educational experience. *See also*: African Americans; Hispanics/Latinos; Socioeconomic status (of students).

Further Reading: W.E.B. Du Bois, *The Souls of Black Folk* (Millwood, KY: Kraus-Thomson, 1953); Carl A. Grant, "Praising Diversity in School: Social and Individual Implications," in Carl A. Grant, ed., *Educating for Diversity: An Anthology of Multicultural Voices* (Boston: Allyn and Bacon, 1995); Sonia Nieto, *Affirming Diversity: The Sociopolitical Context* *of Multicultural Education* (New York: Longman, 2000); Sonia Nieto, *Language, Culture, and Teaching: Critical Perspectives for a New Century* (Mahwah, NJ: Lawrence Erlbaum, 2002).

James M. Frabutt

Dress codes

The term "dress code" often includes not only guidelines for acceptable types of clothing but also grooming guidelines (e.g., regulations regarding hair, cosmetics, jewelry, hygiene, etc.) and regulations regarding school uniforms. Dress codes differ from uniforms in that dress codes specify certain types, styles, and colors of garments that either may or may not be worn, whereas uniforms specify particular garments that must be purchased from a designated source. Dress codes result in similar clothing for students, whereas uniforms result in identical clothing.

Dress regulations of some type have long been part of Catholic school culture, especially at the elementary school level. Images of Catholic school girls in plaid jumpers and white blouses and Catholic school boys in navy blue pants and white shirts are more typical than stereotypical. However, very little has been written about the phenomenon of Catholic school dress codes or uniforms.

School dress regulations may include a combination of uniform garments and garments that meet certain criteria but are not strictly "uniform." For example, a dress code may include a uniform skirt and blouse but specify types of shoes and colors of socks that are within regulations.

Dress codes vary in terms of scope and specificity. These variances have consequences in terms of interpretation, compliance, and enforcement. Some dress code provisions are very general, for example, "no extreme hairstyles" or "shirt with a collar." Other provisions are very specific, for example, "navy blue uniform sweater purchased from the school store." The more vague or general the dress code in general or provisions within the code in particular, the more open the code is to a variety of opinions about whether particular garments are "in dress code" or not.

School uniform policies are easier to enforce because the amount of interpretation and variation is much less than with dress codes. Dress codes allow students a greater degree of self-expression but consume a greater amount of time and energy in determining whether particular garments do or do not fall within the dress code.

In general, elementary schools seem to use uniforms more than dress codes, whereas secondary schools are more likely to have dress codes than uniforms. A number of secondary schools that once had uniforms for girls and dress codes for boys have adjusted their regulations to make the rules for both genders more equitable.

Dress codes generally regulate all outer garments—shirts/blouses, sweaters, pants/skirts/shorts, socks, and shoes. Provisions may address colors, fabrics, and styles that are acceptable or forbidden and manner of wear, for example, "shirts must be tucked in" or "a belt must be worn with pants."

Several reasons are advanced for regulating dress. These include promoting a sense of identity and belonging, reducing peer pressure and competition, setting an appropriate tone for learning, ensuring modesty, facilitating ready identification of students and nonstudents, and reducing costs for school clothing.

Many schools have also adopted different uniforms or dress codes for physical education classes. In addition, alternative dress codes for "out of uniform" days, liturgical celebrations, special events, and various seasons of the year have been developed by a growing number of schools.

While dress regulations, whether of the "dress code" or "school uniform" type, are very prevalent in Catholic schools, the specifics of the school's dress rules are generally developed at the individual school level with the involvement of parents, faculty, and students.

In recent years, public schools have explored and, in a growing number of cases, adopted school uniforms. Such policy decisions have been made with a view toward improving discipline, eliminating garments that may be associated with gangs, reducing the likelihood of theft of expensive articles of apparel, and reducing the likelihood of school violence. *See also*: School uniforms.

Further Reading: David Brunsma and Kerry Ann Rockquemore, "Examining the Effects of School Uniforms on Attendance, Substance Use, Behavior Problems, and Academic Achievement," *The Journal of Educational Research* 92, 1 (1998): 53–62.

Karen L. Tichy

Drexel, Katharine (1858–1955)

Katharine Drexel was the second native-born American to be canonized by the Catholic Church. Drexel founded the Sisters of the Blessed Sacrament for Indians and Colored People. The Sisters of the Blessed Sacrament have established and operated many Catholic schools in the United States, including Xavier University of New Orleans, and the first U.S. mission school dedicated to American Indians. At the time of Drexel's death, the Sisters of the Blessed Sacrament had over 500 nuns in forty-nine different convents operating sixty-three different schools. In addition to her hard work and vision, Drexel donated over $20 million of her own money to fund the operations of the Sisters of the Blessed Sacrament.

Katharine Drexel was born November 26, 1858. She was the second daughter of prominent Philadelphia banker and philanthropist Francis Anthony and Hannah Langstroth Drexel. Hannah Drexel died one year after Katharine's birth; however, two years later Francis married Emma Bouvier. Emma Bouvier quickly became a loving stepmother to Katharine and her older sister, Elizabeth.

Drexel grew up in a comfortable, nurturing, spiritual environment. She was educated by private tutors and afforded the opportunity to travel throughout the United States and Europe. She also spent time with her sisters as a Sunday school teacher in a school established by her stepmother for the poor. During this time Rev. Joseph O'Connor (later Bishop O'Connor), the family's pastor, became Drexel's close friend and spiritual adviser.

In 1883, when Drexel was 21 years old, her stepmother died of cancer. Soon after the tragedy, she sought the counsel of Reverend O'Connor about entering religious life. He advised her to give the idea more thought and prayer. Just two years later in 1885, Drexel's father died. Upon his death, Drexel and her sister Elizabeth inherited an estate valued at more than $1 million. She then dedicated herself to using the income from this estate for charitable causes.

Drexel became particularly interested in the plight of the American Indians. Together with her two sisters and Msgr. Joseph Stephan, she visited several reservations all over the country. She quickly recognized the pressing need for schools not only for American Indians but also for African Americans. Through her research she estimated that there were almost 250,000 American Indians without access to education

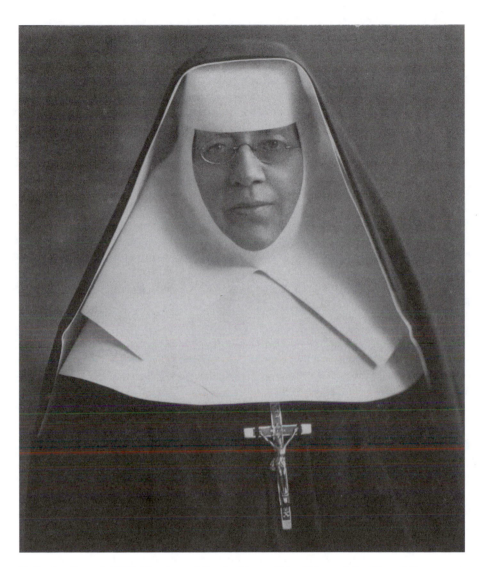

Katharine Drexel, 1895. Courtesy of the Archives of the Sisters of the Blessed Sacrament.

and over nine million African Americans still unable to build substantive lives after the abolition of slavery. Drexel immediately began using her fortune to build schools, supply food, provide clothing and shelter, and even arrange for priests to provide spiritual instruction to both American Indians and African Americans. During this period she realized that while using her money to address these problems certainly helped, in order to make lasting improvements she would have to dedicate her life to this new mission.

In 1889 Bishop O'Connor granted Drexel his consent for her to enter religious life. He encouraged her to establish an organization dedicated to the service of American Indians and African Americans. On November 7, 1891, Katharine received her habit and became Sr. Mary Katharine. In February of the same year she made her vows and became the first sister of the Blessed Sacrament. In 1892 with thirteen other sisters, Sr. Mary Katharine opened the first convent of the Sisters of the Blessed Sacrament in Bensalem, Pennsylvania. "Besides the vows usual in all religious communities, the sisters pledge themselves to work exclusively for the spiritual and temporal welfare of the Indian and coloured races" (Mercedes, http://www.newadvent. org/cathen/02599a.htm). The sisters immediately began their service.

In 1894 the sisters opened an industrial arts school dedicated to the Pueblo Indians of Santa Fe, New Mexico, named St. Catherine's. This was followed by the Institute of St. Francis de Sales in Rock Castle, Virginia. St. Frances was a boarding academy and industrial school for African American females. Drexel and the Blessed Sacrament sisters opened many other schools in this time period in all areas of the country. Perhaps the most significant school started by the Sisters of the Blessed Sacrament in this period was Xavier University of New Orleans. This was the first predominantly African American Catholic University in the country.

Drexel suffered a severe heart attack in 1935 and was forced into retirement. She, however, remained a prayerfully devoted advocate to the missions she and her order founded during her ministry. Drexel died March 3, 1955. She was canonized October 1, 2000. Her feast day is March 3. *See also*: African Americans; Native Americans; Religious orders of women.

Further Reading: Katharine Burton, *The Golden Door: The Life of Katharine Drexel* (New York: Kenedy, 1957); Consuela Marie Duffy, *Katharine Drexel* (Cornwall Heights, PA: Mother Katharine Drexel Guild, Sisters of the Blessed Sacrament, 1966); Bernard L. Marthaler, ed., *New Catholic Encyclopedia*, 2nd ed. (Washington, DC: Catholic University of America and the Gale Group, 2002), 4: 906–907; Ellen Terry, *Katharine Drexel, Friend of the Neglected* (New York: Farrar, Straus, and Cudahy, 1958).

Jeffery M. Boetticher, Jr.

Dropout rates

"Dropout rate" is the term used to describe the percentage of students in a school who leave school before graduating. There are different ways to calculate dropout rate, and there is disagreement on which students should be counted in determining the dropout rate. However, there is no disagreement that school dropout is a problem with serious consequences. These consequences include an underskilled workforce, decreased economic productivity, higher crime rate, lost tax revenue, and increased cost of public assistance. A low school dropout rate or high graduation rate is often used as a benchmark for school success. Catholic schools have a particularly good track record demonstrating a high graduation rate and low dropout rate among their students regardless of socioeconomic background. The reasons attributing to this success are the communal organization of Catholic schools and the high level of social capital within the school community.

James S. Coleman and Thomas Hoffer in their 1987 study reported that the dropout rate in Catholic high schools was one-fourth as high as in public high schools. Specifically, the study found that over 14 percent of high school sophomores attending public schools did not graduate with their class cohort two years later. For Catholic schools only 3 percent did not graduate. In 1993, Anthony Bryk, Valerie Lee, and Peter Holland, using data from *High School and Beyond*, reported similar results, with public high schools and Catholic high schools having a 15.4 percent and 4.0 percent dropout rate, respectively. The Bryk, Lee, and Holland study further demonstrated that the dropout rate for minority students in Catholic schools was lower than the rate in public schools. While the dropout rates in both public and Catholic schools are higher for blacks and Hispanics, the dropout rates for these students were lower in Catholic schools. The dropout rates in public schools were almost 18 percent for Black students and slightly more than 16 percent for Hispanic students. The dropout rates in Catholic school were 7 percent for blacks and approximately 11 percent for Hispanic students. Catholic schools not only have a lower average dropout rate but also reduce the effect of socioeconomic background on dropout rate.

Why are Catholic schools successful in engaging students? Bryk, Lee, and Holland (1993) attributed the success to the communal organization of the Catholic school. From their field studies, they reported a consistent and distinctive community culture. People involved in good Catholic schools see themselves as a community. Their analysis identified three essential elements of communal school organization: (1) values shared among the administrators, teachers, students, and parents, (2) academic and nonacademic activities shared among members of the school community, and (3) a unique set of social relations among school community members that create a caring environment where students and teachers are valued and respected. These social relations were cultivated by teachers having broad responsibilities beyond their classroom duties and faculty collegiality.

Other researchers use the concept of social capital to explain the low dropout rate of Catholic schools. Social capital is the phrase used to describe strong social relationships based on shared values that permit high levels of trust between and among people. The late James S. Coleman explained the low dropout rate of Catholic schools in terms of this definition of social capital. "Catholicism, *per se*, does not account for the low dropout rate. Slowly we come to the conclusion that the relationship between the religious community that surrounds a religious school and the students in the school makes an enormous impact in terms of students dropping out of school" (Coleman, 1987, p. 7). Children who attend Catholic schools typically have more access to social capital than their public school peers. Students in Catholic schools are more apt to have parents who know the parents of their friends, be more involved with their schools, have more interaction with their parents, and be less likely to have changed schools. Jay Teachman, Kathleen Paasch, and Karen Carver (1996) found in their research that families of children who attend Catholic schools are frequently closely connected with the school.

Low dropout rate is an effect of the positive environment within Catholic schools—an environment that is caring and respectful of individuals and engenders trust among administrators, teachers, students, and parents. The social relationships within a Catholic school community warrant closer study as a model for organizational effectiveness. *See also*: *Catholic High Schools and Minority Students*; *Catholic High Schools: Their Impact on Low-Income Students*; *Catholic Schools and the Common Good*; Climate (Catholic school); Coleman, James S.

Further Reading: Anthony S. Bryk, Valerie E. Lee, and Peter B. Holland, *Catholic Schools and the Common Good* (Cambridge: Harvard University Press, 1993); James S. Coleman, "Social Capital and the Development of Youth," *Momentum* 18, 19 (November 1987): 6–8; James Coleman and Thomas Hoffer, *Public and Private High Schools: The Impact of Communities* (New York: Basic Books, 1987); Richard J. McGrath, "Students in Catholic Schools," in Thomas C. Hunt, Ellis A. Joseph, and Ronald Nuzzi, eds., *Catholic Schools Still Make a Difference: Ten Years of Research, 1991–2000* (Washington, DC: National Catholic Educational Association, 2002); Ann Meier, *Social Capital and School Achievement among Adolescents*, a paper prepared for presentation at the 1999 American Sociological Association Annual Meeting in Chicago (Madison, WI: Center for Demography and Ecology, University of Wisconsin-Madison, 1999); Jay D. Teachman, Kathleen Paasch, and Karen Carver, "Social Capital and Dropping Out of School Early," *Journal of Marriage and the Family* 58, 3 (August 1996): 773–783.

Frank X. Savage

E

Edgerton (Wisconsin) bible case

Wisconsin joined the Union in 1848. The state's constitution established public schools, prohibited sectarian instruction in them, forbade making the school a place of worship, and upheld the right of every person to worship Almighty God according to the dictates of his or her conscience. The framers did not consider books of religious doctrine or belief to constitute sectarian instruction, indicating that the Bible was excluded from that category and hence legal to use in public education. The Bible occupied a unique and exalted place in Wisconsin society, as it did nationally at that time.

The public schools of Wisconsin were Protestant-dominated in the years following statehood. The devotional reading of the King James version of the Bible with attendant religious devotions played an important part in public schooling in the state from the outset. Wisconsin's "mainstream" Protestants (Baptists, Congregationalists, Methodists, and Presbyterians) strongly supported the practice. They deemed it nonsectarian, sufficient to make the schools morally and religiously acceptable. The Bible, they believed, was every person's birthright; not only was it indispensable for implanting and maintaining Christian character in the young, but it was also necessary for the republic's survival.

The state's population changed dramatically over the decades, due to immigration. Challenges to the practice of Bible-reading in the public schools grew as the state became more religiously heterogeneous. Then, in the 1880s, in Edgerton, a group of Catholics brought suit on behalf of their children who were pupils in the schools of that city. They charged that the practice violated their children's rights of conscience because it constituted sectarian instruction, which was forbidden by the Wisconsin constitution. The School Board denied their allegations, asserting that the children were free to leave the room during the practice. The board also said that each person had the right to read and interpret the Bible for herself or himself, which, it claimed, made the contention of the plaintiffs sectarian. Further, the board said that it had the right to choose textbooks for use in the schools, and the Bible was on a list recommended by the state superintendent for general, not sectarian, instruction. Finally, the board argued that the vast majority of the people of the district were Protestant and wanted the King James version to be used in school; the Bible, the board averred, was unable to be replaced by any other text.

In 1888, Circuit Court Judge John R. Bennett ruled in favor of the defendant, holding that the practice was legal. He adjudged that "sectarianism" came from "creeds which imperfectly define the great spiritual truths of the Bible," not from the Bible itself. The Bible was a part of the nation's history, and its reading did not make the school a house of worship. Others, besides Catholics, had "rights of conscience," and they made up a majority. The Bible, he contended, was a unique book, a "good, true and ever faithful friend and counselor."

Abetted by the funds raised by *The Catholic Citizen*, the English-language newspaper located in Milwaukee, the plaintiffs appealed to the Wisconsin Supreme Court. Counsel for the plaintiffs averred that the practice violated the Catholic students' rights of conscience and made the school a place of worship. The defendant's counsel concentrated on the crucial role of the Bible in American society and advanced the following points. Counsel denied that the practice violated the Catholics' rights of conscience because they were free to interpret Scripture as they chose. Bible-reading was an expression of the will of the majority. The country had been Christian since its inception; the Bible was the foundation of the Christian religion, which in turn was the basis for the public school system and American civil liberties. The board had no right to exclude such a book, so necessary for the teaching of morals and the fundamentals of the Christian religion from the common schools. Both the framers of the national and state institutions intended it to be an essential part of American civil life, especially its schools.

In a unanimous decision, handed down on March 17, 1890, the Wisconsin Supreme Court ruled that devotional Bible-reading in public schools constituted sectarian instruction and made the school a place of worship. Consequently, the practice was in violation of the Wisconsin constitution on both counts.

Mainstream Protestant reaction to the decision was swift, generally highly critical, and emotional. The decision was regarded as an abandonment of the nation's heritage, which would result in the decay of Wisconsin society. It had outlawed the book that was the "Magna Carta" of the nation's moral and religious influence and the most effective agency, "next to the Church of God," for laying the foundations of popular intelligence, virtue, and freedom in the United States. Protestants decried the description of the Bible as a sectarian book. Some faulted the Catholic Church, with its anti-Bible and abysmal record in protecting the rights of conscience, for the decision. The very book that had created the public schools was now estranged from them. As a result, the schools and their students were bereft of its salutary influence.

Catholics generally rejoiced at the decision, which made the public schools judicially free from Protestant ascendancy. They were joined by Unitarians and liberals. Catholics regarded the decision as a triumph for their rights of conscience. It is well to note, however, that the Catholic bishops in Wisconsin paid scant attention to the Bible-reading controversy compared to the interest they displayed in the Bennett Law strife that was contemporary to it. The Bennett Law was perceived by the bishops as a threat to the existence of Catholic schools, which were paramount in the bishops' educational vision. Nonetheless, the Edgerton decision, the first of its kind by a state supreme court, symbolically ended Protestant domination of the public schools in Wisconsin. It not only reflects the changed demographics of the state but also stands as testimony to the fact that the public schools of Wisconsin had evolved, in the eyes of the law, from "nonsectarian" Protestant Christian to secular institutions. *See also*: Bible-reading in public schools.

Further Reading: J. J. Blaisdell, *The Edgerton Bible Case. The Decision of the Wisconsin Supreme Court* (Madison: State Historical Society of Wisconsin, 1890); Harry H. Heming, *The Catholic Church in Wisconsin* (Milwaukee: T. J. Sullivan, 1896); Thomas C. Hunt, "The Edgerton Bible Decision: The End of an Era," *The Catholic Historical Review* 67, 4 (October 1981): 589–619; W. A. McAtee, "Must the Bible Go?," *Minutes of the Synod of Wisconsin of the Presbyterian Church 1891* (Madison: Tracy, Gibbs, 1891); *Wisconsin Reports*, 76 Wis. 177.

Thomas C. Hunt

Education by Choice: The Case for Family Control

John E. Coons and Stephen D. Sugarman, professors of law at the University of California Berkeley, have devoted much of their scholarly efforts to the examination and remedy of fiscal inequities in public education that result from a dependence on real estate values as the base for tax support of local public schools. Their early work developed the legal framework for the litigation that led to a massive reform of education finance in California. In *Education by Choice*, they went beyond a redistribution of financial resources, to property-poor districts, to advocacy for a voucher system directing funds to parents.

In addition to a wide-ranging diversity of available resources among school districts, they recognized a growing shift of authority away from the locality-specific tax base, to an increasing dependence of schools and local school boards on state and federal funding. Consequently, decisions affecting a child's education become further removed from parental influence.

Education by Choice offers an alternative to the widely accepted model of public education in which the state is the provider of services to schools in which children are assigned according to their place of residency. The main thesis of this book is that children would receive a better education if parents had a greater opportunity to choose their children's educational experiences. They suggest that this can be accomplished by means of a publicly paid voucher that provides equal educational resources to children whose family income cannot afford alternatives. Their proposal, radical and controversial at the time, was indicative of the direction in which the school choice movement would evolve in the ensuing decades.

Education by Choice is a pioneering effort and significant contribution to the research and development of a conceptual framework for advancing family choice in education. As a reaction to the perceived ineffectiveness of the status quo system in which the government was the sole provider of publicly supported education, a movement toward voucherization or privatization of education was proposed in 1955 by the economist Milton Friedman. He advocated a free market economy approach without any role for government. In their book, Coons and Sugarman offer a voucher system under government control that would channel market forces to ameliorate the social inequities attendant upon unequal provision of resources for schooling.

The authors examined the arguments driving the opposition to voucherization. They found that a polarization of public opinion about how to divide authority between the civic authorities and the family has hampered serious examination of the issues. The dialogue is impacted by diverse beliefs and fears about the process of reaching consensus and social cohesion within local communities seeking to make collective decisions about values and desired outcomes in public education. Their exploration of the primary objectives voiced about compulsory education and public schooling led them to conclude that education must serve the best interests of the child, foster civic consensus about ordered liberty, and promote racial integration.

Examining the idea of serving the best interests of the child led the authors to the conclusion that justice requires society to make provisions for the education of all children. In doing so, society must strive for a fairness and rationality in the distribution of choice options that does not subject the nonrich to a politically determined and implemented assignment of students to particular schools. Within the status quo, the wealthy can choose among schools that meet the family's values and goals they envision for their children by moving to neighborhoods that have schools they want or pay tuition for desirable private schools; the rest must accept compulsory assignment. The proposed remedy is a controlled-market approach, using a low-income targeted voucher system that has built-in regulations to assure equity and accountability, balancing the private and social purposes of education.

Coons and Sugarman seek to obtain that balance. They argue that families should have the right to choose the type of education they want for their children that reflects their philosophic and religious values. They should be able to choose the school and a curriculum that meets the needs and learning style of the child. By allowing parents to choose among schools, competition for students would produce more efficient and effective schools and educational experiences for the students. Family choices, however, would have to be reconciled to some extent with the common good that relies heavily on schools to provide an education that supports the nation's democratic ideals and prepares the citizenry to embrace equality of opportunity for all.

Education by Choice proceeds through a methodical analysis of the pitfalls to be avoided and the benefits to be provided by a system of controlled market choice. In Part II, a cogent case is made for a "best-interest-of the child formula" rationale for the primacy of family over the state and professionals as the best judge of what is best in making educational decisions. Part III deals with the concepts and particulars of achieving a desirable social consensus and integration. They explore the issues of ideological pluralism and racial segregation and reflect on the probable effects of choice. They conclude that there is no reason to prefer compulsory public schooling as the only means of attaining integration of personal and societal values. In the concluding chapter, the authors describe a variety of administrative, fiscal, and pedagogical models that could be adopted or adapted to produce a system of controlled-market family choice in education. The authors campaigned, unsuccessfully, to obtain a ballot initiative in California in 1979 to actualize their proposal. However, the basic concepts of controlled choice can be seen in the Cleveland and Milwaukee voucher programs that have been validated by the U.S. Supreme Court. *See also*: Choice, parent and school; Milwaukee Parental Choice Program; Parental rights; Tuition tax credits; Vouchers.

Further Reading: William H. Clune and John F. Witte, eds., *Choice and Control in American Education*, Vol. 1 (London: Falmer Press, 1990); John Coons and Stephen D. Sugarman, *Education by Choice: The Case for Family Control* (Berkeley: University of California Press, 1978); Terry Moe, *Schools, Vouchers and the American Public* (Washington, DC: Brookings Institution Press, 2002); Joseph Viteritti, *Choosing Equality: School Choice, the Constitution, and Civil Society* (Washington, DC: The Brookings Institution Press, 1999).

Dale McDonald, PBVM

Education of Catholic Americans, The

In 1962, two researchers from the University of Chicago began a sociological study that would provide fundamental answers to persistent questions about the value and impact of Catholic education. The authors of the report—Peter Rossi, a professor of sociology, and Andrew M. Greeley, a diocesan priest who had recently completed his doctoral studies—were eager to apply sound social science tools to the evaluation of Catholic schools. Their 1966 book would define the contours of Catholic education for the last quarter of the twentieth century.

Greeley and Rossi were not the first to study the Catholic schools. In fact, the 1950s were a decade of intense American concern about the potentially divisive nature of Catholic schools. Yet much of this concern was based on personal opinion and prejudice; there was little sociological research on the impact of Catholic education.

The study by Greeley and Rossi, titled *The Education of Catholic Americans*, would bring the scholarly study of Catholic schools to a new level. Working through the National Opinion Research Center, Greeley and Rossi studied and interviewed a representative national sample of 2,753 American Catholics and sent an additional 1,000 questionnaires to the homes of other American Catholics. This was to be a sociohistorical study since the respondents had attended school between 1910 and 1960.

They sought answers to three basic questions. Were Catholic schools effective in shaping the religious beliefs of their students? Were Catholic schools a divisive force in American society? Did Catholic schools impede the economic or occupational advancement of its students? All of these questions had been shaped by the debates of the 1950s.

In response to the first question, Greeley and Rossi argued that Catholic schools had their greatest impact on students from very religious families but that "those who come from moderately religious families, or non-religious families, are only influenced in a minimal way." Did this mean that Catholic schools were ineffective as religious educators? Not at all, assured Greeley and Rossi. Survey evidence showed that attendance at mass and the sacraments was significantly higher among moderately religious Catholics if they attended Catholic schools rather than public schools.

The study also revealed that Catholic school students, regardless of their home religious life, were more likely to be informed about church doctrine and accept that doctrine than Catholics who had attended public schools. Given the fact that a stated goal of Catholic schools was to preserve the faith among its congregants, the Catholic schools had done a "reasonably good job." It was hardly a ringing endorsement of Catholic schools as a religious educator, and it was a conclusion that was widely disputed by Catholic educators and critics.

The second question—Are Catholic schools divisive?—was a throwback to earlier studies. It seemed that no matter how hard sociologists tried to inform the public on this matter, the more concerned the general public became that Catholic schools were somehow un-American. Greeley and Rossi confirmed what other sociologists had stated earlier. "We could find no evidence," they wrote, "that the products of such a system were less involved in community activity, less likely to have friends from other religious groups, more intolerant in their attitudes, or less likely to achieve occupationally or academically. On the contrary, we found that they were slightly more successful in the world of study and work, and after the breaking point of college, much more tolerant" (Greeley and Rossi, 1966, p. 299).

The third question—Do Catholic schools impede the economic and occupational achievement of its students?—also elicited a negative response. In fact, among students from the higher socioeconomic groups, Catholic schooling was a distinct asset in academic and career advancement. There was some evidence that even Catholic students from the lowest economic groups were more academically oriented than their counterparts in the public schools. Greeley and Rossi added an interesting observation. The authors hoped that their evidence would put this old and unfounded concern to rest.

Greeley and Rossi speculated on the meaning of their data. Certainly, they argued that Catholic schools were "neither as bad as their most severe critics portray them, nor as good as they might be" (p. 231). It was also true that Catholic education was not the most important element in the value formation and religious attitudes of Catholic children. The religiousness of parents and socioeconomic class were clearly more important. Furthermore, the authors did not find any evidence that Catholic schools were necessary for the survival of American Catholicism. Yet on balance, the schools seemed to have been worth the effort, and they concluded that these schools would continue and might even thrive.

The impact of the Greeley and Rossi study was substantial. The book was widely reviewed and generated a variety of responses. The Catholic press hailed the book as evidence of the value and worth of Catholic schools. But the *New York Times* picked up only the negative implications of the study and claimed that the study proved that Catholic education was "wasted" on a quarter of its students.

Perhaps the most balanced and useful review appeared in the *Harvard Educational Review* in the summer of 1967. Even though the reviewer was disappointed that the authors qualified their conclusions so as not to claim too much for their data or for the Catholic school system, he found the book to be the most useful study that has ever been attempted in the area of American Catholic education.

The impact of *The Education of Catholic Americans* was extraordinary and led to a follow-up study a decade later. Without question, Greeley and Rossi had published a landmark study of the impact of Catholic education. *See also*: Catholic philosophy of education; Effectiveness of Catholic schools; Greeley, Andrew M.

Further Reading: Andrew M. Greeley, William C. McReady, and Kathleen McCourt, *Catholic Schools in a Declining Church* (Kansas City, MO: Sheed and Ward, 1976); Andrew M. Greeley and Peter H. Rossi, *The Education of Catholic Americans* (Chicago: Aldine, 1966); Timothy Walch, *Parish School: American Catholic Parochial Education from Colonial Times to the Present* (New York: Crossroad, 1996).

Timothy Walch

Education: To Whom Does It Belong?

A thirty-two page pamphlet written by Dr. Thomas Bouquillon, published December 1891, stating his theoretical argument for the state's right to educate Catholic children. His pamphlet generated considerable controversy because Bouquillon gave to the state rights to educate beyond the traditional church viewpoint.

Thomas Bouquillon was a noted moral theologian at the Catholic University of America when he was asked by Cardinal Gibbons to write his education paper. Cardinal Gibbons believed that an academic paper from someone of Bouquillon's reputation would help to quell the school controversy. Bouquillon first submitted his argument to the *American Catholic Quarterly*, which refused to publish the paper. Archbishop Ryan of Philadelphia wrote as editor to Gibbons that he did not determine this to be a good time to publish the piece. Ryan apparently believed that Bouquillon's argument was so powerful it would lead to compulsory public education for Catholic children.

Bouquillon then went forward and published his argument as a pamphlet. The publication came just days before the nation's archbishops were to gather in St. Louis. Those opposed to Bouquillon's thesis argued that he purposely timed the release for that date in order to influence the archbishops' discussion of the controversy. Bouquillon denied the accusation, and there was no evidence to support it. Bouquillon's pamphlet claiming that the state had a right to educate drew aggravated attention because Bouquillon, noted for his clarity of thought, built an argument that implicitly supported the position of Archbishop Ireland, who supported the concept of compulsory public education. Bishop Ireland's speech to the National Education Association in St. Paul, Minnesota (1890), praised the state for establishing schools. Ireland noted that the availability of free public schools was necessary for the common good of society.

Ireland further used the occasion of his speech to make two proposals to the state in an attempt to remove the double tax burden from Catholic parents. His first option was the establishment of a denominational system of state-supported schools. If this was rejected, his second option was to supplement public education with religious education referred to as the Poughkeepsie Plan.

The Poughkeepsie Plan allowed for a Catholic school building to be leased by the public school district for a minimal amount. There would be no religious instruction during the school day, but it would be conducted either before or after regular school hours. Catholic school teachers, even religious, would be retained, meet state requirements, and be paid by the public school district.

Ireland received broad criticism for his support of public education that appeared to contradict the position articulated by James Cardinal Gibbons and the spirit of the Third Plenary Council of Baltimore. Gibbons himself supported Ireland throughout the controversy.

Bouquillon's pamphlet provided theological support for Ireland's position. Bouquillon emphasized the primary role of the parent in education but added that education should be directed toward the common good of society. The Church in turn, according to Bouquillon, provides an education for moral and religious preparation. Church education enters into secular subjects only when necessary.

The so-called Bouquillon controversy followed and appeared to contradict the intentions of the Third Plenary Council of Baltimore, 1884, which promoted the establishment of parish schools. Rev. Rene I. Holaind, SJ, professor at the Jesuit Seminary at Woodstock College, Maryland, responded to Bouquillon's argument with his own pamphlet, *The Parent First*.

Opponents of Bishop Ireland's speech and Bouquillon's pamphlet contended that their support of public education affirmed the movement toward secularized public schools and weakened the possibility of Catholic schools to receive state funding. Both sides ultimately appealed to Rome for a resolution to the conflict. In November 1892, Archbishop Francesco Satolli, special representative of Pope Leo XIII to the United States, presented Fourteen Propositions to the American archbishops that were intended to solve the controversy. Fundamentally, the fourteen points, presented with papal approval, supported Ireland's position and vindicated Bouquillon.

In summary, Satolli's points were (Buetow, 1970, p. 174):

1. Catholic schools should be built and made comparable to public schools.

2. If it is impossible to maintain a Catholic school, if all religious distortions are removed, children may attend public school.

3. Catholic school teachers must have adequate preparation and pass diocesan examinations.

4. Teacher preparation schools should be established.

5. Priests are forbidden to excommunicate parents who choose to send their children to public schools.

6. Since the Church teaches faith and morals, children may receive education in secular subjects from state schools.

7. The Church supports the establishment of public schools for the benefit of the people.

8. "If dangers are removed, children are permitted to attend public schools, though pastors and parents must cooperate to see that they receive adequate religious education."

9. Establishing schools will be decided by local ordinaries.

10. Catholic parents who send their children to private schools must provide for their religious education.

11. Representatives of the Church and local school board should work together to provide schools that meet the needs of both the Church and state.

12. "For Catholic students in public schools, the best possible religious education should be provided."

13. It is strongly recommended that Catholic school teachers meet state requirements.

14. Catholic school teachers trained in normal schools should receive state degrees.

Ultimately, those who opposed Ireland and Bouquillon appealed again to Rome questioning the authority of the Apostolic Delegate. Pope Leo XIII indicated in a letter that he supported the building of Catholic schools but gave bishops the right to determine acceptable reasons for attending public schools in their individual diocese. The Pope further asked the bishops to restore harmony to the American Catholic Church by ending the controversy. *See also*: Bouquillon, Thomas; Catholic School Question, The.

Further Reading: Thomas Bouquillon, *Education: To Whom Does It Belong?* (Baltimore: John F. Murphy, 1891); Harold A. Buetow, *Of Singular Benefit: The Story of U.S. Catholic Education* (New York: Macmillan, 1970); Rene I. Holaind, *The Parent First* (New York: Benziger Brothers, 1892); C. Joseph Nuesse, *The Catholic University of America: A Centennial History* (Washington, DC: Catholic University of America Press, 1990); Marvin R. O'Connell, *John Ireland and the American Catholic Church* (St. Paul: Minnesota Historical Society Press, 1989); Daniel F. Reilly, *The School Controversy 1891–1893* (Washington, DC: Catholic University of America Press, 1943).

Merylann J. "Mimi" Schuttloffel

Effective Catholic Schools: An Exploration
The report of research that investigated how Catholic schools are organized and function and what their students were like. The results validated much of what was reported

in the research of the early 1980s, that the academic emphasis and the community-like environment of the Catholic high schools offered a better opportunity to be educated than public high schools.

The study actually began in the fall of 1981 with Peter Holland, a doctoral student in administration in the Harvard Graduate School of Education who brought the request for proposals from the Board of Directors of the National Center for Research in Total Catholic Education of the National Catholic Educational Association to the attention of Anthony Bryk of the Huron Institute of Cambridge, Massachusetts, and the Harvard Graduate School of Education. Peter Holland and Anthony Bryk had been involved in research related to effective public schools and developed a similar proposal to study how Catholic schools are organized and function and who their students were. Data were gathered at two Catholic high schools located in Baltimore and one school in each of the cites of Boston, Cleveland, Louisville, San Antonio, and Los Angeles and in Catholic elementary schools, from which the high school students originated. The research design involved on-site interviews with teachers, students, and parents, observation of classrooms and the functioning schools, and analysis of data of all the Catholic schools that participated in the *High School and Beyond* project of the National Center for Educational Statistics of the U.S. Department of Education.

All of the schools and their faculty emphasized academics and challenged students with high expectations irrespective of their backgrounds. Students' positive involvement was manifested in high levels of attendance and punctuality and a minimum of behavioral problems. Positive student involvement was a result of the influence of family religiousness and social class and the interest of the parents in their children's education. The school settings were regarded by students as positively helpful, with teachers willing to assist students before or after school. Bryk et al. (1984) observed that teachers tended to be "concerned with the kind of persons their students become as well as what they know. Many described their work as a kind of ministry and their role as one of shaping young adults" (p. 16). Catholic high school students with Catholic elementary school training were found to have higher achievement scores on vocabulary, reading, writing, and civics and were similar on mathematics and lower in science than students with public school backgrounds.

Achievement among sophomores was attributable to socioeconomic level and academic preparation prior to high school. Females' achievement scores were higher for writing and lower on mathematics and science. Higher achievement results were observed on reading and writing and lower achievement on science among students with Catholic elementary school training. Students at schools with some emphasis on academic ability grouping were lower in their achievement in mathematics, science, and writing, whereas, achievement among seniors was attributed to choosing academic courses and involvement in cocurriculars. The results that Bryk et al. reported were in accord with the many studies on Catholic education that socioeconomic level was less of an influence on achievement in Catholic schools than it was in public schools. Positive school influences on achievement by both sophomores and seniors were stability of faculty in a larger school with a positive disciplinary environment.

The uniquely Catholic aspect of the schools was a four-year religion program that viewed faith from a maturational perspective. Beginning in the freshman year through the senior year, students were challenged with such topics and issues as who one is in the world and what the role of faith is in a personal God, a Christian's relationship to self and others, Jesus as a model, peer pressure and other challenges teenagers face in living their faith, the sacraments, liturgy, and moral behavior and responsibility. Opportunities to participate in community service programs were also a part of many of the religious education programs.

The research also includes a discussion of the issues of finances and governance that are a considerable burden for many Catholic schools and administrators. To sustain their effectiveness, Catholic high schools require a dependable financial resource, and that has become the tuition fees paid by students' families. Issues that have contributed over time to the increase in financial difficulties are the decline in the availability of contributed services by religious orders, the high cost of the maintenance of older buildings not kept in good repair, a need to adequately finance teachers' salaries, and the need for moneys to cover the cost of improving quality in areas of national concern. Governance of Catholic high schools is best described as decentralized whether it is managed within the context of a religious order, diocesan central office, or school board. The responsibilities and competencies required of principals are quite extensive and include such activities as managing personnel issues, finances, community relations, overseeing curriculum, supervision, teaching, and ensuring the Catholicity of the school.

Instruction in the feeder elementary schools that were studied was focused on what is best described as "the basics" such as skills development for reading, language arts, and mathematics. At the time of the study, there was little, if any, innovation in the elementary schools, and there was no dependable communication or interaction between the Catholic elementary schools and the Catholic high schools. *See also*: *Catholic Schools and the Common Good*; *Catholic Schools Make a Difference: Twenty-five Years of Research*; *High School and Beyond*.

Further Reading: Anthony S. Bryk and Peter B. Holland, "Research Provides Perspectives on Effective Catholic Schools," *Momentum* 15, 3 (September 1984): 12–17; Anthony S. Bryk, Peter B. Holland, Valerie E. Lee, and Ruben A. Carriedo, *Effective Catholic Schools: An Exploration* (Washington, DC: National Catholic Educational Association, Educational Resources Information Center [ERIC] Documentation Reproduction Service No. ED 251 365, 1984); Anthony S. Bryk, Valerie E. Lee, and Peter B. Holland, *Catholic Schools and the Common Good* (Cambridge: Harvard University Press, 1993); John J. Convey, *Catholic Schools Make a Difference: Twenty-five Years of Research* (Washington, DC: National Catholic Educational Association, 1992).

Robert B. Williams

Effectiveness of Catholic schools

In view of the lifelong impact that education has on the citizens of a country, it is essential to know as much as possible about the effectiveness of the schools. The documentation that has been generated on the effectiveness of Catholic schools during the later part of the twentieth century is especially compelling when the scope of the databases is considered. The initial data were derived from the *High School and Beyond* longitudinal study of high school seniors and sophomores that was initiated by the National Center for Educational Statistics of the U.S. Department of Education. The actual study was carried out by the National Opinion Research Center at the University of Chicago and began in 1980 with the administration of standardized tests of reading, vocabulary, mathematics, science, and civics to a sample of 69,662 students attending 1,015 public and private high schools. Eighty-four of the private high schools included in the study were Catholic. Along with the tests a survey about the students and the school was also completed by the students, administrators, teachers, and parents. Follow-ups of both the sophomores and seniors were carried out in 1982, 1984, 1986, and in 1992 another survey of the 1980 sophomores was undertaken.

The first report from an analysis of the *High School and Beyond* data was completed by Coleman, Hoffer, and Kilgore in 1981. Using cross-sectional data, they reported that average private and Catholic school students obtained higher achievement test results on all subjects than average public school students. Higher achievement by students from private and Catholic schools was attributed to their schools' rigorous academic programs involving structured curricula and demanding expectations of teachers and the discipline and order of the school environment. It was also asserted that Catholic schools were as beneficial to students of disadvantaged backgrounds as they were to the advantaged.

A second analysis of the 1980 *High School and Beyond* data on 7,000 Catholic and 7,000 public high school students was undertaken by Greeley in 1982 to evaluate the impact of Catholic high schools on black and Hispanic students. Greeley's analysis revealed that minority students scored over one-half a standard deviation higher on several standardized measures of achievement than students attending public high schools. Catholic high schools were found to be especially effective for the most disadvantaged students of minority origins, for low socioeconomic and familial education levels, and in the general rather than the academic track. These most disadvantaged students manifested the most significant achievement increments noted between Catholic and public school students.

A third study utilizing the *High School and Beyond* data is presented in an investigation of how Catholic schools are organized and function and what their students were like. The study began in the fall of 1981 under the leadership of Anthony Bryk and Peter Holland. Data were gathered at two Catholic high schools located in Baltimore and one school in each of the cites of Boston, Cleveland, Louisville, San Antonio, and Los Angeles and in Catholic elementary schools from which the high school students originated. The research involved on-site interviews with teachers, students, and parents, observation of classrooms and the functioning schools, and analysis of data on all the Catholic schools that participated in the *High School and Beyond* project.

All the Catholic high schools and their faculty emphasized academics and challenged students with high expectations irrespective of their backgrounds. Students' positive involvement was documented in high levels of attendance, punctuality, and a minimum of behavioral problems. Positive student involvement was due to the influence of family religiousness and social class and the interest of the parents in their children's education.

Catholic high school students with Catholic elementary school training had higher achievement scores on vocabulary, reading, writing, and civics, were similar on mathematics, and were lower in science than students with public school backgrounds. Achievement among sophomores was attributable to socioeconomic level and academic preparation prior to high school. Females' achievement was higher for writing and lower on mathematics and science. Higher achievement was observed on reading and writing and lower achievement on science among students with Catholic elementary school training. Students at schools with some academic ability grouping were lower in their achievement in mathematics, science, and writing, whereas achievement observed among seniors was attributed to choosing academic courses and involvement in cocurriculars. The results of the studies of Bryk et al. in 1984 were in accord with other studies on Catholic education that indicated socioeconomic level was less of an influence on achievement in Catholic schools than it was in public schools. Positive school influences on achievement by both sophomores and seniors were the stability of faculty in a larger school and a positive disciplinary environment.

In 1987 Coleman and Hoffer gained access to the longitudinal data of *High School and Beyond* for 1982 and 1984. They reported higher attainment on verbal tasks and mathematics from the tenth to the twelfth grades for Catholic high school students than for those in public school and no differences for science or civics. A one-year-more-grade-equivalent change was noted for the average Catholic school student compared to an average student at public school for reading, vocabulary, mathematics, and writing and a slight benefit in science and civics when family background was controlled in the analysis. The level of verbal achievement by black and Hispanic students attending Catholic schools was more than twice that of white students. A positive impact on achievement among students of lower socioeconomic origins or whose achievement level was lower at the beginning of their school experience than among students with higher socioeconomic and achievement histories was noted. Coleman and Hoffer, comparing private schools in 1987, proposed that the unique religious environment of the Catholic school contributed to the academic success revealed in the research.

Catholic schools' effectiveness was examined not only from the academic perspective but from that of students' values, attitudes, and behavior. A very significant study involved a retrospective analysis of the responses of Catholic students, in their senior year in Catholic and public high schools, to the survey of high school seniors by the *Monitoring the Future* project administered by the Survey Research Center of the Institute for Social Research at the University of Michigan from 1976 to 1985. The results found that the Catholic school context positively influenced students' attitudes toward things related to the military, marriage, educational aspirations, cutting school, a concern for others, frequency of church attendance, and the importance of religion.

To carry out the study, the National Catholic Educational Association commissioned the Survey Research Center to prepare the data so that Catholic students attending Catholic and public high schools between 1976 and 1985 could be identified. The data were drawn from the *Monitoring the Future* project, which submitted questionnaires with 300 to 800 items to 16,000 high school seniors in 125 schools.

The data for 1983–1985 were used to develop the profile of Catholic seniors attending Catholic and public high schools. Catholic high school seniors differed from Catholic public school seniors on all the family and personal background variables. Catholic high school seniors were living in large urban communities, their parents had more education, their mothers were less likely to have worked outside the home, they spent less time at after-school jobs and fewer evenings out during the school week than public high school students, and they were more likely to live in a two-parent family.

Some notable differences between the Catholic and public high school groups were found. Under social and educational values, Catholic high school seniors were higher in their endorsement of pro-marriage attitudes and college plans, whereas public high school seniors were more supportive of things related to the military and reported more cutting of school. Regarding a concern for people, Catholic high school seniors indicated greater community involvement, contributions of money, and concern for others than did Catholic seniors in public high schools. The at-risk behaviors found to be higher among Catholic high school seniors were alcohol use and binge drinking, whereas Catholic seniors attending public high schools reported greater cigarette, cocaine, and illicit drug use. Perceptions of self were more pessimistic among Catholic seniors at public high schools. Regarding religiousness, Catholic seniors at Catholic high schools reported higher church attendance and contributions to the Church and more regard for the importance of religion than did Catholic seniors at public high schools. *See also*: *Catholic Schools and the Common Good*; Coleman, James S.; *Education of Catholic Americans, The*; Greeley, Andrew M.; *High School and Beyond*.

Further Reading: Anthony S. Bryk, Peter B. Holland, Valerie E. Lee, and Ruben A. Carriedo, *Effective Catholic Schools: An Exploration* (Washington, DC: National Catholic Educational Association, Educational Resources Information Center [ERIC] Documentation Reproduction Service No. ED 251 365, 1984); James S. Coleman and Thomas Hoffer, *Public and Private High Schools: The Impact of Communities* (New York: Basic Books, 1987); James S. Coleman, Thomas Hoffer, and Sally Kilgore, *High School Achievement: Public, Catholic, and Private Schools Compared* (New York: Basic Books, 1982); Andrew M. Greeley, *Catholic High Schools and Minority Students* (New Brunswick, NJ: Transaction Books, 1982); Michael J. Guerra, Michael J. Donahue, and Peter L. Benson, *The Heart of the Matter: Effects of Catholic High Schools on Student Values, Beliefs and Behaviors* (Washington, DC: National Catholic Educational Association, Educational Resource Information Center [ERIC] Document Reproduction Service No. ED 317 881, 1990).

Robert B. Williams

Elementary and Secondary Education Act of 1965 (ESEA)

The Elementary and Secondary Education Act (ESEA) was first enacted into law by the Congress of the United States of America in 1965. Since that time, it has been reauthorized and renamed on several occasions but is most commonly referred to as "ESEA." It is the largest and most comprehensive federal law dealing with kindergarten through twelfth grade education in U.S. history. In December 2001 Congress reauthorized the act under the title "No Child Left Behind Act of 2001."

ESEA is divided into nine major areas (Titles) of concern:

Title I—*Improving the Academic Achievement of the Disadvantaged*, which includes improvement of basic programs, student reading skills (Reading First, Early Reading First, Even Start Family Literacy Programs, Improving Literacy through Libraries), and education of migratory children. The purpose of this title is to guarantee that "all children have a fair, equal, and significant opportunity to obtain a high quality education and reach, at a minimum, proficiency on challenging State academic achievement standards and state assessments" (ESEA, Sec. 1001). The title proposes that all components of the educational process—assessments, teacher preparation, curriculum and instructional materials—conform to high standards set by the individual state. As a result of this alignment schools can close the gap between high- and low-achieving students, particularly minority and disadvantaged children. The act endeavors to promote schoolwide reform by ensuring substantial opportunities for professional development for teachers so that enriched and accelerated programs are possible.

Title II—*Preparing, Training, and Recruiting High Quality Teachers and Principals*, consisting of teacher and principal training and recruiting fund, mathematics and science partnerships, innovation for teacher quality (Transitions to Teaching, National

Writing Project, Civic Education, Teaching of Traditional American History, Teacher Liability Protection), and enhancing education through technology. Title II provides grants to state and local educational agencies as well as state agencies for higher education in order to effect student achievement by improving the number and quality of teachers, principals, and assistant principals. Local agencies and schools are to be held accountable for improving student achievement.

Title III—*Language Instruction for Limited English-Proficient and Immigrant Students*, dealing with English-language acquisition, language enhancement and academic achievement, and improving language instruction educational programs. One purpose of this section is to provide assistance to state and local agencies to develop high-quality language programs so that students with limited English proficiency can master the English language and have the opportunity to meet the same achievement standards expected of all students. The act further establishes the need to develop accountability systems and prepare qualified personnel to "work with limited English proficient children" (ESEA, Sec. 3102).

Title IV—*21st Century Schools*, which promotes safe and drug-free schools and communities, twenty-first-century community learning centers, environmental communities, and tobacco smoke policies. The purpose of this part is to provide assistance and support for programs directed at preventing "the illegal use of alcohol, tobacco, and drugs" (ESEA, Sec. 4002), involving parents and communities working together with federal, state, and local agencies to provide a safe environment in which the educational process can be conducted. This support includes both prevention and early intervention programs. Further, the act provides for the establishment of community learning centers where tutorial services, counseling, art, music, recreation, technology, and character education programs can be conducted.

Title V—*Promoting Informed Parental Choice and Innovative Programs*, which addresses innovative programs, public charter schools, magnet schools assistance, and funds for the improvement of education, including elementary and secondary school counseling programs, partnerships in character education, smaller learning communities, gifted and talented students, Star Schools Programs, Ready to Teach, foreign language assistance programs, physical education, community technology centers, educational/cultural/apprenticeship and exchange programs for Alaska Natives/Native Hawaiians and their historical whaling and trading partners in Massachusetts, excellence in economics education, improvement of the mental health of children, arts in education, combating domestic violence, healthy/high performance schools, grants for capital expenses of providing equitable services for private school students, additional assistance for certain local educational agencies impacted by federal property acquisition, and women's educational equity. Title V provides funding to state and local educational agencies to implement innovative improvement programs designed to "meet the educational needs of all students, including at-risk youth" (ESEA, Sec. 5101). It funds the planning, design, implementation and assessment of charter schools as well as desegregation efforts in local school districts.

Title VI—*Flexibility and Accountability*, dealing with improved academic achievement and the Rural Education Initiative. Funds are provided to state and local educational agencies to establish challenging academic standards, develop assessments for those standards, and implement programs targeted at staff development and parental involvement.

Title VII—*Indian, Native Hawaiian, and Alaska Native Education*, concerning Indian education, Native Hawaiian education, and Alaska Native education. This part supports state and local efforts to "meet the unique educational and culturally related academic needs" (ESEA, Sec. 7102) of American Indian, Alaska Native, and Native Hawaiian students so that they have the opportunity to meet the same academic achievement standards expected of all students.

Title VIII—*Impact Aid Program*, dealing with property acquisition and funding of emergency construction and repairs to schools.

Title IX—*General Provisions*, providing for flexibility in the use of administrative and other funds, coordination of state and local programs/plans/applications, waivers from federally established standards, uniform provisions, including equitable distribution of special education services and other benefits to students in private schools, state aid, privacy of assessment results, school prayer, equal access to public school facilities, armed forces access to students and student recruiting information; prohibition on federally sponsored testing; limitations on national testing or certification of teachers; prohibition on nationwide database; unsafe school choice option; prohibition on discrimination; civil rights; rule-making, severability, and evaluations. *See also*: *No Child Left Behind Act—Public Law 107–110.*

Further Reading: 107th Congress, *Public Law 107–110*, Congress of the United States of America (January 8, 2002); Erik W. Robelen, "An ESEA Primer," *Education Week* 21, 16 (January 9, 2002): 28–29; National Association of Secondary School Principals, *NewsLeader* (February 2002).

Joseph D. Massucci

Elementary schools

The National Center for Education Statistics (NCES) defines a school as an elementary school if it has one or more of grades K–6 and does not have any grade higher than grade 8; for example, schools with grades K–6, 1–3, or 6–8 are classified as elementary schools. Therefore, by this definition, elementary schools include schools typically configured as middle schools.

The NCES reported in the *Digest of Education Statistics 2001* that in 1999–2000 almost 20 percent of the public elementary schools in the nation were configured as "middle schools." In addition, approximately 15 percent of the schools classified as secondary schools were "junior high schools" serving typically grades 7–8 or 9. By contrast, the National Catholic Educational Association (NCEA) reported that in 1998 there were only about eighty middle schools among the approximately 6,800 Catholic elementary schools. Because of this small proportion (1%), the NCEA no longer reports data on Catholic middle schools as a separate category.

Nevertheless, a growing trend in Catholic Pre-K or K–8 elementary schools is the incorporation of a middle school program or approach for students in grades 5 or 6–8. Just as does the freestanding middle school, a middle school approach seeks to address the unique needs of the preadolescent student. This approach incorporates features such as departmentalization (i.e., instruction by teachers who specialize in a subject area), advisory and exploratory programs, and cooperative planning among the team of teachers who teach a common group of students.

Research has not identified an optimum grade configuration. Studies have identified more than sixty grade configurations used in American education including about thirty involving seventh and eighth graders. Advocates of traditional K–8 configurations and proponents of newer middle school arrangements argue passionately for the benefits of each. K–8 schools require fewer transitions of students, allow older students to assist younger students, and are more convenient for parents because their children are in one school for more years and are closer to home. Middle schools are able to concentrate on the needs of the preadolescent in particular, offer more elective or exploratory courses and extracurricular activities, and prepare students for the fully departmentalized high school. However, there is also evidence that decisions about what grades to educate together are often driven by school building capacity and economy of scale more than educational philosophy.

The prevalence of the K–8 grade configuration for Catholic elementary schools can be attributed in large measure to its predominant nature as an educational ministry of the parish to its parishioners. A K or Pre-K–8 program enables parishioners to enroll their children in the same school located at their neighborhood parish for a maximum number of years. The parish-based nature of most Catholic elementary schools, in turn, fosters parental involvement and a sense of loyalty arising from the school being part of a larger parish community.

Catholic elementary schools are characterized by an evident child-centered approach. Religious formation is of prime importance, with special emphasis on sacramental preparation and focus on message, community, worship, and service. Academic and intellectual development is promoted in a climate that also emphasizes personal and social development.

Because the Catholic elementary school is generally a part of the educational mission of the entire parish, the entire parish community contributes to the funding of the elementary school, not just the parishioners who have children attending the school. Data provided by the National Catholic Educational Association indicate that the average per pupil tuition in Catholic elementary schools is approximately $2,175 which represents about 60 percent of the total per pupil cost of education of $3,505 in the 2001–2002 school year.

Less than 1 percent of Catholic elementary schools are single-gender schools, a phenomenon more prevalent at the secondary level, where about one-third are single-gender. Approximately 25 percent of Catholic elementary school students are members of minority groups, and approximately 12 percent are not members of the Catholic Church.

Studies drawing upon national databases, such as the results of the National Assessment of Educational Progress, have consistently found higher achievement scores for Catholic school students than for public school students. In addition, such studies have indicated that the difference in achievement often increases in the upper grades. However, the factors contributing to this phenomenon have not, to date, been clearly delineated. *See also*: Parish (parochial) schools.

Further Reading: Joyce L. Epstein, "What Matters in the Middle Grades—Grade Span or Practices?," *Phi Delta Kappan* (February 1990): 438–444; Kathleen M. Fuccaro, "Middle School Direction in a K–8 School," *Today's Catholic Teacher* 33, 1, August–September, pp. 40–41; Thomas C. Hunt, Ellis A. Joseph, and Ronald J. Nuzzi, eds., *Catholic Schools Still Make a Difference: Ten Years of Research, 1991–2000* (Washington DC: National Catholic Education Association, 2002); Dale McDonald, *United States Catholic Elementary and Secondary Schools 2001–2002: The Annual Statistical Report on Schools, Enrollment, and Staffing* (Washington, DC: National Catholic Educational Association, 2002); C. Kenneth McEwin and William M. Alexander, "What Is the Place of the Middle Grades in the K–8 School?," *Middle School Journal* 22, 1 (September 1990): 5–11.

Karen L. Tichy

Elitism

Elitism refers to the real or perceived state of those individuals who enjoy unique privileges not available to the majority of people within a society. These privileges, which are typically bestowed through birth, societal status, or personal wealth, are often institutionalized by those who have power to protect and advance their status. Chief among these privileges is the freedom to choose schools that will ensure the status of the individual and family. Catholic schools have been characterized as elitist. Within Catholic education itself, some schools have been portrayed as elitist.

The history of education in Western civilization can trace many themes from the Greeks and Romans such as various emphases upon philosophy, arts, sciences, and technology. As educational systems developed, important questions surfaced as to who would receive an education. Particular to understanding the antecedents of elitism in Catholic education in the United States are the development of cathedral schools during the Middle Ages and the establishment of such European universities found in Paris and Bologna. The perception or reality of elitism is closely connected to the theme of access to education.

In medieval Europe education was initially provided for the clergy, but education at the great universities was expanded to include degrees not only in theology but also in the disciplines of medicine and law. As these professions developed, laymen who had the time and resources were admitted to complete such studies. Such laymen were usually the sons of the nobility who could provide the necessary means needed to cover the cost of such an education.

The history of Catholic education in the United States parallels, in many ways, the history of other institutional systems. Harvard University, founded in 1636, was initially instituted to prepare leaders, including an educated clergy, for service in the Massachusetts colony. Eventually Harvard admitted students from the gentry for what today would be seen as an education in the liberal arts. Georgetown University, founded in 1789, was also established to prepare a native clergy for the Roman Catholic Church in the colonial system but soon admitted the sons of various families. The shift of expanding educational services from seminarians to the laity demonstrated a growing trend of the accessibility of education. This expansion of accessibility would not be confined to higher education. With the establishment of the common schools, the parochial and private schools such as those established by St. Elizabeth Ann Seton, candidates for education would be expanded beyond the criteria of being male and having money.

Beginning with education limited to males preparing for the ministry, the growth of education was extended to the sons of the gentry. Soon, education would be accessed by women, African Americans, Native Americans, immigrants from every continent, and people with learning and physical challenges.

Catholic education is a tuition-driven school system. It relies primarily upon the resources of those who are able to pay for a significant portion of the total cost of an education. Parish, institutional, and diocesan support, along with limited government programs, augment the remainder of these budgets. Therefore, a family who chooses a Catholic school usually must have financial resources to pay for tuition, books, fees, lunches, and transportation. Because educational services in the United States are administered from each state, some services are provided in some states and not in others.

Generally speaking, a family who uses a Catholic school must provide financial support to two school systems: support for public schools through the payment of property taxes and all the costs involved with a Catholic education. Parishes that are financially stable generally help financially strapped parishes with schools within a diocese, resulting in some people actually supporting three schools, the public schools, their own children's Catholic school, and Catholic schools that are financially challenged.

The Catholic school system was greatly subsidized over the years by the contributed services of religious women, men, and clergy who worked for paltry salaries; this monumental sacrifice allowed vast access to Catholic education from the mid-nineteenth century through 1970. With the increase of lay faculty came the urgency to address the need of paying a just salary. Developments in education, such as computers and adequate facilities for sports and the arts, all necessitated additional financial resources and increases in tuition.

This increase of tuition put many Catholics and other supporters of Catholic schools in a difficult position of not being able to afford a Catholic education or in some cases not being able to make a great sacrifice. The urban poor, new immigrants, and many middle-class people found themselves with little or no choice to access a Catholic education. Hence, some observers believed that Catholic schools were becoming elitist and separatist.

David Baker and Cornelius Riordan (1998) presented a controversial article about the "eliting" of Catholic education in the journal *Phi Delta Kappan*. Within their basic thesis of changing demographics, they maintained that Catholic schools had become more of a private school phenomenon catering primarily to those of abundant financial means. The claims of this article were challenged in a subsequent issue by the distinguished sociologist Fr. Andrew Greeley. The chief rationale of the voucher movement is to provide parents with access to whatever school they choose for their children. Ideologically, the Republican Party supports school choice and vouchers, and the Democratic Party is against them; in practice neither party has delivered much support beyond rhetoric. However, the U.S. Supreme Court ruled in the 2002 case of *Zelman v. Simmons-Harris* that the Cleveland voucher plan was constitutional, opening the door for other states to provide vouchers. Curiously, many politicians and civil rights advocates who are officially against any public support for Catholic and private schools choose these very schools for their own children, thereby perpetuating elitism and limiting choice and access. *See also*: *Catholic High Schools and Minority Students*; *Catholic Schools and the Common Good*; Greeley, Andrew M.; Socioeconomic status (of students).

Further Reading: David P. Baker and Cornelius Riordan, "The 'Eliting' of the Common American Catholic School and the National Education Crisis," *Phi Delta Kappan* 80, 1 (September 1998): 16–24; David P. Baker and Cornelius Riordan, "It's Not about the Failure of Catholic Schools, It's about Demographic Transformation," *Phi Delta Kappan* 80, 6 (February 1999): 462–464; Andrew Greeley, "The So-called Failure of Catholic Schools," *Phi Delta Kappan* 80, 1 (September 1998): 24–26.

Michael P. Caruso

Ellis, John Tracy (1905–1992)

John Tracy Ellis (1905–1992), referred to as the "dean of Catholic Church historians," spent most of his professional life at the Catholic University of America in Washington, DC. He was born in Seneca, Illinois. While an undergraduate at St. Viator's College in Bourbonnaise, Illinois, he developed an interest in history that shaped the

John Tracy Ellis. © CUA University Photograph Collection, The Catholic University of America, Washington, DC.

rest of his life. A Knights of Columbus scholarship enabled him, upon graduation in 1927, to take up advanced work under the guidance of Msgr. Peter Guilday at the Catholic University of America. He received his master's degree in 1928 and his Ph.D. in medieval history in 1930. From 1930 to 1934 he taught courses in European history at two small midwestern colleges, his own undergraduate alma mater and the College of St. Teresa in Winona, Minnesota.

Ellis then decided to enter the diocesan priesthood and returned to Washington for his seminary studies under the direction of the Sulpicians. He was ordained in 1938 and had already begun teaching courses part-time at Catholic University when, in 1938, he was appointed to a regular faculty position, teaching mainly European history.

In 1941, Ellis published *Cardinal Consalvi and Anglo-Papal Relations: 1814–1825*. That same year, Guilday's health began to fail, and Ellis was asked to teach Guilday's courses in the history of the Catholic Church in the United States. This shift in subject matter profoundly affected his scholarship. Some sixteen years later, he acknowledged that he had benefited from the tradition of scholarship that Guilday had established. He also recognized that he was privy to rich archival resources, namely, those of the Library of Congress and of the archdiocese of Baltimore, the nation's premier see.

Shortly after 1941, Ellis became fascinated with the life of Bishop John Lancaster Spalding (1840–1916), the first bishop of Peoria, in particular the critical role he played in the founding of Catholic University. Ellis published *The Formative Years of the Catholic University of America* in 1946. From 1941 to 1961, he also assumed Guilday's position as the executive secretary of the American Catholic Historical Association, and from 1941 to 1963 he edited *The Catholic Historical Review*. His book on the Catholic University led him to study its first chancellor, James Cardinal Gibbons, whose life he researched for seven years, resulting in the 1952 publication of a two-volume *Life of James Cardinal Gibbons*. In 1956, Ellis published two more books, *American Catholicism* and *Documents of American Church History*. In his lifetime, he published over twenty books, received numerous honorary degrees, and was a lifelong lover of the theater. His research concentrated on Catholic institutions and leading Catholic personalities, especially bishops.

Besides books, Ellis also published a number of articles, none of which drew more attention than the address "American Catholics and the Intellectual Life," which he gave in May 1955 to the members of the Catholic Commission on Intellectual and Cultural Affairs. A few years later, Ellis remarked that "the seven years of labor and the 1,442 pages of the final product in the life of the cardinal received nowhere near the attention that was directed to the 37 pages" of the published version of his address. In the address, he set forth reasons to support Denis Brogan's judgment that, despite abundant material wealth of American Catholics, their intellectual prestige was nowhere lower. Among the reasons for this lack of intellectual achievement, Ellis pointed to a poor immigrant Church, the absence of an intellectual tradition among American Catholics, an overemphasis on moral rather than intellectual development, lack of a work ethic for study, an excessive multiplication of mediocre competing graduate schools at Catholic universities, and a ghetto mentality among Catholics. Ellis struck a raw nerve that to this day remains exposed. In more recent years, the debate has turned on whether the criteria for excellence in scholarship should be adopted without modification from secular research universities. In other words, is scholarship informed by faith necessarily different?

In his own time, especially in the 1950s, Ellis could be considered a liberal church historian who, along with Thomas McAvoy of Notre Dame, worked to disassociate Americanism, condemned by Leo XIII, from modernism, condemned by Pius X. By showing that Americanism had a legitimate Catholic form, they helped to open the way for an American Catholicism supportive of the separation of Church and state and of religious freedom. Ellis influenced the American Jesuit John Courtney Murray, who in turn played a key role in shaping Vatican II's document on religious freedom. His many doctoral students have in their own writings enriched the field of U.S. Catholic history.

Ellis' prose was as vivid as his oral presentations were robust. He had an uncanny eye for the idiosyncracies of prominent church personalities but wrote with evident respect for them coupled with a love for the Church. More than any other author, Ellis quoted John Henry Newman, of whom he said "aside from Jesus and His Mother no one has had more influence on my life and thought." *See also*: Catholic philosophy of education.

Further Reading: John Tracy Ellis, *American Catholicism* (Chicago: University of Chicago Press, 1956); John Tracy Ellis, "American Catholics and the Intellectual Life," *Thought* 30 (Autumn 1955): 351–388; "The Intellectual Life: Essays in Memory of John Tracy Ellis, Part One and Part Two," *U.S. Catholic Historian* 13, 1 and 2 (Winter 1995).

James L. Heft, SM

Emotional intelligence

A term used to describe the relationship between emotions and thinking. Definitions range from those relating emotions specifically to intelligence to more general definitions relating them to personal skills. Despite varying definitions, researchers agree that the construct of emotional intelligence is broadly applicable to workplace, classroom, and worship. Recent research has sought to develop measurements of emotional intelligence, an emotional quotient (EQ) that can predict a person's success in many facets of everyday life.

Several implications of emotional intelligence for the classroom have been proposed. Traditional classrooms include aspects of emotion through basic storytelling and literary studies as students must recognize and interpret the feelings and motivations of the characters. Cultural values are also taught through history lessons and in religious education classes. Values such as freedom, equality, and individuality determine emotional reactions. Moral lessons, often grounded in religious thought, further influence interpretation and emotional response. Some schools address emotional intelligence more directly with curriculum designed to teach nonviolence, conflict resolution, democratic principles, and the development of social skills. Such curricula emphasize social engagement and justice. Finally, emotional intelligence is tapped when the importance of positive relationships in both personal and professional aspects of life is stressed as a means for learning in the classroom and beyond its walls.

Many, sometimes conflicting theories of emotional intelligence have been published in both scientific journals and popular publications. The term was first introduced in a doctoral dissertation (Payne, 1985) and subsequent articles appearing in scientific journals by Peter Salovey and John Mayer (1990). Daniel Goleman brought the term to the public in 1995 with the publication of his best-selling book *Emotional Intelligence*. Goleman's popularized definition covers a broad range of skills and areas of interest focusing on knowing one's emotions, managing emotions, motivating oneself, recognizing emotions in others, and handling relationships. Mayer and Salovey propose a more focused definition that is widely accepted in the research literature. It highlights the specific bidirectional relationship between intelligence and emotion:

> Emotional intelligence refers to an ability to recognize the meaning of emotions and their relationships, and to reason and problem-solve on the basis of them. Emotional intelligence is involved in the capacity to perceive emotions, assimilate emotion-related feelings, understand the information of those emotions, and manage them. (Ciarrochi, Forgas, and Mayer 2001, p. 9)

Research on the development of the EQ has brought together studies on cognition, affect, and motivation. Cognition relates to the intelligence component of the quotient, while affect is directly linked to the emotional component. Motivation is a secondary component that relates to goal-directed behavior. Research on EQ is distinct from more general research on cognition and affect because it focuses specifically on how emotion affects thinking and how individuals think about emotions. Ongoing research in the area of social intelligence and multiple intelligences, conducted by Howard Gardner and others, is related to this line of research.

The definition of emotional intelligence proposed by Salovey and Mayer (1990) is referred to as the *ability* approach and includes four distinct components. These four components are arranged in order from simple abilities and psychological processes to more complex levels. The lowest branch is the identification, differentiation, and expression of emotion. These basic skills emerge when infants recognize and respond to facial expressions. From these skills develops the ability to accurately monitor and manage one's own feelings and to recognize and respond appropriately to others' feelings. This component is emotion's influence on action. Emotions are indicators of environmental changes, and individuals with developed skill in this area adapt their actions. They also develop the ability to anticipate how they will feel in different situations and alter and examine their behavior accordingly. The third component involves learning to use emotional knowledge. Individuals apply emotional understanding to situations and relationships with others and also learn to appreciate the complexity of emotions. The fourth component is regulation and control of emotion. Developing skills in this area involves conscious expression of emotions and accurate evaluations of mood and emotions.

In addition to the *ability* approach, other definitions and approaches define emotional intelligence more broadly and in terms of competencies. These definitions tend to be more popularized in nonresearch-oriented media. Goleman's (1995) widely publicized definition divides emotional intelligence into five areas: self-awareness, self-regulation, motivation, empathy, and social skills. Similarly, Bar-On and Parker (2000) have developed a definition of emotional intelligence divided into five areas: intrapersonal, interpersonal, adaptability, stress management, and general mood. Such approaches have served to introduce the idea of emotion as intelligence to a mass audience.

The development of the EQ has attempted to use measurement as a reliable means to predict the relationships between emotion, good adjustment, and adaptation to everyday life events. EQ can be measured through performance tests or self-report questionnaires. Performance tests are more objective than self-reports, measure actual EQ instead of perceived EQ, take more time to complete, and are more closely related to intelligence measures than self-reports. Self-report questionnaires require individuals to have insight into their own EQ, are easier to distort, and relate more closely to personality measures. The Multifactor Emotional Intelligence Scale (MEIS), a performance test, is designed to assess EQ according to the four components of the *ability* approach outlined above. This test is shown to be the most reliable and distinct of the performance tests of EQ. The Bar-On Quotient Inventory (EQ-i) is the most widely accepted of the self-report tests and has demonstrated consistency and reliability in application. *See also*: Gardner, Howard; Multiple Intelligence Theory (MI).

Further Reading: Reuven Bar-On and James D. A. Parker, *The Handbook of Emotional Intelligence: Theory Development, Assessment, and Application at Home, School, and in the Workplace* (San Francisco: Jossey-Bass, 2000); Joseph Ciarrochi, Joseph Forgas, and John Mayer, *Emotional Intelligence in Everyday Life: A Scientific Inquiry* (Philadelphia: Psychology Press, 2001); Daniel Goleman, *Emotional Intelligence* (New York: Bantam Books, 1995); Wayne Leon Payne, "A Study of Emotional Intelligence; Self-Integration; Relating to Fear, Pain, and Desire (Theory, Structure of Reality, Problem-Solving, Contraction/Expansion, Tuning In/Coming Out/Letting Go)," unpublished doctoral dissertation, The Union for Experimenting Colleges and Universities (Cincinnati, OH, 1985); Peter Salovey and John Mayer, "Emotional Intelligence," *Imagination, Cognition, and Personality* 9 (1985): 185–211; Peter Salovey and David Sluyter, *Emotional Development and Emotional Intelligence: Educational Implications* (New York: Basic Books, 1997).

John L. Watzke

Empathy

Empathy, defined by Robert Selman as social role taking, that is, being able to identity with the perspective of another, is considered by the cognitive moral developmentalists as an essential component in the process of moral growth. Empathy is frequently described as "putting on the shoes of another and walking around a mile or two"; the act of empathizing is experiencing as closely as possible the feelings and responses of another.

Empathy differs from sympathy; the former is actually having feelings similar to the other person going through an experience, while sympathy is having feelings *for* another because of what the other is going through. Empathy is a skill that must be developed in persons who will mature morally. Selman suggests, as shown in Table 7, that the skill of empathy develops in a parallel fashion with that of moral growth.

Teachers in Catholic schools, committed to moral growth in children, are encouraged to provide frequent opportunities for their students to practice empathy. For example, in a reading lesson, instead of restricting questions to ascertain whether students have understood the factual data of a given story, teachers should occasionally ask, "How do you think Ellen felt when Jack said that about her dress?" "Why do you think John did that?" "How did he feel about it?"

Older students can develop empathy for literary characters and translate those feelings into a better understanding of others and even self. Consider, for example, Shakespeare's Hamlet. One of the reasons that this character is so compelling is that many people can understand Hamlet's distress and indecision ("To be, or not to be—that is the question: Whether 'tis nobler in the mind to suffer the slings and arrows of outrageous fortune, Or to take arms against a sea of troubles And by opposing end them"—*Hamlet*, III, i) not only abstractly but also empathetically. This ability is of particular value when an understanding of Hamlet's situation helps one understand a parallel situation, for example, between Hamlet's situation and one from one's own life.

Awareness of others' perspectives enables students to analyze their own behavior in a way that is useful for further reflection and subsequent action. The scholars of cognitive moral development (Piaget, Dewey, Kohlberg, Lickona) maintain that it is important for children to explore the thoughts and emotions of both parties in a moral dilemma and to articulate the reason for those feelings if they are to develop the empathy necessary for moral growth. *See also*: Moral education, history of.

Table 7
Parallel Structured and Relations between Social Role-Taking and Moral Judgment

Social Role-Taking Stage	**Moral Judgment Stage**
Stage 0—Egocentric Viewpoint Child has sense of differentiation of self and other but fails to distinguish between thoughts and feelings of either. Child can label other's feelings but does not understand cause-and-effect relation of reason to actions.	*Stage 0—Premoral Stage* Judgments of right and wrong are based on good or bad consequences not on intentions. Moral choices stem from the wish that good things happen to self. Child's reasons for his or her choices simply assert rather than justify.
Stage 1—Social Informational Role-Taking Child is aware that others have a social perspective based on their own reasoning. Child focuses on one perspective rather than coordinate views.	*Stage 1—Punishment and Obedience Orientation* Child focuses on one perspective (i.e., authority of the powerful). Child understands that good actions are based on good intentions. Beginning sense of fairness develops.
Stage 2—Self-Reflective Role-Taking Child is conscious that individuals are aware of the other's perspective. This awareness influences self and other's view. Putting self in other's place is a means of judging intentions, purposes, and actions. Child forms a chain of perspectives but cannot abstract to the level of mutuality.	*Stage 2—Instrumental Orientation* Moral reciprocity is the equal exchange of the intent of two persons in relation to one another. If someone has mean intentions toward self, it is right for self to act in kind. Right is defined as what is valued by self.
Stage 3—Mutual Role-Taking Child realizes that both self and other can view each other mutually and simultaneously. Child can step outside the duality and view interaction as a third person.	*Stage 3—Orientation Maintaining Mutual Expectations* Right is defined as the Golden Rule: Do unto others as you would have them do unto you. Child considers all points of view and reflects on each person's motives to reach mutual agreement.
Stage 4—Social and Convential System Role-Taking Person realizes mutual perspective does not always lead to understanding. Social conventions are seen as necessary because they are understood by all members of the group.	*Stage 4—Orientation to Society's Perspective* Right is defined in terms of the perspective of the generalized other or majority. Person considers consequences of actions for group. Orientation to maintenance of social morality and social order.

Source: Selman, 1976b, p. 309.

Further Reading: Allison Barnes and Paul Thagard, "Empathy and Analogy, 1997," http://cogsct.uwaterloo.ca/Articles/Pages/Empathy.html. Accessed July 21, 2002; Richard S. Peters, "Concrete Principles and the Rational Passions," in Theodore and Nancy Sizer, eds., *Moral*

Education: Five Lectures (Cambridge: Harvard University Press, 1970); Robert L. Selman, "A Developmental Approach to Interpersonal and Moral Awareness in Young Children: Some Educational Implications of Levels of Social Perspective-Taking," in Thomas C. Hennessy, SJ, ed., *Value and Moral Development* (New York: Paulist Press, 1976a); Robert L. Selman, "Social Cognitive Understanding: A Guide to Educational and Clinical Practice," in Thomas C. Lickona, ed., *Moral Development and Behavior: Theory, Practice and Social Issues* (New York: Holt, Rinehart, and Winston, 1976b); Mary Peter Traviss, OP, *Student Moral Development in the Catholic School* (Washington, DC: National Catholic Educational Association, 1985).

Mary Peter Traviss, OP

Endowments

An endowment is a sum of money invested by a nonprofit organization for long-term growth and income, from which a percentage of the profit is allocated to the organization's general operational budget or a specific program. The remaining profits along with the principal dollar amount of the investment stay unused and are continually reinvested so that the endowment grows and lasts into perpetuity. Today 51 percent of Catholic grade schools have endowments that constitute 1.7 percent of their budgets (Kealey, 2001).

Catholic schools typically use endowments to provide annual sources of income to offset the school's operational costs. The other major sources for a Catholic school include tuition, fund-raising, annual giving campaigns, government or corporate grants, and parish and government subsidies. Because the costs of education are steadily increasing, it is important for Catholic schools to maximize their ability to draw revenue from each of these sources. Growing and cultivating a successful endowment have now become an essential component to effectively managing a Catholic school budget.

For example, if a Catholic school were to set up an endowment of $1 million, the revenue stream to the school should develop in the following manner. The school would take this money and place it in a low-risk investment vehicle that provides a reasonable rate of return. For this example, in year one the school realizes a 7 percent return on its money. At the end of year one the school has $1,070,000. Accepted practice is for the school to spend 5 percent of the value of the endowment at the beginning of that year (http://www.donorsforum.org/forms_pdf/0102five.pdf, 2001). Five percent of the value of $1 million equals $50,000. The school could then use the $50,000 for a designated project or to help cover operating expenses. This leaves the endowment account with a value of $1,020,000. In year two the endowment again earns 7 percent. With a 7 percent return the endowment grows from $1,020,000 to $1,091,400. Applying the 5 percent spending rule (5%, $1,020,000), in year two the school has $51,000 to spend. In year three the endowment balance begins at $1,040,000.

The main presumption in this example is that a school will be able to find a low-risk investment that has a rate of return of 7 percent. In good economic times this is not unreasonable. However, in a bad economy this can be quite difficult. If the school's rate of return does not equal the percent of funds that it is spending, gradually the school will begin to erode its endowment's principal. Therefore it is a common practice to cap the annual endowment pay out so that it does not exceed the endowment's interest income for a given year. By adopting this practice, the endowment is assured of continual growth.

There are several misconceptions about responsibly managing an endowment. These misconceptions include the notion that the terms "endowment" and "operational reserves" are synonymous, that having an endowment will hurt other donations, and that planned giving replaces the need for an endowment.

Endowments are different from operational reserves in that operational reserves are moneys that are intended for use in emergency situations; endowments are not. An operational reserve is an investment account that Catholic schools set up to pay for unforeseen expenses. An endowment is not intended to be an emergency fund, but rather an investment account with specific designated purposes and goals that provides interest income in perpetuity to a school. Operational reserve accounts range in size from the equivalent of one to six months of a school's total expenditures. Catholic school endowments are generally much larger, on average ranging in size from $106,218 to $3,311,714 (Kealey, 2001). Lastly, it is foreseeable that a school could in an emergency situation use the majority or all of its reserve account. It is financially irresponsible for a school to use or spend any part of an endowment except a percentage of the endowment's interest income. The general practice for nonprofit organizations is to annually spend 5 percent of an endowment's net value. This allows the endowment manager to reinvest 95 percent of the fund value in addition to any profit that endowment generates so that the endowment's principal is continually growing (http://www.donorsforum.org/forms_pdf/0102five.pdf, 2001).

The second misconception regarding endowments is that by establishing an endowment, a Catholic school will hurt donations and giving to other school fund-raising opportunities. Research has proven that this is not the case. "In fact, the addition of an endowment effort presented to your current donors will encourage them with the foresight of an organization which is planning to stabilize its financial future. Experience demonstrates that dedicated donors do not choose among ways to support their favorite charities, but frequently participate in all of them" (http://www.hcf.on.ca/pages/giving/agencyfaq.html, 2002). A donation to an endowment also has the unique feature of being a lifelong gift. Donors know that if managed properly, the money that they give today will be continually reinvested to benefit the organization into the future. This generally makes contributors feel very good about their giving.

The final misconception regarding endowments is that planned giving replaces the need for a school to establish an endowment. Planned giving is when a donor agrees usually via contract to donate a fixed amount of money to a school each year. There are two main concerns about planned giving versus a gift to an endowment. The first concern is that planned gifts usually are set for a fixed amount of time, usually the lifetime of the donor. A donation to an endowment will last the lifetime of the school. Second, planned giving requires the donor to do significant financial planning. It is the donor's responsibility to manage his or her money to make the required payment each year. By donating to an endowment, the person transfers the investment responsibility to the school. *See also*: Financing of Catholic schools.

Further Reading: Janice Geever, *The Foundation Center's Guide to Proposal Writing* (New York: Foundation Center, 1993); Charlotte Georgi, *Fund-Raising, Grants and Foundations: A Comprehensive Bibliography* (Littleton, CO: Libraries Unlimited, 1985); Regina Haney and Joseph O'Keefe, eds., *Creatively Financing and Resourcing Catholic Schools*: *Conversations in Excellence* (Washington, DC: National Catholic Educational Association, 1999); Jerry Jarc, *Development and Public Relations for the Catholic School* (Washington, DC: National Catholic Educational Association, 1985); Robert J. Kealey, *Balance Sheet for Catholic Elementary*

Schools: Income and Expenses (Washington, DC: National Catholic Educational Association, 2001); Waldenmar A. Nielsen, *The Golden Donors* (New York: E. P. Dutton, 1985); Kerry A. Robinson, ed., *The Catholic Funding Guide: A Directory of Resources for Catholic Activities* (Washington, DC: FADICA, 1998).

Jeffery M. Boetticher, Jr.

Engel v. Vitale

Engel v. Vitale (1962) was the first case wherein the U.S. Supreme Court addressed what has become the highly contentious question of prayer in public schools. In fact, *Engel* stands as the lead case in an unbroken line of opinions under which the Court has prohibited school-sponsored prayer in a variety of settings in public schools.

At issue in *Engel* was a local school board's acting in reliance on a directive from the New York State Board of Regents, the body assigned broad power over public education, to require teachers to have a prayer recited aloud in their classes at the beginning of each school day. The prayer read: "Almighty God, we acknowledge our dependence on Thee, and we beg Thy blessings upon us, our parents, our teachers and our Country" (p. 422). Children whose parents did not wish for them to take part in the activity were excused from participating in the prayer.

Shortly after the board adopted the practice of having the Regents' prayer recited in classes at the start of the school day, the parents of ten children who attended public school filed suit in state court against it both in their own names and on behalf of their children. Alleging that the board's action violated the Establishment Clause, the parents sought an end to the practice on the basis that it was an official prayer contrary to their beliefs, religions, and/or religious practices. The suit also challenged not only the statute authorizing the board to direct the use of prayer but also the prayer itself on the ground that both violated the Establishment Clause. After all three levels of state courts in New York upheld the board's use of prayer, the parents sought further review.

The Supreme Court, in a six-to-one decision, with one justice concurring and two others taking no part in the judgment, reversed in favor of the parents. The Court held that the daily classroom activity of reciting a prayer composed and promulgated by the New York State Board of Regents was a religious activity that was wholly inconsistent with the Establishment Clause. The Court devoted a significant portion of its opinion to a detailed review of the history of state-sponsored prayer in the Anglo-American system of government from sixteenth-century England through the colonial period. Having completed its examination of the role of governmentally endorsed prayer in public life, the Court declared that "[t]here can be no doubt that New York State's prayer program officially establishes the religious beliefs embodied in the Regents' prayer" (p. 430).

The Court next noted that the First Amendment's Establishment and Free Exercise Clauses forbid different types of governmental encroachment against religion. It pointed out that since the Establishment Clause, unlike the Free Exercise Clause, does not depend on any direct government compulsion, public officials violate it by enacting laws that establish an official religion regardless of whether their action coerces nonbelievers. The Court voiced its additional fear that even if there was no overt pressure, placing the power, privilege, and support of the government behind a particular religious belief ran the risk of asserting indirect coercion on others, especially minorities, to conform to the officially approved religion. The Court decided that since the Founders were of the view that religion was "too personal, too sacred, too holy, to permit its 'unhallowed perversion' by a civil magistrate" (p. 432), the practice of state-sponsored prayer ran contrary to their original intent in drafting the First Amendment.

The Court rejected any suggestion that prohibiting state-sponsored prayer in public school evidenced hostility to religion. Instead, the Court characterized its interpretation of the Establishment Clause as rooted in the Founders' awareness of, and repugnance for, how governments had improperly limited the religious freedom of those who held other beliefs. As such, the Court maintained that it was following the Founders' lead in keeping the state out of the business of writing and sanctioning prayer, leaving this religious function to the people themselves and those to whom they looked for guidance. In conclusion, even in conceding "that New York's establishment of its Regents' prayer as an officially approved religious doctrine of that state does not amount to a total establishment of one particular religion to the exclusion of all others" (p. 436), the Court struck it down as inconsistent with the Establishment Clause and its purposes.

The dissent began by reviewing the role of public prayer in the history of the United States and cited presidential support from George Washington to the then current President Kennedy. The dissent contended that since the Court misapplied constitutional principles with regard to prayer, it should have left the statute permitting prayer intact. *See also*: Establishment Clause.

Further Reading: *Engel v. Vitale*, 370 U.S. 421 (1962).

Charles J. Russo

Enrollment

Catholic school enrollment is affected by the political, demographic, and ecclesial forces at work in American society and Catholic Church. In 1880, there were 405,234 students enrolled in Catholic schools (Greene and O'Keefe, 2001). Driven by the great numbers of Catholic immigrants and the mandate of the Third Plenary Council of Baltimore, the number of children attending Catholic schools rose dramatically. By 1900, enrollment increased 111 percent to 854,523 and by 1920 enrollment reached 1,862,213—a 118 percent increase in twenty years. In the forty-year period (1880–1920), Catholic school enrollment increased almost 360 percent (Greene and O'Keefe, 2001).

By the close of the 1920s, the network of Catholic schools was firmly established. The prosperity of the 1920s helped Catholic school expansion. In 1930 there were 10,000 Catholic schools with 2,469,032 students enrolled—an increase of 33 percent in ten years. By 1940, Catholic school enrollment reached 2,581,596 (Greene and O'Keefe, 2001). Table 8 illustrates this increase.

After World War II, the Catholic community continued to grow and enjoy the benefits of a prosperous nation. Expansion of schools and enrollment continued so that by 1950 there were 11,000 Catholic schools enrolling over three million students (Bryk, Lee, and Holland, 1993). In the 1960s Catholics came of age. No longer a persecuted minority, Catholics were among the most powerful and influential people in the country. The need for schools as a safe haven for children of immigrant Catholics was fading. In the fifteen years from 1950 to 1965, Catholic school enrollment increased 81 percent, reaching a peak enrollment in 1965 of almost 5.6 million students in over 13,000 schools (Convey, 1992).

Table 8
Catholic School Enrollment Increase 1880 to 1940 (in thousands)

Year	Enrollment	% Increase	Cumulative %
1880	405		
1900	855	111%	111%
1920	1,862	118%	229%
1930	2,469	33%	262%
1940	2,582	5%	267%

Source: Greene and O'Keefe, 2001.

The 1960s also ushered in sweeping changes in the Catholic Church. The Second Vatican Council (1962–1965) initiated a renewed understanding of the Church and its relationship with the world. Virtually all aspects of church life and ministry changed—Catholic schools were no exception.

In the ecclesial climate following Vatican II, two trends greatly impacted Catholic schools—large numbers of men and women leaving priesthood and religious life and the emergence of new ministries within the Church. With fewer priests and religious, Catholic school staffing shifted from primarily religious and priests to mostly laypeople. The shift resulted in a dramatic increase in the cost of operations. At the same time, Catholic schools found themselves vying with other ministries for the support of the Catholic community. The future need for Catholic schools was called into question. Catholic schools no longer enjoyed the unequivocal support of the Catholic community that had fueled expansion prior to 1965.

The decline in Catholic school enrollment from 1965 to 1990 was precipitous. Over this twenty-five-year period, total Catholic school enrollment decreased 55 percent or by almost three million students. Catholic elementary school enrollment declined 58 percent during this period, while secondary enrollment dropped 43 percent (Convey, 1992). At the peak enrollment in 1965 Catholic schools enrolled over 12 percent of the school-aged population. By 1990, the percentage had decreased to 5.4 percent (Bryk, Lee, and Holland, 1993).

In the latter half of the twentieth century, the Catholic population migrated from the urban areas to the suburbs, leaving empty schools in the cities and not enough schools in the new neighborhoods where Catholics lived. This lack of accessibility to Catholic schools contributed to the overall decline in enrollment.

While Catholic school enrollment was decreasing, enrollment in other private schools, particularly religiously affiliated schools, was increasing. In 1965 Catholic schools enrolled 87 percent of all students attending private schools in the United States (Hunt, 2000, p. 44). By 1975, the percentage dropped to 68 percent, and by 1988 it declined even further to 49 percent. The Catholic school share of private school enrollment has remained fairly constant at 49 percent throughout the 1990s and into the beginning years of the twenty-first century. Table 9 illustrates the decrease in Catholic school enrollment from 1964–1965 to 1989–1990.

Period of stabilization 1990–2002

In the 1990s and the early years of the twenty-first century, Catholic school enrollment exhibited moderate increases overall. The 1992–1993 school year showed the first increase in enrollment since 1965. From 1990 through 2002, Catholic school

Table 9
Decrease in Catholic Elementary and Secondary School Enrollment 1964–65 to 1989–90 (in thousands)

Year	Total	Change	Elem.	Change	9–12	Change
1964–65	5,601	—	4,534	—	1,067	—
1969–70	4,367	−22.0%	3,359	−25.9%	1,008	−5.5%
1974–75	3,504	−19.8%	2,602	−22.5%	902	−10.5%
1979–80	3,139	−10.4%	2,293	−11.9%	846	−6.2%
1984–85	2,902	−7.6%	2,120	−7.6%	782	−7.6%
1989–90	2,499	−13.9%	1,893	−10.7%	606	−22.5%

Source: Convey, 1992.

Table 10
Catholic School Enrollment for Selected Years 1990 through 2001 (in thousands)

Grade level	1990–91	1995–96	2000–01	2001–02
PK–8	1,884	2,029	2,019	1,987
9–12	592	607	628	629
All Schools	2,576	2,635	2,647	2,616

Source: NCEA annual statistical reports on schools 1991, 1996, 2001, and 2002.

enrollment increased by 40,000 students or 1.6 percent. Catholic Pre-K–8 enrollment increased by 3,000 or .2 percent, while Catholic secondary school enrollment increased by 37,000 or 6.3 percent. Enrollment for this period peaked in the 2000–2001 school year with a total student population of 2,647,000—a 2.8 percent increase since 1990— and then declined slightly in the 2001–2002 year. Table 10 illustrates this period of enrollment stabilization.

A number of factors converged to create a favorable climate for increased enrollment to occur. A continued high birthrate, a robust economy, independent research validating Catholic schools as highly effective, and the plight of failing public schools all had an impact on Catholic school growth in the 1990s. In addition, Catholic school leaders at the national and diocesan levels promoted more aggressive marketing campaigns to position Catholic schools as schools of choice.

Challenges affecting Catholic school enrollment

An analysis of Catholic school enrollment trends raises three challenges for Catholic school leaders: (1) maintaining or increasing market share, (2) recruitment and retention of students, and (3) keeping Catholic schools financially and geographically accessible. These challenges require careful planning, consistent marketing, targeted development of secure funding sources, and aggressive advocacy for full and fair parental choice in the selection of schools. *See also*: Admissions; Dropout rates; Religion (of Catholic school students and teachers); Socioeconomic status (of students).

Further Reading: Anthony S. Bryk, Valerie E. Lee, and Peter B. Holland, *Catholic Schools and the Common Good* (Cambridge: Harvard University Press, 1993); John J. Convey, *Catholic Schools Make a Difference: Twenty-five Years of Research* (Washington, DC: National Catholic

Educational Association, 1992); Jessica A. Greene and Joseph M. O'Keefe, "Enrollment in Catholic Schools in the United States," in Thomas C. Hunt, Ellis A. Joseph, and Ronald J. Nuzzi, eds., *Handbook of Research on Catholic Education* (Westport, CT: Greenwood Press, 2001): 161–182; Thomas C. Hunt, "The History of Catholic Schools in the United States: An Overview," in Thomas C. Hunt, Thomas E. Oldenski, and Theodore J. Wallace, eds., *Catholic School Leadership: An Invitation to Lead* (London and New York: Falmer Press, 2000): 34–58; Dale McDonald, *United States Catholic Elementary and Secondary Schools 2001–2002: The Annual Statistical Report on Schools, Enrollment and Staffing* (Washington, DC: National Catholic Educational Association, 2002).

Frank X. Savage

Entitlement

Entitlement programs legally obligate the government to pay benefits to any person who meets the eligibility criteria under the program guidelines established by Congress. These programs guarantee a predetermined level of benefits to eligible recipients and are not subject to the regular appropriations process. These are mandatory spending programs that do not give Congress any discretion on how much money to appropriate. Entitlement programs are funded according to the needs of the pool of eligible recipients. Payments are made by the government to beneficiaries and/or service providers on behalf of the beneficiaries for authorized services. Examples of entitlement programs are Social Security, Medicare, federal child nutrition, education for children with disabilities, and federal student loan programs.

The National School Lunch Act (1946) and the Child Nutrition Act (1960) are permanently authorized entitlement programs that are administered by the U.S. Department of Agriculture. There are five of these programs: School Lunch, School Breakfast, Child Care Food for meals and snacks for children in licensed day-care programs, Summer Food Service to continue provision of meals to students during summer vacation, and Nutrition Education and Training for teachers and food service personnel to support nutrition education in the schools. Schools provide free or reduced-price meals to students who qualify under annually established family income guidelines. The program provides cash and commodity assistance directly to schools that serve meals that meet the dietary requirements of the statute. This financial support includes funding for the purchase of food supplies, personnel, purchase of equipment, and facilities renovation to operate the programs as well as food supplied from the Department of Agriculture surplus food programs. Private and religious schools are eligible to participate fully in the federal nutrition programs and receive the operational funding directly. This is one of the few programs that takes a more expansive view of how the child benefit concept may be exercised by the private and religious institutions directly rather than through a public trustee.

Grants and loans for college expenses are also entitlements. Federal Pell Grants are awarded to undergraduate students according to financial need. Stafford loans are guaranteed by the federal government and paid to the college through the Federal Family Education Loan (FFEL) Program or the William D. Ford Federal Direct Loan (FFDL) Program. Funds for Ford loans come directly from the federal government, while FFEL come from bank and lenders that participate in the program. For those eligible for a subsidized loan, the government pays the interest while they are students and for the first six months after they leave school.

The Individuals with Disabilities Education Act (IDEA) mandates that every child with a disability must be provided with a "free and appropriate public education." The federal government subsidizes part of these costs, and the states and districts must provide the remainder. Unfortunately, individual students parentally placed in private schools are not afforded the same entitlement; only a portion of such students are served under IDEA.

Often confused with true entitlement programs are federal grant programs of educational assistance to states and local school districts. Most programs are funded as discretionary spending items that are determined by the Appropriations Committees and the Congress. This type of legislation provides the funding for programs authorized in various bills for general and categorical aid. These funds are dispersed in the form of grants that are identified as either formula or discretionary.

Formula grants are allocations of specific amounts of money in accordance with a distribution formula prescribed in the law or administrative regulations for each program. Most formula grants are based on targeted categories determined by census data of demographic indicators. Discretionary grants make financial awards to eligible grantees, usually state education agencies or local school districts, on the basis of a competitive review process at the federal or state level. Grant recipients are required to abide by various laws, regulations, and executive orders that apply to recipients of federal funds. For example, standard assurances relate to such items as civil rights or environmental health or safety laws.

Six offices of the U.S. Department of Education are responsible for overseeing the discretionary grant programs established by Congress and administered by the department. These offices are the Office of Bilingual Education and Minority Affairs, Office of Educational Research and Improvement, Office of Elementary and Secondary Education, Office of Post-secondary Education, Office of Special Education and Rehabilitative Services, and Office of Vocational and Adult Education. *See also*: Federal aid to Catholic schools.

Further Reading: Dale McDonald, "Pluralism and Public Policy: Catholic Schools in the United States," in Thomas C. Hunt, Ellis A. Joseph, and Ronald J. Nuzzi, eds., *Handbook of Research on Catholic Education* (Westport, CT: Greenwood Press, 2001): 205–228; United States Catholic Conference, *Making Federal Dollars Work for Catholic School Students and Staff* (Washington, DC: United States Catholic Conference, 1998); U.S. Department of Education, *Serving Private School Students with Federal Education Programs* (Washington, DC: U.S. Government Printing Office, 1996).

Dale McDonald, PBVM

Equality of Educational Opportunity

Equality of Educational Opportunity (1966) is one of the foundational works of educational research of the twentieth century. It is also named the *Coleman Report* after its principal author, James S. Coleman, a noted sociologist. The U.S. Education Commissioner, Harold Howe II, commissioned the report on behalf of the U.S. Congress, responding to the mandate given in Section 402 of the Civil Rights Act of 1964. The purpose of the study was to determine the nature of the lack of educational opportunity for American students in public schools because of their race, color, religion, or national origin.

Coleman attempted to answer four questions in this study. (1) What is the level of segregation among various racial and ethnic groups within public schools? (2) Do the schools offer equal educational opportunities in terms of programs, material, and human resources? (3) Are there variations in student achievement based upon standardized testing? (4) What are the possible relationships that can be posited between students' achievement and the particular school that they attended?

Coleman found that public education in the nation remained effectively segregated ten years after the Supreme Court's *Brown v. Board* decision. 80 percent of white students in grades 1 through 12 attended schools that were 90 to 100 percent white. Comparing white and African American first and twelfth graders, Coleman found that 97 percent of white first graders and 97 percent of white twelfth graders attended a school with a racial population of over 50 percent white. In contrast, 65 percent of African American first graders attended school where 90 to 100 percent of the student enrollment was African American, and 66 percent of all African American twelfth graders attended school where over 50 percent of the enrollment was African American. The typical African American elementary school student attended a school where approximately 65 percent of the faculty would be African American, while the typical white elementary school student would encounter a faculty that was on average 97 percent white. Using the criteria for equality of educational opportunity as defined by the *Brown v. Board* decision, educational opportunity was unequal. Segregation was most prominent in the South, where most schools were either 100 percent white or African American, but patterns of segregation were noted throughout the urban North, Midwest, and West (Coleman, 1966).

Coleman examined the physical, programmatic, and human resources that were available to varying groups of students across the United States. On average, white students tended to be in classrooms with fewer students per teacher (twenty-nine) than students of color (thirty to thirty-three). Student-to-teacher ratios at the secondary level were similar to those of the elementary schools. Schools that were predominantly minority had fewer specialty classrooms, such as science and language laboratories; they had fewer books per pupil in their libraries and were more likely to have an insufficient supply of textbooks for their students. Differences in facilities were more marked when compared by region. While minority students tended to have poorer facilities than the majority, the greater variation in the quality of facilities and resources was from one section of the country to the other. The quality of program that was available to minority students, both African American and Puerto Rican, was inferior to the quality of programs available to white students. The study also demonstrated that both students and teachers were academically and socially tracked, joining students and teachers with fewer resources together (Coleman, 1966).

Coleman reported a significant variation in student achievement between white students and minority students. With the exception of Asian Americans, all other minority groups scored one standard deviation below majority students on standardized achievement tests. The standard deviation between the minority and majority student scores remained the same at each grade level tested. Coleman was quick to point out that this finding was not as benign as it originally looked. For example, as shown in Table 11, a standard deviation of 1.1 on a standardized test means that the higher the grade level, the wider the gap in achievement between the two groups (Coleman, 1966).

Achievement scores, like school facilities, varied across regional boundaries. For example, both African American and white students in the South tended to score lower than their peers in the North. Also, the statistics in Coleman's study did not account for the 20 percent dropout rate among African Americans in the North before

Table 11
Demonstration of the Real Gap in Achievement as
Influenced by the Student's Grade in School with a
Standard Deviation of 1.1 on Standardized Tests

Standard Deviation	Grade in School	Gap in Achievement by years
1.1	6th grade	−1.6 years
1.1	9th grade	−2.4 years
1.1	12th grade	−3.3 years

Source: Coleman, 1966.

they reached the twelfth grade. Overall, Coleman found that schools provided minimal opportunities for minority students to overcome their initial academic deficiencies.

Coleman concluded that the relationship between student achievement and the schools they attend is not as important for white or Asian American students as it is for other minority students. The quality and types of resources that a school provides have a greater impact upon the academic success of minority students. Coleman examined the qualities of good teachers and their relationship to student achievement. While he admitted that he did not do a comprehensive job of qualifying what was meant by good teachers, he found three factors that had an impact on achievement: the teacher's level of verbal skills and the academic background of both the teacher and the teacher's parents. Perhaps the most interesting result in this part of the study was the influence student peer groups had on academic achievement. Students from lower socioeconomic classes who were in classes with a majority of middle class students tended to have higher academic expectations for themselves. Aware of the inherent problems of discrimination, Coleman also noted that minority students who were surveyed tended to believe that they cannot affect either their environment or their future.

Equality of Educational Opportunity provided educators who sought to provide a quality education to minority students a change of paradigm. Rather than looking at equality of opportunity from the perspective of providing equal resources, educators must consider what it will take to provide an equality of educational outcome for all students. *See also*: Catholic Schools and the Common Good; Coleman, James S.

Further Reading: Anthony S. Bryk, Valerie E. Lee, and Peter B. Holland, *Catholic Schools and the Common Good* (Cambridge: Harvard University Press, 1993); James S. Coleman, *Equality of Educational Opportunity* (Washington, DC: U.S. Government Printing Office, 1966); James S. Coleman, Thomas Hoffer, and Sally Kilgore, *High School Achievement: Public, Catholic, and Private Schools Compared* (New York: Basic Books, 1982); Richard D. Kahlenberg, "Learning from James Coleman," *Public Interest* #144 (2001): 54–72.

Anthony J. Dosen, CM

E-Rate

The Telecommunications Act of 1996 provided a means for schools and libraries to have more affordable accessibility to all sorts of telecommunications services, by providing eligible K–12 public and private schools and libraries discounts on approved telecommunications, including Internet access and internal connection costs. The initiation of the fund dramatically increased the use of telecommunications within both public and private schools, including Catholic schools; however, in recent years, applications for moneys have leveled off.

The Universal Service Fund was an outgrowth of a bipartisan amendment to the Telecommunications Act of 1996. By mid-1997, the Federal Communications Commission (FCC) had unanimously ruled to provide up to $2.25 billion per year in discounts to eligible K–12 schools and public libraries for telecommunications services. The funding was to be allocated on a sliding scale from 20 percent to 90 percent, with discounts based on the percentage of students eligible for the National Free Lunch Program, as well as location of school or library (whether in an urban or rural area). Schools and libraries in low-income urban communities and rural areas qualify for higher discounts.

The discounts apply to telecommunications services (wired and wireless), internal connections, Internet access, high-speed data connections, and some equipment necessary to transport information within a school, such as network file servers, hubs, and routers. However, the moneys cannot be used for desktop computers, educational software, or professional development. In addition to completing an application process that has been deemed complex by some school administrators, schools are required to submit a technology plan before funding will be provided.

Statistics related to application for E-Rate funds by Catholic schools varied across surveys. The president of the Schools and Libraries Division of the Universal Service Fund indicated that each year from 1998 through 2000, well over one-third of all Catholic schools had made application. The National Center for Education Statistics (NCES) reported that in 1998, 51 percent of Catholic schools applied for E-Rate, whereas only 9 percent of other religious schools and 15 percent of nonsectarian private schools applied. Quality Education Data (QED), which conducted an independent technology survey for the National Catholic Educational Association (NCEA), reported that 48 percent of Catholic schools made application in year one. The NCEA reported a smaller application rate for the year, indicating that nearly 40 percent of all Catholic schools applied for E-Rate funding, with about 84 percent of those who applied for the funding actually receiving it. In 1999–2000, according to NCEA, the percentage of applicants from the Catholic schools increased only slightly to 42 percent (QED reported an application rate of 44 percent), and about 80 percent of those who applied received moneys from the fund. By 2000–2001, the percentage of applicants dropped to about 38 percent (QED reported 43%). According to QED data published in 2002, the decline was even more pronounced during the 2001–2002 academic year, with only 35 percent of Catholic schools making application for the academic year 2002–2003. Schools that have not taken advantage of the funding have reported that they have been deterred by the complexity of the application process, by the relatively low level of funding they will receive, and by concerns that they are unable to afford the hardware and software that would provide the access to the services within the classrooms and other instructional areas. According to QED, the low application rate in 2001–2002 may have also been attributable to uncertainties after the passage of the *No Child Left Behind Act*. *See also*: Computer accessibility; Internet accessibility; Telecommunications.

Further Reading: Dale McDonald, *United States Catholic Elementary and Secondary Schools 1998–1999: The Annual Statistical Report on Schools, Enrollment, and Staffing* (Washington, DC: National Catholic Educational Association, 1999); Dale McDonald, *United States*

Catholic Elementary and Secondary Schools 1999–2000: The Annual Statistical Report on Schools, Enrollment, and Staffing (Washington, DC: National Catholic Educational Association, 2000); Terian Tyre, *The State of Technology in Catholic Schools* (Dayton, OH: Peter Li, 2000, 2002); U.S. House of Representatives, Subcommittee on Telecommunications and the Internet of the Committee on Energy and Commerce, *Technology and Education: A Review of Federal, State, and Private Sector Programs* Hearing, March 8, 2001 (Washington, DC: U.S. Government Printing Office, 2001). Retrieved July 1, 2002, from http://energycommerce.house.gov/107/hearings/03082001Hearing51/print.htm.

Jeanne Hagelskamp, SP

Establishment Clause

According to the religion clauses of the First Amendment, "Congress shall make no law respecting an establishment of religion, or prohibiting the free exercise thereof." Even though the First Amendment prevents only Congress from making such laws, in 1940 the Court applied its terms to the states through the Fourteenth Amendment in *Cantwell v. Connecticut.*

Appeals to history as to the original intent of the Establishment Clause fail to provide clear answers, stemming largely from the fact that there were close ties between religion and government that began during the colonial period. Rather than engage in a lengthy discussion of the different approaches to the Establishment Clause, two distinct camps emerged: separationists and accommodationists. On the one hand are separationists, supporters of the Jeffersonian metaphor of maintaining a "wall of separation" between church and state, language that does not appear in the Constitution; this perspective is most often associated with the Supreme Court as it limits the amount of governmental aid for students who attend religiously affiliated nonpublic schools. On the other hand, accommodationists believe that the government is not prohibited from permitting some aid or accommodating the needs of children in religious schools by means of the so-called child benefit test.

Unlike its cases involving religious activities in public schools under the Free Exercise Clause, the Court, reflecting changes in its membership, has witnessed shifts in its attitude with regard to aid to students in nonpublic schools. The Court has created confusion over the appropriate judicial standard to apply in disputes involving religion. That is, although it crafted a two-part test in *School District of Abington Township v. Schempp* and *Murray v. Curlett* (1963) to evaluate the constitutionality of prayer and Bible-reading in public schools, the Court expanded it in creating the tripartite Establishment Clause test in *Lemon v. Kurtzman* (1971), a case involving governmental aid to religiously affiliated nonpublic schools. When the Court subsequently applied the *Lemon* test in cases arising under both the Establishment and Free Exercise Clauses, its failure to explain how or why it had become a kind of "one-size fits all" standard in First Amendment disputes leaves commentators and lower courts seeking greater clarity.

The First Amendment became part of the Constitution in 1791 along with the rest of the Bill of Rights. Yet, the Supreme Court did not address a case on the merits of the Establishment Clause until 1947. The only two religion cases that the Court dealt with prior to 1947, both of which were important to Catholic schools, were *Pierce v. Society of Sisters of the Holy Names of Jesus and Mary* (1925) and *Cochran v. Louisiana State Board of Education* (1930), resolved on the basis of the Fourteenth Amendment's Due Process Clause. In *Pierce*, in striking down a state law that would have required parents to send all children between the ages of 8 and 16 in regular education to public schools, the Court affirmed the right of religious schools to function. In addition, the Court decided that while a state may oversee such important features as health, safety, and teacher qualifications in nonpublic schools, it could not do so to an extent greater than for public education. In *Cochran*, the Court upheld a state law that required local school boards to loan textbooks for use in secular subjects to all students in asserting that they, not their religious school, were the beneficiaries and so presaged the child benefit test that would emerge in *Everson v. Board of Education* (1947).

The Court's Establishment Clause jurisprudence with regard to aid to religious K–12 schools has evolved through three phases, each of which is briefly outlined below along with summaries of key Supreme Court cases. During the first stage, which began in 1947 with *Everson v. Board of Education* and ended in 1968 with *Board of Education v. Allen*, the Court enunciated and defined the boundaries of the child benefit test, a legal construct that permits state-funded aid on the basis that it assists children rather than their religiously affiliated nonpublic schools. The years between the Court's 1971 decision in *Lemon v. Kurtzman* and *Aguilar v. Felton* in 1985 were the low point for the child benefit test as the Court largely refused to move beyond the limits it set in *Everson* and *Allen*. However, with its 1993 ruling in *Zobrest v. Catalina Foothills School District*, the Court revitalized the child benefit test and has since handed down rulings consistent with this perspective.

In *Everson v. Board of Education* (1947), the Court upheld the constitutionality of a state statute that allowed local school boards to reimburse parents for the cost of transporting their children to Catholic schools. In *Wolman v. Walter* (1977), the Court addressed the related question of whether a state could permit public funds to be used to provide transportation for field trips by children who attend religiously affiliated nonpublic schools. The Court struck down this law in determining that since field trips are curricular, they had to be treated differently from providing transportation to and from school.

The Court's 1963 ruling in the companion cases of *School District of Abington Township v. Schempp* and *Murray v. Curlett* (1963), although set in the context of a case wherein it struck down prayer and Bible-reading in school, ultimately had a major impact on its Establishment Clause jurisprudence. The significance of these cases stems from the fact the Court used its opinion to enunciate the "purpose and effect" test that evolved into the first two prongs of the *Lemon* test discussed below.

In *Board of Education v. Allen* (1968) the Court upheld the constitutionality of a state law that required local school boards to loan text books for secular instruction to children in grades 7 to 12 who attended nonpublic schools. Relying largely on the child benefit test, the Court reasoned that the purpose of the statute was not to aid religion or private schools and that its primary effect would be to improve the quality of education for all children. The Court upheld similar textbook provisions in *Meek v. Pittenger* (1975) and *Wolman v. Walter* (1977). *Allen* was regarded as the outer limit of the child benefit test prior to *Agostini v. Felton* (1997).

In *Lemon v. Kurtzman* (1971), the Court's most significant case involving the Establishment Clause, the Court struck down state statutes calling for purchases of secular services and providing salary supplements for teachers in religiously affiliated nonpublic schools. In so doing, the Court enunciated the tripartite measure known as the *Lemon* test, according to which:

> Every analysis in this area must begin with consideration of the cumulative criteria developed by the Court over many years. Three such tests may be gleaned from our cases. First, the statute must have a secular legislative purpose; second, its principal or primary effect must be one that neither advances nor inhibits religion; finally, the statute must not foster "an excessive government entanglement with religion." (1971, 612–613)

The Court also noted that "we must examine the character and purposes of the institutions that are benefited, the nature of the aid that the State provides, and the resulting relationship between the government and religious authority" (1971, p. 615). In a kind of catch-22 situation wherein programs often pass the first two prongs of the *Lemon* test, excessive entanglement frequently becomes the basis for invalidating laws providing aid to students in religiously affiliated nonpublic schools.

Over the next fourteen years, the Court largely refused to expand the boundaries of the child benefit test. For example, although it upheld textbook loans in *Meek v. Pittenger* (1975), at the same time the Court struck down provisions dealing with periodicals, films, recordings, projectors, tape recorders, and laboratory equipment on the basis that making these items available had the primary effect of advancing religion because of the religious nature of the schools involved. The Court also invalidated a provision that would have allowed public school teachers to provide auxiliary services including remedial instruction as well as guidance counseling and testing on-site in religious schools on the basis that this would have resulted in excessive entanglement.

Two years later the Court reached a similar result in *Wolman v. Walter* (1977), in upholding a textbook loan program, permitting the state to supply nonpublic schools with state-mandated tests, and allowing public school employees to go on-site in religious schools to perform diagnostic tests to evaluate whether students need speech, hearing, and psychological services. In addition, the Court permitted public funds to be spent providing therapeutic services to students from nonpublic schools as long as they were delivered off-site. However, the Court prohibited the loans of instructional materials and equipment as well as the use of funds to pay for field trips for students in nonpublic schools based on the fear of excessive entanglement.

Mueller v. Allen (1985) represents the one exception during this period when the Court upheld a program under Establishment Clause analysis. The Court ruled that a state could permit state income tax deductions for actual expenses for tuition, textbooks, and transportation of dependents who attended elementary or secondary schools. The Court explained that the deduction was constitutional since it was available to all parents, not only those whose children were in nonpublic schools, and was one among many rather than a single, favored type of taxpayer deduction.

In *School District of City of Grand Rapids v. Ball* (1985), the Supreme Court affirmed that a released time program was unconstitutional because it failed all three prongs of the *Lemon* test. Further, the Court invalidated an after-school program of community education in which teachers from religious schools worked part-time for the public school board teaching students in their own nonpublic school.

On the same day as it decided *Grand Rapids*, the Supreme Court considered a challenge to a school board's permitting public school teachers to provide remedial instruction under the Elementary and Secondary Education Act of 1965 for specifically targeted needy children on-site in their religious, mostly Catholic schools. In *Aguilar v. Felton* (1985), a bitterly divided Supreme Court affirmed that the on-site delivery of services was unconstitutional, even though the board developed safeguards to ensure that public funds were not spent inappropriately. The Court vitiated the program based on its fear that such a system would have resulted in excessive entanglement.

Zobrest v. Catalina Foothills School District (1993) signaled a shift in the Court's Establishment Clause thinking. At issue was a school board's refusal to provide a sign-language interpreter, under the Individuals with Disabilities Education Act (1991), for a deaf student who transferred to a Catholic high school. The Court held that the student was entitled to an interpreter since this form of assistance was neutral insofar as it did not afford financial benefits to his parents or school and there was no governmental participation in instruction because the interpreter was only a conduit to effectuate his learning.

A year later, the Court examined a case where a state legislature created a school district with boundaries that were coextensive with those of a small religious community. The legislature created the district in an attempt to meet the needs of parents of children with disabilities who wished to send them to a nearby school that would honor their religious practices. In *Board of Education of Kiryas Joel Village School District v. Grumet* (1994), the Court affirmed that the law violated the Establishment Clause since it failed all three prongs of the *Lemon* test.

In *Agostini v. Felton* (1997), the Court took the unusual step of essentially dissolving the injunction it upheld in *Aguilar v. Felton.* More specifically, a divided Court, in acknowledging changes in the Court's attitude over the intervening years, concluded that the Title I program at issue did not violate the Establishment Clause since there was no governmental indoctrination, there were no distinctions between recipients based on religion, and there was no excessive entanglement. Perhaps the most significant jurisprudential development in *Agostini* was that the Court modified the *Lemon* test by reviewing only its first two parts, purpose and effect, while recasting entanglement as one criterion in determining a statute's effect.

The Court's most recent case on instructional materials, *Mitchell v. Helms* (2000), further expanded the boundaries of state aid to religious schools. A splintered Court, in a plurality, upheld the constitutionality of Chapter 2 of Title I, now Title VI, of the Elementary and Secondary Education Act (1997), a far-reaching federal law permitting the loan of instructional materials, such as library books, computers, television sets, tape recorders, and maps, to nonpublic schools. In relying on *Agostini*'s modification of *Lemon*, the plurality declared that since the purpose part of the test was not challenged, it had to consider only Chapter 2's effect. The plurality reasoned that the law did not foster religious indoctrination since aid was allocated on the basis of neutral secular criteria that neither favored nor disfavored religion and was available to all schools based on secular, nondiscriminatory basis. Moreover, the plurality explicitly reversed those parts of *Meek v. Pittenger* and *Wolman v. Walter* that were inconsistent with its analysis on loans of instructional materials.

In recent years, considerable controversy has been generated over the use of vouchers. After lower courts reached mixed results in disputes over vouchers, the Supreme Court, in *Zelman v. Simmons-Harris* (2002), a typically fractured Supreme Court upheld the constitutionality of a voucher program from Cleveland, Ohio. The Court was satisfied that the voucher program passed constitutional muster since it involved true private choice wherein parents were able to select where their children attended school without regard to religion. In light of the modifications that the Court enunciated to the *Lemon* test in *Agostini*, it will be interesting to observe how the Court and its ever-changing membership interpret disputes involving aid to Catholic and other religious schools under the Establishment Clause. *See also*: Free Exercise Clause; *Lemon v. Kurtzman*; *School District of Abington Township v. Schempp* and *Murray v. Curlett*.

Further Reading: *Agostini v. Felton*, 521 U.S. 203 (1997); *Aguilar v. Felton*, 473 U.S. 402 (1985); *Board of Educ. v. Allen*, 392 U.S. 236 (1968); *Board of Educ. of Kiryas Joel Village Sch. Dist. v. Grumet*, 512 U.S. 687 (1994); *Cantwell v. Connecticut*, 310 U.S. 296 (1940); *Cochran v. Louisiana State Bd. of Educ.*, 281 U.S. 370 (1930); Chapter 2 of Title I, now Title VI, of the Elementary and Secondary Education Act, Title VI, 20 U.S.C. §§ 7301–73 (1997); *Everson v. Board of Educ.*, 330 U.S. 1 (1947); Individuals with Disabilities Education Act, 20 U.S.C. §§ 1400 *et seq.* (1991); *Lemon v. Kurtzman*, 403 U.S. 602 (1971); *Meek v. Pittenger* 421 U.S. 349 (1975); *Mitchell v. Helms*, 530 U.S. 793 (2000); *Mueller v. Allen*, 463 U.S. 388 (1983); *Pierce v. Society of Sisters of the Holy Names of Jesus and Mary*, 268 U.S. 510 (1925); *School Dist. of Abington Township v. Schempp, Murray v. Curlett*, 374 U.S. 203 (1963); *School Dist. of City of Grand Rapids v. Ball*, 473 U.S. 373 (1985); *Wolman v. Walter*, 433 U.S. 229 (1977); *Zelman v. Simmons-Harris*, 122 S. Ct. 2460 (2002); *Zobrest v. Catalina Foothills Sch. Dist.*, 509 U.S. 1 (1993).

Charles J. Russo

Ethnicity (and parish schools)

Immigrant Catholicism was a conservative, intimate, rural religion. It was a religion that had not changed in hundreds of years, and this continuity gave immigrant Catholics the strength to live in a new world of strangers. The key element in this religion was language, the language of home. Without their native language, their religion would not be the same. Faced with this strong determination to preserve language at all costs, the Church had little choice but to accept these immigrants on their own terms. The response of most bishops was to allow these new Catholics to form national parishes.

The national parish, which is a parish where the liturgy was celebrated in a foreign language and occasionally in English, was very popular in the years from 1890 to 1916, particularly among the Germans, Poles, and Italians. Each of these groups established hundreds of national parishes during these years. The Bohemians, Lithuanians, Slovaks, and Croatians—who emigrated in smaller numbers—each established several dozen national parishes.

By 1916, there were 1,200 Catholic parishes using a foreign language exclusively and nearly 3,000 using a foreign language in addition to English. As part of these parishes, immigrant Catholics established foreign-language parochial schools. These schools were of vital importance to virtually all immigrant Catholic parents.

For many immigrant parents, religious faith and national heritage were treasures to be passed on to the next generation, and measures had to be taken to ensure the treasure was not squandered in the new land. Unlike the local American public school, the ethnic Catholic school offered the promise of educating immigrant children without jeopardizing their spiritual salvation or cultural heritage. For this reason, many immigrant parents contributed their hard-earned dollars toward the establishment and support of parish schools. Support for ethnic parish schools varied from one immigrant group to the next. The Germans had been the first to establish ethnic parish schools in the nineteenth century and were their most ardent supporters. But by the turn of the century, most German parish schools had felt the impact of Americanization and were using English as the main language of instruction. The Poles, who continued to arrive in this country in large numbers during the first two decades of the twentieth century, were enthusiastic supporters of ethnic parish schools. Other Slavic groups also established ethnic parish schools in proportion to their numbers.

Ethnic Catholic schools faced their greatest challenge in the years from 1910 to 1930, the result of a concerted effort to "Americanize" these schools. It was a campaign waged on several different fronts, starting with the government. State law in the early 1920s mandated that all instruction in private schools should be conducted in English and frequently required that private school teachers meet state standards in teacher training.

The Catholic hierarchy also joined in the campaign for Americanization; through their instructions to pastors and diocesan school boards they asserted the right to approve the languages and course of study used in parochial school classrooms. In fact, the hierarchy took a vocal and visible role in this process. Bishops such as James Gibbons, George Mundelein, and John Ireland led the campaign. "Ours is the American Church," noted Ireland, "and not Irish, German, Italian, or Polish—and we will keep it American."

As important as these external forces were, the most important force for Americanization came from within the ethnic Catholic communities themselves. As the older generation of priests and laymen gave way to an American-born generation, the Old World ways were abandoned. Native language and culture were less important to American-born Catholics than to their parents. The new generation did not object to an Americanized curriculum; in fact, they welcomed it. By the 1930s, native language and culture had become extracurricular subjects in most parochial schools and dropped altogether at some of these institutions.

All ethnic schools came in for the same treatment, and perhaps it was inevitable. The ethnic parochial school was tolerated as temporarily expedient by most Americans—both Catholic and non-Catholic. It was assumed by all that national parishes and foreign-language usage would die out as the new immigrants acclimated themselves to American society. But many of these immigrants held on to their native languages and customs with a fierce determination that must have disheartened the American public.

World War I, with its propaganda campaign against all things foreign, ended the tolerance of the American public for ethnic parochial schools. The American public in general and the Catholic hierarchy in particular would no longer accept the argument of ethnic leaders that immigrants could maintain their native languages and cultures and still be loyal to their new nation. The American public rejected this argument as contradictory and pressured the foreign-born to openly pledge their total allegiance to the United States. Ethnic parochial schools were a casualty of this wartime loyalty campaign.

The growing animosity toward ethnic Catholic schools continued to grow in the years after the end of the war. Indeed, it was clear from the proceedings of the Catholic Educational Association (CEA) that the Church was acting quickly to end all things foreign associated with American Catholic parochial education. Flag-waving patriotism was the theme of most meetings as speaker after speaker stressed that Americanization was in the best interest of all Catholic children.

The CEA meeting held in June 1919 was typical in tone. The Parish School Department passed a unanimous resolution that all classes in American Catholic schools must be conducted in the English language. Individual speakers at that meeting expressed similar sentiments that Americanization was in the best interest of the nation. Fr. Joseph M'Clancy of Brooklyn spoke for many at the meeting when he urged all Catholics to work with public officials to instill patriotism in all schoolchildren.

Yet another speaker at that meeting, William J. McAuliffe of Cathedral College in New York, attacked the immigrant claim that Americanization could be accomplished through the use of native languages. McAuliffe, like many Catholic educators, rejected this argument. In its place, he advocated a three-level approach. First, immigrant children were to receive a solid grounding in the English language. Second, the immigrant child should be in a thoroughly American classroom instructed by a teacher who had a thorough command of the English language and an unswerving devotion to American traditions. Finally, McAuliffe hoped that immigrants would choose to extend their education beyond grade school. McAuliffe also advocated the establishment of a network of adult education classes to Americanize those immigrants beyond the influence of the parish school.

M'Clancy and McAuliffe were not alone in their views as educator after educator at CEA meetings throughout the 1920s spoke in favor of Americanization and against ethnic Catholic schools. Additional momentum was provided by the National Catholic Welfare Conference's Civic Education Bureau. Directed by John A. Lapp and Charles A. McMahon, the bureau promoted a variety of measures to Americanize Catholics of all ages. The bureau promoted the Boy Scouts of America because Scouting formed boys into young men who love only one "ism"—Americanism. More important, the bureau published and distributed *The Civic Catechism on the Rights and Duties of American Citizens* for use in Catholic schools across the country. The pamphlet was translated into fourteen languages and published in Catholic and foreign-language newspapers. Within three years after the end of the war, the Church was putting substantial pressure on ethnic Catholic schools to conform to American ways.

Americanizers like M'Clancy and McAuliffe also provided specific blueprints for changing ethnic Catholic schools. These and other educators stressed that history and civics should be the centerpiece of the Catholic school curriculum with the intent of developing a burning love and admiration for all things American. No language other than English could cross the lips of either the teachers or the children in Catholic classrooms. Pastors and principals could contribute toward the Americanization of their schools. They should have the children in their charge salute the flag every morning. Classroom walls should be decorated with pictures of national leaders and heroes, and if need be, Catholic schools should be placed at the disposal of the city, the state, and the nation.

Even though some immigrant Catholic educators did not agree completely with the program developed by the Americanizers, they did accept the basic premise that the value and vitality of ethnic Catholic schools were coming to an end. Foreign-language schools continued through the 1920s particularly among the Poles, but by 1930, these institutions had all but disappeared from the Catholic educational landscape.

The ethnic Catholic school was a key element in the rapid growth of parochial education for the fifty years following the Civil War. More important, these schools served as the bridge from the Old World to the New for many immigrant children. Yet these schools were destined to be temporary and transitional. With the pressure of American nationalism both during and after World War I and the end of mass immigration in 1924, the ethnic Catholic school gradually lost its value to the Catholic

Church. *See also*: Cahenslyism; German American Catholics; Polish American Catholics; Slavic American Catholics.

Further Reading: Dolores Liptak, ed., *A Church of Many Cultures: Selected Historical Essays* (New York: Garland, 1988); Dolores Liptak, *Immigrants and Their Church* (New York: Macmillan, 1989); Timothy Walch, *Parish School: American Catholic Parochial Education from Colonial Times to the Present* (New York: Crossroad, 1996); Howard Weisz, *Irish American and Italian American Views of Education* (New York: Arno Press, 1976).

Timothy Walch

Evangelization

Evangelization is the effort to proclaim the Gospel to the people of today as a service rendered to the Christian community and also the whole of humanity. "For the Church, to evangelize means bringing the Good News to all aspects of humanity and, through its influence, to transform it from within, making humanity itself into something new" (Paul VI, 1975, 18). Evangelization is a complex process that involves the meaningful integration of the Gospel message with current culture. The ultimate goal of evangelization is conversion or *metanoia*. *Metanoia* refers to an interior change or a change of mind and heart that results in an individual embracing Jesus and His message and sharing the message with others. Those who proclaim the good news of Jesus Christ do so not as individuals, but rather as messengers of the Holy Spirit.

The Catholic school is an important and effective ministry of the Catholic Church for evangelization. Catholic schools participate in the overall educational mission of the Church and serve as a highly effective means of providing religious education, faith formation, and a general education in secular subjects so as to enable students to be bonded to Christ and the Church through a holistic education.

For young people, the school is one of the primary ways evangelization takes place. Working together with the family, the Catholic school provides daily opportunities for proclaiming and living the Word of God. Evangelization in the Catholic school is grounded in the relationship between the Gospel message and the Catholic school that is described in the documents of the Church. The threefold ministry of Catholic education is (1) to teach doctrine, the message revealed by God (*didache*); (2) to build community, fellowship in the life of the Holy Spirit (*koinonia*); and (3) to serve the Christian community and all humankind (*diakonia*). These essential elements of message, community, and service are integrated into daily life in the Catholic school. Through religious instruction, catechesis, and liturgy students learn about the Gospel message. The Christian community of the Catholic school teaches students the lived reality of building and maintaining community. Service to others is the third critical component of life in the Catholic school. Service teaches students to reach out to others and share their faith in real and tangible ways.

The Catholic school has, over time, remained a strong and effective vehicle for evangelizing in the world. Despite many changes in American society over the last 200 years, Catholic schools have remained steadfast and responsive to the needs of their students. Through their faithfulness to the Gospel and commitment to the dignity and development of each individual in the school community, Catholic schools have succeeded in keeping an eye on their end purpose—to relate all of human culture to the good news of salvation. This very dedication to their essence assists Catholic schools as they strive to remain a cultural leaven and an evangelizing force for the Church. Through daily activities and voluntary relationships that develop in the Catholic school, students have a unique opportunity to integrate the Gospel message with modern culture. In fact, the bishops have acknowledged the Catholic school as the most effective means available to the Church for the education of young people in the meaning of the Gospel.

In the context of the Catholic school, all efforts at evangelization are by nature Christocentric, because Jesus Himself was the first and greatest evangelizer. As an evangelizer, Christ proclaimed a kingdom, the Kingdom of God. At the center of Christ's message are salvation and liberation from all that oppresses. Through His tireless preaching, the words and actions of Jesus reveal the secret of God, a plan and a promise, thereby changing human destiny. Jesus also teaches us how to build community. Finally, Jesus reaches out to all humankind through signs of service and servanthood. The sick are cured, bread is multiplied, the dead return to life. The Church is called to carry on the evangelizing activity modeled by Christ, and faithfulness to the life of Jesus is the standard of all contemporary ministries of evangelization. Thus, to be an evangelizer is ultimately a call to be Christ-like.

It is important to make proclaiming the Gospel relevant to the culture of the twenty-first century. Evangelization is not to be confused with eighteenth-century European pietism or American Protestant revivalism. Evangelization must be an authentic, meaningful endeavor that remains faithful to both the content of the message and to those who are to receive it. The Gospel message is intended for all people of all times. It is the task of each generation of Christians to assess their own times and carry out the mission of Christ by means suited to the needs and opportunities they perceive. The essential mission of the Church must be carried out to the fullest extent possible in a manner that makes fullest use of available resources in modern society. Evangelists must incorporate the art, music, science, and technology of the culture to successfully convey the meaning of the Gospel message. God's people are immersed in current culture. It is imperative that God's word be related in a meaningful way to those meant to receive it.

The complex process of evangelization involves certain elements that must work in interaction with one another. The Church evangelizes when it seeks to convert both the personal and collective consciences of people through the power of the message of salvation. Evangelization seeks total, deep human transformation within the individuals' cultures. More than anything else, the Gospel must be proclaimed by lived witness. Christians must, in the midst of their own communities, model their capacity for acceptance, understanding, and compassion. This quiet, yet powerful, type of witness, evident through action, is an initial act of evangelization. It stirs important questions and interest in the minds and hearts of those who observe a life of Christian witness.

Explicit proclamation of the Gospel message is another critical component of evangelization. Through active proclamation, the Gospel is explained, justified, and magnified. This proclamation (*kerygma*, preaching or catechesis) is so important in the evangelization process that it has often become synonymous with it. In reality, however, it is only one component of evangelization.

The proclamation reaches full development only when it is listened to, accepted, assimilated, and integrated into daily activity. Persons whose lives have been truly transformed by the Gospel enter into the community of believers, the Church. A person who accepts the Church translates it into adherence to the teachings of the Church and acceptance of the sacraments and the grace they confer.

Finally, a person who has been evangelized reaches out to evangelize others. The evangelized person responds to God's call, bears witness to it, and proclaims it to those who will listen. Those who are evangelized feel compelled to proclaim the Gospel message and make it alive in the hearts of others.

What is the essential content of evangelization? First, to evangelize is to bear witness in a simple and direct way to God and to God's love for the world. In addition, evangelization will always include the clear message that salvation in eternity is offered to all people as a gift from God. Evangelization always includes the preaching of hope in the promises made by God through Jesus Christ. All who work to evangelize must see themselves as messengers of God's word to others and must accomplish their task with ever-increasing love, joy, and zeal.

Evangelization must succeed in relating the good news in a manner that touches life as a whole. The interplay of the Gospel and of people's concrete lives is at the heart of evangelization. This key connection breathes life and meaning into God's word. The work of evangelization, rooted in a basic understanding of and love for the dignity of every individual, extends especially to the oppressed and all who seem condemned to remain on the margins of life. It is the duty of the Church to proclaim the message of liberation to those most in need. Furthermore, one who proclaims the good news must accept the responsibility for promoting justice and peace. This is an important link between the words of redemption and the reality of it. Good works must flow from the Gospel message.

The Second Vatican Council called for a renewal in the Church as it reiterated and expanded ideas previously espoused in Church teaching. This call sparked further Church statements on the role of the laity, specifically youth, in evangelization. *The Decree on the Apostolate of the Laity* (1965), *The Declaration on Christian Education* (1965), and other Church documents make clear that laypersons are called by God to make of their apostolate, through the vigor of their Christian spirit, a leaven in the world. All Christians are called to deepen their own awareness of their responsibility to be of service to others and to work for the sanctification of themselves and others. The Catholic school and its educators are especially well suited to attend to the apostolic formation of youth. The Catholic school educator's relationship with youth provides a unique context in which teachers can give personal witness to the good news and model it in a powerful way. Through participation in the Catholic school community, students learn to accept their responsibility to effect renewal of both Church and society in the next generation. *See also*: Catholic identity; Catholic philosophy of education.

Further Reading: Maria J. Ciriello, ed., *Formation and Development of Catholic School Leaders: The Principal as Spiritual Leader* (Washington, DC: United States Catholic Conference, 1996); Congregation for Catholic Education, *The Religious Dimension of Education in a Catholic School* (Washington, DC: United States Catholic Conference, 1988); National Conference of Catholic Bishops, *To Teach as Jesus Did: A Pastoral Message on Catholic Education* (Washington, DC: United States Catholic Conference, 1972); Pope Paul VI, *Evangelii nuntiandi: On Evangelization in the Modern World* (Washington, DC: United States Catholic Conference, 1975).

Louise P. Moore

Everson v. Board of Education of Ewing Township

Everson v. Board of Education of Ewing Township (1947) was the first case wherein the U.S. Supreme Court addressed a dispute on the merits of the Establishment Clause to the First Amendment of the U.S. Constitution and education. In addition, although not actually using the term, *Everson* marks the genesis of the child benefit test that has served as the benchmark in cases under which public funds can be used to provide a variety of forms of assistance to children who attend religiously affiliated nonpublic schools.

At issue in *Everson* was a state statute from New Jersey that authorized local boards to reimburse parents for the cost of transporting their children to and from any schools other than those that operated in whole, or in part, for profit. A district taxpayer challenged the local board's right to reimburse the parents for sending their children to and from Catholic schools on the basis that its resolution violated the federal and state constitutions. More specifically, the plaintiff alleged that the statute and resolution violated both the Due Process Clause of the Fourteenth Amendment as a taxation of private property bestowed on another for a private purpose and the Establishment Clause by supporting church schools. After a state trial court ruled in favor of the taxpayer, the New Jersey Court of Errors and Appeals reversed its holding in that neither the statute nor the resolution that was passed pursuant to it violated either constitution.

On further review, a closely divided Supreme Court, in a five-to-four decision, affirmed the constitutionality of the statute and the resolution. Just as it had in *Cochran*, the Court rejected the claim that the state violated the Fourteenth Amendment by engaging in a taking for a private purpose, noting that it had to use the power to strike such alleged actions down judiciously. The Court rebuffed this argument by noting that the state decided that the statute served a public purpose by paying the bus fares of all children, including those who attend religious schools. In fact, the Court termed it a coincidence that parental desires to send their children to religious schools was consistent with the state's legitimate public interest in education. As such, the Court maintained that this allegation was insufficient basis on which to say that the state misappropriated public need. The Court added that since it had upheld subsidies and loans to private farmers and homeowners, there was no basis on which to argue that facilitating parents' wishes to send their children to religiously affiliated nonpublic schools failed to further a public purpose.

Turning to the Establishment Clause, the Court briefly traced the history of the Religion Clauses of the First Amendment before beginning its analysis with the declaration, "The 'establishment of religion' clause of the First Amendment means at least this: Neither a state nor the Federal Government can set up a church . . . [or] pass laws which aid one religion, aid all religions, or prefer one religion over another" (p. 15). The Court reasoned that although the statute might have approached the limit of its power under the First Amendment, it did not cross the line because the aid did not go to the schools. Rather, the Court acknowledged that transportation was paid for by all taxpaying parents regardless of where their children attended school. Based on this observation, the Court was unwilling to rule that the First Amendment prohibited the state from paying the fares of children who attend religious schools as part of a general program under which it pays the fares of students who go to school elsewhere. If anything, the Court suggested that should a state be prohibited from conferring other public benefits such as protection afforded by police and firefighters, not to mention connections for sewage disposal, highways, and sidewalks on religious schools, then they might find it much more difficult to operate, a purpose "obviously" not contemplated by the First Amendment. The Court concluded that since parents have the right to satisfy the state's compulsory attendance law by sending their children to religious schools and because the aid in question primarily benefited the students, rather than their schools, the statute was constitutional.

A lengthy dissent was more than three times the majority opinion. In also tracing the history of the Establishment Clause, the dissent conceded that while the statute promoted the general cause of education, it went too far in aiding religious schools. *See also*: Bus transportation; Establishment Clause; Federal aid to Catholic schools; Parental rights.

Further Reading: *Everson v. Board of Education of Ewing Township*, 330 U.S. 1 (1947).

Charles J. Russo

Ex corde ecclesiae

On August 15, 1990, John Paul II promulgated his Apostolic Constitution, *Ex corde ecclesiae*, literally, "from the heart of the Church." The document presents a vision of the nature and mission of Catholic colleges and universities and provides norms for the realization of that vision. An important sequence of events led up to the document.

The Second Vatican Council (1962–1965) invited the entire Church to renewal, and the leaders of U.S. Catholic colleges and universities worked to rethink their nature and mission. The North American meeting of the International Federation of Catholic Universities (IFCU) in 1967 at Land O'Lakes, Wisconsin, issued a declaration that stated that "the Catholic university must have a true autonomy and academic freedom in the face of authority of whatever kind, lay or clerical, external to the academic community" and must be a community "in which Catholicism is perceptibly present and effectively operative."

That 1967 statement marked one of the most important and subsequently most controversial moments in the history of Catholic higher education in the United States, where one-fourth of all Catholic colleges and universities in the world are located. By early 1970, nearly all these institutions had established predominantly lay boards of trustees to which they gave fiduciary responsibility, which created new challenges and opportunities for those concerned with their Catholic identity and mission.

A 1972 congress held in Rome for Catholic universities stated that all Catholic universities shared four characteristics (repeated in paragraph 13 of *Ex corde ecclesiae*): a Christian inspiration of the academic community; continual reflection on expanding knowledge from the perspective of faith; fidelity to the Christian message as it comes through the Church; and a commitment to the service of the Church, to all of humanity, and to the transcendent meaning of life.

Since the early 1970s, the central issue for U.S. Catholic colleges and universities has been how, on the one hand, to understand the necessary institutional autonomy and academic freedom claimed by nonpontifically chartered colleges and universities, and, on the other, how to conceive the appropriate relationship between such institutions and the American bishops and the wider Church. The 1983 revised code of canon law contained for the first time specific legislation for Catholic colleges and universities and affirmed the right of the Church to establish and govern universities, but it was not yet clear to most Catholic educators whether these canons applied to them or only to pontifically chartered institutions.

An international congress on Catholic education soon began to work on a draft document that would answer this question, which was circulated worldwide in 1985.

When the official text of *Ex corde ecclesiae* was promulgated in 1990, the response by the leaders of U.S. Catholic higher education was generally positive to Part I (which described the identity and mission of Catholic universities), but not nearly as positive, and sometimes strongly negative, to Part II (which contained the general norms).

The first part of the document calls for Catholic institutions to show how various types of knowledge relate to one another and to develop a coherent undergraduate curriculum in which philosophy and theology provide integration. It calls for faculty members to learn about each other's work, to search for the ethical and moral implications of both the methods and discoveries of their research, and to promote social justice. In other words, faculty at Catholic institutions are expected to commit themselves to more than their own careers and specific disciplines; they are to commit themselves, in collaboration with others, to the search for ethical and religious wisdom—a truly radical mission for a university.

The document lists four tasks as integral to the mission of a Catholic university. First, a Catholic university is to serve both the Church and the larger society by doing research on "serious contemporary problems," such as "the dignity of human life, the promotion of justice for all, the quality of personal and family life, the protection of nature, the search for peace and political stability." Second, the Catholic university is to offer the opportunity to integrate intellectual and spiritual life. Third, it should be a "primary and privileged place for a fruitful dialogue between the Gospel and culture" (paragraph 43). Fourth, it should evangelize and through its influence transform humanity (paragraph 48).

Since 1990, American bishops and educational leaders have struggled to agree on the most helpful application of the constitution to the American context. The bishops approved in 1996 a mainly pastoral application, as distinct from a legal one, which stressed an open and trusting relationship between the local bishop and the university administration. The Vatican sent the application back to the American bishops requesting that specific legal dimensions, mentioned in the revised code of canon law, be included. In November 1999, the bishops voted to approve another version of the application, which included a number of legal requirements: that Catholic theologians teaching Catholic theology receive a *mandatum* from their local bishop; that the presidents be practicing Catholics and make a profession of faith; that the corporate bylaws explicitly state the institution's Catholic identity and be approved by the local bishop; and that 50 percent of the faculty and the board of trustees be Catholic.

Both *Ex corde* and the bishops' application of it affirm institutional autonomy and academic freedom, but how these characteristics are to be understood remains to be seen. Perhaps most important for the mission and identity of Catholic colleges and universities are Catholic intellectuals. The challenge facing those institutions that desire to deepen their religious identities is broader than the teaching of orthodox theology, as important as that remains. The challenge is no less than to create an academic culture shaped by a Catholic vision of reality. *Ex corde* has provided a daunting and distinctive vision for Catholic universities; its careful and thoughtful implementation will lead to a deeper realization of that vision. *See also*: Bishops; Catholic identity; Catholic philosophy of education; Congregation for Catholic Education, The; Hierarchy; John Paul II, Pope.

Further Reading: The Apostolic Constitution of Pope John Paul II, *Ex Corde Ecclesiae*, 1990; Alice Gallin, *American Catholic Higher Education: Essential Documents, 1967–1990* (Notre Dame, IN: University of Notre Dame Press, 1992); Philip Gleason, *Contending with*

Modernity (New York: Oxford University Press, 1995); John P. Langan, ed., *Catholic Universities in Church and Society* (Washington, DC: Georgetown University Press, 1993).

James L. Heft, SM

Extracurricular activities

School-sponsored activities, such as music, drama, sports, clubs and other programs, are offered to students beyond the scope of the academic curriculum. According to Parkay and Stanford (1995): "When such activities are perceived as additions to the academic curriculum, they are termed *extracurricular*. When these activities are seen as having important educational goals—and not merely as extras added to the academic curriculum—they are termed *cocurricular*" (p. 399). Often, however, these terms are used interchangeably.

Bryk, Lee, and Holland (1993) noted that the extracurriculum provides valuable opportunities to put into practice the school's beliefs. Their research revealed that teachers at the secondary level perceived extracurricular activities as "occasions for moral teaching and for building personal relationships that enhanced classroom work" (p. 136). Moreover, extracurricular/cocurricular programs can and should be a means to infuse Gospel values in students. Teacher moderators and coaches are role models for Gospel values and promoters of student success. Students who are not experiencing success in the classroom can often experience validation through athletics or other school activities.

In a discussion of athletics, McGrath (2000) wrote, "All student-athletes are called to be prophets, to cover new ground consistent with the Gospel, to do new and better things, to create traditions, and to treat people as Jesus would treat them" (p. 15). He referred to athletics as a "character developer" and asserted, "Athletics builds character when coaches and their staffs help to train young people to become great athletes on the field as well as great people off the field" (p. 19). This concept of character building would equally apply to other extracurricular/cocurricular programs in Catholic schools.

McGrath (2000) emphasized the highly influential role of the coach in the lives of student athletes. In delineating the role of the coach, he wrote,

> The opportunity for coaches to inspire young people and channel their lives and energies into a positive direction is overwhelming and unprecedented. No person, including parents, teachers, and clergy, share the position of well-respected coaches who do their job well and are consistent models of responsible adult behavior. The influence of coaches is incalculable and can be an opportunity that is life giving. Players can win for coaches and despise them; they can lose with them and love them. It all depends on the personality and character of the coach. (p. 17)

Thus, the leadership of coaches and other teachers who moderate extracurricular/cocurricular programs is critical to the creation of a community of student learners and a primary determinant of whether or not students develop morally in the process.

Service projects and programs are widespread in Catholic schools. In past generations, students joined after-school organizations through which they helped the aged in rest homes, taught catechism, collected clothes for the poor, and became involved in other good works. Catholic schools today are forcefully urging service as an apostolic goal, a *cocurricular* that is integral to the academic curriculum and, in many instances, a requirement for graduation. In the 1972 pastoral *To Teach as Jesus Did*, the American bishops established the threefold purpose of Catholic education to be that of message, community, and service. In reference to service, they wrote: "Christian service ... helps students acquire skills, virtues, and habits of heart and mind required for effective service to others" (#106). The bishops also stated that students should be inspired to take the initiative in seeking out the needs of individuals and communities. According to Groome (1998), "In American high schools, colleges, and parishes, nothing has done more to educate for justice and to heighten learners' critical consciousness than such programs" (p. 390). He offered two suggestions for their effectiveness: (1) that they provide students with real-life situations, such as feeding the hungry, in contrast to working on a fund-raiser for a charity; and (2) that students be given the opportunity to reflect on their service experience and share their reflections with others.

Bryk, Lee, and Holland (1993) researched a broad range of Catholic high schools and discovered that many teachers either coach a sports team or are involved in other extracurricular activities. In fact, half of the educators in the schools in their study were committed to at least one after-school activity. Half of the teachers also assumed school-related responsibilities such as bingo, fund-raising, and parents' meetings. More than 80 percent of the teachers in the sample reported that they frequently worked with individual students either before or after school hours and also attended extracurricular activities, such as athletics, drama, or music presentations. The researchers acknowledged that principals explicitly seek teachers who are willing to take on this extended role. *See also*: Academics; Curriculum, definitions of.

Further Reading: Anthony S. Bryk, Valerie E. Lee, and Peter B. Holland, *Catholic Schools and the Common Good* (Cambridge, MA: Harvard University Press, 1993); Thomas H. Groome, *Educating for Life*: *A Spiritual Vision for Every Teacher and Parent* (Allen, TX: Thomas More, 1998); Richard McGrath, OSA, *Athletics and the Gospel Mission of the Catholic School* (Washington, DC: National Catholic Educational Association, 2000); National Conference of Catholic Bishops, *To Teach as Jesus Did: A Pastoral Message on Catholic Education* (Washington, DC: United States Catholic Conference, 1972); Forrest W. Parkay and Beverly H. Stanford, *Becoming a Teacher* (Boston: Allyn and Bacon, 1985).

Gini Shimabukuro

F

Faith community

The concept of a faith community is foundational to Catholic schooling. The American document *To Teach as Jesus Did: A Pastoral Message on Catholic Education* (National Conference of Catholic Bishops [NCCB], 1972) offers definition and elaboration of this concept:

> As God's plan unfolds in the life of an individual Christian, he grows in awareness that, as a child of God, he does not live in isolation from others. From the moment of Baptism he becomes a member of a new and larger family, the Christian community. Reborn in Baptism, he is joined to others in common faith, hope, and love. This community is based not on force or accident of geographic location or even on deeper ties of ethnic origin, but on the life of the Spirit which unites its members in a unique fellowship so intimate that Paul likens it to a body of which each individual is a part and Jesus Himself is the Head. In this community one person's problem is everyone's problem and one person's victory is everyone's victory. Never before and never since the coming of Jesus Christ has anyone proposed such a community. (#22)

This document initiated the notion of individual formation within the context of community, that is, the formation of "persons-in-community" (#13), meaning that it is through a faith-based community that students develop their faith. Whitehead and Whitehead (1992) elaborated that Christianity is a community experience, that Jesus' followers have always held to the belief that faith is a communal endeavor, not a private activity.

The church document *The Religious Dimension of Education in a Catholic School* referred to the Catholic school as a "school-home" (Congregation for Catholic Education [CCE], 1988, #27), an extension of students' homes, which promotes a climate that is "humanly and spiritually rich" (#28), which "reproduces, as far as possible, the warm and intimate atmosphere of family life," and which fosters a "common spirit of trust and spontaneity" (#40).

A role of the Catholic educator is to build caring relationships with students, which is foundational to a faith community. The Roman authors of the 1988 document suggested that simple conversations with students is an excellent method for establishing rapport with them. After "a warm and trusting atmosphere has been established, various questions will come up naturally. . . . These questions are serious ones for young people, and they make a calm study of the Christian faith very difficult" (#72). Henri Nouwen (1971) suggested that, perhaps, educators have "paid too much attention to the content of teaching without realizing that the teaching relationship is the most important factor in the ministry of teaching" (p. 5).

Intrinsic to a faith community in the context of Catholic education are the awareness and fostering of individual dignity, in which "the pupil experiences his dignity as a person before he knows its definition" (CCE, 1977, #55). The Christian vision of human dignity embraces the idea that the student "has a dignity and a greatness exceeding that of all other creatures: a work of God that has been elevated to the supernatural order of a child of God, and therefore having both a divine origin and an eternal destiny which transcend this physical universe" (CCE, 1988, #56). A related dimension of a faith community is the appreciation for individual differences. With regard to the non-Catholic student, this implies a demonstration of respect with an openness to dialogue in a context of Christian love.

According to Cowan (in Whitehead and Whitehead, 1992), a faith community is grounded in the experience of mutuality, in which persons participate in direct and nonmanipulative dialogue, with understanding and respect for the other's frame of reference. There are several levels of mutuality, with individual levels of interpersonal skills determining the achievable level of mutuality.

The most fundamental level of mutuality is characterized by two behaviors: self-disclosure and empathy. According to Cowan, self-disclosure signifies "the ability to share directly with another my feelings, thoughts and values" (Whitehead and Whitehead, p. 132). Empathy, on the other hand, denotes "the ability to hear accurately the thoughts, feelings, and values from another's frame of reference" (p. 132). First-level mutuality is evident when the participants share their perspectives with the confidence that they will be heard. Cowan stated that this first level of mutuality is the foundation for succeeding levels of mutuality and that the absence of self-disclosure and empathy in faith communities makes it difficult for them to move into deeper experiences of community.

If a faith community is to function developmentally, according to Cowan, the members' communication must expand beyond first-level mutuality to embrace the possibility of "responsible challenge" (Whitehead and Whitehead, 1992, p. 133), the main component of the intermediate level of mutuality. Responsible challenge involves the ability to invite another individual to constructively examine issues, problems, or crises from a different frame of reference. Self-examination is the reciprocal behavior of the intermediate level of mutuality. Self-examination "depends on my willingness to receive the challenge as an invitation—an opportunity to look at myself or my position on an issue in a new light and to examine the possible validity of this alternative perspective" (p. 134). Faith communities that are not open to responsible challenge, according to Cowan, are predictably limited and superficial, for development cannot occur without challenge.

The third level of mutuality focuses on the exploration of the relationship itself. It involves the ability of individuals to communicate directly with one another about "immediacy issues," that is, ways their behavior adversely affects the relationship or interferes with collaboration. Cowan elaborates this third level of mutuality: "Immediacy issues are potentially powerful sources of developmental change because of their highly personal nature. These issues raise core concerns of how I am experienced in a relationship, not merely my roles, tasks, or skills—but my *self*" (Whitehead and Whitehead, 1992, pp. 135–136).

Thus, mutuality in relationships is necessary to the maturing of individuals and faith communities. Clearly, the depth and intensity of mutuality will differ as appropriate to the specific group. However, Cowan emphatically stated that a faith community cannot be fully effective if the persons involved cannot deal with one another appropriately at each of these three levels. *See also*: *Religious Dimension of Education in a Catholic School, The*; *Catholic School, The; To Teach as Jesus Did.*

Further Reading: Congregation for Catholic Education, *The Catholic School* (Washington, DC: United States Catholic Conference, 1977); Congregation for Catholic Education, *The Religious Dimension of Education in a Catholic School* (Boston: Daughters of St. Paul, 1988); National Conference of Catholic Bishops, *To Teach as Jesus Did: A Pastoral Message on Catholic Education* (Washington, DC: United States Catholic Conference, 1972); Henri Nouwen, *Creative Ministry* (New York: Doubleday, 1971); Evelyn Eaton Whitehead and James D. Whitehead, *Community of Faith, Crafting Christian Communities Today* (Mystic, CT: Twenty Third, 1992).

Gini Shimabukuro

Faith leader (role of principal)

In Catholic schools, "faith leader" generally refers to persons who have responsibilities to foster the integration of Catholic faith in the school's curriculum and all of its other activities. The person usually looked upon to provide leadership is the principal, though many others in the school community exercise initiative.

It has not been particularly difficult for Catholic schools to be characterized by activities and practices that identify them as Catholic. Masses, prayers, clubs, and good works by students are but some of the visible signs of the Catholic faith in schools. What has been challenging is the need for academic subjects in Catholic schools to be distinctive in that they are presented in a manner that reflects the Catholic faith in an intellectually sophisticated and credible manner. The issue becomes, for example, whether history, biology, and so on, which are taught in a Catholic school, are different from those same subjects taught in a public or non-Catholic school. If they are not different, then intellectual faith leadership is lacking.

Parents of students in Catholic schools, while they may not be fully aware of the quality of intellectual faith leadership, are intensely interested in the Catholic school's effectiveness in influencing the behavior of students. Parents expect Catholic schools to have an impact on student discipline, moral behavior, prayer life, church attendance, and so on.

In the past, when Catholic schools were fortunate to have a large number of priests, nuns, and brothers as principals and teachers, it was assumed, rightly or wrongly, that the matter of faith leadership was in good hands. However, various studies indicate a sharp decline in the number of principals and teachers who are members of religious orders. Currently, studies estimate 85 to 90 percent of teachers in Catholic schools are lay. More than 50 percent of Catholic high school principals are lay. The concern appears to be whether faith leadership in Catholic schools will receive proper attention given the rapid and seemingly irreversible shift to lay presence.

This concern has been addressed by massive studies conducted in the United States in general and in Ohio and in Kansas. These studies, which focused on lay leadership and lay leaders in Catholic schools, concluded that lay leaders have strong positive perceptions of themselves as faith leaders. Other major conclusions of these studies are as follows: (1) lay leaders report their academic training as inadequate in the area of faith leadership; (2) more than half have taken no courses beyond their bachelor's degrees related to the faith leadership role; (3) lay leaders indicate high mission motivation, spiritual satisfaction, and spiritual efficacy; (4) lay leaders who engage in spiritual formation activities have higher mission motivation, spiritual satisfaction, and spiritual efficacy than those engaging in lesser spiritual formation activities; (5) those who have received some formal training (graduate or undergraduate course work) in Catholic school philosophy, theology, or history have higher mission motivation, spiritual satisfaction, and spiritual efficacy than those receiving no formal training; (6) religious and former religious have had more formal training in the purposes of the Catholic school than do lay leaders; (7) lay leaders place a high value on religion in their lives; and (8) a high percentage of lay leaders indicated that assuming leadership in a Catholic school was God's choice for their life. Studies also indicate lay leaders are committed to the ministerial aspects of Catholic schools. They frequently attend Eucharistic services and retreats other than those sponsored by their dioceses. Despite these commitments, some lay leaders are not as confident in organizing prayer as they are in other areas, yet a very high percentage feel leading in the spiritual formation of faculty to be a very important function.

Broadly, faith leadership is the attempt to foster Catholic identity by institutionalizing Catholic traditions and doctrinal emphases. Certain competencies peculiar to faith leadership that are unique to the Catholic school have been identified by the National Catholic Educational Association. According to the association, a Catholic school principal should: (1) be familiar with, and create, an environment where the process of faith and moral development as it relates to working with youth and adults can be applied; (2) be familiar with, and create, an environment where the contents and methods of religious education can be applied; (3) know and apply church documents and other religious resources that relate to schools; (4) be capable of providing opportunities that foster spiritual growth of faculty, students, and other members of the school community; (5) be capable of leading the school community in prayer; (6) be capable of integrating Gospel values and Christian principles into the curriculum and the life of the school; (7) be capable of articulating the Catholic educational vision and directing its accomplishments; and (8) be sensitive to the demands of justice in making financial decisions, especially as they relate to the Church's social teachings.

A portion of the sixth competency mentioned above, integrating Gospel values and Christian principles with the curriculum, has been elusive and difficult to accomplish. First and foremost, the Catholic school is an educational institution. Given this, then the issue is, How does the treatment of physics, history, and other subjects in the curriculum differ in the Catholic school as compared to other schools? In Catholic teaching, history is seen to be beyond time. Thus, each event within time is viewed in relation to salvation and disaster. This is different from a simple chronological progression through history, which is common in other schools. The debate in Catholic educational circles centers on whether the Catholic school does very much more than the simple chronological progression through history. Physical science is a search for essences. The same has been true for Catholic philosophy. Has this search been integrated into the way physics is taught in Catholic schools? These questions may be raised with regard to all subjects offered by the Catholic school curriculum. These questions currently are the most challenging for faith leadership.

Given the rapid shift from religious to lay leadership, the concern is not only whether the Catholic identity of Catholic schools will receive proper attention but whether the public would accept increased lay presence and, indeed, whether Catholic schools would survive with so few or no religious leaders and teachers. These concerns have given rise to the importance of faith leadership. Lay leaders, however, feel faith leadership is as strong now as it ever was. *See also*: Administrative models; Catholic identity; Non-Catholic administrators.

Further Reading: Nicholas Compagnone, "Lay Catholic Elementary Principals in the State of Kansas: Self Perceptions of Their Spiritual Leadership and Ministerial Roles," unpublished doctoral dissertation, University of Dayton, OH, 1999; Bruno Manno, *Those Who Would Be Catholic School Principals: Their Recruitment, Preparation, and Evaluation* (Washington, DC: National Catholic Educational Association, 1985); Joseph Massucci, "The Unique Identity of Catholic High Schools: A Comparison of the Church's Expectations and a School Community's Experiences and Beliefs," unpublished doctoral dissertation, University of Dayton, OH, 1993; Louise Moore, "Personal Characteristics and Selected Educational Attainment of Catholic Elementary School Principals in Relation to Spiritual Formation Activities," unpublished doctoral dissertation, University of Dayton, OH, 1999.

Ellis A. Joseph

Family development theory

Family development theory provides a broad framework for explaining the patterned and systematic variations experienced by families as they progress through the family life course. Family development theory is unique in its focus on families as the unit of change. While individual human development is acknowledged as a component of family change, the primary emphasis is on the patterned interactions of the family as a social unit. A formalized definition has described family development as the progressive structural differentiation and related developmental transformations that a family unit experiences as it moves through the life cycle (Dilworth-Anderson and Burton, 1996).

The intellectual lineage of family development theory is traced back to the concept of a *family life cycle*, a notion that appeared in the work of sociologists, genealogists, and social demographers as early as the 1700s. The family life cycle concept essentially likens the family to a biological organism. Analogous processes such as birth, growth, maturation, maintenance, and death are part of a family cycle. More recent scholars have moved away from the term "life cycle" because of its linear, expectable, and ordered connotations. Instead, a less teleological orientation is embodied in the concept of a *family career*, defined as a sequential linking of stages over the life history of a family system (Rodgers and White, 1993). In this view, the process of development is influenced by past developmental stages, "but there is no teleological end to the process that would bring it full circle. A family career is composed of all the events and periods of time (stages) between events traversed by a family" (Klein and White, 1996, p. 30).

Three critical assumptions form the basis for family development theory. First, developmental processes occurring at numerous levels are central to understanding and describing development. Individual family members, relationships among family members, overall family structure, and family roles all change over time. For this reason, family development theorists maintain that families must be analyzed at multiple levels. Klein and White (1996) stressed that the centrality of multilevel analysis for understanding family development is "not just a simple micro-macrosocial distinction that most theorists make but a realization that family as a phenomenon resides at different levels of analysis in different forms. If we leave out a level of analysis and form of family, then the resulting picture we develop is flawed" (p. 124).

Many theorists consider the family as a *social group* as an initial point of analysis. Subgroups are then found at the *relationship* level, a father–daughter or husband–wife relationship, for example. The *individual* level consists of a single family member's experiences and development within the family. Up one level from the family as a social group are *aggregate clusters* of families, relatively homogeneous groups of families that may be structured by social class or ethnicity. Social systems and the general norms and conventions (sometimes upheld as legal expectations) represent the level of analysis of the family as a *social institution*. Importantly, family groups are affected by changes and variations at each of these levels of analysis.

A second critical assumption of family development theory is that the family is a semipermeable or semiclosed group. Inherent in the multilevel nature of the family development theory is the notion of cross-system influence and interaction: "Although the family group sets up distinctive boundaries usually demarcated spatially by household or domicile, these boundaries are permeated by the effects of the larger society" (Klein and White, 1996, p. 124). For example, a poor economic climate of the larger society may exhibit effects on family subgroups, perhaps by increasing marital stress in the husband–wife relationship.

A third key assumption is the multidimensional nature of time in family development theory. Time is a monotonic process measured by the periodicity of a recurring event. Although time has been measured in different ways at different points in history (e.g., sundial, water clocks, mechanical clocks, atomic clocks), family experiences are often used as key markers to divide up time. References such as "before my mother died" or "after your son was born" are examples of an alternative conception of time termed *social process time*. "Social, or family, process time is an important dimension of our conception of time for family scholars because social norms are tied more closely to this social process dimension of time than to calendar or wristwatch time" (Klein and White, 1996, p. 126). Thus, within family development theory, consideration of multiple levels of time ("clock time," biological time, social process time) is a necessary method to fully understand family change. As Catholic married couples have approached a divorce rate similar to that of their non-Catholic peers, and as family life has taken on new meanings in the social context, new ways of supporting Catholic family life and Catholic couples have come into existence. Many parish-based and diocesan-level programs directed to family life, marriage preparation, youth services, and family counseling are based on family development theory, at least implicitly.

Family development theory has been applied to areas of family study such as the transition to parenthood. Family researchers have used the theory to examine the stress and adaptation within families as new roles and expectations emerge with the birth of children. However, family development theory has also been critiqued on some levels. For example, researchers have questioned whether family development theory is adequate to address the "nonlinear paths of development of families whose lives are uniquely transformed by socio-structural forces such as racism, unemployment, and poverty" (Dilworth-Anderson and Burton, 1996, 327). In other words, in response to social forces, many families may forge developmental pathways or engage in life-course transitions that are not comparable to mainstream patterns. Despite criticisms such as these, family development theory is unique in its focus on family as the exclusive unit of development and its breadth provides a framework to understand family patterns of formation, maintenance, and dissolution. *See also*: Parish School of Religion; Total Catholic Education.

Further Reading: Peggye Dilworth-Anderson and Linda M. Burton, "Rethinking Family Development: Critical Conceptual Issues in the Study of Diverse Groups," *Journal of Social and Personal Relationships* 13 (1996): 325–334; David M. Klein and James M. White, *Family Theories: An Introduction* (Thousand Oaks, CA: Sage, 1996); Roy H. Rodgers and James M. White, "Family Development Theory," in Pauline G. Boss, William J. Doherty, Ralph LaRossa, Walter R. Schumm, and Susan K. Steinmetz, eds., *Sourcebook of Family Theories and Methods: A Contextual Approach* (New York: Plenum Press, 1993).

James M. Frabutt

Faribault Plan

Immigration continued in large degree and numbers in the United States in the latter part of the nineteenth century and into the twentieth century. As a result of this phenomenon, questions and controversy arose over the Americanization of these new immigrants and the manner in which the religious education would occur in Catholic as well as state or public schools. Debate ensued between the legitimacy of state schools and the importance of Catholic schools. The School Controversy of 1890–1893 was a struggle within the Catholic Church, of which the Faribault Plan was central.

Catholic parents advocated for a "religiously neutral" public school, supporting the Edgerton Bible decision, in which the Wisconsin Supreme Court ruled that devotional Bible-reading in public schools was sectarian instruction. Although voluntary on the part of the students, it was followed by religious instruction, making the school a place of religious worship, thus violating the Wisconsin Constitution. Catholics advocated religiously neutral public schools because education, at this time, involved a moral aspect, and the state was not equipped to provide this type of education. Historically, there was disagreement over the place and priority of Catholic schools in the United States by many Catholic constituents, including laity, clergy, and prelates.

The motto "Every Catholic child in a Catholic school," although adopted by the Third Plenary Council of Baltimore, was never close to a reality. This was partly the case because conservative bishops accused Archbishop John Ireland of St. Paul, Minnesota, and liberal Catholics of abandoning this sentiment in the Faribault Plan. Some bishops in the United States expressed concern and questioned the legitimacy of Catholic schools in the United States. Ireland pointed out that half of the Catholic children in the United States were not enrolled in Catholic schools and that his compromise plan was a legitimate response to that reality and concern. "Liberal Catholic bishops argued the purpose of the parish school was to preserve the religious faith of children and at the same time prepare them for productive roles in American society. . . . Conservative bishops wholeheartedly accepted the premise that parish schools should protect the religious faith of Catholic children" (Walch, 1996). Archbishop Ireland disagreed with a number of conservative prelates, notably the bishop of Rochester, New York, Bernard McQuaid; Michael Corrigan, archbishop of New York; and Frederick Katzer, archbishop of Milwaukee. Corrigan was the lead prelate among the conservative bishops in the United States in the opposition to Ireland and his Faribault Plan.

John Ireland addressed the annual gathering of the National Education Association (NEA) in 1890, asserting that government authority could make public education compulsory and that the Church and the government should cooperate in this education. Throughout his talk he praised the role of public education in the United States. His hope was that his proposal of combining parochial and state schools would help to rectify the tension that had existed between these two school systems for fifty years. His proposal of the unification of the public and private school was the most liberal of stances and the catalyst for the major controversy at the end of the nineteenth century. Ireland gave permission to the pastors of Faribault and Stillwater, Minnesota, to enter agreements with the local public schools and institute educational programs for Catholic students—hence, the name, Faribault Plan. The plan called for each religion to have its own denominational school system, but if that was impossible, he recommended the adoption of the Poughkeepsie Plan, in which denominational schools would be rented to the public school board, no religion would be taught during school hours, the state would certify and pay the teachers, and the pastor would retain the right to use the school building at hours other than when school was in session. Led by the archbishop of Milwaukee, Frederick Katzer, the bishops of Wisconsin opposed Ireland's stance. Joined by McQuaid and Corrigan, their complaints and concerns made their way to the Vatican.

Calling the NEA speech a "grand opportunity," Ireland defended his position to Cardinal Gibbons of Baltimore, the nation's sole cardinal, claiming it as an opportunity to clarify the misconception that the Church opposed the "education of the people." In a letter to Pope Leo XIII, Gibbons described the pride Americans had in the public schools, yet some bishops thought the public schools promoted immorality. He then asked the Pope not to publicly condemn Ireland as it would lead to greater disagreement within the American Church. Gibbons supported and defended Ireland's proposal and also sought ways to find compromise in the implementation of Ireland's Faribault Plan.

In November 1891, a booklet titled *Education: To Whom Does It Belong?* was published by Thomas Bouquillon, professor of moral theology at the Catholic University of America. In it he asserted that education was the collective responsibility of the family, Church, and state and that the rights of the state, particularly with regard to education, were equivalent to the right of parents. *Education: To Whom Does It Belong?* was responded to in a pamphlet titled, *The Parent First.* Writing on behalf of the conservatives, Rene Holaind, a Jesuit priest and theology professor at St. Francis Xavier College in New York, argued that the parent is primarily responsible in providing for a child's education. These publications by Holaind and Bouquillon became the foundation argument and position for the school controversy and Faribault Plan.

Pope Leo XIII wrote an encyclical, *On the Christian Duties of Christians as Citizens,* in which he exhorted parents to seek education that fosters Christian doctrine and morality. McQuaid, Corrigan, and Katzer relied on this encyclical for the advancement and support of their own position. In time, this issue came to be referred to as the "school question" and in May 1892, the Vatican ruled that cooperation with public schools was allowed. Ireland's Faribault Plan was legitimate in light of this position by the Vatican. Later that year, Pope Leo XIII sent Archbishop Francis Satolli to the United States to meet with Catholic bishops. At the November meeting, Satolli presented fourteen points in which Catholic schools were supported and attendance at public schools was allowed according to the determination of the local bishop. Although the controversy and debate continued after that meeting, in May 1893 Pope Leo XIII sent a letter to Cardinal Gibbons in which he instructed Catholic schools to be encouraged and their preference advanced on the part of the local bishop. *See also*: Catholic School Question, The; Ireland, John; Poughkeepsie Plan.

Further Reading: Thomas Bouquillon, *Education: To Whom Does It Belong?* (Baltimore: John Murphy, 1892); Harold A. Buetow, *Of Singular Benefit: The Story of U.S. Catholic Education* (New York: Macmillan, 1970); Mary A. Grant and Thomas C. Hunt, *Catholic School Education in the United States: Development and Current Concerns* (New York and London: Garland, 1992); Rene I. Holaind, *The Parent First* (New York: Benziger Brothers, 1891); Neil G. McCluskey, ed., *Catholic Education in America: A Documentary History* (New York: Teachers College Press, 1962); Timothy Walch, *Parish School: American Catholic Parochial Education from Colonial Times to the Present* (New York: Crossroad, 1996).

Michael E. Sanderl, FSC

Federal aid to Catholic schools

Following World War II, the federal government began to link education policy with other national interests and carved out a role for the federal government through programs of direct aid to the states. As early as the 1940s, attempts were made to enact federal legislation to provide general assistance to elementary and secondary schools. These attempts failed because of the lack of agreement on several ideological grounds pertaining to state and local autonomy, civil rights, and the inclusion of private and religious schools in programs.

While general aid to schools was being debated, several limited programs of targeted assistance were enacted that included the participation of private and religious schools. The Servicemen's Readjustment Act (GI Bill of Rights) contained provisions for education benefits such as financial support for college tuition, books, and living expenses that could be used at private as well as public colleges. The National School Lunch Program (1946) provided federal food and subsidy to schools to offer meals that were free or at a reduced rate for students from low-income families. The National Defense Education Act (1958), following the launch of the Russian space satellite Sputnik, created a series of categorical federal aid programs to foster scientific and mathematical research at the university level as well as programs to improve the teaching of mathematics, science, and foreign language in elementary and secondary schools.

Traditionally, the American Catholic bishops had vigorously opposed the concept of federalization or nationalization of education but by the 1950s realized that it was inevitable and decided to cooperate and become involved in the formulation of such legislation. The bishops acknowledged the federal role and agreed to offer their support under two conditions: aid was to be equitably distributed to both the public and private educational sectors, and state and local governments were to demonstrate a financial need for the resources to fulfill their obligations to educate their citizens. Today, their basic premise is that when services are available to students and teachers in public schools, equitable services should be made available to their counterparts in religious schools.

The Elementary and Secondary Education Act (ESEA) of 1965 was the first step in the passage of federal general aid legislation directed to elementary and secondary school education. It was a significant component of President Johnson's national priority of declaring a "War on Poverty" and was authorized to provide programs to benefit educationally needy elementary and secondary students living in areas with high concentrations of children from low-income families. This was a shift from the notion of general aid to that of targeted, categorical assistance that has prevailed.

The struggle to overcome the concerns about religion and First Amendment issues that would allow for the inclusion of nonpublic school children in the legislation was resolved through a compromise that established two principles for providing services to students in public, private, and religious schools. These principles were (1) "child benefit" that provides categorical assistance or services primarily for needy students and only incidentally for the school they attended; and (2) the aid would be distributed through public trustees or public authorities who would receive and manage the ESEA funds and act as accountable trustees on behalf of all the eligible children in their community, regardless of the type of school they attended.

ESEA programs provide services only to students and teachers in nonpublic schools. No money is channeled to the schools; thus, Catholic school students and personnel are legally permitted to participate in ESEA programs without compromising First Amendment issues regarding separation of Church and state. Private school officials work through the local public school district to arrange for the delivery of programs and services for the students and faculty.

Federal government programs are usually one of two types: discretionary or formula grants. Discretionary grants are awarded through a competitive process according to established criteria. Grant recipients are required to abide by various laws, regulations, and executive orders that apply to recipients of federal funds. If the listing of eligible applicants does not specify only public schools, private schools may be eligible to apply. Private schools may also be members of a consortium as nonprofit institutions, but religious schools, unlike hospitals and child-care agencies, cannot receive direct grants of public funds. Formula grants are awarded to the state or local education agency based on a predetermined formula, such as the number of children enrolled by grade or the number of children from low-income families. The formula requirements and procedures vary by program, but many provide for the inclusion of private and religious school students and teachers.

Most of the federal programs are targeted to provide assistance to children in need, determined by a poverty count formula. The criterion for determining the level of poverty of a family for federal programs is based on the student eligibility for free and reduced lunch under the guidelines established by the U.S. Department of Agriculture. Schools do not have to offer the lunch program; schools must certify that a student would be eligible if the program were available.

Under the various titles of ESEA legislation, students and faculty members in private schools have received benefits in the form of remedial services to needy students, professional development programs for teachers, technology training and equipment, violence and drug prevention programs and counseling, and instructional and library and media materials.

Private school participation in ESEA has continued through several reauthorizations and Republican and Democratic administrations and U.S. Departments of Education programs. Some problems with implementation have occurred at the local level due to miscommunication or hostility on the part of some of the local school districts that are reluctant to share resources in the spirit of the law and under their obligation to private school students as their public trustees.

While continuing the fundamental philosophy directing federal education aid to benefit children through public trusteeship, subtle shifts in program focus occurred in the 1990s. During the Clinton years, emphasis shifted to improving schools, focusing on programs across the entire school as means of aiding the educationally disadvantaged. This construct excluded private schools that continued with "pull-out" programs that removed students from regular classes to receive remedial aid in neutral settings. The 2002 reauthorization of ESEA, the No Child Left Behind Act, targets federal aid to improve student performance and close the gap between disadvantaged students and their peers. ESEA ties funding to accountability and results, requiring all states that accept funds to set high standards in math and reading and measure progress by annually testing all students in grades 3 through 8. Since private schools do not receive federal funds, and services do not benefit all students, they are exempt from the testing provisions.

Three legal challenges to the participation of private school students in parts of ESEA have reached the U.S. Supreme Court. An attempt to exclude students in religious schools from participation in Title I services was partially remedied in *Aguilar v. Felton* (1985), when the Court ruled that services were permissible as long as they were delivered at a neutral site so as not to give the impression that religion was being endorsed by the presence of public school teachers on religious property. For more than a decade, millions of dollars of program moneys were spent on the acquisition and maintenance of trailers and rental of neutral sites apart from the religious school campus in which children were provided with remedial instruction. This was overturned in *Agostini v. Felton* (1997), when the Court changed its views on the Establishment Clause and allowed services to be delivered back in the religious schools in rooms that would meet the neutrality standard if they were devoid of religious symbols. In *Mitchell v. Helms* (2000) the Court ruled that the use of Title VI funds that supply instructional materials, including computers and software, to both public and private schools did not violate the Establishment Clause. In doing so, it rejected arguments that computers might be diverted for religious purposes to further the religious mission of the schools.

The Individuals with Disabilities Education Act (IDEA) is also available to some private school students. The law requires the local school district to locate, identify, and evaluate those students attending private schools suspected of having disabilities and needing special education and related services. A portion of the federal funds generated by private school students under IDEA must be used to serve private school students. The law does not require the expenditure of state funds in addition to the federal. Consequently, only a small percentage of the private school students eligible for IDEA services receive them due to budget shortfalls. The IDEA mandate that every child is entitled to a free and appropriate public education is not extended to those outside of public schools.

Additional federal assistance is available to Catholic schools through programs administered by the Departments of Agriculture, Health and Human Services, Justice, Labor, and Federal Emergency Management Agency. *See also*: Choice, parent and school; Establishment Clause; Free Exercise Clause; Parental rights; Tuition tax credits; Vouchers.

Further Reading: William Davis, ed., *Making Federal Dollars Work* (Washington, DC:

The Skaggs Catholic Center, half of it pictured Wednesday, April 28, 1999, in Draper, Utah, one of the biggest, most expensive Catholic school complexes ever built in the United States. © AP/Wide World Photos.

United States Catholic Conference, 1999); Dale McDonald, "Education Policy Shifts in the New Law," *Momentum* 33, 2 (April 2002): 73–74; Stephen D. Sugarman and Frank R. Kemerer, eds., *School Choice and Social Controversy* (Washington, DC: Brookings Institution Press, 1999).

Dale McDonald, PBVM

Financing of Catholic schools

Financing of Catholic schools refers to the matter of the source of the money necessary to operate schools established primarily for attendance and participation of students at Catholic schools. In terms of education finance, this concept is commonly referred to as revenue sources. The most common revenue sources for Catholic schools are tuition, parish support, endowments, charitable donations, fund-raising, and public funds for specific services. The relative importance of each revenue source in the overall picture of financing Catholic schools has changed over time.

Parishes operated most Catholic elementary schools during their early history, with the pastor responsible for their fiscal affairs. During these times, services contributed by members of religious orders were the primary source of revenue for Catholic schools. As the number of religious staff decreased and schools were forced to hire more and more lay personnel, the cost of operating schools increased dramatically relative to parish revenue, and thus the ability of parishes to support their schools radically declined. Student tuition dollars became the primary source of revenue. The substantial decline in revenue coming from the parish began in the late 1960s, during the period when many schools were forced to close due to increasing costs, declining parish subsidies as a percent of costs, and increasing tuition, all resulting in declining enrollments. According to data from the National Catholic Educational Association (NCEA), parish subsidies accounted for 63.1 percent of per pupil revenue in Catholic elementary schools in 1969–1970, 60 percent in 1970–1971, 52.9 percent in 1973–1974, more gradually decreasing to 39.6 percent by 1986–1987 (Bredeweg, 1978, 1979, 1984, 1988), and 35 percent in 1992–1993 (Kealey, 1994, p. 15). By 1996, only 33 percent of Catholic elementary school revenue was from parishes (Harris, 1996, p. 66). An NCEA study indicates that the average percent of school revenues from parish subsidy in 1997 was down to 26.2 percent (Kealey, 1998, p. 17).

Although the percent of Catholic elementary school income from parishes has declined over time, about 90 percent of the schools still received some parish financial assistance in 1988–1989. Suburban and rural schools were more likely to receive subsidies than urban schools (Kealey, 1990, p. 10). By 1992–1993, 89.6 percent received parish subsidies (Kealey, 1994, p. 12). During the 2000–2001 academic year, nearly 88 percent of Catholic elementary schools received some parish subsidy (Kealey, 2001, p. 14).

In the 1985–1986 school year, tuition became the main source of Catholic elementary school revenue, surpassing parish subsidies (Bredeweg, 1988, p. 7). (See section on Tuition for more information.) By 2000–2001, only 24.1 percent of total school revenue came from parish subsidies, while nearly 60 percent was from tuition and fees (Kealey, 2001, p. 18).

The proportion of revenue from fund-raisers has increased over time. In 1970–1971, 8.9 percent of school revenue was from fund-raisers and "other" activities (Bredeweg, 1978, p. 8). By 1980–1981, they accounted for 10.3 percent of revenues (Bredeweg, 1982, p. 28), and by 2000–2001, money from fund-raisers and "other" activities contributed an estimated 15.3 percent of total revenue (Kealey, 2001, p. 18). Fund-raising includes activities such as bingo, raffles, festivals, parent activities, candy and magazine sales, and other events designed to generate revenue immediately. All schools in the 2001 NCEA study (Kealey, 2001, p. 16) participated in fund-raising activities.

Endowment funds within development programs are a revenue source with much potential for Catholic elementary schools. Compared to the short-term, temporary nature of fund-raisers, development programs are long-term efforts to raise substantial sums of money that will continue to generate income in the future. Development programs focus on long-term goals and ongoing activities that require strong community relations. Development efforts prior to the 1990s were often included under fund-raising as the "other" category. Nearly 23 percent of the Catholic elementary schools used in the NCEA study for the 1988–1989 school year reported having some type of endowment program (Kealey, 1990, p. 13). By 1994–1995, 40 percent of the schools in the NCEA study had endowment programs; however, an average of only 1.34 percent of total revenue received by these schools was from endowment funds (Kealey, 1996, p. 15). By the 2000–2001 NCEA study, 51 percent of the schools surveyed had endowment programs. The average percent of revenue from endowments was 1.7; the average endowment principal was $1,187,703 (Kealey, 2001, p. 17).

Catholic elementary schools also receive revenue, albeit limited, from both federal and state governments. Assistance for economically disadvantaged students (Title I of 2001 ESEA) is the most common type of federal assistance. Aid in the form of bus transportation is an example of state assistance. Other revenue from government as-sistance is for the school lunch program, textbooks, professional development, and bilingual programs.

With few exceptions, student tuition and fees have been the primary source of revenue for Catholic high schools since the early 1900s. By the mid-1970s, according to an NCEA study of 500 schools, tuition and fees made up 61.8 percent to 80.8 percent of total revenue for private Catholic high schools, 56.5 percent to 74 percent for diocesan high schools, and 42.7 percent to 62.4 percent for parochial high schools; the percent increased as the school size increased. In 1985–1986, NCEA estimated that, on average, 63 percent of Catholic revenue was from tuition and fees. By 1993–1994, 75 percent of revenue was from tuition and fees, and by 1998–1999 the pro-portion was 78 percent.

As tuition was increasing as a component of total revenue, contributed services were decreasing. From 1976–1977 to 1980–1981, contributed services went from con-stituting nearly 16 percent of high school revenues to a little over 10 percent. By 1985–1986, they were only 8 percent of the revenue and by 1998–1999, only 2 percent.

Also with the decline of contributed services by religious staff came an increase in revenue from fund-raising. In 1977–1978 fund-raising averaged 5.9 percent of all Catholic high school revenue: 7 percent for private high schools, 5.3 percent for parochial schools, and 4.8 percent for diocesan institutions. By 1993–1994, NCEA estimates show that fund-raising accounted for 9 percent of total revenue for Catholic high schools.

Along with increased financing through fund-raisers came a growth in development and endowment programs. According to Tracy, "The average Catholic high school opened a development office in 1987, although many schools launched offices well before that year" (p. 28). For the first time, in 1989–1990, NCEA surveys sought information on development programs in Catholic high schools. Of the 200 schools surveyed, 84 percent reported having development offices. Average income from de-velopment sources was $146,100, with private schools raising the most, followed by diocesan schools and then by parish schools. By 1998–1999, 90 percent of the high schools surveyed had development offices. Tracy also notes that average alumni/ae contributions to the annual fund increased nearly 49 percent from 1994 to 1999 (p. 29), while the average parent contribution increased about 45 percent during the same time period (p. 31). The dollars contributed to the fund by others is about the same for the two years, with the median donation about $7,000 (p. 34). Revenue from special events increased 73 percent between 1994 and 1999 (p. 35). Private Catholic high schools have the largest endowments, followed by interparochial schools (schools operated by, and serving, more than one parish), diocesan, and parochial. Independent private schools had a median endowment ($1,350,000) about 650 percent greater than parochial schools ($180,000) in 1999 (p. 36).

Catholic high schools are eligible to participate in several state and federal pro-grams offering financial assistance. Of the schools responding to the NCEA survey, 21 percent participated in the federal program for economically disadvantaged children in 1993–1994, up from 13 percent in 1985–1986. About 77 percent received assistance from a program for consolidation of federal programs for elementary and secondary education, 7 percent participated in Upward Bound, and 21 percent received money for vocational programs in 1993–1994. At the state level, 39 percent of the surveyed schools received bus transportation assistance, down from 47 percent in 1985–1986. Only 9 percent participated in drug education programs in 1985–1986, but this number increased to 54 percent in 1991–1992 and decreased to 50 percent in 1993–1994. More than half the sample participated in library and textbook programs. Health services, guidance and counseling, and programs for low-income and handicapped students also provided revenue for Catholic high schools in 1993–1994. *See also*: Development; Endowments; Subsidies; Tuition.

Further Reading: John J. Augenstein, *Catholic High Schools and Their Finances 1986* (Washington, DC: National Catholic Educational Association, 1986); Frank H. Bredeweg, *Basic Financial Data on Catholic Elementary Schools* (Washington, DC: National Catholic Educational Association, 1978); Frank H. Bredeweg, *Catholic High Schools and Their Finances 1979* (Washington, DC: National Catholic Educational Association, 1979); Frank H. Bredeweg, *United States Catholic Elementary and Secondary Schools & Their Finances 1981–82: A Statistical Report on Schools, Enrollment, Staffing, & Finances* (Washington, DC: National Catholic Educational Association, 1982); Frank H. Bredeweg, *United States Catholic Elementary Schools and Their Finances 1988* (Washington, DC: National Catholic Educational Association, 1988); Michael J. Guerra, *Dollars and Sense: Catholic High Schools and Their Finances 1994* (Washington, DC: National Catholic Educational Association, 1995); Michael J. Guerra and Michael Donahue, *Catholic High Schools and Their Finances 1990* (Washington, DC: National Catholic Educational Association, 1990); Joseph C. Harris, *The Cost of Catholic Parishes and Schools* (Kansas City, MO: Sheed and Ward, 1996); Robert J. Kealey, *United States Catholic Elementary Schools and Their Finances 1989* (Washington, DC: National Catholic Educational Association, 1990); Robert J. Kealey, *Balance Sheet for Catholic Elementary Schools: 1993 Income and Expenses* (Washington, DC: National Catholic Educational Association, 1994); Robert J. Kealey, *Balance Sheet for Catholic Elementary Schools: 1995 Income and Expenses* (Washington, DC: National Catholic Educational Association, 1996); Robert J. Kealey, *Balance Sheet for Catholic Elementary Schools: 1997 Income and Expenses* (Washington, DC: National Catholic Educational Association, 1998); Robert J. Kealey, *Balance Sheet for Catholic Elementary Schools: 2001 Income and Expenses* (Washington, DC: National Catholic Educational Association, 2001); Mary E. Tracy, *Mission and Money: A CHS 2000 Report on Finance, Advancement, and Governance* (Washington, DC: National Catholic Educational Association, 2001).

Barbara M. De Luca

Free Exercise Clause

According to the religion clauses of the First Amendment, "Congress shall make no law respecting an establishment of religion, or prohibiting the free exercise thereof." Even though the First Amendment prevents only Congress from making such laws, in 1940 the Court applied its terms to the states through the Fourteenth Amendment in *Cantwell v. Connecticut*.

As with the Establishment Clause, appeals to history as to the original intent of the Free Exercise Clause fail to provide clear answers, stemming largely from the fact that close ties between religion and government began during the colonial period. While there have been different approaches to the Free Exercise Clause, two distinct camps have emerged: separationists and accommodationists. On the one hand are supporters of the Jeffersonian metaphor of maintaining a "wall of separation" between Church and state, language that does not appear in the Constitution; this perspective is most often associated with the Supreme Court and has limited state-sponsored religious activities in public schools. On the other hand, accommodationists believe that the government is not prohibited from permitting some religious activity in school as long as it does not benefit one religion over another.

Unlike its cases involving governmental aid to religious schools and their students under the Establishment Clause, the Court has more consistently prohibited state-sponsored religious activities, most notably prayer, in public schools, often under Free Exercise Clause analysis. The Court has created confusion over the appropriate judicial standard to apply in disputes involving religion. That is, although it crafted a two-part test in *School District of Abington Township v. Schempp* and *Murray v. Curlett* (1963) to evaluate the constitutionality of prayer and Bible-reading in public schools, the Court expanded it in creating the tripartite Establishment Clause test in *Lemon v. Kurtzman* (1971), a case involving governmental aid to religiously affiliated nonpublic schools. When the Court subsequently applied the *Lemon* test in cases arising under both the Establishment and Free Exercise Clauses, its failure to explain how or why this one test had become a kind of "one-size fits all" standard in First Amendment disputes leaves commentators and lower courts seeking greater clarity. Amid controversy over the place of religion in the marketplace of ideas, this entry offers a largely chronological review of major Supreme Court cases on religious activity in public schools.

The First Amendment became part of the Constitution in 1791 along with the rest of the Bill of Rights. Yet, the Supreme Court did not resolve a case on the merits of a dispute involving religious activities in public schools until 1948 in *People of State of Illinois ex rel. McCollum v. Board of Education of School Dist. No. 71, Champaign County*. At issue here was a program under which a Protestant minister, a Catholic priest, and a Jewish rabbi came to public schools to provide religious instruction during the school day; children whose parents did not wish for them to participate were excused from doing so. The Court struck down the program on the basis that public schools could not be used to assist in teaching religion.

Four years later, the Court upheld a different kind of program that permitted public school students, at the request of their parents, to be released early from school so that they could attend religious classes at other locations. In *Zorach v. Clauson* (1952) the Court affirmed that this released time program was permissible as a means of accommodating parents' religious beliefs.

Engel v. Vitale (1962), the first dispute wherein the Court addressed the question of prayer in public schools, stands as the lead case in an unbroken line of cases in which it prohibited school-sponsored prayer. The Court held that since the daily classroom activity of reciting a prayer composed and promulgated by the state board of regents was a religious activity, it was inconsistent with the Establishment Clause.

A year later, in *School District of Abington Township v. Schempp* and *Murray v. Curlett* (1963), the Court struck down prayer and Bible-reading in school as violating the Establishment Clause. In creating a two-part test to evaluate the constitutionality of prayer and Bible-reading in public schools, the Court declared that "[t]he test may be stated as follows: what are the purpose and the primary effect of the [legislative] enactment? . . . [T]o withstand the strictures of the Establishment Clause there must be a secular legislative purpose and a primary effect that neither advances nor inhibits religion" (p. 222). Insofar as the Court determined that these activities failed both parts of this test, it struck them down.

In 1968 the Supreme Court considered a challenge to a state law forbidding the teaching of evolution in public schools. In *Epperson v. Arkansas* (1968), the Court vitiated the statute in finding that it failed Abington's two-part purpose and effect test. A second Supreme Court case on evolution, almost twenty years later, involved a state law that prohibited the teaching of "evolution-science" in public schools unless accompanied by instruction on "creation-science." In *Edwards v. Aguillard* (1987) the Court vitiated the law because its primary purpose was to change the curriculum in public schools in such a way that it provided a persuasive advantage to the impermissible teaching of "creation-science."

In its most significant case involving the Establishment Clause, but which has had a significant impact on its Free Exercise jurisprudence, *Lemon v. Kurtzman* (*Lemon*) (1971), the Court struck down state laws calling for the purchase of secular services and providing a salary supplement for teachers in religious schools. In ruling that both laws were unconstitutional, the Court enunciated the tripartite measure known as the *Lemon* test. According to this test:

> Every analysis in this area must begin with consideration of the cumulative criteria developed by the Court over many years. Three such tests may be gleaned from our cases. First, the statute must have a secular legislative purpose; second, its principal or primary effect must be one that neither advances nor inhibits religion; finally, the statute must not foster "an excessive government entanglement with religion." (pp. 612–613)

Not unlike under the Establishment Clause, the Court has used this test to strike down most forms of religious activity in schools, especially those that are school-sponsored.

In 1980, in *Stone v. Graham*, the Court decided that posting the Ten Commandments in classrooms, even when they were purchased with private funds, violated the first prong of the *Lemon* test. The Court added that the statute requiring the posting lacked a secular purpose since the Ten Commandments were not integrated into the curriculum.

The Court reviewed its first case on the merits of a moment of silence in a dispute over whether such a practice could be permitted at the start of a school day in *Wallace v. Jaffree* (1985). Here, in examining the legislative history of a statute authorizing silence at the start of the school day for meditation or voluntary prayer, the Court maintained that it was unconstitutional because it lacked a secular purpose insofar as the sponsor's goal was to return voluntary prayer to public schools. Two years later, in *Karcher v. May* (1987), the Court avoided the merits of a case involving a moment of silence. The Court dismissed an appeal filed by two state legislators who sought to defend the law in concluding that they were ineligible to participate in the litigation since they lacked standing by virtue of having lost their leadership positions.

Acting in response to *Widmar v. Vincent* (1981), in which the Supreme Court prevented officials at a state university from refusing to make facilities available to a religious group because of the content of the speech, Congress enacted the Equal Access Act in 1984. The act essentially extended *Widmar* to any public secondary schools that received federal financial assistance and created a limited open forum for students. In 1990 the Supreme Court upheld the act's constitutionality in *Board of Education of Westside Community Schools v. Mergens*.

In *Lamb's Chapel v. Center Moriches Union Free School District* (1993), a rare unanimous decision, the Court extended *Mergens'* rationale in maintaining that since a school board created a limited open forum, it could not prevent a religious group from using its facilities to show a film series on child raising. Eight years later, a dispute arose over a school system's refusal to permit a nonschool-sponsored club to meet during nonclass hours so that members and moderators could discuss child raising along with character and moral development from a religious perspective. Even though the school system prevented the religious club from meeting, officials allowed three other groups to meet because, although they addressed similar topics, they did so from a secular perspective. In *Good News Club v. Milford Central School* (2001), the Court relied on *Lamb's Chapel* in reasoning not only that educators violated the club's rights to free speech when they refused to permit it to use school facilities for meetings but also that such a restriction was not justified by fears of violating the Establishment Clause.

In 1992 the Supreme Court considered whether school officials could invite a religious leader to offer prayers as part of graduation ceremony. At issue was a board policy that permitted principals to invite members of the clergy to offer nonsectarian prayers while providing them with guidelines for prayers on civic occasions prepared by an interfaith organization. In *Lee v. Weisman* (1992), the Court affirmed that school-sponsored prayer at a public school graduation ceremony was unconstitutional. Sidestepping the *Lemon* test, the Court maintained that prayer was unacceptable because the state, through school officials, had a pervasive role in the process not only by selecting who would offer the prayer but also by directing its content. The Court also feared that such governmental activity could result in psychological coercion of students since it viewed them as a captive audience who may have been forced, against their own wishes, to participate in a ceremony that they were not genuinely free to be excused from attending.

In its most recent case on prayer, *Santa Fe Independent School District v. Doe* (2000), a typically closely divided Supreme Court affirmed that a policy permitting student-led prayers prior to the start of high school football games was unconstitutional. In *Santa Fe*, the Court relied on the endorsement test, which asks whether the purpose of a governmental action is to endorse or approve of a religion or religious activity, enunciated in a concurring opinion in *Lynch v. Donnelly* (1984), a nonschool case upholding a display including a creche among secular symbols, rather than *Lee*'s psychological coercion test. Put another way, the Court reviewed the status of prayer from the perspective of whether its being permitted at football games was an impermissible governmental approval or endorsement rather than as a form of psychological coercion that subjected fans to values and/or beliefs other than their own. In striking down the prayer policy, the Court disagreed with the board's claim that the policy furthered the free speech rights of students and that the policy was neutral on its face. The Court also rejected the board's defense that a legal challenge was premature since prayer had not been offered at a football game under the policy. As with *Lee*, controversy over prayer at school events remains even after *Santa Fe*.

In light of how the Court and its ever-changing membership interpret disputes involving prayer and other religious activities in schools, it will be interesting to observe how its Free Exercise Clause jurisprudence evolves in the early part of the twenty-first century. *See also*: Choice, parent and school; Establishment Clause; Parental rights; Vouchers.

Further Reading: *Board of Educ. of Westside Community Schs. v. Mergens*, 496 U.S. 226 (1990); *Edwards v. Aguillard*, 482 U.S. 578 (1987); *Engel v. Vitale*, 370 U.S. 421 (1962); *Epperson v. Arkansas*, 393 U.S. 97 (1968); Equal Access Act, 20 U.S.C.A. §§ 4071 *et seq.*

(1984); *Good News Club v. Milford Cent. Sch.*, 533 U.S. 98 (2001); *Karcher v. May*, 484 U.S. 72 (1987); *Lamb's Chapel v. Center Moriches Union Free Sch. Dist.*, 508 U.S. 384 (1993); *Lee v. Weisman*, 505 U.S. 577 (1992); *Lemon v. Kurtzman*, 403 U.S. 602 (1971); *Lynch v. Donnelly*, 465 U.S. 668, 687 ff (1984); *People of State of Illinois ex rel. McCollum v. Board of Educ. of Sch. Dist. No. 71, Champaign County*, 333 U.S. 203 (1948); *Santa Fe Indep. Sch. Dist. v. Doe*, 530 U.S. 290 (2000); *School Dist. of Abington Township v. Schempp and Murray v. Curlett*, 374 U.S. 203 (1963); *Stone v. Graham*, 449 U.S. 39 (1980); *Wallace v. Jaffree*, 472 U.S. 38 (1985); *Widmar v. Vincent*, 454 U.S. 263 (1981); *Zorach v. Clauson*, 343 U.S. 306 (1952).

Charles J. Russo

G

Gardner, Howard (1943–)

Best known for development of the Multiple Intelligence Theory, which claims there are seven intelligences: logical-mathematical, linguistic, musical, bodily-kinesthetic, spatial, interpersonal, and intrapersonal. Gardner's theory is widely accepted and applied in pedagogical strategies, religious studies, Catholic schools, worship, and sporting events. He is considered a highly influential figure in developmental and educational psychology, and his theory is important to the field of education.

Born in 1943, Gardner received his higher education from Harvard University, completing his Ph.D. in psychology in 1971. His research has focused on human intelligence and education. Dissatisfied with the traditional concept of the intelligence quotient (IQ) as a measure of intelligence based on a singular construct, he looked to other human skills used in everyday life. He studied normal, gifted, and disabled individuals and applied neurological findings in the development of his theory. His research supports his belief that humans possess not a single intelligence factor but a range of skills and levels of competence. His theory was first introduced in his seminal book *Frames of Mind* (1983).

Gardner has since worked to reform traditional education by including the arts, performance-based testing, and more individualized teaching methods. He has published eighteen books on education and his theory. He is currently the John H. and Elisabeth S. Hobbs Professor in Cognition and Education at the Harvard Graduate School of Education. He is also an adjunct professor of psychology at Harvard University and adjunct professor of neurology at Boston University School of Medicine. He has received many honors and eighteen honorary degrees.

Gardner is chairman of the Steering Committee of Harvard Project Zero, a group of cognitive researchers who are focused on the role of the arts in education. The work of this group focuses on the design of performance-based testing and incorporating multiple intelligences into curriculum, teaching, and assessment. His most current project, the Good Work Project, investigates the concept of interdisciplinary institutions. This research examines how modern society, with the influences of a fast-paced environment, technological advances, and powerful market forces, impacts the ability of individuals to produce quality work. *See also*: Multiple Intelligence Theory (MI).

Further Reading: Howard Gardner, *Frames of Mind: The Theory of Multiple Intelligences* (New York: Basic Books, 1983); Howard Gardner, *Intelligence Reframed: Multiple Intelligences for the 21st Century* (New York: Basic Books, 1999); Howard Gardner, *Multiple Intelligences: The Theory in Practice* (New York: Basic Books, 1993).

John L. Watzke

Gaudium et Spes

Gaudium et Spes are the first words in the official Latin version of the Second Vatican Council's document *Pastoral Constitution of the Church in the Modern World*. *Gaudium et spes* means "the joy and hope," referring to the document's conviction that the Church is concerned with the dreams, struggles, and successes of all people. While the formal name of this document is the *Pastoral Constitution of the Church in the Modern World*, theologians and historians have taken to referring to it simply by its Latin opening, *Gaudium et Spes*. It was a groundbreaking document and established a foundation for many changes that occurred in the Church after Vatican II. Soon after John XXIII became Pope in 1959, he convened the Second Vatican Council. Pope John wanted the council to be an opportunity for a spiritual renewal and reinvigoration of the Church that would make it more faithful to Christ's will and for an updating (*aggiornamento*) of its pastoral attitudes, habits, and institutions. *Gaudium et Spes* was supported by the future Paul VI and the future John Paul II, who took part in the discussion and drafting of the document. The positive tone of *Gaudium et Spes* reflected a change in the relationship between the Church and the modern world. Once viewed as sinful and in need of redemption, the world was now seen as grace-filled and as a place of God's ongoing redemptive work.

The document is made up of several parts. The preface stresses the intimate connection between Church and world as the Church makes its own the joys and hopes, the griefs and anxieties of all humanity. The document continues with an introduction and Part I, which outlines a Christian anthropology discussing the dignity of the person and the community of humankind. Part II discusses "Problems of Special Urgency," including marriage and the family, development of culture, economics and politics, and peace and war.

Gaudium et Spes and the changes brought about by Vatican II had a profound effect on Catholic schools. The first impact was greater involvement by the laity. As the number of vowed religious teaching in the schools declined, many more lay teachers were hired. As the Church affirmed the right of individuals to organize into collective bargaining units, teachers began to negotiate with diocesan school boards for better wages and working conditions. Along with the rise of Catholic school boards, there were questions of declining enrollment, minority relations, and changing school demographics. As Catholics moved out to the suburbs, center-city schools were closed, and new suburban schools were opened.

Gaudium et Spes also impacted the philosophy of education that permeated Catholic schools. When adopting a negative view of the world, Catholic schools were often conceptualized as a refuge from the evils of society and as a place of protection from the public schools. With the more open, positive attitude toward society espoused in *Gaudium et Spes*, Catholic schools came to see themselves as participants in the broader social fabric and as contributors to the common good. Thus, even though *Gardium et Spes* was concerned more explicitly with ecclesiology, a development in the Church's self-understanding had noticeable impact in Catholic schools. *See also*: Vatican Council II.

Further Reading: Harold A. Buetow, *The Catholic School: Its Roots, Identity, and Future* (New York: Crossroad, 1988); Mary A. Grant and Thomas C. Hunt, *Catholic School Education in the United States: Development and Current Concerns* (New York and London: Garland, 1992); Michael A. Hayes and Liam Gearon, eds., *Contemporary Catholic Theology: A Reader* (New York: Continuum, 1999).

Jack O'Gorman

General Directory for Catechesis (GDC)

An international document written to clarify the nature, purpose, duties, organizational structure, and some of the desired outcomes the Church seeks to achieve with catechesis or religious education in parishes and schools.

The GDC changed the Church's understanding of catechesis, shifting the focus from an instructional model to one centered in human experience. The document challenged religious educators to see their ministry as consisting of education in both the knowledge of the faith (understanding doctrines, history, the symbolism behind ritual) and the life of faith. The latter includes educating students to participate in the faith community through prayer, liturgy, and sacraments, getting active in the social life of the parish and diocese, making a commitment to works of charity, and promoting the human values of liberty, peace, justice, and environmental protection (#157).

The GDC defines catechesis as "the process of transmitting the Gospel, as the Christian community has received it, understands it, celebrates it, lives it and communicates it in many ways" (#105). The GDC recognizes catechesis as a series of formational activities and experiences that help a child or adult mature the "seed" of an initial conversion of belief in Jesus Christ (#82, 21). Adult catechesis is described as the primary model for all catechesis because of the adult's capability to make a full and permanent commitment to think, judge, and live like Christ (GDC, #59, 53).

This directory created a new type of church document when it was first released in 1971 under the name of the *General Catechetical Directory* (GCD). The earlier edition broke new ground by describing catechesis as a form of ministry closely connected with evangelization, liturgical preaching, and theology, rather than just instruction. In the first year it sold between 30,000 and 40,000 copies in the United States alone and had a profound effect on the way catechesis was done in both Catholic schools and parishes.

The most recent edition of the directory, issued in 1997, changed the name of the document slightly to avoid confusion with the first version. The revision added to the directory the thought of several new documents dealing with aspects of catechesis: the *Rite of Christian Initiation of Adults* (1972), Pope John Paul II's encyclical, *Catechesi Tradendae* (1979), and the *Catechism of the Catholic Church* (1992).

The GDC begins and ends with a parable. The document opens with the Parable of the Sower (#15) and the image of the sowing of the seed of faith. The concluding parable focuses on the harvest, with Jesus describing the various tensions, conflicts, struggles, and preoccupations that impede the growth of faith in the hearts of humans.

The GDC holds up the "pedagogy of God" as a source and model for the pedagogy of faith. This pedagogy is marked by a gradual revelation of God's plan of salvation, meeting people according to their background and readiness to hear, slowly shaping their minds, hearts, memories, and cultures into the plan of salvation (#147).

The directory also includes a careful discussion of the complexity involved in introducing believers to a personal relationship with Christ in a world of diverse cultures. The issues of inculturation—not just finding creative, more acceptable ways to present doctrines, rituals, and teachings but presenting them in a way that really touches the roots of a culture and the deepest heart wishes and concerns of a people— are discussed at great length.

The directory has five sections.

Part One outlines the Church's understanding and theological language for its catechetical and evangelical mission to bring the Gospel to the world.

Part Two describes the sources for catechesis, beginning with the Gospels, the Christian revelations of the person of Jesus Christ and the Trinitarian notion of God, the mystery of salvation through history, and the role of catechisms in the catechetical process.

Part Three explores briefly the methodologies of passing on the faith, following the example of the "pedagogy of God," which has always used the community experience of faith, employed signs, and identified itself as fundamentally a journey to God (#143). The role of inductive and deductive learning and memorization is also discussed.

Part Four discusses issues dealing with the people who are catechized, including the importance of adapting methods and even the message in some ways according to the cultural tendencies of a people, special situations of individuals or groups, and especially the age, social conditions, and psychological maturity of the one being catechized.

Part Five focuses on a description of how catechesis actually happens in a particular parish or diocese. Beginning with an identification of the actual agents who pass on the faith—parents, clergy, lay and religious catechists, and the entire Christian community—this section discusses the importance of the formation and education of the catechist. It also discusses the different places catechesis happens—home, parish, school, associations, movements like retreat programs, and small Christian communities—and the ways in which catechetical efforts should be organized and coordinated in dioceses.

The GCD presents guidelines for the production of national and regional directories and indirectly for catechisms and other catechetical materials. It is the primary source of inspiration for the U.S. catechetical directory, *Sharing the Light of Faith*, which was issued in 1979.

The Church hopes the GDC will increase the level of esteem that parishes, schools, and dioceses have for the role of the catechist and emphasize the importance for all catechists to work at their own spiritual growth and development. *See also*: *Catechism of the Catholic Church, The*; Congregation for Catholic Education, The.

Further Reading: Congregation for the Clergy, *General Directory for Catechesis* (Washington, DC: United States Catholic Conference, 1997); Bill Huebsch, *General Directory for Catechesis in Plain English* (Mystic, CT: Twenty-Third, 2002); Bernard Marthaler, "The Origin, Context and Purpose of the Directory," *Living Light* 9 (1972): 7–19; Daniel S. Mulhall and Maureen Shaughnessy, *New Guide to Teaching the Faith: A Popular Overview of the General Directory for Catechesis* (Cincinnati, OH: Catholic Update, August 1999); Sacred Congregation for the Clergy, *Catechetics in Context: Notes and Commentary on the GCD* (Huntington, IN: Our Sunday Visitor, 1973).

Mark S. Markuly

German American Catholics

No ethnic group embraced parochial education more enthusiastically than did the Germans. Indeed, it is estimated that over two-thirds of the 2,200 German parishes in the United States in the nineteenth century built schools within two years of the establishment of the parish. It is not too much to say that most German Catholic parents were eager and willing to accept the mandate of the bishops that every Catholic child should be in a Catholic school.

What accounts for this uniform devotion to Catholic education? To a significant extent, the German commitment to parish schools was a reflection of a commitment to their native language and culture. In a new land where English ways and words were the norm, German priests and parents quickly established institutions that would protect the institutions they held dear.

The first German immigrants—those who settled in this country in the late eighteenth and early nineteenth centuries—pioneered the German parish school, an institution designed to cultivate and preserve foreign languages and cultures as well as to preserve religious faith and provide literacy. First established in the early decades of the nineteenth century, the German parish school was an important and popular model until the 1930s.

The commitment of German Catholics was almost unanimous and not surprisingly, special emphasis was placed on the preservation of the German language. "Our German language," noted one German American editor "is to us the treasure that is inseparable with our being. We are better citizens, better men, and better Christians if we give expression to our noblest feelings in our own tongue unhindered. We desire to be faithful American citizens; we desire to remain devoted children of the Catholic Church, but we also desire to find an unhindered expression of the soul in our own language (quoted in Shanabruch, 1981, p. 91). As long as native language and culture had meaning for the immigrants, the ethnic parish school played an important role.

It is hard to overestimate the importance that most German immigrants placed on these schools. "The schools they set up," notes historian Philip Gleason, "performed the functions, in addition to intellectual and religious training, of transmitting the ancestral language, orienting the young to the national symbols of the group through successive generations" (Philip Gleason, "Immigration and the American Catholic Intellectual Life," *Review of Politics* 26 [April 1964]: 147–173).

German Catholics dominated the dioceses of Cincinnati, St. Louis, and Milwaukee and were sizable minorities in Chicago, St. Paul, New York, and Philadelphia. They built their schools quickly with no complaint about cost. Funds were raised through pew rentals, voluntary donations, and funds received from mission societies in Europe.

To provide continuing support, many German parishes organized school societies that had the responsibility of raising additional funds. German missionary priests working in America traveled to Europe to convince superiors of religious orders to send a few sisters to the Midwest to teach in the parish schools. By the 1860s, it was hard to find a German Catholic parish without a thriving school. It was an altogether remarkable achievement.

The rapid growth of German Catholic schools in Cincinnati was typical of what was happening in other midwestern dioceses. In 1834, German Catholics established their first parish school in Cincinnati and enrolled an unspecified number of pupils; additional teachers were added in the late 1830s as the enrollment increased. By 1843, with the addition of a second school two years earlier, enrollment was up to 600 pupils. Less than five years later, after an influx of new German immigrants, the number of German Catholic schools had jumped to six, and enrollment was over 1,800. This pattern of growth in the number of pupils and schools continued throughout the years of German emigration to Cincinnati. It is not surprising, therefore, that Cincinnati archbishop J. B. Purcell would note his pride and amazement at the devotion of his German parishioners to parochial schools.

German support for parish education was motivated primarily by the fear that the public schools would "Anglicize" their children and turn them away from "keim und kirche"—home and church. German Catholics firmly believed that language keeps the faith and that one way to ensure the teaching of the German language and culture was to establish their own schools. "Where the Germans had their own German schools and spoke only German," noted one German missionary, "they are as faithful to their Religion as they or their parents were a hundred years ago when they left the ship." The predominantly Irish Catholic hierarchy applauded the German campaign to establish parish schools, but the bishops were not sanguine about the plan to use these schools to preserve their German language and culture. Indeed, concern over this matter would become a major issue within the American Catholic Church in the 1880s and 1890s.

The Germans had been the first to establish ethnic parish schools in the nineteenth century and were its most ardent supporters. But by the turn of the century, most German parish schools had felt the impact of Americanization and were using English as the main language of instruction.

The beginning of the end for German Catholic schools was the onset of World War I. Anti-German hostility swept the United States from 1914 to 1919. All things German were branded as anti-American. In fact, some states and communities went so far as to prohibit the use of the German language in public or on the telephone.

In such a climate, American-born bishops ordered German parishes to cease the use of the German language even for religious instruction. Within a few years, the German Catholic school establishment had been Americanized. By 1930, very few German Catholic schools survived. This may have been a blessing, as anti-German sentiment rose substantially during World War II. This is not to say that the strong German American support for parochial education faded as these schools were closed. In fact, German Catholics shifted their allegiance to nonethnic Catholic organizations that supported Catholic schools. Beginning in 1930 and up to the present, the rosters of organizations such as the Knights of Columbus, the Catholic Youth Organization, and the Holy Name Society, among others, were filled with men of German ancestry. German Catholic support for parochial education changed only in form in the twentieth century. In substance, Catholics of German ancestry remain among the strongest supporters of Catholic education in the United States today. *See also*: Cahenslyism; Catholic School Question, The; Ethnicity (and parish schools); Katzer, Frederick.

Further Reading: Colman Barry, *The Catholic Church and German Americans* (Milwaukee: Bruce, 1953); Josef Barton, *Peasants and Strangers* (New York: Cambridge University Press, 1975); Charles Shanabruch, *Chicago's Catholics: The Evolution of an American Identity*

(Notre Dame, IN: University of Notre Dame Press, 1981); Timothy Walch, *Parish School: American Catholic Parochial Education from Colonial Times to the Present* (New York: Crossroad, 1996).

Timothy Walch

Gibbons, James Cardinal (1834–1921)

James Cardinal Gibbons was the leader of the Catholic Church in America through the late nineteenth and early twentieth centuries. He was a man of his times. Those times spanned the Civil War, Reconstruction, industrialization and labor movement, war with Spain, and World War I. He worked toward a better understanding of Catholicism by Americans and to improve Rome's understanding of American culture. He was a priest for almost sixty years, bishop for fifty-two years, and cardinal for thirty-five years (Ellis, 1963). He was noted for his love of his country, support of separation of Church and state, and good relations with Protestant neighbors (Tehan, 1962).

James Gibbons was born in Baltimore in 1834, the son of Thomas Gibbons, a merchant, and Bridget Walsh. His parents emigrated from Ireland in 1829 but returned there in 1837. His father died in 1847, and the family moved to New Orleans in 1853. Gibbons worked as a clerk until he heard Redemptorist missionaries preach, after which he "resolved to become a priest" (Tehan, 1962, p. 37). Because he was originally from Baltimore, Gibbons enrolled as a student for the archdiocese he would serve for many years.

After he was ordained in June 1861, he was assigned to St. Patrick's in Baltimore. He was quickly named pastor of a poor parish, St. Bridget's, and also pastor of the mission church, St. Lawrence O'Toole (Tehan, 1962). He saw firsthand the effects of the Civil War and served as a chaplain at the prison at Ft. McHenry.

In 1865, Archbishop Martin John Spalding of Baltimore made Gibbons his secretary. Gibbons helped plan the Secondary Plenary Council, held in Baltimore in 1866. Spalding recommended Gibbons for the newly created vicar apostolic of North Carolina. In North Carolina, Gibbons experienced harsh conditions, with few Catholics, religious intolerance, and the effects of Reconstruction. Gibbons traveled throughout the towns and backwoods areas of his diocese, preaching to his parishioners and making converts. In 1876, Gibbons wrote *Faith of Our Fathers*, a popular apologetical work that helped many Americans understand Catholicism.

He attended the First Vatican Council in 1869 and 1870, where he learned about the Vatican's internal workings. In 1872, he became bishop of Richmond, Virginia, while continuing his work in North Carolina. In 1877, he became archbishop of Baltimore. In 1884, Gibbons presided over the Third Plenary Council of Baltimore. This successful council helped manage the growing Catholic Church in the United States and led to the writing of the Baltimore Catechism and to the founding of the Catholic University of America. With the university located in Gibbon's archdiocese, he served as its first chancellor. As chancellor, he worked hard to establish it and weathered a financial crisis in 1904. "In 1886, Gibbons was named a cardinal. He received the cardinal's red hat from Pope Leo XIII in Rome on 17 March 1887" (Spalding, 2000).

Gibbons worked to prevent Rome from condemning the Knights of Labor, a forerunner of the American Federation of Labor. Gibbons also opposed the movement known as Cahenslyism, which called for the Church in the United States to be organized along ethnic lines. Gibbons also communicated with Rome over a controversy called "Americanism," also known as the phantom heresy (Tehan, 1962, p. 218).

The Third Plenary Council of Baltimore called for each parish to have its own parochial elementary school and for parents to send their children there. The permission of the local bishop was required for exemption to these statutes. Gibbons supported the council's desires but also backed the Faribault Plan, proposed by his friend Archbishop Ireland of St. Paul, Minnesota, which existed in Faribault and Stillwater, Minnesota. In this plan, the school board leased parochial schools for one year. Between 9 A.M. and 3:45 P.M., secular subjects were taught by the sisters, all of whom were certified by the state and whose salaries were paid by the state. The sisters dressed in their religious habits, but only after school hours did they give students religious instruction. Gibbons wrote a letter to Rome, which contained "a major statement of American policy on education," in support of Ireland's ideas (Tehan, 1962, p. 210). Rome replied that this plan could be tolerated.

Gibbons was an adviser to several presidents, including Benjamin Harrison, Grover Cleveland, William Howard Taft, William McKinley, Theodore Roosevelt, and Woodrow Wilson. During his tenure as leading spokesman for the Catholic Church in the United States, he witnessed both the rapid growth of the Church and significant gains in acceptance of Catholics by their fellow Americans. "Though he denounced militarism and the arms race as unchristian and urged international arbitration, on the eve of World War I he was a proponent of preparedness and at its outbreak urged an unreserved response to the nation's call" (Spalding, 2000). He also organized relief efforts for war victims in Belgium and France.

Gibbons published several books. In addition to the well-received *Faith of Our Fathers*, he published *Our Christian Heritage* (1889), *Ambassador of Christ* (1896), *Discourses and Sermons* (1908), *A Retrospect of Fifty Years* (1916), and essays for such journals as the *North American Review* and *Putnam's Monthly* (Spalding, 2000). James Cardinal Gibbons died in March 1921 at the age of eighty-seven. *See also*: Bishops, in the nineteenth-century conflict over Catholic schools; Catholic School Question, The; Plenary Councils of Baltimore.

Further Reading: John T. Ellis, *The Life of James Cardinal Gibbons* (Milwaukee: Bruce, 1963); Bernard F. Marthaler, ed., *New Catholic Encyclopedia*, 2nd ed., vol. 6 (Washington, DC: Gale, the Catholic University of America, 2003): 204–207; Thomas W. Spalding, "Gibbons, James," http://www.anb.org/articles/08/08-00538.html, American National Biography Online February 2000, accessed November 21, 2002; Arline Boucher Tehan, *Prince of Democracy, James Cardinal Gibbons* (Garden City, NY: Hanover House, 1962).

Jack O'Gorman

Gifted and talented, education for

PL. 103-382 defines the term, gifted and talented, as "students, children or youth who give evidence of high performance capability in areas such as intellectual, creative, artistic, or leadership capacity, or in specific academic fields, and who require services or activities not ordinarily provided by the school in order to fully develop such capabilities." While this legislation acknowledges the gifted and talented as students who require special services, it does not mandate states to establish such programs. The choice to provide services or not belongs to the state or local education agencies.

To meet this definition of gifted and talented, multiple measures (e.g., intelligence, achievement, and talent) are required for identifying these students. A standardized intelligence test will identify 2–3 percent of the population as meeting the typically accepted 130 IQ benchmark. Standardized academic achievement tests can suffice for identifying individuals who acquire content material at a more rapid rate than their peers. Talent identification, including leadership, can be done through auditions, nominations, and portfolios. The weight given to each of the measures is directly related to the program envisioned by the school. For example, if a performing arts school is selecting students, more weight could be placed on the talent level and less on IQ; perhaps an IQ of 120 would be accepted. The same could be true of a science magnet, where capacities for scientific thinking and problem solving are considered primary selection criteria. As the various measures are weighted, the percentage of students identified as gifted and talented can approach 8–10 percent of the population.

Serving students identified as gifted and talented is done in a variety of ways: by individual, by ability groupings, within the general education classroom, in pullout programs, in resource rooms, and in special schools. Whatever the setting, the curriculum is adapted to the level of the students' gifts and talents. Among the models of curriculum adaptations are the following:

- Acceleration—moving faster through the grades or through mastery of a particular subject area.
- Compacting—providing students with the opportunity to demonstrate what they already know about a subject and eliminating what is known and replacing it with advanced learning experiences.
- Differentiation—modifying the standard curriculum in content, process, product, or effect to meet the needs of the students.
- Enrichment—providing depth to standard content coverage correlated to the students' aptitude and level of sophistication.
- Independent study—allowing the student to work and learn without assistance from others.

Catholic schools most often elect to serve capable students through the acceleration and enrichment models. These models fit within the structure and the fiscal constraints of private school education. Advanced placement (AP) classes at the secondary level are examples of curriculum acceleration and/or enrichment for groups of students who excel academically. An AP class could also be structured around the curriculum compacting model if the individual student's knowledge base is determined and the teacher plans to meet the needs of the various students by deleting from, and adding to, the curriculum a more individually assessment-driven model than the typical enrichment model. Likewise, differentiated instruction requires the teacher to know the interests, abilities, learning styles, and achievement levels of the class members to know how to form learning groups and design instruction around content. Within class ability grouping is more likely to occur at the elementary level.

Students with special gifts and talents can enhance the classroom learning environment as well as pose problems. The following lists of characteristics of students considered gifted and talented show this contrast.

Characteristics with the potential for enhancing the classroom environment:

1. Demonstrates superior abilities to reason, generalize, or problem-solve
2. Has a wide range of interests but develops one or more interests in depth; sustains concentration for lengthy periods on topics of interest

3. Sets high standards for self

4. Learns quickly and retains what is learned

5. Has an advanced sense of social justice

6. Enjoys intellectual challenge; shows an alert and subtle sense of humor

Characteristics that can pose problems in the classroom:

1. Gets bored with routine tasks; ignores details; turns in messy work

2. Resists changing from interesting topics or activities; rejects authority, is nonconforming, stubborn

3. Is overcritical of self and others, impatient with failure, perfectionist

4. Disagrees vocally with others, argues with teachers; dominates or withdraws in cooperative learning situations

5. Be so emotionally sensitive and empathic that adults consider it over-reaction

6. Make jokes or puns adults considered inappropriate

See also: Academics; Curriculum development; Special needs.
Further Reading: Barbara Clark, *Growing Up Gifted: Developing the Potential of Children at Home and at School*, 6th ed. (Upper Saddle River, NJ: Pearson, 2001); Jim R. Deilse, and Barbara A. Lewis, *Survival Guide for Teachers of Gifted Kids* (Minneapolis: Free Spirit, 2002); Leslie S. Rebhorn, "Gifted Education In Catholic Schools," in Thomas C. Hunt, Ellis A. Joseph, and Ronald J. Nuzzi, eds., *Catholic Schools Still Make a Difference: Ten Years of Research, 1991–2000* (Washington, DC: National Catholic Educational Association, 2002).

Mary Frances Landers and Roberta Weaver

Giving Form to the Vision

Following the lead given in the U.S. bishops' pastoral *To Teach as Jesus Did* (NCCB, 1973), the manual *Giving Form to the Vision* is an instrument designed to assist the process by which Catholic educators can implement the message of the pastoral. It provides a means by which the vision of Catholic education could be internalized and implemented.

The book selects the distinguishing principles of Catholic education highlighted in the pastoral, then provides a list of implications according to which educators may assess the quality of their Catholic education program to determine what specific actions need be taken to ensure that the program is in accord with *To Teach as Jesus Did*. The book stresses that the implementation of the "action programs" designed to improve Catholic education is the major goal of the assessment process.

In general, *Giving Form to the Vision* is intended for use by all Christians who function in the teaching ministry, but it is particularly useful for those in decision-making/leadership roles in the total educational program. While it stresses parish institutions, the book indicates its usefulness to diocesan and independent high school administrators, area and diocesan boards of education, and other policy-making groups.

Five groups—Agencies of Educational Policy-Making, Adult Education, Religious Education Outside the School, the Catholic Elementary School, and the Catholic Secondary School—are specifically introduced and offered five instruments designed to facilitate the groups' work in their leadership roles in the teaching ministry. For each of the five groups, the manual suggests a process of implementation that gives direction and structure to the implementation activities. The caution is that those engaged in specific educational activities must be sensitive to the needs of persons working in, and using, other agencies.

The book can be of service in assessing ongoing Catholic educational programs, in revitalizing ailing programs, and in starting new education ventures. The most important aspect of the manual is its emphasis on process and on determining definite means for attaining specific objectives and goals.

Giving Form to the Vision is prepared in a workbook format. The activities of each of the five groups mentioned earlier are discussed separately. The discussions suggest a range of actions to be implemented by the members of each of the five groups following an evaluative activity by the groups. The entire treatment is based completely on the selected distinguishing principles of Catholic education as highlighted in the pastoral *To Teach as Jesus Did*. It reflects the message of the pastoral.

Specific reflections based on the principles from the pastoral are made. Specific questions aimed at written responses by members of the groups are then asked with a view to an evaluation and a revision of existing practices or policies where there is a need to do so. Both the questions and the responses as well as the suggested line of action to be taken use the message of the pastoral as a standard for implementation. In all cases, actions and the implementation of the revised practices are tailored toward the directives in the pastoral.

In some places, questionnaires are used as instruments to ask for agreement or disagreement by the school faculty in his or her school, the conditions described as imperatives drawn from the pastoral do exist and/or should exist (as in the cases of the "Imperatives for Catholic Elementary Schools" [p. 68], and the "Imperatives for Catholic High Schools" [p. 80]). The faculty is then asked to make specific statements on what can be done in the particular school to see that the imperatives of the pastoral are established and observed. In the light of such statements, the faculty and staff and policymakers are able to restate and reaffirm the religious education goals of the school. These statements at least indicate to members of the school community whether an effective process currently exists for reexamination and renewal of the religious mission of the school. Using this instrument could be part of a self-study program for the school. It can also be used as an ongoing or continuing in-service program to alert both the staff and the clientele of the school to the religious imperatives indicated by the pastoral.

In other places (like the out-of-school programs in religious education, p. 37), consciousness-raising checklists are used as instruments to keep respondents thinking about their religious education program and practices on paper. A statement from the pastoral is then cited followed by open-ended questions to provoke more thinking. These open-ended questions are extracted from the pastoral and are used to formulate a series of guidelines for implementation.

As a rule, in each of the five groups, the instruments utilized in *Giving Form to the Vision* restate (sometimes quote directly) the bishops' statements in the pastoral. These quotes/restatements are meant to help the users of the instruments to examine their schools in relation to the imperatives of the pastoral. At the end of each statement is an invitation to indicate how, in the context of the particular school, the goals of the pastoral can be reached. The process, according to the manual, is supposed to result in specific action steps that are accepted and implemented into the ongoing school operation or in the total education program of the parish. The manual stresses that these implementation statements are the critical element in the process of reexamination, renewal, and redesigning of the education program. Throughout the book, there is a re-echo of the central and recurring theme of *To Teach as Jesus Did* on the principles of the educational ministry of the Church. *See also*: National Catholic Educational Association (NCEA); *To Teach as Jesus Did*.

Further Reading: Charles Brady and Mary Sarah Fasenmyer, *Giving Form to the Vision* (Washington, DC: National Catholic Educational Association, 1974); John F. Meyers, "Developments Since the Pastoral: An Educational Perspective," *Notre Dame Journal of Education* 6, 3 (Fall 1975): 205–210; Lawrence Murphy, "The Pastoral as Integrated Ministry: Message, Community and Service," *Notre Dame Journal of Education* 6, 3 (Fall 1975): 222–228; Leo V. Ryan, "To Teach as Jesus Did—A Guide to Educational Ministry," *The Living Light* 2, 3 (Fall 1974): 409–414.

John J. Augenstein

"Godless" schools

One of the goals of Catholic educational policy in the mid-nineteenth century was to rid public schools of the predominant influences of Protestantism, which were evident in the devotional reading of the Bible, with attendant religious exercises, in textbooks, and in personnel. Fundamentally, though, church leaders felt the optimum situation was to have every Catholic child in a Catholic school. The public schools devoid of Protestant influences were at times depicted as secular, or even "Godless," and as the source of moral ruin to Catholic children. The presence of pupils who were "ill-bred, unbelieving, and immoral" who were creedless would lead their fellow students in that environment to become creedless as the schools themselves were. The resulting indifference to God and religion was a precursor to infidelity in practice. Ultimately, it was believed, Catholic youth would be corrupted in that irreligious, or even antireligious, setting. In fact, some of the proponents of this position felt the public school system was the source of all evils and corruption in the United States.

The "Syllabus of Errors" of Pope Pius IX, issued in 1864, demonstrated Catholic animosity to secular schooling. Pius IX wrote this in a time of crucial struggle with secular governments in Europe, with education being one of the chief battlegrounds. The Pontiff proclaimed the basic rights of the Church in the education of its young, rights that were being denied and eradicated by some governments. The Pope pointed out how the Church's view of the purposes of education included humans' eternal destiny and was not limited to mere natural knowledge. If one departed from the word of God in education, he or she must necessarily be guided by error and lies. Education unconnected with the Church must infallibly produce generations that had no guide but their own wicked passions and conceits and be a source of misfortune to the commonwealth and their families. Primary schooling thus constituted was much worse than higher education, because it exposed the young to the greatest of perils.

Indictments of the evils of the "Godless" system of public schooling were forthcoming from individual Catholic bishops and from several of their councils. The decades of the 1870s and 1880s witnessed the most frequent episcopal outpouring of these denunciations. This era was marked by anti-Catholic activities, in the halls of American legislatures as well as in nativistic attacks, sometimes mob-incited.

Public schools were denounced as irreligious and antireligious, as a "social plague," as places that were infidel and "Godless" and hence must be avoided, as poisonous to the soul, as places where Catholic children would imbibe the germs of infidelity and immorality, as causing the loss of faith and depravity in morals, as calculated to destroy Christian principles in the rising generations, and as the responsible agents for infidelity and impiety in society, bringing about contempt for authority, self-seeking and dishonesty, complete disregard for moral obligations, and other kindred evils that were rapidly increasing in American society.

The wickedness of the public school system consisted of the exclusion of religious principles, of the worship of God, and of the teaching of Christianity and was characterized by the selection of bad and pernicious schoolbooks and in the carelessness of teachers with regard to students' language—swearing, cursing, and profanity were marks of public school students. Teachers had an unpardonable lack of watchfulness over the moral conduct of students, especially in boy–girl contact, which was "fraught with most imminent danger." Some bishops declared "without hesitation" that public schools as they exist would prove the ruin of religion and morality in Catholic children. It was the Church's divinely mandated duty to save them from the poisoned atmosphere of these "Godless" institutions. The degenerate environment negated the attempts of parents to raise their children with piety and devotion. It was said that Catholic students were mocked by their classmates who were themselves devoid of religious belief and moral conduct.

It is clear that a number of Catholic bishops in this period were most seriously concerned about preserving the faith and morals of their young. Their denunciations, it should be noted, focused on the system itself and rarely involved individuals. The bishops and others thought that the only way to save Catholic children from this iniquitous system that sought to turn youth into "refined pagans" was to enroll them in Catholic schools. *See also*: Catholic School Question, The.

Further Reading: Thomas J. Jenkins, *The Judges of Faith: Christian versus Godless Schools* (Baltimore: John Murphy, 1886); Michael J. Muller, *Public School Education* (Boston: Patrick Donahoe, 1872).

Thomas C. Hunt

Gospel values

Gospel values are the social principles, standards, and behavioral norms held by Christians that have their origin in the proper exegesis and interpretation of the life, teachings, and salvific action of Jesus Christ.

The term "Gospel," derived from the Old English term "godspel" or "good news," has a dynamic etymology with roots in the ancient Greek word "euangelion" and Hebrew words "bissar" and "besorah." At the time of Christ, "euangelion" referred to the "announcement of the birth of the emperor, the savior of the Empire and protector of the peace" (Stravinskas, 1991, p. 447). The Hebrew terms "bissar" and "besorah," found in the writings of Isaiah, are connected with God's acts of salvation and a degree of reconciliation between God and Israel that surpasses the original exodus experience (Stravinskas, 1991). The early Christian concept of Gospel incorporated both the Greek understanding of the birth of the savior and the Hebrew understanding of God's salvific action. The Gospel or "good news" announced the kingdom of God in the person of Jesus Christ, who purchased for us our salvation through his life, death, and Resurrection. Before the end of the first century, Gospel became associated not only with the message but also with the written accounts of the salvific action of Christ (the Gospel).

Gospel values are evident in the four canonically accepted written accounts of the life of Jesus Christ contained in the Bible. Examples can be found in the beatitudes (Matthew 5:3–12 and Luke 6:20–23); in the reformulation of the law and in the code of conduct offered by Jesus Christ (Matthew 5:20–7:27); in his parables (Matthew 13: 1–52, 18:23–35, 20:1–16, 21:28–32; Mark 4:1–32, 12:1–12; Luke 11:5–8, 13:6–30); in his description of the great eschatological judgment (Matthew 25:31–46); and in the entirety of his mission.

Gospel values are derived from the proper exegesis and interpretation of the life, teachings, and salvific actions of Christ found in the Gospel accounts and their emulation and application to the pressing issues of the day. This understanding is evident in the admonitions of St. Paul in the Epistles, behavioral admonitions found in the Didache, and the writings of the early church fathers. For example, In St. Paul's Epistle to the Galatians, he condemns the behavior of Peter toward the Gentile converts to Christianity as not being true to the Gospel (Galatians 2:14). St. Ignatius of Antioch en route to his martyrdom in Rome in A.D. 110 writes: "I beseech you, therefore, do nothing in a spirit of division, but act according to Christian teaching. Indeed, I heard some men saying: 'If I do not find it in the official records of the gospel I do not believe.' . . . But to me, the official record is Jesus Christ; the inviolable record in His cross, His death, and His resurrection, and the faith which he brings about: in these I desire to be justified by your prayers" (Jergens, 1970, p. 23).

The Second Vatican Council's "Pastoral Constitution on the Church in the Modern World" (*Gaudium et Spes*), citing copiously from Old and New Testament sources, placed the involvement of Christians in social justice issues as a centerpiece of Gospel values:

> One of the gravest errors of our time is the dichotomy between the faith which many profess and the practice of their daily lives. As far back as the Old Testament the prophets vehemently denounced this scandal, and in the New Testament Christ himself with greater force threatened it with severe punishment. Let there, then, be no such pernicious opposition between professional and social activity on the one hand and religious life on the other. The Christian who shirks his temporal duties shirks his duties towards his neighbor, neglects God himself, and endangers his eternal salvation. (Flannery, 1998, p. 943)

The Second Vatican Council's "Declaration on Christian Education" (*Gravissimum Educationis*) articulates the role of the Catholic school in teaching Gospel values. The document notes,

> It is, however, the special function of the Catholic school to develop in the school community an atmosphere animated by a spirit of liberty and charity based on the Gospel. . . . Thus the Catholic school, taking into consideration as it should the conditions of an age of progress, prepares its pupils to contribute effectively to the welfare of the world of men and to work for the extension of the kingdom of God, so that by leading an exemplary and apostolic life they may be, as it were, a saving leaven in the community. (Flannery, 1998, pp. 732–733)

The National Conference of Catholic Bishops developed this concept further in their document *To Teach as Jesus Did*. It notes, "Since the Christian vocation is a call to transform oneself and society with God's help, the educational efforts of the Church must encompass the twin purposes of personal sanctification and social reform in light of Christian values" (NCCB, 1972, p. 3). The document also identifies the mission of Catholic schools to include three connected dimensions: the message revealed by God which the Church proclaims, fellowship in the life of the Spirit, and service to the entire human family.

The U.S. Catholic bishops have recently added more clarity to the essential elements of the Church's social justice teachings (Gospel values) in the document, *Sharing Catholic Social Teaching: Challenges and Directions* (USCC, 1998). It identifies seven major themes: life and dignity of the human person; call to family, community, and participation; rights and responsibilities; option for the poor and vulnerable; the dignity of work and the rights of workers; solidarity; and the care for God's creation. The document also includes recommendations to all engaged in Catholic education at all levels concerning the effective dissemination of these seven essentials of Catholic social teaching. *See also*: *Declaration on Christian Education, The*; *Gaudium et Spes*; *To Teach as Jesus Did*; Vatican Council II.

Further Reading: Austin Flannery, ed., *Vatican Council II: The Conciliar and Post Conciliar Documents* (Northport, NY: Costello, 1987); W. A. Jergens, ed., *The Faith of the Early Fathers* (Collegeville, MN: Liturgical Press, 1970); National Conference of Catholic Bishops, *To Teach as Jesus Did: A Pastoral Message on Catholic Education* (Washington, DC: United States Catholic Conference, 1972); Peter M. J. Stravinskas, ed., *Catholic Encyclopedia* (Huntington, IN: Our Sunday Visitor, 1991); United States Catholic Conference, *Sharing Catholic Social Teaching: Challenges and Directions* (Washington, DC: United States Catholic Conference, 1998).

John T. James

Governance

Catholic education including schools and religious education programs has traditionally been an expression of the teaching mission of the Church and has functioned within the authority structure of the Church. The authority structure of the Church since the early twelfth century has been based on the role of the bishop within his diocese.

Catholic schools and religious education have been closely identified with the parish, a basic unit of ecclesiastical structure. As such, the school and other religious education programs came under the direct authority of the pastor, the administrative officer of the parish.

In 1852, the diocesan school board movement began when Bishop John N. Neuman established a Central Board of Education in Philadelphia. He presided over the board, which was composed of a pastor and two lay delegates from each parish in the city. He reserved the right to approve all resolutions and served as the board's treasurer. Other dioceses also began to establish boards. In 1884 the Third Plenary Council of Baltimore legislated that a "Diocesan Commission of Examination" and "School Commissions" be established in every diocese in the United States. Historically, their role was consultative and advisory to the bishop.

Another dimension of governance was instituted in 1888, when the archdiocese of New York appointed Fr. William Degnan the first diocesan inspector of schools (later superintendent). He had been a member of the archdiocesan board and now represented it and the bishop in the examination of schools, teachers, and students. The position gained acceptance and spread to other dioceses.

In 1904, when the Catholic Educational Association (later, National Catholic Educational Association) was formed, the three founding departments were Catholic colleges, seminaries, and parish schools. The Parish School Department membership included pastors, superintendents, principals, and board members. This vehicle provided the forum for discussion of common concerns and issues across dioceses.

Diocesan offices headed by a superintendent and diocesan boards continued to grow and spread throughout the twentieth century. Education offices began to include more staff to assist the superintendent in areas such as curriculum development and school visitation.

At the 1960 NCEA convention Msgr. John McDowell, superintendent of schools for the diocese of Pittsburgh, proposed a renewal of the role of the laity in education and a strengthening of the office of the superintendent. At this meeting, one of the standing committees on the functions of the superintendents reported that those boards of education that existed were to assist the superintendent and were consultative rather than policy-making in nature. Boards of education were to assist the superintendent by studying the various educational problems to help the superintendent to formulate the programs and policies that were in the best interest of the diocese. In all cases, the bishop was the honorary chairman of the board and gave direction and authority to the decisions made.

Vatican Council II (1962–1965) became the watershed for much change in the Church, including its educational ministry. After Vatican II some leading Catholic educators proposed change in the relationship of parish and diocesan schools to the Church by suggesting that the boards of education should be jurisdictional. One of those was Msgr. O'Neill D'Amour, superintendent of schools for the diocese of Marquette, Michigan, and later secretary of the superintendent's Department of the National Catholic Educational Association (NCEA). This recasting sought to broaden the base of authority and governance in the schools and to create a system of schools.

Also in this era of change, D'Amour and others recommended the establishment of local parish school boards and later regional boards that would be coordinating bodies in an area. These groups were to assist in developing new relationships with public education and the local community as well as the appropriate state education office.

Vatican II also brought change in religious education. That dimension of the Church's educational ministry also expanded and included not only religious education for Catholic children attending public schools (formerly known as the Confraternity of Christian Doctrine, or CCD) but also adult religious education and religious education for those with disabilities.

This expansion of Catholic education also brought change to the governance structure. Diocesan offices initiated positions such as director of religious education, and in some dioceses the chief officer in the education office was titled superintendent or vicar for education. Boards of religious education were established, but soon boards of total education superseded them as well as school boards. These boards oversaw elementary and high schools and religious education and the formation of children, youth, and adults.

Another governance structure also appeared after Vatican II, namely, the parish council. For years parishes had had trustees, usually men who advised the pastor and affirmed with their signatures an annual report to the local bishop. Parish councils had a larger and more diverse membership, including religious and lay members. Such councils also had committees, including one for education. This created a problem, namely, What are the respective responsibilities of the school or total education board and the parish council education committee? Frequently, the school or total education board was subsumed under, or became, the council's education committee.

Finally, as the governance structures were changing at the local parish and diocesan levels, the NCEA structure and services were adapted to meet those changes. The superintendents' department membership expanded to include, among others, directors of religious education, vicars, and superintendents for education and in the early 1970s was renamed Chief Administrators of Catholic Education (CACE). Religious education and boards began under CACE but became separate departments within NCEA to better serve their needs. *See also*: Bishops; Boards of education, diocesan, parish, school; Hierarchy.

Further Reading: Mary-Angela Harper, *Ascent to Excellence in Catholic Education: A Guide to Effective Decision-Making* (Waterford, CT: CROFT-NEI Division of Prentice-Hall, 1980); National Catholic Educational Association, *A Primer on Educational Governance in the Catholic Church* (Washington, DC: National Catholic Educational Association, 2001); M. Lourdes Sheehan, "A Study of the Functions of School Boards in the Educational System of the Roman Catholic Church in the United States." Unpublished doctoral dissertation, Virginia Polytechnic Institute and State University, 1981.

John J. Augenstein

Grand Rapids School District v. Ball

This case, decided the same day as *Aguilar v. Felton*, involved two Grand Rapids, Michigan, programs begun in the 1976–1977 school year. The programs, Shared Time and Community Education, offered classes paid for by the public school district to nonpublic school students in their nonpublic school classrooms, which the district leased for that purpose. The Shared Time program offered classes during the school days that were intended to supplement core courses required by the state. Courses offered included remedial and enrichment mathematics, art, reading, music, and physical education. A student could spend as much as 10 percent of the academic year in Shared Time instruction. All Shared Time teachers were public school employees, but a significant number of them had nonpublic school teaching experience.

The Community Education program offered voluntary classes after school; some of the classes were available during the regular school day at the public school, while other classes were available only through the Community Education program. The Community Education teachers were full-time nonpublic school employees in the nonpublic schools where the Community Education courses were held; they were paid by the public school on a part-time basis. The public school district had a preference for hiring persons already teaching in the school. Courses taught included such subjects as arts and crafts, home economics, newspaper and yearbook production, humanities, and others. The public school district paid for all supplies, materials, and equipment in these classes.

The school district leased classrooms, but the leases did not mention hallways or certain other facilities, although rest-rooms were included. During the duration of the classes, teachers were required to post signs stating that their particular rooms were public school classrooms.

Forty-one private schools participated in these programs, and forty of the schools had a religious affiliation. Taxpayers filed suit in Federal District Court against the district and specific state officials; the suit alleged that both programs violated the Establishment Clause of the First Amendment, as made applicable to the states through the Fourteenth Amendment. The court ruled in favor of the taxpayers, and the Court of Appeals affirmed the decision.

The Supreme Court ruled in 1985 that both programs had the "primary or principal" effect of advancing religion and therefore violated the Establishment Clause. Although the programs had an admittedly secular purpose, the education of children, the fact that the aid had the effect of promoting religion and/or unduly entangled the government in the affairs of religious institutions rendered them unconstitutional.

The majority opinion held that religion was promoted in three ways: (1) there was a possibility that state-paid teachers, working in a sectarian environment, could "subtly or overtly" indoctrinate students in religious beliefs at public expense; (2) the symbolic union of Church and state, found when the state offers program in a church-sponsored institution, could send a message of state support of religion to students and others; and (3) the programs subsidized the religious functions of the private school by assuming responsibility for teaching some secular subjects. Further, there was no monitoring of the courses to ensure that no religious content was introduced.

The opinion also scrutinized the parent handbook of one Catholic school and found that the "God oriented environment which permeates the total educational program" suggested that teachers in religious schools who became "public school" teachers for a period or two would not be able to "change gears" and might well advance some sectarian purpose.

The three-part *Lemon* test was applied to the Grand Rapids facts. To pass the test, the aid: (1) must have a secular purpose; (2) can neither advance nor inhibit religion; and (3) cannot foster excessive entanglement with religion. The Court conceded that the purpose of the programs was secular academic enrichment but that the programs conferred benefits on schools operated by religious institutions. The third part was also violated because the Court found that an unacceptable level of entanglement existed between the public and the sectarian schools in the administration of the programs.

The Court also discussed the concept of a "symbolic union" between Church and state as a result of the public school district-sponsored programs being offered in the religious school and found that such a symbolic union would not pass constitutional muster. Four judges dissented. Chief Justice Rehnquist stated in his dissent: "Not one instance of attempted religious inculcation exists in the records of the school-aid cases decided today, even though both the Grand Rapids and New York programs have been in operation for a number of years." Justice O'Connor made a similar statement in her dissent in *Aguilar v. Felton*, the companion case, which ruled New York's program of providing Chapter One services in religious schools unconstitutional. *See also*: Establishment Clause.

Further Reading: *Aguilar v. Felton*, 105 S.Ct. 3232 (1985); *Lemon v. Kurtzman*, 408 U.S. 602 (1971); Ralph Mawdsley, *Legal Problems of Religious and Private Schools*, 4th ed. (Dayton, OH: Education Law Association, 2000).

Mary Angela Shaughnessy, SCN

Greeley, Andrew M. (1928–)

Andrew Greeley was born on February 5, 1928, in the Chicago suburb of Oak Park, Illinois. Fr. Greeley is an ordained Catholic priest, a distinguished sociologist, and a

Andrew M. Greeley. © University of Notre Dame Archives.

best-selling author. Currently, he serves as professor of social sciences at the University of Chicago and at the University of Arizona. He is also a research associate at the National Opinion Research Center at the University of Chicago. He received his Ph.D. from the University of Chicago in 1962.

Greeley's contributions to Catholic education have resulted primarily from his own work (including some with colleagues) on the effectiveness of Catholic schools. He also has done much to publicize the research efforts of other authors who studied the effectiveness of Catholic schools. In the first extensive research done of parochial schools in the post–World War II era, a study conducted by the National Opinion

Research Center in 1966 (Greeley and Rossi, 1996) reported that the perception of Catholic schools based on earlier research was no longer accurate. Catholic schools had become more effective than public schools in several areas, including the fostering of academic growth. Greeley, McCready, and McCourt reported in a 1976 work that Catholic schools were much valued by laity, and those whose children had attended Catholic schools supported the Church financially at the same level as the average parishioner had prior to Vatican II. The mean contribution of other Catholics had dropped by half after Vatican II. In a controversial "Afterword" to this book, Greeley advocated that the hierarchy get out of the school business and turn the schools over to the Catholic laity.

Fr. Greeley first became professionally interested in Catholic education when he was placed in charge of teaching religion to adolescents in a Catholic parish (Christ the King) in Chicago shortly after his ordination. As an assistant pastor, among other duties, he was charged with teaching youngsters in the parish the *Catechism of the Catholic Church*. From that experience, he found that the curriculum prescribed by the diocese focused on the formal aspects of that document. His students mastered that curriculum well, but as a result of the experience, he judged they were less interested in the Catholic religion than when they entered the course. Since Greeley perceived that the payoff for Catholic education was the residual from such experience in students when they had reached adulthood, he decided to add Catholic stories as the basis for the more formal instruction already in the curriculum. When other priests charged with directing religious education in other parishes observed the impact of Greeley's curriculum, they asked that he publish the stories. This resulted in his first writing about Catholic education.

Greeley, because of his interest in the area of religious education and society, sought and was granted permission to do graduate study in the University of Chicago's Sociology Department. There he became a member of a team at the National Opinion Research Center, which was studying *The Education of Catholic Americans*. The director of that project was Peter Rossi, who became interested in Catholic schools when he was studying the schools of Fitchburg, Massachusetts. In that study, Rossi found that Catholic schools did not fit the stereotypes attributed to them by the educational authorities. For instance, Catholic schools outperformed public schools in academics where the socioeconomic background of the parents was held constant. In researching the impact of Catholic schooling on students, the authors employed what is referred to as Rossi's Law. This concept insisted that the proper subject for research was the residual impact Catholic education had on students in their adult lives.

James Coleman, in his study, the *Adolescent Society*, came to the same conclusion when he discovered that one Polish Catholic high school outperformed Chicago public high schools in academics when background variable factors were held constant. Coleman explained this phenomenon. He asserted Catholic schools required more advanced academic work for those in the college track than did public schools. Even those in the general track in Catholic schools were required to take some advanced academic work. Catholic schools had an institutional philosophy that emphasized the worth of each individual student, and a community spirit seemed to emanate from within the Catholic schools.

Greeley's research also focused on the long-range impact of Catholic schools on the nonacademic impact of participation of students in Catholic schools. Among his findings were that those students who participated for longer periods of time in Catholic schools had greater religious knowledge and were more faithful in religious practices. Their responses to surveys indicated they were more likely to reject social prejudices, including anti-Semitism. Students who attended Catholic schools were more successful, economically and occupationally, than the Catholic youth who did not attend Catholic schools, even when the effects of the social and economic background were held constant. No level of schooling was more important than any other level. What counted was the total number of years in Catholic schools. Catholics who had attended Catholic schools contributed more generously to the Church, as did parents whose children had attended Catholic schools.

Utilizing data gleaned from the *High School and Beyond* study, in a book published in 1982 entitled *Catholic High Schools and Minority Students*, Greeley focused on minority students attending Catholic secondary schools, seeking to discover why black and Hispanic students attending Catholic high schools displayed higher levels of academic effort and achievement than did their counterparts attending public high schools. After consideration of input—demographic, economic, and environmental— and of school effect—discipline and academics—he reported that the Catholic school outcomes were due partially to the kinds of young people attending the schools, to the quality of the schools' discipline, and most important, to the "superior quality of academic instruction" there (Greeley, 1982, p. 71).

In 1998 and 1999, Greeley engaged David Baker and Cornelius Riordan in a debate in the pages of *Phi Delta Kappan*, a well-known journal in education, as to whether Catholic schools were becoming a system of proprietary schools that educated growing numbers of non-Catholics from the wealthiest strata of society and other children who do not consider themselves religious at all. Greeley countered Baker and Riordan's allegations of the growing "elitism" of Catholic schools by pointing out that the presence of non-Catholics in Catholic schools was a major contribution to social justice, since most who were not Catholic were African Americans trying to escape from the horrors of public schools in their neighborhoods. He also questioned Baker and Riordan's rejection of the results of research done on the effectiveness of Catholic schools. In general, he maintained that Baker and Riordan's assertions were not supported by data and that they "twisted" his research on Catholic education. In summary, in his writings on Catholic education, Greeley has stated that he is not a supporter of Catholic schooling but a believer in what research on Catholic schools since 1965 has repeatedly demonstrated, that Catholic schools do make a positive difference in the academic achievement of those students, in their earning power, and in their religious behavior after they become adults. Pupils who have attended Catholic schools more faithfully support the Church than those Catholics who did not. The one factor that positively impacts financial support for the Church is the Catholic school in the parish. Catholic schools have become the successful common schools for the poor and disadvantaged when they have the opportunity to attend those schools. *See also*: *Catholic High Schools and Minority Students*; *Catholic Schools in a Declining Church*; *Education of Catholic Americans, The*; Elitism.

Further Reading: David Baker and Cornelius Riordan, "It's Not about the Failure of Catholic Schools: It's about Demographic Transformations," *Phi Delta Kappan* 80, 6 (February 1999): 462; David Baker and Cornelius Riordan, "The Eliting of the Common American Catholic School and the National Education Crisis," *Phi Delta Kappan* 80, 1 (September 1998): 16–23; Andrew M. Greeley, *Catholic High Schools and Minority Students* (New Brunswick, NJ: Transaction Books, 1982); Andrew M. Greeley, "More Assertions Not Backed by Data,"

Phi Delta Kappan 80, 6 (February 1999): 463; Andrew M. Greeley, "The So-Called Failure of Catholic Schools," *Phi Delta Kappan* 80, 1 (September 1998): 24–25; Andrew M. Greeley and Peter Rossi, *The Education of Catholic Americans* (Chicago: Aldine, 1996); Andrew M. Greeley, William C. McCready, and Katherine McCourt, *Catholic Schools in a Declining Church* (Kansas City, MO: Sheed and Ward, 1976); "One-on-One with Father Greeley," *Chicago Stories*, http://www.networkchicago.com/chicagostories/greeley.htm. Accessed April 24, 2003.

James E. Gay

Groome, Thomas

One of the most influential Christian religious educators in the United States for the last third of the twentieth century. Thomas Groome's theories have deeply impacted the organization of Catholic religion textbooks.

A Catholic theologian, Groome has written several important works. The most famous is *Christian Religious Education: Sharing Our Story and Vision*, which posits a five-step process to more effectively pass on the faith and create more interest among students for learning about religion. This process, which Groome calls *Shared Praxis*, met an important need in Catholicism throughout the 1980s and 1990s.

A lack of agreement on effective religious education methods was one of the indirect results of changes in Catholicism brought about by the Second Vatican Council. Prior to the council, many religious educators still used the methodologies of rote memorization of catechism questions and answers and the use of lecture formats filled with Catholic "facts." Before and after the council, these methods were called into question, but educators could not agree on alternative strategies.

Groome suggested the older methods put too much emphasis on the intellectual or cognitive dimensions of the faith tradition. Synthesizing many trends and insights in Christian religious education for most of the twentieth century, the Shared Praxis approach tries to engage the learner at a deeper level. This is done by moving beyond only academic data and connecting the information of the tradition to real-life situations and reactions, creating a *praxis* (practice or action) way of knowing—a knowing grounded in personal experience.

Groome's Shared Praxis has five "movements":

1. *Experience*: The teacher asks students to share their reactions, feelings, understandings, beliefs, sentiments, or values on a particular topic or activity. For instance, the teacher might ask the students, "What does the Eucharist *mean* in your life?"

2. *Critical Reflection*: The teacher then engages students in a critical reflection on the experiences shared in the first movement through a focused conversation grounded in the students' individual biographies, stories, and visions concerning the topic or activity. Students are asked to get beneath their experiences to understand the social conditioning, norms, and assumptions shaping their worldview and experience of reality.

3. *Sharing the Story and Vision*: Continuing a dialogical rather than lecture format, the teacher shares the Christian story and its vision of the issue. This answers the question, "What does the Church teach about the Eucharist?" It could include relevant stories, history, doctrines and dogmas, rituals, and hopes and dreams of previous generations as it is understood and articulated by the Magisterium, the best in theological thought, and the lived faith of Catholic Christians.

4. *Dialectic between the Meaning of the Christian Story and the Students' Stories*: In this movement the teacher and students engage in a mutual critiquing of their stories

and the story in light of each other. How do the Catholic and Christian story affirm, challenge, or stretch the meaning the students' give to their experiences? On the other hand, how do the students' own personal stories affirm, recognize the limits of, or seek to move beyond the faith community's understanding of the Christian story? For instance, Groome might ask high school students on a unit about the Eucharist: "The Church through the ages has experienced that the Eucharist draws us closer to God and each other. How does it accomplish and fail to accomplish this for you, and what does the experience of our ancestors say to the way you approach the Eucharist?"

5. *Dialectic between the Christian Vision of Life and the Students' Vision*: In this last movement students are asked how their personal experiences or stories fit with the Christian vision and how that vision might challenge them to act in the future.

Because Shared Praxis requires a continuing dialogue with students and has the goal of helping them find the meaning of Catholic teaching in the experiences of their own lives, teachers using this approach must have a great deal of knowledge about their religious tradition.

In the late 1990s, Groome began exploring the philosophical underpinnings of effective Catholic education through the centuries. His *Educating for Life* (1998) attempted to identify the unique spiritual characteristics of the Catholic approach:

1. Recognizing all humans are intrinsically good;
2. Maintaining a "sacramental" conviction that there is always "more" to be found in the ordinary than meets the eye;
3. Approaching humans as relational and community-oriented in nature;
4. Remaining open to the "wisdom" found in the history and traditions of our ancestors;
5. Seeking holiness in life (spirituality);
6. Working for justice and the social values of God's reign;
7. Keeping a "catholic" approach to others and life, by remaining open to truth wherever it can be found.

See also: Religion, teaching of; Total Catholic education.

Further Reading: Thomas H. Groome, *Christian Religious Education: Sharing Our Story and Vision* (San Francisco: Harper & Row, 1980); Thomas H. Groome, *Educating for Life: A Spiritual Vision for Every Teacher and Parent* (Allen, TX: Thomas More, 1998); Thomas H. Groome, *What Makes Us Catholic: Eight Gifts for Life* (New York: Harper San Francisco, 2002).

Mark S. Markuly

Guidelines for Doctrinally Sound Catechetical Material

In the late 1980s, the National Conference of Catholic Bishops decided to develop policy guidelines for the creation of doctrinally sound textbooks (1990). These national guidelines were intended to assist and influence publishers of textbooks for religious education so that the Church's teachings on faith and morals would be faithfully presented while taking into account the characteristics of the children and youth who would be using them to learn the Catholic faith.

The document places its guidance regarding religious education textbooks within the context of the entire task of catechesis with its four dimensions—message, community, worship, and service. It identifies two basic principles of doctrinal soundness:

(1) that the presentation of the Christian message be both authentic and complete and (2) that the presentation recognize that faith is incarnate and dynamic.

The document then identifies four more specific criteria that characterize doctrinally sound materials. Such materials (1) reflect a recognition of the progressive nature of growth in faith and the need for lifelong conversion; (2) highlight fundamental doctrines as central to the faith; (3) present the faith using language and symbols pertinent to the culture of those who will use them; and (4) emphasize that there is one common faith professed by all believers.

Specific fundamental doctrines that need particular emphasis in the life and culture of the United States at this time are identified. These focus on the Trinity, Mary and the Saints, Liturgy and Sacraments, Grace and Morality, and Death, Judgment, and Eternity and certain doctrines within each area.

The document closes with pastoral and practical guidelines for presenting the Church's teaching in ways that are attractive, appealing, and understandable to the people and communities that will use them. This guidance addresses aspects such as the background of those being catechized, the customs and practices of various cultural groups, and the use of catechetical materials in the home.

In 1992 Pope John Paul II approved the *Catechism of the Catholic Church*, and it was published in English in 1994. The bishops of the United States established the Ad Hoc Committee to Oversee the Use of the Catechism and the Office of the Catechism to advise them on matters related to the *Catechism* and to address particular issues regarding its use. Among these issues is the conformity with the *Catechism* of catechetical materials used in the United States.

To address the matter of conformity, a protocol for assessing conformity of, and a review procedure for, materials submitted by publishers to the Office of the Catechism were developed. The protocol focuses only on the doctrinal content presented in the textbooks. It does not address the pedagogical methods for using the textbooks that are suggested or implied in the materials, nor does it address issues such as the manner in which the content is presented in the materials. The protocol and review process are intended to be used for entire series of textbooks or other materials rather than single works or portions of works.

Reflecting the emphasis present in *Guidelines for Doctrinally Sound Catechetical Materials*, the protocol describes specific criteria related to the principles of authenticity and completeness. Detailed listings of key doctrinal concepts are provided for each of the four major parts of the *Catechism*—the Profession of Faith, the Celebration of the Christian Mystery, Life in Christ, and Christian Prayer. The review process is intended to examine whether each of these key concepts is covered adequately in the series.

The Office of the Catechism publishes a list of textbook series and materials that have been reviewed and found in conformity with the *Catechism*. Bishops have directed that only materials that have been found in conformity may be used in school and parish religious education programs in their (arch)dioceses. In many (arch)dioceses, the diocesan offices or departments of religious education have reviewed approved textbooks in terms of their pedagogy and presentation and have issued guidance to schools and parish religious programs to assist them with choosing from among approved series. *See also*: *Catechism of the Catholic Church, The*; National Conference of Catholic Bishops (NCCB).

Further Reading: Archdiocese of Chicago, *The Catechetical Documents: A Parish Re-*

source (Chicago: Liturgy Training, 1996); United States Catholic Conference, *Guidelines for Doctrinally Sound Catechetical Materials* (Washington, DC: United States Catholic Conference, 1990); United States Conference of Catholic Bishops, *The Protocol for Assessing the Conformity of Catechetical Materials with the Catechism of the Catholic Church* (October 2001); http://www.nccbuscc.org/catechism/document/protocol.htm. Accessed July 15, 2002.

Karen L. Tichy

Guiding Growth in Christian Social Living

According to Johnson (1943), in 1939 Pope Pius XI sent a letter to the American hierarchy on the occasion of the fiftieth anniversary of the founding of the Catholic University of America. In the letter, the Pope described the times as being a period of unrest, disorientation, and conflict, with Christian doctrine and Christian morality under attack from several quarters. He asked that the American bishops use the Catholic University to develop "a constructive program of social action fitted in its details to local needs which will command the admiration and the acceptance of all right-thinking men" (Johnson, p. xii). The bishops responded to the Pope's request and charged the Catholic University to "compile at once a more comprehensive series of graded texts for all educational levels. On the foundation of religious training, which is the distinctive characteristic of our schools, these texts will build an enlightened, conscientious American citizenship" (Johnson, p. xii).

To accomplish this task, the rector of the university, Msgr. Joseph Corrigan, established the Commission on American Citizenship in 1939. He appointed Msgr. Francis J. Haas, dean of the School of Social Sciences, as chairperson of the committee and named Msgr. George Johnson of the Department of Education as its director. Also serving on the committee were Sr. Mary Joan, Sr. Mary Nona, Sr. Mary Marguerite, Sr. Mary Charlotte, and Mary Synon as editorial consultant.

In 1943, Msgr. Johnson published *Better Men for Better Times*. This short book contained the principles for designing a curriculum for Catholic schools. In it he noted that the curriculum must keep in mind the child's basic relationships, which were with God and the Church, with his or her fellow human beings, with nature, and with himself or herself. The ultimate goal of Catholic education has always been to help the child to know, love, and serve God so that he or she would be granted eternal salvation. While that is their ultimate goal, Catholic schools also have proximate goals. In his book Johnson listed what the Committee on Citizenship believed to be the five proximate goals of Catholic education in terms of student outcomes. The Catholic school should produce a child who is physically fit, economically literate, embued with social virtues, culturally developed, and in search of moral perfection.

Johnson described what was involved in each of these five goals. In terms of physical fitness, Johnson meant the development of attitudes and habits of healthful living. Economic literacy referred to the understanding of how modern industrialization works, an appreciation for the value of work, and a zeal for social justice. By "social virtues" Johnson meant the understanding of American life, the workings of democracy, and a willingness to make sacrifices of self-interest in order to live in peace and unity. Cultural development has to do with an appreciation for beauty found in art, music, literature, and a quest for the finer things. Finally, moral perfection is achieved through all of the above in a life united with God.

In 1944, drawing on Johnson's work and under his supervision, two members of the Commission on American Citizenship, Srs. Mary Joan and Mary Nona, wrote the three-volume (one for primary grades, one for intermediate, and one for the upper grades) elementary curriculum guide, *Guiding Growth in Christian Social Living*. Johnson also wrote the lengthy introduction to the series. Srs. Mary Joan and Nona describe the curriculum as "a guide for directing the child's living in the light of Christian principles, with a detailed plan of the learning activities that are basic to that living" (p. v). It is not a textbook, nor is it a course of study. It is rather a curriculum guide on how Catholic elementary schools might go about educating children in Christian social living.

In their introduction, the sisters describe the three steps they used in developing this curriculum. Step one was the formulation of the specific objectives that would assist them in designing what they believed would guide the growth of children in Christian social living. These objectives flow from Johnson's earlier description of the child's basic relationships with God and the Church, other men and women, nature, and himself or herself. They are also in accord with Pope Pius XI's 1929 encyclical, "The Christian Education of Youth."

Step two had to do with the life experience of the child. What the authors believed to be the common experiences of the children of America were set out in a series of situations that a child is helped to meet in a Christ-like way. These situations are "assembled according to the fivefold relationships of the child" (p. vi).

Step three involved putting the objectives and the situations together into a development curriculum. "Each subject in the curriculum was carefully considered as a means of strengthening the child's fundamental relationships" (p. vi). There was strong emphasis in each volume on religion, social studies, and science since these three areas most impacted the child's relationship with God, with other human persons, and with nature. There was also a proportionate emphasis on language arts, arithmetic, music and art, and health and physical education. In developing this curriculum, the sisters used the diocesan courses of study in use throughout the United States.

Srs. Mary Joan and Nona note in their introduction that the curriculum guide is "suggestive, flexible and broad enough for the construction of more detailed courses of study from its general plan" (p. vi). They suggested that it might be helpful to diocesan educators in developing their own curricula and courses of study and to teacher training institutions and religious congregations in their teacher training programs.

Along with the *Guiding Growth in Christian Social Living*, the Commission on American Citizenship in the person of Johnson directed the writing of the *Faith and Freedom Series*, a Catholic reading textbook series published first in 1941. Written by Sr. Mary Marguerite, this three-volume collection was to "bridge the gap which has existed for so long a time between the teaching of religious truths and their translation into life situations" (Buetow, 1970, p. 239). It was extremely popular in Catholic schools from the 1940s through the 1960s. *See also*: Johnson, George; Religion, teaching of.

Further Reading: Harold A. Buetow, *Of Singular Benefit: The Story of U.S. Catholic Education* (New York: Macmillan, 1970); George Johnson, *Better Men for Better Times* (Washington, DC: Catholic University of America Press, 1943); Mary Joan and Mary Nona, *Guiding Growth in Christian Social Living: A Curriculum for the Elementary School*, 3 vols. (Washington, DC: Catholic University of America Press, 1944); Mary Marguerite, *Faith and Freedom Series*, Vol. 1 (Boston: Ginn, 1941); Pius XI, "The Christian Education of Youth," in *Five Great Encyclicals* (New York: Paulist Press, 1939).

Patrick J. Riley

H

Heart of the Matter, The: Effects of Catholic High Schools on Student Values, Beliefs and Behaviors

Heart of the Matter is a retrospective analysis of the responses of Catholic students, in their senior year in Catholic and public high schools, to the survey of high school seniors by the *Monitoring the Future* project administered by the Survey Research Center of the Institute for Social Research at the University of Michigan from 1976 to 1985. Results indicate that the Catholic school context had a positive influence on students' attitudes toward militarism, marriage, educational aspirations, cutting school, a concern for others, frequency of church attendance, and the importance of religion.

The Heart of the Matter: Effects of Catholic High Schools on Student Values, Beliefs and Behaviors recounts a research project that was initiated in 1986 by the National Catholic Educational Association (NCEA) to investigate the Catholic high school's impact on nonacademic outcomes. The report begins by providing an introduction to the study and an overview of the extant research on the Catholic high school's impact on academic performance up to 1989.

To carry out the study, the NCEA commissioned the Survey Research Center to prepare the data so that Catholic students attending Catholic and public high schools between 1976 and 1985 could be identified. The data for the research were drawn from the *Monitoring the Future* project that submitted questionnaires with 300 to 800 items to 16,000 high school seniors in 125 schools. Because the National Institute on Drug Abuse funds the *Monitoring the Future* project, more than 40 percent of the items on the questionnaires are about drug abuse, but there were items on attitudes toward education, work, leisure, gender roles, family, religion, social problems, race relations, delinquency, and personality characteristics. To maintain the capacity to include data on values from one of the five questionnaire forms but not the core, the data were clustered into three sets for 1976–1978, 1979–1982, and 1983–1985.

The data for 1983–1985 were used to develop the profile of Catholic seniors attending Catholic and public high schools. Catholic high school seniors differed from their Catholic public school counterparts on all the family and personal background variables. Catholic high school seniors were living in large urban communities, their parents had more education, their mothers were less likely to have worked outside the home, they spent less time at after-school jobs and fewer evenings out during the schoolweek than public high school students, and were more likely to live in a two-parent family.

Three perspectives between Catholic students attending Catholic or public high schools were examined: (1) the differences between the Catholic and public school groups, (2) ten-year data trends regarding background and outcomes from 1976 to 1985, and (3) the unique influences of the school on students' beliefs and values.

Some notable differences between the Catholic and public high school groups were: (1) Under social and educational values, Catholic high school seniors were higher in their endorsement of pro-marriage attitudes and college plans. In contrast, public high school seniors were more supportive of militarism and reported more cutting of school. (2) Regarding a concern for people, Catholic high school seniors indicated greater community involvement, contributions of money, and concern for others than did Catholic seniors in public high schools. (3) The at-risk behaviors found to be higher among Catholic high school seniors were alcohol use and binge drinking, whereas Catholic seniors attending public high schools reported greater cigarette, cocaine, and illicit drug use. (4) Perceptions of self were more pessimistic among Catholic seniors at public high schools. (5) Regarding religiousness, Catholic seniors at Catholic high schools reported higher church attendance, contributions to the church, and regard for the importance of religion than did Catholic seniors at public high schools.

The ten-year data trends for Catholic seniors revealed (1) no change on variables such as living with mother and father, working one to eight hours, pro-school attitude, support of social justice, positive attitude about helping professions, a concern for others, contributing money, avoiding delinquency, happiness, community involvement, racial acceptance, desire to make a difference, church attendance, influence of churches, and church contributions; (2) five variables ending where they began, including materialism, binge drinking, illicit drug use, alcohol use, and pessimism; (3) five declining undesirable outcomes: cutting school, militarism, marijuana use, nights out, cigarette use, and loneliness; (4) two undesirable outcomes with minimal increase: cocaine use and risk-taking; and (5) six desirable outcomes identified, including increase in parents' education, the importance of religion, college plans, pro-marriage attitudes, increased self-esteem, and internal control. The trend of the differences between Catholics attending Catholic or public high schools tended to be minimal.

A multiple regression analysis revealed the unique influence of four variable or attributes as predictors of outcomes. These attributes were the importance of religion, nights out, gender, and attending Catholic high school. Nights out was associated with increases in all at-risk behaviors and decreases in educational values and concern for others. Gender was related to increases in a concern for people, racial acceptance, equal opportunity and the importance of religion, and decreases in militarism and at-risk behaviors, except for cigarette use. Importance of religion was related to increases in a concern for people, faith and church, pro-school, pro-marriage attitudes, and a decrease in at-risk behaviors. Attending a Catholic high school was related to increases in a concern for people, faith and church, pro-marriage, and college plans and to decreases in militarism, a pro-school attitude (attributed to academic demands of the Catholic high school), and cutting school.

Guerra, Donahue, and Benson (1990) conclude: "The evidence gleaned from this reexamination of the *Monitoring the Future* data suggests that when non-academic school effects are found, they favor Catholic schools" (p. 36). *See also*: Effectiveness of Catholic schools; High schools; Outcomes.

Further Reading: John J. Convey, *Catholic Schools Make a Difference: Twenty-Five Years of Research* (Washington, DC: National Catholic Educational Association, 1992); Michael J. Guerra, Michael J. Donahue, and Peter L. Benson, *The Heart of the Matter: Effects of Catholic High Schools on Student Values, Beliefs and Behaviors* (Washington, DC: National Catholic Educational Association, 1990; Educational Resource Information Center [ERIC] Document Reproduction Service No. ED 317 881, 1990).

Robert B. Williams

Hidden curriculum

The hidden curriculum, often referred to as the implicit curriculum, may be defined as the behaviors, attitudes, and knowledge that students learn unintentionally (Parkay and Stanford, 1995). The hidden curriculum has a powerful impact on how students perceive themselves, as well as how they relate to others and to society. This is particularly critical in the Catholic school, as every possible aspect of the curriculum should intentionally educate to the Gospel message, and the school atmosphere should be permeated with Gospel values.

Students may be taught positive or negative behaviors through the hidden curriculum. An example of a positive behavior would be students learning how to cooperate with others; a negative example would be learning how to manipulate the teacher. Attitudes may also be acquired, such as the perception that teachers care or do not care about their students or that school is or is not meaningful or useful. Finally, knowledge about the world is learned through the hidden curriculum, such as the experience, or lack thereof, of consequences for misconduct.

Groome (1998) suggested five functions that are integral to a school community: *word*, *welcome*, *witness*, *welfare*, and *worship*. A school's intentional focus on these functions will enhance its community life and, hence, affect its hidden curriculum.

- *Word*

"Every school is a 'language world' and its quality as a 'house of being' (Heidegger's phrase) greatly affects the 'being' of participants" (Groome, 1998, p. 204). This language world places a great responsibility on teachers and parents to monitor their personal language because of its formative influence on students. According to Groome (1998), "every school should be a language world that teaches the dignity and equality of each person; that nurtures the holistic growth of students and heightens their self-esteem; that encourages respect for society, stewardship of creation, and care for the common good" (p. 205). This includes God's word, as well as human language.

- *Welcome*

The school should demonstrate hospitality toward students, faculty, and staff. In essence, it should be a place where everyone feels at home. The formation of a supportive community of parents, families of students, alumni/ae, and neighbors can provide valuable "social capital" to the school that, Groome maintains, is often left undeveloped.

- *Witness*

Witness implies that the school practices what it preaches. Groome (1998) wrote, "In its explicit curriculum, a school may teach students to live by great personal and social values like honesty, truth-telling, civility, justice, respect, and compassion, but if these values do not permeate the life of the school itself and how it functions daily, it will be ineffective—perhaps even counterproductive—in character formation" (p. 206). Groome cited Thomas Lickona (1991) a renowned author on character education, who asserted, "The way a school is run . . . is the most important kind of character education it provides." Groome recommended that schools routinely examine their environments for integrity between the values the school intends to teach and the reality of daily life in the school.

• *Welfare*

The school must demonstrate care for students, teachers, staff, and all aspects of the community associated with the school, as well as the larger world. This must be consistent, according to Groome (1998), and is "the most effective way to turn students into caring people" (p. 208). Moreover, expressing care nurtures good character in students, which is essential to good education.

• *Worship*

Groome (1998) proposed that every Catholic school should have a vitally active worship life, including student liturgies, opportunities for prayer and reflection, and the presence of religious symbols that foster the faith development of students. In addition, the school should promote students' active involvement in their parishes.

Reimer, Paolitto, and Hersh (1983) reported that some observers have advanced the notion that students learn more, particularly in the areas of moral values and social behaviors, from the hidden curriculum than from formal instruction. In accord with the moral development theory of Kohlberg, these authors claimed that the hidden curriculum provides an invaluable opportunity for the moral learning of students and that, although students can learn a great deal from reading about, and discussing, moral issues, there is no substitute for the involvement in real-life social and moral situations that arise daily in the life of the school. *See also*: Curriculum, definitions of; Extracurricular activities; Null curriculum.

Further Reading: Thomas H. Groome, *Educating for Life* (Allen, TX: Thomas More, 1998); Philip W. Jackson, *Life in Classrooms* (Troy, MO: Holt, Rinehart, and Winston, 1968); Thomas Lickona, *Educating for Character: How Our Schools Can Teach Respect and Responsibility* (New York: Bantam, 1991); Nel Noddings, *The Challenge to Care in Schools* (New York: Teachers College Press, 1992); Forrest W. Parkay and Beverly H. Stanford, *Becoming a Teacher* (Boston: Allyn and Bacon, 1995); Joseph Reimer, Diana Pritchard Paolitto, and Richard H. Hersh, *Promoting Moral Growth, from Piaget to Kohlberg* (Prospect Heights, IL: Waveland Press, 1983).

Gini Shimabukuro

Hierarchy

A term used to describe the three grades or orders of ministry: bishop, priest, and deacon. According to the Council of Trent, these orders owe their existence to divine institution. By comparison, Protestants hold the view that the leaders of the Church receive their power from the community. Consequently, most Protestant denominations do not use the term "hierarchy" to designate their leaders. This Protestant viewpoint implies that the members have the power to influence or shape decision-making. The Catholic Church holds that the hierarchy received their powers from Jesus Christ at the institution of the Church.

"Hierarchy" is used to indicate all those who hold official power within the Church, including cardinals, metropolitans, archbishops, bishops, parish priests, and curates. This group, officially called by their Latin title, *hierarchia jurisdictionis*, hold power by virtue of their office within the Church. Thus, all the ordained bishops, priests, and deacons, because they are ordained, hold office and possess the power of that office.

While all the ordained are technically members of the hierarchy, a more common usage of the term refers to bishops, archbishops, cardinals, and the Pope. Thus, most Catholics consider the hierarchy to comprise only bishops of various ranks.

Jesus Christ is the head of the Church. All power and authority in the Church have their origin in Christ. The Pope is the head of the Catholic hierarchy. The Pope is the jurisdictional and spiritual leader of all Catholic clergy in the world. The College of Cardinals is the Pope's counseling body but is not a legislative entity. The Roman Curia is the structure of government that carries out the Pope's work. It functions like a president's cabinet. The Roman Curia is divided into a collection of dicasteries or offices: congregations, tribunals, pontifical councils, agencies, commissions, vicariates, and the secretary of state. However, the Pope is an ordained bishop, and bishops exercise the fullness of the power of orders.

Cardinals do not hold a jurisdictional position, so "cardinal" is not a hierarchical title. Cardinals are papal electors. All cardinals have one vote, upon the death of a Pope, toward the election of a new Pope. Although most cardinals are bishops, any baptized Christian can be made a cardinal. Only the Pope can appoint cardinals. Although by law cardinals are papal electors, the custom for many years has been that being named a cardinal also means one is a potential candidate for the papacy. Since cardinals typically have elected one of their number to be Pope, a cardinal is by law a papal elector and, by custom, a papal candidate. Bishops who become a cardinal retain their episcopate, whether residential or titular. There are also three types of cardinals: episcopal, presbyteral, and diaconal. These grades correspond to the three grades of clergy: cardinal bishop, cardinal priest, and cardinal deacon.

There are four types of archbishops: metropolitan, titular, coadjutor, and emeritus. Metropolitan archbishops are typically diocesan bishops who preside over an ecclesiastical province or archdiocese. Archbishops receive a pallium, a cotton yoke, from the Pope as a symbol of their unity with the Holy See. Titular archbishops carry the honorary title of archbishop but do not administer a diocese. Coadjutor archbishops function as bishops, but are still under the jurisdiction of another archdiocesan bishop. Coadjutors assume the responsibilities of office at the death, transfer, or retirement of the current archbishop. Coadjutors typically possess this right to succession, to succeed the current archbishop. Emeriti archbishops are retired metropolitan archbishops who carry the honorary title "emeritus" until death.

There are five types of bishops: ordinaries, auxiliaries, coadjutors, titulars, and emeriti. Ordinaries are bishops in the usual sense. They administrate a diocese, or their see. The ordinary hold juridical power in a specific geographical area. Due to a bishop's juridical power, he has oversight of all Catholic schools within the diocese. Bishops typically delegate their authority to the vicar of education or the diocesan superintendent of schools.

Auxiliary bishops assist the ordinary in the diocese. Titular bishops are bishops who only have a titular see; that is, the see no longer exists in a geographical sense. The bishopric is usually an ancient see from the Mediterranean or Holy Land. All auxiliary bishops are titular bishops.

Coadjutor bishops are the same as auxiliary bishops except that they may hold their episcopate with the right of succession. That means that the individual named coadjutor bishop would be named bishop at the death, transfer, or retirement of the ordinary. Typically, this happens only when the ordinary is in very poor health or near retirement. Bishops emeriti are retired bishops. They keep the title as a sign of honor and respect.

Parishes are the smallest unit of diocesan jurisdiction. This includes the geographic area surrounding the parish church. Each diocese is divided into parishes. The pastor is the priest named to head the parish. There may be associate pastors if the parish is too large for one pastor. The laity participate as members of the parish and serve on various councils to assist the pastor. Lay members may also serve as lectors, acolytes, ushers, and extraordinary ministers of the Holy Eucharist. As the bishop's representative, the local parish pastor holds juridical power for an individual parish school.

When considering the hierarchy, it is important to recognize that the Second Vatican Council described the Church as the People of God. The Church is, in a technical, theological sense, the whole people of God, laity, families, priests, religious women and men, bishops, archbishops, cardinals, and Pope. No one group is the Church or is coextensive with the Church. Baptized Christians of whatever vocation and state in life do not simply participate in the Church or belong to it; they constitute the Church. *See also*: Bishops; Governance.

Further Reading: Thomas Bokenkotter, *A Concise History of the Catholic Church* (New York: Doubleday, 1979); Thomas J. Reese, *Archbishop: Inside the Power Structure of the American Catholic Church* (New York: Harper and Row, 1989); Thomas J. Reese, *Inside the Vatican* (Cambridge: Harvard University Press, 1996); George Weigel, *The Courage to Be Catholic* (New York: Basic Books, 2002).

Merylann J. "Mimi" Schuttloffel

High School and Beyond

High School and Beyond is a longitudinal study of high school seniors and sophomores undertaken by the National Center for Educational Statistics of the U.S. Department of Education to monitor changes in academic achievement, attitudes, behavior, and values and to identify what influences them. The study was initiated under the auspices of the National Opinion Research Center at the University of Chicago in 1980 with the administration of standardized tests of reading, vocabulary, mathematics, science, and civics to a random sample of 69,662 students from 1,015 public and private high schools, of which 84 were Catholic. A survey inquiry about the students and the school was also administered to the students, administrators, teachers, and parents. Follow-up surveys of both the senior and sophomore groups were undertaken every two years until 1986, and a further survey was made of the 1980 sophomore group in 1992. Educational researchers interested in determining whether and how Catholic schools are effective considered that the opportunity to utilize the extensive *High School and Beyond* longitudinal database could result in some very compelling evidence about Catholic schools' contributions and value in the educational enterprise.

Coleman, Hoffer, and Kilgore (1982) analyzed the initial data from the representative sample of the total that included 28,240 seniors and 30,030 sophomores. The average private and Catholic school students' achievement test results for all subjects were higher than those of the average public school students. The higher achievement of students from private and Catholic schools was attributed to their rigorous academic programs involving structured curricula and the demanding expectations of teachers and a disciplined and ordered school environment. It was also asserted that Catholic schools were as beneficial to students of disadvantaged backgrounds as they were to the advantaged. These findings led the researchers to propose that public educational policy in the United States ought to consider providing support for a greater role for private education.

Other researchers disagreed with the findings of Coleman and his colleagues due to what they regarded as flaws in the research that involved (1) an emphasis on cross-sectional data, which was later resolved with longitudinal data, (2) selectivity bias that interferes with separating effects due to student differences from those due to the school, (3) using curriculum that is a student difference as a control variable, and (4) the achievement measures were too brief, not curriculum-specific, had ceiling effects, and were inadequate measures of high school achievement. Several issues of *Sociology of Education* were dedicated to critiques and responses to the Coleman et al. research.

By 1987, Coleman and Hoffer had access to the longitudinal data of *High School and Beyond* for 1982 and 1984. The results were higher attainment on verbal tasks and mathematics from the tenth to the twelfth grades among Catholic high school students than among those in public school. No differences were noted for science or civics. A grade-equivalent change of one year more resulted for the average Catholic school student compared to an average student attending public school for reading, vocabulary, mathematics, and writing and a slight benefit in science and civics when control for family background was included in the analysis. Verbal achievement for black and Hispanic students attending Catholic schools was more than twice that of the white students. There was a positive impact on achievement among students of lower socioeconomic origins or whose achievement level was lower at the beginning than among students with higher socioeconomic and achievement histories. In comparing private schools, Coleman and Hoffer proposed in 1987 that the unique religious environment of the Catholic school contributed to the academic success revealed in the research. *See also*: *Public and Private High Schools: The Impact of Communities*.

Further Reading: James S. Coleman and Thomas Hoffer, *Public and Private High Schools: The Impact of Communities* (New York: Basic Books, 1987); James S. Coleman, Thomas Hoffer, and Sally Kilgore, *High School Achievement: Public, Catholic, and Private Schools Compared* (New York: Basic Books, 1982); James Coleman, Thomas Hoffer, and Sally Kilgore, *Public and Private Schools. An Analysis of High School and Beyond: A National Longitudinal Study for the 1980's* (Educational Resources Information Center [ERIC] Document Reproduction Service No. ED 214 314, 1981); John J. Convey, *Catholic Schools Make a Difference: Twenty-five Years of Research* (Washington, DC: National Catholic Educational Association, 1992).

Robert B. Williams

High schools

The first American high school was founded by the Boston School Committee in 1821 as a classical English high school offering a three-year course of studies. High schools came about in several ways other than being established by the community. By the time of Boston's first high school, the proliferation of private academies across the United States was in full swing. Many of these academies would become public high schools due to the interest and needs of the community. Another trend through which high schools came into being was the offering of more advanced course work to students in the upper grades of an elementary school in an anticipation of the development of a secondary program.

Vinovskis (1985) posits that one of the earliest definitions of what a high school was to be and do is found in the 1827 legislation of the Commonwealth of Massachusetts: "[T]owns with at least five hundred families were . . . required to create an upper level public school which would teach American history, bookkeeping, geometry, surveying, and algebra, and only those cities with more than 5,000 inhabitants would be obliged to teach Latin and Greek" (p. 61). The early orientation of the high school was toward a practical curriculum that would benefit students in their pursuit of an occupation. Historians of education contend that the content of curriculum in the early high schools of New England and other communities where there was a concentration of industrial development was shaped to meet the needs of manufacturing and commerce.

During much of the nineteenth century the only thing that differentiated the high school from the elementary school was that one attended high school after elementary school. There was no standard high school curriculum, and the variety of offerings often depended on the financial resources that the community could muster to pay teachers. In the late nineteenth and early twentieth centuries many high school graduates interested in attending college were confronted with rejection because of their high school's inadequate preparatory curriculum. With the interest of the colleges and universities in the preparatory role that high schools were to have, the notion of a "standard high school" emerged. Standardization was initially implemented through an accrediting process by the University of Michigan in 1870. Beginning with the New England Association in 1885, another approach was the creation of the voluntary regional associations of colleges and secondary schools that developed standards for accreditation. Graduates of high schools that met the standards were accepted for admission by the colleges of the association. Meeting the standards meant, in some instances, reintroducing classical and liberal courses that had been abandoned for the more practical subjects when high schools were first established.

In the next phase of their development, high schools were impelled to become more inclusive, which led to the need for more comprehensive offerings that included college preparatory, clerical, commercial and business, and vocational tracks. School districts, especially in the large urban areas, found it more convenient and economical to establish district-wide vocational or technical high schools for students interested in vocational studies. Vocational high schools are also accredited, and many have outstanding academic records and even offer college preparatory course sequences.

The earliest American Catholic high schools were for boys who might be candidates for the seminary. Catholic high schools, whether for boys or girls, were influenced in their offerings by the classical and academic traditions of the Church and the religious congregations that ran them. Some comprehensive Catholic high schools were established at the diocesan level with some programs similar to those of the public schools. A recent trend among Catholic high schools has been to focus on their college preparatory role, which has received much positive recognition. *See also*: Coeducation; Co-institutional high schools; Single-sex schools.

Further Reading: Harold A. Buetow, *A History of United States Catholic Schooling* (Washington, DC: National Catholic Educational Association, 1985); R. Freeman Butts and Lawrence A. Cremin, *A History of Education in American Culture* (New York: Holt, Rinehart, and Winston, 1953); H. G. Good, *A History of American Education*, 2nd ed. (Toronto, Ontario: Macmillan, 1962); Edward A. Krug, *The Shaping of the American High School, 1880–1920* (Madison: University of Wisconsin Press, 1969); Maris A. Vinovskis, *The Origins of Public High Schools: A Reexamination of the Beverly High School Controversy* (Madison: University of Wisconsin Press, 1985).

Robert B. Williams

Hispanics/Latinos

In common parlance "Hispanic," "Latino," and "Chicano" are sometimes mistaken as synonymous. "Hispanic" is a term that refers to people who share a Spanish ancestry; this term has the broadest application in identifying various ethnic groups, including Cubans, Mexicans, Puerto Ricans, and Central and South Americans, and also people from some Caribbean islands such as the Dominicans. "Latino" generally refers to those living in the United States who speak Spanish and trace their heritage to a Latin American country. Chicano identifies people of Mexican descent who live or are citizens of the United States. People who claim Hispanic ancestry are represented by all racial groups.

The U.S. Census 2000 reports that those who identified themselves as Hispanic are represented as follows: Mexican 20,640,711 (58%); Puerto Rican 3,406,178 (10%); Cuban 1,241,685 (4%); Other Hispanic 10,017,244 (28%); for a total U.S. Hispanic/Latino population of 35,305,818.

The most pervasive descriptor that serves as a common denominator of these different groups is the use of Spanish. Within the U.S. Hispanic community is a prevalent diversity that manifests itself in various customs, socioeconomic status, races, and, to some extent, religious affiliation.

A U.S. Census report entitled *The Big Payoff: Educational Attainment and Synthetic Estimates of Work-Life Earnings* (July 2002) presents some critical statistics to set a context for understanding education in the U.S. Hispanic culture: "Among adults 25 years old and over in 2000, 88% of White non-Hispanics, 86% of Asians and Pacific Islanders, and 79% of Blacks had attained at least a high school diploma. Similarly, 28% of White non-Hispanics, 44% of Asians and Pacific Islanders, and 17% of Blacks had received a bachelor's degree. For Hispanics (who may be of any race), only 57% had a high school diploma and 11% a bachelor's degree." These statistics show an improvement in Hispanic educational attainment from previous findings, but Church leaders recognize a need for greater strategies to assist Hispanics in getting an education.

Cuban Americans are generally from professional backgrounds who fled Cuba during Castro's Cultural Revolution. Cuban Americans, by culture and tradition, have valued and supported pursuing an education through college. Puerto Ricans and Mexican Americans are often people from agricultural backgrounds who have migrated to major U.S. cities and urban areas. Coupled with possible language barriers and the need to have cash flow in a household, Puerto Ricans, Mexican Americans, and other Hispanic groups have often sacrificed a formal education to make ends meet.

The Hispanic migration to the United States differs in many ways from that of the various European groups as reflected in the history of Catholic education. There are many examples of European clergy and religious orders setting up schools as the passage to enculturation. Hispanics did not have this luxury of native clergy and religious. Hence, the access and availability of Catholic schools were limited and not eagerly promoted among Hispanics. This lack of access was exacerbated by the cost of tuition.

Statistics generated by the U.S. Census Bureau over the years have illustrated that many Hispanics live at, or below, the poverty level. While this margin has slowly diminished, it remains a fact that many Hispanic families would not be able to afford the expenditures of a Catholic education, despite a strong desire to send their children to Catholic schools. Roughly 10 percent of school-age Hispanic children would attend a Catholic school.

The *United States Catholic Elementary and Secondary School 2001–2002: The Annual Statistical Report on Schools, Enrollment, and Staffing* on ethnic groups and minorities stated that the number of minorities has more than doubled in the past thirty years. The organization's records indicated that of the total U.S. Catholic school student populations in 1970, 1980, and 2002, minorities accounted for 10.8 percent, 19.4 percent, and 26.1 percent respectively. NCEA statistics in 2002 noted that Hispanics in elementary and middle schools numbered 223,187 students, or 11.3 percent of the total elementary and middle Catholic school population of 2,616,330. Hispanic students in Catholic secondary schools numbered at 66,251, representing 10.3 percent of the 644,703 students in these schools.

The presence and culture of Hispanic students, faculty, and administrators are seen as positive contributions to Catholic education. A pressing need remains to find ways to encourage and support a family's desire to provide a Catholic education for their children. Another challenge is for schools to accommodate the rich contributions of Hispanics without assimilating them into a dominant white culture. *See also*: Cristo Rey Schools; Minority students.

Further Reading: Most Reverend Gerald Barnes, *Hispanic Ministry at the Turn of the New Millennium: A Report of the Bishops' Committee on Hispanic Affairs* (Washington, DC: National Conference of Catholic Bishops, 1999). Antonia Darder, Rodolfo D. Torres, and Henry Gutierrez, eds., *Latinos and Education: A Critical Reader* (New York: Routledge, 1997); Eugene E. Garcia, *Hispanic Education in the United States* (Lanham, MD: Rowman and Littlefield, 2001); Suzanne Hall and Carleen Reck, eds., *Integral Education: A Response to the Hispanic Presence* (Washington, DC: National Catholic Educational Association, 1987); Dale McDonald, PhD, *United States Catholic Elementary and Secondary School 2001–2002: The Annual Statistical Report on Schools, Enrollment, and Staffing* (Washington, DC: National Catholic Educational Association, 2002).

Michael P. Caruso, SJ

Holaind, Rene I. (1836–1906)

Jesuit professor of ethics at Woodstock College, Maryland, and author of *The Parent First*, a pamphlet in response to Dr. Thomas Bouquillon's controversial education pamphlet *Education: To Whom Does It Belong?*

During the 1890s the American Catholic Church was gripped by a controversy over parochial schools and the right of the state to educate. Archbishop Corrigan of New York appealed to Rev. R. I. Holaind, SJ, a Jesuit scholar, to write a rejoinder to Dr. Thomas Bouquillon's pamphlet, *Education: To Whom Does It Belong?* In three days, Holaind produced a vigorous response to Dr. Bouquillon's pamphlet. The pressure on Rev. Holaind to respond quickly emphasized anxieties about a general meeting of the American archbishops the following week. There were concerns that Bouquillon's reputation as the major moral theologian of the time would allow his position to prevail. Many, including Corrigan, believed that if that happened, Catholic schools would suffer a staggering blow.

Understanding the urgency, Holaind wrote a powerful rebuttal entitled, *The Parent First*, which stated a counterproposal to Bouquillon's acknowledgment of the state's right to educate. Holaind built his rebuttal on six objections. First, he refused to grant a non-Christian state the right to educate. Second, the state educates only when it is unavoidably necessary. The state may not educate simply because it serves the state's purposes. Third, he restated the traditional position that the Church and parents held the right to educate. Fourth, he questioned whether Dr. Bouquillon clearly gave the

Church authority over moral teaching. Fifth, Holaind conceded that the state may educate when either parents or the Church makes the request. Sixth, the state has no right to control instruction in nonstate schools since this would take away the parents' and Church's right to establish and control their own schools. Holaind drew heavily from European countries to provide other models of Catholic education for the American scene. He was criticized by Archbishop Ireland, leader of Bouquillon's position, for not recognizing how different the American context was from that of Europe.

Holaind argued his position passionately and quickly, which led to more criticism of Dr. Bouquillon's argument. *The American Ecclesiastical Review* and *The Catholic World* became the venue for the continuing debate. Eventually, the controversy migrated to the secular press. Bouquillon's supporters argued that the Jesuits were out to discredit him. The controversy was forwarded to Rome for examination.

The *American Ecclesiastical Review* allowed Rev. Holaind to have a final word. It published an article wherein Holaind matched argument points in a parallel format. Unfortunately, Dr. Bouquillon was not permitted a similar opportunity. In November 1892, Archbishop Francesco Satolli, special representative from Rome to the United States, proposed Fourteen Propositions for a settlement. Fundamentally, the fourteen points, presented with papal approval, supported Archbishop Ireland's position and vindicated Bouquillon. Grumbling continued until Pope Leo XIII issued a letter reiterating the importance of Catholic schooling.

Rene Holaind was born July 27, 1836, in Moulins, France. He entered the Jesuit novitiate at Avignon, France, in 1851. Later he taught at Avignon and Dôle, France. In 1861 he immigrated to the United States. He furthered his education at Boston College and Spring Hill College in Mobile, Alabama. After completing his studies, he then taught for thirteen years in Alabama and Louisiana in Jesuit schools. He also served as a parish priest in Selma, Alabama, for five years.

From 1885 until 1898 Rev. Holaind taught ethics and jurisprudence at Woodstock College in Maryland. During this time he wrote his famous education pamphlet. He also briefly served as a chaplain in the U.S. Army. He was a professor of ethics at Georgetown University in Washington, DC, until 1905. While at Georgetown he authored *Ownership and Natural Right* in 1887, in which he defended the right to own private property. He also wrote a textbook on jurisprudence, *Natural Law and Legal Practice*, which contained a series of lectures he had given at Georgetown. Holaind studied issues related to taxation, capital and labor organizations, strikes, and boycotts. He based his solutions to labor problems on the principles of Christian philosophy. He retired to Woodstock, Maryland, where he died in 1906. *See also*: Bouquillon, Thomas; Catholic School Question, The; *Parent First, The*.

Further Reading: Francis A. Barnum, "Holaind, Rene, SJ, Papers of" (1909), Box 2, Folder 3, Georgetown University Library, Washington, DC; Thomas Bouquillon, *Education: To Whom Does It Belong?* (Baltimore: John Murphy, 1892); Patrick J. Dooley, *Woodstock and Its Makers* (Woodstock, MD: College Press, 1927); John Tracy Ellis, *The Life of James Cardinal Gibbons*, 2 vols. (Milwaukee: Bruce, 1952); Rene I. Holaind, *The Parent First* (New York: Benziger Brothers, 1891); Thomas T. McAvoy, *The Great Crises in American Catholic History, 1895–1900* (Chicago: Henry Regnery, 1957).

Merylann J. "Mimi" Schuttloffel

Holy Office, The Congregation of the

The Congregation of the Holy Office is an administrative office of the Catholic Church whose purpose is to promote and safeguard the integrity of the Catholic Church's teaching in the areas of faith and morals. The administrative office has undergone several name changes throughout its existence and is currently known as the Congregation for the Doctrine of the Faith.

The Congregation of the Holy Office is the oldest of the nine congregations of the Roman Curia. Its origin dates back to the Roman Inquisition, a tribunal created by Pope Innocent III at the beginning of the thirteenth century to investigate the Albigesian heresy in the south of France. Pope Paul III is credited with formally establishing the congregation in his constitution *Licet ab Initio* (1542). The constitution declared the Roman Inquisition to be the supreme tribunal of the whole world whose specific function was to be the prosecution of heresies, the proscription of books, and the nominating of inquisitors for the universal Church. The original congregation comprised six cardinals, including Cardinal Carafa, who later became Pope Paul IV and who produced the first index of forbidden books in 1559.

Recognizing the need for administrative organizations to expedite the governance of the Church, Pope Sixtus V issued his constitution *Immensa Aeterni Dei* (1588), which formally created fifteen congregations including the Congregation for the Holy Inquisition. Pius X, in his constitution *Sapienti Consilio* (1908), identified fourteen congregations, clarified the competency of the congregations, and changed the name of the Congregation of the Holy Inquisition to the Congregation of the Holy Office. Later, Pope Paul VI sought to reform and modernize the entire Roman Curia in his constitution *Integrae Servandae* (1965), which among other things changed the name of the Holy Office to the Congregation for the Doctrine of the Faith. Regarding the function of the congregation, the document states, "Since charity casts out fear, the safeguarding of the faith is better taken care of now by fulfilling the function of promoting sound doctrine. This will result in the correction of errors and at the same time will gently call back to the right path those who are going astray and will provide the heralds of the Gospel with new strength" (Paul VI, 1965, paragraph 7). The document identified the jurisdiction of the congregation to include all questions touching upon doctrine of faith and morals, it opened the door for the consultation with regional bishops in examining new doctrines and opinions, it identified an author's right to defend his or her writings under examination by the congregation before the congregation may issue a decision, it established a body of consultors chosen on the basis of their expertise in a particular field (especially from university faculty), and it provided for the addition of others to the body of consultors whenever the matter being treated required additional expertise. Pope John Paul II added two significant functions of the congregation in his Apostolic Constitution on the Roman Curia, *Pastor Bonus* (1988): fostering studies "so that the understanding of the faith may grow and a response in the light of the faith may be given to new questions arising from the progress of the sciences or human culture" and assisting bishops "in carrying out their office as authentic teachers and doctors of the faith" (John Paul II, 1988, article 48).

The number of congregations, their authority, and their names have changed over time in response to the pressing needs and circumstances of the Church during a particular era. All decisions by the congregations require pontifical approval unless the Pope previously granted special authority to the congregation. At one time there were as many as nineteen congregations, while at present there are only nine.

The congregation is presently composed of between twenty and twenty-five members who include cardinals, archbishops, and bishops from fourteen different countries under the prefecture of Cardinal Joseph Ratzinger of Germany. Another thirty to forty officials, secretaries, and staff currently offer permanent service to the congregation. The congregation is also assisted by twenty-five to thirty consultors from several different countries who are typically professors from various pontifical universities and who are experts in different ecclesiastical fields of study. The Congregation for the Doctrine of the Faith also hosts a visit by the bishops of the world when they make their *ad limina apostolorum* visit to the Pope every five years. This provides an opportunity for an exchange of information and an analysis of problems regarding the doctrinal situation in their various countries and a search for joint solutions to these doctrinal questions. Also, the congregation promotes symposia or scientific meetings on problems that have doctrinal relevance and develops initiatives for the diffusion of sound doctrine. It also works together with the Vatican Publishing House to publish texts of its documents and articles relevant to its work. The prefect of the congregation also serves as the president of the Pontifical Biblical Commission and the International Theological Commission.

Critics note that the congregation's roots date back to the Inquisition, and while it has undergone name changes and has altered its focus in recent years, it still thwarts the free flow of intellectual discourse by issuing a warning (*monitum*) about certain writings and has called for the removal of theologians such as Hans Kung and Charles Curran from positions within institutions of higher learning. Proponents counter that the Church as a function of its teaching authority (Magisterium) has an obligation to articulate the norms of orthodoxy within the Church and to safeguard the faithful from confusion caused by those teaching false doctrines in the name of the Church. *See also*: Congregation for the Doctrine of the Faith, The.

Further Reading: *Annuario Pontifico* (Rome: Libreria Editrice Vaticana, 2001); Charles G. Herbermann, Edward A. Pace, Conde B. Pallen, Thomas J. Shahan, and John J. Wynne, eds., *The Catholic Encyclopedia* (New York: Robert Appleton, 1912); Thomas C. Hunt, Ellis A. Joseph, and Ronald J. Nuzzi, eds., *Handbook of Research on Catholic Education* (Westport, CT; Greenwood Press, 2001); *Integrae Servandae*, L'Osservature Romano (April 14, 1965): 12–23; John Paul II, Congregation for the Doctrine of the Faith (Rome, 2002).

John T. James

Home schooling

The National Center for Education Statistics (NCES) reported in *Homeschooling in the United States: 1999* that in the spring of 1999, an estimated 850,000 students, or approximately 2 percent of children ages 5–17 were being home-schooled. Approximately 20 percent of these students also attended a public or private school part-time. Home schooling is legal in all states; requirements for reporting and documentation vary from state to state.

Home-schooled students are distributed across grade levels in approximately the same proportion as students who attend public and private schools. While home schooling may have begun as a trend among white, middle-class, Christian parents and has been pursued for religious reasons, the most recent research indicates that home schooling is becoming more reflective of American demographics and is being chosen for a wider variety of reasons.

Notable characteristics of parents who choose to home-school include two-parent family configurations, only one parent working outside the home, family sizes of three or more children, and parents who have earned at least a bachelor's degree. Religious reasons were mentioned by approximately 40 percent of parents as a motivation for home-schooling their children.

Trend data reported by Lines in "Home schooling" indicate that the rapid increases in families choosing to home-school may be slowing to rates of approximately 10 percent per year in the late 1990s compared to increases of approximately 25 percent earlier in the decade. At the same time, public attitudes toward home schooling, reported in the *31st Annual Phi Delta Kappa/Gallup Poll*, reflect increasing acceptance of home schooling and willingness to commit public funds to assist home schoolers if standards of educational quality are met. Current legal issues focus on issues of access to public resources such as programs and materials. There has also been a significant increase in commercial enterprises marketing materials and resources to home schoolers and an increase in the number of support organizations devoted to assisting home schoolers and advocating for their rights.

Data on the achievement of home-schooled students indicate performance on standardized tests at higher levels than students educated in public or private schools. However, it is not possible to determine the extent to which such data are representative of all home-schooled students. Concerns about the social development of children who are home-schooled are frequently expressed. However, data show that many home-schooled students participate in extracurricular activities, Scouting, church groups, and support organizations that bring them into social interaction with age-mates.

No data could be found that estimate the number of Catholic parents who choose to home-school their children or describe their characteristics. However, anecdotal data indicate that Catholic home schooling is a significant phenomenon in Catholic education. Catholic home schooling is based on the fundamental principle of parents as primary educators. The right and responsibility of parents as educators of their children have been consistently affirmed in church documents, including the *Catechism of the Catholic Church* (#2223) and Pope John Paul II's apostolic exhortation *Familiaris Consortio* (#36), as well as the Second Vatican Council's *Declaration on Christian Education* (#3). Church documents refer to parents' right and duty to educate in profound terms such as "inalienable" and "incapable of being entirely delegated to or usurped by others."

Despite the fundamental nature of this teaching, there have been conflicts between Catholic parents who home-school and church officials. Many of these conflicts relate to sacramental preparation and access to services from Catholic education institutions. These issues have been raised by Catholic home-school support organizations for attention.

Many dioceses have issued guidelines regarding home schooling, especially related to religious education in general and sacramental preparation in particular. Reactions to these guidelines by parents who choose to home-school range from appreciative to adversarial. Some view such guidelines as helpful clarifications of rights and responsibilities, whereas others view them as attempts to usurp their parental rights given by God and attested to by the Pope and church documents.

Just as commercial enterprises and support organizations have proliferated for home schooling in general, a similar phenomenon exists in Catholic home schooling. Several publishers offer materials designed especially for Catholic home schooling, and both formal and informal networks of Catholic home schoolers have been established. *See also*: Parental rights; Parents as primary educators.

Further Reading: Patricia M. Lines, "Homeschooling," *ERIC Digest* 151, http://eric. uoregon.edu/publications/digests/digest151.html. Accessed September 8, 2002; National Center for Education Statistics, *Homeschooling in the United States: 1999* (Washington, DC: U.S. Department of Education, 2001); Brian D. Ray, *Strengths of Their Own—Home Schoolers across America: Academic Achievement, Family Characteristics, and Longitudinal Traits* (Salem, OR: National Home Education Research Institute, 1997); Roman Catholic Diocese of Pittsburgh, "Faith Education in the Home" (Pittsburgh: Roman Catholic Diocese of Pittsburgh, 1997) http://www.diopitt.org/faith.htm. Accessed November 18, 2002; Lowell C. Rose and Alec M. Gallup, "The 31st Annual Phi Delta Kappa/Gallup Poll of the Public's Attitudes toward the Public Schools," *Phi Delta Kappan* 81, 1 (September 1999): 41–56; Lawrence Rudner, "Scholastic Achievement and Demographic Characteristics of Home School Students in 1998," *Education Policy Analysis Archives* 8 (March 1999) http://epaa.asu.edu/epaa/v7n8/. Accessed August 1, 2002.

Karen L. Tichy

Hughes, John (1797–1864)

John Hughes was born in Ireland in 1797. As a youth he worked as a gardener to help pay his educational expenses to become a priest. Ordained in 1826, he became Bishop Kenrick's right-hand man in Philadelphia, taking the lead in establishing a trustee-less church in 1831 and in working for the founding of Catholic schools in that city. Very early in his career he faced the reality that the United States was a "Protestant country."

In 1838 he was named bishop of New York, where he soon became the champion of the Church's educational rights. The Catholic community was impoverished, so Hughes went to Europe seeking funds to assist him in providing schools for his people. He contended that Catholics should receive their fair share of the common school fund, since they paid taxes. Failing that, they should be exempt from taxes for the public schools.

The Public School Society replaced all denominational schools in New York City in 1824 with the exception of those dedicated to orphans. Allegedly nonsectarian, the schools of the society were Protestant in governance, personnel, textbooks, and practices. In 1840 Hughes delivered "An Address of the Roman Catholics to Their Fellow Citizens of the City and State of New York." In this document Hughes argued that to teach morality without religion inevitably would result in practical infidelity or indifference to religion. The public schools of this sort, he averred, would draw the minds of children away from the religion of their parents. Denominational schools would teach the same secular education as the public schools did, with equal benefit to the state. Additionally, by teaching morality based on religion, they would make their students better citizens than could the public schools. Hughes was rebuffed by the New York City Common Council in his request for funds.

He subsequently took his appeal to the state level. With the cooperation of Gov. William Seward, Hughes sought state support for denominational schools. When that attempt also failed, Hughes intensified his efforts on behalf of parochial schools supported by Catholics themselves. He recruited several religious orders of women to staff the schools, informed pastors of his maxim that building the school came before erecting the church, mobilized the laity into parochial school supporters, and established a diocesan-wide system of parochial schools. Catholic school enrollment grew from 5,000 in 1840 to 20,000 in 1870, and schools moved from church basements to school buildings.

As a result of his efforts in New York, the Public School Society of New York City lost control of public education in that city. The public schools then became "religionless," no longer nonsectarian Protestant as they had been when the school controversy flared up in 1840. They became, and remained, secular, or as some termed, "godless."

Hughes is often credited with launching the parochial school movement that grew rapidly in the nineteenth century. When other bishops failed in their attempts to obtain public funds for their schools, they joined the movement. The concept of the Catholic parish school was supported by the First Plenary Council of Baltimore in 1852 and received the seal of episcopal approval in the Third Plenary Council of Baltimore in 1884. Some Catholic authors have called Hughes the father of Catholic education in the United States. Hughes, who died in 1864, was an aggressive leader of his flock who showed that the Roman Catholic Church could exist in a democracy. He has been said to be the model for what America expected of a Catholic bishop for a century after his death. *See also*: Bishops, in the nineteenth-century conflict over Catholic schools; Parental rights.

Further Reading: Harold A. Buetow, *Of Singular Benefit: The Story of U.S. Catholic Education* (New York: Macmillan, 1970); James A. Burns, *The Growth and Development of the Catholic School System in the United States* (New York: Benziger Brothers, 1912); James A. Burns, *The Principles, Origin, and Establishment of the Catholic School System in the United States* (New York: Benziger Brothers, 1912); John R. G. Hassard, *Life of the Most Reverend John Hughes, D.D., First Bishop of New York* (New York: D. Appleton, 1866); Vincent P. Lannie, *Public Money and Parochial Education: Bishop Hughes, Governor Seward, and the New York School Controversy* (Cleveland: Press of Case Western Reserve, 1968); Richard Shaw, *Dagger John: The Unquiet Life and Times of Archbishop John Hughes of New York* (New York: Paulist Press, 1977).

Thomas C. Hunt

I

✦

Immigration/Immigrants

The system of Catholic schools in the United States that exists today is largely the result of the American Church's response to the needs of Catholic immigrants from European countries in the late nineteenth and early twentieth centuries. The future of Catholic schools in the twenty-first century in all likelihood will be shaped by the American Church's response to needs of new immigrant populations.

From colonial times to 1830, schooling in the United States was closely connected to churches. Both Protestant and Catholic churches established schools to provide for the moral formation of their children and a means to educate children in their particular beliefs. Education was essentially an informal local activity. During this period Catholics were a small minority of the total population—1 percent in 1800 (Hunt, 2000).

As early as 1830, the number of Catholic immigrants had become a problem for the Protestant majority. The influx of people speaking different languages, espousing different religious beliefs, and lacking knowledge of the newfound democracy was perceived as a threat. The suppression of the French Revolution by Napoleon raised doubts about the strength of the fledgling American democracy. A systematic means of transmitting the values of democracy to future generations was needed (Bryk, Lee, and Holland, 1993). Formal schooling was the answer.

Horace Mann espoused the "common school" as the means of providing education to the children of the nation. Mann envisioned children from all religions, social classes, and cultural backgrounds educated "in common." The common school was the means to provide intellectual, social, and moral education necessary to sustain the democracy amid a growing diversity of people.

Since education was primarily viewed as moral formation, it was impossible to separate religion from education in the common school. How to provide moral and religious education in a school populated with children from a variety of religious traditions was problematic. Mann's answer was to develop a nondenominational approach to teach beliefs and values common to all religions. While intriguing in theory, the approach proved impossible in practice. The beliefs and values of the Protestant majority colored the religious content and moral instruction of "the common school." Reading from the Protestant version of the Bible, singing Protestant hymns, and reciting Protestant prayers were intolerable practices for Catholic immigrants. For immigrants to acquiesce to such practices was tantamount to a denial of faith (Bryk, Lee, and Holland, 1993).

The mid-nineteenth century and early twentieth centuries brought mass immigration of people from European countries. Over nine million immigrants, the majority of whom were Catholic, came to the United States between 1880 and the start of World War I (Bryk, Lee, and Holland, 1993). Strong national loyalties developed among these immigrants. People from the same country put aside provincial and village differences and clustered together to preserve their language, culture, and religious heritage (Meagher, 2000).

The public school, offspring of the common school, was a hostile place for Catholic immigrant children. Ethnic Catholic schools were established as an alternative to public schools. They were a safe haven where cultural identity and Catholic faith could be cherished while immigrant children and adults gradually acculturated to a new country. These ethnic Catholic schools led to the establishment and expansion of a system of Catholic schools throughout the United States that is unprecedented in the history of the global church. At the time of peak enrollment (1965), Catholic schools enrolled 12 percent of the school-age population of the United States (Bryk, Lee, and Holland, 1993).

The bishops of the United States, though not of one accord, gradually developed the position expressed in the watershed directive of the Third Plenary Council of Baltimore in 1884. This directive mandated Catholic parents to send their children to Catholic schools and required bishops and pastors to build a school within two years at or near every parish that did not already have a school. The mandate was never fully achieved but did create a climate that fostered rapid growth in the number of schools and enrollment of Catholic children.

With the advent of World War I, an attitude of ethnic intolerance developed in the country. Along with this intolerance was a strong anti-Catholic prejudice. Catholic schools were viewed as institutions that eroded the values of the American enterprise—teaching languages other than English and cultural values of other countries. Some states passed laws requiring compulsory attendance at public schools. In states with such laws, Catholic schools were essentially prohibited. In 1925, the Supreme Court decision *Pierce v. The Society of Sisters* ruled such laws unconstitutional.

To counter the growing anti-American suspicion against Catholic schools and the move of government to control all of education, the American bishops initiated efforts to position Catholic schools as schools that educated children "for God and Country." With these initiatives, immigrant ethnic schools became more American (Bryk, Lee, and Holland, 1993) and Catholic schooling became more systematic.

In the 1960s, American Catholics came of age and were among the most powerful and influential members of society. Catholic schools were no longer needed to provide a safe haven for a minority population. Ironically, at this time Catholic schools started to decline in number and enrollment. In the last decade of the twentieth century and early years of the twenty-first century, the rate of school closings declined, and enrollments stabilized.

A challenge for the Church at the beginning of the twenty-first century is in some ways similar to that of the start of the twentieth century. The United States is experiencing an explosion of Spanish-speaking immigrants from Latin America whose culture and tradition are Catholic. Likewise, there is an increase in immigrants from Asian countries. Will the American Catholic Church be as responsive to these immigrants as it was to the European immigrants a century ago? What place do Catholic schools play in helping these new Americans make the transition to their new land while continuing to hold onto their cultural heritage and Catholic faith? The challenges and opportunities may be as great today as they were in the past. *See also*: Americanization; American Protective Association (APA); Ethnicity (and parish schools); Know-Nothing Party.

Further Reading: Anthony S. Bryk, Valerie E. Lee, and Peter B. Holland, *Catholic Schools and the Common Good* (Cambridge: Harvard University Press, 1993); Jessica A. Greene and Joseph M. O'Keefe, "Enrollment in Catholic Schools in the United States," in Thomas C. Hunt, Ellis A. Joseph, and Ronald J. Nuzzi, eds., *Handbook of Research on Catholic Education* (Westport, CT: Greenwood Press, 2001): 161–182; Thomas C. Hunt, "The History of Catholic Schools in the United States: An Overview," in Thomas C. Hunt, Thomas E. Oldenski, and Theodore J. Wallace, eds., *Catholic School Leadership: An Invitation to Lead* (New York: Falmer Press, 2000): 34–58; Timothy Meagher, "Ethnic, Catholic, White: Changes in the Identity of European American Catholics," in James Youniss, John J. Convey, and Jeffery A. McLellan, eds., *The Catholic Character of Catholic Schools* (Notre Dame, IN: University of Notre Dame Press, 2000): 190–218.

Frank X. Savage

Inclusion

Defining inclusion as a place, for example, the regular classroom with support services brought to the student, is too narrow a focus. Inclusion is not a place; it is an attitude. It is an acceptance and a respect for students who learn differently. Acceptance of different learners means, for example, that the teacher expects to have a range of reading levels in the classroom and plans lessons accordingly. Respect for students who learn differently means that the teacher creates activities that provide students, above-grade level, on-grade level, and below-grade level, an opportunity to access information and to demonstrate what they know at their respective skill levels. All students are not expected to read the same texts, do the same assignments, or complete the same assessments unless they are appropriate for that student based on previous achievement, interests, and abilities.

Where the student receives instruction and what supports are provided are student-dependent. A student with a reading problem could receive specialized service for reading and be in the regular classroom for instruction in the content area (e.g., social studies, science, health). The content area teacher, knowing that reading the text is not something the student can do well, would identify other materials such as videos, reference books at a lower reading level, and/or guided notes that would allow the student access to the content covered in the textbook. On the other hand, a student with a written language problem could receive all instruction in the regular classroom but need adaptations for written assignments. For this student, the classroom teacher might use such strategies as multiple choice and short answers rather than essay tests, have the student provide an oral or pictorial response rather than written, or use word processing technology when a written response cannot be avoided. Both of these teachers are inclusive. They design activities for the demonstration of learning that are compatible with, and respectful of, the student's learning strengths.

Successful inclusion is a pervasive attitude that reflects the culture of the building and the teaching/learning practices. It requires that the principal sets the standard for the building and that the teachers working with parents and others who know the student as a learner make the classroom accommodations.

The principal can support inclusion in the following ways:

- Attitude—Support of students with special learning needs is measured by how closely the resources allocated for special learners and general learners are equitable to the needs of the respective students. The principal needs to make sure that the focus is always on what each student needs. The same, sometimes identified as fair, is not always equitable or appropriate.

- Lead by Example—Remembering that not everything will work, be willing to fail, regroup, and try a different approach. Let the staff know that failure is something to be learned from, not something to be punished. The principal can empower the staff by establishing child study teams or teacher assistance teams to explore learning and behavioral accommodations for individual students.

- Collaborate—Work with teachers and parents on building a philosophy of inclusion. Principals who know the needs of their students don't have a difficult time setting policy that allows for alternative grading systems or preferential scheduling of classes.

- Staff Development—Since students with special learning needs are not the usual student, teachers need to expand their repertoire of teaching/learning strategies. The principal needs to acknowledge, by providing staff development opportunities, that teachers may not be prepared to teach every special learner but that they are expected to acquire the skills needed to serve the students enrolled in the school.

Classroom teachers can support inclusion by providing accommodations in the following ways:

- Input—Use videos, computer programs, field trips, job shadowing, and visual aids to support active learning and to augment or supplant the textbook.

- Output—Have students demonstrate understanding and knowledge by writing a song, telling a story, designing a poster or brochure, or performing an experiment as an alternative to the traditional test or written paper.

- Size—Reduce the length of report to be written or spoken, reduce the number of references needed, or reduce the number of problems to be solved by the student with language or motor-processing difficulties.

- Time—Individualize a timeline for project completion or allow more time for test taking for students slow at processing information but capable of learning the information.

- Difficulty—Tier assignments (advanced, on-grade level, and below-grade level) so the outcome is the same but with varying degrees of concreteness and complexity.

Specific programs such as *Dreams Are Free*, Diocese of Venice, Florida; *FIRE*, Archdiocese of Kansas City, Kansas; and *Success Central*, Catholic Central in Springfield, Ohio, exemplify models of inclusive practice in Catholic elementary and secondary schools. Others of inclusive thinking are the Archdiocese of Washington in Washington, D.C., with a director of inclusive education and the University of Dayton in Dayton, Ohio, which produces a quarterly newsletter, *Network for Inclusive Education*, and holds an annual conference, *Inclusive Catholic Education*, in October. *See also*: Special needs.

Further Reading: Pat Carter, ed., "Spirit of Full Inclusion Thrives at Purcell Marian," *NICE Inclusion Quarterly* 1, 4 (1997): 3; Council for Exceptional Children, *Implementing IDEA: A Guide for Principals* (Arlington, VA: Council for Exceptional Children, 2001); Antoinette Dudek, *Is There Room for Me?* (Washington, DC: National Catholic Educational Association, 1998); James McLeskey and Nancy L. Waldron, *Inclusive Schooling in Action: Making Differences Ordinary* (Alexandria, VA: ASCD, 2000); H. Roberta Weaver and Mary F. Landers, guest eds., "Focus Section," *Catholic Education: A Journal of Inquiry and Practice* 3, 3 (2000): 325–396.

Mary Frances Landers and Roberta Weaver

Index of Forbidden Books, The

The Index of Forbidden Books constituted a list of books identified and forbidden by the Church because their contents were determined to be in conflict with, or a danger to, faith and morals. In 1559, Pope Paul IV published the first *Index*. This explicit *Index* was maintained by the Church for slightly over 400 years until 1966, when the Sacred Congregation for the Doctrine of the Faith announced the cessation of any further editions of the *Index*.

The enthusiasm of believers to divest themselves of books whose contents were in conflict with faith is encountered for the first time during St. Paul's ministry at Ephesus. *The Acts of the Apostles* documents: "A good many of those who formerly practiced magic collected their books and burnt them publicly" (19:19). Providing guidance for believers by preparing lists of texts as edifying and acceptable or banning others that were not was initiated very early in the history of the Church. The earliest precursor document in a series of such documents was the *Muratorian Fragment* or *Canon*, dating from the second century, which was a list of the recognized Scriptures of the New Testament. The *Thalia* by Arius, whose teachings were the basis of the heresy of Arianism, was the very first book to be censured by the Church at the Council of Nicaea in A.D. 325. Betten (1909/1920) observes, "[I]ndeed, at all times the condemnation of a heresy by the Church entailed the prohibition of the works propagating it" (p. 7). Prior to the fifteenth century, councils and Popes censored and prohibited many books whose contents were in conflict with orthodox Catholic teaching. By the fifteenth century, Johann Gutenberg's press with movable type resulted in an extraordinary increase in the production of books and tracts. This influenced the Church to require that books and other printed materials be submitted for review to local ecclesiastical authorities. By 1559, Pope Paul IV responded to the proliferation of what has been referred to as "heretical" and "pernicious" publications by having them scrutinized and listed as unacceptable items on the first *Roman Index of Forbidden Books*.

The *Index* provided guidance for educators and families to avoid books whose contents were a danger to faith and morals until it was discontinued in 1966. In discontinuing the *Index*, the Church did not abandon its concern about books that might pose a danger to faith or morals. The responsibility of the Church to scrutinize writings and publications regarding faith and morals continues to be affirmed in the present *Code of Canon Law*. Canon 823:1 states: "In order to safeguard the integrity of faith and morals, pastors of the Church . . . have the duty and the right to condemn writings which harm true faith or good morals." Further delineation of the Church's accountability for writings is developed in Canons 825:1, 826:3, 827:1, 827:2, 830:2, and 831:1.

By the middle of the twentieth century, books and publications that had constituted the primary means of mass social communication were overwhelmed by mass media in the form of radio and television. In 1963, prior to the discontinuation of the *Index*, Vatican Council II issued the Decree on the Means of Social Communication (*Inter Mirifica*) that relates to "the press, the cinema, radio, television and others of a like nature" (p. 283). This decree explicates the responsibility that the Church, clergy, and the laity have regarding the use of mass media. Parents are especially reminded to protect children from media that might endanger faith and morals.

In 1971, the Pontifical Council for the Instruments of Social Communication issued the Pastoral Instruction on the Means of Social Communication (*Communio et Progressio*), which "sets out basic doctrinal principles and general pastoral guidelines. It carefully refrains from going into minute details on a subject which is continually changing and developing and which varies so much according to time and place" (p. 294). This instruction includes guidance for developing the ability to make informed decisions about the content of media. Since the discontinuation of the *Index*, the trend of the Church's instruction has focused on the importance of the individual's fidelity to conscience in the face of challenges to faith and morals. Jelen, citing Pope John Paul II's encyclical *Vertatis Splendor*, notes that "now as ever, the primary business of Catholicism is the shaping and development of individual consciences . . . to maximize human freedom, understood as voluntary obedience to God's law" (p. 49). *See also*: Holy Office, The Congregation of the.

Further Reading: Francis S. Betten, *The Roman Index of Forbidden Books* (St. Louis, MO: B. Herder Book Co., 1909/1920); Canon Law Society of America, *Code of Canon Law: Latin-English Edition* (Washington, DC: Canon Law Society of America, 1983); Ted G. Jelen, "Catholicism, Conscience, and Censorship," in Daniel A. Stout and Judith M. Buddenbaum, eds., *Religion and Mass Media: Audiences and Adaptations* (Thousand Oaks, CA: Sage, 1996); Pontifical Council for the Instruments of Social Communication, *Communio et Progressio*, January 29, 1971 [Pastoral Instruction on the Means of Social Communication], in Austin Flannery, ed., *Vatican Council II, Volume 1: The Conciliar and Post Conciliar Documents*, new rev. ed. (Northport, NY: Costello, 1996); Vatican Council II, *Inter Mirifica*, December 4, 1963 [Decree on the Means of Social Communication], in Austin Flannery, ed., *Vatican Council II, Volume 1: The Conciliar and Post Conciliar Documents*, new rev. ed. (Northport, NY: Costello, 1996).

Robert B. Williams

Indoctrination

Indoctrination is a teaching approach to moral education often used by teachers, and often by parents, to pass on to the next generation specific parental, societal, and religious norms, the differences between right and wrong. Sometimes referred to as "telling," indoctrination employs lecture, memorization, admonition, correction, punishment, repetition, praise, and approval. It includes didactic instruction, and it is at times given in a formal setting, but it may also be transmitted informally. It is a focused exposure to tradition and cultural heritage with a view to imitation. Thus, modeling, for example, may also be indoctrination.

Indoctrination does not ordinarily use such practices as critical thinking, discernment, discussion, and dialogue about the possibility that basic values held by society may change. Indoctrination looks to authority for guidelines and stresses the importance of standing firm and without question to what one was taught.

During the twentieth century the term "indoctrination" acquired a negative connotation associated with anti-intellectualism and close-mindedness. As an approach to moral instruction, it is often dismissed by other schools in the field, particularly the developmentalists, who consider it excessive socialization and believe it to be opposed to interactionism and eventually to internalization. Kohlberg himself, however, later modified his views on the negativity of indoctrination declaring that while stage development is essential to moral maturity, it is not the only aim of moral development. Specific values content must also be taught, he claimed, and teachers do this at some level by indoctrination. Kohlberg wrote, "I no longer hold these negative views of indoctrinative moral education and now believe that the concepts guiding moral education must be partly indoctrinative" (Barry Chazan, *Contemporary Approaches to Moral Education: Analyzing Alternative Theories* [New York: Teachers College Press, 1985], p. 83). The philosopher Richard Peters (*Authority, Responsibility and Education* [London: George Allen and Ubwin, 1973]) considered an indoctrinative approach to be "a special type of instruction . . . [that] consists in getting children to accept a fixed body of rules in such a way that they are incapacitated from adopting a critical attitude toward them" (p. 155). The main distinction, for Peters, was not on what was taught, but the way in which it was taught. It is a difficult distinction for teachers and requires great care and delicate execution but seems particularly important for Catholic educators.

This is the educational belief of the Catholic Church, which has long used indoctrination as a means of introducing commonly accepted moral teachings to the young. It views indoctrination as one of the essentials of teaching the young of a certain age, intellectual maturity, and in a particular stage of development. Philip Jackson's now famous concept of "hidden curriculum" (*Life in the Classroom* [New York: Holt, Rinehart, and Winston, 1968]) is indoctrination. The curriculum is called "hidden" because it is not explicit, but it is a value nonetheless and teaches effectively, in its own way. Developmentalists have frequently lauded the "hidden curriculum" when it meets the criteria of what they call "moral atmosphere."

Used without care and attention to appropriateness, a stress on indoctrination and didactic instruction in general can result in the teacher becoming authoritarian. Instead of fostering moral development in the young, an authoritarian teacher inhibits its growth. There is a vast difference, however, between authoritarianism and authority. The scholars in the field of moral development do not suggest that the teacher abdicate authority, but rather that the teacher exercise authority in a way that encourages critical thinking on the part of the student. There are several ways in which the teacher may accomplish this. The nonauthoritarian teacher will, for example, help students see the inadequacy of their moral thinking, rethink a situation, and come up with a better solution. This kind of teacher may teach didactically, but she or he also supports students in the use of skills necessary to improve their responses to moral issues and restructure their thinking about moral dilemmas.

The nonauthoritarian teacher is also attentive to consistency in the student's suggestions. The ability to illustrate this flaw in the student's moral thinking takes skillful questioning. The teaching act also requires the skills of active listening and the habitual practice on the part of the teacher in using the student's own thinking to demonstrate inadequacy and inconsistencies in moral thinking.

While passing on factual data, the nonauthoritarian teacher might encourage cooperative learning, that is, students working together toward a common goal. The give-and-take of shared learning creates natural disequilibrium and raises a felt need to resolve conflict. The teacher might teach didactically, while at the same time she or he builds a social community so necessary for moral development. The point is that didactic teaching, even indoctrination, and moral development are not mutually exclusive in the classroom. It is authoritarianism that inhibits moral growth. *See also*: Moral education, history of.

Further Reading: Lawrence Kohlberg, "Revisions in the Theory and Practice of Moral Development," in William Damon, ed., *Moral Development: New Directions for Child Development* (San Francisco: Jossey-Bass, 1978): 83–88; Lawrence Kohlberg, "Stage and Sequence: The Cognitive Developmental Approach to Socialization," in David A. Goslin, ed., *Handbook of Socialization Theory and Research* (Chicago: Rand McNally, 1969): 347–480; William M. Kurtines and Jacob L. Gewirtz, *Moral Development: An Introduction* (Needham Heights, MA: Allyn and Bacon, 1995); Joseph Reimer, Diana P. Paolitto, and Richard Hersh, *Promoting Moral Growth: From Piaget to Kohlberg* (Prospects Heights, IL: Waveland Press, 1983); Mary Peter Traviss, *Student Moral Development in the Catholic School* (Washington, DC: National Catholic Educational Association, 1985).

Mary Peter Traviss, OP

Inner-City Private Elementary Schools: A Study

Inner-City Private Elementary Schools was a seminal study of inner-city private elementary schools sponsored by the Catholic League for Religious and Civil Rights. Prior to this study "no systematic description of the family backgrounds" (p. 3) of pupils in inner-city private elementary schools had been published. It was the first in-depth study on Catholic and other inner-city private elementary schools that at the time were serving primarily African American and Hispanic children.

Data from a preliminary study of Milwaukee's St. Leo School, which at the time was 98 percent black, convinced the Catholic League to pursue a national study. The St. Leo study showed students were performing above the national norm in some areas and making dramatic progress in areas of "deficiency" (Cibulka et al., 1982, p. ii). As such, the Catholic League saw the urgent need to conduct research on a larger scale in order to "assess the educational impact these schools have had—and the impact state or federal assistance might have—on the education of children in the inner city" (Cibulka et al., 1982 p. ii). Data for this national study of fifty-four elementary schools in eight cities were collected during the 1978–1979 academic year.

Common characteristics of the schools were as follows: the schools selected had a student body that was at least 70 percent minority, tuition was charged, and the schools were Title I institutions.

The study documented the types of families using inner-city private schools. Blacks were predominant in Washington, D.C., New Orleans, Chicago, and Milwaukee, representing 85 percent or more of the student body at participating schools. Hispanics were predominant in New York and Los Angeles. Almost half of the families had household incomes of less than $10,000, which was below the poverty level. These incomes were earned by one wage earner in 51 percent of the families, several of which were single-parent families (35%). Despite income, 55 percent of the families had more than one child in the schools. Lastly, the religious affiliations of families also differed. Not all families were Catholic; in fact, 31 percent were Protestant, and 2 percent had no church membership. Blacks had the lowest proportion of Catholic affiliation (44%); most blacks were Protestant (53%). In contrast, the affiliation of most whites (92%) and Hispanics (98%) was Catholic.

The study reported several groundbreaking findings related to why parents chose private education. Parents chose private education because they expected that their children would receive a better education than in public schools. Parents were not solely motivated by religious reasons. In fact, parents made clear distinctions between the educational quality of private schools and the "religious element" of schools. Seventy-nine percent of parents had neutral or positive attitudes toward public schools.

An important conclusion was the emergence of the inner-city private school as a functional alternative to inner-city public schools. Families who could not afford to, or chose not to, move to the suburbs were afforded the quality of suburban schools in their existing communities. Along with this conclusion was the finding that low- and moderate-income parents would make significant financial sacrifices to send their children to private schools.

Findings also debunked long-held beliefs about inner-city private schools. First, the data showed that inner-city private schools families did not represent elite strata of the community. The parental level of education ran the gamut, and household incomes were varied. Second, inner-city private schools were shown not to be draining public schools of the best and brightest. Students entered these private schools at various performance levels. Lastly, one of the more profound findings was that the evidence refuted the idea that private inner-city schools encouraged "white flight" from urban public schools.

The study documented the backgrounds of school personnel and how the inner-city private school functioned. Among the findings of the evidence were that (1) schools were decentralized politically and administratively, (2) 92 percent of the principals believed that challenging relevant class work diminished and eliminated discipline problems, and (3) 93 percent of teachers reported a school climate that "stimulated learning." The administrators and teachers in these private schools generally rejected beliefs that children from poor homes created disciplinary problems that impeded the learning environment. Additionally, a significant amount of agreement among teachers, administrators, and parents about the educational goals of their respective schools was revealed. *See also*: *Catholic High Schools and Minority Students*; Minority students.

Further Reading: James G. Cibulka, Timothy J. O'Brien, and Donald Zewe, *Inner-city Private Elementary Schools: A Study* (Milwaukee: Marquette University Press, 1982); James S. Coleman, Thomas Hoffer, and Sally Kilgore, *High School Achievement: Public, Catholic, and Private Schools Compared* (New York: Basic Books, 1982); Andrew M. Greeley, *Catholic High Schools and Minority Students* (New Brunswick, NJ: Transaction Books, 1982).

Yolanda Hart

Inner-city schools

Inner-city Catholic schools are schools usually located in the central core of a city. Inner-city Catholic schools represent a specialized subset of urban schools. They exhibit particular unique characteristics. These schools report a student population that is primarily non-Catholic, minority, and economically disadvantaged. Today many inner-city Catholic schools face crises in enrollment and financial viability. Maintaining inner-city Catholic schools currently represents one of the biggest challenges facing Catholic education.

Examining the history and development of Catholic schools in the United States provides a context for understanding the current challenges facing Catholic education, particularly those of Catholic schools located in the inner city. The first Catholic schools in the United States were built in cities, where most Catholic immigrants settled in the early 1800s. When Catholics came to America from Europe, they often found that their children were unwelcome in the largely Anglo-Protestant schools of the time. Catholic schools were a necessity if Catholic children were going to become educated. Catholic schools in America were opened with the threefold purpose to assure the development of the Catholic faith, to educate Catholic children academically, and to prepare children to become contributing members of society. Catholic schools were originally supported as a missionary activity by religious orders and were staffed by religious men and women from around the world who came to the United States to serve these immigrant children. For many years, these courageous religious worked for little salary.

Through the years, Catholic schools in America grew and prospered. As Catholics became more educated and successful in society, Catholic parishes were better able to support Catholic schools. Enrollment in Catholic schools continued to grow through the 1950s. At that time, every Catholic child was expected to attend a Catholic school. Many new Catholic schools were built during this period. Often, in fact, a Catholic school was built before the parish church was built. The late 1960s, however, brought many changes to Catholic schools. Notably, there was a substantial decrease in the number of religious men and women available to teach in Catholic schools. In addition, many Catholics moved from cities to the suburbs. This reduced the Catholic population and drained the financial resources of cities. These social conditions along with reduced birthrates posed serious financial problems for urban schools, particularly inner-city schools.

Overall enrollment in Catholic schools fell from 5.5 million in the mid-1960s to under three million in 2002. Population shifts, lower birthrates, the shift from religious to primarily lay faculty, and increased costs are cited as reasons for this decline in enrollment. The composition of the Catholic school population has also undergone dramatic change. Overall Catholic school enrollment has changed in terms of race, ethnicity, and religion. For example, in 1970 minority enrollment was 12.2 percent of the total enrollment. By the year 2002 minority enrollment in Catholic schools had more than doubled to 26.1 percent. Non-Catholics represented 2.7 percent of all Catholic school students in 1970, and by 2002 this group had grown to 13.2 percent. These demographic shifts have been even more pronounced in inner-city schools.

Inner-city Catholic schools face particular challenges as more Catholics move to the suburbs. With more diverse student populations and the rapid depletion of economic resources, inner-city schools are in crisis. What is the future of inner-city Catholic schools? Is there a future for them?

Although there has been a decrease in the total number of Catholic schools in the past thirty-five years, the Church has not lost sight of its commitment to educate children, particularly those of the poor, within the inner cities and urban areas. In 2001–2002, 45.6 percent of all Catholic schools were located in urban areas, with 13 percent of those schools located in the inner city. Maintaining Catholic schools in the inner city continues to be an important ministry of the Catholic Church. Despite the diminishing number of Catholics in urban areas, the call to serve the poor remains. Some inner-city Catholic schools now show a more than 90 percent non-Catholic student population. Most students are nonwhite minority, with blacks and Hispanics representing the largest groups. The number of economically disadvantaged students is large and continues to grow.

Researchers have pointed to the astonishing success of inner-city Catholic schools. An independent study of Catholic schools and public schools in New York City by the Rand Corporation in 1990 found Catholic secondary school students achieved higher results on several scholastic measures. All schools studied were located in inner-city neighborhoods and drew from a pool of seriously disadvantaged youth. James Coleman, Thomas Hoffer, and Sally Kilgore concluded in their study, *High School Achievement: Public, Catholic, and Private Schools*, that Catholic school students, especially minority students, scored significantly higher on standardized tests even after controlling for differences in family characteristics. They also found that Catholic schools were less racially segregated in comparison to public schools. In *Catholic Schools Make a Difference: Twenty-five Years of Research*, John Convey reports that Catholic high school students received consistently higher scores than public school students and that whites, blacks, and Hispanics received higher scores in every single category studied (reading, science, and mathematics). Recent studies continue to support the effectiveness and efficiency of Catholic schools, particularly for minorities and disadvantaged inner-city youth.

Several issues are closely related to the future viability of inner-city Catholic schools. Parental choice is considered by many to be a key ingredient in improving education, especially in inner-city areas. Parental choice allows parents to have a voice in where their children attend school. Since inner-city Catholic schools have demonstrated success in educating children, these schools stand to benefit by advances in the area of parental choice.

Educators have long recognized parental involvement as essential to the success of schools. John Convey (1992), in his analysis of twenty-five years of research, identified the commitment and involvement of parents as a distinguishing characteristic of Catholic schools. Hunt, Joseph, and Nuzzi (2002) found that current research continues to support parental involvement as key to the success of Catholic schools. Inner-city Catholic schools must work to sustain a high level of parental involvement for the good of their students.

Maintaining financial viability is a major challenge for inner-city schools. Schools must carefully analyze their current financial position and degree of efficiency in operation. They also need to study recommendations for organization, strategic planning, and development efforts. New and creative approaches to financial management may offer financial stability to inner-city schools in order that they may continue to carry out their mission. *See also*: *Catholic High Schools and Minority Students*; Minority students; Urban schools.

Further Reading: James S. Coleman, Thomas Hoffer, and Sally Kilgore, *High School Achievement: Public, Catholic, and Private Schools* (New York: Basic Books, 1982); John J. Convey, *Catholic Schools Make a Difference: Twenty-five Years of Research* (Washington, DC: National Catholic Educational Association, 1992); Paul T. Hill, Gail E. Foster, and Tamar Gendler, *High Schools with Character* (Santa Monica, CA: Rand Corporation, 1990); Thomas C. Hunt, Ellis A. Joseph, and Ronald J. Nuzzi, eds., *Catholic Schools Still Make a Difference: Ten Years of Research, 1991–2000* (Washington, DC: National Catholic Educational Association, 2002); National Catholic Educational Association, *Catholic School Highlights 2001–2002* (Washington, DC: National Catholic Educational Association, 2002).

Louise P. Moore

Institute for Catholic Educational Leadership (ICEL)

The Institute for Catholic Educational Leadership (ICEL) is a program based at the University of San Francisco (USF) designed to educate and form leaders and administrators of Catholic and private education. ICEL's mission is "to offer a scholarly educational program relevant for private school personnel, to build a sense of community among the students and faculty who pray together and serve others, and to prepare highly competent, effective, and dedicated educators for Catholic schools" (www.soe.usfca.edu/icel/index.htm, December 2002). Its programs include the doctorate in Catholic educational leadership, the master's in Catholic educational leadership, the administrative services credential, and the master's in Catholic school teaching. ICEL also cosponsors the St. Ignatius Credential Project, which is a credential program for California teachers and certification program for religion teachers. In addition to the degree and credential programs, ICEL sponsors school community services that include in-service development for faculties, symposia, conferences, and workshops on current topics in private education. ICEL is also dedicated to research. ICEL publishes its doctoral studies and participates in the publication of *Catholic Education: A Journal of Inquiry and Practice*.

Allen Calvin, Rev. Pierre Du Maine, and Michael O'Neill founded the Institute for Catholic Educational Leadership at USF in 1976. At the time Calvin was dean of the School of Education at USF, Du Maine was superintendent of Catholic schools in the archdiocese of San Francisco, and O'Neill was superintendent of Catholic schools in the diocese of Spokane, Washington. These three men recognized the great need of the Church for scholarly and ministerial preparation of Catholic school personnel.

Prior to Vatican II, Catholic school teachers and administrators came almost exclusively from the ranks of religious congregations. With the decline in the available number of vowed religious women and men in the period following Vatican II, Catholic education experienced a pursuant need for leadership preparation and succession.

Many Church leaders became concerned that the identity of Catholic schools would suffer. Catholic officials were concerned that if future leaders of Catholic schools did not understand the philosophical and historical backgrounds of Catholic schools, they could not possibly become effective school leaders. Catholic school teachers and administrators did indeed require specialized formation.

In 1975, as O'Neill began the exploratory work of creating ICEL, he surveyed the 741 Catholic elementary and secondary school principals in the state of California. He asked the principals to rank thirty-seven previously identified needs of Catholic schools. The needs that ranked highest were incorporated into ICEL courses. O'Neill wanted to offer high-quality academic programs that were strongly based in theory and taught by the best instructors at a low cost.

The board of trustees of the University of San Francisco officially approved ICEL in June 1976. ICEL began with the offering of a master's degree and a national symposium of 120 prominent Catholic school leaders. The symposium was focused on the central cause of ICEL, the future of Catholic schools. In May 1977, the board of trustees approved the doctorate of education program. At the time this was the only doctoral program specifically focused on Catholic education in the United States.

In 1978, Edwin J. McDermott, SJ, replaced Michael O'Neill as director of ICEL. O'Neill assumed the position of dean. In 1989 Mary Peter Traviss, OP, became the third director of ICEL.

Also in 1978, ICEL began its first off-campus educational program in the archdiocese of Los Angeles. In this program participants received a California teaching credential with an emphasis in Catholic school teaching. In 1991, a similar program was started in the diocese of Honolulu.

ICEL has grown substantially since its first graduating class in 1978. In 1978, ICEL had one graduate, Br. Anthony Pistoni, who received a master's degree in private school administration. In 1998–1999, ICEL conferred thirty-seven master's degrees and six doctoral degrees. ICEL has also initiated a number of new programs such as outreach activities, distant learning initiatives, Web resources, and conferences and collaborated in the founding of the journal *Catholic Education: A Journal of Inquiry and Practice.*

Due to the success of ICEL and the manifest national need for leadership preparation, a number of other Catholic colleges and universities have also begun programs dedicated to the education of Catholic school teachers and administrators. These colleges and universities include Australian Catholic University, Barry University, Boston College, the Catholic University of America, Christian Brothers University, Fordham University, Manhattan College, Marywood College, Rosary College, Saint Mary's College, Loyola College, Seton Hall University, Ursuline College, the University of Dayton, the University of Notre Dame, the University of Rochester, and the University of Saint Thomas. The University of Rochester is the first non-Catholic institution to offer a program dedicated to educating Catholic school personnel. This entire group of institutions became a consortium in 1989, the Association of Catholic Leadership Programs (ACLP). ACLP is affiliated with the National Catholic Educational Association (NCEA) through its Chief Administrators of Catholic Education (CACE) division.

Currently, ICEL offers three main degrees: a master's of arts in Catholic school teaching, a master's of arts in Catholic school administration, and a doctorate of education in Catholic educational leadership (Ed.D.). The institute has three main goals: to maintain an academically challenging program, to stimulate an appreciation for research in its students, and to promote the building of community among faculty and students in order to enhance scholarship and faith formation. Additionally, ICEL believes that its graduates should possess the following characteristics: they should be open to growth, academically and professionally competent, religious leaders, community builders, and committed to doing justice. *See also*: Staff development; Total Catholic Education.

Further Reading: Margaret Cadigan, ed., *Directory of Catholic Colleges and Universities* (New York: Paulist Press, 2001); Edwin J. McDermott, "Overview of the ICEL Symposium," *Momentum* 18, 2 (May 1987): 52–54; Agnes Jean Vieno, "The Institute for Catholic Educational Leadership: An Analysis of Student Expectations and Goal Achievement, 1976–1988," unpublished doctoral dissertation, University of San Francisco, 1989; John Watzke, "Teachers for Whom? A Study of Teacher Education Practices in Catholic Higher Education," *Catholic Education: A Journal of Inquiry and Practice* 6, 2 (December 2002): 138–167.

Jeffery M. Boetticher, Jr.

In Support of Catholic Elementary and Secondary Schools

A statement of the United States Catholic bishops issued on November 21, 1990, as an expression of their shared interest in, and advocacy for, Catholic schools in the United States. In 1972, the bishops had published a widely acclaimed pastoral statement on Catholic education, *To Teach as Jesus Did*. This earlier pastoral statement addressed the overall educational mission of the Church and contained high praise for Catholic schools. While *To Teach as Jesus Did* remains the most thorough development of the bishops' position on Catholic education, this 1990 statement was an effort to recommit to the teachings expressed in the earlier pastoral statement and to continue the development of the bishops' own thinking on the value of Catholic schools for the Church.

One important area of development is the articulation of a fourth purpose of Catholic schools. Earlier, the bishops had settled on a threefold purpose that was the organizational theme of the 1972 pastoral statement *To Teach as Jesus Did*. Calling upon both Scripture and tradition, the bishops announced these purposes: message (*didache*), community (*koinonia*), and service (*diakonia*). In the 1990 statement, the bishops added a fourth purpose, worship, so that official documents now speak about the fourfold purpose of Catholic schools—message, community, service, and worship. The bishops first advanced this addition in the National Catechetical Directory, *Sharing the Light of Faith*, published in 1979.

In Support of Catholic Elementary and Secondary Schools is a brief statement and was published in pamphlet form. In addition to being a reaffirmation of the teachings of *To Teach as Jesus Did*, the statement serves as a preparatory document to anticipate its twenty-fifth anniversary. The bishops begin the 1990 statement by recognizing that 1997 will mark the twenty-fifth anniversary of *To Teach as Jesus Did*. While still then seven years away, the statement articulates a seven-year plan of goals that the bishops hope will serve as a sign of their commitment to the principles laid down in the earlier pastoral message. Specifically, the bishops committed themselves "unequivocally" to the following goals: (1) that Catholic schools will continue to provide high-quality education for all their students in a context infused with Gospel values; (2) that serious efforts will be made to ensure that Catholic schools are available for Catholic parents who wish to send their children to them; (3) that new initiatives will be launched to secure sufficient financial assistance from both private and public sectors for Catholic parents to exercise this right; and (4) that salaries and benefits of Catholic school teachers and administrators will reflect the social justice teaching of the Church as found in the bishops' pastoral *Economic Justice for All*. To accomplish these goals, the bishops further committed to the following initial actions: a clear teaching focus on the need for stewardship, the establishment of diocesan educational development offices, the formation of diocesan, state, and national organizations to ensure parental rights, and the development of a long-term strategic plan for Catholic schools in the United States.

The bishops align themselves with other important Catholic teachings in making their case for support of Catholic schools. They make ample use of quotations from other church documents that espouse similar positions, including an address of Pope John Paul II to Catholic educators in New Orleans in 1987 called *Catholic Education: Gift to the Church*, documents from the Congregation for Catholic Education such as *The Catholic School* (1977) and *The Religious Dimension of Education in a Catholic School* (1988), and their own statements such as *To Teach as Jesus Did, The Hispanic Presence: Challenge and Commitment* (1983), and *What We Have Seen and Heard: A Pastoral Letter on Evangelization from the Black Bishops of the United States* (1984).

The bishops strike a sad note in their detailing of some of the statistics chronicling the struggling of some Catholic schools. They noted that in the period 1970–1990, the cost of operating Catholic schools skyrocketed, increasing 500 percent, an increase twice the pace of the consumer price index, which measures inflation nationally. They leave unmentioned the primary reason for this dramatic cost increase or an analysis of the overall financial picture, but schools, like most organizations, make primary investments in their human resources, thereby making teaching personnel and staff the most significant and important costs in operating the school. Throughout this period, Catholic schools continued to experience a steady decline in the numbers of available vowed female and male religious, thereby necessitating a shift from vowed religious to lay staffs. This shift and the concomitant need to pay just salaries to lay teachers contributed to the increased costs of operating Catholic schools during this period. The bishops also noted that the percentage of potential Catholic students attending Catholic schools had dropped consistently from 1980 to 1990, mostly due to shifting demographics. *See also*: Bishops; National Conference of Catholic Bishops (NCCB); *To Teach as Jesus Did*.

Further Reading: Congregation for Catholic Education, *The Catholic School* (Washington, DC: United States Catholic Conference, 1977); Congregation for Catholic Education, *The Religious Dimension of Education in a Catholic School* (Washington, DC: United States Catholic Conference, 1988); Thomas C. Hunt, Ellis A. Joseph, and Ronald J. Nuzzi, eds., *Handbook of Research on Catholic Education* (Westport, CT: Greenwood Press, 2001); John Paul II, *Catholic Education: Gift to the Nation* (Washington, DC: National Catholic Educational Association, 1987); National Conference of Catholic Bishops, *Sharing the Light of Faith: National Catechetical Directory for Catholics of the United States* (Washington, DC: United States Catholic Conference, 1979); National Conference of Catholic Bishops, *The Hispanic Presence: Challenge and Commitment* (Washington, DC: United States Catholic Conference, 1983); National Conference of Catholic Bishops, *To Teach as Jesus Did: A Pastoral Message on Catholic Education* (Washington, DC: United States Catholic Conference, 1972); National Conference of Catholic Bishops, *What We Have Seen and Heard: A Pastoral Letter on Evangelization from the Black Bishops of the United States* (Washington, DC: United States Catholic Conference, 1984); United States Catholic Conference, *In Support of Catholic Elementary and Secondary Schools* (Washington, DC: United States Catholic Conference, 1990).

Ronald J. Nuzzi

Integration in Catholic schools

Integration is most widely defined as enrolling students of different racial groups in the same schools. Integration in schools promotes diversity by bringing students of different backgrounds together. In 1954, the *Brown v. Board of Education* court case concluded that separate education received by different racial/ethnic groups is unequal. Since then, the government, school administrators, citizens, and parents have attempted to facilitate racial integration of schools through a variety of means, perhaps the most infamous of which is busing.

Integration in Catholic schools must be considered within the context of the extensive and growing racial diversity in Catholic schools. The proportion of ethnic minority students served by Catholic schools has more than doubled over the last thirty years, with 10.8 percent minority enrollment in 1970, 19.4 percent in 1980, and 24 percent in 2000. The 2001–2002 annual statistical report on Catholic elementary and secondary schools reported minority student enrollment at 682,136, or 26.1 percent of total enrollment (2,616,330). Table 12 provides enrollment statistics across racial/ethnic groups for elementary and secondary schools. As summarized in Table 13, regional variability in minority enrollment ranges from 8.8 percent in the Plains

Table 12
Enrollment and Percentages by Ethnic Background

Category	Elementary/Middle		Secondary		All Schools	
	Number	*%*	*Number*	*%*	*Number*	*%*
American Indian/Native Alaskan	6,875	0.3	2,262	0.4	9,137	0.3
Asian	71,311	3.5	24,226	3.7	95,537	3.7
Black	158,855	8.1	48,850	7.6	207,705	7.9
Hispanic	223,137	11.3	66,251	10.3	289,388	11.1
Native Hawaiian/Pacific Islander	15,454	0.8	5,480	0.9	20,934	0.8
Multiracial	39,070	2.0	10,476	1.6	49,546	1.9
White	1,451,298	73.7	482,896	75.4	1,934,194	74.0
Unknown	5,540	0.2	4,262	0.1	9,899	0.3
Total	**1,971,440**	**100.0**	**644,703**	**100.0**	**2,616,33**	**100.0**

Source: MacDonald, 2002.

Table 13
Minority Enrollment Percentages
by Region (2000–2001)

Region	Percentage
New England	14
Mideast	27
Great Lakes	17
Plains	9
Southeast	21
West–Far West	48

Source: Savage, 2002.

to 48 percent in the West–Far West region. A high percentage of minority enrollment is typically found in large urban areas—Newark, Los Angeles, Detroit, New York, Chicago, Cleveland, and St. Louis, for example.

To assess the level of integration in schools, however, requires more information than simply the percentage of minority students being educated. For example, a school that has 100 percent minority enrollment is clearly not well integrated; it is a segregated school consisting entirely of one racial group. Measuring integration requires the consideration of "how well distributed students are across schools with different proportions of white and minority students in them. If a system were well integrated it would have virtually all its students attending schools whose racial composition resembled the racial composition of the broader community in which those schools were located" (Greene, 1999, p. 5).

Even with that operational definition, it is challenging to find definitive evidence concerning the relative integration level of Catholic schools. Much has been written, however, about the racial integration of private versus public schools, often within the context of the school choice debate. Researchers have arrived at separate conclusions regarding public versus private school integration, likely traced back to a diversity of methodologies, data sets, samples, analysis strategies, and perhaps political agendas as well.

A body of evidence supports the notion that private schools are more integrated than public schools. The underlying assumption for this argument is that public schools assign students to schools based on where they live, a practice that often replicates racial segregation in housing patterns. Private schools, in contrast, are able to attract students without regard to geographical boundaries, thereby transcending segregated housing patterns.

Coleman's research from the early 1980s found that racial integration within private schools was greater than within public schools (Coleman, Hoffer, and Kilgore, 1982). Using data from the 1992 National Educational Longitudinal Study (NELS), Greene (1998) calculated that the national average of minority students in classrooms was 25.6 percent. A classroom was then considered racially integrated if its racial composition was within ten percentage points of the national average. Based on that definition, 18 percent of public school students were in integrated classrooms compared to 37 percent of private school students. The same inquiry also indicated that twelfth grade private school students (55%) were also less likely to be in segregated classrooms—more than 90 percent or less than 10 percent minority—than their public school counterparts (41%). In another investigation, Greene and Mellow (1998) utilized a distinctly different methodology to arrive at the same conclusion. The researchers observed school lunchrooms and recorded where students sat by race, resulting in an Index of Integration (IOI). The IOI was greater for private school lunchrooms (63.5%) than for public school lunchrooms (49.7%). Finally, research on the racial integration question has been conducted in cities that have implemented school choice/voucher programs. For example, Fuller and Mitchell (1999), analyzing Milwaukee school data after implementation of its school choice program, reported greater levels of integration for private (38% of students in segregated classrooms) versus public schools (58% in segregated classrooms).

Despite this evidence, inquiries have considered the very same question and arrived at the opposite conclusion. Using data from a nationally representative sample of 23,000 kindergartners (the Early Childhood Longitudinal Study), Ritter, Rush, and Rush (2002) reported that slightly more public than private schools students were likely to attend integrated classrooms. The authors, noting that their findings contrasted with Greene's 1992 NELS data (1998), question the current applicability of the earlier results given the highly dynamic racial composition of students in the United States. The Civil Rights Project at Harvard University issued a report on racial enrollment and segregation that drew on data from the National Center for Education Statistics and the Bureau of the Census. The report concluded, "The most significant finding in this report is that segregation levels are quite high among private schools, particularly among Catholic and other religious private schools, where the levels of segregation are often equal or greater than levels of segregation among public schools" (Reardon and Yun, 2002, p. 3). In particular, black-white segregation was found to be greatest among Catholic schools, with black students attending Catholic schools that are 31 percent white, versus non-Catholic religious schools (35%) or secular private schools (41%). *See also*: *Catholic High Schools and Minority Students*; Enrollment; Minority students.

Further Reading: Howard L. Fuller and George A. Mitchell, "The Impact of School Choice on Racial and Ethnic Enrollment in Milwaukee Private Schools," *Current Education Issues* 5 (Institute for the Transformation of Learning: Marquette University, 1999); Jay P. Greene, "Civic Values in Public and Private Schools," in Paul E. Peterson and Bryan C. Hassel, eds., *Learning from School Choice* (Washington, DC: Brookings, 1998); Jay P. Greene, "The Racial, Economic, and Religious Context of Parental Choice in Cleveland," Paper presented at the Annual Meeting of the Association for Policy Analysis and Management (Washington, DC, 1999); Jay P. Greene and Nicole Mellow, "Integration Where It Counts: A Study of Racial Integration in Public and Private School Lunchrooms," paper presented at the Meeting of the American Political Science Association (Boston, 1998); Dale MacDonald, *United States Catholic Elementary and Secondary Schools, 2001–2002: The Annual Statistical Report on Schools, Enrollment and Staffing* (Washington, DC: National Catholic Educational Association, 2002); Sean F. Reardon and John T. Yun, "Private School Racial Enrollments and Segregation," commissioned paper, the Civil Rights Project, Harvard University, 2002; Gary W. Ritter, Alison Rush, and Joel Rush, "How Might School Choice Affect Racial Integration in Schools? New Evidence from the ECLS-K," *Georgetown Public Policy Review* 7, 2 (Spring 2002): 125–136; Frank X. Savage, "Catholic School Demography: Changes from 1990–2000," in Thomas C. Hunt, Ellis A. Joseph, and Ronald J. Nuzzi, eds., *Catholic Schools Still Make a Difference: Ten Years of Research, 1991–2000* (Washington, DC: National Catholic Educational Association, 2002).

James M. Frabutt

Intentionality

Michael O'Neill of the University of San Francisco in the late 1970s coined the term "intentionality." According to O'Neill, the "permeation" of religious influence had marked Catholic schools prior to the Second Vatican Council. Intentionality was the key ingredient that enabled Catholic schools to be different from their public counterparts and marked them as unique.

Three layers marked the school as a "faith community," according to O'Neill. The first of these was content. This layer comprised the curriculum, textbooks, and the explicit "teaching product" of schools. The presence of black and ethnic studies in curricula constitutes content permeation in Catholic schools, all the while respecting the integrity of the disciplines.

The second layer was methodology. Teaching methods, discipline, decision-making styles, staff relationships, and the way students are treated made up this layer. They display a faith community in action.

The third and final component, the heart of permeation, was intentionality. O'Neill described it as when people in a school share a certain intentionality, a certain pattern of "values, understandings, sentiments, hopes and dreams, that deeply condition everything that goes on, including the math class, the athletic activities, the dances, coffee breaks in the teachers' lounges, everything" (1979, p. 49). The whole of intentionality was greater than the sum of its parts, created by the intentions of all in school life, and once created takes on a certain existence and momentum of its own, carrying along the very people who created it. The power of collective intentionality was strong enough to withstand some in the school who do not share in it, and those nonparticipants may indeed stimulate others to broaden their own perspectives and hence strengthen their own commitment, resulting in an even greater presence of intentionality in the school.

Catholic elementary schools, often known as the "sisters' schools" in pre-Vatican

II days, are to be faith communities and are not seen as automatically Catholic because they are staffed exclusively or overwhelmingly by religious. It is what people involved in them believe and profess in their lives that makes them faith communities. Intentionality is at the heart of a truly Catholic school. *See also*: Catholic identity; Catholic philosophy of education.

Further Reading: Michael O'Neill, "Catholic Education: The Largest Alternative System," *Thrust* 7 (May 1978): 25–26; Michael O'Neill, "Toward a Modern Concept of 'Permeation,'" *Momentum* 10, 2 (May 1979): 48–50.

Thomas C. Hunt

Internet accessibility

Although significant increases in the amount of computer hardware in Catholic schools occurred in the last few years of the twentieth century, the growth in Internet accessibility accelerated even more dramatically, particularly in the years from 1995 to 1999. After the academic year 1998–1999, the growth in Internet access continued, but statistics about Internet availability in Catholic schools varied significantly across surveys.

Until 1995, very little data about Internet accessibility had been collected, due to the relative newness of the Internet as a telecommunications technology in schools. Beginning in 1995, the National Catholic Educational Association (NCEA) and the National Center for Education Statistics (NCES) began acquiring that data for K–12 schools at regular intervals. Quality Education Data (QED) also gathered technology data for NCEA.

In 1995, 35 percent of all Catholic schools had some access to the Internet, with 43 percent of all Catholic school students in attendance at one of these schools. While the percentage of nonsectarian private schools with Internet access (32%) was nearly comparable to that of the Catholic schools, the percentage of Catholic schools with access to Internet was more than double that of other religious schools (16%). However, the mean number of computers with Internet access in nonsectarian schools (twenty-three) far exceeded that in the Catholic or other religious schools, each of which had a mean of five Internet-accessible computers. In comparison, half of all public schools were connected and had, on the average, twelve computers that were Internet-accessible.

In 1995, among Catholic schools with Internet access, nearly half (48%) had only one computer connected for Internet access; 37 percent had between two and five computers so equipped; 3 percent had between six and nine computers Internet-ready; and 12 percent reported ten or more computers available with Internet access. However, very few schools (7%) had five or more instructional rooms (e.g., classrooms, computer labs, media centers) with access; 39 percent had only one instructional room with Internet access; 18 percent had two or three rooms so equipped; and 35 percent had no instructional access to the Internet.

In 1995, within the Catholic school community, administrators were most apt to utilize the Internet. Only 7 percent of administrators indicated that they did not access the Internet at all; however, 35 percent reported that they did so to a moderate or large extent. Teachers were the second most frequent users of the Internet, with 27 percent doing so relatively frequently; however, 30 percent indicated that they never accessed the Internet. Students were least apt to use Internet resources; 44 percent reported that they never used the Internet, while 24 percent did so to a moderate to large extent.

According to NCES, by 1998, about 80 percent of Catholic schools nationwide had some access to the Internet, with 86 percent of all Catholic schools in attendance at a school with Internet accessibility. The average number of Internet-accessible computers per school in the Catholic sector had increased more than fourfold, from five to twenty-two. In contrast, the percentage of other religious schools with Internet access had increased to 54 percent, while that of nonsectarian schools with Internet access had risen to 66 percent. All private schools lagged behind the public schools, which boasted an 89 percent access rate.

Although Catholic schools were more likely than other private schools to be connected to the Internet by 1998, nonsectarian private schools were much more likely than Catholic schools to have instructional computers connected. Typically, nonsectarian schools averaged forty instructional computers with Internet access, more than double the eighteen Internet-accessible instructional computers in Catholic schools and more than triple the twelve such computers in other religious schools. The nonsectarian schools also outpaced both the Catholic schools and other religious schools in ratio of students to instructional computers with Internet access. On the average, nonsectarian schools boasted a 7:1 ratio of students per Internet-accessible instructional computer, compared with a 19:1 ratio for Catholic schools and an 18:1 ratio for other religious schools. The public school ratio was 12:1.

Between 1995 and 1998, dramatic improvements were made in the number and percentage of instructional rooms with Internet access. According to NCES, by the 1998–1999 academic year, about 27 percent of all instructional rooms in Catholic schools were Internet-accessible. Of the Catholic schools that reported any Internet access, 31 percent had access in five or more instructional rooms; 16 percent reported access in two to four rooms; 41 percent indicated that only one instructional room was Internet-accessible; and only 12 percent reported that no instructional rooms were so equipped. These impressive gains brought Catholic schools more closely into alignment with the percentages reported by the private nonsectarian schools: 36 percent with Internet access in five or more instructional rooms; 17 percent with access in two to four instructional rooms; 32 percent with access in only one room; and 15 percent with no instructional access to the Internet.

Since 1998, there have been no large-scale surveys conducted by the National Center for Education Statistics to obtain private school data about technology. However, QED surveys suggested that by the 1999–2000 academic year, nearly all Catholic schools provided Internet access from media centers/libraries and computer labs, and about 84 percent of classrooms had at least one computer with Internet access. These statistics closely paralleled those of the public schools, who reported 98 percent of schools with some Internet connections and 77 percent of instructional rooms with Internet access. NCEA annual survey data was less impressive, citing school Internet accessibility as nearly 74 percent in the 1999–2000 academic year. However, they noted that not every diocese reported the information.

The 2002 QED report noted that 98 percent of Catholic schools provided Internet access, with over three-fourths (76%) of classrooms having Internet access. If QED's data were accurate, then between 2000 and 2002 there was a significant decrease in the percentage of classrooms connected to the Internet (from 84% in 2000 to 76% in 2002). This phenomenon was not explained. However, 69 percent of all computers in Catholic schools were connected to the Internet by academic year 2001–2002. Data gathered directly by NCEA were less encouraging. In their 2001–2002 survey of Catholic elementary and secondary schools, they found that only about 85 percent of Catholic schools had Internet access, with those in New England least apt to provide connections. As in 1999–2000, NCEA noted that not every diocese provided this information.

According to NCES surveys, public schools reported even greater Internet access by 2001–2002. In their Digest of Education Statistics, 2002, NCES reported that during the 2001–2002 academic year, 99 percent of public schools had Internet access, with 85 percent of classrooms having at least some access. In a different survey (Internet Access in U.S. Public Schools, Fall 2001) NCES reported that 87 percent of classrooms had Internet access.

The earliest Internet connections in most schools were dial-up connections. In 1995, 95 percent of Catholic schools were using modem/dial-up connections; 97 percent of other religious schools were doing likewise. However, 14 percent of nonsectarian private schools had already begun to invest in dedicated lines such as 56Kb or T1 lines. Nonsectarian schools were four times as likely as Catholic schools (8% vs. 2%) to use ISDN. Within three years, there was a significant shift in type of Internet connections across all sectors of education. In the Catholic schools, dial-up connections had dropped from 95 percent to 65 percent. By 1998, 27 percent were using dedicated lines such as 56Kb or T1; 13 percent had at least some cable modem access; and 17 percent had ISDN connections.

In their 2002 report, QED noted that by academic year 2001–2002, 69 percent of connections were high bandwidth, while only 31 percent were low bandwidth. Only 1 percent of Catholic K–12 campuses reported utilizing wireless Ethernet networks. According to NCES, in 2001, 85 percent of public schools used broadband connections. At time of publication, other updated statistics about Internet connectivity were not available.

Catholic schools' large increases in Internet availability occurred at the same time that federal funding became available for such uses. In 1998–1999, over 80 percent of Catholic schools that applied for the E-Rate moneys made available by the Telecommunications Act of 1996 received them. However, by 2001–2002, QED reported that only about two-thirds of Catholic schools that made application actually received funding. These moneys helped to fund Internet connections and facilitated accessibility of Internet in instructional rooms. *See also*: Computer accessibility; E-Rate; Telecommunications.

Further Reading: Sheila Heaviside and Elizabeth Farris, *Advanced Telecommunications in U.S. Private Schools, K–12, Fall 1995* (NCES Rep. No. 97394) (Washington, DC: U.S. Department of Education, National Center for Education Statistics, 1997); Anne Kleiner and Elizabeth Farris, *Internet Access in U.S. Public Schools and Classrooms: 1994–2001* (NCES Rep. No. 2002-018) (Washington, DC: U.S. Department of Education, National Center for Education Statistics, 2002); Basmat Parsad, Rebecca Skinner, and Elizabeth Farris, *Advanced Telecommunications in U.S. Private Schools: 1998–99* (NCES Rep. No. 2001-037) (Washington, DC: U.S. Department of Education, National Center for Education Statistics, 2001); Thomas Snyder and Charlene Hoffman, *Digest of Education Statistics 2002* (NCES Rep. No. 2003-060) (Washington, DC: U.S. Department of Education, National Center for Education Statistics, 2003); Terian Tyre, *The State of Technology in Catholic Schools* (Dayton, OH: Peter Li, 2000, 2002).

Jeanne Hagelskamp, SP

Interpersonal intelligence

One of seven intelligences identified in Howard Gardner's Multiple Intelligence Theory—a theory that has gained wide acceptance in education and instruction since the
middle of the 1980s. Interpersonal intelligence involves a high ability to understand
and work with other people. Its core elements are the capacity to observe and analyze
distinctions in others' moods, temperament, intentions, and desires. Individuals with
high interpersonal intelligence work well with others, are effective communicators,
and thrive in different social situations. Teachers, counselors, and salespeople are
examples of individuals who display high ability in this intelligence. This intelligence
has also been applied as a means to understand and participate in religious studies
and the mass.

According to Gardner, interpersonal intelligence meets the criteria for an independent intelligence because it is culturally significant and has biological origins. The
core element of this intelligence is the ability to observe and interpret the actions of
others. Every normally functioning individual develops some level of competence in
this area. Studies of the connections between the brain and interpersonal skills show
that the frontal lobe controls interpersonal knowledge. Brain damage to this region
affects an individual's personality without affecting other abilities. The independence
of this intelligence is demonstrated by individuals with brain lesions to this region.
Such individuals cannot communicate with and react to other people but maintain
other skills. Other individuals have lost linguistic and visual skills but maintain the
ability to relate interpersonally. Additionally, autistic children often show a propensity
for math or music but have no sense of self or communication skills. Alzheimer's
patients also show a decline in all areas of functioning while remaining socially capable.

The development of interpersonal abilities follows a pattern in normally functioning
individuals. The bond between the child and the mother is the beginning of interpersonal development. Infants first learn to imitate and recognize facial expressions, make
distinctions among people, and associate emotions and experiences. Next, children
show that they are self-aware as they recognize their name, use pronouns to distinguish
different people, and engage in role play. Older children have a more developed sense
of self and a more advanced ability to relate to others as they learn to empathize and
cultivate friendships. Some develop basic interpersonal skills, while others come to a
more fully developed and integrated sense of self and relationship to the greater social
world.

Studies of primates show connections to human social development. Chimpanzees
have a prolonged attachment to their mothers that is essential to their interpersonal
development. Evolutionary studies show that in hunting and gathering societies, group
cohesion, leadership, and communication were necessary for the maintenance of society. Although interpersonal intelligence is identified as an independent intelligence,
it relates closely to intrapersonal intelligence because understanding of the self is
necessary for understanding and communicating with others.

Interpersonal intelligence can be easily incorporated into religious education. Group
work, used more often in classrooms, can be an instructional practice in religious
classes as well. Developing a cooperative atmosphere can enhance the experience in
any classroom. Peer teaching, small group discussions on church issues, group projects, and service learning are some ways to develop and use interpersonal intelligence.
Interpersonal intelligence is highly valued in pastoral ministers, vowed religious,

clergy, teachers, and principals. Persons with high interpersonal intelligence relate to others well, are comfortable with self-expression, and have a certain clarity of expression that enables them to work cooperatively with others.

The environment of the Catholic mass fosters interpersonal communication skills. Throughout the mass, participants sing, listen, recite prayers, and reflect as a united community. Ushers greet parishioners to welcome them to the celebration. The Liturgy of the Word and the Liturgy of the Eucharist involve dialogue and communication between the priest and the congregation. The petitions bring forth a united response and a call to remember and pray for the greater community. The Rite of Peace invites parishioners to address each other with a handshake and spoken message of peace. *See also*: Gardner, Howard; Multiple Intelligence Theory (MI).

Further Reading: Howard Gardner, *Frames of Mind: The Theory of Multiple Intelligences* (New York: Basic Books, 1983); Howard Gardner, *Intelligence Reframed: Multiple Intelligences for the 21st Century* (New York: Basic Books, 1999); Howard Gardner, *Multiple Intelligences: The Theory in Practice* (New York: Basic Books, 1993); Ronald J. Nuzzi, *Gifts of the Spirit: Multiple Intelligences in Religious Education* (Washington, DC: National Catholic Education Association, 1999).

John L. Watzke

Intrapersonal intelligence

One of seven intelligences identified in Howard Gardner's Multiple Intelligence Theory—a theory that has gained wide acceptance in education and instruction since the middle 1980s. Intrapersonal intelligence relates to the ability to know one's own self and access one's own feelings. Individuals high in intrapersonal intelligence are aware of their abilities, desires, and motivations and regulate their behavior accordingly. Engaging in self-analysis, self-regulation, and self-reflection utilizes this intelligence. This intelligence has also been applied as a means to understand and participate in religious studies and the mass.

According to Gardner, intrapersonal skill meets the criteria for an independent intelligence because it is culturally significant and has biological origins. Every normally functioning individual develops some degree of competence in intrapersonal skill. Studies show that the frontal lobe of the brain controls this skill. Brain damage to this region alters an individual's personality without disrupting other functioning. The independence of this intelligence is shown by individuals who have difficulty with personal skills but show otherwise normal functioning. Additionally, autistic children often lack the ability to refer to themselves while displaying high mathematical and artistic abilities.

The development of intrapersonal abilities follows a pattern in normally functioning individuals. Infants first learn to imitate and recognize facial expressions, make distinctions among people, and associate emotions and experiences. Next, children show that they are self-aware as they recognize their name, use pronouns to distinguish different people, and engage in role play. Older children have a more developed sense of self. Some individuals develop basic intrapersonal skills, while others come to a more fully developed and integrated sense of self.

Evolutionary studies show that intrapersonal skills can develop only in more advanced societies. Individuals must be able to focus on more than merely surviving to become personally aware and must have a language or symbol system. Although intrapersonal intelligence is identified as an independent intelligence, it relates closely to interpersonal intelligence because understanding of the self is necessary for understanding and communicating with others.

Intrapersonal intelligence can be easily incorporated into religious education. Traditional classrooms often do not include elements relating to this intelligence. By incorporating reflection and encouraging personal awareness, the educational experience can be enhanced in religious classes. Self-assessment, journal writing, moments of silence, composing prayers, and examination of conscience are ways to encourage the development of intrapersonal awareness. Intrapersonal intelligence includes the skills of being quiet, of learning to reflect in silence and in prayer on the events of the day, the course of one's life, and the successes and failures of everyday life. Examining one's conscience, a common preparation for celebrating the Sacrament of Reconcilation (confession) engages the intrapersonal intelligence.

The Catholic mass is an excellent environment for intrapersonal development. Although there is an important community aspect of the mass, there are also moments of silence to encourage reflection. Upon entering church, congregants usually kneel and pray as a way to focus on the mass. The homily is usually followed by a short time to reflect on the priest's message and the message of the Gospels. The petitions call for reflections on important global and personal issues. *See also*: Gardner, Howard; Multiple Intelligence Theory (MI).

Further Reading: Howard Gardner, *Frames of Mind: The Theory of Multiple Intelligences* (New York: Basic Books, 1983); Howard Gardner, *Intelligence Reframed: Multiple Intelligences for the 21st Century* (New York: Basic Books, 1999); Howard Gardner, *Multiple Intelligences: The Theory in Practice* (New York: Basic Books, 1993); Ronald J. Nuzzi, *Gifts of the Spirit: Multiple Intelligences in Religious Education* (Washington, DC: National Catholic Education Association, 1999).

John L. Watzke

Ireland, John (1838–1918)

John Ireland was born in Ireland in 1838. He emigrated to the United States with members of his family in 1850. He was ordained a priest on December 21, 1861. He served as a chaplain with the Union army in the Civil War. He was made a bishop in 1875 and became coadjutor of the archdiocese of St. Paul. In 1888, he was installed as archbishop of St. Paul.

A forceful personality, Ireland made a number of enemies within the Church in this country over his support of the founding of the Catholic University of America, because of his opposition to "nationalism," the establishment of ethnic churches in this country, to his stance on the "school question" within the Church in the United States and, to a lesser extent, because of his advocacy of temperance.

In July 1890 Ireland addressed the annual meeting of the National Education Association (NEA) that was held in St. Paul. Describing himself as "a friend and an advocate of the State school," Ireland went on to say, "The free school of America! Withered be the hand raised in sign of its destruction" (Rippley, 1988, p. 8). These words, along with his expressed statement that he wished the parochial schools did not have to exist, incurred for him the wrath of many prelates, a majority of whom were German American, who had gone to great lengths to establish and support parochial schools. Ultimately, Ireland, defended by Cardinal Gibbons of Baltimore, was called to Rome to defend his speech. Upheld, Ireland continued in his support of gradual Americanization.

John Ireland. © University of Notre Dame Archives.

Responding to the needs of several of his hard-pressed parishes, Ireland applied a form of the Poughkeepsie Plan in Faribault and Stillwater, Minnesota. Basically, the plans as implemented in the archdiocese of St. Paul called for the school board of those cities to manage and control for one dollar annually the school building and all the equipment of Immaculate Conception Parish in Faribault and of St. Michael's in

Stillwater. The plans met with strident opposition from several groups of Protestant clergy; for example, a group of Baptist ministers warned of the "subtle encroachment" of the Roman Catholic Church on the "integrity of our public schools" (Reilly, 1969, p. 83) and with members of the Catholic hierarchy, Archbishop Katzer of Milwaukee termed the plans a "surrender of a Catholic school to state authorities" (p. 138).

Ireland also became embroiled in the controversy over the pamphlet authored by Dr. Thomas Bouquillon of the Catholic University of America. Entitled "Education: To Whom Does It Belong?," Bouquillon maintained that the civil state had a basic right in educational matters. Opposed by many German American prelates and some leading laymen of German nationality and by the Jesuits (a Jesuit, Fr. Rene Holaind, had written a response to Bouquillon's piece), Ireland again found himself in the center of a controversy.

Ireland also was at center stage over the educationally related issue of ethnic churches, which was brought to bear by Cahenslyism (Peter Paul Cahensly led the movement to have ethnic, rather than territorial dioceses and parishes) and the subsequent claim by St. Raphael Verein that sixteen million immigrants had lost the faith in the United States, a fact that made ethnic parishes and dioceses necessary.

Sometimes known as the "Consecrated Blizzard" (Reilly, 1969, p. 99), Ireland's position on the school question led to ongoing and heated opposition among some of his fellow bishops. Indeed, Cardinal Gibbons wrote to Pope Leo XIII on Ireland's behalf, attesting to Ireland's orthodoxy.

The Vatican's answer to the conflict came in May 1892 with the statement, "The sound decrees of the Baltimore Council as to parochial schools remaining fully in force, the agreement made by the Most Rev. John Ireland with regard to the Faribault and Stillwater schools, all the circumstances being taken into consideration, can be allowed" (McCluskey, 1962, p. 151). The words "can be allowed" ("tolerari potest"), did not settle the conflict, whereupon the Pope sent a personal legate, Archbishop Francis Satolli, to end the controversy among the American bishops over the school question. Satolli's attempt at a solution, advanced through fourteen propositions that were presented at a meeting of the American archbishops, even though he served as Pope Leo's personal legate, was unsuccessful. Finally, the Pope himself wrote to the American bishops on May 23, 1893, ending the controversy.

Following the Pope's condemnation of "Americanism" in a late nineteenth-century encyclical, Ireland agreed with the Pontiff as to the errors the Pope had identified but denied he had held any of them.

Ireland was very influential in American circles outside the Church. Known as a liberal within the Church, he was a leader in Catholic circles advocating a positive relationship with American institutions. He died on September 23, 1918. *See also*: Catholic School Question, The; Faribault Plan.

Further Reading: Harold A. Buetow, *Of Singular Benefit: The Story of U.S. Catholic Education* (New York: Macmillan, 1970); Neil G. McCluskey, SJ, ed., *Catholic Education in America: A Documentary History* (New York: Teachers College Press, 1962); James H. Moynihan, *The Life of Archbishop Ireland* (New York: Harper Brothers, 1955); Daniel F. Reilly, *The School Controversy 1891–1893* (New York: Arno Press and the New York Times, 1969); LaVern J. Rippley, "Archbishop Ireland and the School Language Controversy," in F. Michael Perko, ed., *Enlightening the Next Generation: Catholics and Their Schools 1830–1980* (New York: Garland, 1988).

Thomas C. Hunt

Irish American Catholics

Irish Americans have always been ambivalent about parochial education. To be sure, the Irish were the leaders of the movement to establish parish schools in the United States. But at no time in the history of American Catholic parochial education did a majority of Irish Catholic children attend parish schools. It is an incontrovertible fact of American history that a significant majority of Irish Americans graduated from public schools.

The source of this Irish ambivalence was a lack of motivation to support parochial schools. Many ethnic groups such as the Germans and the Poles eagerly established parochial schools in America to preserve their native language and cultural traditions, but not the Irish.

Ireland had been under British domination for more than a century when the Irish began to immigrate to the United States in the 1820s. In truth, the Irish came to America not so much to find cultural freedom as to escape the poverty of their native land. Few gave much thought to preserving what little was left of their language and culture.

The Irish who did join the parochial school movement in the United States did so to preserve the Catholic faith of their children. In all the decades of oppression at the hands of the English, the Irish never abandoned the Church. Indeed, attending mass and harboring priests were acts of defiance against the hated English oppressors. More to the point, the Irish could well recall English efforts to use all manner of temptations—including education—to entice them to become Protestants. American public schools, many using the King James Bible as a text, seemed very much like the English institutions that the Irish remembered from their native land.

It is surprising, therefore, that the Irish American leadership, as reflected in the Catholic hierarchy, was not uniform in its support for parochial schools. Even though the majority of nineteenth-century American Catholic bishops had been born in Ireland, each responded to the issue of parochial education in his own way. Some bishops chose to minimize their involvement in educational matters. Others were able to do very little because ethnic conflict and poverty had created far larger problems than the establishment of parish schools. Still other bishops were tireless advocates of parochial education, and in their dioceses, their word was church doctrine.

The personification of this last group was Bishop John Hughes of New York. Hughes' self image was that of an Irish chieftain. "I had to warn them against the dangers that surrounded them," he wrote of his flock, "to contend for their rights as a religious community." Hughes articulated and typified the ghetto mentality that set the tone for Irish American Catholicism throughout the nineteenth century.

The post–Civil War growth of Catholic parochial schools caused serious concerns among Irish Catholics. Most Irish American leaders were pleased with the rapid growth of their parish schools, but some—conservatives for the most part—were not satisfied. In fact, conservatives such as Archbishop Michael Corrigan of New York were appalled with the large number of Irish American parents who continued to send their children to public schools in spite of warnings to the contrary. The conservatives looked for a way to force reluctant pastors to build more schools and require recalcitrant Catholic parents to send their children to these schools. It was a frustrating experience with many false starts and few results except for an increase in acrimony.

The last two decades of the nineteenth century were years of upheaval and social change within the Irish community and the Catholic Church. A new generation of

American-born Irish Catholics were attracted to the fruits of American life and hoped to prepare their children for increasingly productive lives in American society. The strong desire of these Irish Americans to participate fully in American society provided a challenge and dilemma for Irish American educators well into the twentieth century: Could parochial schools be both secular and Catholic? That was the salient question put to Catholic educators in the first two decades of the twentieth century.

It was a laudable goal fraught with difficulties. As Irish American Catholic schools became increasingly similar to public schools, their independence and very reason for existence were threatened. In fact, growing similarities between parochial and public schools caused concern among some Irish Catholics. One editor, Patrick Hickey of the *Catholic Review*, argued that the Irish American parochial school, in its effort to Americanize, had strayed from the true path; to Hickey's way of thinking, the worst thing that could be said of parochial schools was that they were similar to public schools.

Even though Irish American Catholic schools remained distinct from the public schools in one important area—intensive religious instruction—they became increasingly similar in other areas. As Irish Catholic parents became concerned about their children's economic future, they pressured parochial school educators to emulate the curriculum used in public schools. Like all parents, Irish American parents wanted the best for their children.

Yet the development of the Irish American model for parochial education, the norm in every diocese by 1930, would be undermined in the coming decade by economic conditions beyond the bishops' control. The hardship of the Great Depression stopped the progress of Irish Catholic school construction in dioceses large and small. To be sure, this did not stop a sizable core of committed Irish Catholics who continued to send their children to these schools whenever possible. Classrooms were crowded, and by 1950 it was not surprising to find major metropolitan areas in which 50 percent or more of the schoolchildren were enrolled in Catholic parochial schools.

In looking back on the Irish contribution to parochial education, one must conclude that the idea of a distinct Irish American Catholic education is something of a misnomer. In truth, Irish Americans never thought of their parish schools as anything but Catholic. In truth, Irish American educators—priests and nuns, for the most part— did not see a need to stress Irish American cultural values in the classroom. They simply assumed that Irish values and Catholic beliefs were intertwined. The former was subsumed into the latter. When Irish Americans began to establish and promote parochial schools, their stated goals were to prepare their children for useful, productive roles in American society without compromising their religious faith. There was little mention or concern about Irish culture or language. Without doubt, they achieved their stated goals. Irish Americans are among the most successful ethnic groups in the United States today. Parochial schools were an important building block in that achievement. *See also*: Ethnicity (and parish schools).

Further Reading: Jay P. Dolan, *The American Catholic Experience: A History from Colonial Times to the Present* (Garden City, NY: Doubleday, 1995): 262–293; Charles Fanning, *The Irish Voice in America* (Lexington: University Press of Kentucky, 1990); Timothy Walch, *Parish School: American Catholic Parochial Education from Colonial Times to the Present* (New York: Crossroad, 1996); Howard Weisz, *Irish American and Italian American Views of Education* (New York: Arno Press, 1976).

Timothy Walch

Italian American Catholics

Italian American Catholics took a different course from that of other ethnic groups when they turned away from the ethnic parish school. In spite of their large numbers and their willingness to build extraordinary churches, the Italians showed little interest in parish schools. This unique response to education—one so different from the German, Polish, and Slavic response—perplexed the stolid, Irish-born bishops of the American Church.

Certainly, the Italians posed the biggest challenge for these church leaders. In fact, the unwillingness of the Italian immigrants to support the common goals of the hierarchy became known as the "Italian problem." The bishops' "solution" to this Italian streak of independence was to cultivate the allegiance of Italian children. "If we cannot get the adults," noted one bishop, "let us try for the children."

But this "solution" did not solve the Italian problem. In fact, it was but one aspect of the problem. "Experience has amply proved that the Italians will not send their children to parochial schools if they have to pay for them," noted one Italian priest. Even when the bishops built and paid for Catholic schools in Italian parishes, the classrooms were not full.

What accounted for the Italian intransigence? The answer lay in the relationship between the Church and the laity in Italy and the economic circumstances faced by most Italians arriving in the United States at the turn of the century. These factors played a major part in the determination of Italians not to build or support parochial schools. This determination marked the Italians as unique among Catholic immigrants.

Catholicism as a philosophy of life and as a world religion was unknown to the typical nineteenth-century peasant, known in their native land as *contadini*. These peasants knew of the Church only through the personality of their local parish priests. Before the unification of Italy as a nation-state in the 1870s, local priests came almost exclusively from the upper classes known as the *galantuomo*. Not surprisingly, the *contadini* respected the *galantuomo* as leaders of a Church of immense wealth and power.

But with the nationalization movement, known as the "Risorgimento," the Church and its priests lost control over temporal affairs in Italy. With nationalization, the priesthood was a less attractive career for the *galantuomo*, and the Church was forced to recruit large numbers of new priests from among the middle classes and even from among the *contadini*. By the turn of the century, therefore, the relationship between Church and peasant had been turned upside down. The parish priest was no longer the leader of the local community. Indeed, the priest could not even count on the respect normally accorded to a representative of the Church.

More important, many priests were suspected of being traitors to their social classes. Because their material well-being was determined by the *galantuomo*, parish priests were often defenders of the privileges of the upper classes and opponents of change. Many of these priests were seen as sycophants at best and often seen as traitors to their people.

This Italian tradition of anticlericalism was transported to the United States by the *contadini*. In many Italian American neighborhoods, local ethnic newspapers attacked the Church generally and local priests in particular. Letters published in these papers indicated that many immigrants also were anti-Catholic. This tension was exacerbated by the presence of non-Italian priests in many Italian parishes. These Irishmen made Italian Catholics all the more wary of the American Church and its parochial schools.

But anticlericalism was not the major reason for the low numbers of Italian American children in parochial schools. The *contadini* perceived the child as a useful, productive member of the family. Children were needed to support the family. Italian parents were shocked and amazed at the "imposed idleness" of the American children enrolled in school. Not surprisingly, Italian parents actively opposed any effort to have their children attend school. When school attendance became mandatory, the *contadini* grudgingly complied, but many turn-of-the-century Italian Americans agreed with the New York Italian who noted that the attendance of his children at school "ruined all our hopes of a decent living, kept us poor, and destroyed the sanctity of the home."

Italian Catholics opposed education in general and parochial education in particular. In spite of their large numbers and their willingness to build extraordinary churches, the Italians showed little interest in parish schools. This unique response to education—one so different from the German and Polish response—perplexed the stolid, Irish American bishops of the American Church. If the majority of Irish bishops failed to reach their Italian congregants through the establishment of parish schools, they did find a measure of success through special missions and apostolates. Bands of Italian priests would travel from one diocese to the next reinvigorating the spirituality of Italian immigrants and reminding them of their obligations to Holy Mother Church. This form of religious education was not a suitable alternative to the parish school, but the bishops accepted success where they could find it.

Yet, the Italian American contribution to parochial education should not be dismissed or minimized. Small clusters of Italian Catholics in every diocese did choose to support Catholic schools, and religious leaders such as Mother Frances Xavier Cabrini and Bishop Giovanni Battista Scalabrini symbolized the Italian American commitment to the preservation of Catholic values in the New World. If the majority of Italian Catholics did not support parish schools, there is no question of their commitment to their own unique form of Catholic education. *See also*: Ethnicity (and parish schools).

Further Reading: Richard M. Linkh, *American Catholicism and European Immigrants, 1900–1924* (New York: Center for Migration Studies, 1975); Timothy Walch, *Parish School: American Catholic Parochial Education from Colonial Times to the Present* (New York: Crossroad, 1996); Howard Weisz, *Irish American and Italian American Views on Education* (New York: Arno Press, 1976).

Timothy Walch

J

John XXIII, Pope (1881–1963)

Elected Pope on October 28, 1958, and chose the name John XXIII. Noted for convening the Second Vatican Council in 1959, which opened in October 1962.

He was born Angelo Roncalli, November 25, 1881, at Sotto il Monte near Bergamo, in northern Italy. His parents were tenant farmers until his adult life. Angelo was the fourth of twelve children and the first male.

Angelo had a close relationship with all of his family, as was typical of Italian peasantry. He always remembered his mother's religious devotion and her proclamation that she had consecrated his life to the Madonna. As a priest and teacher, he often spoke of how the Madonna gave the peasants kindness and hope. At the age of 8 his father took him to Saint Peter's Bridge to observe a parade in honor of the foundation anniversary of Catholic action, a lay social movement. Because he was too small to see over the crowd to the parade route, Angelo's father lifted him onto his shoulders, a gesture Angelo fondly remembered years later as Pope. Throughout his lifetime, Angelo's sisters served him as housekeepers and cooks at several of his assignments. His most difficult moments were the loss of each family member, especially when he was in Foreign Service and could not minister to them.

These warm family relations are often credited for the abilities Roncalli later used as a diplomat. Roncalli had a delightful personality, warm and overtly affectionate, which allowed him to move comfortably among new people. He often noted how deeply he was also influenced by a parish priest, the calm and compassionate Francesco Rebuzzini.

Roncalli studied at the seminary in Bergamo, later earning a scholarship to the Pontifical Seminary in Rome. He was ordained in 1904 at the Church of Santa Maria on the Piazza del Popolo and said his first mass in St. Peter's.

After his ordination he returned to his diocese as secretary to Bishop Radini-Tedeschi. Roncalli was enormously fond of Radini-Tedeschi and learned many of his leadership skills from him. He also served as professor of church history and apologetics at the Bergamo seminary. He included in his busy schedule time to work with a diocesan organization of Catholic women and at a residence hall for students.

When World War I began, Roncalli became Sergeant Roncalli of the medical corps

Pope John XXIII. Courtesy of the Library of Congress.

and, later, Lieutenant Roncalli of the chaplains' corps. After the war he returned to his former work in the diocese.

Benedict XV called him to Rome to work for the Congregation for the Propagation of the Faith. In 1925 Pius XI made him an archbishop and appointed him Apostolic Visitor to Bulgaria. At first he disliked the idea of leaving Italy and his family; some even suggested that he had been exiled by the move. Roncalli always saw the hand of God in events so quickly he used his post to improve relations between Catholicism and orthodoxy, one of his dearest objectives.

In 1935, as Apostolic Delegate to Greece and Turkey, Roncalli moved to Istanbul. There he spent most of World War II earning his reputation for relieving the Greeks from the suffering of famine and occupation. Meanwhile, he initiated many contacts with separated Eastern Churches. He was also part of a secret program to give Jews safe passage out of Germany and other occupied countries. Roncalli did not seek to gain credit for these actions, and only after the war's conclusion did the public learn of the thousands he saved.

Roncalli was aware of the entangled nature of Italian politics and the Church, and he most often reacted as a peasant, willing to ignore structural failures if human relations were handled with care. He often dealt with the Church's institutional structures the same way.

Pius XII named Roncalli as nuncio to France following the war. Tensions existed between the Church and French factions, Gaullists and Vichyites. A clever Roncalli managed to minimize antagonisms. He also became an observer for the United Nations Educational, Scientific, and Cultural Organization (UNESCO), increasing his awareness of international relations. In 1953, Pius XII made him a cardinal. He received his red hat from French president Auriol, a socialist, demonstrating Cardinal Roncalli's ability to make friends and win respect for the Church in France.

Subsequently, Cardinal Roncalli was made patriarch of Venice, a prestigious post in the Church. He again won the love of his flock as he guided them with openness and kindness. As he aged, Roncalli cared less about how others might interpret his actions and continued to exert a warm, pastoral image as he mingled with Venetians.

Roncalli was seldom credited for the depth or originality of his thoughts. Throughout his career, Roncalli's interpretation of the Church's role in modern society was under suspicion by Vatican conservatives. Often, they underestimated him and failed to recognize his subtle strategies for reform. During his tenure in France, his perception of the Church's role was influenced by progressive French theologians and other modern thinkers. His writings and preaching continued to demonstrate his efforts to develop a role for the Church in a changing, modern world.

Surprising many in the Church, Cardinal Roncalli was elected Pope on October 28, 1958. At the age of seventy-seven, most considered Roncalli's term an honor and a reward for his successful ecclesiastical career. Pope John XXIII recognized the power of his position and amazed the world when he announced plans for the Second Vatican Council on January 25, 1959. He opened the council on October 11, 1962, amid worldwide anticipation and media coverage.

John XXIII died on June 3, 1963, after a long illness. His death evoked a huge wave of sympathy from those inside the Catholic Church and many outsiders who were touched by his warm personality and enthusiastic energy. *See also*: *Gaudium et Spes*; Vatican Council II.

Further Reading: Thomas Cahill, *John XXIII* (New York: Viking Press, 2002); Richard Cushing, *Call Me John: A Life of Pope John XXIII* (Boston: St. Paul Editions, 1963); Lawrence Elliott, *I Will Be Called John: A Biography of Pope John XXIII* (New York: Reader's Digest Press, 1973); Christian Feldman, *John XXIII: A Spiritual Biography* (New York: Crossroad, 2000); Alfred McBride, *A Retreat with Pope John XXIII: Opening the Windows to Wisdom* (Cincinnati, OH: St. Anthony Messenger Press, 1996).

Merylann J. "Mimi" Schuttloffel

John Paul II, Pope (1920–)

Karol Jozef Wojtyla was born May 18, 1920, in Wadowice, Poland. He was the youngest of three children born to his father, Karol Jozef Wojtyla, and mother, Emilia (Kaczorowska), who died when Karol was 9 years old. His father was a pious man and set a good example for his son in learning and practicing his Catholic faith.

Hallmarks of young Wojtyla's education that remained a part of his entire life included his athletic agility, passion for drama, and appreciation of literature. He studied literature at the Jagiellonian University in Krakow, where he was involved in theater and literary activities. He pursued seminary studies underground during the Nazi occupation in Poland.

Wojtyla was ordained a priest on All Saints Day, November 1, 1946. After completing various pastoral assignments in Poland, he went to Rome for further theological studies. Wojtyla was a student at the Pontifical Angelicum University sponsored by the Dominicans. When he completed his doctorate and postdoctoral studies, he returned to Poland for several pastoral assignments, which included his appointment of teaching ethics at the Catholic University of Lublin.

In 1958 he was ordained auxiliary bishop of Krakow and became archbishop of this see in 1964. Three years later in 1967, Pope Paul VI made Wojtyla a cardinal. As cardinal archbishop he distinguished himself as an indefatigable leader, working tirelessly against the oppressive encroachments that communism made upon the dignity and the political rights that his people so desired.

The year 1978 would prove to be a dramatic time of transition for the Roman Catholic Church. On October 16 of that year, Karol Wojtyla was elected as the third Pope to serve that year, following the deaths of Paul VI in August and John Paul I in September. Wojtyla chose the name of John Paul II and so began his long pontificate. John Paul II's election and pontificate established numerous precedents. He was the first non-Italian Pope elected in 456 years; he was the first Slav ever chosen as successor to Peter; he was the first Pope to visit many continents and countries around the world; during the presidency of Jimmy Carter, he was the first Pope to visit the White House, on October 6, 1979. His legendary command and finesse of numerous languages opened countless doors for him.

John Paul II is perhaps the most prolific writer ever to serve as bishop of Rome. Drawing upon his literary studies and mastery of linguistics, he has written plays, poetry, encyclicals, exhortations, sermons, and letters. In *Crossing the Threshold of Hope* (1994), the Pope as pastor and teacher prepared the world for the coming millennium.

Three documents written and promulgated during the pontificate of John Paul II are noteworthy for their impact and influence upon Catholic schools: the revised *Code of Canon Law* (1983), the Apostolic Constitution *Ex Corde Ecclesiae* (1990), and the *Catechism of the Catholic Church* (1992).

The revised code of canon law brought to completion a project initiated by Pope John XXIII. *Book III The Teaching Office of the Church* (canons 793–821) comprises specific legislation related to Catholic schools. Several familiar themes are enshrined in these canons such as the role of primacy that parents have in educating their children, the value of Catholic schools, and the various duties, rights, relationships, and responsibilities involved with Catholic schools, pastors, religious communities, parishes, and local churches.

The Apostolic Constitution *Ex Corde Ecclesiae* (1990) sought to contextualize can-

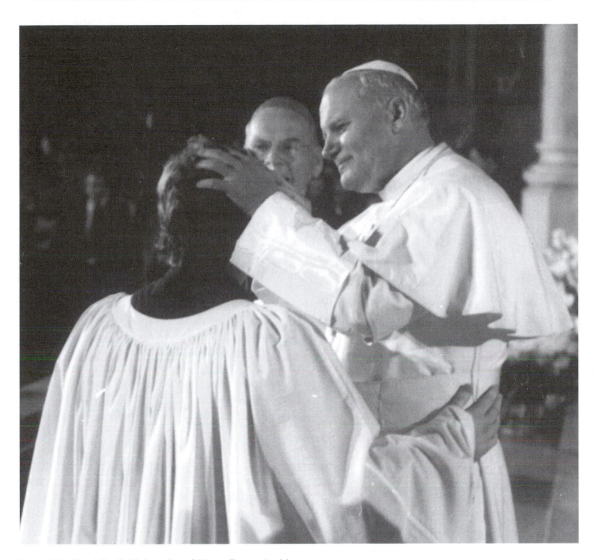

Pope John Paul II. © University of Notre Dame Archives.

ons 807–814. Part I, *Identity and Mission*, sets the tone of the document, identifying "essential characteristics" of Catholic higher education. In Part II, *The General Norms*, the document stipulates how Catholic higher education must conform to various relationships with the local church. In the United States, the 236 Catholic colleges and universities encountered many thorny issues to be resolved, particularly with the areas of academic freedom and the mandate to teach theology granted by bishops to professors.

The *Catechism of the Catholic Church* (1992) is a summary of beliefs and practices in the Roman Catholic Church. Catechetical textbooks and religious education programs in all Catholic elementary and secondary schools undertook revisions of curriculum that would reflect the content of the *Catechism*.

John Paul II has made several pastoral visitations to the United States (1979, 1987,

1993, 1995, 1999). These sojourns often provided opportunities for him to visit various Catholic educational institutions. John Paul II met with 19,000 young people at Madison Square Garden in New York on October 3, 1979. He affirmed that most of them were students from Catholic high schools. He noted that the purpose of Catholic education is to create encounters with Jesus Christ so that the students in turn will bring Christ's presence to the world. The students presented the Pope with a T-shirt, a pair of blue jeans, and a guitar as tokens of their affection and way of life.

On September 12, 1987, the Pope visited the only historically black, Catholic college in the United States, Xavier University in New Orleans, Louisiana, where he delivered a major address on Catholic higher education. During this second visit to the United States (1987), he met with representatives from Catholic schools and religious education programs at the Louisiana Superdome in New Orleans on September 12, 1987. In his address, the Pope expressed gratitude to the educators for sharing in the teaching ministry of Jesus. He emphasized the role of parents in educating their children at home and being involved at their children's schools. The Pope stressed the right of parents to choose the schools that best serve their needs. John Paul II noted the reputation of academic excellence of U.S. Catholic schools. He reminded Catholic school leaders to be knowledgeable about the U.S. bishops' pastoral letter *To Teach as Jesus Did* (1972) and the Vatican documents *The Catholic School* (1977) and *Lay Catholics in Schools* (1982).

The Pope took this opportunity to cite the ultimate goal in Catholic education as knowledge and redemption in Jesus Christ. He emphasized the role of community as the context of the Catholic school's mission, mirroring the life and love of the Holy Trinity. He also noted the importance of the wider community beyond that of the parish or diocesan structures, which elicit engagement and respect as students encounter cultural diversity.

At World Youth Day in Denver, Colorado, he met with President William Clinton at Regis University on August 12, 1993. Shortly before leaving Denver on August 15, 1993, the Pope visited Mount St. Vincent's Home; this facility is home and school to children aged 5 to 14 with various learning and emotional challenges. The Pope commended the Sisters of Charity of Leavenworth who staff the home and used this visit as a time to underscore the rights of children. *See also*: *Catechism of the Catholic Church, The*; *Ex corde ecclesiae*.

Further Reading: Peter Hebblethwaite, *Pope John Paul II and the Church* (Kansas City: Sheed and Ward, 1995); John Paul II, *Crossing the Threshold of Hope* (New York: Knopf, 1994); George Weigel, *Witness to Hope: The Biography of John Paul II* (New York: HarperCollins, 1999).

Michael P. Caruso, SJ

Johnson, George (1889–1944)

George Johnson was the consummate organization man in the history of Catholic education. He was born on February 22, 1889, in Toledo, Ohio. Following a parochial school education and preparatory and collegiate courses of study at St. John's University in Toledo, Johnson studied for the priesthood at St. Bernard's Seminary in Rochester, New York, and at the North American College in Rome. He was ordained in 1914, enrolled at the Catholic University of America (CUA) in 1916, and received his Ph.D. from CUA in 1919. He became superintendent of the Toledo parochial schools that year and joined the faculty at the Catholic University of America in 1921, where the prominent Catholic educator, Thomas Edward Shields, mentored him.

Johnson was practical, pragmatic, and self-effacing, yet he also had strong convictions about the purpose of Catholic schooling in a free society. He combined native organizational and political skills with the intellectual drive and Shield's educational philosophy. During the years from 1929 until his sudden death in 1944, Johnson reflected the consensus of opinion on parochial education.

Because of this gift, Johnson served as a Catholic representative on a number of public commissions and at the time of his death was secretary of the American Council of Education. He did all this in addition to serving as secretary of the National Catholic Educational Association (NCEA), director of the education department of the National Catholic Welfare Conference (NCWC), and professor of education at CUA.

Johnson's ideas on education had been influenced by Shields, but not entirely formed by him. Like his mentor, Johnson was receptive to progressive ideas on education, but he was always careful to draw distinctions between his own views and those of his more liberal colleagues. Throughout his career, Johnson was committed to the total integration of Catholic education in a free society. His service on government commissions reflected this commitment. Johnson's philosophy also was reflected in his 114 articles, two books, and the laboratory school that he founded at CUA in 1935.

Many biographers and friends referred to Johnson as a "bridge builder." Indeed, he broke down the barriers that had grown between the NCEA, the NCWC, and the CUA Department of Education. Moreover, he opened the association up to new ties with secular organizations such as the U.S. Office of Education, the National Education Association, and the American Council of Education.

Johnson was an articulate, thoughtful opponent of federal involvement in education but a persuasive proponent of the civic responsibilities of Catholic schools. He channeled his views through several mediums. Service on two federal committees on education and speeches and reports at the NCEA meetings were his two major forums.

Johnson's ideas were shaped by many factors, particularly by his service on various government commissions and committees. Between 1929 and 1944, he served on President Hoover's Advisory Committee on Education, President Roosevelt's Advisory Committee on Education, the Wartime Commission of the U.S. Office of Education, the Education Advisory Committee of the Coordinator of Inter-American Affairs, and the Advisory Committee on Education of the Joint Army and Navy Committee on Welfare and Recreation. On most of these committees Johnson was the principal representative of Catholic education, and in this capacity he was often called upon to explain the Catholic position on educational issues.

Johnson also influenced general opinion on Catholic education through his 1943 book, *Better Men for Better Times*. The volume was written for Catholic educators and encouraged them to develop the child's basic relationships with himself and others. Published by the Catholic University of America Press, the volume was aimed at a rather narrow spectrum of Catholic educators. But the book caught the attention of David Lawrence, publisher of *United States News*, who reviewed the book in his popular magazine. *Better Men for Better Times* became a best-seller for the university press, and orders came in from thousands of individuals in the armed forces and other organizations. Once again, Johnson's influence extended beyond his expectations.

Johnson's premature death in 1944 came as a shock to all who knew him. He suffered a fatal heart attack while speaking to the graduates of Trinity College in Washington, DC. It was an untimely death for a man who had done so much for Catholic education but who had so much more to do. As the consummate organization man, Johnson was the authoritative, if unofficial, spokesman for America's Catholic schools during the 1930s and 1940s. He was eulogized in many national publications starting with the *Congressional Record*. Long after his death, however, Johnson's ideas continued to live on in his many contributions to Catholic educational organizations. *See also*: *Guiding Growth in Christian Social Living*; Shields, Thomas Edward.

Further Reading: Harold L. Buetow, *Of Singular Benefit: The Story of U.S. Catholic Education* (New York: Macmillan, 1970); Mary Giovanni Vidoni, "Monsignor George Johnson: His Principles and Their Application to the Curriculum of the Catholic Schools," unpublished master's thesis, Catholic University of America, 1952; Timothy Walch, *Parish School: American Catholic Parochial Education from Colonial Times to the Present* (New York: Crossroad, 1996).

Timothy Walch

Jurisdiction

The power or authority vested in an individual or entity to act or carry out its required functions. While the bishop retains ultimate jurisdiction over all Catholic schools within the diocese, the jurisdiction of school officials such as superintendents, presidents, and principals and school entities such as boards or councils is dependent upon to whom the bishop has delegated certain authority within the diocese, upon whether the Catholic school is parochial, interparochial, diocesan, or private, and upon the governance model used within the particular school type.

Canon law provides a framework for understanding jurisdiction as it is applied to Catholic schools. According to Canon law, no school can claim the title Catholic without supervision or written recognition by an ecclesiastical authority (Canon 803). Furthermore, it is the responsibility of the bishop to regulate and to be vigilant over the Catholic education within the diocese (Canon 804). This vigilance includes approving those who are entrusted with teaching religion, and if necessary, calling for their removal for religious or moral reasons (Canon 805). The bishop's responsibility of vigilance extends even to private schools run by religious orders operating within the diocese (Canon 806). Since the bishop's legislative authority cannot be delegated (Canon 466), the jurisdiction of all school officials and school entities is consultative in at least the areas cited above. Unlike the bishop's legislative power, his executive and judicial power can, and is, delegated among a number of functionaries, including pastors, the superintendent of schools for the diocese, and other various administrators within the diocese.

Just as our civil law recognizes corporations as having the legal status of personhood, canon law recognizes certain entities as having the particular legal status of juridic persons. Dioceses, parishes, and religious congregations are all juridic persons. Canon law requires juridic persons to have administrators who are responsible for the care of all goods under their jurisdiction (Canons 1281–1288). Accordingly, "where the school is part of an existing juridic person the responsibility of the canonical administrator must be respected as the ultimate authority" (O'Brien, 1987, p. 14).

The bishop of a diocese typically delegates to the superintendent of schools the responsibility for the administration of all diocesan schools and as a coordinator of all parochial and interparochial schools. Pastors serve as the canonical administrators of parochial schools. For the interparochial schools, the bishop typically names a pastor from one of the sponsoring parishes as the canonical administrator. Diocesan, parochial, and interparochial schools also have principals and, in the larger high schools, presidents, who serve as site-based administrators of the school.

Catholic schools sponsored by a religious community do not fall under the direct authority of the bishop except in those areas specifically identified in canon law. The religious congregations are juridic persons separate and distinct from the juridic person of the diocese, and therefore the governance of their schools is aligned with the dictates of the religious orders' constitution and governance structure. Religious congregations typically have a member of their order serving as the canonical administrator for a school or schools.

In light of canon law, it follows that all Catholic school boards, councils, and committees are either consultative to the appropriate canonical administrator, for example, the bishop, bishop's delegate, or pastor, or are of limited jurisdiction as outlined in their constitution and bylaws that have been approved by the bishop or religious congregation.

There are effectively three basic models of boards used within Catholic schools: the consultative board, the board with limited jurisdiction, and the corporate board. A consultative board usually takes on the responsibilities of planning, policy development, financing, public relations, and evaluation. The canonical administrator or delegate typically sits on this board. The board serves as a policy-making body, while the administration of the educational program is left to the president, principal, or administrative team. The board with limited jurisdiction takes on specific governance responsibilities enumerated in the board constitution and bylaws that have been duly approved by the appropriate ecclesiastical authority. A board with limited jurisdiction has more authority than the consultative board, including the responsibility for the hiring, evaluation, and dismissal of the chief administrator (president or principal), subject to the final review by the canonical administrator. The corporate board typically takes on all the responsibilities articulated in its corporate charter and bylaws and serves as the ultimate governing authority except for those areas specifically reserved for the bishop in accordance with canon law. *See also*: Bishops; Governance; Hierarchy.

Further Reading: J. Stephen O'Brien, ed., *A Primer on Educational Governance in the Catholic Church* (Washington, DC: National Catholic Educational Association, 1987): John Paul II, *Code of Canon Law* (Washington, DC: Canon Law Society, 1983); Mary Shaughnessy, *A Primer on Law for Administrators and Boards, Commissions & Councils of Catholic Education* (Washington, DC: National Catholic Educational Association, 2000).

John T. James

K

Katzer, Frederick (1844–1903)

Frederick X. Katzer was born in Austria in 1844. Educated in Austria, he initially wanted to become a Jesuit. He emigrated to the United States in 1864, entered St. Francis Seminary in Milwaukee, and was ordained as a diocesan priest in 1866. Following a stint as professor of theology at the Salesianum in Milwaukee, he was made secretary to the bishop of Green Bay. In 1886 he was consecrated as bishop of Green Bay.

Katzer was said to consider Germany his mother and the United States his bride. He was described by Archbishop John Ireland of St. Paul, a longtime adversary, as "a man thoroughly German and thoroughly unfit to be an archbishop," yet was considered the best friend to the Polish American Catholics among the hierarchy of Wisconsin.

While still head of the see of Green Bay and prior to his assuming the archbishopric of Milwaukee, Katzer became embroiled in the Bennett Law strife. Along with the ailing Archbishop Michael Heiss of Milwaukee and Bishop Killian Flasch of La-Crosse, he coauthored the "Manifesto" of the Wisconsin Catholic bishops in opposition to the Bennett Law in March 1890. (The most objectionable features of the Bennett Law were the requirement that the language of instruction in schools be English and that a youngster had to attend school in the public school district in which he or she lived.) The bishops declared the law "unnecessary," because there were but a few Catholic parochial schools in the state that did not use English as their language of instruction; as "offensive," because the Catholics had built and maintained their schools without any state assistance; and as "unjust," because the law interfered with the sacred, inalienable rights of parents to educate their children. It was the responsibility of the state to assist parents in carrying out their God-given duty, not interfere with them. Catholic education promoted the welfare of the state by making good, virtuous citizens; the state should not molest parents in their God-given mission. Parental obligation to provide a religious education for their children stemmed from the natural and divine law; mere secular education was not sufficient. Katzer and his fellow bishops saw the hand of the Masons in the law, noting that similar measures existed in Europe at that time, which were products of Masonry. He maintained that the law constituted state aggression and was an encroachment of Antichrist that was inimical to the interests and welfare of those who took Christianity seriously.

But two months later, Katzer delivered the keynote address to representatives of sixty-seven German American Catholic societies gathered at the German Catholic Convention in Milwaukee. Averring that the proper order in education was the individual, then the family, and lastly the state, Katzer contended that it was the responsibility of the state to protect the rights of individual and family, not assume them as was the case in the Bennett Law. Describing the Bennett Law as one of a group of "gag laws suggested by the union of devils," Katzer again blamed the Masons for this incursion into the rights of parents to choose a religious education for their children. Regarding the law as the entering wedge for the suppression of Catholic schools, Katzer called on the delegates to defend the schools, terming it their "highest duty" and an "honor."

Katzer became archbishop of Milwaukee in 1891 over the objections of Ireland and other American archbishops whose first choice was John Lancaster Spalding. His elevation was regarded as a victory for the German party. Katzer and several of his allies did not accept Archbishop Ireland's controversial Faribault Plan (nor did their suffragan bishops), which called for cooperation with public schools. Katzer regarded this plan as a "surrender of Catholic schools to State authorities." Indeed, Katzer and others were unhappy with the compromise offered in the internal Catholic "school war" of the early 1890s by the papal delegate, Archbishop Francis Satolli. Katzer held that the correct position on the school question was the one taken by the American bishops at the Third Plenary Council of Baltimore, which called for the erection of a parochial school for each parish and attendance at those schools by Catholic children, unless, in both instances, exemptions were granted by the local bishop.

Portrayed by Ireland as a "man who knows as little of America as a Huron," Katzer was a staunch advocate of Catholic schools and a formidable adversary on their behalf. He remained so until his death. *See also*: Cahenslyism; Catholic School Question, The; German American Catholics.

Further Reading: Colman J. Barry, *The Catholic Church and German Americans* (Milwaukee: Bruce, 1953); Harry H. Heming, *The Catholic Church in Wisconsin* (Milwaukee: T. J. Sullivan, 1896); Anthony J. Kuzniewski, *Faith and Fatherland: The Polish Church War in Wisconsin, 1895–1918* (Notre Dame, IN: University of Notre Dame Press, 1980); Daniel F. Reilly, *The School Controversy 1891–1893* (New York: Amo Press and the New York Times, 1969).

Thomas C. Hunt

Know-Nothing Party

The Know-Nothing Party, also known as the American Party, was an anti-Catholic and anti-immigrant party that rose to political power in the 1850s. Preventing state funding for Catholic schools and advocating the use of the King James Bible in common schools were among key Know-Nothing issues. The Know-Nothings' fall from power was as quick as their ascent. By 1860, the Know-Nothings were no longer an effective political force. As a result, many former Know-Nothing party members were absorbed into the growing Republican Party.

The Know-Nothing Party, founded in the early 1850s, began as a secret society called the Supreme Order of the Star Spangled Banner. Charles Allen, of New York, founded this secret order, which was a patriotic fraternal society whose membership was limited to native-born Protestants. When members were asked about their secret order and activities, members replied "I know nothing," hence the origin of the group's popular name. The Know-Nothing Party was a reaction to, and result of, anti-Catholic and anti-immigrant sentiments that were flourishing in the United States.

The Know-Nothings capitalized on the environment of the time. There was an exponential growth in the United States immigrant population, particularly the Catholic immigrant population (by 1850 Catholics were the largest single religious denomination in the nation). Simultaneously, there was a growing and intense wave of nativism, particularly among the Protestant population.

The party's political platform contained anti-Catholic and anti-immigrant provisions. For example, Know-Nothings advocated that immigrants live in the United States for twenty-one years before they were allowed to vote. Along the same lines they declared that immigrants should not hold public office and that children of immigrants not have any rights unless they attended common (public) schools.

The party wanted to diminish what members felt was the growing political power of Catholics and immigrants in the United States. Know-Nothings were particularly suspicious of the Roman Catholic Church and the Jesuit order. According to Know-Nothing claims, the Roman Catholic Church and the Jesuit order held allegiance to the Vatican and the Pope, not to the United States. Initially, the group tried to pressure existing political parties to nominate only native-born Protestants for political offices. The Know-Nothings felt political offices should be limited to native-born Protestants.

In 1855 and 1856 the Know-Nothings removed their cloak of secrecy and held open conventions on the state and national level. The Know-Nothings claimed to be a reform movement. The formal name for the Know-Nothing Party in these conventions was the American Party. As a result of their formalization there were three U.S. political parties during that period: Democratic, Republican, and American.

Although they were a national party, the Know-Nothings flourished in the North, dominating state houses in the 1850s. Once it gained political power, the Know-Nothing Party began to attempt to legislate its anti-immigrant and anti-Catholic platform. It attempted to diminish Catholic schools legislatively by promoting Protestant values in public schools. For example, in Massachusetts a law was enacted requiring public school students to read Scripture daily from the King James version of the bible. Similar activities continued after the 1854 Massachusetts election, when the Know-Nothings won all the state senate seats, all but three of the state representative seats, all the congressional seats, and all state offices including the governorship. The Know-Nothings by far were most successful politically in Massachusetts. Once in office, these party members pursued and passed a constitutional amendment barring the use of common school funds for religious schools.

Know-Nothings also passed a "nunnery inspection" law, which targeted Catholic schools. Schools were subject to surprise visits by committee members responsible for the investigation of "certain unnamed practices allegedly taking place within" Catholic schools.

Know-Nothings' actions against Catholics and immigrants were not limited to legislative action. Know-Nothings used public opinion, word of mouth, and physical force to implement their agenda. For example, non-Catholics were told that the Catholic attempts to get a share of the common school funds for their own schools and to eliminate the Protestant Bible from the public schools "were a concerted attack on the foundations of the Republic." The environment the Know-Nothings created through their words placed them in the midst of violent controversies. In 1854 and 1855 Know-Nothings were in the midst of bloody Election Day riots. Members of the party were blamed for singling out Catholic voters and forcibly preventing them from voting. Ridicule and harassment were also used. For example, in Milwaukee, Know-Nothing harassment made it unsafe for Catholic sisters (vowed religious women) to wear their religious garb on the street. In Philadelphia, sisters from St. Michael's in Philadelphia decided to move their entire community to Dubuque, Iowa, because of obstacles to their work in Philadelphia that were attributable to the Know-Nothing agitation. Lastly, six Xaverian brothers, who came to Louisville, Kentucky, to open parish schools were pursued, ridiculed, and insulted as a result of Know-Nothing agitation. Ultimately, this harassment forced all but one brother to abandon their home and return to Europe. *See also*: Anti-Catholicism.

Further Reading: Tyler Anbinder, *Nativism and Slavery, The Northern Know Nothings & the Politics of the 1850s* (New York: Oxford University Press, 1992); James A. Burns, *The Growth and Development of the Catholic School System in the United States* (New York: Benziger Brothers, 1912); James W. Fraser, *Between Church and State: Religion and Public Education in a Multicultural America* (New York: St. Martin's Press, 1999); Michael F. Holt, "The Politics of Impatience: The Origins of Know Nothingism," *The Journal of American History* 60, 2 (September 1973): 309–331; Neil G. McCluskey, *Catholic Viewpoint on Education* (Garden City, NY: Doubleday, 1959).

Yolanda Hart

Ku Klux Klan

The Ku Klux Klan was a secret society formed in the aftermath of the Civil War to terrorize former slaves and ensure that a white power structure would remain in control of southern society. The Klan's activities lessened with the end of the military occupation of the South in 1877.

The Klan returned to national prominence in 1915 in response to a large influx of immigrants from Southern and Eastern Europe and the movement of African Americans to northern cities. This renewed Klan took as one of its missions the abolition of all things Catholic, including parochial schools.

The principal mission of the Klan was to support "100 percent Americanism" and to take action against all groups that the Klan defined as un-American. Among the groups that came under attack by the Klan were African Americans, Jews, and Catholics.

The Klan chose Michigan and Oregon as the battlefields for its campaign to abolish Catholic schools. In Michigan, for example, the Klan mounted a campaign to require the attendance of all children in public schools. Even though the Klan was vociferous and predicted victory, its confidence was not enough to overcome the opposition of the state's large Catholic population. The proposal was soundly defeated by a margin of nearly two to one in 1920. A second effort in 1924 also went down to defeat. There is little doubt that Michigan Catholics, galvanized by the fearful consequences of such a measure, held the balance of power on this issue.

But in Oregon, a state with a small Catholic population, the Klan was more successful than in Michigan. The Oregon campaign emerged out of a strong tradition of nativism in the state. As in other states, the concern over foreigners and the need to reinforce American values intensified in Oregon in the years after World War I. The public school was seen as a bulwark of these values, and the Klan molded this concern into an attack on Catholic schools.

The 1922 election campaign was intense, with the Klan leading a vociferous and vituperative attack on the Catholic Church as well as its schools. Klan members toured the state labeling Catholic schools as un-American. It was a twisted logic that appealed to the hundreds of thousands of non-Catholics in the state.

Oregon Catholics and other opponents of the bill found themselves defending their patriotism but having little impact on public opinion. On November 7, 1922, the Klan won the day. They elected Walter Pierce, a pro-amendment advocate, as governor, they sent pro-amendment legislators to the state house, and most important, they passed the school initiative abolishing Catholic schools.

Compulsory attendance at public schools was to begin in September 1926, but opponents of the measure were determined to test the constitutionality of the new law. They appealed to the U.S. District Court in Portland early in 1923, and in March 1924 the Court ruled unanimously that the state of Oregon had exceeded its powers, unlawfully taken constitutional rights from the Catholic schools, and deprived them of their property under the due process of the law. Newspapers and educators across the country applauded the decision.

Press opinion and district court decisions were not enough to convince Pierce and the Klan that the law was unconstitutional. In fact, the court decision seemed to make the Klan even more determined. Immediately after the district court decision was announced, Pierce announced the state's decision to appeal the case to the U.S. Supreme Court.

The Supreme Court heard a refinement of the controversy that had been going on in Oregon for the previous three years. The state argued that only a compulsory system of public school education could preserve patriotism and train young citizens to become defenders of their country. In response, the attorneys for the Catholic schools argued that the issue was tyranny versus liberty.

On June 1, 1925, the Supreme Court handed down a unanimous decision in favor of parochial education. Known as *Pierce v. Society of School Sisters*, the written opinion noted that the Oregon law was a clear violation of the Fourteenth Amendment to the Constitution. The Court did not dispute the right of the state to regulate schooling or the right to require all children of a certain age to attend some school.

But the rights of the state did not extend to dictating the *choice* of schools. In other words, the state of Oregon had no right to abolish parochial schools or force Catholic parents to send their children to public schools. The decision in the Pierce case was widely hailed as the "Magna Carta" of private education.

The Supreme Court decision was a landmark in constitutional law. "The Oregon decision," noted historian Lloyd Jorgenson, "provided for the non-public schools a protection very similar to that which had been extended to the non-public colleges, under different circumstances to be sure, by the *Dartmouth* decision a century earlier" (Jorgensen, 1968, p. 466). Ironically, the Klan had precipitated a course of action that would secure the legal right of Catholic schools to exist and thrive in this country.

The *Pierce* decision undercut the Klan's campaign against Catholic education. To be sure, the Klan did not abandon its attacks on parochial schools, but the efforts were without power or the force of law. The Klan remained active throughout the 1920s and was particularly effective in the campaign to defeat Al Smith's candidacy for president in 1928. After 1930, the Klan was largely discredited and had become a fringe group in American society. *See also*: Anti-Catholicism.

Further Reading: David H. Bennett, *The Party of Fear: From Nativist Movements to the*

New Right in American History (Chapel Hill: University of North Carolina Press, 1988); Lloyd P. Jorgenson, "The Oregon School Law: Passage and Sequel," *Catholic Historical Review* 54 (1968): 455–466; William G. Ross, *Forging New Freedoms: Nativism, Education, and the Constitution, 1917–1927* (Lincoln: University of Nebraska Press, 1994).

Timothy Walch

L

Lalanne Project

Lalanne is a Catholic teacher service program sponsored by the Center for Catholic Education at the University of Dayton, a Catholic and Marianist University. The program is named after Fr. Jean Baptiste Lalanne (1795–1879), one of the original seven members of the Society of Mary or Marianists, who was a distinguished educator in France. During a two-year commitment, Lalanne teachers serve in urban Catholic schools while living in the community. Teachers pursue a master's degree during the summers at the University of Dayton. Throughout the school year and during the summer, the teachers engage in spiritual formation activities including retreats and times of prayer in their communities. There are two main goals of the program: (1) to provide support for teachers who wish to minister in Catholic schools as they begin their careers and (2) to assist urban Catholic schools to attract and retain highly qualified faculty members.

In 1996, the Center for Catholic Education surveyed Catholic school superintendents across the United States. Over 65 percent of the responding superintendents indicated that one of their greatest needs was finding committed and qualified teachers who were able to pass on the faith tradition. In response to this survey, the Center for Catholic Education began Lalanne in 1997, under the direction of Dr. Theodore Wallace and Rev. Ronald Nuzzi.

Lalanne accepts applications from those who have completed a teacher education program as well as degrees in the arts and sciences. Religious studies/theology majors are also encouraged to apply for the program. At the completion of the program, those who did not have a teaching credential when they began the program complete a course of study that results in a provisional license from the state of Ohio or, in the case of religious studies/theology majors, a teaching certificate through the archdiocese of Cincinnati. Those who enter the program with a teaching certificate or license take classes through the graduate education program. Areas of concentration are Teacher as Leader, Reading Credential, School Psychologist, and Educational Leadership.

The community life of the Lalanne teachers centers around supporting each other in their service. Teachers decide on times of prayers, meals, and a meeting on a weekly basis. Teachers also commit themselves to engage in a faith sharing and a social activity together at least once per month. These times of gathering provide the teachers with opportunities to engage in discussions about their ministry in the classroom both from a professional viewpoint as well as from a spiritual perspective. Making connections between their chosen career and personal faith provides Lalanne teachers with a concrete example of how to build communities in their classrooms and schools.

Besides the times of prayer within community, Lalanne teachers engage in other activities designed to develop their spiritual lives. Two retreats are held each year. One retreat is conducted during the summer. The emphasis of this retreat is on the coming year of ministry and community life. The second retreat of the year is geared toward helping teachers identify the ways in which Christ has made His presence known in their experience of teaching and community living.

Course work at the University of Dayton and associated activities make up the bulk of the formal professional development component of Lalanne. Through the academic component Lalanne teachers reflect on their experiences in the classroom and their previous academic preparation in order to improve their ability to educate young people. The mentoring program is another aspect of the professional development. Lalanne teachers are assigned a mentor who works with them at their school. Additionally, staff members from the Center for Catholic Education conduct classroom visits, which are designed to help teachers improve their teaching.

The three components of the program interact synergistically. While no one teacher has all of the pieces of the puzzle, each brings a set of skills and experiences to community living, teaching, and faith sharing. Coincidentally, the three components of Lalanne correspond very closely with the call of a National Catholic Educational Association committee in 1982 for Catholic colleges and universities to develop programs to prepare teachers for Catholic schools with an emphasis on course work, faith development, and field experiences.

Funding for the program comes from multiple sources including benefactors, the University of Dayton and the schools that participate in the program. Lalanne teachers are paid a stipend below the entry-level salary for beginning teachers at the school. Most of the difference between the stipend and the beginning salary is contributed to Lalanne.

The dioceses participating in the program make a commitment to find affordable housing for the teachers, to provide mentors for each of the teachers, and to designate a local contact person who visits the teachers on a monthly basis for dinner and prayer.

The program placed its first six teachers in Dayton, Ohio, in August 1999. In the fall of 2002 the program had twenty-nine teachers in six cities located in six different dioceses. Of the eight teachers who have finished the program, all have remained in education, and six have continued to teach at the schools where they were originally placed.

The application process for Lalanne is competitive. Prospective Lalanne teachers must complete standard application questions, three essays—one on each of the following areas: community living, personal spirituality, and professional development—and submit official transcripts and three letters of recommendation. These written applications are reviewed by the staff of the Center for Catholic Education. Criteria used in the review are academic performance, readiness to live in community, flexibility, commitment to service, and evidence of activities that indicate a strong and active faith life. Applicants judged to be strong in these areas are then invited to participate in an interview process. Interview teams consist of three to four persons representing the University of Dayton School of Education and Allied Professions,

Campus Ministry, and the dioceses and/or schools served by Lalanne. Each member of the interview team offers written feedback on each interviewee to the Lalanne director.

Lalanne is a member of the consortium of teacher service programs sponsored by the University of Notre Dame's Alliance for Catholic Education.

Through the Catholic Network of Volunteer Service (CNVS), most Lalanne teachers are enrolled as AmeriCorps members. As such, they receive an AmeriCorps Education Award, a voucher for each year of their service, which can be used to continue their education or pay back student loans.

Fr. Jean Baptiste Lalanne (1795–1879), for whom the program was named, was one of the original members of the Society of Mary or Marianists. He was a noted educator in France, and his success was due in large measure to his devotion to education as both a ministry and a profession, to his great love of children, and to his sympathetic understanding of their problems. His career as an educator spanned more than sixty years. Besides the founder of the Marianists, Fr. William Joseph Chaminade, no one played a more important role in establishing and developing the Marianist educational tradition than Fr. Jean Baptiste Lalanne. *See also*: Alliance for Catholic Education (ACE); Christian service; Teacher shortage; Teaching as ministry.

Further Reading: National Catholic Educational Association, *The Pre-Service Formation of Teachers in Catholic Schools: In Search of Patterns for the Future* (Washington, DC: National Catholic Educational Association, 1982).

Edward M. Brink, SM

Lay Catholics in Schools: Witnesses to Faith

The 1982 Roman document *Lay Catholics in Schools: Witnesses to Faith* raised the issue of the lay teacher, initially put forth in the Second Vatican Council's document *Declaration on Christian Education*, with the intent to "expand on its contents and deepen them" (Congregation for Catholic Education [CCE], 1982, #1). This document put forth a challenge to the soul of the Catholic school lay teacher. It called for a deeply felt recognition of continuous self-development, with a firm commitment to personal action, acknowledging the causal relationship between the development of the teacher and his or her contingent effectiveness in the area of student formation.

> The teacher under discussion here is not simply a professional person who systematically transmits a body of knowledge in the context of a school; *teacher* is to be understood as *educator*—one who helps to form human persons. The task of a teacher goes well beyond transmission of knowledge, although that is not excluded. Therefore, if adequate professional preparation is required in order to transmit knowledge, then adequate professional preparation is even more necessary in order to fulfill the role of a genuine teacher. It is an indispensable human formation, and without it, it would be foolish to undertake any educational work. (#16)

The use of the phrase "genuine teacher" in this document is noteworthy. "Educator" is derived from the Latin root *educere*, which means *to draw out*. The "genuine teacher," the true educator, successfully *draws out* the person in the learner in a loving and respectful context. This is possible only after the teacher internally experiences his or her own personhood as a learner, with love and respect for self. By so doing, the teacher is able to recognize what it is he or she is attempting to *draw out* of his or her students. The "genuine teacher" typifies one who is dedicated to the task of forming students who will make the "civilization of love" (CCE, 1982, #19) a reality. The more a teacher gives concrete witness to modeling the ideal person to students, the more students will believe and imitate it.

The combination of spiritual with human formation constitutes "an appropriate professional competence" (CCE, 1982, #62) for the Catholic school teacher, which "does not come to an end with the completion of basic education" (#65). It is an ongoing, holistic, formational process, reflective of new-paradigm thinking, which supports the concept of the lifelong learner in contrast to a static view toward education.

The spiritual/religious formation of the teacher consists of personal sanctification and apostolic mission. "Formation for apostolic mission means a certain human and well-rounded formation, adapted to the natural abilities and circumstances of each person" and requires "in addition to spiritual formation . . . solid doctrinal instruction . . . in theology, ethics and philosophy." In addition, teachers should receive "adequate formation in the social teachings of the Church, which are "an integral part of the Christian concept of life," and "help to keep intensely alive the kind of social sensitivity that is needed" (CCE, 1982, #65). The authors stated that the effects of ongoing teacher formation is immeasurable. "Without it, the school will wander further and further away from its objectives" (#79).

This document exhorted the Catholic educator to routinely engage in self-evaluation on the authenticity of his or her vocation to Catholic education. The authors encouraged educators to self-reflect to awaken such a consciousness. "To what extent they [lay Catholic teachers] actually do have such an awareness [of their vocation of teaching] is something that these lay people should be asking themselves" (CCE, 1982, #61).

Emphatic in this document is the role of the teacher as a builder of community, with a profound elaboration on the meaning of community in a school context: "[T]he educational community of a school is itself a *school*. It teaches one how to be a member of the wider social communities; and when the educational community is at the same time a Christian community—and this is what the educational community of a Catholic school must always be striving toward—then it offers a great opportunity for the teachers to provide the students with a living example of what it means to be a member of that great community which is the Church" (CCE, 1982, #22). This "school" of the Christian faith community within the formal school was claimed a distinctive feature of Catholic education and possible only in circumstances where "there is a sharing of the Christian commitment among at least a portion of each of the principal groups that make up the educational community: parents, teachers, and students" (#41).

Paramount to the Christian vision is that the teacher recognize the dignity of each student. The authors asserted that it must never be forgotten that, in the context of crises which most affect the younger generations, the most important element in the educational endeavor is "always the individual person: the person, and the moral dignity of that person which is the result of his or her principles, and the conformity of actions with those principles" (CCE, 1982, #32). The value placed upon the individual, an outgrowth of Vatican II thinking, continued to surface in this document.

Direct and personal contact between teachers and students is crucial, identified by the Church as a privileged opportunity for giving witness. True education steps beyond the imparting of knowledge, as it promotes human dignity and fosters genuine human relationships. These Roman authors emphatically stated that the atmosphere of a Catholic school should be marked by sincere respect and cordiality, that it should be a place where authentic human relationships flourish. Openness and a readiness for dialogue with students, with an awareness that the enrichment is mutual, are key factors in the building of student relationships. Not simply a methodology for their formation, direct and personal contact with students constitutes "the means by which teachers learn what they need to know about the students in order to guide them adequately" (#21). *See also*: Congregation for Catholic Education, The; Lay teachers; Teaching as ministry.

Further Reading: Congregation for Catholic Education, *Lay Catholics in Schools: Witnesses to Faith* (Boston: Daughters of St. Paul, 1982).

Gini Shimabukuro

Lay teachers

Lay teachers are teachers in Catholic schools who are not members of religious congregations or diocesan priests. From their foundation until the 1950s, the Catholic schools in the United States were almost exclusively staffed by members of religious congregations, that is, by sisters, brothers, and priests. In the 1960s, when the number of religious vocations began to decrease, the number of lay faculty members in Catholic schools increased. In 1967, the percentage of lay teachers was 42 percent. By 1983 the percentage had increased to 76 percent. During the 2000–2001 school year, 93.5 percent of the faculty members in Catholic schools were laypeople. The changes in faculty statistics in the past forty years have resulted in many changes, notably shifts in financial operations for the school and changes in the hiring and professional development of teachers. What has also become evident is a need to articulate the unique spiritual component that lay teachers incorporate into their ministry of teaching.

The shift in the majority of faculty members in Catholic schools being members of religious congregations to being laypeople occurred at approximately the same time as the Second Vatican Council. The Decree on the Apostolate of the Laity affirmed the ministry of laypeople. The decree urged laypeople to give a willing and enthusiastic response to the voice of Christ. This same conviction impels many of the lay teachers to serve in Catholic schools today. With salaries consistently below those of teachers in neighboring public schools, those teachers who consciously choose to stay in Catholic education do so at a personal economic cost. They continue to serve because they believe that their ministry is a vocation.

The financial impact on Catholic schools cannot be underestimated. The religious sisters, brothers, and priests who served as the majority of teachers before 1950 worked for minimal compensation. Religious orders sponsored schools, and the sponsorship resulted in unrealistically low operating expenses. The religious congregation contributed the services of most of the teachers in the school, asking only a fraction of what it would cost for each teacher to subsist if living outside a religious community. An increase in the number of lay teachers necessitated the paying of salaries, even though most were not competitive with public schools. Retirement and health care costs were no longer absorbed by the congregation but became the responsibility of the parish or dioceses that sponsored most of the schools. The need to charge tuition to attend became more widespread, and those tuition costs have continued to increase. Prior to the 1960s Catholic school tuition was relatively rare.

Other changes were more positive and less of a financial burden but were not always as easy to implement. Members of religious orders were no longer assigned to a school by a religious superior. Hiring became the responsibility of the principal and/or pastor, as did discerning which candidate possessed the qualities that would make her or him a successful teacher of secular subjects and religion while instilling values consistent with the faith. Once positions were filled with the best-qualified candidates, the continued professional development of the teachers was now the responsibility of the administration instead of the religious superior. This formation, which for the most part took place within the walls of the religious community, now needed to be done in new ways to meet the framework of the lives of the lay teachers.

The question of effectiveness of lay teachers to instruct in areas of faith and to pass on the traditions of the faith is often raised by those who attended Catholic schools when the faculty was largely religious. The implication seems to be that lay teachers are less effective in instilling values and teaching matters of faith. Even the question of whether a school can be genuinely Catholic in the absence of members of a religious order on the staff has been raised. These questions, while not always asked with the best of intentions in mind, have led Catholic schools in general to look at the issue of Catholic identity more consistently.

In the midst of this transition, many have asked whether a lay spirituality has developed among teachers or if there is a need to develop a system of spirituality that meets the needs of lay teachers in Catholic schools. The underlying theme is that as members of religious congregations had set practices for developing their spiritual lives, laypeople may also have unique methods and practices that will help and support them in their ministry of Catholic education. Vatican II recognized that lay spirituality would take its particular character from the circumstances in one's life (married and family life, celibacy, and widowhood), from one's state of health, and from one's professional and social activity. It seems that the profession of teaching and, in particular, teaching in a Catholic school, would provide a fertile ground for development of a unique form of spirituality. *See also*: *Lay Catholics in Schools: Witnesses to Faith.*

Further Reading: Harold A. Buetow, *The Catholic School: Its Roots, Identity, and Future* (New York: Crossroad, 1988); Anthony S. Bryk, Valerie E. Lee, and Peter B. Holland, *Catholic Schools and the Common Good* (Cambridge: Harvard University Press, 1993); Austin Flannery, ed., *Vatican Council II: The Conciliar and Post Conciliar Documents* (Northport, NY, Costello, 1975); National Catholic Educational Association, *Sharing the Faith: The Beliefs and Values of Catholic High School Teachers* (Washington, DC: National Catholic Educational Association, 1985); Sacred Congregation for Catholic Education, *Lay Catholics in Schools: Witnesses to Faith* (Vatican City: Author, 1982).

Edward M. Brink, SM

Learning styles

Learning style refers to the unique way an individual concentrates on, processes, internalizes, and remembers new information. A learning style is a biologically and developmentally determined set of personal characteristics for learning. Differences in learning style among individuals account for the range of effectiveness of instruction across students in the classroom. The identification of various learning styles evolved from research on cognitive styles, or ways of organizing and processing information. As the focus in education has shifted from a single measure of intelligence to multidimensional intelligence, comprehensive models of learning have incorporated the need for different teaching techniques attuned to varying styles of learning.

Learning styles have been identified as varying across such factors as age, gender, achievement level, culture, and information-processing style. Learning styles change in all individuals as they age. However, each developmental transformation is unique to the individual. Males and females frequently learn differently from each other; males tend to be more nonconforming and in need of more mobility within an informal learning environment than their female counterparts. Achievement level is also related to learning style. High and low achievers have significantly different learning styles and do not tend to perform well under the same instructional methods. Cultural differences in learning styles occur within five areas associated with instructional delivery: cognitive style, emotional stimulus, environmental stimulus, sociological stimulus, and physiological stimulus. Differences in the way individuals process new information also account for variation in learning style.

A large number of theoretical models propose categorizations for learning styles (Dunn and Griggs, 2000). One of the best known is associated with Howard Gardner's Theory of Multiple Intelligences. Rita Dunn and Kenneth Dunn (1998) propose that for each of the eight intelligences of this theory (kinesthetic, verbal/linguistic, logical/mathematical, visual/spatial, musical/rhythmic, interpersonal, intrapersonal, and naturalistic) there is a corresponding learning style that promotes optimal learning. The five-dimensional model consists of associated learning preferences: environmental preferences; emotional preferences; sociological preferences; psychological preferences related to perception; and psychological preferences based on analytic mode. David Kolb proposes a model based on experiential learning theory. This model regards learning as a four-stage cycle: concrete experience, reflective observation, abstract conceptualization, and active experimentation. Charles Claxton and Patricia Murrell identify four levels of learning style: personality, information-processing, social interaction, and instruction. Herman Witkin approaches learning styles from a field-dependent versus field-independent perspective and proposes a fourth model. Field-dependent students are strongly influenced by the environment and prefer interpersonal interactions, rather than the analytical areas of study that a field-independent student would prefer. Anthony Grasha and Sheryl Riechmann identify six learning styles: competitive, collaborative, avoidant, participant, dependent, and independent. Finally, James Anderson and Maurianne Adams distinguish analytical learners from relational learners. Analytical learners focus more on details associated with knowledge; relational learners focus on overarching themes among knowledge.

These theoretical models have important implications for general and religious education. Their cumulative effect has led to the implementation of different teaching styles to adapt to the unique learning styles of students. Traditionally, classrooms have been teacher-focused, requiring students to adapt to the teaching method of the particular instructor. Developments in learning style research have shifted pedagogy to student-focused classrooms in which teachers adjust to the needs and styles of their students. This research suggests that educators can affect academic performance significantly by responding to the diverse learning styles in the classroom. In the religion classroom, the preparation for sacraments, and the celebration of mass, learning styles theory support multisensory and participatory learning experiences designed to immerse students in the rites, traditions, and celebration of religion.

Although teaching styles may differ across educators, there is reason to believe that teachers tend to teach in one unique style with little variation. For this reason, learning style theories also have implications for teacher education. If future teachers are to be familiar with the various learning styles in their classroom, it is important that they receive training in the implementation of various teaching styles as well. Rita Dunn and Kenneth Dunn (1998) have developed *The Teaching Style Inventory* to assist teachers in identifying their own teaching style.

Although students benefit from learning in their natural learning style, it is equally important for them to be challenged to learn within alternative methods of information processing. Learning new information would be easiest for a student being taught within his or her learning style, but a student who has been taught through a wide range of teaching styles benefits by becoming proficient in multiple learning styles. This proficiency better prepares students for their academic and professional careers. *See also*: Multiple Intelligence Theory (MI).

Further Reading: Ann C. Baker and David A. Kolb, *Conversational Learning* (Westport, CT: Quorum Books, 2002); Rita Dunn and Kenneth J. Dunn, *Practical Approaches to Individualizing Staff Development for Adults* (Westport, CT: Praeger, 1998); Rita Dunn and Shirley A. Griggs, *Practical Approaches to Using Learning Styles in Higher Education* (Westport, CT: Bergin and Garvey, 2000); Howard Gardner, *Multiple Intelligences: The Theory in Practice* (New York: Basic Books, 1993); Ronald J. Nuzzi, *Gifts of the Spirit: Multiple Intelligences in Religious Education* (Washington DC: National Catholic Educational Association, 1999); Eugene Sadler-Smith, Christopher Allinson, and John Hayes, "Learning Preferences and Cognitive Style: Some Implications for Continuing Professional Development," *Management Learning* 31, 2 (2000): 239–256.

John L. Watzke

Lemon v. Kurtzman

This case, decided in 1971, actually consisted of two cases consolidated on appeal. Both cases challenged the constitutionality of state aid to, or for the benefit of, private schools. A Rhode Island statute authorized the payment of salary supplements to teachers of secular subjects in nonpublic elementary schools, and the Rhode Island Supreme Court had declared the statute unconstitutional. Pennsylvania statutes provided direct aid to private schools through reimbursement for teacher salaries, instructional materials, and textbooks used for approved secular subjects. The Pennsylvania Supreme Court upheld the statute. The two cases were heard together on appeal. The U.S. Supreme Court ruled that both schemes were unconstitutional and violated the First Amendment to the U.S. Constitution.

The Rhode Island statute authorized payment of a 15 percent salary supplement to teachers in nonpublic schools at which the average per pupil expenditure on secular education was below the public school average. Teachers receiving the supplement could teach only courses that were offered in public schools, could use only public school materials, and had to agree to refrain from teaching courses in religion. At the time of the case, only Catholic school teachers and no other private school teachers received the supplement. The lower court's finding that the parochial school system was "an integral part of the religious mission of the Catholic Church" (p. 2107) was upheld by the U.S. Supreme Court.

The Pennsylvania Nonpublic Elementary and Secondary Education Act allowed the state superintendent to purchase "secular educational services" from nonpublic schools by directly reimbursing those schools for teacher salaries, textbooks, and instructional materials. The reimbursement was limited to secular subjects. The appellate court did not accept the complainant's argument that the act propagated a particular religious faith. In 1971 the U.S. Supreme Court struck down the Pennsylvania program because of the restrictions and oversight that such a program would have required. Additionally, the Supreme Court held that direct reimbursement to religious schools constituted state aid to religion.

This combined case became famous for the establishment of the *Lemon* test in determining the constitutionality of aid to religious schools. There are three prongs to the *Lemon* test: (1) the statute or aid must have a secular purpose; (2) the statute or aid can neither promote nor hinder religion; and (3) the statute or aid cannot foster excessive government entanglement with religion.

The Court suggested that the first prong is generally easily met. States and lawmakers do not pass laws that provide funds to purchase religious materials, for example. Both the Rhode Island and the Pennsylvania laws had secular purposes, providing secular education to children of the state. The second prong presented difficulty in both states because paying a salary supplement to teachers in a religious school or reimbursing such a school for salary costs clearly benefited the religious sponsors of the school as the aid enabled school administrators to attract and retain teachers.

The Court suggests that all teachers in a Catholic school are somehow teachers of religion, a premise supported by the 1983 *Code of Canon Law, Canon* 804, which states, "The local ordinary is to be careful that those who are appointed as teachers of religion in schools, even non-Catholic ones, are outstanding in true doctrine, in the witness of their Christian life and in their teaching ability." This canon demonstrates that Catholic Church officials will consider all who teach in Catholic schools, even if they do not formally teach religion, as religion teachers.

The Supreme Court opinion holds that Catholic school teachers, by the very fact of teaching in Catholic school, have loyalty to the Catholic Church. In Rhode Island, then, the justices believed that it would be difficult for Catholic school teachers to disregard religion and avoid mentioning any religious topics in secular class.

The third prong, "does not foster excessive government entanglement with religion," presents serious problems. The bookkeeping involved in paying salary supplements or making reimbursement payments certainly involves government officials in the financial business of a religion, in these cases, primarily the Catholic religion. The majority did not believe that there existed a rational way to overcome the entanglement problems.

The Supreme Court also considered the plaintiff's argument that the statutes were no different from ones that granted tax-exempt status to religious institutions. Tax-exemption for places operated by institutions of religion had a 200-year history in the United States, while the statutes under consideration were relatively recent, as the majority noted: "Indeed, the state programs before us today represent something of an innovation" (p. 2117).

The majority opinion made clear that the justices valued the existence of Church-related elementary and secondary schools and the savings their operation represented for taxpayers. The question they decided was whether the state aid to religious schools contested here violated the Establishment and Free Exercise Clauses of the First Amendment. The Court found that the aid did violate the First Amendment.

Justice O'Connor in the more recent *Aguilar v. Felton* and *Agostini* cases has suggested that the *Lemon* test may no longer be useful. Nonetheless, *Lemon* is still considered good law.

Catholic school administrators, who are often asked to support legislative action that would aid religious and other private schools, should keep the three prongs of the *Lemon* test in mind, particularly the third prong. The *Lemon* case provides a standard that has stood for over thirty years. Proponents of vouchers and other choice programs, under present law, must ensure that whatever is done does not foster excessive government entanglement with religion. It is the Court's task to determine the point at which government entanglement is "excessive." *See also*: Establishment Clause; Federal aid to Catholic schools.

Further Reading: *Agostini v. Felton*, 117 S.Ct. 1997 (1997); *Aguilar v. Felton*, 105 S.Ct. 3232 (1985); Canon Law Society of Great Britain and Ireland, ed., *The Code of Canon Law in English Translation* (Grand Rapids: William B. Eerdmans, 1983).

Mary Angela Shaughnessy, SCN

Leo XIII, Pope (1810–1903)

Leo XIII was born in 1810 to a noble family in central Italy. Baptized Joachim Pecci, he was ordained a priest in 1837; he served in several leadership capacities in the Church before he was elected to succeed Pius IX as Pope in 1878.

Leo's pontificate was noted for many achievements, among them his teaching on social issues, including education. Author of many important encyclicals, Leo wrote on the relations of capital and labor in his groundbreaking *Rerum Novarum*, his most important social encyclical. In it he condemned the excesses of socialism and economic liberalism and upheld the rights of workingmen. He opened the Vatican archives to scholars; called for the renewal of Thomistic thought in philosophy; and encouraged biblical study, which included the founding of the Biblical Commission. In *Testem Benevolentiae*, issued in 1899, he condemned what he termed the errors of "Americanism." Subsequent events showed that he was criticizing those who called on the Church to adjust its doctrines to modern life, not attacking the Church in the United States, which he praised but three years later.

Pope Leo is justly renowned for his social teaching, enunciated in other encyclicals. He regretted the loss of the influence of the Church from public institutions, which resulted in "unbridled freedom" in teaching. He called on the world's bishops to work to make all education in accord with the Catholic faith. He urged parents to pay watchful attention to the education of their children and raise them virtuously. Civil states were urged to operate according to the dictates of the natural or divine law, including recognizing that the Catholic Church is the one true faith.

In *Immortale Dei*, written in 1885, he taught that the authority of the Church superseded that of the state in "mixed matters," that is, those affairs in which each institution had a legitimate stake (such as marriage and education). The Church, he maintained, was the true and sole teacher of virtue and the guardian of morals in society. Catholics, he pointed out, were to accept the Church's teachings and to do what they could to see to the instruction of the young in religion and true morality. In a letter that year to the English bishops, who were involved in a struggle with the government over education, he insisted on the absolute necessity of religion in schools because schools were the instruments whereby the Catholic faith was preserved whole and entire. It was the responsibility of government, he penned, to recognize the rights

Pope Leo XIII. Courtesy of the Library of Congress.

of parental choice in education, because there would be no better citizen than one who is a practicing Christian.

The relationship and relative rights of civil and ecclesiastical societies continued to occupy the Pontiff's mind. The state was bound to recognize the natural moral law in its actions and legislation. Civil authorities were obliged by God to consider the welfare of humans' souls in enacting legislation and be concerned with their citizens reaching the end for which they were created by God.

In 1890, the Pope authored yet another influential encyclical, *Sapientiae Christianae*, which had a bearing on education and which called on Catholics to follow the teachings of the Church, which represented God, when Church and state positions conflicted. Parents were enjoined to "absolutely oppose their children frequenting schools where they are exposed to the fatal poison of impiety" (Husslein, 1940, p. 162). He praised Catholics worldwide, who "at the expense of much money and more zeal, have erected schools for the education of their children" (p. 162).

The strife between and among the American Catholic hierarchy over the support of, and necessity of, attendance at Catholic schools reached the Vatican in the later years of the nineteenth century. Attempting to put an end to the dispute, Leo sent his personal delegate, Archbishop Francis Satolli, to a meeting of the American archbishops in the fall of 1892. Satolli's Fourteen Propositions failed to end the turmoil. Some prelates resented Satolli's work as overturning their hard work in establishing and supporting Catholic schools. Ultimately, after several other instances of opposition to his efforts had occurred, the American archbishops voted unanimously in November 1893 to accept the substance of his mediating efforts, and peace was achieved. Catholic schools were to be promoted, but attendance at public schools by Catholic children was to be accepted when dangers to the children's faith were rendered remote. Internal peace had been restored.

Pope Leo XIII died on July 20, 1903. *See also*: Catholic School Question, The; *Rerum Novarum*; Social justice.

Further Reading: William B. Friend, "Leo XIII, Pope (1878–1903)," *Social Justice Review* 92, 3–4 (March/April 2001): 53–55; Joseph Husslein, ed., *Social Wellsprings*, I (Milwaukee: Bruce, 1940); Bernard F. Marthaler, ed., *New Catholic Encyclopedia*, 2nd ed., Vol. 8 (Washington, DC: Gale and the Catholic University of America Press, 2003), pp. 490–493; J. Martin Miller, *The Life of Pope Leo XIII* (Philadelphia: National, 1903); Daniel F. Reilly, *The School Controversy 1891–1893* (New York: Arno Press and the New York Times, 1969).

Thomas C. Hunt

Linguistic intelligence

One of seven intelligences identified in Howard Gardner's Multiple Intelligence Theory—a theory that has gained wide acceptance in education and instruction since the middle 1980s. Linguistic intelligence includes the written and spoken word, the capacity to develop linguistically, and the use of language for communication. Its core operations include the awareness of semantics, phonology, syntax, and pragmatics. Individuals with high linguistic ability demonstrate an awareness of the meaning and order of words, as well as sensitivity to phonetic distinctions and innate command of the pragmatic uses of language. Poets, writers, and homilists are examples of individuals who often display a high ability in this intelligence. This intelligence has also been applied as a means to understand and participate in religious studies and the mass.

According to Gardner, linguistic skill meets the criteria for an independent intelligence because it is culturally significant and has biological origins. Four culturally significant aspects of linguistic knowledge, which represent a wide range of ability, are the rhetoric of language, the mnemonic potential of language, the use of language for explanation, and the use of language to reflect upon itself. Every individual develops some degree of competence in linguistics. Studies of the connections between the brain and language show that normal linguistic development is centered in the left temporal lobe. Brain lesions to specific regions cause dysfunction in the production of phonemes, in the pragmatic aspects of speech, and in the semantics and syntax of language. The independence of this intelligence is demonstrated by individuals who have difficulty with language but function normally otherwise and by individuals who struggle in many areas but have normal language functioning. Some children have a good grasp of the essential features of language, although they are mentally handicapped. Some autistic children can read at a very young age, although they cannot communicate verbally. Deaf children are also able to communicate with gestures that represent the core elements of language.

Linguistic intelligence emerges early in human development and follows a pattern in normally functioning individuals. Within the first four years of life, children progress from babbling to more complex use of the language. Children begin with single words, then learn to pair words together, create sentences, tell stories, and pose questions. Although all children follow a similar developmental pattern, each individual child develops linguistic skills with a different speed and level of difficulty. Some develop basic levels of functioning, while others show a strong command of the language from an early age.

Across cultures, language is used as a tool for communication. The wide variety of language function is due to the diversity of cultures. Verbal communication and memory are essential in preliterate societies because of the dependence on oral expression. Modern society places a greater emphasis on writing and reading. Different skills are developed through communication with the written word such as organization and word choice. Although linguistic skill is identified as an independent intelligence, it overlaps with other intelligences in certain areas. The syntactic and phonological processes relate specifically to linguistic intelligence, while pragmatic and semantic functions cross over into other intelligences, such as logical-mathematical, interpersonal, and intrapersonal intelligence.

Linguistic intelligence can be easily incorporated into religious education. Although verbal and written expression is a traditional component of classrooms, linguistic intelligence can be emphasized through equal focus on reading, writing, and speaking about religious topics. Word games and puzzles on church issues, biblical readings, storytelling, and studying the etymology of religious terms are some interactive ideas to develop and use linguistic skills.

Prayer, however, written and spoken, is clearly the strongest presence of the linguistic intelligence in Catholic tradition. Part of every religious education program and Catholic school is the reading and memorization of traditional prayers, a practice that engages the linguistic intelligence. That most Catholics can recite a variety of prayers (Our Father, Hail Mary, Act of Contrition) from memory is an indication of the use of the linguistic intelligence in Catholic education.

Each component of the Catholic mass incorporates linguistic intelligence. The Introductory Rites includes unified greeting and response, dialogue, and prayer. The Liturgy of the Word involves listening to the words of God through Scripture readings. The Profession of Faith unites the congregation verbally through the recitation of the creed. The Liturgy of the Eucharist requires active listening. The Communion Rite has important dialogue between the priest and the congregation. *See also*: Gardner, Howard; Multiple Intelligence Theory (MI).

Further Reading: Howard Gardner, *Frames of Mind: The Theory of Multiple Intelligences* (New York: Basic Books, 1983); Howard Gardner, *Intelligence Reframed: Multiple Intelli-*

gences for the 21st Century (New York: Basic Books, 1999); Howard Gardner, *Multiple Intelligences: The Theory in Practice* (New York: Basic Books, 1993); Ronald J. Nuzzi, *Gifts of the Spirit: Multiple Intelligences in Religious Education* (Washington, DC: National Catholic Educational Association, 1999).

John L. Watzke

Logical-mathematical intelligence

One of seven intelligences identified in Howard Gardner's Multiple Intelligence Theory—a theory that has gained wide acceptance in education and instruction since the middle of the 1980s. Logical-mathematical intelligence encompasses deductive reasoning, mathematical ability, and scientific investigation. Individuals with high logical-mathematical abilities demonstrate an innate understanding of patterns, calculations, and logic. Physicists, mathematicians, and scientists are examples of individuals with high ability in this intelligence. This intelligence has also been applied as a means to understand and participate in religious studies and the mass.

According to Gardner, logical-mathematical skill meets the criteria for an independent intelligence because it is culturally significant and has biological origins. Studies of the brain show that language and calculation are not connected. Brain-damaged patients can retain linguistic abilities while lacking the ability to understand numeric symbols or operational signs. Brain lesions to the left parietal lobe affect math and logic abilities. The independence of this intelligence is also demonstrated by idiot savants who are able to make complex calculations but lack other normal abilities. Other individuals possess normal functioning but show marked weakness with numbers.

The development of logical-mathematical ability follows a pattern in normally functioning individuals. This intelligence is centered on the relationship between the individual and objects. Infants first observe the objects around them but are aware of them only when they are physically present. Children next realize that objects exist even when they are not in sight, group objects together, and learn to count. Next, children learn to compute numerical operations with the objects and finally grasp abstract operations. Although all normally developed adults reach the cognitive level of formal operations, only individuals with high ability in this intelligence are oriented toward the ways of reasoning and thinking demonstrated by mathematicians and scientists.

Across cultures, systems and numbers are important. Although Western culture demonstrates complex mathematical systems and scientific findings, all cultures display basic operations, numerical systems, and logical thinking. While logical-mathematical ability is identified as an independent intelligence, it overlaps with, and is often seen as an underlying component of, the other intelligences. Logic is central to language, music, and spatial relationships—concepts that may take on varying degrees of cultural significance.

Logical-mathematical intelligence can be easily incorporated into religious education. While education traditionally emphasizes this ability, religion classes can also include numbers and logic to enhance the classroom experiences. Ritual behavior is also related to the logical-mathematical intelligence. In learning to repeat certain behaviors in a proper sequence, such as participating in mass, students use the logical-mathematical intelligence. Highlighting the numbers of biblical significance, creating story problems, playing number games, and celebrating important dates on the church calendar are some interactive ideas to develop and utilize logical-mathematical skills. Classes involving measurements, calculations, predictions, and experiments also engage the logical-mathematical intelligence.

The structure of the Catholic mass follows a set pattern and logical order. Each component of the mass further incorporates logical-mathematical intelligence. The priest's homily logically explains the readings and necessitates interpretation by the listener. The Apostle's Creed and the Nicene Creed are in chronological order of important events. The Liturgy of the Eucharist has logic and order on which the assembly depends. Comfort in liturgical settings often develops in response to the familiarity of the order of worship, a familiarity based in the logical-mathematical intelligence. *See also*: Gardner, Howard; Multiple Intelligence Theory (MI).

Further Reading: Howard Gardner, *Frames of Mind: The Theory of Multiple Intelligences* (New York: Basic Books, 1983); Howard Gardner, *Intelligence Reframed: Multiple Intelligences for the 21st Century* (New York: Basic Books, 1999); Howard Gardner, *Multiple Intelligences: The Theory in Practice* (New York: Basic Books, 1993); Ronald J. Nuzzi, *Gifts of the Spirit: Multiple Intelligences in Religious Education* (Washington, DC: National Catholic Educational Association, 1999).

John L. Watzke